W9-BYP-827

BEHEMOTH

THE STRUCTURE AND PRACTICE OF
NATIONAL SOCIALISM

BEHEMOTH

THE STRUCTURE AND PRACTICE

OF NATIONAL SOCIALISM

1933-1944

FRANZ NEUMANN

1963

OCTAGON BOOKS, INC.

NEW YORK

TO MY WIFE

NOTE ON THE NAME BEHEMOTH

IN THE Jewish eschatology—of Babylonian origin—Behemoth and Leviathan designate two monsters, Behemoth ruling the land (the desert), Leviathan the sea, the first male, the second female. The land animals venerate Behemoth, the sea animals Leviathan, as their masters. Both are monsters of the Chaos. According to the apocalyptic writings, Behemoth and Leviathan will reappear shortly before the end of the world. They will establish a rule of terror—but will be destroyed by God. In other versions Behemoth and Leviathan will fight each other incessantly, and finally will destroy each other. The day of the righteous and just will then come. They will eat the meat of both monsters in a feast which announces the advent of a realm of God. Jewish eschatology, the Book of Job, the prophets, the apocryphal writings are full of references to this myth, which is often differently interpreted and often adapted to political circumstances. St. Augustine saw in the Behemoth the Satan.

It was Hobbes who made both the Leviathan and the Behemoth popular. His *Leviathan* is the analysis of a state, that is a political system of coercion in which vestiges of the rule of law and of individual rights are still preserved. His *Behemoth*, or the *Long Parliament*, however, discussing the English civil war of the seventeenth century, depicts a non-state, a chaos, a situation of lawlessness, disorder, and anarchy.

Since we believe National Socialism is—or tending to become—a non-state, a chaos, a rule of lawlessness and anarchy, which has 'swallowed' the rights and dignity of man, and is out to transform the world into a chaos by the supremacy of gigantic land masses, we find it apt to call the National Socialist system

The Behemoth.

PREFACE

THE MANUSCRIPT was finished when Germany attacked Russia; the book was being set up when Germany, to save her face, declared war on the United States. Since the author never believed in the possibility of Russian-German collaboration, and since war with the United States—whether declared or not—had been a fact since 1939, the two events did not affect his book.

Yet even at the present writing the two events have deeply affected Germany's domestic situation, both military and psychological.

During the First World War, Germany had to fight on two fronts not only on the battlefield, but, since 1917, psychologically as well: the two enemies were Bolshevism and Wilsonianism. Her defeat in 1918 signified the victory of these two doctrines over the semi-absolutism of the Empire, and, in the final competition between democracy and Bolshevism, Wilson's New Freedom remained victorious. Today's constellation is almost identical. National Socialism is again fighting a psychological two-front war. For the older generation of the German people, America still is the land of unlimited industrial possibilities; it represents a mode of life infinitely superior to a manipulated and terrorized culture. To large groups of workers, whether communist or not, Soviet Russia is the realization of old dreams—this time combined with a military efficiency as high and perhaps even higher than that of National Socialism.

A military defeat of Germany is necessary. Whether National Socialism can be crushed without a military defeat, I do not know. But of this I am certain: a military defeat will wipe it out. The military superiority of the democracies and of Soviet Russia must be demonstrated to the German people. The philosophy of National Socialism stands and falls with its alleged 'efficiency.' This must be proved untrue. The stab-in-the-back legend of 1918 must not be allowed to arise again. More and better planes, tanks, and guns and a complete military defeat will uproot National Socialism from the mind of the German people.

But that is not enough. The war must be shortened by dividing Germany and divorcing the large masses of the people from National Socialism. This is the task of psychological warfare, which cannot be disassociated from the domestic and foreign policies of Germany's opponents. Psychological warfare is not propaganda. It is politics. It consists in demonstrating to the German people that military superiority can be achieved by a democracy which does not claim to be perfect but which rather admits its imperfections, and does not shun the long and arduous task of overcoming them.

I have endeavored throughout the book to use only original German sources for my analyses, which frequently differ sharply from current interpretations of National Socialism. The Introduction is not intended as a history or full critical analysis of the Weimar Republic; it seeks merely to bring out the structural defects of the system. I hope before long to publish a social history of the Republic.

The idea for the present book came from studies made at the London School of Economics and Political Science, where I had the great pleasure of working for three years. I am deeply indebted to many suggestions I received from my friend Harold J. Laski and from Professor Morris Ginsberg.

I am obligated to many friends, above all to my colleagues in the Institute of Social Research and to its directors, Dr. Max Horkheimer and Dr. Frederick Pollock. My friend Herbert Marcuse went through some parts of the manuscript; Dr. Otto Kirchheimer gave me valuable suggestions on questions of criminal law; Dr. A. R. L. Gurland placed his comprehensive knowledge of German industry at my disposal. My friend D. V. Glass helped me in the section on population problems. My former assistant, Dr. O. K. Flechtheim, now an instructor at Atlanta University, spent much time in research on the history of the Weimar Republic. Professor E. J. Gumbel, now at the New School for Social Research, lent to me his many publications on republican justice.

The Honorable Thurman W. Arnold, Assistant Attorney General of the United States, kindly permitted me to use a memorandum originally prepared for him and the lectures on the German cartel system which I delivered before the members of the Anti-Trust division in 1938 and 1939.

The Research Institute on Peace and Post-War Problems of the

American Jewish Committee kindly permitted me to incorporate my memorandum on Germany's New Order. Professor Robert M. MacIver went through the final chapter and made a number of valuable suggestions.

Professor Alfred E. Cohn of the Rockefeller Institute for Medical Research was kind enough to place at my disposal a sum for editing expenses. The editing was done by Messrs. D. V. Glass, M. I. Finkelstein, and Norbert Guterman, who, together with Dr. Felix Weil, also assisted me in reading the proofs.

Acknowledgments are gratefully made to the following publishers for permission to reprint:

Little, Brown & Company, Boston, from Douglas Miller, *You Can't Do Business with Hitler.*

Houghton Mifflin Company, Boston, from Adolf Hitler, *Mein Kampf* (published by Reynal and Hitchcock).

Alfred A. Knopf, New York, from William L. Langer, *The Diplomacy of Imperialism.*

The Brookings Institution, Washington, from Cleona Lewis, *Nazi Europe and World Trade.*

The Viking Press, New York, from Thorstein Veblen, *Imperial Germany and the Industrial Revolution.*

W. W. Norton, New York, from Alfred Vagts, *A History of Militarism,* and Emil Lederer, *State of the Masses. The Threat of a Classless Society.*

Columbia University Press, New York, from Mildred Wertheimer, *The Pan-German League.*

A. J. Holman Company, Philadelphia, from their edition of Martin Luther's *Works,* Vol. I, from pp. 250 and 271, Vol. IV from pp. 240, 249, and 272.

FRANZ NEUMANN

23 December 1941

PREFACE TO THE SECOND EDITION

UNDER NORMAL CONDITIONS, the author would have written a new book. This would have made early publication impossible, as would also the present difficulties of manufacture. For these reasons, publisher and author decided to add to the first edition a comprehensive appendix. The appendix brings the development of National Socialism up to date. It also fills certain omissions of the first edition, especially in four major fields:

> German administration, especially the Police
> the structure of the Party
> the German theory and practice of military government
> the structure of economic controls

The appendix is thus a small book in itself and only the courage of the Oxford University Press made it possible to publish a much enlarged book at the old price.

Each chapter of the appendix is prefaced by a note indicating which major chapter of the book it supplements. Since, in addition, the new material is listed in detail in the table of contents and the index, it should be fairly easy to correlate the book and the appendix.

After the appendix had been completed, German generals plotted Hitler's assassination. The attempt of 20 July 1944 failed, but it led to the complete concentration of political, legislative, and administrative powers in the hands of Göring and Goebbels under the direction of Himmler, who also controls the home (reserve) army. Himmler is thus not only the undisputed master of the home front, but through his control of the home army and of the Combat S.S., reaches deep into the fighting front.

The Hitler Edict of 25 July 1944 by which Göring was charged with the adaptation of the home front to total war and Goebbels made his deputy may lead to the disappearance of the still existing dualism of State and Party. The Party would then altogether destroy the remnants of the rational and administrative state and substitute for it the amorphous, shapeless Movement, thus transforming the little that remains of the state into more or less organized anarchy.

F. N.

1 *August* 1944
Washington, D. C.

CONTENTS

PART TWO

TOTALITARIAN MONOPOLISTIC ECONOMY

PART THREE

THE NEW SOCIETY

BEHEMOTH

APPENDIX

PART ONE

THE POLITICAL PATTERN OF NATIONAL SOCIALISM

PART TWO

TOTALITARIAN MONOPOLISTIC ECONOMY

PART THREE

THE NEW SOCIETY

INTRODUCTION

THE COLLAPSE OF THE WEIMAR REPUBLIC

1. THE EMPIRE

FOR HALF A CENTURY or more, the history of modern Germany pivoted around one central issue: imperialist expansion through war. With the appearance of socialism as an industrial and political movement threatening the established position of industrial, financial, and agricultural wealth, fear of this challenge to imperialism dominated the internal policy of the empire. Bismarck tried to annihilate the socialist movement, partly by enticement and even more by a series of enactments outlawing the Social Democratic party and trade unions (1878-90). He failed. Social Democracy emerged from this struggle stronger than ever. Both Wilhelm I and Wilhelm II [1] then sought to undermine the influence of the socialists among the German workers by introducing various social reforms —and also failed.

The attempt to reconcile the working class to the state was carried as far as the ruling forces dared; further efforts in this direction would have meant abandoning the very foundation on which the empire rested—the semi-absolutistic and bureaucratic principles of the regime. Only political concessions to the working classes could bring about a reconciliation. The ruling parties were unwilling, however, to abolish the Prussian three-class franchise system and to establish a responsible parliamentary government in the Reich itself and in the component states. With this recalcitrance, nothing remained for them but a war to the death against socialism as an organized political and industrial movement.

The methods of struggle selected took three basic forms: (1) the re-organization of the Prussian bureaucracy into a stronghold of semi-absolutism; (2) the establishment of the army as a bulwark of monarchical power; and (3) the welding together of the owning classes.

The absence of any liberal manifestation in this program is significant. The liberals had been defeated in Germany in 1812, in

3

1848, and again in the constitutional conflict of 1862. By the last quarter of the nineteenth century, liberalism had long ceased to be an important, militant political doctrine or movement; it had made its peace with the empire. On theoretical grounds, furthermore, the spokesmen of absolutism rejected liberalism as a useful tool against socialism. Take the doctrine of inalienable rights. What was it but an instrument for the political rise and aggrandizement of the working classes? Rudolph Sohm, the great conservative legal historian, expressed the current conviction this way:

From the circles of the third estate itself there have arisen the ideas which now . . . incite the masses of the fourth estate against the third. What is written in the books of the scholars and educators is nothing other than what is being preached in the streets . . . The education that dominates our society is the one that preaches its destruction. Like the education of the eighteenth century, the present-day education carries the revolution beneath its heart. When it gives birth, the child it has nourished with its blood will kill its own mother.[2]

The reorganization of the bureaucracy was undertaken by Robert von Puttkamer, Prussian minister of the interior from 1881 to 1888. Contrary to common belief, the earlier bureaucracy of the eighteenth and early nineteenth centuries was far from conservative and made common cause with the champions of the rising industrial capitalism against feudal privilege. The transformation of the bureaucracy set in when the nobility itself began to participate extensively in capitalist enterprise. In a thorough-going purge, Puttkamer dismissed the 'unreliable' elements (including even liberals). The civil service became a closed caste, and the campaign to inject a spirit of thorough conservatism was as successful as in the army. The king was finally able to demand by edict that the 'civil servants to whom the execution of my governmental acts is entrusted and who,, therefore, can be removed from office by disciplinary action,' support his candidates in elections.[3]

Puttkamer brought still another weapon into the fight against socialism. Inspired by the conviction that 'Prussia is the special favorite of God,'[4] he made religion a part of bureaucratic life.[5] Bureaucracy and religion together, or rather the secular and clerical bureaucracies, became the primary agencies against socialism. The ideological accompaniment was an unceasing denunciation of materialism and the glorification of philosophical idealism. Thus Heinrich von Treitschke, the outstanding German historian of the period, clothed his eulogies of power, of the state, and of great men in the same language of modern idealism that was being repeated in every university, school, and pulpit. A firm union was cemented between the Conservative party, the Protestant church, and the Prussian civil service.

The second step was the transformation of the army into a solid tool of reaction. Ever since Frederick II of Prussia, the officer corps was drawn predominantly from the nobility, who were supposed to possess the natural qualities of leadership. Frederick II preferred even foreign-born noblemen to Prussian bourgeois, whom he—together with the men serving in his armies—regarded as 'canaille' and brutes.[6] The Napoleonic Wars shattered this army and demonstrated that troops held together solely by brute discipline were far inferior to the revolutionary armies of France. Under Gneisenau and Scharnhorst, the German army was then reorganized and even democratized to a limited extent, but this development did not last long. In 1860, when Manteuffel had finished his purge, fewer than a thousand of the 2,900 line infantry officers were non-nobles. All the officers' commissions in the guard cavalry and 95 per cent in the other cavalry and in the better infantry regiments were noblemen.[7]

Equally important were the adaptation and reconciliation of the army to bourgeois society. In the '80s, with the defeat of liberalism among the bourgeoisie and the rising threat of the socialist movement, the bourgeoisie abandoned its earlier opposition to the army-extension program. An alliance developed between the two former enemies and the 'feudal bourgeois' type appeared on the scene. The institutional medium for this new type was the reserve officer, drawn largely from the lower middle classes to meet the tremendous personnel problem created by the increase of the army to a war strength of 1,200,000 in 1888 and 2,000,000 (3.4 per cent of the total population) in 1902. The new 'feudal bourgeois'[8] had all the conceit of the old feudal lord, with few of his virtues, little of his regard for loyalty or culture. He represented a coalition of the army, the bureaucracy, and the owners of the large estates and factories for the joint exploitation of the state.

In France during the nineteenth century, the army was fused into the bourgeoisie; in Germany, on the contrary, society was fused into the army.[9] The structural and psychological mechanisms that characterized the army crept steadily into civilian life until they held it in a firm grip.[10] The reserve officer was the key actor in this process. Drawn from the 'educated' and privileged stratum of society, he replaced the less privileged but more liberal *Landwehr* officer. (Reactionaries had always distrusted the *Landwehr* and considered its officers 'the most important lever for an emancipation of the middle class.') [11] In 1913, when the supply of reserve officers from the privileged strata proved too small for the larger army that had been projected, the Prussian army ministry calmly cancelled its plans for an increase rather than open the doors to 'democratization' of the officer corps.[12] One lawyer lost his commission in the reserve for defending a liberal in a *cause célèbre;* so did a mayor who had not stopped a tenant of city property from holding a socialist meeting.[13] As for socialists, it was decided that they lacked the necessary moral qualifications to be officers.

The third step was the reconciliation between agrarian and industrial capital. The depression of 1870 had hit agriculture hard. Additional difficulties were created by the importation of American grain, the rise of industrial prices,[14] and Chancellor Caprivi's whole trade policy, which was dominated by a desire to keep agrarian prices low. Driven to the point of desperation, the agrarians organized the *Bund der Landwirte* in 1893 and began a fight for protective tariffs on grain,[15] arousing the resentment of industrial capital.

A historic deal put an end to the conflict.* The industrial groups were pushing a big navy program and the agrarians, who had been either hostile or indifferent before, agreed through their main agency, the Prussian Conservative party, to vote for the navy bill in return for the industrialists' support for the protective tariff. The policy of amalgamating all the decisive capitalist forces was finally completed under the leadership of Johannes von Miquel, who, first as leader of the National Liberals in 1884 and later as Prussian minister of finance from 1890 to 1901, swung the right wing majority of his party behind Bismarck's policies and inaugu-

* See pp. 204, 209 for a more detailed discussion.

rated his famous *Sammlungspolitik,* the concentration of all 'patriotic forces' against the Social Democracy. The *Sammlungspolitik* received its supreme expression in the direct coupling of grain tariffs with naval construction in 1900. The National Liberals, the Catholic Center, and the Conservative party had arrived at a common material basis.

The conclusion and aftermath of the First World War soon showed that the union of reaction was too fragile a structure. There was no universally accepted ideology to hold it together (nor was there a loyal opposition in the form of a militant liberal movement). It is strikingly evident that Imperial Germany was the one great power without any accepted theory of the state. Where was the seat of sovereignty, for example? The Reichstag was not a parliamentary institution. It could compel neither the appointment nor the dismissal of cabinet ministers. Only indirectly could it exert political influence, especially after Bismarck's dismissal, but never more than that. The constitutional position of the Prussian parliament was still worse; with the help of his specially devised 'theory of the constitutional gap,' Bismarck had even been able to get along without parliamentary sanction for his budgets.

The sovereign power of the empire resided in the emperor and princes assembled in the second chamber (the *Bundesrat*). The princes derived their authority from the divine right of kings, and this medieval conception—in the absolutistic form it had taken during the seventeenth century—was the best Imperial Germany could offer as its constitutional theory. The trouble, however, was that any constitutional theory is only an illusion unless it is accepted by the majority of the people, or at least by the decisive forces of the society. To most Germans, divine right was a patent absurdity. How could it have been otherwise? In a speech at Königsberg on 25 August, 1910, Wilhelm II made one of his frequent divine-right proclamations. This is what he said:

It was here that the Great Elector made himself sovereign Duke of Prussia by his own right; here his son put the royal crown upon his head . . . Frederick William I here established his authority like a rocher de bronze . . . and here my grandfather again put the royal crown on his head by his own right, definitely stressing once again that it was granted to him by God's Grace alone and not by parliaments, popular assemblies, and popular decision, and that,

therefore, he considered himself a selected instrument of Heaven
. . . Considering myself an instrument of the Lord, I go my
way . . .

The innumerable jokes and cartoons that appeared deriding this
particular restatement of the theory leave little doubt that no political party took it seriously except the Conservatives, and they
only to the extent that the emperor identified himself with their
class interests. The justification of sovereign power is the key question of constitutional theory, however, and German writers had to
avoid it. There was no alternative in a country split along so many
lines—Catholic and Protestant, capitalist and proletarian, large land
owner and industrialist—and with each so solidly organized into
powerful social organizations. Even the most stupid could see that
the emperor was far from being the neutral head of the state and
that he sided with specific religious, social, and political interests.

Then came the test of a war that called for the greatest sacrifices in blood and energy on the part of the people. The imperial
power collapsed and all the forces of reaction abdicated in 1918
without the slightest resistance to the leftward swing of the masses
—all this not as the direct consequence of the military defeat, however, but as the result of an ideological debacle. Wilson's 'new
freedom' and his fourteen points were the ideological victors, not
Great Britain and France. The Germans avidly embraced the 'new
freedom' with its promise of an era of democracy, freedom, and
self-determination in place of absolutism and the bureaucratic machine. Even General Ludendorff, virtual dictator over Germany
during the last years of the war, acknowledged the superiority of
the Wilsonian democratic ideology over Prussian bureaucratic efficiency. The Conservatives did not fight—in fact, they had nothing
with which to fight.

2. THE STRUCTURE OF THE WEIMAR DEMOCRACY

Constitutions written at the great turning points of history always
embody decisions about the future structure of society. Furthermore, a constitution is more than its legal text; it is also a myth
demanding loyalty to an eternally valid value system. To establish
this truth we need only examine characteristic constitutions in the

history of modern society, such as the French revolutionary constitutions or the Constitution of the United States. They established
the organizational forms of political life and also defined and chan-
nelized the aims of the state. This last function was easily accomplished in the liberal era. The charters of liberty, whether they
were embodied in the constitution or not, had merely to provide
safeguards against encroachment by the constituted authorities. All
that was necessary for the free perpetuation of society was to
secure freedom of property, of trade and commerce, speech and
assembly, religion and the press.

Not so in post-war Germany. The constitution of 1919 was an
adaptation of Wilson's new freedom. Confronted with the task of
building a new state and a new society out of the revolution of
1918, however, the framers of the Weimar Republic tried to avoid
formulating a new philosophy of life and a new all-embracing and
universally accepted value system. Hugo Preuss, the clear-sighted
democratic constitutional lawyer who was entrusted with the actual
drafting of the constitution, wanted to go so far as to reduce the
document to a mere pattern of organization. He was not seconded.
The makers of the constitution, influenced by the democrat, Friedrich Naumann, decided on the opposite course, namely, to give a
full elaboration of the democratic value system in the second part
of the constitution, to be headed the Fundamental Rights and
Duties of the German People.

Simply to take over the tenets of political liberalism was out of
the question. The revolution of 1918 had not been the work of the
liberals, but of the Socialist parties and trade unions, even though
against the will and inclination of the leadership. True, it had not
been a socialist revolution: property was not expropriated, the large
estates were not subdivided, and the state machine was not destroyed, the bureaucracy was still in power. Nevertheless, working-
class demands for a greater share in determining the destiny of the
state had to be satisfied.

Class struggle was to be turned into class collaboration—that was
the aim of the constitution. In point of fact, the ideology of the
Catholic Center party was to become the ideology of Weimar, and
the Center party itself, with a membership drawn from the most
disparate groups—workers, professionals, civil servants, handicraftsmen, industrialists, and agrarians—was to become the prototype of

the new political structure. Compromise among all social and political groups was the essence of the constitution. Antagonistic interests were to be harmonized by the device of a pluralistic political
structure, hidden behind the form of parliamentary democracy.
Above all, there was to be an end to imperialistic expansion. Republican Germany would find full use for its productive apparatus
in an internationally organized division of labor.

The pluralist doctrine was a protest against the theory and practice of state sovereignty. 'The theory of the sovereign state has
broken down' and must be abandoned.[16] Pluralism conceives of the
state not as a sovereign unit set apart from and above society, but
as one social agency among many, with no more authority than the
churches, trade unions, political parties, or occupational and economic groups.[17] The theory originated in Otto von Gierke's interpretation of German legal history, fused in a curious combination
with reformist syndicalism (Proudhon) and the social teachings
of neo-Thomism. Against a hostile sovereign state, the trade unions
and the churches demanded recognition of their assertedly original,
non-delegated right to represent autonomous groups of the population. 'We see the state less as an association of individuals in a
common life; we see it more as an association of individuals,
already united in various groups for a further and more embracing
common purpose.' [18]

Underlying the pluralist principle was the uneasiness of the impotent individual in the face of a too-powerful state machine. As
life becomes more and more complicated and the tasks assumed
by the state grow in number, the isolated individual increases his
protests against being delivered up to forces he can neither understand nor control. He joins independent organizations. By entrusting decisive administrative tasks to these private bodies, the pluralists
hoped to accomplish two things: to bridge the gap between the
state and individual, and give reality to the democratic identity
between the ruler and the ruled. And, by placing administrative
tasks in the hands of competent organizations, to achieve maximum
efficiency.

Pluralism is thus the reply of individual liberalism to state absolutism. Unfortunately, it does not accomplish its self-imposed tasks.
Once the state is reduced to just another social agency and de-

prived of its supreme coercive power, only a compact among the dominant independent social bodies within the community will be able to offer concrete satisfaction to the common interests. For such agreements to be made and honored, there must be some fundamental basis of understanding among the social groups involved, in short, the society must be basically harmonious. However, since the fact is that society is antagonistic, the pluralist doctrine will break down sooner or later. Either one social group will arrogate the sovereign power to itself, or, if the various groups paralyze and neutralize one another, the state bureaucracy will become all-powerful—more so than ever before because it will require far stronger coercive devices against strong social groups than it previously needed to control isolated, unorganized individuals.

The compact that is the basic device of pluralism must be understood in a literal sense. The Weimar Democracy owed its existence to a set of contracts between groups, each specifying important decisions on the structure of the state and public policy.

1. On 10 November 1918, Field Marshal von Hindenburg, who had supervised the demobilization of the army, and Fritz Ebert, then leader of the Social Democratic party and later the first president of the Republic, entered into an agreement the general terms of which were not divulged until some years later. Ebert is quoted as having said afterwards: 'We allied ourselves in order to fight Bolshevism. The restoration of the monarchy was unthinkable. Our aim on 10 November was to introduce as soon as possible an orderly government supported by the army and the National Assembly. I advised the Field Marshal not to fight the revolution . . . I proposed to him that the supreme army command make an alliance with the Social Democratic party solely to restore an orderly government with the help of the supreme army command. The parties of the right had completely vanished.' [19] Although it was consummated without the knowledge of Ebert's party or even of his closest collaborators, this understanding was in full accord with the Social Democratic party's policy. It covered two points: one negative, the fight against bolshevism; the other positive, the early convening of a national assembly.

2. Nothing was said in the Hindenburg-Ebert agreement about the social structure of the new democracy. That was covered by

the Stinnes-Legien agreement of 15 November 1918, establishing a central working committee between employers and employees. Stinnes, representing the former, and Legien, the leader of the Socialist trade unions, agreed on the following points. Henceforth, employers would withdraw all support from 'yellow dog' organizations and would recognize only independent trade unions. They accepted the collective-bargaining agreement as the means for regulating wages and labor conditions and promised to co-operate with the trade unions generally in industrial matters. There could hardly have been a more truly pluralist document than this agreement between private groups, establishing as the future structure of German labor relations a collectivist system set up and controlled by autonomous groups.

3. The agreement of 22 and 23 March 1919 between the government, the Social Democratic party, and leading party officials contained the following provision:

There shall be legally regulated workers' representation to supervise production, distribution, and the economic life of the nation, to inspect socialized enterprises, and to contribute toward bringing about nationalization. A law providing for such representation shall be passed as soon as possible. It must make provision for the election of Industrial Workmen's and Employee's Councils, which will be expected to collaborate on an equal footing in the regulation of labor conditions as a whole. Further provision must be made for district labor councils and a Reich labor council, which, in conjunction with the representatives of all other producers, are to give their opinion as experts before any law is promulgated concerning economic and social questions. They may themselves suggest laws of this kind. The provisions outlined shall be included in the Constitution of the German Republic.

Article 165 of the constitution did then incorporate the provisions of this joint resolution, but nothing was done to carry out the promise except for the 1920 law establishing the works councils.*

4. The relation between the Reich and the various states was fixed by an agreement of 26 January 1919. The dream of German unification was abandoned, as was Hugo Preuss's demand for the dismemberment of Prussia as the first step in the unification of

* See pp. 406, 423 for a discussion of the works councils.

Germany. The federative principle was again made part of the constitution, though in a milder form than before.

5. Finally, all earlier agreements were blanketed by an understanding among the parties of the Weimar coalition: the Social Democrats, the Catholic Center, and the Democrats. This understanding included a joint decision to convene a national assembly as early as possible, to accept the existing status of the bureaucracy and of the churches, to safeguard the independence of the judiciary, and to distribute power among the various strata of the German people as later set forth in that section of the constitution devoted to the Fundamental Rights and Duties of the German People.

When it was finally adopted, the constitution was thus primarily a codification of agreements already made among different sociopolitical groupings, each of which had demanded and received some measure of recognition for its special interests.

3. THE SOCIAL FORCES

The main pillars of the pluralistic system were the Social Democratic party and the trade unions. They alone in post-war Germany could have swung the great masses of the people over to democracy; not only the workers but also the middle classes, the section of the population that suffered most from the process of monopolization.

Other strata reacted to the complex post-war and post-revolution situation exactly as one would have expected. The big estate owners pursued a reactionary policy in every field. Monopolistic industry hated and fought the trade unions and the political system that gave the unions their status. The army used every available means to strengthen chauvinistic nationalism in order to restore itself to its former greatness. The judiciary invariably sided with the right and the civil services supported counter-revolutionary movements. Yet the Social Democracy was unable to organize either the whole of the working class or the middle classes. It lost sections of the former and never won a real foothold with the latter. The Social Democrats lacked a consistent theory, competent leadership, and freedom of action. Unwittingly, they strengthened the monopolistic trends in German industry, and, placing complete reliance on formalistic legality, they were unable to root out the reactionary elements in the judiciary and civil service or limit the army to its proper constitutional role.

The strong man of the Social Democratic party, Otto Braun, Prussian prime minister until 20 June 1932 when he was deposed by the Hindenburg-Papen *coup d'état*, attributes the failure of the party and Hitler's successful seizure of power to a combination of Versailles and Moscow.[20] This defense is neither accurate nor particularly skilful. The Versailles Treaty naturally furnished excellent propaganda material against democracy in general and against the Social Democratic party in particular, and the Communist party unquestionably made inroads among Social Democrats. Neither was primarily responsible for the fall of the Republic, however. Besides, what if Versailles and Moscow had been the two major factors in the making of National Socialism? Would it not have been the task of a great democratic leadership to make the democracy work in spite of and against Moscow and Versailles? That the Social Democratic party failed remains the crucial fact, regardless of any official explanation. It failed because it did not see that the central problem was the imperialism of German monopoly capital, becoming ever more urgent with the continued growth of the process of monopolization. The more monopoly grew, the more incompatible it became with the political democracy.

One of Thorstein Veblen's many great contributions was to draw attention to those specific characteristics of German imperialism that arose from its position as a late-comer in the struggle for the world market.

The German captains of industry who came to take the discretional management in the new era were fortunate enough not to have matriculated from the training school of a county town based on a retail business in speculative real estate and political jobbery . . . They came under the selective test for fitness in the aggressive conduct of industrial enterprise . . . The country being at the same time in the main . . . not committed to antiquated sites and routes for its industrial plants, the men who exercised discretion were free to choose with an eye single to the mechanized expediency of locations . . . Having no obsolescent equipment and no out of date trade connections to cloud the issue, they were also free to take over the processes at their best and highest efficiency.[21]

The efficient and powerfully organized German system of our time was born under the stimulus of a series of factors brought into the forefront by the First World War. The inflation of the early '20s permitted unscrupulous entrepreneurs to build up giant economic empires at the expense of the middle and working classes. The prototype was the Stinnes empire and it is at least symbolic that Hugo Stinnes was the most inveterate enemy of democracy and of Rathenau's foreign policy. Foreign loans that flowed into Germany after 1924 gave German industry the liquid capital needed to rationalize and enlarge their plants. Even the huge social-welfare program promoted by the Social Democracy indirectly strengthened the centralization and concentration of industry, since big business could far more easily assume the burden than the small or middle entrepreneur. Trusts, combines, and cartels covered the whole economy with a network of authoritarian organizations. Employers' organizations controlled the labor market, and big business lobbies aimed at placing the legislative, administrative, and judicial machinery at the service of monopoly capital.

In Germany there was never anything like the popular anti-monopoly movement of the United States under Theodore Roosevelt and Woodrow Wilson. Industry and finance were of course firmly convinced that the cartel and trust represented the highest forms of economic organization. The independent middle class was not articulate in its opposition, except against department stores and chains. Though the middle class belonged to powerful pressure groups, like the Federal Union of German Industries,* big business leaders were invariably their spokesmen.

Labor was not at all hostile to the process of trustification. The Communists regarded monopoly as an inevitable stage in the development of capitalism and hence considered it futile to fight capital concentration rather than the system itself. Ironically enough, the policy of the reformist wing of the labor movement was not significantly different in effect.[22] The Social Democrats and the trade unions also regarded concentration as inevitable, and, they added, as a higher form of capitalist organization. Their leading theorist, Rudolf Hilferding, summarized the position at the party's 1927 convention: 'Organized capitalism means replacing free com-

* See pp. 236-7.

petition by the social principle of planned production. The task of the present Social Democratic generation is to invoke state aid in translating this economy, organized and directed by the capitalists, into an economy directed by the democratic state.' [23] By economic democracy, the Social Democratic party meant a larger share in controlling the monopolist organizations and better protection for the workers against the ill effects of concentration.

The largest trusts in German history were formed during the Weimar Republic. The merger in 1926 of four large steel companies in western Germany resulted in the formation of the *Vereinigte Stahlwerke* (the United Steel Works). The *Vereinigte Oberschlesische Hüttenwerke* (the United Upper Silesian Mills) was a similar combination among the steel industries of Upper Silesia. The *I. G. Farbenindustrie* (the German Dye Trust) arose in 1925 through the merger of the six largest corporations in this field, all of which had previously been combined in a pool. In 1930 the capital stock of the Dye Trust totaled 1,100,000,000 marks and the number of workers it employed reached 100,000.

At no time in the Republic (not even in the boom year of 1929) were the productive capacities of German industry fully, or even adequately, utilized.[24] The situation was worst in heavy industry, especially in coal and steel, the very fields that had furnished the industrial leadership during the empire and that still dominated the essential business organizations. With the great depression, the gap between actual production and capacity took on such dangerous proportions that governmental assistance became imperative. Cartels and tariffs were resorted to along with subsidies in the form of direct grants, loans, and low interest rates.[25] These measures helped but at the same time they intensified another threat. The framework of the German government was still a parliamentary democracy after all, and what if movements threatening the established monopolistic structure should arise within the mass organizations? As far back as November 1923, public pressure had forced the Stresemann cabinet to enact a cartel decree authorizing the government to dissolve cartels and to attack monopolistic positions generally.* Not once were these powers utilized, but the danger to privileges inherent in political democracy remained and obviously became more acute in times of great crisis.

* See pp. 261-3.

4. The Decline of Organized Labor

The whole process of rationalization, concentration, and bureaucratization had serious repercussions on the social structure. Certainly one of the most significant was the serious weakening of the power of the trade unions, best illustrated by the decline of the strike. The strike weapon has its greatest effectiveness in a period of comparatively free competition, for the individual employer's power of resistance is relatively low. It becomes more difficult to strike successfully as monopolies develop and the strength of employers' organizations grows, and still more so when monopolies reach the scale of international cartels, as in steel. Even stoppage of production on a nation-wide scale can be compensated by the cartel. These are rules of general application.

The pluralism of Weimar led to additional factors in Germany. Growing state intervention in business enterprises gave labor disputes the taint of strikes against the state, while governmental regulation led many workers to consider it unnecessary to join unions. The unions for their part were not eager to fight a state in which they had so much at stake. Above all, monopoly was making major —and for the unions deleterious—changes in the social stratification. The increasing percentage of unskilled and semi-skilled workers (and particularly of women workers); the steady increase in foremen and supervisory personnel; the rise in the number of salaried employees in office positions and in the growing distribution apparatus, many organized in non-socialist unions with a middle-class ideology [26]—all these factors weakened the trade-union movement. The great crisis made matters worse, first because of the tremendous decline in production and the creation of large masses of unemployed, and secondly because the accompanying political tension tended to make every strike a political strike,* which the trade unions flatly opposed because of their theories of revisionism and 'economic democracy.'

The close collaboration between the Social Democracy and the trade unions on the one hand and the state on the other led to a steady process of bureaucratization within the labor movement. This development and the almost exclusive concentration on social re-

* On strikes, see pp. 411-12.

form rendered the Social Democratic party quite unattractive to the younger generation. The distribution of party membership, according to length of membership and by age group, is very revealing.

Length of Membership	Per Cent	Age Group	Per Cent
5 years and under	46.56	25 years and under	7.82
6 years to 10	16.26	26 years to 30	10.34
11 years to 15	16.52	31 years to 40	26.47
16 years and over	20.66	41 years to 50	27.26
	100.00	51 years to 60	19.57
		61 years or over	8.54
			100.00 [27]

What little freedom of action Social Democracy retained was further restricted by the Communist party. Except for the revolutionary days of 1918 and 1919 and the heyday of inflation and foreign occupation reaching a peak in July 1923, the German Communist party was not a directly decisive political force. At one time it sought to be a small sect of professional revolutionists patterned after the Bolshevik party of 1917; and at other times a 'revolutionary mass organization,' a kind of synthesis between the early Russian model and a structure such as the Social Democratic party. Its real significance lay in the fact that it did exert a very considerable indirect influence. A close study of the Communist party would probably reveal more about the characteristics of the German working class and of certain sections of the intelligentsia than would a study of the larger Socialist party and trade unions.

Both the Communists and the Socialists appealed primarily to the same social stratum: the working class. The very existence of a predominantly proletarian party, dedicated to communism and the dictatorship of the proletariat and stimulated by the magic picture of Soviet Russia and of the heroic deeds of the October Revolution, was a permanent threat to the Social Democratic party and to the controlling forces in the trade-union movement, especially in periods of depression and social unrest. That this threat was a real one though its magnitude was never constant is clear from the election and membership figures. True, the Communists failed to organize a majority of the working class, smash the Socialist party, or capture control of the trade unions. The reason was as much their inability to evaluate correctly the psychological factors and sociological trends operating among German workers as it was their inability to break the material interests and ideological links that bound the workers to the system of pluralistic democracy developed by reformism. Nevertheless, the reformist policy was always wavering simply because of the threat that the workers might desert the reformist organizations and go over to the Communist party. An excellent example is offered by the Social Democratic party's hesitating tolerance of the Brüning cabinet (1930-32) as compared with its definite opposition to the Papen and Schleicher cabinets (1932). The Communist party had attacked all three as fascist dictatorships.

Reactionaries found in the Communist party a convenient scapegoat, not only in the attack against communists and Marxists but against all liberal and democratic groups. Democracy, liberalism, socialism, and communism were branches of the same tree to the National Socialists (and Italian Fascists). Every law aimed supposedly against both Communists and National Socialists was invariably enforced against the Socialist party and the entire left, but rarely against the right.

The policy of the Communist party itself was strikingly ambivalent. On the one hand, it gave the workers sufficient critical insight to see through the operations of the economic system and thus left them with little faith in the security promised by liberalism, democracy, and reformism. It opened their eyes quite early to the transitory and entirely fictitious character of the post-inflation boom. The fifth World Congress of the Comintern had declared on 9 June 1924 that capitalism was in a stage of acute crisis. Though this analysis was premature and the consequently 'leftist' tactics of the Communist party completely erroneous, it did prevent the complacency that developed among the Socialists, who saw in a boom financed by foreign loans the solution of all economic problems and who considered every Social Democratic mayor or city treasurer a first-rate financial wizard if he succeeded in securing a loan from the United States. Even at the very peak of the boom Communist leaders predicted that a severe depression was in store for the world and their party was thus immunized from the dangers of reformist optimism.

On the other hand, the creditable features of the Communist

analysis were more than balanced by the profoundly backward character of their policy and tactics: the spread of the leadership principle within the party and the destruction of party democracy, following the complete dependence on the policy of the Russian party; the strong prevalence of revolutionary syndicalist tactics; the 'National-Bolshevist line'; the doctrine of social fascism; the slogan of the *Volksrevolution;* and finally, the frequent changes in the party line.

The one other potential ally, the Catholic Center party, proved completely undependable. Under Erzberger and for a time under Josef Wirth, it had provided the most inspiring democratic leadership the Republic experienced. With the growth of reaction, however, the right wing became more and more predominant in the party, with Brüning as the exponent of the moderate conservatives and Papen of the reactionary section. Of the other parties, the Democratic party disappeared from the political scene, and numerous splinter groups tried to take its place as spokesman of the middle class. Houseowners, handicraftsmen, small peasants formed parties of their own; revaluators organized a political movement. They could all obtain some political expression because the system of proportional representation allowed every sectarian movement a voice and prevented the formation of solid majorities.

5. The Counter-Revolution

On the very day that the revolution broke out in 1918, the counter-revolutionary party began to organize. It tried many forms and devices, but soon learned that it could come to power only with the help of the state machine and never against it. The Kapp Putsch of 1920 and the Hitler Putsch of 1923 had proved this.

In the center of the counter-revolution stood the judiciary. Unlike administrative acts, which rest on considerations of convenience and expediency, judicial decisions rest on law, that is on right and wrong, and they always enjoy the limelight of publicity. Law is perhaps the most pernicious of all weapons in political struggles, precisely because of the halo that surrounds the concepts of right and justice. 'Right,' Hocking has said, 'is psychologically a claim whose infringement is met with a resentment deeper than the injury would satisfy, a resentment that may amount to passion for

which men will risk life and property as they would never do for
an expediency.' [28] When it becomes 'political,' justice breeds hatred
and despair among those it singles out for attack. Those whom it
favors, on the other hand, develop a profound contempt for the
very value of justice; they know that it can be purchased by the
powerful. As a device for strengthening one political group at the
expense of others, for eliminating enemies and assisting political
allies, law then threatens the fundamental convictions upon which
the tradition of our civilization rests.

The technical possibilities of perverting justice for political ends
are widespread in every legal system; in republican Germany, they
were as numerous as the paragraphs of the penal code.[29] Perhaps
the chief reason lay in the very nature of criminal trials, for, unlike
the American system, the proceedings were dominated not by counsel but by the presiding judge. The power of the judge, furthermore, was strengthened year after year. For political cases, the
favorite statutory provisions were those dealing with criminal libel
and espionage, the so-called Act for the Protection of the Republic,
and, above all, the high treason sections (80 and 81) of the penal
code. A comparative analysis of three *causes célèbres* will make it
amply clear that the Weimar criminal courts were part and parcel
of the anti-democratic camp.

After the downfall of the Bavarian Soviet Republic in 1919, the
courts handed down the following sentences:

> 407 persons, fortress imprisonment
> 1737 persons, prison
> 65 persons, imprisoned at hard labor

Every adherent of the Soviet Republic who had the slightest connection with the unsuccessful coup was sentenced.

The contrast with the judicial treatment of the 1920 right-wing
Kapp Putsch could not possibly have been more complete. Fifteen
months after the putsch, the Reich ministry of justice announced
officially on 21 May 1921 that a total of 705 charges of high treason
had been examined. Of them,

412 in the opinion of the courts came under the amnesty law of
4 August 1920, despite the fact that the statute specifically excluded
the putsch leaders from its provisions

108 had become obsolete because of death or other reasons
174 were not pressed
 11 were unfinished

Not one person had been punished. Nor do the statistics give the full picture. Of the eleven cases pending on 21 May 1921, only one ended in a sentence; former Police President von Jagow of Berlin received five years' honorary confinement. When the Prussian state withdrew Jagow's pension, the federal supreme court ordered it restored to him. The guiding spirit of the putsch, Dr. Kapp, died before trial. Of the other leaders, some like General von Lüttwitz and Majors Papst and Bischoff escaped; General Ludendorff was not prosecuted because the court chose to accept his alibi that he was present only by accident; General von Lettow-Forbeck, who had occupied a whole town for Kapp, was declared to have been not a leader but merely a follower.

The third significant illustration is the judicial handling of Hitler's abortive Munich putsch of 1923.[30] Hitler, Pöhner, Kriebel, and Weber received five years; Röhm, Frick, Brückner, Pernet, and Wagner one year and three months. Ludendorff once again was present only by accident and was released. Although section 9 of the Law for the Protection of the Republic clearly and unmistakably ordered the deportation of every alien convicted of high treason, the Munich People's Court exempted Hitler on the specious argument that, despite his Austrian citizenship, he considered himself a German.

It would be futile to relate in detail the history of political justice under the Weimar Republic.[31] A few more illustrations will suffice. The penal code created the crime of 'treason to the country' [32] to cover the betrayal of military and other secrets to foreign agents. The courts, however, promptly found a special political use for these provisions. After the Versailles Treaty forced Germany to disarm, the Reichswehr encouraged the formation of secret and illegal bodies of troops, the so-called 'black Reichswehr.' When liberals, pacifists, socialists, and communists denounced this violation of both international obligations and German law (for the treaty had become part of the German legal system), they were arrested and tried for treason to the country committed through the press. Thus did the courts protect the illegal and reactionary black

Reichswehr. Assassinations perpetrated by the black Reichswehr against alleged traitors within their ranks (the notorious Fehme murders), on the other hand, were either not prosecuted at all or were dealt with lightly.[31]

During the trials of National Socialists, the courts invariably became sounding boards for propaganda. When Hitler appeared as a witness at the trial of a group of National Socialist officers charged with high treason, he was allowed to deliver a two-hour harangue packed with insults against high government officials and threats against his enemies, without being arrested for contempt. The new techniques of justifying and publicizing National Socialism against the Weimar Republic were defended as steps designed to ward off the communist danger. National Socialism was the guardian of democracy, they shouted, and the courts were only too willing to forget the fundamental maxim of any democracy and of every state, that the coercive power must be a monopoly of the state through its army and police, that not even under the pretext of saving the state may a private group or individual take arms in its defense unless summoned to do so by the sovereign power or unless actual civil war has broken out.

In 1932 the police discovered a National Socialist plot in Hessen. A Dr. Best, now a high official in the regime, had worked out a careful plan for a *coup d'état* and documentary proof was available (the Boxheimer documents).[33] No action was taken. Dr. Best was believed when he stated that he intended to make use of his plan only in the event of a communist revolution.

It is impossible to escape the conclusion that political justice is the blackest page in the life of the German Republic. The judicial weapon was used by the reaction with steadily increasing intensity. Furthermore, this indictment extends to the entire record of the judiciary, and particularly to the change in legal thought and in the position of the judge that culminated in the new principle of judicial review of statutes (as a means of sabotaging social reforms). The power of the judges thereby grew at the expense of the parliament.*

The decline of parliaments represents a general trend in post-war Europe. In Germany it was accentuated by specifically German

* See also pp. 442, 446.

conditions, especially by the monarchist-nationalist tradition of the bureaucracy. Years before, Max Weber pointed out that sabotage of the power of parliament begins once such a body ceases to be just a 'social club.' [34] When deputies are elected from a progressive mass party and threaten to transform the legislature into an agency for profound social changes, anti-parliamentary trends invariably arise in one form or another. The formation of a cabinet becomes an exceedingly complicated and delicate task, for each party now represents a class, with interests and views of life separated from the others by sharp differences. For example, negotiations went on for four weeks among the Social Democratic, Catholic Center, Democratic, and German People's parties before the last fully constitutional government, the Müller cabinet, could be formed in May 1928. The political differences between the German People's party, representing business, and the Social Democratic party, representing the worker's party, were so deep that only a carefully worked out compromise could bring them together at all, while the Catholic Center was always at odds with the others because of its dissatisfaction over insufficient patronage.

So precarious a structure could not permit its delicate balances to be upset too easily and it became necessary to modify whatever parliamentary principles might tip the scales. Criticism of the governing parties had to be toned down, and the vote of censure was actually used on but two occasions. When no agreement could be reached among the parties, 'cabinets of experts' were set up (like the famous Cuno cabinet in 1923), allegedly standing above the political parties and their strife. This travesty on parliamentary democracy became the ideal of the reactionaries, for it enabled them to conceal their anti-democratic policies beneath the cloak of the expert. The consequent impossibility of applying parliamentary controls to the operation of the cabinet was the first sign of the diminution of parliamentary strength.

The Reichstag's actual political power never corresponded to the wide powers assigned to it by the constitution. In part the explanation lies in the striking social and economic changes that had taken place in Germany, resulting in an enormous complexity of economic life. Growing regimentation in the economic sphere tended to shift the center of gravity from the legislature to the bureaucracy and growing interventionism made it technically impossible for the

Reichstag fully to control the administrative power or even to utilize its own legislative rights in full. Parliament had to delegate legislative power. Democracy might have survived none the less— but only if the democratic value system had been firmly rooted in the society, if the delegation of power had not been utilized to deprive minorities of their rights and as a shield behind which anti-democratic forces carried on the work of establishing a bureaucratic dictatorship.

It would be wrong to assume that the decline of parliamentary legislative power was merely an outcome of the last, pre-fascist, period of the German Republic, say from 1930 to 1933. The Reichstag was never too eager to retain the exclusive right of legislation, and from the very beginning of the Republic three competing types of legislation developed side by side. As early as 1919, the Reichstag voluntarily abandoned its supremacy in the legislative field by passing an enabling act that gave sweeping delegations of power to the cabinet, that is, to the ministerial bureaucracy. Similar measures were enacted in 1920, 1921, 1923, and 1926.

The enabling act of 13 October 1923, to cite but one example, empowered the cabinet to 'enact such measures as it deems advisable and urgent in the financial, economic and social spheres,' and the following measures were promulgated under this authority: a decree relative to the shutting down of plants, the creation of the Deutsche Rentenbank, currency regulation, modifications in the income tax law, a decree introducing control of cartels and monopolies. In the five years from 1920 through 1924, 450 cabinet decrees were issued as compared with 700 parliamentary statutes. The legislative power of the cabinet thus had its beginning practically with the birth of the German parliamentary system.

The second index of parliamentary decline is to be found in the character of the statute itself. The complexity of the legislative set-up led the Reichstag to lay down only vague blanket principles and to give the cabinet the power of application and execution.

The third and final step was the presidential emergency decree, based on article 48 of the constitution. While the Reichstag did have the constitutional right to repeal such emergency legislation, that was small consolation, since the right was more apparent than real. Once measures are enacted, they affect social and economic life deeply, and though parliament may have found it easy to abolish an emergency decree (the lowering of the cartel prices and of wages, for example), it could not so easily pass a substitute measure. This consideration played some part in determining the attitude of the Reichstag to the Brüning decrees of 1930 introducing profound changes into the economic and social structure of the nation. Mere repeal would have disrupted the flow of national life, while a substitute was impossible to achieve because of the antagonisms among the different groups in parliament. As a matter of fact, much as the parties may have decried the delegation of legislative power to the president and the bureaucracy, they were often quite happy to be rid of the responsibility.

The keystone of any parliamentary system is the right of the legislature to control the budget, and this collapsed during the Weimar Republic. The constitution had restricted the Reichstag somewhat by forbidding it to increase expenditures once they were proposed by the cabinet, except with the consent of the federal council. Apart from this limitation, however, all the necessary safeguards of the budgetary rights of parliament had apparently been written into the budget law (*Reichshaushaltsordnung*) of 31 December 1922 and into articles 85, 86, and 87 of the constitution. But enough loopholes remained for the bureaucracy to encroach steadily. The matter of auditing and accounting was taken away from the Reichstag entirely and transferred to the *Rechnungshof für das Deutsche Reich,* an administrative body independent of both cabinet and parliament, to which no member of parliament could belong. Finally, the minister of finance occupied so strong a position in relation to his colleagues that he could veto any minor expenditure alone, and he and the chancellor together could veto other expenditures even against a majority decision of the whole cabinet. Ultimately the president of the Reich enacted the budget by emergency decrees, against the advice of constitutional lawyers.

Once again we find in Germany only the specific working out of a general trend. Parliament's budgetary rights always tend to decline in interventionist states, as the English example shows. Fixed charges increase at the expense of charges for supplies. Where there is a huge permanent bureaucracy and increasing state activity in many economic and social fields, expenditures become fixed and permanent, and, in fact, fall outside the jurisdiction of the parliament. In Germany, furthermore, only the income and expenditure of the Reich proper were recorded in the budget. The financial operations of the independent federally owned corporations, whether organized under public or private law, lay outside budgetary control. The post and railways, mines, and factories owned by the Reich were not dependent on the budget. Only their balances appeared, either as income to the Reich or as a subsidy demanded from it.

This entire trend was in full conformity with the wishes of German industry. Their major lobbying organization, the Federal Union of German Industry, demanded ever greater restrictions upon the Reichstag's budget rights. The German People's party took over their proposals in its platform. They insisted that all expenditures should have the approval of the cabinet and that the auditing body, the *Rechnungshof*, should be given a decisive position in determining whether or not the budget was to be accepted. The reason for this attempt to sabotage the budget rights of the Reichstag was frankly stated by Dr. Popitz, the foremost expert on public finance in the federal ministry of finance. Universal suffrage, he said, had brought into the Reichstag the strata of society that do not pay high income taxes and surtaxes.[35]

The decline of parliamentary supremacy accrued to the benefit of the president and hence to the ministerial bureaucracy. Following the American model, the Weimar constitution provided for popular presidential election. The similarity between the two constitutional systems ended right there, however. In the United States the president is the independent head of the executive branch of the government, whereas the German president's orders had to be countersigned by the appropriate cabinet minister or by the chancellor, who assumed political responsibility for presidential acts and pronouncements. The German president was relatively free, nevertheless. For one thing, the popular election gave him a position of some independence from the various parties. He could appoint the chancellor and ministers at his discretion; he was not bound by any constitutional custom, such as the English tradition of calling upon the leader of the victorious party. Presidents Ebert and von Hindenburg both insisted on making their selections freely and independently. The president's right to dissolve parliament gave him further political power. The provision that he could not do so twice for the same reason was easily evaded.

Nevertheless the president could not be termed the 'guardian of the constitution,' as the anti-democratic theorists would have it. He did not represent democracy and was far from being the neutral head of the state, standing above the squabbles of parties and special interests. Throughout the Weimar Republic and especially under Hindenburg, the presidency was eminently partisan. Political groups arranged for and financed the president's election; he remained dependent on partisan groups surrounding and advising him. He had preferences and a political alignment, which he attempted to carry far beyond constitutional limits. When Communists and Socialists tried to expropriate the princely houses through a popular initiative, President von Hindenburg condemned the attempt in an open letter (22 May 1926) for which he did not even bother to get the signature of the chancellor, insisting that such a letter was his private affair. On the occasion of Brüning's second appointment, Hindenburg demanded that two of his conservative friends (Treviranus and Schiele) be included in the cabinet. Then he betrayed them.

Ebert's authority had been limited. Being a Socialist, he could not command the respect due the head of the Republic. But Hindenburg was the Field Marshal, the great soldier, the old man. That was different, especially after Brüning had created a veritable Hindenburg myth to assure the former's re-election in 1932. Hindenburg's strength lay predominantly in his close connections with the army and large estate owners of East Prussia. From 1930 on, when the presence of 107 National Socialist deputies made ordinary parliamentary legislation well-nigh impossible, he became the sole legislator, using the emergency powers of article 48 of the constitution.[86]

The Reichswehr, reduced to 100,000 men by the Versailles Treaty, continued to be the stronghold of conservatism and nationalism. With army careers now closed to many and promotion slow, there is little wonder that the officers' corps became militantly anti-democratic, despising parliamentarianism because it pried too closely into the secrets of army expenditure, and detesting the Socialists because they had accepted the Versailles Treaty and the destruction of the supremacy of German militarism. Whenever a political crisis arose, the army invariably sided with the anti-democratic elements. Hitler himself was a product of the army, which had made use of him as far back as 1918 and 1919 as a speaker and propaganda officer. None of this is surprising. What is surprising is that the democratic apparatus tolerated the situation.

The Reichswehr ministers, the inevitable Gessler and the more loyally democratic General Groener, were in an extremely ambiguous constitutional position. As cabinet ministers they were subject to parliamentary control and responsibility, but as subordinates of the president, the commander-in-chief, they were free from parliamentary control. The contradiction was easily solved in practice: the Reichswehr ministers spoke for the army and against the Reichstag. In fact, so completely did they identify themselves with the army bureaucracy that parliamentary control over the army became virtually non-existent.

6. The Collapse of the Democracy

The Social Democracy and the trade unions were completely helpless against the many-sided attacks on the Weimar democracy. Moderate attempts were made to spread the idea of an economic democracy, but this new ideology proved even less attractive than the old Socialist program. Salaried employees remained aloof; the civil-service organization affiliated with the Socialist trade unions declined in membership from 420,000 in 1922 to 172,000 in 1930, while the so-called neutral, but in fact Nationalistic, civil-service body organized 1,043,000 members in 1930, primarily from the middle and lower ranks. The significance of these figures is obvious.

The Social Democratic party was trapped in contradictions. Though it still claimed to be a Marxian party, its policy had long been one of pure gradualism. It never mustered the courage to drop one or the other, traditional ideology or reformist policy. A radical break with tradition and the abandonment of Marxism would have delivered thousands of adherents into the Communist camp. To have abandoned gradualism for a revolutionary policy, on the other hand, would have required cutting the many links binding the party to the existing state. The Socialists therefore retained this ambiguous position and they could not create a democratic consciousness. The Weimar constitution, attacked on the right by Nationalists, National Socialists, and reactionary liberals, and on the left by the Communists, remained merely a transitory phenomenon for the Social Democrats, a first step to a greater and better future. And a transitory scheme cannot arouse much enthusiasm.*

Even before the beginning of the great depression, therefore, the ideological, economic, social, and political systems were no longer functioning properly. Whatever appearance of successful operation they may have given was based primarily on toleration by the anti-democratic forces and on the fictitious prosperity made possible by foreign loans. The depression uncovered and deepened the petrification of the traditional social and political structure. The social contracts on which that structure was founded broke down. The Democratic party disappeared; the Catholic Center shifted to the right; and the Social Democrats and Communists devoted far more energy to fighting each other than to the struggle against the growing threat of National Socialism. The National Socialist party in turn heaped abuse upon the Social Democrats. They coined the epithet, November Criminals: a party of corruptionists and pacifists responsible for the defeat in 1918, for the Versailles Treaty, for the inflation.

The output of German industry had dropped sharply. Unemployment was rising: [37] six million were registered in January 1932, and there were perhaps two million more of the so-called invisible unemployed. Only a small fraction received unemployment insurance and an ever larger proportion received no support at all. The unemployed youth became a special problem in themselves. There were hundreds of thousands who had never held jobs. Unemployment became a status, and, in a society where success is paramount, a stigma. Peasants revolted in the north while large estate owners cried for financial assistance. Small businessmen and craftsmen faced destruction. Houseowners could not collect their rents. Banks crashed and were taken over by the federal government. Even the stronghold of industrial reaction, the United Steel Trust, was near collapse and its shares were purchased by the federal government at prices far above the market quotation. The budget situation became precarious. The reactionaries refused to support a large-scale works program lest it revive the declining power of the trade unions, whose funds were dwindling and whose membership was declining.

* See also pp. 45-6.

The situation was desperate and called for desperate measures. The Social Democratic party could choose either the road of political revolution through a united front with the Communists under Socialist leadership, or co-operation with the semi-dictatorships of Brüning, Papen, and Schleicher in an attempt to ward off the greater danger, Hitler. There was no other choice. The Social Democratic party was faced with the most difficult decision in its history. Together with the trade unions, it decided to tolerate the Brüning government when 107 National Socialist deputies entered the Reichstag in September 1930 and made a parliamentary majority impossible. Toleration meant neither open support nor open attack. The policy was justified ideologically in the key address of Fritz Tarnow, deputy and head of the Woodworker's Union, at the last party convention (1931):

Do we stand . . . at the sick-bed of capitalism merely as the diagnostician, or also as the doctor who seeks to cure? Or as joyous heirs, who can hardly wait for the end and would even like to help it along with poison? . . . It seems to me that we are condemned both to be the doctor who earnestly seeks to cure and at the same time to retain the feeling that we are the heirs, who would prefer to take over the entire heritage of the capitalist system today rather than tomorrow.[88]

This was the policy of a man who is hounded by his enemies but refuses either to accept annihilation or to strike back, and invents excuse after excuse to justify his inactivity.

Continuing the policy of the lesser evil, the party supported the re-election of Hindenburg in April 1932.

CANDIDATE	FIRST BALLOT		SECOND BALLOT	
	VOTES	PER CENT	VOTES	PER CENT
Düsterberg (Stahlhelm)	2,577,729	6.8	. . . .	. . .
Hindenburg	18,657,497	49.6	19,359,983	53
Hitler	11,339,446	30.1	13,418,547	36.8
Thaelmann	4,983,341	13.2	3,706,759	10.2

Hindenburg promptly re-paid his debt by staging the *coup d'état* of 20 June 1932, replacing the legally elected Prussian government of Otto Braun by his courtier, Papen. All that the Social Democratic party did in opposition was to appeal to the Constitutional Court, which rendered a compromise verdict that did not touch the political situation. Papen remained as Reich commissioner for Prussia. The Social Democratic party became completely demoralized; the last hope of resistance against the National Socialists seemed to have vanished.

The Communists had been no less optimistic than the Socialists, but for different reasons. 'We insist soberly and seriously,' said Thaelmann, 'that the 14th of September was, so to speak, Hitler's best day; that no better will follow but rather worse.' [39] They looked forward to a social revolution in the immediate future, leading to the dictatorship of the proletariat.

In the November elections of 1932 the National Socialists lost 34 seats. The Social Democrats, thinking only in parliamentary terms, were jubilant: National Socialism was defeated. Rudolf Hilferding, their leading theorist and editor of the party journal, *Die Gesellschaft*, published an article in the January 1933 issue entitled 'Between Two Decisions.' He argued that National Socialism was blocked by parliamentary legality (Malaparte's idea).* Hilferding became bold. He refused collaboration with Schleicher, Hitler's immediate predecessor, and he rejected the united front with the Communist party. The primary aim of the Socialists, he said, was the fight against communism. He ridiculed Hitler's attempt to get dictatorial power from President von Hindenburg: 'To demand the results of a revolution without revolution—this political construction could arise only in the brain of a German politician.' [40] Hilferding forgot that the Italian politician Mussolini had held the very same idea and had carried it out successfully.

Only a few days after the publication of Hilferding's article, Hitler took power. On 4 January 1933 the Cologne banker Kurt von Schroeder, whose name looms large in National Socialist history, arranged the conference between Papen and Hitler that brought about a reconciliation between the old reactionary groups and the new counter-revolutionary movement, and paved the way for Hitler's appointment as chancellor on 30 January. It was the tragedy of the Social Democratic party and trade unions to have had as leaders men with high intellectual qualities but completely devoid of any feeling for the condition of the masses and without any insight into the great social transformations of the post-war period.

* See p. 41.

The National Socialist German Workers Party was without an ideology, composed of the most diverse social strata but never hesitating to take in the dregs of every section, supported by the army, the judiciary, and parts of the civil service, financed by industry, utilizing the anti-capitalist sentiments of the masses and yet careful never to estrange the influential moneyed groups. Terror and propaganda seized upon the weak spots in the Weimar democracy; and from 1930 to 1933 Weimar was merely one large weak spot.

'The man with power,' said Woodrow Wilson in his Kansas address of 6 May 1911, 'but without conscience, could, with an eloquent tongue, if he cared for nothing but his own power, put this whole country into a flame, because this whole country believes that something is wrong, and is eager to follow those who profess to be able to lead it away from its difficulties.' [41]

7. A Tentative Summary

Every social system must somehow satisfy the primary needs of the people. The imperial system succeeded to the extent and so long as it was able to expand. A successful policy of war and imperialist expansion had reconciled large sections of the population to the semi-absolutism. In the face of the material advantages gained, the anomalous character of the political structure was not decisive. The army, the bureaucracy, industry, and the big agrarians ruled. The divine-right theory—the official political doctrine—merely veiled their rule and it was not taken seriously. The imperial rule was in fact not absolutistic, for it was bound by law, proud of its *Rechtsstaat* theory. It lost out and abdicated when its expansionist policy was checked.

The Weimar democracy proceeded in a different direction. It had to rebuild an impoverished and exhausted country in which class antagonisms had become polarized. It attempted to merge three elements: the heritage of the past (especially the civil service), parliamentary democracy modeled after Western European and American patterns, and a pluralistic collectivism, the incorporation of the powerful social and economic organizations directly into the political system. What it actually produced, however, were sharpened social antagonisms, the breakdown of voluntary collaboration, the destruction of parliamentary institutions, the suspension of political liberties, the growth of a ruling bureaucracy, and the renaissance of the army as a decisive political factor.

Why?

In an impoverished, yet highly industrialized, country, pluralism could work only under the following different conditions. In the first place, it could rebuild Germany with foreign assistance, expanding its markets by peaceful means to the level of its high industrial capacity. The Weimar Republic's foreign policy tended in this direction. By joining the concert of the Western European powers the Weimar government hoped to obtain concessions. The attempt failed. It was supported neither by German industry and large landowners nor by the Western powers. The year 1932 found Germany in a catastrophic political, economic, and social crisis.

The system could also operate if the ruling groups made concessions voluntarily or under compulsion by the state. That would have led to a better life for the mass of the German workers and security for the middle classes at the expense of the profits and power of big business. German industry was decidedly not amenable, however, and the state sided with it more and more.

The third possibility was the transformation into a socialist state, and that had become completely unrealistic in 1932 since the Social Democratic party was socialist only in name.

The crisis of 1932 demonstrated that political democracy alone without a fuller utilization of the potentialities inherent in Germany's industrial system, that is, without the abolition of unemployment and an improvement in living standards, remained a hollow shell.

The fourth choice was the return to imperialist expansion. Imperialist ventures could not be organized within the traditional democratic form, however, for there would have been too serious an opposition. Nor could it take the form of restoration of the monarchy. An industrial society that has passed through a democratic phase cannot exclude the masses from consideration. Expansionism therefore took the form of National Socialism, a totalitarian dictatorship that has been able to transform some of its victims into supporters and to organize the entire country into an armed camp under iron discipline.

PART ONE

THE POLITICAL PATTERN OF NATIONAL SOCIALISM

Introductory Remarks on the Value of National Socialist Ideology

THE ideology of National Socialism offers the best clue to its ultimate aims. It is neither very pleasant nor simple to study. When we read Plato and Aristotle, Thomas Aquinas and Marsilius of Padua, Hobbes and Rousseau, Kant and Hegel, we are fascinated as much by the inner beauty of their thinking, by their consistency and elegance, as by the way their doctrines fit in with socio-political realities. The philosophical and sociological analyses go hand in hand. National Socialist ideology is devoid of any inner beauty. The style of its living writers is abominable, the constructions confused, the consistency nil. Every pronouncement springs from the immediate situation and is abandoned as soon as the situation changes.

The immediate and opportunistic connection between National Socialist doctrine and reality makes a detailed study of the ideology essential. Ordinarily, we must reject the notion that sociology can determine the truth or falsity of a system of ideas by examining its social origin or by associating it with a certain class in society. But in the case of National Socialist ideology, we must rely on sociological methods. There is no other way of getting at the truth, least of all from the explicit statements of the National Socialist leaders.

World domination may not be the conscious aim of National Socialism, but economic and social antagonisms will drive it to extend its realm far beyond Europe. The doctrinal elements of the ideology make this conclusion inevitable, despite all disclaimers, even despite the fact that Hitler himself denounced as 'a stupid and infamous lie' a widely publicized speech by Minister of Agriculture Darré that proclaimed world domination as the National Socialist aim. (See his New Year's message to the German people as printed in the *Frankfurter Zeitung*, 1 January 1941.) To prove the charge, we must analyze each doctrinal element in turn.

Behind a mass of irrelevant jargon, banalities, distortions, and half truths, we can discern the relevant and decisive central theme of the ideology: that all traditional doctrines and values must be rejected, whether they stem from French rationalism or German idealism, from English empiricism or American pragmatism, whether liberal or absolutist, democratic or socialist.* They are all hostile to the fundamental goal of National Socialism: the resolution by imperialistic war of the discrepancy between the potentialities of Germany's industrial apparatus and the actuality that existed and continues to exist.

The values and concepts that National Socialism has negated are the philosophical, legal, sociological, and economic concepts with which we operate daily and which characterize our society. Many of them, such as the notion of state sovereignty, which is often thought to be reactionary, reveal their progressive character under analysis and thereby demonstrate their incompatibility with National Socialism. Our study of National Socialist ideology will take up each element in turn and show its actual operation within the political, sociological, juristic, and economic structure of the regime. The categories that will be developed do not necessarily correspond to definite stages in the growth of National Socialist ideology, although some of them coincide.

In its external form, as propaganda, totalitarian ideology differs from democratic ideologies not only because it is single and exclusive, but because it is fused with terror. In the democratic system, an ideology is one among many. In fact, the term 'ideology' itself implies a competitive relation among several thought structures in society. The National Socialist doctrine may be called an 'ideology' only because it competes in the world market of ideas, as it were, with other ideologies, though it is, of course, sovereign and single in the domestic market. The democratic ideology is successful if it can persuade or attract; the National Socialist ideology persuades through its use of terror. To be sure, in democracies, too, material benefits accrue to those who accept the prevailing ideologies, and those who do not suffer occasional violence, but the democratic system at least allows for criticism of such alliances and offers an opportunity for competing elements and forces.

National Socialism has no theory of society as we understand it, no consistent picture of its operation, structure, and development. It has certain aims to carry through and adjusts its ideological pro-

* See p. 459.

nouncements to a series of ever-changing goals. This absence of a basic theory is one difference between National Socialism and Bolshevism. The National Socialist ideology is constantly shifting. It has certain magical beliefs—leadership adoration, the supremacy of the master race—but its ideology is not laid down in a series of categorical and dogmatic pronouncements.

Moreover, changes in its ideology permit us to determine whether or not National Socialism has succeeded in gaining the sympathy of the German people. For, where there is an immediate connection between the declared ideology and the political reality, the shifts in doctrinal formulation must be occasioned by the fact that specific strata of the German population have not been attracted by the earlier doctrine.

I

THE TOTALITARIAN STATE

1. The Techniques of Anti-Democratic Constitutional Thought

The failure of the Kapp putsch in 1920 and of the 1923 Munich putsch taught the National Socialists that in our world the *coup d'état* is not the proper technique for seizing political power. Curzio Malaparte wrote a widely read book in defense of the *coup d'état.*[1] He argued that the way to bring about a successful revolution is for a small group of shock troops and highly trained conspirators to seize the key places in the public services. As proof, he cited the Russian Revolution of 1917, the Kapp putsch, the Fascist seizure of power in Italy, the *coups* of Pilsudski in Poland and Primo de Rivera in Spain. His choice of examples could hardly have been worse. The success of the Bolshevik revolution may be attributed in part to Malapartian practices, but even more to the fact that the Kerensky government was weak and Russian society was in full disintegration. The Kapp putsch was a failure; Mussolini's march on Rome, a myth. Related and equally invalid is the military theory that a highly skilled army, equipped with the most advanced weapons, is necessarily superior to a large mass army. The German victories in the present war have been the result of the immense military superiority of a mass army combined with highly mechanized shock-troop divisions—and also of the moral decomposition of their opponents.

Unfortunately for Malaparte, in 1932 he predicted that Hitler, whom he labelled 'a would-be leader,' 'merely a caricature of Mussolini,' would never come to power because he relied exclusively on opportunist parliamentary methods. The National Socialists were right, of course, and Malaparte wrong. In his commemoration speech of 8 November 1935, Hitler himself admitted the error of his early putsch: 'Fate has meant well for us—It did not let an action succeed which, had it succeeded, must finally have foundered

41

because of the inner immaturity of the movement and its faulty organizational and spiritual foundations. We know this today. Then, we acted with courage and manhood. Providence, however, acted with wisdom.'

After the Munich fiasco, the National Socialist party became 'legal.' It solemnly promised not to incite to high treason or to a revolutionary overthrow of the constitution. As a witness at a trial of National Socialist Reichswehr officers charged with high treason, Hitler on 25 September 1930 took his famous 'purity oath.' The Storm Troops (S. A.) became harmless sport and parade bodies. Few political parties insisted more loudly than the National Socialists on the preservation of civil liberties and democratic equality.

Every device of parliamentary democracy, every liberal institution, legal provision, social and political tie became a weapon against liberalism and democracy; every opportunity was taken to heap abuse on the inefficiency of the Weimar Republic. Following is a modest selection of charges against liberalism and democracy drawn solely from the writings of National Socialist professors (the invective of party orators can be left to the imagination):

The liberal state is 'neutral and negative,' mere machinery; to use Lassalle's phrase, it is 'a night watchman's state.' Therefore it is 'without substance'—unable to reach decision or to determine what is good or bad, just or unjust. The idea of freedom has degenerated to the point of anarchy. Disintegration and materialism are rampant. And the Marxist ideal, which is only a variation of liberalism, is no better.

Democracy is the rule of the 'unorganized mass,' an aggregate of Robinson Crusoes rather than of people. Its principle is 'nose-counting,' and its parliaments, dominated by private groups, are arenas of brute struggles for power. The law serves only private interests; the judge is nothing but a machine. Liberalism and law are in fact mutually exclusive, though they have been temporarily allied through expediency. In sum, liberalism and democracy are monsters, 'negative' Leviathans, one might say, so strong that they have been able to corrupt the racial institutions of the Germanic heritage.

It would be wrong, however, to assume that during the 'twenties and early 'thirties National Socialism simply set out to prove democracy worthless or to propose a substitute: monarchy or dictatorship or anything else. Quite the contrary, it paraded as the salvation of democracy. Carl Schmitt, the ideologist of this sham, developed it as follows.

Weimar democracy contains two elements, one democratic and the other liberal (*rechtsstaatlich*), not to be confused with each other. Democracy applies the principle that there is an identity between the rulers and the ruled. Equality is its substance, not liberty. Equality can exist only within a given community, and the basis of both community and equality may vary. We may have equality derived from the physical or moral homogeneity of the community, like the virtue Montesquieu called the principle of a republic. Or it may stem from a religious solidarity, such as lay at the base of the democratic ideology of the Levellers in the Puritan revolution. Ever since the French Revolution, the basis has been national homogeneity. Rousseau, who formulated this notion and built upon it the only truly democratic system, held that national homogeneity meant unanimity.[2] His conception of the general will therefore does not admit political parties, for parties, as their very name indicates, express only partial wills. A truly democratic system will express the complete identity between the rulers and the ruled.[3]

Parliamentarianism is not identical with democracy but is merely one of its historical forms. The basic principles of parliamentarianism are public debate, separation of powers, and the universality of law. Debate requires the agencies of political power to engage in discussion as a means of arriving at the truth. Public debate allows the body of citizens to check up on and control their agents. But, says Schmitt, practice no longer conforms to theory. Parliamentary discussion is today nothing more than a device for registering decisions previously reached on the outside. Every deputy is bound by rigid party discipline. He would not dare let himself be swayed by an opponent. The debate is a fraud. The speeches are made for the record. Since the major decisions are reached in secret committees or in informal negotiations among the controlling groups, even the publicity of the debate is a sham.

The principle of the separation of powers restricts parliament to legislation—in other words, to the enactment of abstract general rules. Again practice has run away from the theory. Parliament is no longer exclusively a legislator; it is even more an administrator, and an inefficient one at that. In the era of monopoly capitalism, general laws have become devices to conceal individual decisions.

The homogeneity of the people is almost nonexistent. The pluralistic system has substituted many loyalties for the one basic loyalty to the nation. The polycracy, that is, the conjunct body of independent public agencies (social-insurance institutions, control boards, publicly owned corporations, and so forth), subject to no parliamentary supervision, has destroyed the unity of political decisions. It has torn many of the vital limbs from the body politic. The federative principle, by protecting particularist interests, has made a mockery of the idea of the sovereignty of the one people.

Civil liberties and inalienable rights, finally, negate democracy. Rousseau had already indicated this point, at least by implication; for the social contract theory means that the citizen surrendered his rights upon entering into the contract. The traditional personal and political liberties were a product of competitive capitalism. That era has now passed and capitalism has entered a phase of interventionist, monopoly capitalism and collectivism. Since freedom of trade and freedom of contract have disappeared, their corollaries, freedom of speech and assembly, freedom of press and of trade-union organization, have become meaningless.[4]

By an interesting paradox, this anti-democratic analysis, designed to minimize the meaning of fundamental rights, enormously over-evaluated them at the same time, transforming them into bulwarks for the defense of private property against state encroachment, and assigning them a constitutional function completely alien to the German tradition.[5] Innumerable books, pamphlets, and speeches denounced parliamentary institutions for their inefficiency, their undemocratic character, their corruptibility. Bureaucratic ideology was the immediate beneficiary. The judiciary was raised to a supreme political function and, for all the attack on the pluralistic, polycratic, and federative causes of disunion, any criticism of the independent political status enjoyed by the army was scrupulously avoided. Fundamental rights were denounced as incompatible with democratic philosophy, while the fundamental rights of property and equality were given an extent and depth they never had before.

The logical outcome of this deliberate manœuvre was a demand for a strong government, culminating in the slogan, 'All power to the president.' The president, it was claimed, is a truly democratic institution: he is elected by the people. The only true *pouvoir neutre et intermédiaire*, he should have the legislative and executive powers concentrated in his hands. The president's neutrality is not mere lack of color, but true objectivity above the petty quarrels of the numerous interests, public agencies, and states.[6]

The underlying sentiment that came forth was thus the decisionism of Carl Schmitt,[7] the demand for action instead of deliberation, for decision instead of evaluation.

Decisionism rests on a peculiar, yet highly attractive, doctrine of the nature of politics, strongly resembling the revolutionary syndicalism of Georges Sorel. Politics, Schmitt declared, is the relation of friend to foe. The foe is in the last resort anyone who must be exterminated physically. Every human relation can become a political one in this sense, for every opponent can become a foe subject to physical extermination. The New Testament's command that one should love even one's enemies refers only to the private foe, the *inimicus*, not to the public foe, the *hostis*.[8] This is a doctrine of brute force in its most striking form, one that sets itself against every aspect and act of liberal democracy and against our whole traditional conception of the governance of law.

Opposing theories were either without influence or else they played into the hands of the anti-democratic thesis. The communists, for example, denounced the constitution as a veil for capitalist exploitation and as the political superstructure of a monopoly capitalist economy. As a matter of fact, the Weimar constitution concealed nothing. Its compromise character, the bargaining of the interests, the independent status of the Reichswehr bureaucracy, the openly political role of the judiciary were all clearly discernible. Constitutional theory and practice disclosed the weakness of the democratic forces and the strength of their opponents. By the same token, they revealed that the Weimar constitution owed its existence far more to the tolerance of its enemies than to the strength of its supporters. The lack of any accepted constitutional doctrine, even if it had been merely a camouflage and pure fiction, and the consequent public character of the fundamental antagonisms were precisely the factors that rendered the constitution transitory and prevented the formation of one solid loyalty.

Socialist constitutional theory failed to evolve a specifically socialist doctrine. It agreed with Carl Schmitt in condemning the Weimar constitution for its lack of decision.[9] It did not even grant the constitution a compromise quality, but maintained that the incompatible interests and positions stood side by side without any integration. Every constitution enacted at a turning point of history, the socialists reasoned, must state a program of action and evolve a new order of society. Since the Weimar constitution had no aims of its own, it admitted every conceivable value-system.

Their destructive criticism challenged the socialists to reformulate the value-system of the Weimar democracy. So they developed the doctrine of a social *Rechtsstaat* that combined the heritage of civil rights, legal and political equality with the requirements of collectivism.[10] Stressing constitutional provisions for socialization of industry and trade-union recognition, they demanded the establishment of an economic constitution that would provide for an equal share of labor representation. The social *Rechtsstaat* was thus the rationalization of labor's demand for an adequate share in the political life of the nation. As a political theory, it was admittedly transitory (along with the corresponding doctrine of economic democracy), for the social *Rechtsstaat* was conceived merely as the first step toward a fully socialized society. And it had as little effect as the rest of Social Democratic and trade-union policy.

Still another opponent of decisionism was the so-called Austrian school: the 'pure science of law.' State and law it declared to be identical provinces. There is but one law, the law of the state. Since every political phenomenon must be explained in terms of law, every political form is a *Rechtsstaat*, a state based upon law. Not even the most absolute dictatorship could avoid falling into this category, because the dictator's power can be conceived only as explicitly or implicitly delegated to him by a basic law that stands at the top of the legal system. The legal order is a hierarchy, a system of imputations running from the basic norm at the top to the individual contract and specific administrative act at the bottom. There is thus no categorical distinction between public and private law, between a natural and a legal person.[11]

The critical impact and debunking force of the Austrian school cannot be denied. Its insistence on the sole validity of positive law and on the complete ejection from the science of law of all moral considerations of a sociological or political character make it impossible to cover political demands with the cloak of law. At bottom, the theory is relativistic and even nihilistic; no wonder its founder and untiring exponent, Hans Kelsen, identified democracy with parliamentarianism and defined it merely as an organizational framework for reaching decisions without recourse to any universally accepted values.[12] This relativistic conception of democracy is precisely the ground for the decisionist and socialist attacks.

Though a debunking doctrine may be a useful tool in scientific analysis, it cannot provide the basis for political action. The pure science of law, furthermore, shares the defects of logical positivism and every other 'pure science': it is virginal in its innocence. By throwing out of account all relative problems of political and social power, it paves the way for decisionism, for the acceptance of political decisions no matter where they originate or what their content, so long as sufficient power stands behind them. The pure science of law has done as much as decisionism to undermine any universally acceptable value-system.

It was the liberals who represented in the legal field the great cultural tradition of Germany—profound historical knowledge, sharp and precise power of analytical thought, and a firm adherence to the values of German idealist philosophy. They attempted to bring the democratic structure into harmony with liberal guarantees. The Weimar system, supposedly the constitutional expression of this harmony, was the embodiment of their failure.

Little need be said of the conservative constitutional doctrines. Their dream of monarchical restoration shared with decisionism the longing for a strong state, united within and powerful without. The state was to be the highest moral value. As critics of the liberal democracy, the conservatives played directly into the hands of the anti-democratic movement and prepared the first stage of National Socialist ideology.

2. THE TOTALITARIAN STATE

The idea of the totalitarian state grew out of the demand that all power be concentrated in the hands of the president. Immediately after Hitler's accession to power, political theorists began to make much of the totalitarian idea as elaborated by the constitutional lawyers. All power was to be vested in the state; anything less was sabotage of the National Socialist revolution. The totalitarian state was described as an order of domination and a form of people's community. It was anti-democratic because democracy, with its notion of an identity between the ruler and the ruled, undermined the necessary authority of leadership. Leadership, the National Socialists declared, is not delegated by the people—'authority presupposes rank and is valid against the people's will because the people do not bestow but recognize it.' [13]

Hitler's accession to power gave rise to a vast literature re-examining the traditional forms of state and government. Distinctions were drawn between the *liberaler Rechtsstaat,* born in the French Revolution and embodied in the English constitution, and the *nationaler Rechtsstaat* first developed by Italian fascism and later victorious in National Socialist Germany. The latter was characterized as a state that reconciles justice with political necessity.[14] The essence of the National Socialist revolution was believed to lie in its revival and further development of the best conservative tradition (formerly exemplified by the rule of Frederick II of Prussia), a tradition that had been 'desecrated and degraded' by the liberals with their 'night watchman's state.' [15] For some theorists, Hegel's idea of the state was the model for National Socialism.

In order to avoid identification of the totalitarian state with the absolutisms of the seventeenth and eighteenth centuries, the theorists insisted further that the state was more than a mere system of coercion: it was a form of life of the racial *Volk*. Various types of totalitarian states were distinguished in order to mark off the National Socialist brand from the others, whether Italian or Russian.[16]

The totalitarian doctrine, it is important to recognize, was once espoused by the top party leadership. Goebbels declared that 'our party has always aspired to the totalitarian state . . . The goal of the revolution must be a totalitarian state pervading all spheres of public life.' [17] Frick, minister of the interior and a leading figure in the party, signed a circular letter on 11 July 1933, admonishing the federal regents 'to guard the state authority under all circumstances.' [18] Hitler addressed the S. A. leaders in a similar vein in Bad Reichenhall on 1 July 1933. The third phase of the revolution, he said, 'must be the establishment of the totality of the state, as we understand it; the National Socialist movement must make this state the bearer of its spiritual goods.' [19] At the 1933 Lawyers Conference, he exhorted his listeners 'to guard the authority of this totalitarian state.' [20] And again as late as 15 November 1934, Frick, speaking to army officers, stressed the need for absolute authority, for 'a strong government unhampered by individual persons, groups, classes, estates, parties, and parliament.' [21]

Such glorification of the state was abandoned a short time later (it is absent from *Mein Kampf*, by the way). Why was it stressed so heavily through 1934? Three factors appear to have been decisive. First, the political theorists and lawyers of the previous era had retained their positions of prominence in the matter of formulating ideology. These men looked upon the National Socialist revolution as a new edition of the imperial system, with its basis in the authority of the bureaucracy and the army. Now that it was back in the hands of reliable leaders, the German state would again embody the highest values. Italian fascism had developed a doctrine of the totalitarian state, and since the differences between the two had not yet manifested themselves, the natural attempt was made to tie the Italian doctrine in with the earlier German tradition.

A special twist given the totalitarian doctrine by Carl Schmitt, the most intelligent and reliable of all National Socialist constitutional lawyers, helped greatly. He made it palatable even to big industry, something he had set out to do as early as 1932. In an address—significantly entitled 'A Strong State and Sound Economics' —before the *Langnam Verein** (literally the 'Long Name Association' or northwestern industries), he invented a distinction between two kinds of totality, the Roman and the Germanic.[22] Roman totality was quantitative; the Germanic, qualitative. The former regimented all spheres of life, interfering with every human activity. In sharp contrast, the Germanic remained content with a strong and powerful state that demanded full political control but left economic activities unrestricted. Schmitt's doctrine is, of course, no more Germanic than its opposite is Roman. In fact, it had been formulated much more clearly and realistically by an Italian, Vilfredo Pareto, who espoused political authoritarianism and economic liberalism simultaneously and who influenced the early economic policies of Mussolini.

Both considerations—the appeal to the monarchic tradition of a strong state and to private property and private initiative—loomed large in the last speech Hitler delivered to a (relatively) freely elected Reichstag (23 March 1933). Hitler declared that a monarchi-

* See p. 137.

cal restoration was not subject to discussion at present because the chief task was to establish the unconditional authority of the government. At the same time, he promised the strongest stimulus to private initiative and the recognition of private property.[23]

The totalitarian doctrine of the state thus satisfied the various traditional partisans of German reaction: university professors, bureaucrats, army officers, and big industrialists. It was also acceptable to the western world in general. For, any political theory in which the state is central and dominant and entrusted with the guardianship of universal interests is in line with the tradition of western civilization, no matter how liberal that tradition may be. The western tradition does not regard the state as an oppressive machinery opposed to the rights of man, but as an entity watching over the interests of the whole and guarding those interests against infringement by particular groups. State sovereignty expresses the need for security, order, law, and equality before the law, and the National Socialist emphasis on the totality of the state had not yet broken with this European tradition.

Totalitarianism also served the practical needs of the moment. During the first months of the regime, every Brown and Black Shirt functionary tried to grab all the spoils and offices he could. Rank and file members of the party began to grumble about the betrayal of the revolution; one wing even called for a second revolution. Röhm's Brown Shirts eyed the new power of the Reichswehr enviously.

The situation was difficult and Hitler was prompt to use the weapon of the totalitarian doctrine. The revolution was to proceed in an orderly fashion—in so far as property, the civil service, and the army were concerned. Section 26 of the Army Act and a Prussian decree of 4 May 1933 ruled that party members must surrender their membership while serving in the armed forces or the police, since they were subject to a different disciplinary power.* On 20 November 1933, Rudolf Hess, then deputy leader, came out with a forceful declaration that party leaders had no right to issue ordinances and decrees.[24] Above all, local and provincial party bosses must keep their hands off business. That is the meaning of Dr. Frick's circular letter warning high federal officials, to whom it was

* See also pp. 65, 369, 378, 382.

addressed, against allowing the party machine to infringe upon the authority of the bureaucracy. Dr. Frick had no intention of interfering with the terrorization of Jews; the beating of defenseless prisoners in the Brown Shirt barracks; the kidnapping of communists, socialists, and pacifists; or the murder—'shot while trying to escape'—of political enemies. But the party must not interfere in business and administration.

3. THE SYNCHRONIZATION OF POLITICAL LIFE

The totalitarian theory was also the instrument for co-ordinating all public activities. Absolute control from the top—the famous *Gleichschaltung* (synchronization) of federal, state, provincial, and municipal activities—was justified in the doctrine of the state's total right and total power. In contrast to the pluralistic and federalistic Weimar Republic, the new state could not and would not brook the existence of autonomous public bodies within it; and during the years 1933 and 1934, which Hitler called the period of stabilization of power, a whole series of enactments took care of all the necessary details. Unlike Italy, full concentration of power and *Gleichschaltung* were accomplished in a very short space of time.

The basic statute was the enabling act of 24 March 1933, entitled 'An Act to Relieve the Distress of the People and of the Reich,' passed by a Reichstag elected less than three weeks before, on 5 March. It has also been called 'the preliminary constitution of the Reich.' [25] This Act gave the cabinet unlimited legislative power, with the right to depart from constitutional provisions and to interfere everywhere except in parliamentary institutions or with the federal council (*Reichsrat*). It further decreed that the powers of the president were not to be curtailed. A new and 'simplified' legislative procedure was instituted. Although the legislative power of the Reichstag was not expressly abolished, that power became obsolete in effect, to be used only in exceptional situations and then only for ornamental purposes.

The Reichstag that is left today, composed of party officials, is a mere ornament, and after his flight from Germany Mr. Fritz Thyssen, himself a member of that august body, revealed [26] that the Reichstag session on 1 September 1939 (the war meeting) was attended by only one hundred members, while the remaining seats were simply filled at random with party secretaries.

The cabinet became the normal legislator. This wiping out of the separation between legislative and administrative functions—a characteristic development in nearly all modern states—means that political power is no longer distributed among different strata of society and that minorities can no longer oppose legislative proposals.[27] The state power is not only unified but is absolute. (It is also unified under liberal democracy, of course, for separation of powers does not mean that three different powers exist. It would be more accurate to speak of separate and distinct functions rather than powers.)

The enabling act represented a most radical departure from the principles of liberal constitutionalism, from the system of norms and customs that limits the state's legislative power. As one writer put it, 'the federal administration received the power of leadership over Germany; under Adolf Hitler this is by far the most extensive political power.' [28]

The history of the enabling act gives the lie to the National Socialist claim that they came into power by constitutional means. It is true that the act was passed by a vote of 441 to 94 and thereby received the necessary two-thirds majority of the members present (Article 76 of the Weimar Constitution). But the meeting took place in an atmosphere of terror. The eighty-one Communist deputies and many Social Democrats had been arbitrarily arrested and were therefore absent. (The Social Democrats present voted against the measure.) If the Centrists had not capitulated and given their support to the bill, a reign of terror would unquestionably have been unleashed.

Furthermore, Article 5 provided that the enabling act was to lose its validity if 'the present federal cabinet is replaced by another.' The circumstances surrounding this provision, demanded by Hindenburg, are significant. The world has forgotten that in this first Hitler government, which took power on 31 January 1933, there were only three National Socialists out of twelve. (In effect, this cabinet was a revival of the Harzburg Front of October 1931, organized by Hitler and Hugenberg with Schacht's blessing, in order to forge a 'national' opposition to the Brüning cabinet.[29]) It was to protect the majority of his own reactionary friends in the new

government of 'national concentration,' and particularly three of
them (Vice-Chancellor von Papen, Hugenberg, minister of economics, and Gerecke, minister of employment), that Hindenburg
insisted on Article 5. In other words, the enabling act gave full
legislative power to the cabinet as then constituted and to no
other.

Hugenberg soon resigned as minister of economics; Gerecke was
arrested for embezzlement; the Nazi Darré was appointed minister
of agriculture; and Deputy Leader Hess began to attend cabinet
meetings though not a member. Legally, that should have ended
the enabling act. It goes without saying that in fact nothing of the
sort occurred. Here is how one constitutional lawyer, a high official
in the ministry of the interior, defended retention of the act: 'It
would belittle the significance of the great event of national concentration if we were to enter upon a discussion of what would
constitute the premature end of the simplified legislative process,
whether the replacement of one person by another in the cabinet
or an alteration of the political composition of the cabinet.' [30]
Another commentator, less reticent, contended that the act retained
its validity because the National Socialist party had always had a
majority in the cabinet.[31] This was a manifest lie.

Because of the obvious violation of Article 5, the political and
legal theorists of National Socialism prefer to speak of the enabling
act as 'the corner-stone of a new constitution.' To call it an enabling
act after all would be tantamount to recognizing its roots in the
despised Weimar constitution. From an exceptional delegation of
power under the constitution, and hence a measure the validity of
which must be judged in terms of the constitution, they turned the
act into a *Reichsführungsgesetz*, a statute creating the Reich leadership. As such, it marks the end of Weimar and the beginning of the
National Socialist system.[32]

In any event, National Socialism is not concerned with legal conformity to the prevailing constitutional system. It substitutes the
claim of 'legitimacy.'[33] A system is 'legitimate' when it has an intrinsic justification for existence, in this case, the success of the
National Socialist revolution. In other words, the justification of the
new constitution lies in its success—an argument that is neither new
nor convincing.

Nor did violations of the enabling act stop with Article 5. As

we have seen, the act ostensibly preserved parliamentary institutions and the federal council, and promised to guarantee the rights
of the president. In less than two years, however, the federal council was abolished (statute of 14 February 1934) and the posts of
chancellor and president merged immediately after Hindenburg's
death on 1 August 1934. The merger was defended by reference
to Hindenburg's will, in which he is supposed to have nominated
Hitler as his successor, and by the 89.9 per cent approval in the
popular referendum of 19 August. Even according to National
Socialist theories, the referendum had no constitutional status, but
only a possible moral significance. The Weimar constitution distinguished between referendum and initiative. In the former, the
people acted as arbiters in legislative conflicts between the president and parliament—a situation that never arose in practice. The
initiative, on the other hand, gave political groups an opportunity
either to force legislation or to prevent parliamentary enactment.
Initiatives had been attempted three times in the entire history of
the Republic: the Left-inspired initiative to confiscate princely
properties; the Communist initiative against battleship construction;
and the initiative started by the reactionaries against the Young
Plan. They failed; inevitably so in view of the way in which public
life was thoroughly organized and the rigidity of the party system.
Nevertheless the initiative was a potential instrument for correcting
the petrified state of political and parliamentary life. The initiative
started by the Communists to expropriate the princely houses, although it failed, so aroused the Socialist masses that the Social
Democratic executive was forced to change its policy and lead the
popular movement.

In contrast to the republican forms, the National Socialist Plebiscite Act of 14 July 1933 is a matter of propaganda rather than of
constitutional law. The statute gives the cabinet the exclusive right
to submit an intended enactment to the people. National Socialist
lawyers have arbitrarily interpreted the statute to mean that the
people can also be asked to approve a legislative enactment after it
has been passed and published. In a one-party system, lacking liberal
guarantees, the plebiscite is something entirely different from the
democratic referendum. According to the official release accompanying the plebiscite act, it stems from 'old Germanic legal forms'
and its function is to express the people's voice 'in an ennobled

form.' What if the people should reject an intended or already enacted measure of the cabinet? Apart from the fact that such an outcome is inconceivable, the experts all agree that the Leader is not bound by the popular decision. 'Even if the voting public turns against him, he remains the one who represents the objective mission of the people.' [34]

The process of unifying and concentrating legislative power was completed once the referendum was politically and juristically reduced to the level of a mere ornament and once legislative power was vested entirely in the cabinet. *Gleichschaltung* could now be freely extended far into the administrative realm. The next step was to abolish the independent status of the states (*Länder*). The first blow fell with the co-ordinating act of 31 March 1933, giving state cabinets the right to legislate alongside the state diets. The existing state diets were then dissolved by federal statute. In subsequent elections, the so-called 'national opposition,' composed of National Socialists and Nationalists, won majorities in all the diets. The majorities became still larger when the Social Democrats were unseated on 7 July 1933. On 30 January 1934, a statute 'to reconstruct the Reich' (*Reichs-Aufbaugesetz*) transferred to the Reich all sovereign powers still held by the states, thereby destroying their state character and wiping out the diets. The same process was repeated in the municipalities; the municipal diets were abolished by statute of 30 January 1935 (*Gemeindeordnung*). Authoritarian control was complete from top to bottom.

A second co-ordinating act, passed on 7 April 1933, introduced the office of federal regent, appointed by Hitler. In Prussia, Hitler himself took this office. A statute of 30 January 1935 (*Reichsstatt-halter-Gesetz*) made the regents subject to cabinet order and thus transformed them into civil servants of the Reich. They were deprived of their right to appoint the state governments and could merely propose names to the Leader. The federal regents thus became figureheads. The post was well paid, however, and went to deserving party officials. Even National Socialist lawyers now find it impossible to determine precisely what is the constitutional position of the states. The best they have been able to do so far has been to say that the states continue to exist as transitory institutions awaiting the final territorial reorganization of the Reich.[35]

The same theorists who had demanded that all power be concentrated in the president's hands were now equally eager to reduce his position to that of a figurehead. One lawyer put it very nicely: 'Owing to the failure of Parliament, the center of gravity shifted to the president. Now, after National Socialism's seizure of power, the Reich president can once again free himself from his entanglements with daily politics and return to his *constitutional* position as the representative of folk unity and as the protector of the nation.' [36] Another writer, a bit more careful, declares that the president has not surrendered his authoritarian leadership to Hitler, but has assumed a new function, that of representative.[37] The rapid decline of presidential power was given clear legislative expression, especially in the statute creating the office of federal regent. The regents were not made subject to the president's command but to that of the chancellor [38]—'the federal regent's task is to provide for fulfilling the principles of politics laid down by the federal chancellor.' And the president, once the strong man, now became a mere front behind whom stood the unlimited power of the Führer.

4. THE TOTALITARIAN STATE IN THE WAR

Before the outbreak of the present war, the concentration of political power in the hands of the federal cabinet had attained a very high stage. The institution of federal regents and the destruction of municipal self-government that reduced the status of the municipal organs to that of federal agents, gave the federal cabinet full power over the whole political structure of Germany down to the lowest territorial unit. This power was restrained only by the administrative tribunals and the judiciary.

The outbreak of the war has, however, seen an even greater concentration of political power. The Ministerial Council for the Defense of the Realm was formed out of the Federal Council for the Defense of the Realm (nothing is known of the composition or tasks of this council, as even the *Frankfurter Zeitung* was forced to admit in its issue of 1 January 1941). The ministerial council has virtually taken over the legislative power of the cabinet. It consists of Reich Marshal Göring, who is its head; the Leader's deputy; the director of the federal chancellery, Lammers; the chief of the supreme command of the armed forces, Keitel; the general commissioner for administration, Frick (also minister of interior); and the general commissioner for economics, Funk (also minister of economics). In special cases, it also allows for the addition of other persons. The creation of the Ministerial Council for the Defense of the Realm is tantamount to the establishment of a general staff for civil defense and for economics. The general commissioner for economics (Funk) is the superior in power to the ministers of economics, labor, food, forestry, and even finance; while the ministers of justice, interior, culture, and church affairs are subordinate to the general commissioner for federal administration (Frick). Nothing gives a clearer picture of the reversal of outworn liberal forms than the degradation of the minister of finance. Fiscal considerations can no longer prevent the carrying out of necessary administrative and economic measures. The paramount influence that the treasury had and still has in England has always been an obstacle to the execution of many necessary tasks. In the new administrative set-up, the minister of finance has become purely a subordinate official.

The ministerial council is the normal legislator for all practical purposes. Its decrees have the power of law and do not have to be countersigned by the Führer, for, as the *Frankfurter Zeitung* puts it, 'during the war he often stays in his headquarters outside the capital' (10 January 1941). The ministerial council regulates all matters that are directly or indirectly connected with the defense of the state. This stipulation, of course, in no way limits its authority.

The decrees of the ministerial council, however, do not and cannot take care of all details, and in the ordinary or simplified legislative process details are normally left to executive decrees promulgated by the minister under whose jurisdiction the particular matter falls. Similar but more far-reaching power attaches to the executive decrees that can be enacted to carry out or go beyond the legislative acts of the ministerial council.

The commissioners for economics and for administration and the general deputy for the Four Year Plan (Göring) may, each in his own domain but with the consent of the other two and with that of the chief of the supreme command of the armed forces, issue executive decrees that may—and this is the new step—even contravene existing legislation. The commissioners' authority is thus far wider than that of the ministerial bureaucracy that usually formulates the executive decrees. As a result, the commissioners have altered the penal code and the code of civil procedure.

Even this development, however, is not the last in the process of concentrating legislative power. In January 1941, the Führer issued an edict empowering the Reich Marshal independently to enact any legislation or administrative decree that he deemed necessary for air-raid protection. This empowering edict goes further than any other known.

Thus the Leader has the following legislative powers at his disposal:

1. His direct acts, either in the form of statute, decree (*Verordnung*), or edict (*Erlass*). The last-named form is increasingly resorted to, as in the incorporation of Eupen-Malmedy and Moresnet into the Reich and as in the appointment of federal commissioners for Norway and the Netherlands. Another example is the extension of the Four Year Plan. Direct legislative activity on the part of the Leader has diminished, however.

2. The simplified legislative acts of the federal cabinet, based on the emergency statute of 1933. This has been virtually abandoned during the war.

3. Parliamentary statutes. These have not been used since 1936, but may be revived for propagandistic purposes.

4. The referendum. Again a means of propaganda.

5. The legislative power of the Ministerial Council for the Defense of the Realm—the normal legislator.

6. Decrees of the triumvirate of commissioners, part of them executive decrees carrying out legislative acts of the ministerial council, part of them going beyond. Falling within this category is the decree power of the commissioner of the Four Year Plan.

7. The legislative powers of the Reich Marshal in the matter of air-raid protection.

8. The legislative power delegated to the federal ministers in their respective jurisdictions, based upon specific authorizations, and, of course, the large amount of other delegated legislation.

The concentration of political power has not stopped short at the top, but has also been extended to the provincial level. A decree issued by the ministerial council on 1 September 1939 appointed 18 national defense commissioners domiciled at the seats of the 18 provincial commands of the armed forces (*Wehrkreiskommando*). They are the executive agents of the ministerial council for the provinces. Their task is the unification of civil defense. They have no apparatus of their own, but have to utilize the existing machinery of the provincial presidents (in Prussia), the federal regents, or the state ministries, according to where the provincial command of the armed forces is located. The national defense commissioners are, therefore, the superior administrative officials in the provinces, entitled to give orders to every administrative agency in their region, unless exempted. Their deputies, who, in fact, often carry out the actual work, are the chiefs of those administrative agencies that the national defense commissioners utilize for carrying out their tasks. This regulation entails a complete destruction of the traditional hierarchical structure of the German Civil Service and at the same time testifies that the need for administrative efficiency is esteemed more highly than are traditional conceptions and values. To give an instance, National Defense Commissioner Number XII, for the command of the armed forces domiciled at Wiesbaden, utilizes for its activities the office of the sub-provincial president in Wiesbaden. His deputy, therefore, is by law the *Regierungspräsident*, the sub-provincial president at Wiesbaden. Ordinarily, this sub-provincial president is subordinate to the provincial president, but as a deputy of the national defense commissioner, he is in fact placed above his superior officer.

According to a further decree of the ministerial council of 22 September 1939, the national defense councils may appoint special deputies for specific regions.

On the same date 18 national defense committees were set up to aid the national defense commissioners. They are composed of the federal regents, the party district leaders, the provincial presidents, the prime minister and ministers of the state, the high S.S. leaders, the sub-provincial and provincial presidents, the presidents of the labor exchanges, the trustees of labor, and such other men as may be called upon. The function of these committees is of a merely advisory nature.

War, therefore, has brought the reality of the totalitarian state to completion. Political power resides exclusively in the Ministerial Council for the Defense of the Realm.

Immediately before the outbreak of the war, the restrictions imposed by administrative tribunals were largely abolished. By an edict issued by the Leader on 28 August 1939, the simplification of the administration was made the order of the day. Under this misleading title, restrictions upon the authoritarian power of the administrative agencies were largely abolished. In the administrative procedure of the Reich, of the states, of the municipalities, and of public corporations, the right to a second appeal was abolished. The judicial appeal before administrative tribunals was replaced by a mere complaint to the superior administrative agency. Only if the lower administrative tribunal permitted an appeal to the higher administrative tribunal could such an appeal be made.

The second decree for the simplification of the administration, issued on 6 November 1939, simply abolished all the lower administrative tribunals, and another decree of 26 September 1939 abolished the lowest judicial administrative agencies in the counties. According to the Leader's edict, public corporations have become simply organs of the state. They are now not only controlled by it, but have become part and parcel of the administrative apparatus. They can be closed down at the discretion of the federal authorities. Only the party and its affiliated organizations are exempt from this possibility.

The edict of 3 April 1941 set up a new federal administrative tribunal. It combines the Prussian administrative tribunal, the former Austrian administrative tribunal, the former federal disciplinary tribunal, and so on. The members are appointed by the Leader, but they can be transferred to other offices at the end of each year. Extraordinary members for dealing with special problems may be appointed for fixed periods by the minister of the interior, and even outsiders may be appointed. The new federal administrative tribunal is, therefore, not an independent agency, and the judges do not enjoy a guarantee of independence. Thus, in reality, the power of the Ministerial Council for the Defense of the Realm and of its inferior agencies, the eighteen national defense councils, is completely unrestrained and unlimited. It is subiect to no institutional control.

During the present war, the reality of the totalitarian state has, therefore, been extended to such a degree that there can hardly be scope for further extension.

But this reality does not correspond to the ideology. To the extent that the political power of the state has increased, the idea of the totalitarian state has been rejected.

II

THE REVOLT OF THE PARTY AND THE 'MOVEMENT' STATE

1. The Ideological Protest against the Totalitarian State

THE claims of the party and the claims of the totalitarian state were obviously conflicting. If the state was to be supreme, the party could only be one of its arms, such as the civil service or the army, and perhaps less important than either. National Socialism, however, had triumphed primarily through the efforts of the party and its political groups and military affiliates, its handicraft organizations, its agricultural branches, even its working-class wing. The party officials were hungry for spoils and clamored for the posts held by civil servants, most of whom had not joined the party or had joined it out of convenience, not conviction; the small middle class demanded its share of department stores and co-operatives; and the Brown Shirts, led by Captain Röhm, thirsted for equality with the Reichswehr, whose leaders they contemptuously dubbed 'desk generals.' Alfred Rosenberg, the philosophical oracle of the party, was impatient with Baron von Neurath's cautious foreign policy. Grumbling spread. The party tried to end the dissatisfaction by launching a vast propaganda campaign bolstered by the threat of concentration camps. But the talk of a second revolution led by the Brown Shirts did not subside, and ominous rumblings were discernible in the general murmur. The Brown Shirts, an army of uprooted proletarians and small middle-class people, were disillusioned when Hitler appointed von Fritsch to succeed Hammerstein as chief of the army and allowed von Blomberg to retain the ministry of war. Röhm saw his ambitions frustrated. Tension increased; there was constant friction between the Brown Shirts and the nationalistic Steel Helmets and the army. Illegal interference with business assumed serious proportions. On 17 June 1934, Vice-Chancellor von Papen delivered his famous speech at Marburg, in which he upheld the citizen's right to criticize the regime.[1] Hitler decided to get rid of his 'Mountain.' The result was the massacre of 30 June 1934, comparable to the events of St. Bartholomew night in 1572. State authority had bloodily reasserted its rights; the second revolution was dead.

During the same period the idea of the totalitarian state was nevertheless thrown overboard. Alfred Rosenberg opened the attack upon it with an article in the *Völkische Beobachter*, central organ of the party (9 January 1934).[2] The totalitarian, or the 'abstract' state, he declared, belonged to the period of liberalism, in which it had served as a technical instrument of power. Under liberalism, the state was above the nation: its representatives claimed pre-eminence over the rest of the citizens. 'The revolution of 30 January 1933 does not continue the absolutist state under a new name; it places the state in a new relation to the people . . . different from that which had prevailed in 1918 or 1871. What has taken place in 1933 . . . is not the establishment of the state's totality but of the totality of the National Socialist movement. The state is no longer an entity juxtaposed to the people and the movement, is no longer conceived as a mechanical apparatus or an instrument of domination; the state is a tool of the National Socialist philosophy of life.' Rosenberg clearly indicated the reasons for which he denounced the supremacy of the state. Idealization of the state, he said, implies the glorifying of its officials at the expense of the movement. He recommended discontinuance of the talk about the totalitarian state and emphasis on the totality of the National Socialist view of life, with the National Socialist party as its bearer and the National Socialist state as its tool.

Rosenberg's article protesting against the supremacy of the state was in full accord with his long treatise entitled *The Myth of the Twentieth Century*, in which he denounced the state, refusing to 'kneel in dust' before it, and attacked Hegel.[3] In *Mein Kampf*, published long before his advent to power, Hitler expresses similar sentiments, gives full rein to his contempt for the Weimar democracy, and prophesies the coming of a new era. Constitutional lawyers and political theorists, who in 1933 and 1934 had declared themselves converts to National Socialism, apparently neglected to read this book in which every claim made by and for the state is rejected. The state, Hitler says, is not a moral concept or the realization of an absolute idea, but is the servant of the racial people. It is 'not an end but a means. It is indeed the prerequisite for the formation of a higher human culture, but not its cause. On the contrary, the latter lies exclusively in the existence of a race capable of culture.' At another place he says that 'the state is a means to an end. Its end is the preservation and the promotion of a community of physically and psychically equal living beings.' It enables them better to maintain their kind. As a result, 'not the cultural achievements or relative power of a state but the part assigned to its people is the decisive factor in its evaluation . . . A state is bad, no matter what its degree of culture, if it leads the racial bearers of this culture to their doom.' For these reasons, Hitler rejects unconditional obedience to the state and affirms a biological right to resist. 'Not the preservation of a state or a government,' he writes, 'is the highest aim of existence, but the preservation of the people . . . Once the latter is in danger of being oppressed or abolished, the question of legality plays only a subordinate part . . . The ruling power may use a thousand so-called "legal" means, yet the instinct of self-preservation of the oppressed is always the most sublime justification for their fighting with all weapons . . . Human rights break state rights.' [4]

Hitler says elsewhere that 'if a people is led to destruction by its government, rebellion on the part of each and every member of this people is not only a right but a duty . . . If a man is not ready or able to fight for his existence, righteous Providence has already decreed his doom.'

The theory is unmistakably a kind of perverted liberalism, based on a biological conception of natural law and in which the purity of the race replaces the innate rights of the individual. Liberalism, too, conceives of the state as a tool or mechanism, and Hitler's appeal to Providence recalls the liberalist deist philosophers who invoked the aid of Providence to guarantee social harmony. The differences, however, are immense. The liberal doctrine has been one of state protection without regard to race, creed, or class. This has given way to the doctrine of the racial élite.

The doctrine according to which the position of the state is subordinate was resurrected after the blood purge of 30 June 1934. The party congress of September 1934 supplied the occasion for reformulating the relation between party and state, and the Führer's proclamation emphasized that the National Socialist revolution was a thing of the past.[5] Hitler rejected the idea of permanent revolution, declaring that it would lead to disintegration in racial, political, and economic life. Permanent revolutions, he went on, are nothing but 'struggles for power among politicians greedy for spoils.' Success could not be achieved without stability. The National Socialist revolution had to be ended because the people had already been infused with the National Socialist philosophy of life and because the army had become an eternally reliable bulwark of the National Socialist state. During the immediately preceding stage, the supreme task had been to strengthen the authority of the state. The future task was to consolidate the party and its old Brown Shirt and Elite Guard fighters into a single community, bound by a solemn oath to purify and mobilize the whole people and strengthen faith in the party. Another speech, delivered at the conclusion of the convention, was the most aggressive attack yet launched on the theory of the totalitarian state. The party, Hitler declared, supplies the political élite; 'The state is not our master; we are the masters of the state.' [6]

2. THE TRIPARTITE STATE

Political and constitutional theorists, whose conformist instincts were roused, at once proceeded to reformulate National Socialist doctrine. The decisive contribution was again made by Carl Schmitt.[7] The German political structure, he wrote, rests on a tripartite foundation of state, movement, and people. The state is the 'static political part,' the movement 'the dynamic political element,' and the people 'the non-political sector living in the protective shade of political decisions' (p. 12). Though Schmitt rejects any attempt 'sophistically to play off one element against the others,' the pattern he sets up implies a hierarchical structure. Within the National Socialist or fascist tradition, the 'dynamic' (whatever it may mean) ranks higher than the 'static,' and the non-political lower than the political. Indeed, Schmitt's book repudiates any attempt to identify the state with its bureaucracy and judiciary—the 'movement' 'carries the state apparatus as well as the social and economic order' (p. 14).

Carl Schmitt sharply distinguishes his theory of the tripartite structure of the state from the dualistic theory of liberalism, in which the state and society confront each other as two separate entities. In the new theory, the state has no monopoly of political decisions. Schmitt concludes that the state no longer determines the political element but is determined by it, that is, by the party.

The exact relation, however, between the state and the movement remains vague. Though indissolubly bound to the state, the party is not identical with it. It gives directions to the state but acts only through its leader. Leadership, in turn, must not be confused with supervision, command, dictatorship, or bureaucratic rule. The part to be played by the people is even less clear. By definition, the people is the non-political sector, that is, has no say in the making of political decisions. But this part of Schmitt's thesis was not accepted; for its frank implication that the people existed only to be ruled aroused passionate protests. It was argued against Schmitt that the people is not non-political but political, that it is the *Urkraft* or primeval force from which all individuals derive their rights. 'The political totality of National Socialism is founded on one all-pervading political idea born of one unified political people and realized in one political movement. The living and perpetual form of the state is the embodiment of this idea.' [8]

As we shall see, National Socialism takes pride in having placed the people in the center of its social and political philosophy. Carl Schmitt's tripartite theory was retained with one significant change: the people was declared to be part of the political structure. How the people could act politically was not explained; only the leadership of the 'movement' was recognized. Innumerable theorists and pamphleteers stepped forward, calling the people the fountainhead of the state, but none was able to indicate how the people could serve as such, especially since the leader was not bound by plebiscites. Bad metaphysics replaced any rational discussion of the problem.

3. THE PARTY AND THE STATE

Concerning the relation between the party and the state, National Socialist political theory is equally vague. In his speech at the party convention of 1935, Hitler himself attempted a definition: 'The task of the state,' he said, 'is to continue, within the existing framework, legally to administer the state organization which has historically developed.' The party's task is 'first, to direct the efforts of its entire organization toward the establishment of a stable self-perpetuating and eternal cell for the National Socialist doctrine; second, to educate the whole people to this idea; and third, to hand over the people, thus educated, to the state for its leadership . . . As to the rest, the principle of mutual respect must be observed by both juris-dictions.' [9] This leaves us exactly where we were before, for the problem was to determine precisely where the state's jurisdiction ends and where the party's begins.

One-party states reveal three types of relation between party and state. In Italy, the party is 'incorporated' in the state; the party is an organ of the state, a 'state party.' Soviet Russia gives the party full command over the state, and the periodic purges are to a con-siderable extent aimed at preventing the accumulation of autono-mous political power in the hands of the state bureaucracy. The German type stands somewhere between the two and is difficult to analyze. The analysis, however, must be undertaken—not so much to satisfy the curiosity of constitutional and administrative lawyers as to elucidate the fundamental problems of where political power resides and how strongly National Socialist ideas have penetrated the army and the civil services.*

Let us begin our search for clarification with an analysis of rele-vant legislative, administrative, and judicial practices. The constitu-tional basis of the party-state relation rests on the 'unity of party and state' statute of 1 December 1933, supplemented by the Leader's ordinance of 29 March 1935. According to this statute, the party is 'the bearer of the Germanic idea of the state and is indissolubly united with the state.' It was made a corporation under public law, its charter to be issued by the Leader. In order to cement this union organizationally, Hess, then deputy leader, and Röhm, then chief of the Brown Shirts, were made members of the federal cabi-net. Under the terms of the same statute, party members and Brown Shirts were given independent jurisdiction. The 'unity' statute was the logical conclusion to all those acts that had destroyed the com-peting political parties: the police rules issued under the presidential emergency decree of 28 February 1933; the statute of 26 May 1933 confiscating Social Democratic property; the decree of 23 June 1933, signed by the Prussian minister of the interior, prohibiting all activity of the Social Democratic party, of its deputies in parlia-

* The sociological implications of the relation between party and state are discussed on pp. 369, 378, 382.

ment, in the diets, state councils, provincial councils, and municipalities; the prohibition of the Nationalist fighting rinks (*Kampf-
ringe*), 1 June 1933; the voluntary dissolution of the German
Nationalist People's party (27 June 1933), of the Bavarian People's
party (4 July 1933), and of the Catholic Center party (5 July
1933), all culminating in the statute of 14 July 1933, which prohibited the formation of new parties and threatened imprisonment
for any attempt to revitalize or organize any party except the
National Socialist.

Taken at face value, the statute does not differ greatly from the
Italian law of 1932 regulating the relation between the National
Fascist party and the Italian state. It does not place the party above
any other public corporation, such as a church, municipality, or
board administering a health insurance fund. Under German public
law, the corporation is but a relatively free institution. No corporations exist in public law that are not under the control of the
state.[10] Their tasks are clearly defined by law, the extent of their
authority is strictly limited, and their activities come under the control of courts, administrative tribunals, and other agencies. In fact,
public corporations have no general autonomy in the modern state.
Each receives its power by delegation from the state, and some
theorists have quite logically been led to reject the concept of
autonomy as incompatible with the legal system of the modern
state. By describing the party as a public corporation, we imply
that the tasks and authority of the party are circumscribed by law
and that its activities are supervised by the state. The party would
then be on an equal footing with any other relatively independent
state institution.

Such considerations, however, did not seem to dovetail with the
claim that the 'movement' represented and led the state. As a result,
constitutional and legal theory and practice discarded the wording
of the unity statute of 1933 and so rephrased it that the party
became fully independent of the state and even stood above it.[11]

The actual development of the relation between the party and the
state indicates that the concept of public corporation does not
apply here. The party not only co-operates in matters of legislation,
administration, and the judicial process, but occupies a position
superior to that of the state. This is especially true of the S.S. and
the Hitler Youth.

4. THE S.S. AND THE HITLER YOUTH

The S.S. or Elite Guard is the police and hence the state in its most important domestic function. It serves as a protective police and provides personnel for the secret state police. Since its establishment in 1925 and its extension in 1929, the S.S. has constituted a closed group living under laws of its own. Selection of its personnel has taken place primarily on the basis of biological principles such as the 'seed cultivator' employs—the purpose is 'to select those who most closely resemble the ideal of the Nordic man.'[12] The main element in the ideology of its members are faith, honor, and unconditional obedience. Their élite consciousness is upheld in a decree of 9 November 1935, which entitles and compels every S.S. man to defend his honor with his weapon. According to the same decree, he has to be at least twenty-one years old, serve an apprenticeship of eighteen months, take an oath to his Leader, and have his labor and army services behind him. He is inducted on receipt of his dagger. The privileges granted to the S.S. were further extended by the federal supreme court. Section 53 of the penal code permits the ordinary citizen to use weapons only in necessary self-defense, but a court decision established that S.S. men were free to use their weapons even when the attack could be warded off by other means. 'The bearer of an S.S. uniform cannot offer the spectacle of a tussle to his folk comrades. Such a spectacle is incompatible with the S.S. uniform.'[13]

A ruling of 26 May 1939 defines the S.S. in its relation to the police.[14] Its task is to defend the state against open and hidden foes. The three S.S. sections are so different, however, that they have little but the name in common.[15] The 'general' S.S. is a pure party organization, administered by the party treasurer (he is also chief of the party administration).* Out of the general S.S. two special groups are constituted: the Troops on Hand (*Verfügungstruppen*) and the Death Head formations (*Totenkopfformationen*), both controlled by the minister of the interior.[16] The party troops are at the state's disposal, and the leader of the S.S. (Himmler) is also chief of the federal police (statute of 17 June 1936).

The police comprises two organizations: the *Ordnungspolizei*

* See p. 81.

(headed by S.S. Sub-Leader Daluege) and the *Sicherheitspolizei* (protective police, headed by S.S. Sub-Leader Heydrich). The police leadership is the same as the S.S. leadership and the S.S. formations the same as the police formations—in other words, the state has in this field abdicated in favor of the party.

The Hitler Youth, which originated in the *Jugendbund der NSDAP* (founded in 1922 and given its present form in 1926) is another example of party supremacy. In its early period it was only a section of the Brown Shirts, directly controlled by the S.A. leader. Baldur von Schirach, who was appointed youth leader on 30 October 1931, was an S.A. group leader. Because the Hitler Youth was a section of the S.A., the ban pronounced against the latter on 13 April 1932 had to be applied to the former as well. Following the ban, the Hitler Youth was disaffiliated from the S.A. But the process was slow; though Baldur von Schirach was appointed *Reichsleiter* * of the party in June 1933, and thereby admitted to the highest circle of leadership, it was not until 29 March 1935 that an executive decree made the Hitler Youth independent of the S.A. and recognized it as one of the groupings of the party.

The Hitler Youth comprises several groups: the Hitler Youth proper (boys between 14 and 18 years of age); the *Jungvolk;* the *Bund Deutscher Mädel;* the *Jung Mädel;* and the Faith and Beauty (*Glaube und Schönheit*) organization formed by the *Bund Deutscher Mädel*. The entire body is represented and financially controlled by the party treasurer.†

When Baldur von Schirach was appointed youth leader of the German Reich, he became the highest state agent for youth organizations, functioning both as party and state leader. He used his new powers to co-ordinate the entire youth movement and thus put into effect the party's claim to complete control. He dissolved the *Grossdeutscher Bund*, consolidated the Scharnhorst youth, Labor Front youth, and Agrarian youth into the one movement, and reached a working agreement with the religious youth organizations.

Despite his political monopoly over all youth organizations, the youth leader is not regarded as a state official; he does not belong to the civil service and is not subject to its disciplinary regulations.

* See p. 373.
† See p. 81.

The union between the Hitler Youth and the state rests solely on the fact that one person holds two offices. Nevertheless, the Hitler Youth receives financial assistance from the state and enjoys innumerable political privileges.

On 1 December 1936 the government issued the 'Hitler Youth statute,' which proclaimed that 'the entire German youth within the Reich territory is organized in the Hitler Youth.' The same statute elevated the national youth leader to a supreme federal office directly under Hitler. And a decree of 11 November 1939 gave the national youth leader superiority in all youth matters over regional officials in Prussia, state governments, and federal commissioners in occupied territories. Despite all this, the youth movement is not regarded as 'state youth' (such as the Italian *Balilla*, for example) but as 'party youth.' [17] Federal and state agencies are simply means through which the national youth leader fulfils party needs. The Hitler Youth has a legislative, administrative, and judicial power of its own, especially documented in the youth service decree (*Jugenddienstverordnung*) of 25 April 1939, which made it the duty of every youth between the ages of ten and eighteen to serve in the Hitler Youth. In imitation of Carl Schmitt's 'tripartite' theory, the home, the school, and the Hitler Youth are described as the three pillars of youth training.

When the Hitler Youth was expanded to comprise the entire youth of Germany, it lost its party character. A new organization intended to mold future leaders became necessary, and an executive decree (25 March 1939) provided for the creation of such an élite, a *'Stamm' Hitler Jugend* within the organization. Membership in it is voluntary and this central group is again a party organ in the strict sense of the term.[18]

5. THE PARTY AND THE OTHER SERVICES

The relation described in the preceding section is reversed with regard to the labor service, the army administration, and the civil services: here the state is placed above the party. Section 26 of the *Reichswehrgesetz* (army statute) provides for the abrogation of party membership during the period of a man's service. Section 17 of the Labor Service Act (26 June 1935) prohibits party activities during labor service, with a few minor exceptions. It is true that

Section 11 of the Civil Service Act suspends the principle of incompatibility and allows civil servants to accept unsalaried positions in the party and its affiliated organizations without special permission; but the true relation between the civil services and the party is best illustrated in the *Anordnung über die Verwaltungsführung in den Landkreisen* (regulation for the administration of small rural units), 28 December 1939. This ruling entrusts the *Menschenführung*, that is, the manipulation of the people, to the party sub-leader, who is responsible to his superiors for 'the mood and attitude of the people in the small administrative units.' But the responsibility for the administrative functions rests exclusively with the *Landrat*, who is not subject to any interference by party officials—they may only make suggestions. This ruling clearly demonstrates that despite the ideological degradation of the state, the absolute and exclusive commanding power of the state executive has in no way diminished. Except for the police and the youth movement, the civil service is supreme, the state is still totalitarian.

The difficulties arising from the extremely equivocal relation between the party and the state are legally solved by the leadership principle; moreover, many high party leaders are at the same time high state officials. In this context, we shall discuss only the legal framework; the sociological and political implications will be analyzed later.*

At the top, the unity of the party and the state is embodied by Adolf Hitler, who is both leader of the party and chief of state. The deputy leader of the party is a cabinet member, though he is not a state minister in the proper sense.[19] All federal regents and most Prussian provincial presidents are also provincial leaders of the party (Gauleiter). The chief of the party's foreign division (Bohle) occupies the same post at Foreign Affairs (30 June 1937). There are variations, however. For instance, an order of 29 February 1937 directs that the *Kreisleiter* of the party should not hold any full-time administrative position in the state or municipalities. On the other hand, both state and party organizations are subject to the commands of the chief of road construction (Todt) and the chief of the Four Year Plan (Göring).

Not only do leaders of the party frequently occupy high govern-

* See pp. 369, 378, 382.

ment posts, but the party's jurisdiction has been given an official status. The deputy leader of the party helps to frame legislative and executive orders (for example, the decrees of 25 July 1934 and 6 April 1935) and to select civil servants directly appointed by the Leader (Section 31 of the Civil Service Act of 26 January 1937). The same is true of labor service leaders (3 April 1936). In municipal administration, the party's delegate is and remains a party official (Section 6 of the *Reichsgemeindeordnung*).

We may conclude that it is impossible to describe the party as a public corporation. The fact becomes clearer when we examine the problem of judicial control, the crucial problem for any public corporation. Unanimous opinion holds that the party is not subject to any control whatever. The party's property may not be attached for a public or private debt.[20] Moreover, the inner administration of the party, its legislative structure, and its judiciary are not comparable to those of any other public corporation. Documents issued by the party leaders are public documents and party political leaders are public servants. Party courts have powers identical with those of ordinary courts: they are entitled to hear witnesses and experts under oath; a lower party official is not allowed to give evidence before any state court or administrative organ without the consent of the party chiefs. State prerogatives enjoyed by civil servants are thus extended to the party hierarchy, and party uniforms and institutions enjoy the same protection as the uniforms and institutions of the state (statute of 20 December 1934). Party property is free of taxation (statutes of 15 April 1935 and 1 December 1936).

The autonomous position of the party is best expressed in the fact that it is not liable for the torts of its officials, although such liability holds in German law for officials of private corporations and civil servants (Article 131 of the Weimar constitution). Some Prussian courts of appeal and the federal supreme court have declared the party liable for torts of its officials, especially in non-political matters,[21] but the majority of the lawyers and most of the lower courts accept no liability at all. The party expressly claims all the privileges of the civil service but rejects the liabilities. It cannot be sued for the torts of its agents unless it voluntarily accedes the state's jurisdiction in a particular case.[22] The party thus occupies the position usually assumed by one sovereign state toward another.

Should this situation extend in all fields, the party will ultimately stand above the state.

The party is not an organ of the state. Its position cannot be defined in terms of our traditional constitutional jurisprudence. Walter Buch,[23] supreme party judge and, as such, one of those holding mastery over life and death, compares the party to the state itself. If his comparison were true, an absurd situation would exist, for it would mean the existence of a dual system, two co-existent sovereign powers, both claiming allegiance and creating a dual jurisdiction. To solve the dilemma, Frick, the federal minister of the interior and an old party member—one who has not been able to rid himself completely of the tradition of conservative think-ing he absorbed as a Bavarian civil servant—employs the following analogy: the party and the state apparatus are like two pillars sup-porting the roof of the state, but the state official can and must accept orders only from his superior in the state hierarchy.[24] Vio-lent protests arose against this interpretation, because it again made the state supreme. Reinhardt, the secretary of state in the federal ministry of finance and a high party official, insisted that the 'fundamental basis of unity is not the state but the National Socialist party.'[25] His view would make the state an agency of the party; this is contradicted by the fact that the army and the civil service are subject only to the command of the appropriate state authori-ties.

And if Carl Schmitt should try to solve the puzzle by invoking his formula that 'party and state are different but not separate, com-bined but not merged,'[26] he would be shedding little light indeed —as little as is shed by those intelligent National Socialist theorists who hold that the party and the state live in a 'constitutional com-munity,' by virtue of which the idea of the party is that of the state.[27] Many competent observers have come to the conclusion that since National Socialist political and constitutional theory are in a state of flux, nothing definite can be asserted.[28] Our task will be to show that this is not quite true, that there is a definite pattern of political and constitutional theory, although this pattern does not fit the rational categories of political thought as we know it, whether liberal, absolutist, democratic, or autocratic.*

Before we proceed to develop the structure of the new National

* See pp. 459-67, 473-5.

Socialist theory, we must examine the significance of the National Socialists' denunciation of the state. The whole matter will be clarified by a comparison of National Socialist and Fascist theories.

6. PARTY AND STATE IN ITALY

In Italy, the Hegelian theory of the state is still dominant, though in a distorted form. 'The foundation of fascism,' according to Mussolini, 'is its conception of the state, its character, its duty, its aim. Fascism conceives of the state as an absolute in comparison with which all individuals or groups are relative . . . For us Fascists, the state is not merely a guardian . . . nor is it an organization with purely material aims . . . Nor is it a purely political creation . . . The state, as conceived and created by fascism, is a spiritual and moral fact in itself, since its political, juridical, and economic organization of the nation is a concrete thing; and such an organization must be in its origin and development a manifestation of the spirit.' [29]

Mussolini's pronouncement, profoundly influenced by the doctrines of the Italian Nationalists, has been fully adopted by official constitutional theory in Italy. Everything is 'encompassed by the state.' [30] The state is an organism; it has a life of its own.[31] Giovanni Gentile gave this doctrine its philosophical form. The state is an ethical state, an embodiment of the national consciousness, and it is endowed with a mission. The state is in fact the individual, freed from all 'accidental differences'; the state is action and spirit.[32] In accordance with this doctrine, the Fascist party is a subordinate part of the state, an institution within the state.[33]

At an earlier period in his career, when he was an opponent of the government, Mussolini had denounced this apotheosis of the state, which he was later to make the official political doctrine. 'I start from the individual,' he had said, 'and strike out at the state. Down with the state in all its forms and incarnations. The state of yesterday, of today, of tomorrow. The bourgeois state and the socialist state. In the gloom of today and the darkness of tomorrow, the only faith which remains to us individualists destined to die is the at present absurd but ever consoling religion of anarchy.' [34] An about-face such as this is nothing new in Mussolini. His attitude has undergone a number of profound changes on the subject of

private property, the monarchy, the church, the senate, the stabilization of the lira, and so on.

Gentile's sophisms proved helpful in these metamorphoses—with
their aid almost any opposites can be reconciled. Even anarchism
and state absolutism can be made compatible by calling the state
the true and only individual. We are not concerned, however, with
the ramifications of Fascist ideology, but seek rather to learn why,
in contrast to National Socialism, the official Italian ideology places
the state above everything. In a speech to the Liberal Conservatives,
delivered in Milan, 4 April 1924, Mussolini himself gave the answer.

'Throughout the kaleidoscopic changes of government that have
taken place, the bureaucracy has remained the sole stable element.
Without the bureaucracy we would have had absolute chaos. It has
represented the continuity of the nation's administrative and political life amid the eternal and rotating instability of governments.' [35]

Fascism exalted the state because throughout Italian history the
state was always weak. The unification of Italy, which took place
at about the same time as the unification of Germany, did not lead
to the creation of a strong state power. Italy remained a country
split by sharp geographical, economic, and social antagonisms.[36]
The political unity that had been achieved was sorely threatened.
The Holy See and its 70,000 priests violently opposed the new
Italian state for having robbed the church of its territories. As late
as November 1914, von Bülow, the German ambassador, could
threaten Italy with the restoration of the pontifical state unless she
joined the German-Austrian alliance. Moreover, the mass of the
Italian people was opposed to the War of 1914, and the opposition
was not merely confined to small revolutionary groups, as was the
case in Germany. Unlike Germany, Italy stood at the brink of civil
war immediately before the outbreak of the First World War. The
decade from 1890 to 1900 had been packed with strikes, revolts,
scandals in finance and industry, rising prices, growing unrest among
the industrial proletariat of the north and the peasantry of the
south.[37] On the eve of the First World War, the Italian workers
were able to proclaim and organize a Red Week. It is not commonly
known that by the end of the war 1,100,000 trials were pending
against deserters.[38] One fifth of the Italian army had deserted the
flag.

The requirements of competition in the world market imposed

on Fascism the task of strengthening Italian state power. A democratic Italy would have been faced with the same necessity, though it would have employed different methods and acted from different motives. All this, however, does explain why the paeans to the state are so central in the Fascist ideology.

In contrast with Italy, the German state machine was never seriously threatened, not even during the revolutionary days of 1918 and 1919. The bureaucracy continued to operate under its own chiefs, although seemingly under the orders of the workers' and soldiers' councils. The new democratic governments formed in the Reich and in the states interfered little with the old personnel, and the steps they did take to replace the old civil service with new democratic officials were slow and faltering. When, as in Thuringia and Saxony, the workers' governments speeded up the process of democratizing the administration, the Reich stepped in and deposed the governments. The constitution of 1919 finally guaranteed the status and individual rights of civil servants. The ensuing period of state intervention added new fields to the activities of the state bureaucracy, and, as parliamentary democracy disintegrated, power gradually shifted to the ministerial bureaus and the army.

The National Socialists were thus faced with an accumulation of state power centralized in a bureaucracy of high skill and long experience. Their attempt to erect a competing party machine side by side with the bureaucratic state machine and embracing all the activities of the state came to naught. At an early period there was a party foreign office (Alfred Rosenberg), a party ministry of justice (Hans Frank), a party ministry of labor (Hierl), and a party ministry of war (Röhm). Hitler himself put an end to these attempts on 30 June 1934.

7. THE RATIONAL BUREAUCRACY

The doctrine of state supremacy had to be abandoned in Germany because the claims of the party conflicted with the claims of the state. Had this situation not existed, nothing could have prevented Hitler from holding to the totalitarian state theory. Today, the doctrines exalting the state, notably Hegelianism, have been thrown overboard.

It may be true, as Hobhouse tried to prove, that Hegel's glorification of the state was the strongest ideological factor responsible for Prussian militarism and the First World War.[39] But Hegel cannot be held responsible for the political theory of National Socialism. A number of Hegelians are still active within the National Socialist movement; among them some even try to adjust Hegel's theory to the new National Socialist ideology.[40] Their efforts, however, are laughable. For no one can doubt that Hegel's idea of the state is basically incompatible with the German racial myth. Hegel asserted the state to be 'the realization of reason,' and compared to the theories of Haller and the allegedly liberal doctrines of the *Burschenschaften* (student unions led by the philosopher Fries), his political theory was progressive. Hegel despised them both, for Haller represented a reactionary political move to justify the political power of the most backward strata in society, while the 'liberal' doctrine of the *Burschenschaften* contained the germ of racism, Anti-Semitism, and Teutonic egotism, as even Treitschke could see.[41] Hegel's theory is rational; it stands also for the free individual. His state is predicated upon a bureaucracy that guarantees the freedom of the citizens because it acts on the basis of rational and calculable norms.[42] This emphasis on the rational conduct of the bureaucracy, which is, according to Hegel, a prerequisite of proper government, makes his doctrine unpalatable to National Socialist 'dynamism.'

A few words are required to clarify the notion of 'rational' bureaucracy, as Hegel meant it, and the relation between it and a democratic system. Bureaucratic encroachments are today resented in almost every country as a threat to individual liberty.* And if we define democracy solely as an organizational pattern that distributes political power among freely elected representatives, we can readily see that a bureaucracy that is permanent, hierarchically ordered, and subject to arbitrary command must appear as the contradiction of democracy. But democracy is not merely an organizational pattern. It is also a system of values, and the goals it pursues may change. Competitive capitalism aimed exclusively to protect the freedom of society from government interference. In the era of collectivism, which replaced competitive capitalism as a result of profound economic changes, and in which the masses demand recog-

* On the process of bureaucratization, see pp. 367, 385, 412, 418.

nition of their material status, the system of values represented by liberal democracy proves inadequate. Unemployment insurance, health and disability insurance, housing programs become necessary and must be accepted as part of the paraphernalia of democracy. In addition, some kind of control over economic activities must be established. Two methods are apparently open for the realization of these new aims. One, a pluralistic solution, involves self-government through private interested parties; the other, a monistic solution, involves bureaucratic regimentation. The choice between the two methods is not easy, all the less so since the ultimate in bureaucratic power is reached only when public and private bureaucracies interpenetrate. Preference for self-government does not necessarily follow from the nature of democracy. It would follow, and indeed it would be the ideal solution, if the private bureaucracies could reach agreement on all major issues without harming the interests of society as a whole. But the expectation is Utopian. Whenever private groups agreed, it was at the expense of society as a whole; the consumer usually suffered, and government interference proved indispensable. Our society is not harmonious, it is antagonistic, and the state will always be the *ultima ratio*. In Germany, as I have tried to show, the pluralist system of private administration sooner or later compelled the government to intervene, and as a result the power of the state bureaucracy increased. Moreover, the parties concerned, such as trade unions, cartels, trade associations, and political groups, tend to become bureaucratic bodies,* whose purpose is either to keep their organizations running or to keep themselves on top. Inevitably, the spontaneous desires of the rank and file are sacrificed.

Faced with the choice between two kinds of bureaucracy, the citizenry might prefer the public bureaucracy to the private. For private bureaucracies pursue egoistic group interests, whereas public bureaucracies, even when they are dominated by class interests, tend to serve the general welfare. The reason is that public bureaucracies obey fixed and ascertainable rules, while private bureaucraies follow secret instructions. The public servant is selected by a merit system based on the principle of equal opportunity for each competitor, even though the principle is often perverted in practice. Private

* See pp. 81, 390, 412.

bureaucracies co-opt their members and there is no public control of this process.

Max Weber's sociological analysis of bureaucracy, though based on an ideal case, contains a certain amount of truth that applies to any bureaucratic body. Precision, permanency, discipline, reliability, and rationality characterize the bureaucrat who acts 'impersonally,' that is, *'sine ira et studio,'* without hate or passion . . . ; he is motivated by a simple idea of duty, without regard to the person, with formal equality for everyone.[48] It is true that bureaucracy may turn into an anti-democratic force, but whether it does so or not will depend much more on the strength of the democratic forces than on its inner tendencies. Even if it should become reactionary, the bureaucracy will incline toward carrying out its policies legally, in line with the fixed rules according to which it must behave. It will preserve a minimum of liberty and security and thus support the contention that all rational law, regardless of content, has an incontestable protective function.

The rational practices of bureaucracy appear incompatible with National Socialism for the reasons mentioned. The rejection of state supremacy is therefore more than an ideological device intended to conceal the party's betrayal of the army and the civil service; it expresses a real need of the system to do away with the rule of rational law.

We must not be deceived into assuming, however, that centralizational of bureaucratic machinery has in any way lessened in Germany, that the party's existence has in any way restricted bureaucratic powers. On the contrary, preparedness and war have noticeably strengthened authoritarian control in the federal, state, and municipal bureaucracies.

8. The Party as a Machine

We are confronted by two simultaneous trends: enormous growth of the public bureaucracy in number and function; and an ideological campaign of denunciation waged against the bureaucracy, accompanied by a campaign to aggrandize the party. The party itself represents a huge bureaucracy, and the party's struggle against the state apparatus has in no way retarded the process of bureaucratization within the party. On the contrary, quite in keeping with the general rule, private bureaucratization has increased with state intervention. As public regimentation has advanced, the private organizations have taken on a bureaucratic aspect. Because of the complex character of the state's activities, individuals are compelled to join organizations without which they could not hope to find their way through the maze of regimentation. The same process has compelled the organizations to appoint experts, to create a division of functions among their personnel, and to adopt fixed rules for their activities. As a result, the party is not only a body of faithful followers but a bureaucracy as well. It represents a fusion of two kinds of rule: 'charismatic' and bureaucratic,[44] and the size of its administrative apparatus rivals that of a state. As a result, party jurists distinguish sharply between party leadership and party administration; according to one lawyer on the treasurer's staff, the distinction between leadership and administration is symbolized by the contrast between two party buildings: the *Führerbau* (Leadership Building), characterized by 'artistic manifoldness,' and the Administration Building, characterized by a rigid functionalism.[45] We shall return to this allegorical reference. For the present, it is significant to note that since 16 September 1931 complete control of the party administration has been in the hands of the treasurer. This has been reaffirmed in the decrees of 2 June 1933 and 23 March 1934. 'The party administration lies wholly in my hand,' remarks Franz Schwarz, the chief party treasurer, 'because it has to be unified.' [46] Schwarz controls the entire party, its groupings, namely the S.A., the S.S., and its affiliated organizations (the German Labor Front; the organizations of the physicians, lawyers, engineers, teachers, university professors, civil servants; the motor corps, the Hitler Youth, the students' union). A third category, the so-called *betreuten* (protected) organizations,[47] are similarly subject to party supervision. These are the *Deutsche Gemeindetag* (the association of German municipalities), *Deutsche Frauenwehr, Reichsbund der Kinderreichen,* and *Reichsbund für Leibesübungen.*

Hitler's decree of 29 March 1935 determines the extent of the treasurer's financial control, declaring that the party and its groupings constitute one financial unit under the control of the treasurer, who may also call on any state agency for legal assistance in carrying out his tasks. The treasurer has financial command over the property of the party and its groupings, and also supervises the finances of all affiliates; in fact, he fixes the amounts each affiliate must raise from among its members. The party's financial control is not restricted to party organizations, but extends to non-party activities such as the Winter Relief collections (decrees of 1 December 1936 and 24 March 1937), although most of the contributions are made by non-members. Organizations exempt from the treasurer's control are the labor service and the National Socialist Aviation Corps (decree of 17 April 1939). This general trend in exemption is also observable in the S.S. organization: those National Socialist formations that in effect serve as coercive arms of the state are gradually freed from party control.

The party funds are made up of membership fees, with a flat rate for old members (those who joined prior to 1 April 1933) and a graduated scale for new ones; of service fees (entrance fees, registration fees, etc.); of license fees for the manufacture of party uniforms, emblems, and the like; of monies raised through special collections (statute of 5 November 1934), lotteries (decree of 6 March 1937), and government subsidies. Huge sums are involved, as may be inferred from the size of the party membership (at the end of 1934 it was about 2,400,000, remaining at about that figure until 1 May 1937, when it rose sharply). The increase has been even greater since 10 May 1939, when the requirements for joining were made less strict. According to Hitler's wish, the ideal ratio of party members to the rest of the population is approximately ten per cent. The regulations of 11 August 1937 provide that new members should be recruited from Hitler Youth who have belonged to their organization for four uninterrupted years and have reached the age of 18. Induction of these recruits takes place at the yearly party convention. The party has not only an enormous top machine, but also 760 sub-district leaders, 21,354 local leaders, 70,000 leaders of party cells, and 400,000 party block leaders.[48] As a result, the state and the party stand side by side. Legally neither controls the other, each is sovereign in its own field—a constitutional situation which is self-contradictory.

III

THE CHARISMATIC LEADER IN THE LEADERSHIP STATE

1. The Constitutional Function of the Leader

According to current National Socialist ideology, the Leader, Adolf Hitler, is the unifying link that joins state, party, and people. In German etymology, as one National Socialist philosopher has been forced to admit, the term 'leader' has a rather prosaic background.[1] No 'leaders' exist in the army (except in the lowest ranks), the model hierarchy that the National Socialist theorists are fond of invoking; but there were plenty of 'leaders' in the very unheroic professions: the tram conductor, the railway engineer, and the pilot of a vessel were usually called 'leaders,' though they are not allowed so to call themselves today.

The principle of leadership points first of all to an organizational pattern that operates from the top to the bottom and never inversely. It dominates all social and political organizations, except the judiciary, who, as National Socialist lawyers like to say, still vote in accordance with 'Germanic' principles, although it is difficult to see why this allegedly Germanic democratic practice should begin and end at the bench. The leadership principle does not operate in industrial corporations, combines, or cartels.* An understanding of the leadership function is essential for an understanding of National Socialist ideology.

Leadership is alleged to be entirely different from domination: according to German ideology, the character of leadership is precisely what distinguishes the regime from absolutist domination. Similarly, Germany's rule over Europe is not described as domination. The New Order is, rather, one of 'leadership' by Germany and Italy. 'Germany and Italy do not claim domination [*Herrschaft*] but leadership,' says an editorial in the *Frankfurter Zeitung* on 5 January 1941.†

* See pp. 241, 245, 270, 288, 419.
† See p. 130.

Adolf Hitler is top leader. He combines the functions of supreme legislator, supreme administrator, and supreme judge; he is the leader of the party, the army, and the people. In his person, the power of the state, the people, and the movement are unified.[2] Originally, the Leader was merely the chancellor, more ruthless than any that had gone before, and, by virtue of the enabling act of 1933, more powerful, but nevertheless only one agent among several; his decrees had to be countersigned by his ministers and he was often able to act only through President von Hindenburg. After Hindenburg's death, the president's office was fused with that of the chancellor (then Leader and Federal Chancellor, now, since July 1939, simply Leader), and the state was turned over to a single person. This person is Leader for life,[3] although no one knows whence his constitutional rights are derived. He is independent of all other institutions, so that he has not had to (and did not) swear the constitutional oath to parliament, as required by Article 42 of the constitution. He cannot be deposed by a popular initiative, such as is provided for in Article 43. He does not administer the three offices of president, chancellor, and party leader; he merely uses them to demonstrate his power. The federal cabinet is not a cabinet; the fifteen ministers are responsible only to the Leader. They are purely and simply administrative chiefs appointed and dismissed at his pleasure. Cabinet meetings, therefore, need not be convoked and are in fact quite infrequent, leaving the Leader as the sole legislator. Cabinet statutes enacted on the basis of the enabling act of 1933 are not cabinet acts in the sense of decisions made within the cabinet, but acts of the Leader. Ministers need not be consulted. The same is true of plebiscites and statutes enacted by the Reichstag. The law is what the Leader wills, and legislation is an emanation of his power. Similarly, he embodies the administrative power, which is carried out in his name. He is the supreme chief of the armed forces (statute of 21 May 1935) and, as we shall have occasion to see,* the supreme and infallible judge. His power is legally and constitutionally unlimited; it is futile to attempt to describe it. A concept that is boundless cannot be rationally defined.

On the day of Hindenburg's death every member of the army had to take the following oath: 'I swear this holy oath to God: that I shall give unconditional obedience to Adolf Hitler, Leader of

* See p. 440.

the Reich and the people, supreme commander of the army, and that, as a brave soldier, I shall be ready to risk my life at any time for this oath.' [4] Cabinet members have to swear as follows: 'I swear that I shall be faithful and obedient to Adolf Hitler, the Leader of the German Reich and people, that I shall give my strength to the welfare of the German people, obey the laws, and conscientiously fulfil my duties, so help me God.' (Statute of 16 October 1934.) The civil service oath runs as follows: 'I swear that I shall be true and obedient to Adolf Hitler, the Leader of the German Reich and the people, that I shall obey the laws and fulfil my official duties conscientiously, so help me God.' (Section 4 of the Civil Service Act of 26 January 1937.) These oaths show that supreme leadership is not an institution regulated by rules and precedents, or an office with delegated authority, but the investiture of power in one person, Adolf Hitler.[5] The justification of this principle is charismatic: it rests on the assertion that the Leader is endowed with qualities lacking in ordinary mortals. Superhuman qualities emanate from him and pervade the state, party, and people. It is not necessary to quote here the idolatrous utterances made by party members, cabinet ministers, army officers, university professors, and a number of Protestant clergymen.

Max Weber [6] has directed attention to the general phenomenon of charismatic rule and has clearly marked it off from all rational and traditional theories of domination. His discovery is in fact a rediscovery of a phenomenon as old as political life itself. Charismatic rule has long been neglected and ridiculed, but apparently it has deep roots and becomes a powerful stimulus once the proper psychological and social conditions are set. The Leader's charismatic power is not a mere phantasm—none can doubt that millions believe in it. Here we propose to examine three aspects of the problem: the origin of charismatic leadership; the psychological make-up of those who believe in it; and its social function. We shall have to question history for our answer.

2. LUTHER AND CALVIN

Medieval political thought was superseded by the irrationalist philosophies of absolutism, which held sway for a time before they were, in turn, swept away by modern rationalism. Both the Lutheran and Calvinist reformations offered irrational theoretical justifications for unlimited sovereign authority, and were not, as is commonly assumed, among those movements that initiated the era of liberalism, natural rights, equality, and rationalism. In the periods of religious wars and civil insurrections, the rising middle classes had great need of peace and tranquillity; merchants and industrialists yearned for equality with the clergy and the nobility. As a result, a central secular authority was established and its sovereign power was justified as that of an institution to which men owed not only outward obedience but sincere inner devotion. Charismatic justification of existing authority thus found a place at the beginning of bourgeois society; today, in the throes of its gravest and deepest crisis, European society has returned to its earliest theoretical views.

The early Tudor Puritans used all sorts of justifications for the king's authority—the Scriptures, divine natural law, reasons of state; they pointed with solemn warning to the terrible fate of revolutionary and millennial movements on the continent, such as the peasant insurrections or the Taborite and Anabaptist movements. The apologists of Henry VIII invoked the Calvinist and Lutheran doctrines to recommend obedience to the king's person. Their argumentation was predominantly anti-rational, even charismatic. 'The king,' wrote Tyndale, 'is, in this world, without law and may at his lust do right or wrong and shall give accounts to God only.' [7] Henry VIII is likened to the 'sun of man'—one 'dares not cast [his eyes] but sidewise upon the flaming beams [of the king's] bright sun which he in no wise can steadfastly behold.' [8] Obedience to him was a civil, more, a religious duty. The king had to be obeyed because he was endowed with superior human qualities. He was the Leader. One can readily see that these doctrines were opportunistic in character, devised to meet the needs of England's domestic and international position. A central and unchallengeable authority was required, free from the grip of the Catholic Church and able to resist foreign aggression—an authority that would subordinate and, if necessary, even exterminate the autonomy of local, feudal, and ecclesiastical domains. All this made it impossible to resort to a social-contract theory, with its revolutionary implications. The Lutheran and Calvinist political doctrines supplied a solution to the problem.

Luther, it is true, postulated an individual freedom, but his idea of freedom was profoundly different from ours. As set forth in his important treatise, 'On Christian Freedom,' Luther's concept of freedom actually combines our own idea and its exact opposite. 'A Christian man,' Luther says there, 'is the most free of all and 'subject to none; a Christian is the most dutiful servant of all and subject to everyone.' The antinomy could hardly be expressed in more definite terms. Both postulates, freedom and subservience, claim equal validity and universality.

The concept of 'inner freedom' resolves the contradiction. Freedom and bondage belong to two different spheres; the former to the internal, the latter to the external world. The first statement of Luther concerns the inward man and his freedom; the second, the outward man who must obey. Such a dichotomy between the inner and outer life, each governed by different laws, was alien to Greek and medieval philosophy. All classical Greek thinkers held that inner freedom was not possible without outer freedom, and the medieval thinkers looked upon man as a rational being whose essence and activities were ordered according to natural law. Luther divorced the inner realm from the outer, and negated the value of 'works,' that is to say, of external influences. 'No external thing can make a Christian free or pious' and no external relation can affect 'the soul, whether to free or enslave it.' The poor is as free as the rich, the indentured peasant as free as the king, the prisoner as free as his jailer. The oppressed already possess freedom; why should they strive for it?

True, the world as it is does not conform to the Christian ideal. Brotherhood, justice, and love do not prevail here, and Luther originally did not hold up this world as an embodiment of Christian principles. He only accepted the world and the sovereign power of the state as regrettable facts. But this resigned acceptance soon gave way to a full-blown justification. 'This article [referring to the peasant demand of 1525 that serfdom be abolished] would make all men equal and so turn the spiritual kingdom of Christ into a worldly, external kingdom; and that is impossible. For a worldly kingdom cannot stand unless there is an inequality of persons, so that some are free, some imprisoned; some lords, some subjects, etc. And St. Paul says . . . that in Christ master and servant are one thing.' [9] This was Luther's reply to the demand that villeinage be abolished.

According to Luther, there are two kinds of justice, an inner and an outer. True inner justice can only be fulfilled in inner freedom, and outer justice through carrying out one's duties in a given station. An attack against a ruler is an attack against his office. 'In the first place, a distinction must be made between an occupation or a work and the man who is in it, between a work and the doer of it. An occupation or a work can be good and right in itself and yet be bad and wrong if the man in the occupation or the doer of the work is not good and right or does not do his duty rightly.' [10] The office as such has absolute authority. It is divorced from the officeholder, and this foreshadows the abstract character of ·human relations.* The relations between master and servant and king and subject become abstract and anonymous. The institution of bondage is eternal and immutable. Even if a Christian should fall into the hands of heathen Turks, he should not flee from his new masters: 'because if you run away you rob your master of your body, which he bought or obtained in some other way; it no longer belongs to you but has become his, like cattle or other property.' [11] All relations involving power over men and things, whether private or public, are thus sacrosanct. 'Disobedience is also a greater sin than murder, unchastity, theft, or dishonesty.' 'Obedience is the duty of subjects, that they direct all their diligence and effort to do and to leave undone what their overlords desire of them, that they do not allow themselves to be torn or driven from this, whatever another do.' [12]

The outer world not only requires no brotherhood, justice, and love; it need not even be harmonious. Authorities demand not love but obedience, and mete out not mercy but relentless punishment. 'The ass will have blows, and the people will be ruled by force; God knew that full well and so He gave the rulers, not a feather duster but a sword.' [13] 'Therefore, let everyone who can, smite, slay, and stab, secretly or openly, remembering that nothing can be more poisonous, hurtful, or devilish than a rebel. It is just as when one must kill a mad dog.' [14]

Luther's political theory, to the extent that he had one, contained very little, however, that might be termed a charismatic justification of power. Despite the ruthlessness of its thesis, the Lutheran doctrine, in so far as it allowed of inner freedom, set forth a harmonious inner world to oppose the wickedness and corruption of the outer one. To this extent, it contained revolutionary seeds that came to

* See pp. 385, 397, 402.

blossom in the teachings of the Taborites and Anabaptists. Moreover, by divorcing the office from the officeholder, by making
human relations impersonal, it inaugurated and bolstered the doctrines of a rationally operating bureaucracy.

The charismatic doctrine was fully developed by Calvin.[15] His
writings constitute the political theory of the bourgeoisie of the
time, which was chiefly concerned with establishing a strong coercive state machine. The Calvinist doctrine makes a clean break with
medieval thought in all its aspects, theological, philosophical, political, and social; whereas Luther at least confronted the wickedness
of the world with the justice of the evangelical order, as the latter
contained the kernel of possible protest and revolution, Calvin
brought temporal and religious realms into harmony by imposing
his new creed upon the state. The new creed was not that of the
Sermon on the Mount but of the Decalogue, and the theology was
not scholastic but positivist. According to Calvin, man is not a rational being endowed with the light of reason; he is unable to perceive and guide his life according to any rational precepts. His
reason is corrupt, 'enveloped and blinded by innumerable errors.' [16]
His 'intelligence and reason is perverted through the fall' and his
'integrity of understanding' [17] has been destroyed, so that it is impossible for him to attain truth. He can reach it in a very limited
field only. This 'limited field' makes for an intrinsic connection
between Calvinism and the empiricist, experimental attitude of the
period that followed. Calvin allows for a certain capacity 'to perceive earthly matters, those which do not teach either God or his
kingdom or true justice or the immortality of future life, but are
connected with the present life.' [18] Truth can never be attained
through the rational process. Man has to restrict himself to 'the
political doctrine, the art to rule well, to mechanical arts, to philosophy, and all those professions which one calls liberal.' [19] Philosophy and political doctrines can never attain ultimate truth; one
would say in our time, they are concerned solely with finding the
right means to revealed ends. Calvin's positivism is even more clearly
revealed in the fact that the only methodological principles he recognizes as valid are induction and generalization from daily experience.[20] Certainty and universality never result from such scientific
procedures.

Yet each man has in him the seed of reason, and this distinguishes

him from beasts. After the fall, humanity would have been lost had
not God left within us a modicum of reason, which we may call
'the communal grace of God.' [21] How can this ripen and grow?
Not through man's reasoning process—this much is certain—but
solely through special election to grace. The universal grace that
potentially envelops all men alike becomes actualized only through
God's appointment of men to special stations. Calvin here leads us
back to our birth in order to show us that the reason we possess is
a gift of God and not a natural possession. 'When the infant leaves
the womb of its mother, what wisdom does it possess? . . . A child
is less than the poorest beast . . . How is it that we possess the
spirit of intelligence when we come of age? It is necessary that
God give it to us.' [22] Election to grace is not an award for a pious
life or for good works; it may even be conferred upon a pagan.[23]
Though God's ways are inscrutable, they do not follow an accidental course—everything is inexorably predestined, willed by God.

But how are men to recognize whether their fellow men are
endowed with God's grace? The answer is, by their success. The
ruler, the magistrate, the successful businessman, the political leader,
the lawyer, doctor, factory foreman, the slave owner, all owe their
position to God's grace. They are therefore to be obeyed. The
charisma flows to everyone in power, in every sphere of life, every
profession and condition.

The political and social theory follows logically from the theological premises, the whole constituting the most radical departure
from the scholastic position. No precept can exist, no natural law,
that binds anyone. If man's conscience is corrupt, so is natural law,
and God's justice may not be conceived through it. 'If he [man]
had remained in the state of natural integrity as God created him
. . . each would bear in his heart the law, so that there would have
been no constraint . . . Each would know his rule and . . . would
follow what is good and just.' [24] But conscience and natural law
cannot teach us how to behave. Natural law is not the creative principle of the state, which is neither a natural institution nor the product of man's needs. The state is a coercive institution, antagonistic
to the nature of man.[25] It is created by God and is part of His plan
to save us from deprivation. 'Because the order of nature has been
perverted, it is necessary that God . . . show us . . . that we are
not capable of liberty, that it is necessary for us to be kept in a state

of subjection.' [26] Thus Calvin breaks with the Aristotelian and Thomist tradition and embraces political Augustinianism, establishing 'the divine right of the established order.' [27]

Sanctity extends not only to the state as such (as Luther contended), but to all persons in the hierarchy of the state who share in the exercise of its power. No distinction is made between the bearer of sovereignty and its organs. To our superiors we owe unconditional obedience, not merely as a duty to man but to God, and beyond obedience we owe humility and reverence. Those who disobey invoke not only the severity of earthly law but the wrath of God. Obedience and reverence to authority are demanded not out of constraint but out of volition. The medieval notion of the governmental contract is implicitly and explicitly repudiated. According to Calvin, it is seditious to judge a king by his obligations or services to the people, for the king is under obligation to none but God. Calvin does sometimes speak of a 'mutual obligation' between the king and the people, but he never understands it to mean a contract; the duties God imposes upon the ruler and the people are never mutual ones.

Any institutional limitation of the ruler's power is of course incompatible with such a view. This does not mean that Calvin advocates or defends tyranny and despotism—on the contrary, he admonishes rulers to steel themselves against vanity and to fulfil their duties in a benevolent spirit. Otherwise they will meet the wrath of God.[28]

Historians of political thought have made much of Calvin's statement that the magistrates may resist the king if they are constitutionally empowered to do so. 'In case there are representatives of the people who have been established to restrict the despotism of the kings, as, for instance, the tribunes of the people in Rome, or in our kingdoms the estates assembled, it is their duty to resist the presumptions of the rulers. If they yield, they betray the liberty of the people, which has been entrusted to them by God.' [29] This short paragraph, which has received enormous attention, has been regarded either as a vestige of medieval natural-law doctrine or as the beginning of democratic ideology. The interpretation is entirely unjustified and contrary to the spirit of the entire work. It has arisen because French Huguenots like Francis Hotman and Du Plessis Mornay expounded pseudo-revolutionary regicidal doctrines on the basis of Calvin's theory. The writings of these monarchomachs, however, should not be used as a basis for such an interpretation. For one thing, Calvin was not directly responsible for their doctrines, and for another they were not revolutionaries in any sense of the term, but opportunists who used every juristic and theoretical argument to fight the king and the Catholic league. Calvin's statement, quoted above, is conservative: it denies the individual's right to resist and describes the actual situation in France and many other European countries in which the estates restricted the king's power.[30] Calvin insists that where such powers exist they must not be surrendered, for they are as much an emanation of God's grace as is the power of the king.

The same chapter of the *Institutions* [31] speaks of one other means of deliverance from oppressive burdens, and the passage is much more characteristic of Calvin's theory than is his statement about the rights of the estates general. It has received little attention. God, Calvin says, may send a providential savior to his people. God manifests his miraculous power, goodness, and providence by appointing one of his servants as a savior and arming him so that he may punish an unjust ruler and deliver the people from oppression. However, people must not be too credulous when such a savior appears. The charismatic leader is announced here, the man who, in the name of God's providence, is authorized to overthrow the government and free the people.

3. THE THAUMATURGIC KINGS

At the birth of modern capitalism, allegedly initiating a system of rationality, calculability, and predictability, stands this social doctrine, which is in every respect the opposite of rationalism, though it fulfils certain psychological needs of the people that are older than capitalism. Anthropologists have directed attention to the mana of kings, the magic power that radiates from the person of the ruler and reaches the people. Touching the king or being touched by him gives strength to the weak and health to the sick. The king is the hero, the embodiment of the tribal totem; he wards off demons that threaten the people, their property, and their health. Such were the beliefs of the primitives. Their views were not irrational; the belief in the ruler's magic power had a rational basis. Rulers had to guarantee success. When floods threatened or epidemics and wars decimated the tribe, the king had to save and deliver his people. If unsuccessful he was deposed and killed.[32] The royal charisma was based on a mutual bargain.

The more we approach modern civilization, the more the charisma is divorced from the king's social and political obligations.

The oriental idea of kingship, even the messianic idea of the Old Testament, was based on the charismatic doctrine. The root idea was that a primeval monster had existed who incarnated the principle of evil and was inimical to God and man (Tehom myth).[33] Jahwe, the savior, had finally defeated this monster and brought temporary blessings upon the people. This, the basic idea not only of the Old Testament but of all other oriental religions, lies at the root of the belief in the divine and magic power of kings. The king is not only God's deputy on earth, he is God. Heroes, if genuine, were originally not men but gods.[34] 'Earliest known religion is the belief in the divinity of kings.' [35]

The oriental idea of kingship was imported into Europe by Alexander of Macedonia. Prior to him, the Greek rulers had been entirely political figures, their relation to the people purely rational in character. Since Alexander kings have been worshipped as gods.[36] The ideological distance between the empires of Alexander and Augustus is short. Augustus was regarded as a Messiah,[37] as Horace's description indicates: 'the son of Maja who descended to the people of the Quirites.' [38]

In German history, the charisma was attached to the tribe and not to the king's person,[39] yet it was never regarded as the sole source of authority and law, and popular consent was as important as the aura of the selected tribe. In the Frankish tradition, the charisma manifested itself in the flowing locks of the Frankish kings, which gave them unusual power and luck. The belief was definitely not of Christian origin; this is clear from the fact that the church opposed the Germanic view of blood legitimacy. Yet, by a fatal historical accident, the church made an extraordinary contribution to the revival of the charismatic belief. After the overthrow of the Merovingian kings and the establishment of the Carolingian dynasty, the church, by anointing Pippin, transferred the charisma from the Merovingians to the Carolingians. In confirming the Carolingian *coup d'état*, the pope, oracle of natural law, even made unction a sacrament, thus conferring God's grace upon the new ruling house. By this act, the church, for reasons of expediency, abandoned its old policy of opposing the veneration of kings as gods, a policy it had vigorously asserted in the case of the Byzantine kings, especially against the Proskynesis.

Shortly afterward, however, the church had to renew its fight against royal deification. Since Robert the Pious, the French kings, as well as the Plantagenets of England, had claimed the power to heal. The king's touch could cure scrofula, and, on fixed ritual occasions, thousands thronged around the ruler for this boon. The Gregorian dispute between the papacy and the kingdom was not only a struggle for supremacy between secular and spiritual power, but a struggle waged by the church against the magic and supernatural powers claimed by the kings.[40] From that period on, unction was no longer regarded as a sacrament and the emperor became a layman.

Despite this opposition, the regal healing power lived on in popular belief. Barbarossa, the German emperor, attempted to endow the German Reich with sacred attributes in order to combat the pope; he considered himself a *numen* with oracular power. His laws were *sacer*, the *res publica* was *diva*. Under the influence of oriental conceptions, Frederick II of Hohenstaufen was looked upon as a personified god, and John of Salisbury, the great English humanist, quite correctly saw this entire trend as marking a retrogression to paganism.[41] Superstitious belief in the healing power of kings had an extraordinarily long heyday, lasting far into the age of rationalism. Philip the Fair of France and his entourage re-established the king's power to heal as a means of offsetting the claims of Pope Boniface VIII,[42] and, incidentally, of facilitating the expropriation of the order of Templars. The fourteenth century witnessed a reawakening of thaumaturgic practices and beliefs; Luther reports them without a single critical word,[43] and dozens of pamphlets issued in France and England dealt with the healing power of the king. The protectorate of Cromwell is the only period during which this healing was not practiced. After the Restoration, the belief was revived, with an amazing amount of apologetic literature pouring forth under Charles II.[44] In France, the belief disappeared shortly after the Revolution.

In the history of thaumaturgic practices in the Occident, the significant fact is that magic powers are invoked every time the sovereign tries to assert independence of religion and social forces. Alexander needed deification for his imperialist conquests. Since he ruled over people of many religions, identifying himself with any one of these would have involved the danger of having to repudiate all others. By raising his own person to the status of divinity, he transcended all the existing religions. Other forms of justification, such as the rational doctrine of Aristotle or the democratic doctrine urged by the sophists, were out of the question. Augustus, too, felt the need of deification for similar reasons,[45] and the Carolingians resorted to it because they had established the new monarchy through unconstitutional means. Frederick Barbarossa and Frederick II invoked the charisma to help them defend the secular power from church encroachment. In France and England, where the king's power to work miracles was defended by versatile apologists, apotheosis of the monarch also served as a preventive of popular resistance. The Bourbons, Plantagenets, and early Tudors alike claimed to be little gods as a means of investing their persons with the power necessary to awe recalcitrant subjects.

4. The Psychology of Charisma

We are not concerned with anthropological theories of the charismatic claim, and yet a few words are necessary to explain why it has been revived. Without doubt, the alleged supernatural endowment of the ruler is an adulterated form of the messianic idea, the antecedents of which can be traced back to the 'primeval monster who incarnated the principle of evil and stood opposed to God and man.' Such antecedents, however, do not explain the psychology of charisma, which is far more important than its objective analysis. As for the charismatic claim itself, it is not enough to describe it as an 'outcome of the innate human characteristics of dependence on a higher power,' as a natural quest 'for someone to help in view of present distress.' [46] Such statements do not explain why the doctrine arises in specific periods of history or why specific social strata rely on it rather than on rational considerations.

The problem requires an analysis of the psychological processes that lead to the belief in one man's power to perform miracles, a belief that characterizes certain pre-religious dispositions of the human mind.[47] The analysis can also lead to an understanding of the psychological process that underlies man's adoration of man. As Rudolf Otto has shown, the state of mind and the emotions involved are those of an individual who feels himself overwhelmed by his own inefficacy and who is led to believe in the existence of a *Mysterium Tremendum*. The mystery creates awe, dread, and terror. Man shudders before the demon or God's wrath. But his attitude is ambivalent—he is both awed and fascinated. He experiences moments of extreme rapture during which he identifies himself with the holy.

This entirely irrational belief will arise in situations that the average man cannot grasp and understand rationally. It is not only anxiety that drives men to embrace superstition, but inability to understand the reasons for their helplessness, misery, and degradation. In periods of civil strife, religious turmoil, and profound social and economic upheavals productive of misery and distress, men are often unable, or deliberately rendered unable, to perceive the developmental laws that have brought about their condition. The least rational strata of society turn to leaders. Like primitive men, they look for a savior to fend off their misery and deliver them from destitution. There is always a factor of calculation, often on both sides. The leader uses and enhances the feeling of awe; the followers flock to him to attain their ends.

Obedience is a necessary element in charismatic leadership—obedience both subjectively, as an onerous burden, and objectively, as a means of exacting the performance of duty. Consequently, there can be no equality among the followers, for power is derived from the leader. He has to distribute it in unequal doses, so that he has an élite to rely upon, one that shares his own charisma and through it helps him to dominate the mass. Charismatic organization is always based on strict obedience within a hierarchical structure.[48]

But if the genuinely religious phenomenon of the charisma belongs to the sphere of the irrational, its parallel political manifestation is purely a ruse for the establishment, maintenance, or enhancement of power. It would be a fatal mistake to claim that it controverts any rational justification of state sovereignty. The charismatic claim of modern leaders functions as a conscious device, intended to foster helplessness and hopelessness among the people, to abolish equality, and to substitute a hierarchical order in which the leader and his group share the glory and advantage of the *numen.* It has even more efficacy than the charisma of primitive kingship: leaders are not deposed or killed if they fail to deliver their people from evil. *Do ut das* no longer applies. The charisma has become absolute, calling for obedience to the leader not because of his useful functions, but because of his alleged superhuman gifts.

IV

THE RACIAL PEOPLE, THE SOURCE OF CHARISMA

THE Leader's charismatic power has to derive from somewhere, from God or the tribe. In National Socialist theory its source is in the racial people. Rare is the National Socialist utterance that does not claim that all power is derived from the people. We have seen that Carl Schmitt's 'tripartite' political scheme aroused sharp criticism because it deviated on this point, assigning an inferior, unpolitical part to the people.

1. NATION AND RACE

What, then, do the German National Socialists understand by the 'racial people' and why do they stress its supremacy? Why do they so deliberately avoid using the current term 'nation'?

Races exist, there is no denying it, and a race may be defined as a group of individuals possessing in common certain traits transmitted by heredity, which are sufficiently clear to mark off one group from others.[1] As we are not concerned with anthropological problems, we can pass over the question what these distinctions are and when they are sufficiently marked. Nor are we interested in adopting any specific classification of races; we agree with the large majority of anthropologists that there are no superior or inferior races, and that there is no scientifically determinable connection between racial and cultural attributes. 'The so-called racial explanation of differences in human performance and achievement is either an ineptitude or a fraud.' [2] We also agree that there are no pure races, that 'every civilized group of which we have record has been a hybrid group, a fact which effectively disposes of the theory that hybrid people are inferior to purebred ones.' [3]

Scientific arguments contribute little to an understanding of German racism. It is of little avail, for example, to attack racism by pointing out that the term 'Aryan' does not denote a common bone structure or blood composition, or any other physical or biological similarity, but merely a common linguistic origin. Even the discoveries of National Socialist anthropology are not to any great extent incorporated into the body of National Socialist philosophy, which merely speaks of Aryan races or of Nordic and Germanic superiority. Instead of refuting the racial theory, we shall try to understand its social, political, and cultural significance. The attempt has already been made. Scholars have drawn attention to the intimate connection between racism and the persecution of minorities, that characterized the Inquisition, the Albigensian crusade, and the campaign against the French Huguenots, and have interpreted race persecution as a modern form of religious intolerance and heresy-hunting. On this basis, racism has been described as an ideology designed to defend and justify 'unequal citizen rights.' [4] This theory is certainly correct, but does it help us to understand why racism supersedes nationalism and why Anti-Semitism, which is the German form of racism, is accepted not merely as a device for persecution but as a genuine philosophy of life pervading the whole National Socialist outlook? We shall be able to solve the problem only by analyzing the functions of the various concepts involved.

Race is an entirely biological phenomenon: the concept of 'the people' contains an admixture of cultural elements. Common descent, common geographical location, common customs, common language and religion—all play a part in the making of a people, although the particular significance of the various elements may vary according to the historical situation.[5] The concept of a *racial* people, a term the Germans are fond of, is, however, based primarily on biological traits; the cultural elements serve only to distinguish various groups within one race.

In contrast, the nation is primarily a political concept. It involves the idea of the state, without which the nation cannot be conceived. A people becomes a nation if it possesses a consciousness of common political aims, if it is capable of achieving and maintaining a unified political will. As eminent a political leader as Disraeli rejected the very concept of the people. 'The phrase "the people" is sheer nonsense. It is not a political term. It is a phrase of natural history. A people is a species; a civilised community is a nation. Now, a nation is a work of art and a work of time.' [6]

Nation and nationality are intrinsically connected with the state.[7]

The modern state, however, has not been created by the nation, but resulted from the introduction of commodity production, which has preceded the appearance of modern nations. When the product of labor is a commodity convertible into money, this money can be used to build the state and to establish a bureaucracy and standing army. The first modern states were the Italian city-states, created not by national feeling and national striving but by capitalists who hired soldiers and bureaucracies to build up a centralized machine. In Italy, France, and Germany these states were even established by foreigners with whose help the French kings, the Italian *podeste*, and the German princes broke down the feudal opposition.[8] Seen in this light, the early modern state was not only not national, but profoundly anti-national. Its governments had no legitimacy. The political theory evolved during this period, if it was not oppositional, was concerned solely with devising *arcana dominationis*, techniques with which to establish and maintain the rule of the absolutist dictators. Machiavelli's *Prince* is the prototype of them all.

In its decisive function, the nation is the ideological ground that justifies a central coercive authority over the feudal, local, and ecclesiastical powers. It serves as a mechanism for unifying the vast network of individual and group interests—this in the period when the middle classes become conscious of their own objectives and succeed in impressing them upon the whole people.

The social-contract theory, as Hobbes had developed it, was inadequate to satisfy the need for a unifying mechanism and ideology, and Rousseau quickly detected its deficiencies. Hobbes had held that selfish interest could somehow keep society together and that the state, as an aggregate of individual wills, could exist even though no common aim pervaded its individual members. In opposition to this doctrine, Rousseau declared that society must be 'a moral, collective body.'[9] The transition from natural society to political society, he said, must produce 'a very remarkable change' in man 'by substituting justice for instinct in his conduct and giving his actions the morality they formerly lacked.'[10] The right of the stronger, so fundamental for Hobbes's and Spinoza's political doctrine, could not provide a basis on which society might rest; such right, Rousseau declares, is either superfluous or nonsensical.[11]

The nation creates common aims and common loyalties; it makes the general will concrete and renders the state independent of divine sanction, establishing exclusive links between the individual and his secular community. The nation, moreover, gives every state a legitimate basis, differing in this respect from the universalism of medieval doctrine. Finally, it does away with the dynastic principle of legitimation that identified the state with the ruler.

It was during the French Revolution that the nation revealed itself as the decisive political force. At that time, the subjective factor, national consciousness, the will to political unity, turned into an objective reality,[12] and one class, the bourgeoisie, constituted itself as the nation, so that the nation became the property, so to speak, of that class. Through the nation the bourgeoisie impressed its system of values on all of the people.

The fusion of the theory of nationalism with the much older doctrine of popular sovereignty had revolutionary implications,[13] permitting the emergence of an essentially secular society with a universally accepted system of values. The French Revolution illustrates the revolutionary impact of the new concept. Abbé Sieyès was the first to propound the view that the third estate, the middle class, was the nation, because it was the sole productive sector of society. The nation, in his view, was the aggregate of those individuals who stand under a common law and are represented through the same legislative assembly. The nation is sovereign, its existence its complete justification, and its will the supreme law. The state is in its service; state power is legitimate only through and by it. Such a conception, directed against the aristocracy and the monarchy, was clearly revolutionary. Its influence was so strong that even the counter-revolutionaries did not deny the existence of the nation but tried painstakingly to turn it to the advantage of the monarchy or of the alliance between the monarchy and the aristocracy (de Maistre and Montlosier).[14]

The French Revolution determined the entire course of ideological discussion among European states before Hitler's advent to power: the nation as an entity composed of free and equal citizens, the Jacobin concept of the nation. According to Ernest Renan, the nation is a plebiscite, daily renewed, established by the free decision of free men.[15]

The sociological function of this new concept is self-explanatory. Large, thickly populated economic regions emerged, unified by common currency, tariffs, and transportation; annihilating, or at least weakening, intermediate autonomous powers; and demanding a new allegiance. The French revolutions of 1791, 1793, and 1848 all declared that the nation's sovereignty is indivisible and inalienable. The new nation jealously guarded its rights; deputies were elected in its name and not in that of any group or class, and no one was allowed to come between the individual and the nation. This was dramatically and drastically demonstrated in the *Lex Le Chapelier* passed during the French Revolution, a law that forbade the organization of unions. 'The individual,' Le Chapelier declared, 'owes allegiance solely and exclusively to the state and to no one else.'

The concept of the nation, furthermore, serves to individualize a society by marking it off from all others. This can occur only when societies confront one another, each with specific traits that can be readily distinguished. After the breakdown of medieval universalism, the dynastic principle offered a basis for individualization. But when this principle broke down and was succeeded by the liberalist state, no integrating or individualizing factor was at hand. The liberalist state itself could perform this function. Its aim was only negative: the protection of life, liberty, and property. States, that is to say bureaucratic, police, and military machines, show more similarities than differences. Consequently, the national concept had to fill the gap left by the dynastic principle. It supplied the individualizing factor in a world of competing states.

2. RACISM IN GERMANY

In contrast to France, the German development never stressed national sovereignty. In fact, the concept of the nation never took hold in Germany. It is true that Fichte, one of the forerunners of racial nationalism,[16] formulated the idea of a German nation, but this concept referred to 'the people' and stressed the racial and biological affinities produced by common descent at the expense of the political affinities or the conscious, free decision of equal citizens. Even Wilhelm von Humboldt, a great liberal, denied the sovereignty of the nation,[17] while Heinrich von Treitschke regarded the national principle as a mere 'abstraction,' a 'Napoleonic phrase,' 'an empty figure.' [18]

The national idea usually goes hand in hand with the democratic principle and popular sovereignty, and both were extremely distasteful to German theorists and politicians. German disunity and the rivalries among the various states and their princes may have had much to do with this distaste. In any case, whenever German theorists and political figures did speak of the nation, they divorced it from any Jacobin, democratic, or political implications, that is, from any doctrine of popular sovereignty. A biological race theory replaced the political theory of nationality. Long before Hitler, the political bond among free men tended to give way to the natural bond among racial Germans.

There is another reason why the national idea did not play a decisive part in imperial Germany. Emphasis on the sovereignty of the nation as such equalizes all nations and constitutes a barrier against the assertion of national superiority. If the nation rests on the free decision of free men, no nation is superior to any other. National sovereignty handicaps imperialist expansion. Indeed, whenever democratic states resort to such expansion, they almost invariably abandon the national concept and glorify racial and biological traits that allegedly make them superior to the conquered. The doctrine of the white man's burden illustrates this point, and is true of the United States. We need only cite the writings of Josiah Strong. 'It is manifest,' he declared, 'that the Anglo-Saxon holds in his hands the destinies of mankind, and it is evident that the United States is to become the home of this race, the principal seat of its power . . .' [19] This racial theory was as much a foundation for imperialist expansion as it was a spurious solution of class antagonisms.

Still, racial theories have had no basic significance in shaping the ideology of the English and American people. The rapid growth of such theories in England and America during the nineteenth and early twentieth centuries served as an aid to the conquest of colonial, semi-colonial, or very weak states, but their services were never required to organize the total power of the nation for war. Not so in Germany. German expansion was and is directed against powerful states. When Germany came forward as an active imperialist force, it found the earth divided among the various military machines. Redistribution, where it could not be achieved peaceably, required the force of arms and an enormous outlay in blood and money. It required an ideology that could justify the huge effort in the eyes of the people. The alleged superiority of the German Nordic race performed this function.*

As a result, the belief in German racial supremacy is deeply embedded in the history of German thought. Herder, the first outstanding philosopher of history, wrote of 'a people, who, by their size and strength of body, their enterprising, bold, and persevering spirit in war . . . have contributed more than another race to the weal and woe of this quarter of the globe. It was the Germans who defended Christianity against the incessant invasions of Huns, Hungarians, Mongols, and Turks. By them, too, the greater part of Europe was not only conquered, planted, and modelled, but covered and protected.' [20] The same view is held by a large number of Germany's historians, philosophers, and economists. Friedrich von Schlegel invoked racial qualities to explain the superiority of the Germanic tribes over the Romans.[21] Heinrich von Treitschke, the historian of the Bismarck period, though he held a somewhat equivocal position on the race question, interpreted history as a process characterized by the emergence and decay of races,[22] and made a comparison between the racial attributes of the Germans, and those of the Dutch, English, Russians, Italians, and Americans, showing all non-Germans to be inferior in generosity, feeling for beauty, and the 'simple fidelity' of nature. In brief, Treitschke made a catalogue of German virtues, which is still the stock-in-trade of all German propagandists. At the same time he fought against the racial Teutonic philosophy of the student unions (Burschenschaften).[23] He idolized state power, denied that it could ever be wrong, and asserted that the most healthy and vigorous expression of that power was war.[24]

The influence of the so-called state or *Katheder* socialists upon the ultimate development of National Socialist racism seems far more important. The writings of Friedrich List and Adolph Wagner clearly show the factors that contributed to the triumph of racial ideas. These men † were attempting to counteract socialist theories of class struggle by repudiating liberal political thought and by setting up a state capitalist scheme that would 'incorporate' the working classes and imbue the whole people with the spirit of their racial superiority. The aim was to organize society for imperialist

* See pp. 184-218.
† See also pp. 195, 209.

adventures. Adolph Wagner recognized that Prussian efforts to annihilate the political and industrial labor movement were insufficient and doomed to failure. He also thought that the Western concept of *Nation* was dangerous for Germany, since it implied giving the working classes equal rights, thereby delivering to them the fate of the nation and of the state.

Friedrich List, the first articulate National Socialist—he was not just a forerunner but a full-fledged National Socialist—urged the establishment of a system of state capitalism. His *National System of Political Economy* [25] outlined the plan, and his *Memorandum on the Value and the Conditions of an Alliance between Great Britain and Germany* gave it further elaboration.[26] The latter work clearly reveals the reasons underlying the acceptance of racial theories and state capitalism.

The ruling section of the peoples of this earth has for some time been segregating itself according to descent . . . One speaks of a German, a Romanic, a Slavonic race in a political aspect. This distinction alone seems destined to exercise great influence upon the practical politics of the future. At the head of the three races stand England, France, and Russia . . . There is hardly any doubt that the Germanic race has, by virtue of its nature and character, been preferentially selected by Providence for the solution of the great task—to lead the affairs of the world, to civilize the wild barbaric countries, to populate those still uninhabited, for none of the others has the capacity to emigrate *en masse* and to found more perfect communities in foreign lands . . . and to keep free of the influences of barbaric and semi-barbaric aborigines.

England, inhabited by a Germanic race and equipped with a mighty fleet and vast empire, has the mission of reorganizing the world. But she can do so only with Germany's aid. 'Alliance with Germany will remain the only true means whereby England can make Asia and Africa serviceable for her future greatness, alliance with Germany not as she is today but with Germany as she ought to be and as she could become, with England's help.' [27] England must recognize, List declares, that Germany cannot become strong on the basis of free trade. Free trade is a fit doctrine only for a nation that is already powerful. Germany is disunited and weak, and only protective tariffs can assure her political unity and economic power. Germany has to become so strong that she is able to keep England's competitors, France and Russia, at bay. Besides, as the past has amply demonstrated, Germany's industrial growth is to the benefit of England, because England supplies the German market.

List was thus the first to develop the theory that Hitler brought to full flower in *Mein Kampf* and that National Socialist foreign policy attempted to realize during the years preceding the German-Russian non-aggression pact of 1939: a redivision of the earth between Germany and England on the basis of German racial doctrines of superiority.

Similar motives appear in the writings and political activity of Adolph Wagner, leader of the academic socialists.[28] The fundamental problem he sets himself is: how can Germany become powerful? It cannot be done, he thinks, by accepting the British system of economics, that is, free trade and free competition. Nor can Germany become great by accepting Marxist socialism, which is a materialist doctrine that incites class warfare and negates the right of property.[29] Wagner is willing to admit, however, that there is a grain of truth in the Marxist critique of liberalism. The solution lies in building German economy along the lines suggested by List.[30] The economy must be subordinated to the community, and all egoistic interests must be subordinated to the state. The community that acquires supremacy in this way is racial, conceived on the model outlined by Herder and Schlegel.[31] German culture, as created by the Germanic race, is superior to all others. Wagner put his aggressive doctrine of racial imperialism to practical use during the Franco-Prussian war of 1870, when he bitterly denounced France as a once powerful but now decadent state, which would finally succumb because its Gallic race was biologically inferior to the Germanic.[32] Germany cannot win the place she deserves if she adheres to the principles of Manchester liberalism. The *Verein für Sozialpolitik* (1872) offered Wagner a powerful medium for denouncing liberalism and socialism alike and for indoctrinating the academic world (and through it the civil service) with his state-socialist idea. State regimentation, as he foresaw and acclaimed it, would utilize and enhance the productive power of industry and thereby weaken the industrial and political might of the proletariat.

It was but a step from this racial imperialism to Anti-Semitism, which we shall discuss later.

The great popularity of the racial doctrine dates from the publication of Houston Stewart Chamberlain's dilettante concoction, the *Foundations of the Nineteenth Century*,[33] which was an adaptation of Count Gobineau's *Essay on the Inequality of Human Races*,[34] published in 1854. Gobineau's work repudiated the French revolutions of 1789 and 1848 and all they stood for. His doctrine was designed to combat political liberalism and the labor movement, and the book in which he stated it was dedicated to the king of Hanover, who had only recently abolished the liberal constitution by unconstitutional means. Gobineau sought an ideological basis for a state form that would exclude the proletariat from political rights and insure a stable foundation for aristocratic rule, and that would also improve upon the French counter-revolutionist theories of Bonald and de Maistre. Gobineau regards aristocracy as racially conditioned. He develops a hierarchy of races in which the Negro represents the lowest type and the white race the only civilized, with the fair, blond, Germanic race holding a special position of leadership. Again it is England, not Germany, that typifies the characteristics of the Germanic race. A special Gobineau association was established and did much to propagate the teachings of the master.[35] Gobineau, however, was not concerned with justifying any kind of imperialism, French, German, or English. His primary interest was to preserve, or rather to restore, the privileges of an aristocracy whose political power had been shattered by a series of revolutions and whose rule could no longer be justified by tradition.

Gobineau's doctrine was re-worked by Houston Stewart Chamberlain and his father-in-law, Richard Wagner; in their hands it became a powerful instrument for racial imperialism and Anti-Semitism. It would be wearisome to repeat Chamberlain's arguments. In brief, he held that the Teutonic race comprises those who genuinely shape 'the destinies of mankind, whether as builders of the state or as discoverers of new thoughts and of original art . . . Our whole civilization and culture of today is the work of one definite race of men, the Teutonic.' [36] Chamberlain went far beyond Gobineau, criticized him, in fact, for having accepted the creative function of mixed races. Pure races, he held, would evolve through a long historic process that would ultimately create a race of super-men.

Richard Wagner had met Gobineau in Rome in November 1876 and had been deeply impressed by him,[37] becoming an ardent advo-cate of his theories. When Chamberlain joined the Wagner circle and later married Wagner's daughter, his father-in-law's enthusiasm for Gobineau was soon transferred to Chamberlain. Letters that passed between him and his mother-in-law, Cosima Wagner,[38] clearly show the evolution of the racial doctrine and the influence of Gobineau's personality and thought upon the Wagner circle. Strangely enough, Chamberlain refutes the idea that a pure race is superior to a hybrid one (letter of 15 November 1893). He ascribes the opposite thesis to Gobineau and even declares that 'the shadow of Gobineau's teaching would hang like a cloud over some discus-sions [of Richard Wagner] in the tenth volume [of Wagner's works].'[39] The correspondence, moreover, makes it increasingly clear that the entire elaborate structure of the *Foundations* was sheer embellishment of Chamberlain's Anti-Semitism, the central thesis of which was his assertion of a Jewish conspiracy to defeat the Germanic races.[40] In a letter of 11 November 1902 [41] he insists that 'the chapter on Semitism is for me the most important one.' This idea of a Jewish conspiracy recurs over and over in the dis-cussions of the Wagner circle, especially in Richard Wagner's own statements. Wagner held to the idea with amazing tenacity, in spite of the fact that one of his most influential champions in the musical world was Hermann Levi, the Jewish conductor of the Royal Munich Opera Company, who devoted all his energies to Wagner's operas. Wagner, however, was always suspicious of Levi, invariably imagining a Jewish conspiracy whenever something went wrong in the performance of his works. This is especially clear in the correspondence between him and King Louis II.[42]

3. ANTI-SEMITIC THEORIES

Racism, then, increasingly became unadulterated Anti-Semitism, so that as the doctrine of German racial superiority developed, Anti-Semitic sentiment developed with it. Here again scientific dis-cussion of the truth of National Socialist Anti-Semitic utterances would be futile, for Anti-Semitism has had deep roots in German history. The whole history of German intellectual life is shot through with Jew-baiting, and Anti-Semitic organizations played a leading part even during the imperial period.

With the exception of Lessing, Goethe, Schelling, and Hegel, nearly all the great poets and thinkers of Germany, even if they were not outspoken Anti-Semites, often unconsciously betrayed Anti-Semitic sentiments that contrasted sharply with the humanitarian philosophies they advocated.

Martin Luther was the first outspoken and passionate Anti-Semite. Christians, he warns, should not debate with Jews over the Articles of Faith. Better, he declares, drive the Jews from Germany. His ironical remarks on how they should be expelled sound much like those of *Der Stürmer*, Streicher's Anti-Semitic sheet, in which advertisements appear offering the Jews one-way tickets to Palestine. 'Country and streets,' Luther says, 'are open to them so they might move to their country if they like. We shall give them gifts, with pleasure, in order to get rid of them, because they are a heavy burden like a plague, pestilence, misfortune in our country.' This statement is followed by others expressing bitter hatred and resentment. When the Jews go, they should be deprived of 'all their cash and jewels and silver and gold.' 'That into the hands of the young, strong Jews and Jewesses be placed flails, axes, mattocks, trowels, distaffs, and spindles, and they are made to earn their daily bread by the sweat of their noses as it is put upon the shoulders of the children of Adam.' 'That their synagogues or schools be set on fire.' 'That their houses be broken up and destroyed . . . and they be put under a roof or stable, like the gypsies . . . in misery and captivity as they incessantly lament and complain to God about us.' [48]

The two special treatises in which these outbursts of fanatic hatred appear typify the sentiments of a small section of the German middle classes throughout modern German history and have formed the basis for Anti-Semitic acts up to the time when National Socialism made them part of official policy.

Fichte was an avowed Anti-Semite, and his Anti-Semitic feelings took sharpest form during the period in which he was developing his near-anarchist theory of the state. It is important to realize that these Anti-Semitic statements occur during the liberal period of his development. The connection was not accidental, as we can recognize when we remember that in the period following the French Revolution and the wars of liberation, it was the liberal movement that took up and carried forward Anti-Semitism. Napoleon's rule had brought legal emancipation to the Jews in Germany, and the fight against Napoleon there became a struggle against all that his reforms had achieved. Under liberal and patriotic slogans, mobs destroyed Jewish homes and synagogues, and mal-treatment of Jews became an almost daily occurrence.

Anti-Semitism has been a political force in Germany ever since the wars of liberation. The Bismarck period made it a popular movement. The Jews were blamed for the financial crisis that terminated the economic upswing of the years following the War of 1870. In 1873 Wilhelm Marr, a Hamburg journalist, published a pamphlet called *The Victory of Judaism over Germany*,[44] which incited violent Anti-Semitic hatred. In the same period, an aggressive imperialism justified by racial arguments joined hands with the Anti-Semitic wave.

The two last-mentioned trends merged when Adolph Wagner joined Court Chaplain Stöcker in the *Christlich Soziale Arbeiter-partei*, founded in 1878.[45] This organization, whose original aim was to enlist the workers' support for the imperialist program, soon became an out-and-out Anti-Semitic party that carried on wide-spread propaganda and gained representation in the Reichstag. A whole stream of Anti-Semitic writers marks the period: Eugen Dühring, the famous critic of liberal capitalism whom Engels attacked in his *Anti-Dühring;* Max Stirner, the anarchist; Hermann Ahlwardt, who incited pogroms and succeeded in staging a ritual murder trial at Xanten, near Düsseldorf. Ultimately, the movement entered into political alliance with the Conservative party.

Although Anti-Semitism was nowhere so actively propagated as in Germany, it failed to strike root in the population; the agitation became so vigorously fanatic that it defeated itself. The workers' movement remained immune from it, and Bebel, pre-war leader of the German Social-Democratic party, was acclaimed when he denounced Anti-Semitism as the 'socialism of fools.' In 1885 the Conservatives dropped Anti-Semitism from their platform and sev-ered their connections with the Anti-Semitic party, causing its parliamentary defeat.

Anti-Semitism was also the basic policy of the Pan-German

Union, which raised the demand for a greater German empire, especially for a Middle Europe under German hegemony.*

Three major themes recur in these Anti-Semitic writings. First, the identification of capitalism with Judaism, especially in the writings of Adolph Wagner. This thesis has been submitted to scientific investigation in Werner Sombart's famous book, *The Jews and Economic Life*. The second thesis is that the Jews are also the leaders of Marxist socialism. Both themes are incessant in the National Socialist propaganda scheme and thoroughly pervade Hitler's autobiography.[46] The third and most potent theme combines the two others: the leaders of world Jewry (the Elders of Zion) have organized a Jewish world conspiracy for the destruction of 'Aryanism.' In the conspiracy, some Jews have been singled out to lead world capitalism, others to conduct the operations of the international socialists and bolsheviks. The evidence for this conspiracy consists of the infamous Protocols of the Elders of Zion, the history of which is too well known to require discussion here.[47]

4. Blood Purification and Anti-Jewish Legislation

National Socialism is the first Anti-Semitic movement to advocate the complete destruction of the Jews. But this purpose is only part of a wider plan defined as 'the purification of German blood,' in which barbarism and a few progressive features combine to form a repellent whole. Prophylactic measures have been enacted to insure the propagation of Nordics in sufficient number.[48] Marriage is permitted only after thorough medical and eugenic examination. S.S. men must have special permits for marriage. Even more important are the measures intended to prevent the propagation of physically and biologically unfit persons: the castration of habitual criminals and the sterilization of hereditary defectives. The term 'habitual criminal' refers to persons over twenty-one years old who have been twice sentenced to prison terms of six months each for sex crimes, or to persons sentenced for murder or manslaughter committed to incite or satisfy sexual lust. The agency that orders the castration is the criminal court.

The basic text of eugenic legislation is a statute 'to prevent hereditarily diseased offspring' (issued 14 July 1933). It permits

* On the Pan-German Union, see below, pp. 204-7.

sterilization in cases of (1) hereditary imbecility, (2) schizophrenia, (3) manic depression, (4) hereditary epilepsy, (5) Huntington chorea, (6) hereditary blindness, (7) hereditary deafness, (8) extreme physical malformation. The patient, the medical officer, or the director of the institution in which the patient is confined may apply to a special sterilization court (*Erbgesundheitsgericht*), which is composed of a judge, a medical officer, and a medical practitioner. Appeal from its decision may be taken to an appeals court (*Erbgesundheitsobergericht*), which has a similar composition and whose decision is final.[49]

The courts have given an exceedingly broad and brutal interpretation to the sterilization statute.[50] If we are to believe the statements of Mr. William Shirer in his articles in *Life* magazine,[51] Himmler, chief of the German police and leader of the S.S., has ordered the execution of about 50,000 mental deficients during this war alone. Since Himmler is a most articulate racial fanatic and is master of life and death in Germany, Shirer's report has a *prima facie* probability.

The National Socialist population policy—part of which is discussed in the chapter entitled *The Grossdeutsche Reich*—is, perhaps, the most revolting of National Socialist policies. It is so completely devoid of Christian charity, so little defensible by reason, so fully opposed to pity and compassion, that it appears as a practice of men utterly pagan. It centers around the two commandments issued by the National Socialist leaders: to the German women, whether married or not, the commandment to produce children; to the S.S., the commandment to kill those who are not fit to live. Produce as many children as possible so that the earth can be ruled by the master race; kill the unhealthy so that the masters need not be burdened by the care of the weak.

In this respect, National Socialism and bolshevism are utterly divergent. Not the persecution of political opponents—which is practiced in both countries—but the extermination of helpless individuals is the prerogative of National Socialism.

The same spirit pervades the entire anti-Jewish legislation, which we can here consider only in its broad outlines. The process of urbanization, which had affected the whole population, was accentuated among the Jews, especially during the Hitler regime. For years before the advent of Hitler, however, the Jewish population had been on the decline because of the falling birthrate among Jews, frequent mixed marriages, and many desertions from the Jewish community.[52]

Jewish influence was unquestionably strong in the free professions and in big cities. Outside the free professions, Jews were engaged mainly in trade and transport, though their share in industry was not inconsiderable. In agriculture they played a very small part, if any. Most of the department stores were owned by Jews; Jews were also predominant in the metal trades (57.3 per cent Jewish), though the influence of the free-metal trades had declined rapidly as a result of the monopolist process mentioned in a previous chapter. Jews controlled 18.7 per cent of all the banks and most of the clothing industry. The economic significance of the banks was on the wane, however, since financial capital had long been declining in favor of industrial capital.[53]

In industry proper, Jewish influence was not very significant. Only one of the electro-technical concerns can be said to have been Jewish. Of course, there were Jewish members of boards of managers and of supervisory boards in a few giant industrial enterprises. Where Jews held high positions in the field of industrial management, however, they did so by virtue of their efficiency and ability; otherwise they would not have been tolerated by the industrial leadership, which was thoroughly Anti-Semitic. Paul Silverberg, for example, was the organizer of the Rhenish lignite industry, and Oscar Oliven was outstanding in the field of electrification. Most of the so-called Jewish industrial leaders, however, had in fact severed their connection with the Jewish community and, more often than not, were active and ardent Catholics or Protestants and political reactionaries, who would gladly have joined the National Socialist party had that party not been so overwhelmingly Anti-Semitic.

The Anti-Semitic laws affect the position of Jews as citizens. The so-called Nuremberg laws of 15 September 1935, which were promulgated to 'maintain the purity of German blood,' prohibited marriages between Jews (including persons having one Jewish grandparent) and German citizens of German 'or racially similar blood.' Non-Aryans who had one or more Jewish grandparents were permitted to marry among each other only with the consent of the federal minister of the interior and the deputy leader. Marriages performed against the law, as well as extra-marital sexual relations, were made punishable by hard labor. Jews were not permitted to display official flags or to exhibit their colors in any way. They could not employ any female servant of German blood unless she was over forty-five years old.

These 'blood purification' laws are among the most infamous in the repertory of National Socialism. They not only play into the hands of blackmailers but they have completely shattered the last vestiges of legal protection previously granted by the penal code. Though the statute clearly prohibits only extra-marital cohabitation, and though Section 3 of the penal code affirms the principle of territoriality, according to which only crimes committed in German territory are punishable in Germany, the courts extended the act far beyond the original wording and today race betrayal and race defilement are punishable even if committed by Germans living outside Germany.[54] The new interpretation was based upon Section 2 of the penal code, as amended by act of 28 June 1935, which provides that 'any person who commits an act which the law declares to be punishable or which is deserving of penalty according to the fundamental conceptions of a statute and sound popular feeling, shall be punished. If no penal law exists that directly covers the act, it shall be punished under that statute the fundamental conception of which applies most nearly to the act.' Drastic as it is, this section is clearly not applicable to the matter under discussion, and an old, highly reputable professor of criminal law at once denounced the decisions based upon this section.[55] He pointed out that the federal supreme court's decision contained not a word of proof and that Section 2 did not permit it to abandon the territorial principles upon which the very structure of the penal code depended.

Increasing cruelty has been shown in the decisions dealing with extra-marital sex relations between Jews and non-Jews. The federal supreme court, for example, deemed it an aggravating rather than an extenuating circumstance that an old Aryan living with a Jewish woman, whom he was prepared to marry, continued the relation after the enactment of the 'blood purification' act. Such behavior, the court declared, was expressive of 'a specially stubborn rebellion against National Socialist legislation.'[56] The same rigor has been applied in cases where the unmarried couple had a child for whom they were fully providing.[57]

The complete abandonment of legality by the courts is even more clearly revealed in their interpretation of the term of 'impermissible cohabitation.' A large number of acts that in no way constitute sexual cohabitation have been declared to be punishable,[58] and even an oral request to cohabit has been construed and punished as 'attempted racial defilement.'[59] It is a mystery how such decisions could be reconciled with the aim of the statute, which according to a definition by the federal supreme court is 'to protect the blood as a living organism circulating in the German people.'[60] The decision has with equal cruelty been applied to racial defilements (committed by Jews and non-Aryans) and to race betrayal (committed by Germans).

A systematic effort was made to create a legal Ghetto, and many enactments and court decisions have pared away the political rights of Jews and non-Aryans. The decree of 17 August 1938 and the executive order of the federal minister of the interior of 23 August 1938 concerned Jewish first names. Every Jew, unless he had a name which was listed as permissible, was compelled to add 'Israel' or 'Sarah.' Jews born after the enactment of the law could be given only such names as were provided for in the minister's ruling. Names like David, Abraham, Jacob, Daniel, Gabriel, Judith, Eve, and Ruth, all of which have historical or religious significance, were not listed and were therefore forbidden to Jews; the names permitted were spelled in the Yiddish manner so as to stamp them as foreign and ridiculous in the eyes of Germans. Unintentional or negligent violation of the ruling was made punishable by fine or imprisonment up to one month. On 5 October 1938, a decree imposed special Jewish stamps on passports issued to Jews. An earlier ruling (23 July 1938) compelled Jews to apply for special identification papers, which they were to carry on their persons at all times and which they had to attach to applications they made to an official or party agency.

Expulsion of the Jews from the German commonwealth began with the nationality act of 15 September 1935, which made a distinction between 'state subjects' (*Staatsangehörige*) and citizens (*Reichsbürger*). State subjects were those who belonged to the protective association of the German Reich; and citizens were those 'of

German or racially similar blood who by their behavior demonstrate that they are willing and able faithfully to serve the German
people and the Reich.' Citizenship was to be acquired by means of
a citizen's charter, and only citizens possessed political rights. An
executive decree of 14 November 1935 made without charter every
national of German or racially similar blood a citizen, provided
he possessed the right to vote or was granted citizenship by the
federal minister of the interior. The same citizenship act expelled
all the remaining Jewish civil servants.

This step was the last in a series of legislative measures aiming
to expel non-Aryans from the civil services, free professions, and
all cultural fields. The opening piece was an act promulgated 7 April
1933, for the purpose of 'restoring the civil services,' according to
which only those Jews who were war veterans, or whose parents
or sons had been killed in the First World War, or who had already
been employed in the service in August 1914 could remain at their
posts. By the end of 1938, however, Jews were completely eliminated from the civil services and free professions, and the destruction of the economic position of the Jews was ready to begin in
full force. The occasion for this next step was the murder of
vom Rath, counsellor at the German Embassy in Paris. The assault
on the economic position of the Jews coincided, significantly
enough, with the purge of 'inefficient' personnel from retail and
handicraft business: that is to say, with the repudiation by National
Socialism of its pledge to protect the old middle classes. It is virtually certain that the vom Rath murder was merely a pretext and
that the economic persecution of the Jews was a mere diversion
intended to conceal the assault on the middle classes as a whole.

5. ARYANIZATION OF JEWISH PROPERTY

The elimination of Jews from economic life was carried out in
three forms: contractually, illegally, and by statute. 'Legal' elimination took the form of forced sales, especially of small Jewish businesses, thus satisfying the appetites of National Socialist officials and
small Aryan competitors. One of the methods used was that of
handing over the Jew's share of a business to his Aryan partner—the
National Socialist district leader often put pressure on the Aryan
partner to get rid of his Jewish associate.[61] Jews were increasingly

denied the protection of German labor legislation.[62] The practices, which have little economic significance, merit attention only in a study of the methods of National Socialist persecution and their so-called 'purity in business.' On 8 May 1935 the *Frankfurter Zeitung* was forced to admit that far from benefiting the German middle classes, Aryanization chiefly served the interests of the giant enterprises, which used the opportunity to 'round off and extend' their holdings by buying out Jewish owners. Small concerns had neither the capital nor the equipment required to take over Jewish concerns. Thus Aryanization became a powerful stimulant to capital concentration and monopoly, a development we shall discuss below.*

Monopolist growth by way of Aryanization was particularly marked in the banking field. Between 1932 and 1939 the number of private banks decreased from 1350 to 520.[63] Aryanization not only assisted the interests of powerful banking institutions; it also became a means for industry to acquire banks of its own and extend its activities in the banking field.[64] For example, the powerful banking firm of S. Hirschland of Essen, which had played such a considerable part in the industrial development of the Ruhr basin and which had given financial support and aid to Thyssen, was Aryanized by a group controlled by Thyssen and Flick. (The same process probably contributed to Thyssen's downfall, since it made his most powerful rival a part-owner in a bank that had formerly served Thyssen's interests.)

We lack the space to tell the whole story of the Aryanization of Jewish business. Wherever powerful Jewish firms could not be swallowed by competing Aryan enterprises, they were taken over by banks, as was the Schocken department store, a family enterprise that is now a joint stock corporation owned by banks; or the machine shops and wagon factory of Orenstein and Koppel. Aryanization strengthened 'predatory' capital at the expense of 'productive' capital. It also harmed retail business as a whole. For example, a number of Jewish factories, among them the three largest shoe factories, all of which had retail outlets of their own, were consolidated, and the hold of the monopolists over the retailers and the entire field was thereby strengthened. The huge increase of power and profits that Aryanization brought to the big banks and big

* See pp. 275, 289-90.

business was further enhanced when Austria, the Sudetenland, the protectorates, and France were acquired.

The German material on which the contents of this book are based does not supply documentary proof of illegal seizures, although the testimony of refugees offers ample evidence that the practices were widespread. We do, however, find a great deal in the documents pertaining to legislative expropriations. In Germany, there are a number of professions the practice of which requires a license. A number of lawyers and administrative tribunals held that the Jew *per se* was not unreliable and that for this reason the administrative agency could not refuse a license to a Jew solely because of his race.[65] Consequently, the factory code, in which most of the provisions on this point appeared, was amended by a statute of 6 July 1938, so as to make Jews ineligible for licenses in a number of trades (watchmen, information and inquiry agents, real-estate agents, real-estate administrators, loan-commission agents, marriage agents, guides, etc). From this statute German lawyers now deduce that the principle of freedom of trade no longer applies to the Jew.

Legislative and administrative acts endeavor everywhere to make the concealment of a Jewish business impossible. Any merchant may request an injunction against any Jewish firm that even allows the impression that it is Aryan,[66] and every Aryan has the right to warn a customer against buying from a Jewish competitor if such warning is in the interests of the public.[67] Slowly and reluctantly, the courts have granted Aryans the right to withdraw from long-term contracts with Jews.[68]

Complete legislative exclusion of Jews from economic life was initiated by a decree of 26 April 1938, which compelled Jews to 'register and evaluate their total domestic and foreign properties' and (by executive decree of the same date) forbade them to acquire by purchase or lease any industrial, agrarian, or forestry enterprise; at the same time, Jews were prohibited from establishing any new business without permit. The fact that an inventory of Jewish property was ordered as early as April 1938 again makes it extremely unlikely that the expropriating legislation of November of that year was simply a retaliatory measure against vom Rath's murder or a response to the 'spontaneous anger of the enraged populace.' It was rather part of a long-nurtured plan. The discontent among small businessmen because of their elimination from business had to be diverted.

A decree of 12 November 1938, enacted about a week after vom Rath's death, forbade Jews to carry on retail, handicraft, or mail-order business, or to sell their goods at fairs and markets. It eliminated Jews from plant management (1 January 1939) and authorized employers to dismiss more important Jewish employees; it also authorized co-operatives to expel all their Jewish members. The executive decree of 23 November took great pains to insure that compulsory liquidation of Jewish business would not profit the Jewish owners. Goods could not be sold out to consumers, but had to be handed over to the group in industry or trade for safe-keeping. Such goods had to be appraised by officially appointed persons, and liquidators for the business were often appointed.

This enactment, which struck only at retail and handicraft businesses, was supplemented by another, dated 3 December 1938, which affected every Jewish industrial and trade enterprise that could be put up for compulsory liquidation or sale. Trustees could be appointed for such enterprises so that the owner lost all authority to dispose of his enterprise or any part of it. The decree also authorized the government to order any Jew to sell his agricultural or forest land holdings and real estate within a period to be designated. It forbade Jews to acquire such holdings, by purchase or auction. Jews could not dispose of their holdings without special consent; they could not mortgage them. The last provision was so broadly interpreted that in the end Jews had no security whatever for their claims. For example, a Jewish beneficiary of a will could not secure his claim to an estate by placing a mortgage on it.[69]

The Jews were further denied protection by being excluded from the benefits of a decree regulating the maturity of old mortgages (22 December 1938), although the wording of the decree did not discriminate against them.[70] Trustees appointed to liquidate or sell Jewish businesses completely replaced the owner, so that he was not even permitted to delete his firm from the commercial register. (The name of the firm often enjoyed wide repute and thus constituted a considerable asset.) [71] The same decree compelled Jews to deposit all stocks and bonds with a recognized bank. These could not be disposed of without special permission of the federal minister of economics. Gold, platinum, silver, jewels, and similar possessions had to be surrendered to special purchasing agencies established by the Reich (executive decree of 21 February 1939). The basis of appraisal was fixed by the government.

The vom Rath murder was made the occasion for a special assessment of 1,000,000,000 marks to be paid by all Jews of German nationality whose property exceeded 5,000 marks. The levy was to be raised by a tax of 20 per cent on all property belonging to such Jews, and was made payable in four equal instalments running to 15 August 1939 (decree of 12 November 1938 and executive decree of 21 November 1938). As a further reprisal, a special decree (12 November 1938) compelled the Jews to pay costs for all damages to Jewish businesses and houses resulting from the riots of 8, 9, and 10 November 1938, staged by the National Socialist party. The tax and the other laws were of course linked to one another. The liquidation of Jewish business, real estate, stocks, and bonds was hastened by the need to pay the levy; the value of Jewish holdings was depreciated and many holdings were wiped out.

Even the anti-Jewish economic legislation cannot be reviewed in detail here. Taxation exemptions enjoyed by charitable organizations were not extended to Jews, and laws intended to alleviate the debtor's burden were made inapplicable to them. Tax exemptions allowed to people with children were suspended if the children were Jewish (citizen tax law of 31 October 1938). Jewish tenants do not enjoy any protection against notice from the landlord (30 April 1939). Thus, segregation, political enslavement, economic extinction, and the cultural ghetto go hand in hand.

6. The Philosophy of Anti-Semitism

This enslavement was not accomplished at one stroke. There are a number of reasons for the so-called official leniency shown until 1938 regarding the economic position of Jews. Foreign pressure was undoubtedly very important. The speech which Federal Minister of the Interior Dr. Frick,[72] gave before the diplomatic corps and the foreign press on 15 February 1934, justifying the anti-Jewish legislation, clearly shows how much Germany cared for public opinion. The insistence upon legality instead of outright expropriation is also to be explained by purely economic reasons. A precipitate liquidation of Jewish holdings would have disrupted German economic life.

Political and psychological factors in the anti-Jewish economic legislation seem to have played a decisive part. The economic legislation against the Jews was one of the most important methods for distributing spoils; it performed the same function as the expropriation of ecclesiastical property under Henry VIII and during the French Revolution. It redistributed property among those strata of the population whose support is vital for the regime: the powerful financial and industrial capitalists.

Expropriation of Jewish property is also a method of satisfying the anti-capitalistic longings of the German people. Since property has generally been left untouched by National Socialism, it is vital for the regime to show that it has the power of taking it away. In the eyes of the anti-capitalistic masses, the expropriation of one section of the people makes it appear possible that some day the regime may resort to outright and wholesale nationalization, an expectation shared by many foreign observers who are prone to denote the National Socialist regime as an anti-capitalist one.

Instead of exterminating Jewish economic life at one blow, the National Socialist administration proceeded gradually. The reasons for this were political. The administration kept a number of anti-Jewish measures up its sleeve and enacted them one by one, whenever it was necessary to stimulate the masses or divert their attention from other socio-economic and international policies. Spontaneous, popular Anti-Semitism is still weak in Germany. This assertion cannot be proved directly, but it is significant that despite the incessant propaganda to which the German people have been subjected for many years, there is no record of a single spontaneous anti-Jewish attack committed by persons not belonging to the Nazi party. The writer's personal conviction, paradoxical as it may seem, is that the German people are the least Anti-Semitic of all.

To understand the roots of Anti-Semitic terrorism requires a distinction between the various types of Anti-Semitism and a brief discussion of prevalent Anti-Semitic theories.

Anti-Semitism can be totalitarian or non-totalitarian. For the totalitarian Anti-Semite, the Jew has long ceased to be a human being. He has become the incarnation of evil in Germany, nay, in the entire world. In other words, totalitarian Anti-Semitism is magic and beyond discussion.

Non-totalitarian Anti-Semitism preserves remnants of rationality and can, therefore, be analyzed. It exists in four forms: religious, economic, political, and social.

Religious Anti-Semitism derives its strength from the accusation leveled against the Jews that they were responsible for the crucifixion of Christ. Such feeling, still powerful in certain Catholic countries (for instance, Catholic Canada and South America) had very little influence in Germany. It could be found among the impoverished Catholic masses, particularly in Upper Silesia, but even there religious Anti-Semitism was fused with Polish nationalism. It largely expressed the opposition against the Germanization of the province during the imperial period, a process in which German Jews played an important, perhaps the most important part. Polish nationalism was directed against the Prussian bureaucracy, who represented political power, and against the German Jews, who represented cultural Germanization. And since Polish nationalism was largely carried on by the lower ranks of the Catholic clergy, the fusion of religious Anti-Semitism and Polish nationalism was inevitable. The Catholic Church, as a whole, is not Anti-Semitic. On the contrary, it recognizes that Anti-Semitism is incompatible with the spiritually Semitic origin of Christianity.[73] Anti-Semitism within the church is far more a matter of political expediency than a basic element of faith or politics.

Anti-Semitism in its other forms was restricted to the new and old middle classes: the free professions, university teachers, farmers, white-collar workers, artisans, shopkeepers, and civil servants. Their Anti-Semitism certainly had an economic basis: it was both competitive and anti-capitalistic. That the competitive position of the Jewish lawyers, doctors, bankers, retailers, university teachers, and civil servants caused Anti-Semitism requires an explanation. Jews occupying primarily intermediary positions were, so to speak, the concrete manifestation of capitalism for the old and new middle classes. The small farmer went to the Jewish banker, to the Jewish grain or cattle dealer, or to a Jewish mortgage agent. The retailer who resented the existence of Jewish department stores still had to buy from a Jewish wholesaler and still had to obtain loans from a Jewish pawn shop or a Jewish banker. His creditors were Jews.

The average German did not and could not see that the Jewish middlemen were, in fact, merely middlemen—representatives of an impersonal and anonymous power that dictated their economic activities. The recognition that the middlemen acted on behalf of a non-Jewish financial and industrial capitalism would have driven the farmers, retailers, and handicraftsmen into the socialistic camp, a step they could not take without abandoning their traditions. Moreover, the socialist program disregarded the interests of these groups. The Anti-Semitic white-collar worker employed by a Jewish retailer or wholesaler, a Jewish banker or a department store, could have joined forces with the manual workers to attack, improve, or overthrow capitalism. But he refused to be proletarized. He rejected the claim of the industrial proletariat to leadership and tried to work out his own *Standesbewusstsein*, a consciousness of his own calling. Industry and labor legislation supported him in this endeavor. His anti-capitalist longings were thus concentrated in his hatred for and resentment against the Jewish employer, no matter how good his conditions of employment might be.

For these groups, Anti-Semitism created 'an outlet for resentment arising from damaged self-esteem,' [74] and also made possible a political collaboration of the old and the new middle classes with the landed aristocracy. In addition, anti-Jewish hatred expressed the anxiety of those groups whose traditional patterns of culture were threatened by the intellectual vanguard that was to a considerable extent composed of Jews. The modern theater, atonal music, expressionism in painting and literature, functional architecture, all these seemed to constitute a threat to the conservatives whose cultural outlook was basically rural, and who thus came to identify the city and its culture, its economics, and its politics with the Jew.

Anti-Semitism is also a means of throwing the guilt for the last war upon 'alien enemies so that self-accusation was no longer necessary.' [75] The Jews are to blame, and the German sacred ego is spared.

Anti-Semitism in present-day Germany is, however, more than a mere device utilized when necessary and discarded when it has fulfilled its aims. We must not forget that National Socialism re-writes German history and even world history in terms of fighting, exposing, and destroying Jewish influence. The Federal Institute for the History of the New Germany has demanded the re-writing of history in all its aspects. Wilhelm Grau [76] has drawn up the program and has already begun to apply the new postulates in his study of Wilhelm von Humboldt,[77] the founder of the Berlin University, who is, for Grau, one of the arch pro-Jews. Walter Frank, the president of this institute, is concerned almost exclusively with the Jewish question. He is the author of the leading biography of Adolf Stöcker. He has denounced the Jewish character of the Third French Republic.[78] His latest book [79] deals exclusively with Jewish figures of the Weimar Republic, such as Walter Rathenau and Maximilian Harden (Harden was a Jewish journalist and advocate of the imperial expansionist policy, who, as may be readily admitted, was not exactly an ornament to his profession).

The National Socialist lawyers' organization has already published nine pamphlets dealing with the influence of Jews upon legal theory and legal practice and holding them responsible for the rationalism in legal theory.[80] There is an enormous number of contributions showing the perversion of Germanic institutions by Jewish influence, and there is hardly a book, a pamphlet, or an ideological pronouncement that does not attack Jewish conspiracy, Jewish immorality, the Jewish disintegrating spirit, Jewish capitalism, Jewish rationalism, Jewish pacifism, and Jewish militarism. There is almost no vice that is not attributed to Jews. It is scarcely surprising that National Socialism should do this. But the almost complete moral corruption of the German intelligensia, especially of the academic world, is a depressing fact.

How seriously National Socialism takes the 'scientific research' in the Jewish problem is illustrated by the opening in Frankfort on 26 March 1941 (*Frankfurter Zeitung*, 27 March 1941) of the Institute for Jewish Research, the first outside agency of the party (*Hohe Schule der Partei*). Slovak, Hungarian, Rumanian (Cuza), Italian, Bulgarian, Norwegian (Quisling), and Dutch (Mussert) guests, as well as party, army, and civil service officials, attended the ceremony. Alfred Rosenberg again dwelt on his favorite theme, 'Science and Party.' The party university would create new room for science—especially for the natural sciences—but must concentrate on the 'biological laws . . . of peoples and races' and lay bare the poisonous influence of the Jews. The new director, Wilhelm Grau, explained the task of the new institute in the same terms as he had done before—the figure of the Jew thus becomes the dominating figure of German, nay, European history. The institute disposes of the greatest European Jewish libraries that the conqueror had confiscated: the Rothschild library in Frankfurt a. M., the library of the Warsaw Theological Seminary of the Tlomacky synagogue, the library of the Yiddish-Scientific Institute, and that of the Alliance Israélite Universelle (Paris). Publications and speeches made it clear that the institute regards Anti-Semitism as the fundamental ideology of German imperialism. According to one expert, Dr. Gross, the term Anti-Semitism should be avoided, for the Jews are not Semites, but a mixed race and cannot be settled either in Europe or in Arabic countries outside Europe (*Frankfurter Zeitung*, 28 March 1941). The servility of that 'scientific organization' to German imperialism is obvious. German racism has never given serious consideration to the findings of their own anthropologists. If it is necessary to win over the Near East, Jews will not be Semites, and the name of Semites will again be reserved for a friendly nation of Arabs.

Three factors seem to play a fundamental part in the present all-pervading Anti-Semitism.[81]

First, racism and Anti-Semitism are substitutes for the class struggle. The officially established peoples' community superseding the class struggle needs an integrating element. Carl Schmitt has maintained that politics is a struggle against a foe who must be exterminated.* The theory is true if the society is aggressive. The new enemy is the Jew. By heaping all hatred, all resentment, all misery upon one enemy who can easily be exterminated and who cannot resist, Aryan society can be integrated into a whole. The internal political value of Anti-Semitism will, therefore, never allow a complete extermination of the Jews. The foe cannot and must not disappear; he must always be held in readiness as a scapegoat for all the evils originating in the socio-political system.

Secondly, Anti-Semitism provides a justification for eastern expansion. Both Hitler's autobiography [82] and the party program demand a liberation of all racial brethren from the foreign yoke (Articles 1 and 2 of the party program), and this implies foreign eastern expansion. Though the party program also demands the restoration of the colonial possessions, Hitler himself, in his autobiography, advocates Friedrich List's foreign policy—that is, collaboration with England; consolidation of the European empire,

* See p. 45.

especially by acquiring eastern territories; and rejection of colonial expansion. But it is precisely in the east and the southeast that Jews form compact minorities.[83] Were there no racial theory, the incorporation of these territories would have meant giving the Jews, who have a much closer affinity to German culture than have Poles, Czechs, Slovaks, Croats, Rumanians, and Bulgars, a status equal to or even superior to the non-Jewish inhabitants. The theory of German racial superiority and Jewish racial inferiority permits the complete enslavement of the eastern Jews and thereby the playing off of one minority against the other. It actually establishes a hierarchy of races—giving no rights to the Jews, a few to the Poles, a few more to the Ukranians (since they, too, live in Soviet Russia and must be flattered), and full rights to Germans.

The administration of the General Gouvernement (of German-occupied Poland) cleverly distinguishes between the various minorities.[84] The racial Germans, i.e. those who 'by descent, language, attitude, education or other circumstances are Germans,' are on top, although they do not acquire German citizenship. They receive identification cards (decree of 26 January 1940) describing them as German *Volkszugehörige*. They are employed in the administration and are to a large extent placed on the same footing as German citizens. Their children can be educated only in German schools. Only they and German citizens may receive hunting licenses. They enjoy the collective wage regulations for German workers and salaried employees, and receive social insurance benefits although they have no legal claim. Finally, they have formed a *Volksdeutsche* community, an organization endowed under public law with legal personality by a decree of 19 April 1940.

Next to these Germans are the Ukranians, the Gorales, and the White Russians, who all receive preferential treatment. They may, although they have not yet done so, establish judicial administrations of their own (decree of 19 February 1940). They are even allowed to keep their radio sets.

Next to them are the Poles and next to the Poles, at the bottom of the scale, are the Jews. The cultural, economic, legal, and political ghetto has been gradually transformed into a physical ghetto, as in Warsaw and Cracow. German Anti-Semitic legislation is largely applied in Poland. By a decree of 28 November 1939, every Jewish community has to set up a Jewish council, which is to collaborate with the German authorities. While Poles have merely a duty of work (*Arbeitspflicht*), all Jews between 14 and 60 years old are subject to compulsory labor (*Arbeitszwang*), i.e. to convict labor under orders of the higher S.S. and police officials. They have to wear a white arm-band bearing the star of Zion (decree of 23 November 1939). Their property (1 April 1941) has been or will be confiscated.

Finally, Anti-Semitism in Germany is an expression of the rejection of Christianity and all it stands for.[85] Anti-Christian trends in Germany have two roots and two opposite directions. One rejects Christianity because it is Christian; the other because it is not Christian enough. The free thinkers' movement rejected Christianity not only as scientifically untenable, but also because, in their view, the churches had betrayed the Sermon on the Mount. The free thinkers did not substitute race hatred, leadership veneration, or terrorism for Christian love, *caritas*, and the brotherhood of man, but the evolution of a scientifically tenable rational theory of justice and morality. Christian socialism in Germany (Protestant and Catholic) tried to integrate socialism with Christian morality.

The second anti-Christian trend does not reject the churches because of their alleged betrayal of Christian principles, but rejects the Christian principles themselves because they seem incompatible with the specific tasks that Germany has to undertake, or because those principles mutilate and fetter man.

Religious Anti-Semitism is, then—and to this extent I share Maurice Samuel's view—the articulate rejection of Christian morality, but is restricted to the Semitic origin of Christ because Christianity is too deeply rooted in the German people and the uprooting of Christianity would be so gigantic a task that National Socialism can only fulfil it by the long process of education.

The most powerful ideological anti-Christian influence in imperial Germany was that of Nietzsche. But Nietzsche was no Anti-Semite and every attempt to stamp him as such must end in failure. Even the National Socialists finally admitted that his pro-Semitic statements are too numerous to be neglected.[86] Nietzsche denounced Anti-Semitism as mere jealousy against spirit and against money and the Anti-Semites as the most recent 'speculators in idealism.'[87] Nietzsche's work is a most powerful attack upon the philosophy of the nineteenth century. His hatred is concentrated on Christianity, liberalism, democracy, and socialism, i.e. on those trends which, in his view, had initiated and accomplished the enslavement of man. According to Nietzsche, only a total revolution of values can remedy the situation. The will to power is the vehicle of the new order. The old order implies the enslavement of man's healthful and vital instincts, initiated by Judaism and Christianity, but far more by the New than by the Old Testament. Religion has introduced the idea of equality, has taught man to 'stammer the words of equality'; [88] democracy is merely a secularized Christianity, 'a kind of return to nature.' [89] 'The poison of the teaching, equal rights for all, Christianity has sowed it.' [90] 'The equality of souls before God, this lie, this screen for the *rancunes* of all the base-minded, this anarchist bomb of a concept, which has become the last revolution, the modern idea and principle of destruction of the whole social order—this is Christian dynamite.' [91] St. Paul, Rousseau, and socialism all express the same perversion. 'The gospel that the low and the poor have equal access to happiness, that one has nothing to do but to free one's self from the institutions, the tradition, the authorities of the higher estates, in this respect the rise of Christianity is nothing but the typical teaching of the socialist.' [92]

But just as much as he rejects democracy, liberalism, socialism, and Christianity, he also denounces nationalism and imperialism. So deep was Nietzsche's conviction that Christ had mutilated the healthy instincts of men that he never forgave his friend Richard Wagner the opera *Parsifal*, in which Wagner returned to Christianity. His hatred of Christianity shows, especially in his *Zarathustra*, sadistic features. Christianity, as a negation of nature, is unnatural and therefore contemptible.

Though Nietzsche's philosophy and the National Socialist ideology contain a good many similarities, there is an unbridgeable gulf between the two, since Nietzsche's individualism transcends the pattern of any authoritarian order.

Whatever the ultimate meaning of Nietzsche may have been, his reception in Germany favored the growth of National Socialism.[93] It provided National Socialism with an intellectual father who had greatness and wit, whose style was beautiful and not abominable, who was able to articulate the resentment against both monopoly capitalism and the rising proletariat. It was especially the Free Youth Movement, the so-called *bündische* youth, which protested against the mustiness of the bourgeois culture, against the complacency of the protestant clergy, against the traditional forms of nationalism, against the rule of the bureaucrats and desk-generals, trade-union bosses, industrial barons, financial jobbers—in short, rejected the whole world of bourgeois culture. But just as Nietzsche was unable to replace this condemned reality and the Christian teachings by anything but a more refined naturalism, a Darwinian doctrine of natural selection, so the Free Youth Movement, which furnished a good many National Socialist leaders, failed to elaborate any new philosophy except a moral and religious nihilism that, as does any nihilistic movement, ultimately leads to the acceptance of any power strong enough to crush all opponents. It was again the middle classes who were most deeply affected by Nietzsche's anti-Christianity. The protest against a world that did not satisfy their ambitions and against a value system that imposed moral restraints upon them is expressed in the anti-Christian and anti-Jewish movement.

V

THE GROSSDEUTSCHE REICH

FOR a believer, the racial theory justifies the 'liberation' of Germans from foreign sovereignty and the incorporation into greater Germany of territories largely inhabited by Germans. Racial self-determination brought Danzig, Memel, Upper Silesia, the Polish Corridor, the Sudetenland, and the province of Posen into the Reich. In its more recent stages, racism could even serve as an ideological weapon against England and the United States, for the National Socialists announce the new World War to be a struggle between a proletarian race and the plutocratic democracies.*

By no stretch of the imagination, however, can racism or the doctrine of social imperialism justify Germany's 'new European order,' the conquest of unquestionably non-German, backward states. Poland, Czechoslovakia, Bulgaria, Rumania, and Yugoslavia are even more 'proletarian' than Germany and their peoples are not German by 'race' or by history. Their incorporation into the Reich requires other ideological weapons, the doctrine of living space (*Lebensraum*). Hitler himself expounded this notion in an address to the Reichstag on 28 April 1939. The occasion was President Roosevelt's peace telegram, expressing the belief that all international problems can be amicably settled by discussion. In the twelfth point of his reply, Hitler said:

I answer: Theoretically, we should believe that this is feasible, for in many cases common sense would indeed plainly show the justice of the demands made by one side and the compelling necessity for concessions by the other side. For example, according to common sense, logic, and all the principles of human and of higher justice, nay, even according to the laws of a Divine will, all nations ought to have an equal share in the goods of this world. It should not be the case that one nation claims so much living space that it

* See page 184 for a detailed discussion.

cannot get along when there are not even 15 inhabitants to the square kilometer, while other nations are forced to maintain 140, 150, or even 200 on the same area. But in no case should these fortunate nations further curtail the living space of peoples who are already suffering, by robbing them of their colonies, for example. I should, therefore, be happy if these problems could really be solved at the conference table.[1]

Living space has been the major slogan of German political thinking ever since the partition of Czechoslovakia. 'The revolt of the continent,' says the influential *Frankfurter Zeitung*, 'consists in the final exclusion of England from Europe. Europe has begun to emancipate itself from the economic and political hegemony of England.'[2] Living space is a very complicated notion, requiring important changes in population policy and a complete revision of traditional conceptions of international law. It derives an allegedly scientific dress from geopolitics, and its roots in German tradition go back to Middle Ages.

1. THE MEDIEVAL HERITAGE

Closely linked with the idea of living space is the concept of the *grossdeutsche Reich*. In characteristic fashion, the National Socialists seized upon this concept, with its traditional and romantic appeal, and developed it into the ideological basis of their new order.

The appealing qualities of this slogan are undeniably strong. Through all the struggles of the past six or seven centuries of European history, men have never abandoned their longing for a unified Europe, under one political leadership, united not by brutal military strength and economic exploitation but by a common philosophy. The manifestations of this yearning have changed from period to period and from country to country. But its basic appeal has been fundamentally unchanged.

One of the earliest and most profound expressions is Dante's idea of an imperial rule that would be the expression of a *humana civilitas*.[3] Humanity is a political unity based on the conscious devotion of the individual to this unity, embodying a common culture and a common philosophy of life. The incarnation of unity should be an emperor, residing in Rome and directing his efforts to the achievement of peace and order. He would embody the *vis coactiva;*

the pope the *vis contemplativa*. Under completely different circumstances, the nineteenth-century German poet Novalis (Friedrich von Hardenberg) sought a similar escape from the contradictions, disharmonies, and pettiness of the real world. In a beautiful
essay, 'Christianity or Europe,' he too found the possibilities for an
orderly, unified world in a romantic revival of the medieval idea of
universalism embodied in the person of the Christian emperor.

The greatest twentieth-century German poet, Stefan George,
made the same theme the center of his work. The activity of the
George circle, which had great influence upon post-war German
culture (upon historical writing, for example; the school produced
important biographies of Caesar, Shakespeare, Goethe, Napoleon,
Nietzsche, Kleist, and Frederick II Hohenstaufen), was an unceasing protest against the mechanization and commercialization of contemporary life, against bourgeois civilization with its shopkeeper's
spirit and its cheap pleasures and satisfactions. With Dante and
Novalis as their recognized predecessors, they dreamed of the revival of an empire combining the universalism of the church and
the authority of the Roman Empire. George's long poem, *The
Seventh Ring*, idealizes the return to the days of the greatest of
German emperors, Frederick II Hohenstaufen.[4]

All this was grist for the National Socialist mill. The imperial
idea goes back to the Holy Roman Empire, it found new expression among the greatest literary works of modern Germany, and it
inspires the common man. What better weapon could there be,
ready to hand to be transformed and adapted to the aims of the
new empire?

The going has been extremely rough, however, for the idea of
the Reich is actually incompatible with National Socialism. Alfred
Rosenberg was once honest enough to say so. National Socialism,
he wrote, is not the heir of the Holy Roman Empire: quite the
contrary; it is the heir of the struggles of the German people against
the universalism of that empire.[5] And even in its own day the
medieval empire foundered in a maze of contradictions. There could
be no unity of the Christian concept of world order, the hegemony
of the German emperor, and the democratic strivings of the Italian
communes. Against the papal claims of universal authority, resting
upon the Thomist notion of a hierarchy of orders culminating in
one universal order, the emperors presented the 'constitutional' au-

thority of ancient Rome. Both claims conflicted with the Roman idea of popular sovereignty. In actual fact, the Holy Roman Empire as the organizing force of a German nation remained a myth except for a few brief years.[6]

The case of Stefan George offers a striking illustration of the inability of the National Socialists to resolve this age-old conflict. At first sight, George seems a true precursor of National Socialist ideology; and that characterization of his work is a common one. The organ of the George circle, the *Blätter für die Kunst*, carried on an unceasing struggle against naturalism and realism in literature.[7] Not a struggle against the hated real world, however, for that very process would amount to contamination with reality. Instead, George and his followers fled into the realm of art for art's sake. The heroic individual must transform himself, not the world. He should put his trust in faith instead of reason, in blood rather than intellect, in nature and not society.[8]

The kinship of this heroic figure with National Socialist ideas is obvious. More than that, it was George who revived the term the *Third Reich* (his last work, and, ironically, one of his poorest, is entitled *The New Reich*). For him, however, the concept is exclusively a cultural one. It does not imply the acceptance of Prussian hegemony over Europe. When it came to the final test, Stefan George could not accept National Socialism. He left Germany for Switzerland in the company of a close friend, the poet Karl Wolfskehl, a Jew. He never returned. When he died in Locarno in 1935, he exacted a pledge from his friends, according to one account, never to permit his body to be returned to a National Socialist Germany.

After George, German writers became increasingly preoccupied with the idea of the Third Reich. It was Moeller van den Bruck who adapted it to the needs of the new German imperialism.[9] Though he insisted that the 'continuity of German history' must not be forgotten in the program of the Third Reich, Moeller van den Bruck cannot properly be classed with the revivalists of the old imperial idea. He was, rather, the most articulate spokesman for the new theory of social imperialism.*

With the publication in 1938 of Christoph Steding's posthumous

* Discussed in the next chapter. See page 198.

work, *The Reich and the Sickness of European Culture*,[10] with a preface by Walter Frank, president of the Institute for the History of New Germany, Stefan George's concept of the Third Reich was completely reversed. Steding was driven by an almost pathological hatred for culture and 'neutrality.' His book is a wholesale attack upon knowledge, education, and the intellect, upon the endless 'palaver' of the democracies. There is a reality—the Reich—which is more powerful than any philosophy or theory. Any cultural contributions that do not recognize the imperial idea must be rejected as worthless and often dangerous. And since, Steding argues, unpolitical culture is a foreign importation from the neutrals, the neutrals must share the onus. Neutrality means avoidance of political decisions. The neutral is a born Pharisee; like a commission agent, he protests against the barbarism of the Reich and withdraws his own 'culture.' 'It is not virtuous [for the neutral] to stand on both feet. It is virtuous rather to limp on both feet' (p. 71).

Steding's book thus conceives the whole of European culture as a gigantic conspiracy against the Reich and its destiny. And this hostility to the Reich is the sickness of European culture. Cultural historians—men like the Swiss Jakob Burckhardt or the Dutchman Huizinga—are enemies; they discuss table manners and the history of the Reich with the same earnestness. Did not Burckhardt reduce the state itself 'to a mere work of art, a mere neutralizing expression' by his endless concentration on 'intimate things, on internal processes,' rather than on politics (p. 207)? Along with the cultural historians and with Nietzsche and the Scandinavian playwrights, Ibsen and Strindberg, Steding's hatred is directed particularly against the exponents of dialectical theology (Barth, Overbeck, Thurneysen, Brunner, Kierkegaard). 'The Young and Dawes Plans,' he writes (p. 97), 'the bank for international settlements and the dialectical theology of Karl Barth are one and the same.' Such crushing criticism leaves one speechless. After all, not only is the culture of the neutrals dualistic and mediating, it is also deviationist (p. 201). In other words, to be neutral is to deviate from everything that is essential for the Reich.

Only a strong Reich can guarantee the reality of Germany and of Europe, can guarantee 'that an English consul general will not do as he pleases with a country like Norway' (p. 269). Only the Reich can restore to science its proper character—objectivity. By 'objective' is meant political in character, for only thus does science 'live from the polis, the state, the Reich' (p. 299). This Reich, it is true, rests on the tradition of the Holy Roman Empire; as a political reality, however, and not as a cultural idea (p. 350). It is no wonder therefore that Steding relegates Stefan George, and Moeller van den Bruck too, to the philosophy of the Second Reich. They are not sufficiently integrated for the reality of the Third. Even a National Socialist like the psychologist Jung (not to mention Nietzsche) is condemned for the dualism of his thinking (p. 127).

Just what Steding himself means by the Reich is entirely obscure. Since the book was published in 1938, the editor Walter Frank carefully announces in the Preface that Steding 'is not concerned with the revision of political frontiers but with the revision of spiritual horizons' (p. xlvii). This obvious distortion, stemming from equally obvious motives, would have been rejected by Steding as intellectual nonsense, of course. It is precisely the incorporation into Germany of Europe, or at least of the ancient territories of the Holy Roman Empire, with which he is supremely concerned.

We thus have one more illustration of the difficulties raised by the concept of the Reich for National Socialist ideology. Racism fares badly in Steding's book. Though he throws an occasional compliment to the official philosophy, he has nothing but contempt for the anthropologists burrowing in the past in the search for specific racial traits. 'They who often speak of the folk hate the state; the "politicals" do it just as their opponents who speak of the state and hate the people' (p. 555). Race is not the creative element; it is only the raw material from which the Reich must be formed.

What is left as justification for the Reich? Not racism, not the idea of the Holy Roman Empire, and certainly not some democratic nonsense like popular sovereignty or self-determination. Only the Reich itself remains. It is its own justification. The philosophical roots of the argument are to be found in the existential philosophy of Heidegger. Transferred to the realm of politics, existentialism argues that power and might are true: power is a sufficient theoretical base for more power. Germany lies in the center, it is potentially the greatest power in Europe, it is well on its way toward becoming the mightiest state. Therefore, it is justified in building the new order. An acute critic has remarked about Steding: 'From the remains of what, with Heidegger, was still an effective transcendental solipsism, his pupil constructs a national solipsism.' [11]

Even the 'national solipsism,' however, creates difficulties for the National Socialists. This is well illustrated in a recent work, *Hegemony: A Book about Leading States*, by Heinrich Triepel.[12] The book presents a realistic analysis, by a reactionary but by no means National Socialist constitutional lawyer, of the legal and sociological characteristics of hegemony. Hegemony is defined as the leading character of one state against another (p. 343), and thus stands midway between influence and outright domination. Starting with an entirely different approach, Triepel none the less parallels Steding in defining hegemony in straight power terms, stripped of all cultural props. The medieval empire was a dual hegemony; the Third Reich is largely a continuation of the Prussian tradition. Because it is the most powerful state in Europe, the new Germany can legitimately claim still more power.

As a good conservative, steeped in the tradition of German idealism, Triepel must nevertheless seek a moral basis for leadership and hegemony. He finds it in the voluntary consent of the followers (p. 44). Leadership is simply the exercise of 'energetic but moderate might' (p. 41); the political leader is merely one among many (p. 16). The phenomenon of leadership and free consent permeates all social and political relations. Triepel's silence on the racial identification between leader and follower and on the metaphysical qualities of leadership is devastating. He creates a simple equation: hegemony is power. Hence the great value of the book lies in its debunking function. Official National Socialism, with its grotesque metaphysics and its pseudo-anthropology, greeted the work coldly.[13]

2. Geopolitics

A second, and far more important, ideological prop for the expansionist program of National Socialism is geopolitics. Geopolitics is supposed to be the scientific basis for the concept of living space. The term *Lebensraum*, as matter of fact, was apparently first used by the father of geopolitics, the geographer Friedrich Ratzel, in a little work with that title published early in the present century. Even with Ratzel, however, this 'science,' which he called anthropogeography, was not so much geography as a philosophy of history.

Subsequent developments have succeeded in stripping away every scientific element and substituting political arguments, metaphysical considerations, and a lot of meaningless verbiage.

The complete subjugation of political geography to the needs of German imperialism was the work chiefly of two men: Rudolf Kjellen and Karl Haushofer. Kjellen was a Swedish political scientist (died 1922) whose works were widely translated and circulated in Germany. He coined the term geopolitics and made it fashionable. One scholar reports the following story: 'At the Leipzig fair in the spring of 1924 one could see an effective poster in the exhibition hall of the publishing houses: a hard working man was drilling into a globe lying below his knee and above was the caption, "Political Geography—Good Business." ' [14] Good business not merely for publishers but also for German imperialists! For that poster attests to more than merely the new popular interest in geopolitics. In 1924 Germany overcame the devastating post-war inflation and her imperialists began to put the fashionable new 'science' to use. It was in that year, too, that the geopolitical school began to organize into a working group and that the first number of the *Zeitschrift für Geopolitik* appeared.

The most tireless spokesman of the geopolitical school is Karl Haushofer, professor of geography at the University of Munich, founder of the German Academy, retired major general, world traveler—and teacher and friend of Rudolf Hess. Beginning before the First World War, Haushofer had written a stream of books and articles on frontiers, power and earth, space-conquering powers, the geopolitics of the Pacific, and on general theoretical questions.[15] His most popular book is *Weltpolitik von Heute*, published in 1934 with a dedication to Hess and another friend. The preface defines its purpose as 'thinking in large spaces.' The *Zeitschrift für Geopolitik* is a house organ for Haushofer and his disciples. There is also available to them *Raumforschung und Raumordnung*, monthly organ of the government agency, *Reichstelle für Raumforschung* (Federal Bureau for Space Research).

The history of geopolitics has more than passing interest for us because it offers another excellent illustration of the way in which the National Socialists have twisted and altered already existing doctrines to fit them into their own scheme of ideas and actions. They did not invent geopolitics any more than they invented the idea of a *grossdeutsche Reich.* What they have done is to exploit it far more successfully than earlier German imperialists.

Ratzel coined the term anthropogeography to designate the subject that deals with the natural factors in man's life. The interest in climate and other geographical factors was always considerable in historical writing. It is very tempting to fall back upon Mother Earth, permanent, stable, unchanging, as the outstanding element in the making of human culture. What Ratzel sought was a 'mechanical anthropogeography,' [16] laying bare the laws regulating the 'simple relation of the static earth surface and the changing humanity on it.' [17] Its main theme is the relation between mobile man and the immobile earth: 'Life is movement.' [18]

Two geographical factors, location and space, play a major role in determining the laws of anthropogeography, and both of these factors have a categorical character in National Socialist ideology. Location is by far the more important of the two for Ratzel.[19] The term covers the size and form of a given territory, its attributes, such as climate or vegetation, and its relation to neighboring spaces, its separating and connecting properties. Location will determine whether a territory should be on friendly or hostile terms with its neighbors. It helps determine culture: isolated location offers security but also makes for cultural sterility; central location alone makes a strong country most influential; it places a weak country like Germany in mortal danger.[20] And the paramount importance of the sea in this connection is obvious.

Though far less significant,[21] the concept of space also gives rise to certain important laws. Ratzel lays great stress on the law of the growth of spaces, that is, the trend toward giant empires. Like location, space too is correlated with culture. The smaller the space the more intensive the culture on the one hand, whereas in large spaces culture is slow to penetrate toward the center. Large races with specific characteristics must inhabit large spaces, however, to prevent the inevitable race mixture from corrupting the racial kernel at the center.

Special mention must be made of Ratzel's idea of the 'inrooting' (*Einwurzelung*) of the people in the soil. In its historical and political implications, this is one of the most significant of the laws regulating the relation between man and the earth. People with lower cultural standards, Ratzel says, are generally far less dependent on

the earth than people of higher levels. The more intensive the cultivation (in its broadest sense, including, but extending beyond, mere
agricultural cultivation), the more the population becomes 'inrooted.'

Traditional conceptions of the state are shattered by Ratzel's
anthropogeography. The laws of movement, location, and space
cannot be reconciled with the notion of a unified legal and political
sovereignty over a specific area. For then space would be nothing
more than the object of rule, whereas for Ratzel space and location
become the very essence of the state. The union between man and
the earth is an organic bond; [22] not merely an analogy, as in the
various biological organic theories of society, but as a real union, a
scientific truth. Ratzel's working out of this theory need not concern us. The absurd lengths to which he went are sufficiently illustrated by one example. To justify the continued existence of Prussia after its territorial mutilation in 1806, he compared the state with
organisms of the lower order: only on lower levels of life can the
body continue to live even after the destruction of a vital organ.

Of major political significance is the implication of Ratzel's organic theory for the theory and practices associated with the concept of nationality. A frontier is not an arbitrarily fixed line, but a
strip or band marking the meeting between a movement and a
counter-movement. It is the result of a long process of 'inrooting,'
during which space becomes increasingly valuable. A frontier may
even form an independent organism within the state. Furthermore,
the fundamental law of the growth of spaces—illustrated by the in-
comparably greater extent of Russia or the British Empire as against
Persia or Rome, for example—runs counter to the principles of nationality.[23] Even the high seas are subject to this law. The Atlantic
has displaced the Mediterranean; some day it may be dethroned in
turn.

The policies of nationality are thus regressive. They may be
retained only where they can serve as an aid to territorial acquisition. In our day we have developed 'space-conquering forces'
(raumüberwindende Mächte), a term of Ratzel's that has become
part of the official National Socialist language. One of the great
tasks before us is to develop a popular consciousness of large spaces.
A people whose horizon remains that of the small space will inevitably decay.

Kjellen [24] provides the bridge from Ratzel to National Socialism.

He had a knack for popular, concretely documented presentation, which gave him a much more important role in the development of geopolitical ideology. And at one point he makes a significant departure from Ratzel's analysis: he restores nationality, or rather, he combines the national and territorial elements. Not the nineteenth-century nation, however, but the folk. Nationality, says Kjellen, is the manifestation of the 'folk individuality' of the state. The national state is therefore the natural, organic form of the state. Folk and state, organically different, are merged into one union.

For all its 'empiricism' and supposed realism, and despite certain important departures, Kjellen's theory remains basically a re-hash of the organic theory of Ratzel. States, he writes, are 'super-individual organisms that are as real as individuals, only far bigger and mightier in their developmental processes.' [25] The state is a biological phenomenon, a 'form of life' (p. 44). The individuality of the state is a natural unity, expressed in the economic field as autarky, demographically as nationality, socially as the solidarity of all groups, and politically as loyalty to the rulers (pp. 142-3).

Anyone can see that Kjellen's theory is not simple geopolitics, but a composite. It is equally obvious that he has anticipated the National Socialist theory of European expansion. His state is an autarkic economy within which the masses are incorporated under the slogan of a people's community. It demands unconditional allegiance to the ruling class and it justifies Germany's expansion and foreign conquests by her central location in Europe and her need for living space. The organic theory stands revealed as pure Machiavellianism. As a class, organic theories of society are absurdities if they are conceived as anything more than analogies. Biological laws are not reproduced in social life. As ideology, however, organic theories can be powerful instruments, for all their absurdity. Kjellen, as we may note finally, insists that political expediency, determined by natural factors, is the sole determinant of a state's policies (p. 38). Legal and moral reasons have no validity.

Two other names deserve mention in the pre-history of National Socialist geopolitics: 'Sir Halford MacKinder and Friedrich Naumann. Their major contribution—one that Haushofer openly recognizes—is the formulation and popularization of the notion of a Central Europe (Mittel Europa). According to Haushofer, MacKinder actually coined the phrase shortly after the turn of the century,[26] and stimulated Partsch, the world renowned German geographer, to design a map of Central Europe, made up of Germany, the Netherlands, Switzerland, Austria-Hungary, and Rumania. In 1919, MacKinder published a book under the title, *Democratic Ideas and Realities*, urging the Peace Conference to discard sentimental ideas of democracy and to recognize geographical realities. He wanted especially to prevent a joining of the Russian and German spaces, because such a union could rule not only Europe but the entire world.

In Germany, the idea of a Central Europe naturally became very popular during the First World War.

We may mention Paul de Lagarde (Bötticher) 1827-91, professor of oriental languages at Göttingen University. Lagarde was primarily responsible for shaping Rosenberg's ideology, and Rosenberg frequently acknowledges his indebtedness to him and shares with him a hatred of Catholics and Jews, of popular franchise and enlightenment, and demands the eradication of all Semitic and Roman elements from the German language and culture. Lagarde was also the precursor of the Central Europe concept; he saw Germany's future in its expansion into Poland and West Russia and advocated a Middle Europe reaching from the mouth of the Ems to the mouth of the Danube, from Memel to Trieste, from Metz to the River Bug.[27] Even Rosenberg's idea of deporting the Jews to Madagascar derives from Lagarde.

Perhaps the chief popularizing agent was Friedrich Naumann's book, *Mitteleuropa*, published in 1915.[28] Though not a geopolitical treatise properly speaking, the work falls very definitely within the trend we are discussing. Its significance was tremendously enhanced by the position the author occupied in Germany. A member of the Reichstag, Naumann was the founder of the Democratic party in 1918 which framed the Weimar constitution. His great prestige as a 'democratic' leader lent a halo of liberalism and democracy to the social imperialism he had learned in his early training under the crudely Anti-Semitic Stöcker.

Naumann's major proposal was the establishment of a federated superstate (*Oberstaat*), completely integrated economically and surrounded by a tariff wall (p. 289). It would be called Central Europe. Its spirit would be the spirit of a new Germany (*Neudeutsches Wesen*), in which all economic activity would be collectively organized. As one justification for his proposal, this liberal democrat alleged the existence of a peculiarly German economic psychology. If a French businessman, he argued, were to receive an order requiring the enlargement of his plant employing fifteen men, he would sub-contract rather than enlarge. And if he did the latter, it would inevitably turn out that he was no real Frenchman but an Alsatian or Swiss. The German, on the other hand, would invariably enlarge his plant in these circumstances. The German businessman is enterprising, scientific in his approach, and disciplined. His workers support him loyally, for are not the German workers the most educated in the world, trained in the trade unions and the Social Democratic party?

English capitalism is doomed. Germany's time will come. 'For this our time, Frederick II, Kant, Scharnhorst, Siemens, Krupp, Bismarck, Bebel, Legien, Kirdorf, and Ballin have educated us. For this Fatherland our dead have died in battle. Germany must go forward in this world!' (p. 113). A new economic era will arise. Hungary will be the granary of Central Europe, and other products will be allocated to each section. Jewish businessmen will play an important role in extending the already predominantly German character of Central European economy. In the end, world power will have been concentrated in a few centers, London, New York, Moscow (or St. Petersburg), and perhaps China or Japan (p. 161). Other states will be mere satellites, reinforcing 'the leading group to which they belong.' Today the neutrals are like 'asteroids or comets' outside the constellation. They must be drawn in, for there is no place for neutrality in a world of giant sovereigns (p. 172). This is the mission of the new Germany. 'In this task all economic organizations of entrepreneurs and workers will help us. That will become our political, world-economic socialism' (p. 197).

All these strains reach their ultimate formulation with Karl Haushofer.[29] His ideas can be studied briefly in his most popular work, the book he dedicated to his friend Rudolf Hess, *Weltpolitik von Heute.* Let us follow them in Haushofer's own sequence.

To begin with, a German who wishes to understand the geopolitical basis of contemporary world politics must place himself in the center of the 'folk' and cultural space. Here Haushofer is of course much closer to Kjellen than to Ratzel. Racial determinants, the 'racial will,' are dynamic elements within the 'static world of international agreements' (pp. 16-17). But within what 'folk' space shall one stand? The Germany of 1932 was the product of Versailles, and the treaty was based on gross geopolitical errors. In fact, geopolitics is one weapon in the fight to correct such errors as the division of Europe into colony-possessing powers in the West, space-possessing powers in the East, and strangulated states in the center.

It was the Versailles Treaty, too, which brought about the autonomous development of America, the weakening of the British Empire, the return of Russia to Asia, and the gradual revival of self-determination in southern and eastern Asia. Ultimate political decisions will be made within these groups, and they will depend upon a clear insight into the relations between power and state. 'Primal geopolitical drives' (*geopolitische Urtriebe*) are at work within this spatial framework, thrusting from the continent to the coast and beyond the coast to the domination of the opposite coast. Ratzel's law of growing spaces is not limited to continental masses: it also crosses the sea (p. 49).

From the German standpoint, the central space must be Central Europe (Haushofer would prefer the term 'Inner Europe' as more precise geopolitically). The first political task is to restore the space of the German Reich. There are five different German spaces: (1) the military space, which in 1934 was even smaller than the territory of the Reich; (2) the territory of the Reich; (3) the compact mass of the German 'folk' soil—Germany, the Polish Corridor, the Sudetenland, Upper Silesia, Teschen, Austria, Alsace-Lorraine, and southern Denmark; (4) the sphere of influence of German language and culture; and (5) the independent Dutch-Flemish spaces.

The main powers of the world fall into distinct categories. The fundamental opposition is between the 'renaissance' powers, Germany, Italy, and Japan, and the powers of 'perseverance,' England and France. The United States, Russia, Brazil, and China operate 'between the tides' (p. 76). In addition, there are spaces like India and Mongolia, which possess a future but no present, and like the Baltic sea space, Spain, and Portugal, which are mere remnants of the past. The solution to these oppositions and political conflicts does not lie in internationalism. The League of Nations, the British Commonwealth of Nations, the Federation of Soviet States, Pan-America, Pan-Europe, Pan-Pacific, Pan-Africa—they are all of no avail. An old German proverb says: *Wer auf sich selber ruht, steht gut* (Self-help is the best help) (p. 105). In 1931, the Sudeten deputy Hans Krebs, writing in a National Socialist publication, attacked Coudenhove-Kalergi's idea of a Pan-Europe with similar arguments. Against Pan-Europe he sets Central Europe. A federation of Europe within the League framework is incompatible with National Socialist ideas of space and living space.

Turning to immediate practical considerations, Haushofer's first problem is to work out the spatial margin necessary for a state to live. His solution justifies the destruction of France and England and the incorporation of the smaller states. On the one hand, there is the law of growing spaces. The space of the British Empire has reached its maximum and therefore decay is inevitable. France has lost the will to live, for a country that has begun to surrender is through (pp. 110-11). On the other hand, there is a minimum spatial limit. Therefore small states must be incorporated into larger spaces. Two exceptions—the Vatican City and Switzerland—are allowed because of their long tradition of independence.

The category of great power must be replaced by world power. A great power is determined solely by the 'will to power'—otherwise China and Brazil would be great powers. It was a category of the era of the 'concert of powers,' when the great powers co-operated in dividing up the world among themselves (p. 129). Now that co-operation has given way to antagonism, world powers have become geopolitically decisive. Since Germany has not yet attained the status of a world power, it need not be concerned with the frictions between the powers. Germany must work carefully, utilizing the existing antagonisms by 'a surprisingly decisive interference of counsel and action': everything will fall into the lap of him who waits (p. 135). This analysis of Germany's role in the struggle of world powers is the kernel of the book, according to Haushofer.

A further invaluable weapon in Germany's struggle for living space is racism, and Haushofer presents an amazingly frank analysis. 'Master races' must remain pure; race mixture has brought about the decay of many a great empire (p. 151). France, for example, carries the seeds of its own destruction. Among non-Germanic people, significantly enough, race and class become synonymous and it is essential to prevent the rise of lower classes and races to the level of the master race.

Today we see the suppression of racial minorities everywhere—a golden opportunity for political and propagandist manipulation of the slogan of self-determination. 'A far-seeing policy opens enormous possibilities to us . . . if we esteem the principle of self-determination of the large and small peoples . . . with the slogan "honor, freedom, equality" . . . The condition, however, is superior knowledge of the state of pressure upon the people [*Volksdruckverhältnisse*] and of the forms of political domination throughout the world, which long ago became a unified power field' and within which nothing can happen without producing repercussions elsewhere (p. 152). Nothing could be more frank. Self-determination is merely a weapon. Take advantage of every friction growing out of the minority problem. Stir up national and racial conflicts where you can. Every conflict will play into the hands of Germany, the new self-appointed guardian of honor, freedom, and equality all over the world.

Ethical and military considerations are weapons too. Germany has the right to base its policy on the immorality of territorial acquisitions by other powers. They were robberies concealed and justified by international law. The mandates, for example, were nothing other than 'spatial fraud' (p. 155). The redistribution of space will be accomplished in new and entirely different ways. Germany will make use of 'spiritual warfare' (propaganda); new military techniques including the use of aeroplanes and tanks as loosening (*auflockernde*) forces against both troops and civilians; and morale-destroying lightning blows by small highly specialized bodies of soldiers; supplementary weapons like the boycott now practiced in India and China and capable of greatly intensified force if co-ordinated into the National Socialist movement. By such means, 'culture-people without colonies' may even be able to acquire tropical territories without bloodshed (pp. 158-9). Frontiers are not 'soulless lines'—they are organisms and they too will be changed at will.

Germany's world mission can be understood only in terms of the long-term aims of the world powers.[30] Great Britain's long-term aim is merely conservation of what she now possesses. The British Empire will therefore be dismembered. France, too, will fall. Only Russia and the United States, Japan and Germany, and, to a lesser extent, Italy will remain as world powers. Just what

Germany's short-term aims are is never clearly revealed, but it is not hard to deduce them from the rest of the discussion.

One example will suffice to illustrate the hold of geopolitics in official German circles (especially in the army and navy). 'Today we must choose,' wrote Alfred Rosenberg in 1927, 'between Crusade politics and space politics; between world imperialism and the racial will of the state; between Barbarossa and Henry the Lion; between the Stresemann-League of Nations and the racial National Socialist Germanic state.' [31] It is geopolitics *versus* medieval universalism as the base of the new Reich.

The most outspoken representative of geopolitics mixed with racism is the famous Ewald Banse, who quite naively stated the need for imperialistic war and, from geography, racism, military science, and the Reich idea, elaborated *Wehrwissenschaft* as that academic discipline which 'is the systematic application of every branch of human thought and human endeavor to the end of increasing the defensive strength of our people.' [32] This new science receives the rank of a 'national philosophy.' In a little-known book [33] written for the layman, Banse analyzed the whole world, each country in turn, its geography, its 'blood and character,' its political organization, according to the tenets of geopolitics of learning and utilizing every conflict of whatever nature in each part of the world for German aims.

Much of the general popularity of geopolitics can be found in the same element that underlies the success of any pseudo-scientific theory of society or politics: the possibility of attributing all evils to a single and seemingly objective factor. In Hans Grimm's novel, *Volk ohne Raum* (A People without Space), for example, we are given a popular emotionalized treatment of geopolitics.[34] The entire 1200 pages constitute one long outcry against British power and a preparation for German imperialist expansion. This is an adequate description of Haushofer's book, too. In one map (p. 120), England is depicted as an enormous spider seated in the British Isles and sucking up blood from all corners of the earth. Toward Russia, on the other hand, Haushofer is rather ambivalent. He speaks of Germany squeezed between France and the Soviet Union. Yet the reference to MacKinder's notion of the Russo-German space as the geographical pivot of history could equally be preparation for the signing of the non-aggression pact or for war against Russia.

In the final analysis, geopolitics is nothing but the ideology of imperialist expansion. What little intelligible geography it has retained, as in the arguments for certain frontier rectifications, is neither new nor particularly important within the whole structure. The bulk of geopolitics is a hodgepodge of ethical, military, economic, racial, demographic, historical, and political considerations. It offers a fine illustration of the perversion of genuine scientific considerations in the interests of National Socialist imperialism.

As a scientific justification for expansion, geopolitics is nonsense, of course.[35] It could have validity only if the entire world were centered around one focal location. Since more than one central location does in fact exist, however, how do we determine which shall swallow which? Why should Alsace-Lorraine be incorporated into Germany rather than have France swallow Germany up to the Rhine? Should Germany or the Soviet Union incorporate Poland? Or to put it more generally, from the argument that the frontier is a band or organism and not a line, how does one determine in whose favor the frontier should be rectified? Canada or the United States? The United States or Mexico? Obviously, the answer does not lie in geography—it lies in power.

3. Population Pressure

Both Germany and Italy have made extensive use of a pro-natalist population policy as a further basis for their claim for more living space. The very success of the policy—despite the difficulty in obtaining official statements regarding its purpose, especially for Germany, birth rate statistics leave no doubt as to its success[35]—at once exposes the fraudulent nature of the claim, however. In his reply to President Roosevelt, Hitler complained bitterly about the overcrowded population of countries without living space. Yet his regime moved heaven and earth to increase the size of the German population.

Republican Germany had already taken steps to increase the birth rate. Article 119 of the Weimar constitution promised special protection to large families. Private organizations like the League of Large Families (founded in 1919) put constant pressure on the legislature. Wage differentials based on family status were universal for civil service employees and common among some of the salaried employees. On the other hand, the manual workers' unions opposed family allowances partly for ideological reasons (desire for a class wage) and partly from fear lest the differential drive heads of families out of jobs. Birth-control information was widely disseminated. Fifteen organizations were active in this field and many of the sick funds gave their members advice on contraceptives.[36] Leniency by the courts, especially in the Protestant regions, helped bring the number of abortions to an estimated 800,000-1,000,000 yearly. In general, pro-natalism was very much on the defensive under Weimar.

The National Socialists lost little time in reversing the picture. Minister of the Interior Frick announced the change in a speech in June 1933.[37] Birth-control centers were closed, leniency toward abortion was brought to a sharp halt, and the advertising of contraceptives stopped.[38] The party took over the League of Large Families, making it a section of the race-policy department. It now has a membership of some 300,000 families. By a law of 1 June 1933 (taking effect within two months), couples about to marry could obtain interest-free loans up to 1,000 marks if they fulfilled certain conditions. They must be politically reliable and racially, physically, and morally eligible citizens. The bride must have been gainfully employed for at least six months during the two years preceding marriage. She must cease working and must pledge not to take another job unless her husband is unable to support the family. The loans are given in the form of coupons to be used in purchasing furniture and household equipment and are to be repaid in small monthly instalments over a period of eight years. One-quarter of the loan is cancelled at the birth of each child. The purposes of the law are clear from its provisions: reduction of unemployment by eliminating married women whose husbands are employed (a continuation of the reactionary policy introduced over widespread protest toward the end of the Republic), and stimulation of the birth rate.

As the military preparedness program brought full employment in its wake, the program of stimulation of marriages and large families was directed more and more exclusively toward pro-natalism. By act of 3 November 1937, the requirement that women who receive marriage loans cease working was dropped. A measure adopted about one month earlier provided that the money turned back in repayment of the loans be used to provide special allowances and grants to families with dependent children, and particularly as settlement grants to build up the rural population. Other measures discriminated in favor of large famiiles in income tax rates and in various other ways.

National Socialist pro-natalism has undoubtedly been successful. By the end of 1938 there had been 1,121,707 marriage loans granted and 980,365 cancellations because of births.[39] These stimulants together with a general economic improvement pushed the birth rate up, though it is impossible to say which factor played the more important part.

Now what does the demand for an 'adequate space for the population' really mean? Its supposed scientific basis is virtually non-existent.[40] It would be absurd to argue that because Germany (including Danzig and the Sudetenland) has 4 per cent of the world population, her 0.5 per cent of the world area should be increased to a corresponding 4 per cent. There are tremendous variations in the value of different sections of the earth. Furthermore, an industrial nation may need less territory than an agricultural or nomadic country. If the argument is that a nation requires enough space to overcome structural employment, Germany has herself answered by attaining full employment at a time when many 'have' nations were unable to do so. And even ascribing Germany's success to the temporary panacea of armaments and war does not save the population argument. Colonies are notoriously unfit for large-scale settlement. Eastern and southeastern Europe is overcrowded so that German settlement there is possible only by driving out the present inhabitants. What is really responsible for overpopulation is a non- or mal-functioning economic system. Therefore it can be overcome only by a functioning international division of labor, not by acquisition of more territory. To hold overpopulation responsible for unemployment is sheer demagogy designed to conceal the inner antagonisms produced by capitalism.

The inescapable conclusion is that regarding population the living-space doctrine has a merely ideological function in the interest of imperialism. A comparison with earlier population theories is very revealing. The early nineteenth-century policy was dominated by a single fear, succinctly expressed by the Prince of Oettingen-Wallerstein before the Bavarian Second Chamber in 1834: 'One must close the road to revolution by making it difficult for those without property to marry.' [41] By a series of acts (1828, 1833, 1852), the duchy of Württemberg required governmental permission for marriage and enumerated a long list of prohibitions. This marked a sharp reversal from early mercantilism, which had repealed marriage restrictions and even encouraged illegitimate children in order to build up the labor supply. Many other states, including Bavaria, followed the example of Württemberg.

One writer in 1827 even went so far as to make the cynical proposal that all young men be required to submit to infibulation, the metal rings preventing sexual intercourse not to be removed until the man could prove his ability to support a wife and children.[42] Even the famous liberal constitutionalist Robert von Mohl found it necessary to argue against unrestricted marriages, though he himself included marriage among the original rights of man.[43] Others proposed measures discriminating against illegitimate children or requiring various financial guarantees for permission to marry.[44] Anything to prevent a further growth of the population and its supposed threat to the safety of the ruling classes.

How different is National Socialism's technique. By its racial imperialism, it seeks to incorporate the masses into the new authoritarian structure of society, promising them a share in the coming profits of world conquest. The living-space doctrine prepares the way ideologically, while the population policy prepares the way materially by increasing the size of the master race.

4. THE NEW INTERNATIONAL LAW

The ideology of expansion is not complete with tradition, geopolitics, and pro-natalism. A new international law is needed too; more correctly, perhaps, a new one at each stage in international relations. National Socialism has made many contributions to international law, to the surprise of those who believe that National Socialist political theory is simply state absolutism. Why not, after all? National Socialism has, prior to 1933, always utilized liberal democratic forms where they could be useful in attaining certain objectives. Before seizing power, did not the National Socialists take full advantage of civil rights, especially freedom of the press and of parliamentary government? After coming to power, having destroyed civil rights at home, they could still make use of international law in their dealings with the outside world. And they were nothing if not frank. One National Socialist international lawyer wrote: 'For specific reasons, international lawyers of repute should prove that the old concept of international law is compatible with the National Socialist philosophy of life.' 'At present,' he continued, 'Germany must still try, using international law among other means, to make certain that the dictates imposed upon her give way to a better order.' [45] What is surprising is that outside Germany, especially in England, experts in international law were seemingly unaware of the game that was being played.

The alternative for the National Socialists would have been to revive the old Prussian doctrine of Philipp and Andreas Zorn, that international law does not exist, that the body of alleged international law is merely external state law subject to the sovereign power of the state. Alternatively, they might fall back on the *clausula rebus sic stantibus:* fundamentally changed circumstances allow a country to withdraw from all existing international obligations. One attempt was actually made in this direction by a National Socialist lawyer named Schecher.[46] He undertook to prove that the National Socialist philosophy inevitably gave the internal law of the state unlimited precedence over international law. The latter is valid only in so far as it forms part of the domestic legal system, and the state alone determines that. The official theorists were much more clever than Schecher, and his views have been rejected almost unanimously.

Equally unsuccessful was the notion of geo-jurisprudence,[47] worth mentioning because it has been strongly supported by Haushofer. Geo-jurisprudence seeks to reformulate international law in terms of vassals, dependencies, protectorates, and federations worked out on geopolitical principles. The crux of the argument is that space can make juristic independence meaningless. When one can shoot clear across a state, Austria or Switzerland for example, the independence of such a state has no meaning. On the other hand, Danzig, Memel, the Saar, and even the southwestern neck of Bavaria are spatially insecure for the same reason and need added protection. (The only comment necessary is that this is a military argument, with space drawn in as a blind.)

THE BREAKING OF THE FETTERS OF VERSAILLES

The use of international law to overcome the 'dictates imposed upon' Germany, to break the 'fetters of Versailles,' is, then, officially approved. Germany must regain equality with other great powers by re-arming, militarizing the Rhineland, removing 'colonial injustice' and 'territorial shame.' That is what most German international lawyers have been saying ever since the end of the First World War, as a matter of fact. 'Wiping out the shame of Versailles' was a stock phrase in the Weimar Republic. They always believed that the Versailles Treaty was invalid because it was a dictated peace, arguing either on the analogy of civil law, where contracts made under duress are null and void, or by invoking the *clausula rebus sic stantibus*, or by charging non-fulfilment of the promises of the Fourteen Points and of Lansing's note of 5 November 1918. Others said that the Treaty ran counter to the eternal ideas of justice. After Hitler took power, of course, the wraps were taken off and the attack gained enormously in vigor and vituperation.[48] The overwhelming majority of the German people unquestionably supported the revisionist demands, provided that they could be achieved peaceably.

The leading voice in the Nationalist Socialist revisionist chorus is Carl Schmitt's.[49] As the leitmotif he introduces natural law, a concept that the National Socialists rigorously excluded from their domestic law. 'It is not man's will and man's rules,' writes a colleague of Schmitt's, 'but nature which is man's law and the limit of his powers.'[50] The term 'natural law' is generally avoided for rather obvious reasons, but the insistence upon justice and morality and the very form of the argument is nothing but the rationalistic natural law that goes back to Grotius.

The rationalist element is dressed in the terminology of irrationalism.[51] Not man but the community is placed in the center of the system. Since the essence of the community is to prevent one member from prevailing over another, and since international society is a community, the argument runs, international inequality violates the essence of international law. Germany rightly claims her rights to equality. The trick and the sham of the argument lie in the word equality. There can be no quarrel with the argument that by their very sovereignty all states are equals. International law could not exist without recognizing this principle, provided equality is understood as a juristic category. In the same way, equality of all men in our legal system means legal equality, that is, the illegality of slavery and so forth. The National Socialists, however, do not stop with this formal concept. For them, equality also means the right of each state to adequate living space. It has all sorts of moral and political implications.[52] Carl Schmitt enumerates a whole catalogue of rights, such as the eternal right to existence, self-determination, defense, and so on.[53]

The whole chain of reasoning is neither very original nor essentially valid. Its exponents admit that they are wiping out the boundary between ethics and law.[54] If we agree with a recent American work that holds this to be progress,[55] then we can refute the National Socialists in political or ethical terms, not in terms of law. However, if we retain the traditional separation between law and morals as essential,*—as I do—the purely arbitrary character of the reasoning becomes clear. Perhaps Germany should have been allowed to rearm, militarize the Rhineland, and occupy the Corridor and Danzig. That is not the question. To justify these acts by international law makes law a mere prostitute of politics.

The argument unquestionably has a popular appeal. It duped the civilized world quite successfully. The National Socialist propaganda machine knew how to get the writings of its international lawyers into respectable foreign periodicals. That helped. Their trick of excluding Soviet Russia from the international community helped too. They maintained that membership in the international community requires homogeneity, a number of common features and beliefs.[56] This argument is obviously borrowed from the doctrine that a democracy can function only if there is a certain degree of homogeneity within its borders.[57] Just what the elements of this international homogeneity are is never made clear. What is made crystal clear is the fact that the Soviet Union shares none of the features of the civilized world, and so stands outside the pale of international law.[58]

The excommunication of Soviet Russia was decreed by Hitler in his speech to the 1936 party congress. That speech brought a

* See p. 443.

flood of literature in its wake.[59] Absurd as the arguments are, they were an unquestioned aid to the success of National Socialist foreign policy. Statesmen in parliaments and in the League loudly denounced the militarization of the Rhine and the introduction of universal conscription in Germany. These denunciations did not come from the heart, however, and were not followed by action. Neither British labor nor liberals or appeasers denied the validity of the German claims.

THE NEW NEUTRALITY AND THE JUST WAR

In other situations, notably on the neutrality question, the blending of law and ethics led to the wrong solution. Then the National Socialists reverted to strict traditionalism. Recently English and American international lawyers have revived the medieval and early liberal concept of a just war and they separate the rights and duties of neutral states according to the character of the war. Perhaps the best expression of this view was given by the then Attorney-General, Robert H. Jackson, in his address before the International Bar Association on 27 March 1941. Mr. Jackson attacked those who have 'not caught up with this century which, by its League of Nations Covenant with sanctions against aggressors, the Kellogg-Briand treaty for renunciation of war as an instrument of policy, and Argentine Anti-War treaty, swept away the nineteenth-century basis for contending that all wars are alike and all warriors entitled to like treatment.'[60] Neutrals must assist those nations who are fighting to ward off aggression—a just war. In the same vein, there is a considerable body of literature holding that neutrals may discriminate against any nation violating the Kellogg-Briand pact. Two important contributions in the 1936 British Yearbook of International Law, for example, go even further.[61]

This new theory, especially in the Jackson formulation, ought to be quite acceptable to German philosophy of law. Yet they attack it, invoking the oldest and most rationalistic arguments in existence. The same Carl Schmitt who invented 'thinking in concrete words,' to replace abstract, rationalistic thought, has devoted many articles to combating the new theory of war and neutrality. He denies the distinction between just and unjust wars, and that neutrality can be 'halved.' [62] Either war is still a legal institution, he argues, in which case preference for either side on the part of a neutral makes it a belligerent; or war is simply a police measure taken by some supernational agency.

German lawyers maintain further that the English declaration of war on Germany violated the League Covenant and that the Kellogg-Briand pact is rendered invalid by the many reservations that destroy its universality.[63] No legal basis exists, therefore, for discrimination against Germany. It is with great satisfaction that they cite the views of Borchard and Lage on the British reservations to the Kellogg-Briand pact.[64] We might note, finally, that the opposing view has not won universal approval in the United States by any means. In a lengthy and widely discussed communication to *The New York Times*, for example, Hyde and Jessup maintained that the repeal of the old Neutrality Act was unneutral and violated the principle of impartiality.[65]

While the Germans were developing their new theories of international law, the French and British governments destroyed the League of Nations. In a speech on 10 October 1936, Leopold II of Belgium announced the severance of 'one-sided' obligations and the adoption of a policy of absolute neutrality patterned after the Dutch and Swiss models. English public opinion clearly recognized this as the death blow to collective security. But at least one English international lawyer was sufficiently pleased to indicate his approval in a German journal to which he contributed frequently.[66] England, he thought, would still fight to maintain Dutch and Belgian independence—not for the sake of international law or the League of Nations, however, but solely to protect the interests of the empire. He was equally confident that Britain would not take part in any conflict arising out of the Franco-Soviet pact.

Elsewhere on the continent we find Switzerland—never too friendly to the League and partly exempt from the obligations of the Covenant after the London declaration of 13 February 1920— returning to a position of absolute neutrality on 22 December 1937/ 14 May 1938. A similar development took place in Scandinavia.[67]

German theory had scored another victory, not on its merits but for reasons of political expediency. It goes without saying that the neutral states were not the beneficiaries, except perhaps Sweden

and Switzerland for a brief time. The German attack on the theory
of just war and discriminatory neutrality was nothing more than
part of the preparation for the new World War.

THE GERMANIC MONROE DOCTRINE

With the coming of the present war, however, a completely new
pattern of international law has been developed: the Germanic
Monroe Doctrine. Geopolitics and international law have been
joined.

The 'large space' theory need not necessarily bring about a transformation of accepted international law. If one holds that states are
the sole subjects of international relations, it does not matter
whether the subjects are small- or large-space states, whether they
give themselves the fancy title of *Reich* or remain content with
mere 'state.' That is still the view of many German international
lawyers.[68] But the dominant school has abandoned both traditional
concepts, state and international law. One writer posed the problem
this way: 'If the development really tends toward large spaces, is
"international law" then that concerned with the relation between
the large spaces or is it the law of the free people living in one
common large space?' [69] The very framing of the question reveals
the basic motive. It not only stamps Poles, Czechs, Dutch, Belgians,
and Jews as 'free' people, but it also justifies the hierarchy of races
within the German realm by a body of rules, called international
law but in fact nothing other than the law governing the empire.
In other words, the relation of individual states to one another no
longer comes within the scope of international law. On the contrary,
the sanctity of international law is rejected as applying only to the
position within each of the empires.[70]

This scholastic strategy has still further consequences. The trend
toward large spaces, conceived by Ratzel merely as a geographical
phenomenon, now becomes an historico-political process. Large-
space economics precedes large-space politics. Large spaces have
been made mandatory, it is argued, by the trustification, monopolization, electrification, and rationalization of German industry.[71]
The integrating function of technology is not seen within the
framework of a program of territorial division of labor but within
a program of territorial expansion great enough to absorb the prod-

ucts of the economic giants. The intrinsic connection between a monopolistic economy and territorial conquest stands fully revealed.

Traditional international law is condemned as the creation of Jews [72] and as a cloak for British imperialism. Space must become the primary basis of international order [73]—in other words, a return of regionalist ideas. It is National Socialist regionalism against the universalist international law of British imperialism and interventionism. 'Behind the façade of general norms [of international law] lies, in reality, the system of Anglo-Saxon world imperialism.'[74] Universalism works on the assumption that the equality of all this is implied in the very notion of sovereignty. Since states no longer stand in the center of international law, the ideas of state sovereignty and state equality must fall. Universalism must be replaced by thinking in 'concrete orders' and the most concrete of all orders existing is the *grossdeutsche Reich*. Steding's book comes close to this conception, and, though it has found few other echoes in Germany, the National Socialist international lawyers have given it much attention.[75]

As precedents for their new regionalism, the Germans point to such spatial consequences of modern warfare as the idea of danger zones expressed in the American Neutrality Act and of security zones in the Panama Convention of 3 October 1939. In the German view, the former is particularly significant because it abandons the freedom of the seas, the basic principle of international universalism, and substitutes the principle of zones. Similarly, the three-hundred-mile zone proclaimed in the Panama Convention is regarded as a necessary consequence of the large-space idea underlying the Monroe Doctrine, as irreconcilable with neutrality.[76] German theorists are gleeful over the new elaboration of the Monroe Doctrine into Pan-Americanism. 'This principle of order,' writes one, 'has been declared valid for the whole world.' [77] After all, it was an American expert, Quincy Wright, who said of the Havana Pact: 'Whereas formerly the Monroe doctrine dealt only with land areas in the Western hemisphere, it is now proposed to extend it to the seas. Formerly the Monroe Doctrine was linked with the general assertion of the freedom of the seas, but in its new form, it has some resemblance to the doctrine of *mare clausum* by Spain and Portugal in the sixteenth century against which Grotius launched the principle of *mare liberum*.' [78] That, National Socialists claim, is identical with the basic idea of the German-Italian-Japanese pact of 27 October 1939.

German doctrine thus contrasts two approaches: the regional, anti-universalist space principle and the universalist British principle of securing the life lines of the empire in every part of the world. The Monroe Doctrine becomes 'the most successful example of a large-scale principle in international law.' [79] Arguing that what is sauce for the goose is sauce for the gander, Ribbentrop made good use of the Monroe Doctrine in replying on 1 July 1940 to Secretary Hull's warning that the United States cannot 'acquiesce in any attempt to transfer any geographic region of the Western Hemisphere from one non-American power to another non-American power.' [80] Ribbentrop first denied the validity of such an interpretation of the Monroe Doctrine, and then closed with the following: 'The government of the Reich would like to take this opportunity to point out that, as a matter of principle, non-interference by European states in the affairs of the American continent cannot be justified unless the American states, for their part, likewise refrain from interference in the affairs of the European continent.'

Ever since the first Hague Peace Conference of 1909, the United States has insisted that the Monroe Doctrine occupies an exceptional position.[81] American jurists have always questioned whether it may properly be classed as international law at all. They have preferred to regard it as an expression of the right to self-defense, in no way conflicting with the universality of international law. In German hands, the exception now becomes the rule. There is no longer one international law but as many as there are empires, that is, large spaces. The *grossdeutsche Reich* is the creator of its own international law for its own space. Interventionists must keep their hands off.

The postulates of the Germanic Monroe Doctrine seem convincing at first sight. Hardly any other ideological element is held in such profound contempt in our civilization as international law. Every generation has seen it break down as an instrument for organizing peace, and a theory that disposes of its universalist claims has the obvious advantage of appearing to be realistic. The fallacy should be equally obvious, however. To abandon universalism because of its failures is like rejecting civil rights because they help legitimize and veil class exploitation, or democracy because it conceals boss control, or Christianity because churches have corrupted Christian morals. Faced with a corrupt administration of justice, the reasonable person does not demand a return to the war of each against all, but fights for an honest system. Likewise, when we have shown that international law has been misused for imperialistic aims, our task has begun, not ended. We must fight against imperialism.

That what is sauce for the goose is sauce for the gander is, indeed, what we understand by justice. But are the sauces really identical? No one can deny that the Monroe Doctrine was once an ideological basis for American imperialism. In his presidential message of 1904, Theodore Roosevelt claimed for the United States the position of supreme arbiter for the whole American continent. Frequent intervention, especially in the Caribbean, has made the doctrine unpopular in Latin American countries. With the administration of Secretary of State Charles Evans Hughes, however, the Monroe Doctrine began to lose its interventionist and imperialistic sting, and during the present Roosevelt administration it is being merged with the principle of Pan-American solidarity. Secretary of State Hull formulated the new conception in his press release commenting on the exchange of notes with the German government:

It [the Monroe Doctrine] contains within it not the slightest vestige of any implication, much less assumption, of hegemony on the part of the United States. It never has resembled and it does not today resemble policies which appear to be similar to the Monroe Doctrine, but which, instead of resting on the . . . respect for existing sovereignties, seem to be only a pretext for the carrying out of conquest by the sword . . . and of complete economic and political domination by certain powers.[82]

We may be readily prepared to admit that Pan-American solidarity is not merely a lofty ideal. Nevertheless, economic penetration of a country is still very different from complete political and economic control by another nation. The resistance of a number of Latin American countries to American leadership at all the recent hemispheric conferences offers ample proof. Once the United States fully understands Pan-American solidarity, she will realize that it must be rooted in co-operation among large masses of workers, peasants, and middle classes, and not merely in dealings with

Latin-American ruling groups, ready to ally themselves with a great
power willing to guarantee their political status, prerogatives, and
luxuries. Solidarity between the governments must be cemented
by a solidarity of the peoples. That is America's greatest political
task. And even in its present rudimentary form, Pan-Americanism
is utterly different from the Germanic concept of a Monroe Doctrine. The American basis is democratic consent by sovereign states;
Germany knows nothing but conquest and domination.

THE FOLK GROUP VERSUS MINORITY

At first sight, one might suppose that there would be no place
for the racial theory in the large space doctrine of international
law. It is precisely here, however, that the concepts of Reich and
race merge.

There is a popular notion that the National Socialist insistence
on a racial law is mere ideology with practical consequences only
for the Jews, that the German practice of international law operates
with the old concepts. A similar idea is widely held about German
political theory. Both are dead wrong. The decline of the state in
domestic as well as international law is not mere ideology; it expresses a major practical trend. We have already seen that Carl
Schmitt and his followers refuse to call the legal relations between
the rival empires international law but restrict that term to the law
between the racial groups within each empire. This theory, in other
words, takes the denial of the state and of state sovereignty
seriously. The ideological aim is clearly to give the German solution of the problem of racial minorities the sanctity of international
law. The main political consequence is the abandonment of the
principle of minority protection for the so-called *Volksgruppenrecht*, the law of 'folk groups.'

The way religious, national, racial, and cultural minorities are
treated can be taken as an index of the moral and cultural level
of a state. It became evident during the Paris Peace Conference
that the Wilsonian principle of self-determination, by itself, was not
sufficient to solve this most pressing of European problems. Military, economic, geographic, and historical considerations interfered. Minorities remained. Their protection could not be left to
the discretion of the states in which they lived. The framers of the

Treaty of Versailles and of the League of Nations Covenant therefore established a system of international regulations under the
guardianship of the League. As a matter of fact, provision for international protection first appeared in the treaty concluded by the
Allied and Associated Powers with Poland, and this agreement served
as a model for all other eastern European states, who had to accept
similar obligations before they could gain admission to the League.

The idea of minority protection reflects the best heritage of
liberalism.[83] The legal and political equality of all citizens is guaranteed 'without distinction as to birth, nationality, language, race, or
religion.' There shall be unrestricted use of any language in private
life and adequate facilities for its use in the law courts. Wherever
a minority constitutes 'a considerable proportion of the inhabitants,'
the state is obliged to provide elementary education in the language
of the minority and to defray the cost of educational, religious, and
welfare services. At their own expense, minorities may establish
and conduct their own schools and other social and cultural institutions. Freedom of worship must be unrestricted. Disputes could be
brought before the League and ultimately to the World Court at
the Hague.

The minority treaties thus aimed primarily at equality and only
secondarily at the protection of any specific national character and
culture. The chief practical difficulty in carrying out their provisions was that the minorities had no collective rights, and could
not act as the guardians of their own interests. At its best, therefore, international protection was not really the protection of a
national minority as such, but of each of its members.[84] Moreover,
the League too often found it expedient to side with the sovereign
states. Even so brutal an action as the Polish punitive expedition
against the Ukrainians in eastern Galicia, the aftermath of which
I had the opportunity of witnessing personally, did not evoke serious League protests. In the final analysis, legal protection by treaty
was no more successful than the efforts by the minorities to organize and hold annual conferences in all European countries except
Soviet Russia. The effort broke down completely with the decline
of the League, and its underlying principles were finally abandoned
by the British government during the Sudeten crisis of September
1938.

Needless to say, National Socialist theory and practice have a completely new approach—the folk group law.[85] Its aims may be summarized by contrasting them with the abortive pattern of international minority protection.

INTERNATIONAL MINORITY PROTECTION	THE FOLK GROUP LAW
1. Aims at the equality of all members of the minorities with other citizens;	1. Aims at differentiating the political and legal status of each group according to its specific character;
2. protects minorities by an international guarantee;	2. anchors the protection solely in the mother country;
3. is individualistic in that it does not recognize minorities as legal entities but recognizes the individual rights of members of the group;	3. recognizes the group as an entity and does not recognize individual rights of its members;
4. sees the determinant character of a minority in an objective factor (race, religion, language) or in the subjective factor of the conscious adherence of individuals to a group.	4. sees the determinant character of the folk group in the objective factor of race or the subjective factor *and* in the acceptance of the member by the group.

The National Socialist rejection of egalitarianism is unquestionably a backward step, a denial of the very principle that has distinguished Western civilization from preceding societies. The National Socialists seize upon the obvious inadequacy of mere legal and constitutional equality, and charge that formal equality tends only to conceal socio-economic privilege and exploitation. We must concede some justice to their accusations. The 'concrete personality' of a folk group must certainly be taken into account. Legislators and governments must consider the actual economic, cultural, and social situation of each minority, without, however, sacrificing the basic principle of legal and constitutional equality. The idea of the folk group might imply, furthermore, the right of the minority to appear before national and international tribunals as counsel for its members or even on behalf of the group as whole. And there is the characteristic trick of every National Socialist criticism of traditional Western conceptions. For they make no attempt to transform the socio-economic structure so as to make the formal equality real. Instead, they use a legitimate critique to abolish even legal equality. This technique characterizes the whole conceptual and intellectual framework of National Socialism. In their hands, the 'concrete personality' of the folk group really means differentiation among the groups so as to play one off against the other. The conqueror imposes a hierarchy of races. The folk-group idea is nothing but a device to hold some groups down while inviting others to share in the spoils of the conquest.

The abandonment of international guarantees and the substitution of protection from the mother country were accepted by Lord Runciman and Neville Chamberlain in the sinister autumn days of 1938.[86] It was a crime against international law and minority protection, though an inevitable consequence of the collapse of the League. Were it only a temporary measure, the loss of rights by minorities might be accepted without great objection. National Socialism, however, considers the new system to be the permanent solution. Carl Schmitt denies the very existence of international law among the rival empires. Hasselblatt, who had the greatest share in drafting the proposals of the Sudetendeutsche party, calls his draft bill of 27 April 1937 'inner state international law.' [87] We are clearly faced with one of the most ominous aspects of the new German theory. Acceptance of the principle that the mother country is the political guardian of the minorities means not only the rejection of rational international relations but also the end of internal unity in every state having sizable minorities. It makes the mother people the arbiter of disputes between the state and the minorities living therein. Instead of intervention by the international community based on rational norms and procedures, the National Socialists demand the arbitrary intervention of the mother state—racial imperialism, in other words. The alleged racial ties shall be stronger than juristic or political allegiance. Descent takes precedence over citizenship. Racial Germans throughout the world remain Germans, members of the folk group, subject to its law. The fifth column is elevated to an institution. (Minority groups inside Germany are the exception, of course.)

Recognition of the racial German group as a corporation under public law is coupled with the demand for full autonomy and an equal share in the government. That was the explicit meaning of the Sudetendeutsche party proposals of 27 April 1937.[88] The six bills they introduced, especially the draft penal statute against the 'misuse of denationalization,' subjected the Czechoslovak state to the pressure of its German minority. The Runciman proposals went still further and actually removed the Germans from Czechoslovakian sovereignty.[89] Recognition of the minority as a public corporation, as the Germans understand it and have applied it in Czechoslovakia, Hungary, and Rumania,[90] thus creates a state within a state and exempts the German group from the sovereignty of the state.

In the Netherlands, Dutch penal law and administration have been replaced by German law in all cases of crimes committed by Germans, former German citizens, or citizens of the protectorates of Bohemia and Moravia.[91] German penal law also applies to anyone who commits a crime against 'the *grossdeutsche Reich*, the German people, the National Socialist party, its groupings or affiliated organizations,' against a German citizen, against anyone employed by the Reich or in the service of German authorities; or if the crime is committed in buildings and plants serving the Reich, the party, and so on.

It might be argued that the regulations for Holland are special measures originating in the harsh conditions of occupation. Unfortunately, identical provisions exist for the protectorate of Bohemia and Moravia,[92] and these areas are not occupied zones, but, so we are led to believe, 'a dependent, original territory within the *grossdeutsche Reich* created solely by the will of the Leader.' [93] The constitutional basis derives from Hitler's edict of 16 March 1939. The protectorate is thus not the successor to the Czechoslovak Republic and its pre-incorporation law is not valid as part of Czechoslovakian law. Of course, the Leader has left intact that body of law which does not 'contradict the essence of the assumption of protection by the *deutsche Reich*.' Nevertheless, the exemptions granted to Germans in the protectorate far exceed the infamous capitulations, the privileges enjoyed by foreigners in the Ottoman Empire, Egypt, China, and Morocco.[94]

Hitler's edict (article II, section I) makes 'every folk-German inhabitant of the protectorate' a German citizen and subject to the German administration of justice exclusively. The penal system has been set up by a series of decrees, the aim of which is not to protect the folk-German groups but rather 'to bring the Germans in the protectorate into a close and direct relation with the Reich, and thereby to strengthen the development of their racial characteristics.' [95] A completely German administration of justice has been created, which is simply a copy of the system prevailing in the Reich itself.

The German civil judiciary has jurisdiction over all Germans, whether they are plaintiffs or defendants. By a significant fiction, all partnerships, limited liability companies, joint stock corporations, foundations, and institutions are classed as German citizens if their central office is in the Reich and sometimes even if their headquarters are in the protectorate. German courts have jurisdiction in all marital disputes if the wife is a racial German, even if the husband is a citizen of the protectorate. Only in the most exceptional cases can a German be a party to an action before a protectorate court. Much of the substantive law of the Czechoslovak Republic has been retained, yet even here a number of exceptions have been made for racial Germans. The most important is the introduction of German marriage law and certain changes in labor and patent law.

Criminal law in the Netherlands follows closely after the protectorate system. There is a noticeable tendency to extend German substantive penal law into the protectorate (a list of the relevant statutes would fill many pages). Finally, the protector has the discretionary right to set aside any decision of a protectorate court and bring the case before a German tribunal.

What folk-group law means in countries dominated by Germany is quite clear from these illustrations. The German minority receives the status of a dominant majority, while the majority, Bohemians and Moravians for example, acquire the impotence of a minority. The view that Germans are racially superior and Czechs inferior, that each folk group is a legal entity, an 'autonomous unit' as the Germans call it, living under a law adapted to its specific character, has completely destroyed what little protection had been given by the international minority treaties. The anti-rationalist, anti-egalitarian, anti-normative theory that considers only the 'concrete personality' and refuses to accept the universalist principle of equality before the law, has reduced the majorities in the conquered territories to the status of slaves.

What determines a folk group anyway? A minority was constituted by race, religion, nationality, or language. The conscious decision of the individual was decisive, as in the admirable 1922 German-Polish treaty relating to Upper Silesia, which expired in 1937. The National Socialists reject this method of determining a minority. In the recent treaties with Hungary and Rumania, both objective and subjective criteria are deemed insufficient. The former were rejected because the state in which the minority lives might scrutinize each case to see whether or not the objective conditions were fulfilled, might deny their existence in certain cases and thereby jeopardize the rights of a minority member. The subjective test is invalid because it admits many who have nothing in common with the folk group and who join it merely for material gain. The protocol to the German-Hungarian treaty introduces a combination of two conditions for membership in the German folk group in Hungary: desire and acceptance.[96] The leadership of the group thus becomes the arbiter, and the composition is ultimately determined by the mother country, which exercises complete control over the folk group through the leadership principle, money, propaganda, and terror. It is thus possible to stifle at birth any divergent political opinions within the German folk groups, and the group can be transformed into an obedient tool of the mother country.

FOLK INTERNATIONAL LAW AND STATE SOVEREIGNTY

This imperialistic trend is not bound by any international law and needs no justification. The Reich exists, and that fact is sufficient justification. That is the second consequence of the new doctrine of international law.

The German word for international law is *Völkerrecht*. The new National Socialist theory takes this word in its literal meaning, 'law of the peoples.' Rejecting the idea that states are the subjects of international law, they maintain that only the people are subjects. As long as the state is considered the subject of international law, it is still part of the tradition of Western civilization.[97] Even restrictive qualifications, such as the claim that the vital interests of a state may supersede international obligations, or that immoral treaties are void, or that the *clausula rebus sic stantibus* dispenses with international obligations—all devices clearly artificial—imply a continued recognition of the two fundamental concepts of international law, state sovereignty and state equality.

Liberal international lawyers are accustomed to blame the present world chaos on unlimited national sovereignty. They believe that a rational international order cannot be established until state sovereignty is either restricted or abolished altogether. Some even maintain that the individual citizen is already—or ought to be—a subject of international law, and is thereby bound to two organizations, the state and the international community.[98] If the international community should apply sanctions, for example, in this view the punitive action would be directed not against the state but only against a law-breaking government. The citizens could then rise against the government without violating their allegiance to the state.[99] By creating divided loyalties, the dichotomy will provide the psychological basis for international solidarity.

We need not dwell on the methodological difficulties arising from the theory of dual sovereignty. We can readily admit that any future international order set up after the destruction of fascism must have a proper psychological basis as well as the material means of maintaining an international community. That is not the present problem, however. However passionately we may desire the elimination of fascism, we cannot close our eyes to the possibility that it may not be wiped out. It is therefore of the utmost importance to lay bare the propagandist character of National Socialist conceptions of international law and the dangers inherent in the doctrine of dual loyalty. The following pages might well be entitled: *In Defense of State Sovereignty*.

It is still useful, even though tautological, to define sovereignty as the highest power. Since highest power and highest right are incompatible, the limits of sovereignty do not lie in the law, but in the bases on which sovereignty rests, in the area in which it is effective, and in the people from whom the state can command obedience. Sovereignty is a polemical notion, directed against other equally sovereign powers. A more complete definition would therefore be the potentially highest power over a specific territory and over a specific category of people. Conceived in this manner, the notion of sovereignty is today a progressive one for two negative reasons: the juristic equality of all states and the consequent rationality of international relations. If every state is sovereign, all states are equal. As a juristic category, equality is, of course, incomplete and lame. Nevertheless, it prevents the misuse of international law for imperialist expansion. Sovereignty thus establishes formal rationality in an anarchic world, creates a clear-cut delineation of the spheres of power, and subjects to the power of the state only those who live within its territory and a select few (citizens) outside. It creates a barrier, so to speak, which, though hindering the establishment of a just international order, seriously limits the extent of state power at the same time.

In international relations, sovereignty can be attributed only to the state as such, as a legal entity, never to its organs. It is logically impossible to speak of the sovereignty of the monarch or of the government. This approach is also progressive in a negative way, more progressive than the institutional, sociological, and pluralistic theories that reject the concept of state sovereignty and attribute power only to organs or social groups within the state. It is true that talk of the state as such has the ideological function of concealing the ruling power of specific social groups. But that does not prevent us from detecting the real bearers of power behind the mask, whereas abolition of the sovereign state does. If the state is no longer an abstract legal entity but merely the structure of the folk or the race, if sovereignty no longer resides in the state but in race or folk, as in the National Socialist theory, two consequences are apparent. In the first place, the negatively progressive character of the concept of state sovereignty is destroyed. The sovereign race knows no territorial limits, and there are then no barriers to the highest power. The sovereignty of the Germanic race exists wherever there are racial Germans. The juridical fact of citizenship cannot abrogate the natural fact of membership in a race. The sovereignty of the race is the ideological basis for the fifth column and for imperialism. National Socialism points to the fact that when circumstances require it, other states, too, pay far more regard to racial descent than to the juridical fact of citizenship. They refer to the fact that Australia, for instance, in 1914, imprisoned 3,866 Australian citizens born in Germany and 61 German-Australians born in Australia.[100] That regrettable fact may or may not have been justified by political expediency. Nevertheless, it has not induced Australia to raise the exception to the rank of a principle.

By removing the mask of the state, furthermore, we can no longer detect the actual focus of political power. The race does not rule, of course, nor has the folk any political power. Who does rule in Germany? Where does the political power actually reside? The answers to these questions are difficult enough to find within the framework of traditional jurisprudence. They are even harder to find in the National Socialist ideology, and precisely that difficulty is the essential purpose of the doctrine. Its aim is to hide the fact that the new German state has amassed enormous political and social power without the limits traditionally imposed on the powers of the state.

National Socialism similarly rejects the state as the subject of international law and substitutes the sovereign racial people. This development was prepared in stages, becoming more and more audacious as German power expanded. In 1934, one of the leading younger theorists, for example, announced international law to be nothing but the law of war.[101] Since war is the central phenomenon of inter-state relations, he argued, all doctrines that regard international law as an instrument for peace are Utopian.[102] The sole function of international law is to regulate and discipline war according to the principles of honor and the duel.[102] This approach is a timid step toward the complete rejection of international law, by denying its major function, the organization of peace. As a matter of fact, there is nothing fundamentally wrong in it from a narrowly 'realistic' point of view. When we examine the consequences of the underlying premise, however—the rejection of collective security, of sanctions, of pacts of mutual assistance, of mediation and arbitration—it becomes apparent that the theory is no more than a peculiar formulation of Hitler's foreign policy, directed against the League and the Franco-Russian and other non-aggression pacts.

A closer approach to the racial theory is found in the famous book, *Die rassengesetzliche Rechtslehre* (the Race-Law Theory of Law), written by the now deposed but still relevant National Socialist lawyer, Helmuth Nicolai.[103] As the title indicates, Nicolai sought to develop a race-law theory embracing the whole field of law (not merely international). He was unsuccessful because he lacked both knowledge and imagination and did not go beyond the assertion that law derives its validity from a common feeling of right, which, in turn, springs from common racial traits. The possibility of international law is thus still affirmed, though its content is reduced to a minimum.

The next step toward a pure racial doctrine was taken by Norbert Gürke,[104] the most original of the National Socialist international lawyers. He too begins with the same assumption that community of racial descent produces, and racial differences condition, international law. He does not fully eliminate the concept of the state, but retains it as the historic form that a race gives itself.[105] There still remains the possibility of international law between different racial states.

The radical implications of the racial doctrine were finally and fully drawn by Werner Best,[106] a high S. S. functionary who was responsible during the Weimar Republic for the attempted *coup* that resulted in the discovery of the so-called Boxheimer documents. Law is a fact of life, says Best. Since life is organic and hostile to abstract norms and since it means life within a people, law always appears as a concrete rule, the sole aim of which is the furtherance of life, or, in his own terms, the regulation of 'the inner folk processes of life.' Law can be posited only by the Leader, who is the concrete head of the people. The external field of the operation of law is not humanity (the liberal conception), but the concrete people. 'On the basis of the racial concept of law, the relations between states, hitherto called international law, cannot be called law.' [107] In the internal field of operation, the liberal finds an enormous variety of forms of law, based on the assumption that man is free. For the racialist, on the other hand, the internal efficacy of law depends upon the 'transpersonal and transtemporal' structure of the people. International law is therefore inconceivable from this approach as well. Best admits that there may operate from time to time certain rules in international relations. Since they can be abandoned at any time, however, it would be mere verbal formalization to call these rules international law.

In sum, the National Socialist theorists agree that obstacles to imperial aggrandizement cease to exist when the people demand it. By furnishing the basis for expansion, the racial theory is fundamentally different even from those conservative and absolutistic doctrines that construe international law merely as external state law. The latter are reactionary doctrines, but they still retain remnants of rationality in so far as they place legal limits on the sovereignty of the state. The racial theory is dynamic: Its function may be summarized as follows:

(1) By denying that states are subjects of international law, it denies the equality of all states and allows differentiation among them. (2) By denying that states have sovereignty, it destroys the last element of rationality in international relations. The spatial and functional limits inherent in the notion of state sovereignty disappear. (3) By proclaiming the sovereignty of the race, it subjects all racial Germans, whatever their nationality, to the law of the Germanic race. (4) By denying that international law exists among rival empires, it rejects any legal frontier to aggression, while at the same time it defends its own empire by a perverted Monroe Doctrine. (5) By applying the term international law to the relations between the folk groups within its empire, it destroys the last remnants of minority protection and invests minority oppression with the sanctity of international law.

5. The Scope and Character of the Grossdeutsche Reich

The ideology and structure of the *grossdeutsche Reich* are relatively easy to determine from the plans of National Socialism, but not the ultimate scope of the Reich. It would be fatally wrong to assume that National Socialist leadership has pre-determined the final limit to German domination over Europe or the eventual form of its empire. The boundaries are being determined by the political situation, by military success, by strategic motives, by economic considerations, which may or may not coincide.

An illustration will suffice—the work of Werner Daitz. His name is unknown to the American public, but he has great influence within the National Socialist party, as well as with industry and banking. A chemist and engineer by profession, Daitz [108] has always been closely connected with private industry, at present with the Possehl combine and the Blast Furnace Works, both in Lübeck. He is one of the few men whose picture and biography had been published in 1934 as exerting decisive influence in the National Socialist party on economic questions.[109] He works closely with Kurt Weigelt, one of the managers of the Deutsche Bank, a member of the supervisory board for the German Asiatic Bank, of the German East African Corporation, and others, and a member of the colonial office of the National Socialist party. Daitz has been a member of the party leadership since 1931, as the deputy for economic questions and now in the foreign political office of the party. He is obviously a man whose theories reflect important elements at the top of the present German regime.

Daitz's plan for European organization is a synthesis of racism, geopolitics, and large-scale economics. Thus, he holds that living space is determined not merely by geographic but equally by racial considerations. It serves to extend the European orbit of German domination to the utmost limit. The key of the theory is his definition of 'racial kernel' or 'nuclear spaces.'

The world of today is divided into various racially determined living spaces. 'The basic law of a racial order of life' is 'that a race cannot abandon its original living space without more or less abandoning itself.' [110] This decisive original space is the racial kernel, or nuclear space. Colonial and frontier spaces can never take its place. Blood, soil, and law are the constituent elements of the new order, which requires the destruction of universalism and its replacement by continental orders. The future division of the world is expressed in the 'fanfares of a racial Monroe Doctrine,' in the slogans: Europe for the Europeans, America for the Americans, India for the Indians. Whereas the European, the Japanese, and Indian Monroe Doctrines are properly biological, the American is also imperialistic, because of its exclusively geographic character. Just why that should be the case is never made clear in Daitz's analysis. It would seem much more reasonable to argue the reverse, that geographic limits are genuine and natural and are violated by biological considerations.

The definition of the European nuclear space is most revealing. 'Considered as an indispensable nucleus space of the white race, Europe reaches from Gibraltar to the Urals and from the North Cape to North Africa.' [111] Its natural supplementary and colonial spaces extend far into northern Asia to the Okhotsk and the Behring seas and far into Africa to the south. Italy and Russia are the doorkeepers of the white race in the south and east, a position formerly held by Italy and England. That regard for the whole of Europe alone induced the Leader to attempt to establish good relations with England.

The obvious question then arises: Who has the responsibility for this new huge space? The answer is equally obvious. 'Germany is responsible not only for itself but, because of its natural weight, for Europe and the European community of people.' (This is Friedrich List's idea with one important change—Germany replaces England.) 'Under Adolf Hitler, the great Germanic Empire rises anew with its spatial political basis in the north Baltic sea space, its soldierly style of life, and its foreign political duty.' By German political duty, Daitz means the establishment of a continental policy. The North and Baltic Sea spaces, the Mediterranean space led by Italy, and the Russian space join into a unit for the 'strengthening of Europe.' By concluding the German-Soviet non-aggression pact, Russia has returned to Europe.

This interesting theory brings out three leading ideas: Europe is a unit comprising the whole European geographic area joining the African and north Asiatic regions. The leadership of Europe belongs to Germany. Russia and Italy, so long as they play ball with Germany, may share in this task. But should her allies disagree with Germany, then Germany will naturally assume exclusive guardianship of the whole of Europe, together with its supplementary and colonial spaces.

Daitz's thesis is the clearest expression of the scope of Germany's ambitions. It is as concrete as National Socialism can be. Whether Germany will extend its grasp beyond the space he has defined will depend upon both strategic opportunities and the internal antagonisms within the new Reich.

At this time it is also impossible to predict whether or not the forms of political rule which the National Socialists have worked out before and during the war will be retained afterwards. The following political patterns in the relation between Germany and the rest of her empire can be distinguished:

1. Military rule is particularly characteristic of northern France and Belgium.[112] Power is vested in the military authorities. In northern France, they are set up in an hierarchical structure, *Oberfeldkommandanturen*, *Feldkommandanturen*, and *Ortskommandanturen*, though the military distinction between the first two was largely abolished on 1 December 1940. Each now administers a province,[113] whereas the third is only a local military agency. National Socialist military administration far exceeds the scope of traditional military occupation. Its aim is to transform the structure and policies of the occupied territories so as to synchronize them with those of the

Reich itself. That is especially noticeable in the handing of the Jewish question (decree of 28 August 1940, establishing a Jewish registry, requiring registration of Jewish property, and levying a special Jewish property tax), and in the close ties between German and French business.

2. The second type is best represented by the Netherlands and Norway. The highest authority in the Dutch territory is a federal commissioner appointed under the Leader's edict of 18 May 1940. The commissioner (Dr. Seyss-Inquart for Holland, at present) exercises all constitutional functions of the king and his government. He legislates, appoints, and dismisses, utilizing Dutch officials for the execution of his orders. His immediate subordinates are four German general commissioners, one for administration and judiciary (Dr. Wimmer), one for security (S.S. Leader Rauter), one for finance and economics (former minister Dr. Fischboeck), and one without portfolio (S.S. Leader Fritz Schmidt), who carries out the anti-Jewish and anti-Freemason policies among other duties. The general commissioners could be compared to cabinet ministers. The Leader's edict retains Dutch law in so far as it is compatible with German needs; in part it has been superseded by German law,* and, for political purposes, the German S.S. may be used wherever needed. The actual policy is one of a still closer incorporation of the Netherlands into the orbit of the German Reich.[114]

The administration of Norway differs only slightly.[115] When the attempt of Quisling to form a Norwegian government failed because of lack of support not only from the Norwegian people but apparently also from the German military authorities, Hitler, by an edict of 20 April, installed the National Socialist district leader Josef Terboven as federal commissioner. He was faced with an already existing and popularly supported administrative council composed entirely of anti-Quisling Norwegians. Terboven and Quisling first tried to institute a kind of indirect rule whereby the Germans would merely assume the role of protector. They asked the Storting to call a meeting to depose the king and elect a state council. The whole effort was a failure. Thereupon Terboven dissolved all the existing parties (25 September 1940) and the old council of administration, and appointed commissioners, chosen exclusively from the

* See p. 164.

ranks of the Quisling National Union party, as directors of the thirteen government departments. According to Terboven's decree of 28 September 1940, the department heads have absolute control over their divisions and are responsible only to the commissioner. They may issue and implement administrative decisions that previously would have been promulgated by the king, the Storting, or the council of state. They are the leaders of their departments in the German sense. The federal commissioner himself is, of course, the supreme legislator and administrator. His commissariat is organized into three functional departments and eight regional offices. In addition, the German terroristic machinery has been introduced—not only the S.S., which exercises the political power in all the occupied territories, but also the people's courts.[116] By September 1940, authoritarian control became almost complete from top to bottom, and the Germans boast of it.[117]

The difference between the military and civil types of administration is considerable. The latter exercises a much stronger form of authoritarian control and is far more concerned with the complete synchronization and assimilation of the whole of political and social life.

3. The Germans regard the protectorate of Bohemia-Moravia as the model for the eventual administrative system of the *grossdeutsche Reich*. The type they have in mind rests on a perversion of Lord Lugard's famous principle of 'indirect rule': give the natives a semblance of independence but retain the key positions in the hands of the whites. This principle works out badly enough in colonial countries, keeping the native population at a given social and economic level and preventing them from advancing. When applied to a nation that in Europe is second only to the Germans in industrial efficiency, the result is stark tragedy. The Germans have run into one serious difficulty. Lugard's formula can only be . applied if at least one important section of the population is willing to run the government under outside tutelage. In Czechoslovakia, the leading industrialists and agrarians were always anti-democratic and ready to sell themselves to the highest bidder. They have co-operated very willingly with the National Socialist regime and the Germans were fortunate to find in Hacha a man weak enough to undertake the task of governing. In no other country, however, has the attempt been successful. Not even in Poland were the Germans

able to find a political group willing to act as their tool; that is a
sure sign among other things that the scorned Wilsonian principle
of self-determination is deeply rooted in the consciousness of the
people.

4. Colonial methods have been introduced in their worst form
in Poland in the *Generalgouvernement*, as it is called by the Nazis.[118]
Those portions of Poland that were formerly German were incorporated into the Reich proper (9 October 1939; in force since 26
October): West Prussia, Poznan (later called Warteland), Upper
Silesia, and the region of Zichenau in East Prussia. The rest has
become a German colony, covering 100,000 square kilometers and
including 10,000,000 people. The constitutional basis is the Leader's
edict of 12 October 1939, creating the post of *Generalgouverneur*
and appointing to the office Dr. Hans Frank, minister without portfolio and leader of the National Socialist lawyers' union. Occupied
Poland is now merely an occupied territory, in both German theory
and practice. The Polish state has ceased to exist and the *Generalgouvernement* is 'a constitutional structure completely dissolved
from the former Polish state.' [119] The very name of the territory
was changed in August 1940 from '*Generalgouvernement* of the
occupied Polish territory' to simple '*Generalgouvernement*.' The
territory is under German sovereignty, though not part of the
grossdeutsche Reich. In contrast to the Bohemian protectorate, the
Generalgouvernement is considered a foreign country and is excluded from the German customs and currency area.

The administration, most recently fixed by decree of 16 March
1941, is carried on by the governor general and a government that
is an executive organ as well as an advisory body. The government
is headed by a secretary of state and is divided into two sections,
the secretariat of eight officials (office of the governor general,
of the government, of legislation, of price formation, of spatial order, of personnel, of management, and of archives), and twelve
departments: interior, finance, justice, economics, food and agriculture, forests, labor, propaganda, building, railroads, and post.

In its advisory capacity, the government is composed of the governor, the secretary of state, the directors of the currency bank and
of the auditing office, the twelve departmental chiefs, the directorate
of the state monopolies, and the chiefs of the order and security
police.

The colony is divided into four districts headed by district chiefs (governors). Each region is in turn divided into rural and urban units. The police power is in the hands of a high S.S. leader directly responsible to the governor. Within the lower administrative ranks, a special police force has been created (6 May 1940) of racial Germans between eighteen and forty years of age.[120] Until 31 July 1940 the governor was also head of the Four Year Plan office for the area; thereafter, he has utilized the general framework of his administration to carry out the tasks of the Four Year Plan. He is assisted in that work by an economic council for the *Generalgouvernement*, which he also heads. In addition, he is head of the council for the defense of the realm and leader of the party in the *Generalgouvernement*. There is thus no Polish administration. All that is left to the Polish people is a 'natural autonomy,' as Frank formulated it,[121] without legal or constitutional rights. The administration of the 1148 cities and villages is, on paper, left to Poles, but it is subject to the discretion of the governor general and is actually under German control.

A typical example of the colonial status of the territory is the decree of the governor general on 13 September 1940, instituting a system of administrative penal law.[122] S.S. and police leaders have power to assess fines up to 1000 zlotys and impose terms up to 3 months. The accused need not necessarily be heard. Appeal can be made only if the sentence emanates from the lowest administrative chief. All other officials are simultaneously prosecutors, judges, and executors, and there is no appeal from their decisions. Authoritarian administration in Poland is thus thorough and complete, the status of the territory is that of a colony pure and simple, and there is no indication that this territory will ever become a new independent or even semi-independent Poland.

The variety of patterns in the political organization of the *grossdeutsche Reich* does not follow any predetermined plan, but reflects the different problems the conquerors have faced. Every pattern is one of conquest, even in those states that, like Slovakia, Hungary, Bulgaria, and Rumania, retain their legal independence. Propaganda, economic penetration, corruption of the ruling groups, fifth columns, and military intervention were all utilized. The seedbed had long been made fertile by the sharp racial and social antagonisms that prevented the growth of a strong democratic consciousness in eastern and southeastern Europe. Small ruling cliques, often composed of absentee owners, needed dictatorship and outside assistance and they supported anyone who could pay better and ensure their rule. The agrarian problem, particularly acute in these regions, had never been dealt with adequately. Save in Czechoslovakia, minorities were handled with bayonets, not gloves. The French and British had made the fatal error of not basing their policies in eastern Europe upon the support of the masses and the minorities. The way was therefore clear for German propaganda among the oppressed sections of the population. (The parallels with Latin America merit serious considerations.)

The economic pattern of the *grossdeutsche Reich* is not so clear as its political set-up. It is here that the lack of a rational conception of the New Europe becomes most apparent. One wing of the National Socialists insists that the German Reich proper must be the productive center of Europe; that within this area the process of industrialization should be intensified; that by becoming the sole producer for the whole of Europe, the Reich will raise the living standards of its own people; that the surrounding countries should supply raw materials and labor and produce agricultural goods. The former Jugoslav minister of agriculture, Otto von Frangés, on the other hand, argues in a detailed discussion of the relation of southeastern Europe to the German Four Year Plan, that the southeastern countries are dangerously overpopulated and must be industrialized.[123] The former Rumanian minister of trade, M. Manoilesco, had, in his book, *Théorie du protectionisme et de l'échange international* (Paris, 1929), insisted on the utilization of protective tariffs for industrializing Rumania.

Frangés represents a whole school of southeastern European economists.[124] Though they agree that by an intensification of agricultural cultivation, the Danube states could readily supply Germany with most of its wheat, corn, wool, cattle, and vegetable oils, they insist on industrialization of the region as the central need. As early as 1929, former Rumanian Minister of Trade Manoilesco argued, for example, that the Danube states should not export ores but only semi-refined or fully refined metals. Obviously these economists wish to raise the living standards of their own people, although in more recent years their demands have become rather moderate. They now limit their program to the establishment of industries in which unskilled labor with low productivity and with but little training can be set to work. They even admit that although the incorporation of the Danubian states into the large space might lead to further industrialization, 'no high expectations can be placed upon it.' [125]

The Heidelberg economist, Carl Brinkmann, rejects industrialization.[126] He wants a solution like Friedrich List's economic theory, or Hamilton's 'American plan.' Napoleon's continental blockade failed, he argues, because Russia was not incorporated in it and because the plan did not repay the effort. The economic structure of southeastern Europe was based upon the exploitation of the 'peasantry for unnatural experimentation in industrialization,' especially in Rumania. On the other hand, Brinkmann also rejects the notion of mono-cultural states with the sole function of supplying raw materials and food stuffs for Germany. He demands the highest amount of 'autonomous industrialization' warranted by the specific character of each country. Only exchange of goods should be centralized within the one large area of Middle Europe.

As a matter of fact, there is little point in searching for discussion of the way the *grossdeutsche Reich* should be organized economically. The economic position of the conquered states will not be determined by a preconceived plan but by the inner dynamics of totalitarian monopoly capitalism. Present German policies give no indication of the future economic structure. They are conditioned by the immediate requirements of warfare and aim at the highest productivity of all those industries that are essential for the prosecution of the war, while cutting down on consumption or luxury goods industries unless necessary for export.

The one feature common to all conquered territories is the treatment of Jewish business. Apart from the many problems raised by the process of Aryanization, which are solved in the same way as in Germany proper, the economy of the *grossdeutsche Reich* is devoted exclusively to supplying the needs of the German Reich proper. In nearly all the occupied territories increasingly large numbers of workers are being sent into the Reich, and thus compulsory or formally voluntary labor service has been introduced.* Direct requisitioning of goods and exploitation by exchange manipulation

* On the problem of foreign labor, see also page 341.

is an equally important method of utilizing the occupied territories. Wherever sale is resorted to, the rate of exchange for foreign currencies is fixed arbitrarily.[127] The protectorate is incorporated into the currency union of the *grossdeutsche Reich,* but Poland is not (currency decree of 15 November 1939 [128]), so German currency in the *Generalgouvernement* must be exchanged through the currency office in Cracow.

Two problems remain to be discussed: the control of business in the occupied territories and structural economic changes. There is not the slightest doubt that German business has acquired and extended its control over foreign enterprises in the occupied areas. German newspapers and periodicals conscientiously report the new acquisitions, but without indicating the methods used. Four techniques stand out.* One is the incorporation of foreign business into the German cartel structure. In some cases, German cartel legislation, especially concerning compulsory cartellization, has been introduced into the new territories (protectorate, 10 January 1940); [129] elsewhere foreign firms have simply been joined to the German cartels. Since all the important cartels are quota cartels, this means that the production or sales quotas allocated to foreign plants are determined by the German majority. On occasion, the German writers even admit that they have considerably strengthened their influence in specific industries through this device.[130] A foreign enterprise can be killed in this way or blackmailed until it surrenders to its German competitors. The final effect is an intensification of the process of monopolization within Germany proper.

This steady Germanization of business is frequently referred to as 'simplifying the structure of the combines.' A large and ever increasing number of foreign enterprises have found their way into German combines.[131] The Bohemian coal and iron industry has thus been consolidated. Banks have been merged.[132] Large holdings of foreign, especially French, banks in southeastern Europe have been taken over, often with the consent of the owners in return for a share in the victor's spoils. Where that is not possible a very ingenious device has sometimes been used. (This is the second technique.) The Dutch Philips Bulb factory in Eindhoven, Holland, which controls many German corporations, was and still seems to

* On the Continental Oil Corporation, see pages 276, 356. On Germanization, see also pages 180, 275.

be inaccessible to German business. The Germans proceeded to establish the *Alldephi* limited liability corporation, exclusively German, and then by law gave it a proxy for all the shares in German corporations held by the Dutch Philips group. As a result, the Dutch or other foreign owners were represented by a German corporation in the meetings of the shareholders of the German corporations.[133] The dominating influence of the Dutch Philips corporation has been effectively eliminated. (One of the firms profiting most from economic Germanization in Austria and protectorate is, of course, the Hermann Göring Works.) Increasingly (this is the third technique) Germans have been appointed trustees for foreign property, such as over the world famous Unilever combine in Holland [134] or the Lorraine iron and steel works.[135] The fourth major technique, the establishment of special corporations for the exploitation of conquered territory, will be discussed later.*

As for state property, clear reports are available only from Poland. State monopolies of alcohol, salt, tobacco, matches, mineral oil, sugar, and lotteries have been re-established and even extended, and the profits accrue to the conquerors.[136] The *Generalgouvernement* has established its own currency bank (*Emissionsbank* in Poland), directed by a governor responsible only to the governor general of Poland. Property owned by the former Polish state is distributed as spoils. A decree of 15 November 1939 first attached all Polish state property; and in 24 September 1940 it was transferred to the *Generalgouvernement*. Since the new administration is not regarded as the successor to the Polish state, it refuses to assume any liability for obligations upon this property.[137] A special corporation has been founded (*Werke des Generalgouvernements, A.G.*), with a capital of 1,000,000 zlotys, to administrate some portions of the former Polish state property. Other portions are administered directly by the governor general, while still others have been leased to German private business. And it is announced that 'the subsequent transfer of one or the other work into private property is not excluded.' [138]

We can therefore conclude definitely that business in the occupied territory has been largely acquired by German industrialists, and that Germanization, like Aryanization, has accelerated the process of concentration of capital. For the masses of the people in these

* See p. 276.

territories, one problem is crucial. Will Germany carry on the process of industrialization, accelerate, perfect, and rationalize industry and thereby raise the standard of living; will it allow only such productive efforts as will supplement German production; or will it reverse the trend of industrialization and throw the populations back to the level of a starving peasantry supplying the needs of the master race? The answers to these questions cannot be based on the ideological prono ncements of National Socialism. After all, does not the National Socialist ideology of 'blood and soil' envisage a country of peasants, while the urbanization of the German population has proceeded more rapidly under this slogan than ever before?

The structure of the *grossdeutsche Reich* will be determined by the inner antagonisms of the German economy. These inner antagonisms, inherent in every capitalistic system, will become even more apparent in Germany and will be further complicated by the national antagonisms produced by the policy of the *grossdeutsche Reich*. Germany will not be able to carry out the tremendous task of transforming a war economy into an economy of peace except by transforming conquered Europe into a vast reservoir of man power, of producers of food stuffs and raw materials. The standard of living of the inhabitants will thereby be lowered in order to keep the German working class satisfied.* Little can be learned from today's experience. Some industries have been closed down, chiefly those in direct competition with German industry or producing only consumers' goods. Others have been rebuilt and expanded. There is no doubt that water power will be fostered in Norway [139] and oil production in Poland. Roads are being built.[140] These steps are necessary for military efficiency. We have no way of knowing if the Germans have carried out a wholesale destruction of industrial enterprises, though it would seem unlikely.

Should it be victorious, the *grossdeutsche Reich* will be based upon the most gigantic economic and political exploitation of all history. It will be impossible, at least for many decades, for a future German government to justify her influence in Middle Europe. Germany, as the most highly developed industrial machine in Europe, must, of course, play a decisive role in the European economic

* See also p. 329.

structure. How Germany will be able to justify this claim after National Socialism has reduced millions to starvation is a question to which we cannot now foresee the answer. Exploitation—and nothing else—is the common denominator of all economic, political and social measures taken in the conquered territories. Hitler, on 27 January 1932, in the speech which he delivered at Düsseldorf before Western industrialists on Thyssen's invitation, made this crystal clear. 'The white race,' so he said, 'can maintain its position in practice only if the differences in the living standards in the world are retained. Give to our so-called export markets the same living standards that we have, and you will find that the preponderance of the white race, which is expressed not only in the political might of the nation but also in the economic position of the individual, can no longer be retained.' [141] The promise which Hitler held out to Western industry has been fulfilled to a degree which exceeds the expectations of probably the most aggressive industrialists.

VI

THE THEORY OF RACIAL IMPERIALISM

Up to this point we have simply accepted imperialism as the most significant trend in German politics. In fact, our whole analysis has centered on the problem of Germany's expansion.

The imperial period confined its preparations for expansion to establishing an army, navy, and a reliable bureaucracy, and to merging the interests of state, industrial, and agrarian leadership. The working classes were excluded. For a time, their political and industrial organizations were suppressed, and when that experiment failed, their ideological isolation and their complete exclusion from public service kept them outside the state and the ruling groups.

1. DEMOCRACY AND IMPERIALISM

The World War of 1914-18 saw the first attempt to incorporate the working classes into an imperialistic system. The Social Democrats and the trade unions actively co-operated. In doing so, they partly betrayed the principles of their party program, but some of them honestly believed that the war was defensive and that they would be able to carry out the socialist mission of overthrowing Czarist Russia, thereby setting free the forces of revolution. But despite an initial success, the attempt to incorporate the masses ultimately failed. The Independent Social Democratic party and the *Spartakus Bund* grew at the expense of the Social Democrats and the trade unions. The imperialist goal of German industry became so clear that the problem of the peace aims could no longer be sidestepped. At the end, the terrific impact of the Wilsonian ideology completely shattered the ideological basis upon which German imperialism rested.

The Weimar democracy—that is, the Social Democrats, Democrats, and Left-wing Catholics—attempted to build a society that was not imperialistic but was concerned with the internal reconstruction of Germany and its participation in the concert of western European powers. This attempt also failed, because the three partners could not destroy the monster that lay within the German economic system. In fact, instead of smashing the power of the industrial monopolists, they unwillingly strengthened it.

The imperialistic sections of German society found in the National Socialist party the ally needed to provide the mass basis for imperialism. This does not mean that National Socialism is merely a subservient tool of German industry, but it does mean that with regard to imperialistic expansion, industry and party have identical aims.

But how can an aggressive imperialistic policy be carried out today? Not within the framework of a political democracy. General Ludendorff and J. A. Hobson, the leading English authority on imperialism, are in complete agreement on this point. 'Peoples do not understand aggressive wars, but they have a very good understanding of a fight for the preservation of their own lives . . . Neither a nation nor each individual within it will support the war to the utmost unless there is a sure conviction that the war is for the preservation of their lives.' [1] For Hobson, the outstanding phenomenon of our period is that imperialism and democracy have become incompatible. 'A political democracy in which the interests and will of the whole people wield the powers of the whole state, will actively oppose the whole process of imperialism. Such a democracy has now learned the lesson that substantial economic equality in income and ownership of property is essential to its operation. The defense of capitalism is, therefore, bound up in every country with the destruction or enfeeblement of the public franchise and representative government.' [2] History amply proves the truth of Ludendorff's and Hobson's views. The First World War is an excellent illustration of this, as we have already indicated. What little democracy and few civil liberties still remained in the Germany of 1914-18 were effective agents in promoting anti-imperialist propaganda, a propaganda that was not imposed from above but sprang from the innermost feelings of the masses. In Italy, the longing for peace and the hatred of war has increased by leaps and bounds since the Abyssinian war of 1896. The history of American foreign relations also provides ample material. The first attempt to annex Hawaii (16 February 1893), undertaken by President Harrison, was a failure.

Then President Grover Cleveland withdrew the annexation treaty. The second and successful attempt (16 April 1897) was carried out under great difficulties, although no sacrifice in blood or money was required. Once again, the primary justification of the acquisition was the old slogan of the white man's burden. The acquisition of the Philippines in 1898 was similarly hazardous. Although 'innumerable voices now called for an assumption of the armored imperial garb which European powers had just made the fashion,'[3] the opposition was so strong that it nearly prevailed.

The history of English imperialism shows similar developments. It may be admitted that popular feeling for imperialist acquisition can often be aroused. Skilful propaganda, such as invasion scares of the kind current during the Boer War in England, the coalescence of what Mr. Weinberg calls humanitarianism and force,[4] and concessions to the masses, such as the extension of the franchise or material benefits, can for a time succeed in securing mass support. But such a mass basis is never stable. Opposition may arise and has always arisen. Besides, the imperialistic wars of the nineteenth century did not require high sacrifices in blood and energy. The Spanish-American War is one example, and the Boer War another. No imperialistic war in the nineteenth and the beginning of the twentieth centuries required anything approaching the total mobilization of man power and productivity that have characterized the wars since 1914. None of them made it necessary to transform a nation into an armed camp; none completely changed social life; none revolutionized habits. Still, it is possible, even within a liberal democracy, so to intensify nationalism by skilful propaganda and the granting of material benefits to the lower classes that the war actually appears as the outcome of spontaneous demands by the masses and not as the deliberate policy of a single group.

2. THE PROLETARIAN FOLK AGAINST PLUTOCRACIES

Throughout the history of modern imperialism, imperialistic propaganda always tried two different approaches: first, to present any war as a defensive one, as a fight for life; secondly, ideologically and organizationally to incorporate the masses into the war.[5] The white man's burden, the mission of a people, manifest destiny are examples of the second kind of approach.[6] This kind has never been able to produce support for a large-scale aggressive war. People will not voluntarily decide totally to organize themselves for imperialistic expansion when colossal sacrifices in blood and energy are required. They must be compelled to do so. They must be organized in such a way that they cannot resist. They must be submitted to such propaganda that they do not express open resistance. Their democratic convictions must be uprooted and other ideologies must be implanted.

Nor can such wars any longer be organized in the old framework of counter-revolution and absolutism, where only the war machine is centralized and where it relies simply upon the dictatorial powers of the military command. The war is a total one; no sphere of life remains untouched. Every activity must be subordinated to it; the individual must become completely immersed, must become part and parcel of it. Such incorporation is particularly necessary because a society that has passed through the phase of large-scale democracy can no longer exclude the masses. Organizational, ideological, and propagandistic patterns must be elaborated for this purpose. The new ideology must be democratic, at least in appearance. The rulers and the ruled must be represented as pursuing identical interests; the internal social antagonisms must be utilized and transformed into external aggression.

The new National Socialist doctrine of a racial proletarian imperialism is the culmination of this method. This doctrine fuses two basic elements: hatred of England and hatred of Marx.

The essence of the theory is extremely simple. Germany and Italy are proletarian races, surrounded by a world of hostile plutocratic-capitalistic-Jewish democracies. The war is thus a war of proletarianism against capitalism. 'This war is the war of the money power against labor and against the creative human being, the embodiment of labor.' Creative human beings must combine. 'For all awakening peoples who make labor the focus of their lives, the watchword must henceforth be: workers of all lands, unite to smash the rule of English capitalism.' With these words, Dr. Robert Ley,[7] head of the German labor front, initiated the new propaganda campaign that culminated in Hitler's speech of December 1940. This speech contrasted capitalistic liberty, namely the freedom 'for everybody to grab for himself, free from state control,' with 'the power of work.' 'I built up my entire economy on the basis of work. Our German mark unbacked by gold is worth more than gold.' The war is depicted as a war for a 'world of co-operative labor' against 'selfishness . . . capitalism . . . individual and family privileges,' against 'the accursed plutocracy, against those few dynastic families which administer the capitalistic market for the few hundred persons who, in the last analysis, direct those families.' [8]

According to National Socialism, capitalism is a Jewish invention; hence, the opponents of National Socialism must be Jews. The *Schwarze Korps*, the organ of the S.S., repudiated the whole National Socialist racial theory and declared that the English are a nation of white Jews.[9] Scholars were at once set to work to prove that English culture and civilization are predominantly Jewish. One such scholar [10] has devoted two large books to show how the Jews have conquered and how they rule England. By completely perverting Max Weber's thesis, he presents the Puritan revolution and the rise of Puritanism generally as the victory of Judaism over Christianity.[11] For the purpose of anti-English propaganda, a special periodical against plutocracy and the incitement of peoples, called *Die Aktion*,[12] was launched in August 1940.

Racial proletarianism is the genuine theory of National Socialism and its most dangerous expression. It is its most fallacious and yet most attractive doctrine. Its fallaciousness is obvious. If gold constitutes wealth, then Germany is indeed poor. But National Socialism insists that gold is not wealth, that all wealth derives from the productivity of man. If that is so, then Germany is the richest country in the world. There is no doubt that the doctrine is attractive. It exploits the hatred of England, a powerful motive in Germany, in many parts of the British Empire, and in many of the Latin-American countries. It exploits hatred of the Jews, aversion to capitalism, and, finally, utilizes Marxist phraseology and symbolism to an ever increasing extent. It is clear that the very purpose of the doctrine of racial proletarianism is to entice the working classes. This point requires further discussion.

The labor theory of value, the class struggle, and the classless society are the three categories basic to the development of Marxist theory in Germany. However much revisionists and orthodox Marxists may have transformed or even abandoned Marxism, there is no doubt that from these three concepts spring the fundamental impetus of the Social Democratic and Communist parties. Marxist theory had spread through the masses. It formed the focus of all political discussions between and within the two parties. Every tactical measure was argued in terms of Marxist theory, and quotations from Marx and Engels were used in every discussion that touched fundamental problems. No leading socialist dared to throw out the theory of the class struggle; no one dared deny the *ultima Thule* of a classless society. Even collective bargaining was conceived as a form of the class struggle, and the participation of trade unionists in labor courts and arbitration bodies was hailed as the recognition of that principle. To a foreigner, such discussions may seem ridiculous, dogmatic, and the cause of the so-called 'immaturity' of the German labor movement. We do not intend to argue this point. It is indisputable that Marxist theory and symbolism completely permeated the Social Democratic and Communist labor movements and molded their character, and it is in this setting that the theory of proletarian racism must be understood. This theory is an attempt to eradicate Marxism by a process of transmutation. The complete collapse of the German labor movement, resulting in the destruction of the Social Democratic and Communist organization, has facilitated this difficult task. Whether the basic impetus has collapsed too is quite another question.

In the eyes of Social Democrats and Communists, the goal of a classless society and of a higher form of life is not achieved by the enslavement of foreign nations, but by the transformation of the capitalist system and the destruction of oppressive bureaucracy. To achieve such a goal requires supreme courage, willingness to make sacrifices, patience, and intelligence. The struggle against one's own ruling class is, as history shows, much more strenuous than foreign wars, and international proletarian solidarity is acquired only in a long, arduous political struggle. But National Socialism offers the worker everything offered by Marxism, and without a class struggle. National Socialism offers him a higher form of life, 'the people's community,' and the rule of labor over money, without compelling him to fight against his own ruling class. On the contrary, he is invited to join the ruling classes, to share in their power, glory, and material benefits by being a part of a colossal machine. He need no longer be isolated or strive against the current. He is not asked to show more courage and make more sacrifices than anybody else. On the contrary, Germany's victory is his victory, the victory of labor over money, of the people's community over class rule, of true freedom over a liberty that was merely a cloak for exploitation. This doctrine has not been abandoned even after the attack on Russia.

Is the National Socialist ideology successful? Has the theory of proletarian racism really permeated the ranks of labor? Has it definitely destroyed the belief in a democratic socialism or in communism? This is the decisive question, for upon the answer to it depends the fate of Europe. Upon it also depend, to a great extent, the methods of psychological warfare that must be used against Germany. If every German, even every German worker, is a potential Hitler, if the masses stand solidly behind the Leader, if the people are united behind the doctrine of racial proletarian imperialism, then Germany's opponents can have but one war aim: to destroy Germany, divide her, and keep her enslaved. For if this is the case no attempt to drive a wedge between Hitler and the German people can be successful.

That, indeed, is a view held by many, in particular by those foreign statesmen who did most to destroy German democracy and to support National Socialism in every international crisis. It is these statesmen who wish to shift the responsibility for the victory of National Socialism from their own foreign policy exclusively to the German people. It is true that this argument cannot be lightly dismissed. And it is much more difficult to substantiate the contrary view that the German people do *not* stand behind National Socialism. Germany's culture is now nothing but propaganda; public opinion in Germany is manipulated and controlled; and to express oppositional views would mean death or a concentration camp. We have no direct means of ascertaining the real attitude of the German people, and we must develop indirect methods. We shall try to find out to what extent National Socialism has permeated the German people by analyzing the function of the new ideology in more detail, by discussing the origin of this type of social imperialism, by examining those social strata that are most responsible for German aggressive imperialism, and, finally, by investigating the character of National Socialist social organization to see how far it is based on terror and how far on consent. Much of this discussion will be found in the final chapter.

3. Pseudo-Marxist Elements in the Social Imperialist Theory

The new National Socialist ideology is clearly a perversion of the Marxist ideology, aimed at ensnaring the Marxist working class. I know of only one instance in which this incorporation of the Marxist workers is explicitly admitted as the aim of the social policy and that is in the 'Mecklenburg theses of the Union of National Socialist Pastors' (Protestant) of 29 May 1933. The first thesis begins: 'Influenced by Marxism and having embraced National Socialism, our people no longer recognizes the old ecclesiastical forms.' It is, therefore, impossible to retain these old forms, they have to be changed and adapted to this social stratum.[13] This concern has resulted in many different attempts, all of which have failed. The ideology of proletarian racism is the new answer to this old challenge.

When we read the new ideological pronouncements, we might almost take them for Marxist analyses embellished with a touch of Spengler, Moeller van den Bruck, and Rosenberg. For example, an editorial in the *Frankfurter Zeitung*,[14] entitled 'The Sinking World,' is, in fact, a Marxist criticism of Great Britain. Although, it says, there are rich people in Germany, 'they have no say in affairs,' in contrast to England, which is 'the home of a decaying bourgeois world.' 'The bourgeois social system was essential for the destruction of feudalism,' and thus had great historical merits, but it has outlived its usefulness. 'Within this world . . . a solemn roar could be heard for more than a century. It grew ever louder and the more one closed one's ears, the louder and more menacing it became.' It was the roar of the masses 'living without free light and air.' The liberties these masses had were 'not even sufficient to give them work and daily bread.'

The British upper class secured its own position much more firmly and stubbornly in this so-called democracy . . . In England you find no trace of the new ideas . . . The labor party does not want to overthrow the bourgeois world . . . In England, the capitalist world is not menaced by any danger from within. The British are not against a great and powerful Germany because they are afraid that such a Germany would diminish England's power. They are against the . . . German ideas because they are afraid that their own world will collapse before them.

This article is in the tradition of Marx, Engels, and Lenin, and is almost indistinguishable from well-known denunciations of the British social and political system. It is constructed around a class analysis of British society, a society in which the ruling classes use the outward forms of democracy for preserving their privileges, in which the Labor party has become a petty-bourgeois organization. The whole system is in a process of decay, desperately fighting against the attraction that the new theory, the new economy, the new society exert upon the deceived masses of the British people.

The part played by the Marxist labor theory of value in criticizing the English economic system is clearly illustrated in a speech by Dr. Dietrich, the federal press chief, entitled: 'The Spiritual Foundation of the New Europe.' [15] 'National Socialism has recognized that the best foundation of every currency is confidence in the leadership of the state and in the productive forces of the nation.' German socialism, although it starts from the natural inequality of man, demands that everyone should have an equal opportunity to rise in the social scale. 'Within the finely spun web of the economic process and behind the veil of money,' National Socialism has discovered 'the center of economic power, namely, human labor as the all-animating basis . . . Within the maze of economic concepts, it has found the thread of Ariadne which leads our economic thought along the path to clarity: productive labor. It has dethroned the liberal dogma of the primacy of profits for the capitalists and replaced it by the principle of national productivity.'

This statement, and a similar one made by Alfred Rosenberg at the opening of the Party Institute for Jewish Research,* even echo the Marxist doctrine of the fetishistic character of bourgeois society. It goes without saying that this analysis is not genuinely Marxist, but pseudo-Marxist. It is directed exclusively against money and disregards the fetishistic nature of the commodity. But the phraseology is definitely shaped by the need for conquering the Marxist masses to whom the terms would be familiar.†

* Cf. p. 124.
† Cf. p. 193.

These examples may suffice. We may, by way of contrast, show the adaptation and the transformation of Marxist slogans to meet the needs of national socialist policy.

MARXIST FORM	NATIONAL SOCIALIST FORM
Class struggle	Proletarian war against capitalistic states
Labor theory of value	Money as the fetish of the nation's productive power
Classless society	People's community
The proletariat as the bearer of truth	The German race as a proletarian race is the incarnation of morality

The formulation of the new doctrine is thus in line with the adoption of Marxist symbols, such as the red flag (although adorned with the swastika), the elevation of the Marxist May Day to a national holiday, and the acceptance of many proletarian songs, though with new texts. All this serves the same purpose: to make the theory of racial imperialism the ideological basis of a war of the German people against the surrounding world, this war having as its object the attainment of a better life for the master race through reducing the vanquished states and their satellites to the level of colonial peoples.

4. NATIONALIST FORERUNNERS OF SOCIAL IMPERIALISM

The new doctrine was first fully developed by the Italian Enrico Corradini, the founder of the Nationalist party, which had the greatest influence upon Italian Fascism. The Nationalist party and its Blue Shirts were taken over *en bloc* by the Fascist party, which then changed its name to the National Fascist party.[16] The Nationalists were only a small minority but they had more highly trained men than the Fascists and their theories were accepted by the new party. Luigi Federzoni, Alfredo Rocco, Scipio Sighele, R. Forges-Davanzati all derive from the Nationalist party. Corradini, a high school teacher, developed the first consistent theory of a social imperialism based entirely on the incorporation of the masses.[17] The theory is, in itself, a hodgepodge of various elements, especially of French 'integral nationalism' and of revolutionary syndicalism. The argument is simple. Italy is a great proletarian country. Between Italy and the surrounding states there is the same relation as between the working classes and the satiated bourgeoisie. Italy is imprisoned in the Mediterranean without industrial resources and without a colonial empire. Her nationalism must therefore be social, and Corradini even coined the term *socialismo nazionale*.[18] He went beyond the mere assertion of a need for war and for heroism. He incorporated into his own work the doctrines of Georges Sorel and transformed them into means of ensnaring the working classes.[19] The adaptation was not very difficult, since Sorel, the most brilliant and the most contradictory critic of Marxism and liberalism, had never hidden his sympathies for French 'integral nationalism' and for the *Action française*.[20] Sorel believed that the proletariat could only achieve its aims by violence, that is, by the general strike, the highest manifestation of solidarity. For Corradini, the highest expression of solidarity is war.[21] Sorel maintained that the new classless society could be established only on the basis of the free incorporation of all producers in syndicates; for Corradini, the new order is one of corporations.[22] But whereas Sorel understood by producers only dependent workers, for Corradini, as for Fascism and National Socialism later, producers included everyone—employer and employee, master and servant, jointly organized in a corporative system that would replace parliamentary democracy. Corradini, therefore, was the first to advocate the marriage of nationalism and revolutionary syndicalism, a marriage later consummated by Fascism.

It is significant that the development of Corradini's doctrine took place between 1909 and 1912, culminating in the congress of the Nationalist party at Florence in 1910.[23] It was a period of high tension between the contending great powers, marked by the Morocco crisis, the Agadir incident, the Turkish-Italian war of 1911, and the acquisition of Tripoli in 1912. Shortly before the peace treaty in 1912, Italy introduced universal, adult male franchise. The imperialistic ventures of 1911 and 1912 were opposed by the populace. It is characteristic that Antonio Labriola, a Socialist leader with many syndicalist tendencies, defended the Libyan war and considered the annexation of Tripoli good business for the bourgeoisie and, in consequence, a boon to the Italian proletariat. But the Socialists opposed the war even though their opposition was timid. Spontaneous opposition was more powerful; Mussolini himself, then a revolutionary Socialist, passionately attacked Corradini and the Nationalist party, denounced the national flag 'as a rag to be planted on a dung hill,' [24] initiated a propaganda campaign against the Turkish-Italian war, and was sent to prison for a year.

Corradini's theory is probably the first attempt to utilize the forces making for class struggle to develop an imperialistic socialism.

We have already mentioned the attempts made by Friedrich Naumann in his book, *Middle Europe*,* to stress the identity of capitalist and working-class interests and the educational influence of the Social Democratic party and the trade unions. We have also mentioned the unbroken line from Friedrich List to Adolf Wagner.† But the most articulate German expression of this theory of social imperialism can be found in the works of Oswald Spengler and Moeller van den Bruck. We are not concerned with Spengler's attitude toward National Socialism or with the National Socialists' attitude toward Spengler. These are, for the most part, accidental phenomena. Spengler had a great influence on all German anti-democratic movements and ideologies. Whatever experts may say against his factual statements, his brilliance cannot be denied. *The Decline of the West* contains observations that, like lightning flashes, illuminate the landscape and bring out new aspects we tend to overlook in the mass of detail. We do not intend to deal with Spengler's philosophy of history, his morphology, or his cyclical theory, but with two problems formulated in his political philosophy: the emergence of caesarism from the conditions of political democracy, and the need for imperialistic expansion in the form of a Prussian socialism.

The emergence of a Caesar from the womb of democracy has been predicted time and again by French, German, and Spanish counter-revolutionaries. This prophecy derives from a specific theory of human nature, according to which man is utterly corrupt, ignorant, wicked, and incapable of freedom.

* See p. 140.
† See p. 104.

The world moves at a great pace towards the constitution of a despotism, the most gigantic and the most destructive that men have ever seen. The road is prepared for a gigantic, colossal, universal tyrant. Everything is prepared for it. Mark it well; there is no longer any moral or material resistance. There is no longer any material resistance: statesmen and rulers have abolished frontiers and the electric telegraph has abolished distance. There is no longer any moral resistance: all spirits are divided, all patriotism is dead. It is a question of choosing between the dictatorship from below and dictatorship from above [God]. I choose the one from above, because it comes from regions which are pure and more serene. In the last resort, however, it is a question of choosing between the dictatorship of the dagger and that of the saber: I choose that of the saber, because it is nobler.[25]

This was the future that Donoso Cortes, the Spanish Catholic counter-revolutionist, foresaw for humanity during the period of liberal revolutions in Europe in 1848. He did not believe in any hope for a rule from above, namely, the rule of God. The whole issue seemed to be between two kinds of dictatorships: the military on the one hand and the demagogic from below on the other. He preferred military rule. He thus stood in the tradition of Bonald and de Maistre, who, as a protest against the French Revolution, had also denounced liberalism and democracy as the carriers of Caesarism.

This is also Spengler's mood. His philosophy of man is profoundly pessimistic: 'Man is a beast of prey.' He 'knows the intoxication of feeling when the knife pierces the flesh of the enemy, bringing to the triumphant senses wails and the odor of blood.' [26] Democracy breeds parties and parties breed a party machine that controls and incorporates the masses and thereby gives rise to a new Caesar. Popular franchise is a fake; the more it is extended, the less is the actual power of the voter. It thereby plays into the hands of the caesaristic tendencies within the political organizations.[27] Freedom of the press keeps man in submission. The press and the electric news services bully him by phrases and catch-words that pour out in an unending stream of propaganda. Spengler would subscribe to Lord Salisbury's description of the English sensational press and extend it to the press in general, namely, that Harms-worth (Lord Northcliffe) 'had invented a paper for those who could read but not think and another for those who could see but not read.' [28] 'Three weeks of press work and the truth is acknowl-edged by everybody.' 'This is the end of democracy.' [29] In the first place, money destroyed democracy, its weapons of destruction being the political parties and universal franchise, the very liberties that it so highly esteems. With the destruction of democracy begins the era of contending states, led and organized by Caesars who completely control man. [30]

What is the internal structure of these contending states, espe-cially of Germany? The answer is given in Spengler's most signifi-cant political work: *Prussiandom and Socialism*,[31] first published in 1920. The major concern of this book is once more the incorpora-tion of the Social Democratic party into Prussian socialism for the purpose of imperialistic wars. This is done primarily by redefining socialism. Socialism is freed from Marxism and identified with the Prussian tradition of duty, authority, and hierarchy. Socialism is not international; it is German-Prussian. It is not class struggle, but co-operation under the authority of the state. No parties, no pro-fessional politicians, no periodic elections; economic organization in a hierarchic structure must be the order of society. Only by discipline, hierarchy, authority, and obedience can the working class be incorporated.[32] According to Spengler, cartels and syndi-cates betray the coming structure of such an authoritarian corporate state. Once more it is the antagonism between Germany and Eng-land that determines the policy of the contending states. In conse-quence, the question for Spengler is, 'in the future shall trade rule the state, or shall the state rule trade?' and the answer is: 'Prus-sianism and socialism stand jointly against the influence of the British spirit in Germany, against that philosophy of life which permeates our whole life as a people, paralyzes it and makes it soul-less.' This 'socialism means power, power, and again power. Plans and ideas are nothing without power.' [33]

This is Spengler's program of social imperialism. The kind of socialism he had in mind is very clearly set forth in his numerous smaller essays: 'The Human Vermin,' that is, the laboring classes, should toil at least twelve hours a day, as under early capitalism.[34]

Increases in wages and in taxes mean a plundering of the real productive forces.[35] The slave state depicted by Hilaire Belloc is the state advocated by Spengler.

What are the ideals motivating this new era of Prussian state socialism, a socialism of war and of imperialism? There are none. 'The age of theory is drawing to an end.' Its place is taken by a 'second religiousness,' [36] which is the counterpart of the era of caesarism and which consists in the 'unchained might of colossal facts.' [37]

This doctrine is a pagan positivism, and more than anything else in his book it reveals his complete break with the whole of Western civilization. It is significant that the Protestant critics [38] of Spengler did not recognize the pagan character of his book, whereas the Catholics clearly saw and denounced it.[39] Except for the racial theory, which he regarded as too crude, Spengler's book contains nearly all the elements of the National Socialist philosophy. The contempt for man and for the masses, for culture and intellect, the insistence on hierarchy and leadership, on discipline and obedience, the elevation of the 'productive forces' are as present in Spengler as in Ley or Hitler.

The very same endeavor, the ideological preparation for imperialistic war, is operative in Moeller van den Bruck's [40] work. Once again we cannot say with absolute certainty whether or not Moeller van den Bruck was a forerunner of National Socialism. Alfred Rosenberg emphatically rejects this claim.[41] However, Rosenberg believes that the only genuine forerunners of National Socialism were Nietzsche and Richard Wagner, Paul de Lagarde, and Houston Stewart Chamberlain. He regards Moeller van den Bruck, in spite of some compliments he pays him, as a mere *littérateur*, and his theory as bloodless and artificial. His theory was also rejected because it was the philosophy of the Black Front (Strasser's group) and of conservative clubs that National Socialism took pains to destroy. To be rejected by National Socialism redounds to van den Bruck's honor, for he was indeed a *littérateur* of high merit, translator of Flaubert and Dostoievski, and path breaker for modern French novelists and poets.

We cannot consider the whole of van den Bruck's theory. We

shall stress only two closely connected aspects of it: hatred of
England and social imperialism. The leitmotif of the Third Reich
is Clemenceau's ill-famed statement that there are 20,000,000 Germans too many in the world (p. 17). Germany's claims to expansion are developed around this statement. There are a number of
geopolitical formulations (p. 65), but they are not of basic importance. The paramount question is a social one. The whole book is
one passionate attempt to divorce the German worker from Marx,
to uproot the doctrine of class struggle, and to supplant it by that
of war. 'Before the social problem can be solved for the classes,
it must be solved for the nation' (p. 67). English and French
workers can live, whereas Germans and Russians cannot. Neither
settlement programs nor emigration, nor Malthusianism nor class
struggle, can solve the social question. Settlement programs are
insufficient. Neo-Malthusianism is unnatural because 'nature has
willed overpopulation' (p. 70). The Marxist parties have completely
failed, but the idea of socialism is a reality. Socialism must be national, not international, and must think in terms of foreign policy.
The class struggle must therefore be replaced by 'world politics'
(p. 188). Moeller van den Bruck draws the final inference from
social imperialism. He is sympathetic to the doctrine of national
bolshevism as advocated by the Communist party in certain periods
and by Otto Strasser's Black Front. This conservative revolutionary,
who made the term 'Third Reich' popular, was driven by a boundless nationalist passion. He is the most articulate, most cultured, and
most important representative of the doctrine that culminates in the
theory of proletarian racism.

The aim of the doctrine is clear, but there is still the question
whether it is successful. Has it really permeated the bulk of German
society? The answer will be made easier by an analysis of those
social strata that actively supported imperialist expansion.

5. GERMAN IMPERIALISM

German imperialism enjoys the benefits of a late-comer * and of
a have-not state. It is this fact that gives German imperialism its

* See p. 14.

efficiency and its brutality. In countries like England, Holland, or France, which have outgrown the stage of mere investment and have passed on to colonial and protectorate imperialism, internal anti-imperialistic trends have inevitably arisen. Large-scale capital export creates a capitalistic stratum completely disinterested and even hostile to further expansion, the stratum of the *rentier* group.[42] The *rentier*, whose income is not derived from productive work and from business activities but from stocks and bonds, is not an aggressor. On the contrary, he is an appeaser, who wants to keep what he possesses and who refuses to incur new risks. The antagonism between the *rentier* and the activistic imperialist has pervaded British foreign politics since the time of Joseph Chamberlain, and ended with the victory of the *rentier* under Balfour, Baldwin, and Neville Chamberlain. This antagonism is shown very clearly in Sir Austen Chamberlain's letters: *Politics from Inside.*[43] It is expressed in the conflict between the Tory Democrats and the old Conservatives. Disraeli and Joseph Chamberlain may be called the forerunners of social imperialism. They were democratic imperialists, basing the expansion of the empire on the working classes, to whom the franchise and material benefits were granted; but ever since Balfour, the *rentier* class has pressed forward within the Conservative party. It is no longer concerned with expansion; it detests risks. The conflict between the Conservative party became an open one with the issue of free trade against protection. While Joseph Chamberlain clearly saw the impossibility of competing with expanding Germany on the basis of free trade and wanted to create a wall of tariffs around the empire, the *rentier* group refused to undertake an experiment that would have necessitated the complete reorganization of English industrial machinery involving full concentration and trustification. Balfour was finally overthrown in 1911, but Austen Chamberlain did not succeed him. Bonar Law became the leader of the party and the spokesman of the *rentier* group. Thus, the imperialistic group had lost the leadership within the Conservative party as early as 1911; regained it only during the First World War under Lloyd George within a coalition government; and finally lost it again under Baldwin and Neville Chamberlain. Germany was acutely aware of this conflict manifest in the English social structure and in English foreign policy. In all forms the German hatred of England assumes, whether derived from geopolitics or German imperialism, England is depicted as a decaying country, the country of a bourgeoisie no longer willing to expand which has violated the primary law of life in a competitive society: the law that one must expand or die.

Germany's *rentier* class was wiped out during the inflation. The war had already destroyed foreign investments; the inflation wiped out domestic savings. The annihilation of a prosperous middle class turned out to be the most powerful stimulus to aggressive imperialism, for it was the section of the middle class having but little to lose that whole-heartedly supported the drive by heavy industry for rearmament and for imperialism.

The problems faced by German imperialism were different from those of Great Britain in still another respect. British imperialism in the nineteenth and early twentieth centuries was directed against colonial, semi-colonial, or weak powers; and Great Britain had its colonial wars fought primarily by native armies under British command. Germany was faced with the world already divided among states possessing large armies or navies. As no peaceful redistribution could be achieved, as international cartels and the carving out of economic spheres of interest were not sufficient, only war remained. The first attempt was 1914; 1939 the second. But Germany fully learned the lessons of 1914, that the preparation for war has to begin in peace, that war and peace are no longer two different categories, but two expressions of one and the same phenomenon, the phenomenon of expansion. The domestic structure of society must be transformed in order fully to utilize all the productive forces of society for war. In particular, labor must be incorporated, must become part and parcel of the totalitarian structure. Material benefits, terror, and propaganda must uproot any pacifist or socialist convictions.

There exist two basic types of imperialism, popularly known as 'haves' and 'have-nots.' Each of these must be subdivided. Each is different in its ideology, technique, and aim. The following diagram will facilitate an understanding of these types, which, however, do not mean that a 'have' state must eternally remain satiated. It can, under certain conditions, turn into an aggressor, but will then, today, inevitably become fascist.

IMPERIALISM OF SATIATED POWERS

PURE ECONOMIC IMPERIALISM:

Trade (Commercial) Imperialism—free trade—universal international law—competitive structure of economy—no changes in the domestic political system—retention of independence by the object of expansion combined with certain rights for the imperialist power, trading zones, port privileges, etc.

Investment imperialism—protective tariffs—beginnings of regionalism (spheres of interest)—monopolization and trustification—no changes in the domestic political system—independence of the desired territory economically undermined.

POLITICAL-ECONOMIC IMPERIALISM:

Colonial Imperialism—attempted ideological incorporation of the masses ('democratic' imperialism: Disraeli, Joseph Chamberlain, Italy in 1912) but no change in the domestic system—incorporation of the needed territory into the imperialist power with colonial status.

Protectorate Imperialism: attempted ideological incorporation of the masses (white man's burden, etc.)—monopolization and trustification—capital export—political protection of investments by curtailing the independence of the subdued state.

IMPERIALISM OF THE 'HAVE-NOTS'

'SOCIAL' IMPERIALISM:

Continental Imperialism—ideological and organizational incorporation of the masses—autarky—highest stage of monopolization and trustification—new Monroe Doctrine—transformation of subdued states (civilized) into colonies.

World Imperialism—ideological and organizational incorporation of the masses—the continent as the kernel—proletarian racism as the ideology and the lever for world imperialism.

Our contention is that Germany's imperialism is primarily the policy of its industrial leadership, fully supported by the National Socialist party; that the other classes merely follow that leadership or even resist it. This contention must be proved. Such proof can only be given by showing the historical growth of imperialism in Germany, by analyzing the attitudes of the various classes of society toward aggressive war. Such an analysis will in turn strengthen our contention that imperialistic war is the outcome of the internal antagonisms of the German economy.

As a key to the attitude of the German people toward war, we may use their behavior toward Great Britain.[44] We have already stressed the fact that hatred of England is present in all doctrines that enter into the National Socialist ideology. Neither Friedrich List's desire for alliance with Great Britain, nor Adolf Hitler's hope for collaboration with Great Britain as expressed in his autobiography changes our view. This collaboration was demanded primarily on the assumption that England is still a world power of enormous strength and that it is better jointly to exploit the world than to risk a war against England.

The configuration of the hatred of England within German society shows a curious picture, which was for the first time laid bare by the late, extremely gifted, German historian, Eckart Kehr.[44] In German society, England was the object of both veneration and hatred. The conservative agrarians, primarily concerned with securing protection for their grain production, had no economic objections to the bulk of British trade and industry. They were merely out to preserve the German economic structure so as to retain their socio-economic and political influence. They did not strive for world domination but for protection and security. Politically, however, England appeared to the conservative agrarians as the incarnation of evil, that is, of parliamentary democracy and universal franchise. England represented that type of government that was most opposed to the conservative form of life.

The attitude of the conservative agrarians toward Russia was just the opposite. In the latter part of the nineteenth century, Russia appeared increasingly as the competitor of Germany's agrarian production and thus became to the agrarians the object of economic hatred. But politically, Russia appeared to the conservatives as the ideal. Its absolutism was venerated and admired.

The attitude of German industry was diametrically opposed to that of the conservative agrarians. England was the feared and hated competitor, arousing all the resentment that a 'have not' feels against a 'have.' At the same time, German industry admired English constitutionalism, which ever since Montesquieu had been the model according to which all liberal movements in Europe molded their policies. German industry, on the other hand, liked cheap imports of foodstuffs and grain from Russia, since cheap imports would prevent the raising of wages. It despised the Russian absolutistic system. Graphically presented, the picture looks like this:

Liberals (industry)—politically against Russia; economically against England.

Conservatives (agrarians)—economically against Russia; politically against England.

But instead of the 'hatred of England' and the 'veneration of England' cancelling each other, the political aversion of the agrarians and the economic resentment of the industrialists merged into one all-comprehensive and decisive 'hatred of England.'

The occasion for this merger was Tirpitz's naval building program.

The Conservative Agrarians were never very much in favor of the Tirpitz naval building program. So much is clear after the perusal of the two large volumes of memoirs by Count Westarp,[45] for many years leader of the Conservative party. This is never explicitly stated, for the book was published in 1935 under the National Socialist regime. On the contrary, admiration for Tirpitz is frequently expressed. Nevertheless, Count Westarp clearly distinguishes Conservative policy from the policies pursued by the National Liberals and the Pan-German League. According to Westarp, the Pan-German League, about which we shall have to say a few words later, represents western Germany, free conservatives and national liberalism, but not the Conservative policy.[46] Westarp rejects, for instance, the policy of the Pan-Germans during the Morocco crisis of 1911, takes pains to keep aloof from what he calls the 'Utopian war aims'[47] of the Pan-Germans from 1914 to 1918 and constantly stresses the national liberal influence on the policy of aggressive imperialism and annexation.[48] Throughout his memoirs, this true Conservative reveals a considerable dislike of the National Liberal party, the out and out annexationists, though for obvious reasons he does not dare openly to attack them, especially because, after 1900, conservatives and liberals reached an understanding.

It is, indeed, the most striking phenomenon of Germany's history that the industrial bourgeoisie, unable or unwilling to fight for parliamentary democracy and submitting to the semi-absolutistic system of the empire, directed all their political energy toward an aggressive imperialism. German political liberalism was never mild and humanitarian; it was aggressive and brutal—even if the form seemed democratic. As early as the bourgeois revolution of 1848, Pan-German and annexationist programs and ideas become fully apparent. Georg Herwegh, a genuine democratic leader of 1848, and a poet of considerable distinction, wrote a poem in 1844, in which he expressed the dream of a German navy as the bearer of Germany's greatness: 'Und in die Furchen die Kolumb gezogen, geht Deutschland's Zukunft auf' (Germany's future takes the course plotted by Columbus).[49] The wide freedom won by this navy will, so he maintains, liberate Germany from England's 'grocer spirit.' [50]

Alfred Vagts,[51] with his keen sense of the social basis of foreign policy, has drawn our attention to two such famous liberals. Varnhagen von Ense in 1836 expressed his hope for the incorporation of Holland into Germany, and as early as 1848 formulated an outline of a democratic or social imperialism. 'It may come to pass that we shall demand Alsace and Lorraine from France, the Baltic countries from Russia. Such things Black-Red-Gold can do. Up to now, this has just been a beginning.' Vagts also reports that in 1861 a liberal and a creator of Prussian public opinion advocated an aggressive policy toward France and Denmark: 'Only in the field of facts and deeds can the German question be solved, and only our absolutist inactivity and our endless gabbling [sic] have failed to do so.' [52] In 1914 Franz von Liszt, outstanding criminologist and international lawyer, demanded the incorporation of the Scandinavian countries and of Turkey within the German orbit.[53]

In his well-known pamphlet *Händler und Helden* (Traders and Heroes, Munich and Leipzig, 1915), Werner Sombart contrasted the commercial and utilitarian spirit of the English to German heroism. England's spirit is that of the trader whose attitude toward life is summed up in the question: 'What can life give me?' (p. 15). English society is plutocratic; English morality is characterized by Bentham's '*hundsgemeine*' (vile) maxims (p. 19); the English state is nothing but a giant commercial enterprise. In contrast, Germany has a mission to fulfil, she has to spread the German heroic spirit, the German idea of the state.

Ever since its foundation in 1866, German national liberalism has advocated an army and navy, expansion, and colonial acquisition. The fight that Eugen Richter, as the representative of the Left Liberals, undertook against army expansion was unsuccessful even

within his own party, especially because Richter's hostility was
primarily based on fiscal reasons. From 1893 on, German Liberalism
has never actively fought against the expansion of the German
military machine.

In the field of naval construction, German liberalism was even
the originator. This aspect of the history of German liberalism and
of the whole problem of the social bases of German naval policy
is admirably presented by Eckart Kehr [54] in a book that is indispensable to an understanding of German imperialism. It proves convincingly that the stimulus to naval construction came from the
industrial bourgeoisie, and not from the crown, the civil service, or
the Conservative party. The National Liberal party, as the party
of the industrial bourgeoisie, gradually abandoned liberalism, which
was still fully evident in the program of 12 June 1867, and concentrated primarily on military and naval rearmament.[55] But perhaps
even more characteristic are those men who were considered the
true representatives of German liberalism: Theodor Barth, Max
Weber, and Gerhart von Schulze-Gävernitz. They represented
democratic liberalism in its hopes of breaking down the privileges
of the conservative agrarians by supporting a navy and advocating
an imperialistic foreign policy. Emil Rathenau, father of Walther
Rathenau, founder of the General Electric Corporation, as well as
Georg von Siemens, his great competitor, both belonged to that
group.

These trends merged or culminated in the Pan-German League [56]
founded in 1890 (actually bearing that name since 1894). This
league was the direct result of Germany's colonial policy and the
direct ideological forerunner of the National Socialist party. Of
all the patriotic associations set up in imperial Germany, the Pan-
German League was undoubtedly the most aggressive and the most
repulsive. Although never strong numerically, it had an extraordinary propaganda apparatus, continually agitating for land and sea
rearmament, for colonial expansion, and for an aggressive anti-
English policy. The League never hesitated to attack the monarchy when the foreign policy of Wilhelm II did not fit into its
plans. It utilized Anti-Semitism whenever and wherever this appeared necessary. During the First World War it was, of course,
the most radical annexationist group. The political affiliations of the
members of the League [57] are extraordinarily interesting:

47 per cent of the members belonged to the National Liberal party.
15 per cent to the Conservative party.
15 per cent to the *Deutsch Soziale* and Reform party (violently Anti-Semitic).
14 per cent to the *Reichspartei*.
 9 per cent to the *wirtschaftliche Vereinigung* (Anti-Semitic agrarians).

Included among the members of the League were such illustrious German national liberals as A. Bassermann, Heinze, and Gustav Stresemann. The two leaders of the League both came from the liberal camp. The League closely collaborated with all the other patriotic organizations, such as the Navy League, the Colonial League, the Society for Germans Abroad, the National Security League (*Wehrverein*), the Society of German Students, and so on. The statistics of the social composition of the group are not very revealing. In 1914, for instance, 24 per cent belonged to the teaching profession, 31 per cent were businessmen, 12 per cent were officials, 8 per cent were physicians, and the businessmen came primarily from small and medium-sized businesses. The conclusion that 'there seems to have been no connection before the war between big business and the Pan-German League either financially or in membership' [58] may be correct. But this does not tell the whole truth, for there is not the slightest doubt that the League's propaganda served the interests of big business, whatever may have been the motives of the other members of the League.[59]

The internal connection between naval propaganda and the needs of German business was clearly established in a resolution of the national liberal youth movement in 1902, that is, immediately after the passing of the new naval construction bill. 'Even after the implementation of the last naval building program, the German navy does not seem commensurate with the importance of German shipping and does not seem adequate for a powerful, independent, foreign policy.' [60]

At no time was the aggressive part played by the industrial leadership—so reluctantly accepted by the agrarians—clearer than between 1900 and 1902, on the occasion of the adoption of the Tirpitz naval program. Tirpitz himself, with masterly clarity, stated the aims of a German navy in his famous memorandum of 16 June 1894. 'The starting point for the development of a fleet must be the maritime interests of the nation . . . A state which . . . has . . . maritime or world interests must be able to . . . give expression to them and must be able to make its power felt . . . within its territorial waters. Rational world trade, world industry, to a certain extent deep sea fishing, world communications, and colonies, are impossible without a fleet capable of asssuming the offensive.' And in his memoirs he adds, 'The navy never seemed to me to be an end in itself, but always a function of these maritime interests. Without sea power Germany's position in the world resembled that of a mollusc without a shell.' [61] Here the role of the navy as the guardian of German commerce and as an instrument of offensive, that is, of aggression, is clearly stated, and it is characteristic that in order to achieve such an aim, Tirpitz always supported Wilhelm's continental alliance, an alliance with Russia, so as to have Germany's eastern flank free against England.[62] For his purpose Tirpitz never hesitated to utilize all available propagandist machinery,[63] to collaborate with all existing patriotic organizations, and even to set up a propaganda agency of his own. In order to foster navy-mindedness, the Naval Society was founded in 1898. It was the creation of Tirpitz and of the two most powerful armament manufacturers, von Stumm-Halberg, who owned the newspaper Die Post, and Krupp, who owned the newspaper Neueste Nachrichten.[64] After some propagandist preparation, industry opened the campaign for a new naval expansion (1899), fully supported by Tirpitz. The promoters, too, believed that the naval bill was an excellent outlet for the deep resentment aroused by the government's unsuccessful policy of oppression against the Social Democratic party. This first propagandist campaign, initiated by Stumm's Post and backed by the patriotic groups, petered out. It was taken up a second time when, in his famous speech of 18 October 1899, the emperor publicly demanded a strong fleet. The two newspapers we have mentioned at once reopened the campaign for a strong fleet, with the result that the first draft of a new naval bill was published. So strong, so open became the relation between patriotism and big business that many honest nationalists, especially Berlin university professors, began to attack this miscegenation. Yet in spite of this denunciation, industry held fast to its program. In a meeting of the central union of German industry on 13 February 1900, the resolution to go on with the program was openly proclaimed and the only change made was to substitute a patriotic ideology for the business theory.[65]

Yet it was just this naval bill that threatened to overthrow Miquel's concentration policy, the union between industry and the agrarians. The conservative agrarians attacked the bill, trying to induce the Catholic Center to vote against it. The agrarian organization, the *Bund der Landwirte*, remained if not openly hostile, at least extremely skeptical. The naval bill was finally passed as a result of a shameless bargain between industry and the agrarians. On 1 May 1900, the naval bill and the grain tariffs were interlocked, and Miquel's policy of concentration triumphed. 'To industry, the fleet, world politics, and expansion; to the agrarians, tariffs, the maintenance of the social supremacy of the conservatives; and as a consequence of this settlement, to the Center party, political hegemony.' [66] Theodor Mommsen, the great liberal historian, denounced this bargain as the 'union of Junkerdom and Chaplainocracy' (rule of Catholic priests) [67] and even Adolph Wagner, himself a convinced imperialist, lashed out at the merger of patriotism and business, attacking the boundless greed for profits.[68]

Just at this period the expansionists recognized the need for incorporating the masses and letting them share in this huge business venture. For this purpose, the economist Ernst von Halle, a hireling of the naval ministry, appointed to issue propaganda on behalf of the naval program, formulated the social imperialistic policy in the following words: Germany 'can successfully undertake political competition with other nations only if she really has behind her the support of the great masses.' Such support can only be secured by a progressive social policy. The primacy of foreign policy must therefore determine social reform. 'If we do not succeed in merging social reform policy and world policy into a higher unity, the German people of the future will no longer possess the right of self-determination in its domestic and in its foreign policy, but will have them determined by other, foreign nations.' [69]

The higher unity into which social reform and world politics merged was National Socialism and it is ironical that this decisive formulation of the National Socialist ideology emanates from Ernst von Halle, who was born with the name of Levy.[70]

We may thus say that while expansion into the sphere of British influence was demanded by German industry and the Liberal party, the Conservatives and Catholics, though at first reluctant, ultimately subscribed to it as a part of the bargain that secured their social and political power.

It was during the elections of 1907 [71] that the extent to which imperialistic ambitions had permeated the German people became manifest. The parliament of 1906 had been dissolved by Chancellor von Bülow, because his colonial policy had been attacked by the Catholic Center and the Social Democratic parties, who sharply criticized the military rule in German southwest Africa and the corruption of the colonial policy, especially through monopolistic contracts. The government and its party went to the poll with a slogan that this election must determine 'whether Germany is capable of developing from a European power into a world power.' [72] The gospel of imperialism was preached by the colonial secretary, Dernburg—significantly enough a banker and a Liberal—by the whole Liberal movement, by the many nationalistic leagues, and, last but not least, by the central league of German industrialists. But the election campaign also developed into a bitter fight against Catholicism and Socialism. This counter-attack on the Center party soon had its desired effect. The party became frightened into continually asserting its nationalistic, patriotic, and even imperialistic aims, and restricted its own attack to the abuses in the German colonial administration. The elections of 1907 resulted in a defeat for Socialism but not for the Catholic Center, and in the victory of all the imperialistic parties.[73] The Socialists, though losing but few votes, lost about half their deputies. The Liberal-Conservative block began to rule, and the Center party, as a consequence of the elections, shifted more and more to the right and practically displaced its radical leadership.

The attitude of the bourgeois parties is, therefore, clear: they either strove for, or at least supported the imperialist leadership of the industrial groups.

6. The Social Democrats and Imperialism

But there is still the important question whether world politics and social reform merged into a 'higher unity,' as von Halle demanded. It was precisely over the issue of imperialism that there was dissension within Socialist theory and within the Socialist movement. It was over this problem that a section of the revisionists within the Social Democratic party attacked orthodox Marxism; it was primarily over this issue that Lenin attacked all social demo-

cratic movements throughout the world. The attitude of the working classes toward imperialism not only was the paramount political
question, but the Social Democrats were conscious of the fact.
Formulating the issue in a very crude way, the question was really
whether the German worker should actively support, or at least
tolerate, Germany's expansion in order to share in the material benefits that might possibly be derived from it.

The elections of 1907 gave rise to an overproduction of articles,
pamphlets, speeches, and debates on imperialism and colonialism,
and all leading Social Democrats participated in the debates. The
conflict came to the fore at the international socialist conference at
Stuttgart in 1907 and at the Social Democratic party congress at
Essen in the same year. Three trends emerged in this discussion:
the revisionist, the anti-imperialist-orthodox, and the social-imperialist.[74] Parvus, a leading orthodox Marxist who became one of the
chief social imperialists during the First World War, had attacked
colonialism during the election campaign and republished his pamphlet after the defeat in 1907.[75] His pamphlet is remarkable in many
respects: in its denial that monopolization and cartellization automatically further the interests of the working classes; its insistence
that colonies, far from raising the standard of living of the German
worker, would on the contrary reduce it; and its analysis of the
German ruling groups, which he even then depicted as composed
of cartel leaders, bank directors, and high state officials. He was
supported in his criticism by Rudolf Hilferding, the leading party
theorist.[76] Colonialism, for Hilferding, was the necessary outcome
of capitalism. Though the rate of profit in German industry was
then very high because of cartellization and protective tariffs, he
argued it was threatened by over-accumulation. In consequence,
German industry had to expand beyond Germany's frontiers. For
Germany as a late-comer this expansion was difficult to achieve.
Four such previous attempts, in Brazil, East Asia, Morocco, and
Turkey, had been frustrated. But German industry would not hesitate to repeat the attempt. It would, for this purpose, strengthen its
domestic domination. It had already succeeded, or was on the point
of doing so, in winning the conservative agrarians, the Catholic
Center, and the whole liberal movement, and would finally organize
the whole of public opinion. If it succeeded in this task, it would
turn against the proletariat, for in contrast to England, German

imperialism was reactionary and 'must be reactionary, because the resistance of the working classes is already too great' (p. 163).

That, however, was not the view of the whole party.[77] While the party's official scientific periodical, *Die neue Zeit*, mainly expressed the view of the orthodox section, the *Sozialistische Monatshefte*, edited by Josef Bloch, was the organ of the social imperialists and of the group that demanded a continental orientation of Germany against England.[78] This group abandoned the attack on capitalism, and tried instead to get as much as possible for the worker. But this revisionist attitude split into two separate wings. The first, led by the theoretical spokesman Eduard Bernstein[79] sought to shift the social basis of the Social Democratic movement by including in it the lower middle class, represented by left liberals, and worked to promote a union of these two groups. It therefore tried to incorporate into the Social Democratic movement those strata of society that suffered most, perhaps even more than the worker, from the monopolistic structure of society. In consequence, Bernstein became the leader of the pacifist group within the Social Democratic party, going over during the war to the anti-war Independent Social Democratic party.

The other wing, however, was definitely 'social imperialistic,' and we use here the term in its original meaning, of an imperialistic policy desired by and for the working classes. This group despised the left liberals and the petty bourgeoisie,[80] and sought an alliance with the captains of industry. It fully accepted colonial expansion as a boon for the working classes, expecting rising wages and a quickening of the natural life of capitalism, which would hasten the coming of socialism.[81]

At the two congresses, it became clear that the adamant hostility of the German delegations to colonialism had lessened and views were expressed that distinguished between good and bad, human and inhuman imperialist policies. The enraged orthodox majority pointed out what was perfectly true, that the German delegation to the international congress consisted mostly of trade-union delegates who were more susceptible to social imperialist ideas than was the party leadership and membership. Nevertheless, even among the orthodox party leaders, unconditional rejection gave way to conditional rejection.[82]

It was during the First World War that the social imperialist tendencies within the Social Democratic party became particularly virulent. The classic expression of this trend is Heinrich Cunow's book, *Is the Party Bankrupt?* [83] Cunow, a professor in the University of Berlin during the Weimar Republic and an economic historian of great merit, made the jump from revolutionary opposition to the full acceptance of imperialism, arguing that the imperialist development of capitalism was a natural process that could no more be resisted than the introduction of labor-saving machinery. Antiimperialism was therefore as nonsensical as was machine wrecking in earlier days.[84] Paul Lensch [85] became the most ardent propagandist of that group. He was aided by the former revolutionary, Parvus.

It is often maintained that the social imperialist trend became a powerful movement within the Social Democratic party. This incorrect assertion is based on the fact that the huge majority of the party and of the trade unions were patriotic and supported the war. But the social patriotism of the majority of the party was directed against Russia, against Tsarist absolutism, while the hostility of the social imperialists was primarily directed against England.[86] To distinguish between the two trends is imperative, despite the fact that they overlapped and often coincided in practice. There is no doubt that the huge majority of the party remained uncontaminated by social imperialism, and never accepted the fallacious reasoning that class interests can best be served by warfare against imperialist competitors.

How little headway was made by social imperialism in the party was amply proved by the party's development under the Weimar Republic. Not social imperialist revisionism triumphed, but the pacifist and petty bourgeois outlook of Eduard Bernstein. It was English Fabianism that, under the Weimar Republic, triumphed over orthodoxy, although the orthodox formulas and slogans were retained. Throughout the history of the Social Democratic party during the Weimar Republic, no responsible labor leader went the way of social imperialism except August Winnig,[87] a former trade-union chairman, who, as provincial president, sided with the *Kapp Putsch*, had to leave the party, devoted his literary abilities to advocating the social-imperialist gospel, and finally joined the National Socialist party.

How little headway was made by social-imperialist doctrines

within the Social Democratic party can also be seen from its Russian policy. At Rapallo, in 1922, under the aegis of Foreign Minister Walther Rathenau, Germany concluded her first treaty of friendship with Russia—a clever counter-thrust to French diplomacy. The idea of using Russian help in the fight against Versailles belonged to the stock-in-trade of many groups in Germany. Count Brockdorff Rantzau, the German ambassador to Russia, who had refused to sign the Versailles treaty, was one of the first. Alliance with Russia was regarded as a means of fighting capitalism and imperialism, the 'God-fathers of Versailles.' Hugo Stinnes, the leading German industrialist, as a protest against the Ruhr occupation, painted at the Spaa conference the picture of a proletarian revolution. National-Bolshevik groups, especially the *Widerstand* group of Ernst Nieckisch, up to 1935 advocated a fight of the East against the West. The German Reichswehr secretly collaborated with the Red Army—partly in order to gain experience with new weapons that were forbidden to Germany by the treaty of Versailles, partly because the Bismarckian tradition of establishing friendly relations with Russia was still strong.

The Social Democratic party never supported Russo-German friendship as a means of breaking the power of England and France. For them, the League of Nations represented the very last word of rational international relations. That, of course, did not imply hostility to Russia. On the contrary, they never supported the foreign policy that sought an alliance with Soviet Russia against the Western powers.

Within the ruling classes hatred of Russia was as powerful as hatred of England. The vastness of the Soviet territory, the masses of men, the gigantic wheat fields, the iron ore, the oil fields were always a great attraction to European capitalism. As early as 1917, General Max Hoffmann, who signed the treaty of Brest-Litowsk, conceived the idea of a fight of the Western powers against Bolshevism. In 1920, he suggested this to the Social Democratic party in Berlin, and was rebuked. In 1922, he prepared a memorandum offering Germany's assistance to the Western powers in a fight against Bolshevism.[88] During the First World War, the imperialists were as hungry for Russian wheat and oil, and for the Baltic 'settlement' space as for Longwy, Briey, Alsace, Lorraine, Belgium, and British

colonies. Friedrich Naumann's view has already been mentioned.*
Paul Rohrbach was one of the apostles of Ukrainian autonomy
under German sovereignty. The geopoliticians held the same views.
We have already seen that the implication of MacKinder's theory is
not necessarily a German-Russian alliance; it can just as logically
be the incorporation of Russia into Germany.†

Both England and Russia appeared as the objects of German expansion—against Russia, one could join the anti-Bolshevik chorus;
against England—one could make imperialism social. The Social
Democrats were immune to hatred of England and hatred of Russia.
Much as the party hated bolshevism, it never lent its help to any
interventionist crusade against Soviet Russia.

7. RACIAL IMPERIALISM AND THE MASSES

So deep is the abyss between National Socialism and the old
Social Democratic spirit that only a handful of Social Democratic
labor leaders went over to National Socialism—a few in the central
organization of the Social Democratic trade unions, here and there
an editor of a socialist paper, here and there a party and a trade-
union secretary. But the great majority of all party and trade-union
functionaries remained either aloof or in opposition. This attitude
is the really lasting merit of Social Democratic education. The defensive mentality that the party and trade unions had developed
from 1914 to 1932, though it turned out to be catastrophic for the
existence of the Weimar Republic, prevented the party officials from
actually supporting the regime. Compared with the French trade
unions and with the French Socialist party, the German movement
died a heroic death.

The latest phase of National Socialist theory, the doctrine of
proletarian racism, of social imperialism, has failed to gain a complete hold over the masses. The old party and trade-union bureaucracy does not collaborate with the regime. The large majority of
trade unionists and Social Democrats are not National Socialists.
Throughout their history they have resisted the seductive theory
of social imperialism; there is no reason to believe that they support
it today. The repressive social policy of the National Socialist re-

* See p. 140.
† See p. 146.

gime gives additional substance to our contention. But we cannot, of course, say that Social Democrats and trade unionists are openly hostile to National Socialism. That would be asking too much of them. They are waiting. Their old organizations have been destroyed. Their belief in the usefulness of their organizations has gone. But even the younger generation, which was not indoctrinated by the Social Democratic party and by the trade unions, shows just as little National Socialist sympathy.

When we discuss the social structure of National Socialism, we shall draw attention to an outstanding phenomenon: thorough indoctrination of the masses is always accompanied by almost complete terrorization. This is necessary because of the contradiction between the enormous capacity of the productive apparatus and the destructive uses to which it is actually put. Even the most unenlightened worker is forced to ask himself whether it is possible to reconcile the flattery of the masses, the aping of Marxist ideology, high productivity, and terrorism. Even the most self-centered worker will, almost every day, come up against the question why so developed an industrial apparatus as the German has to be kept together by terror. Unlimited productive power, terror, and propaganda cannot create National Socialism among the workers. On the contrary, the workers are more likely to move along revolutionary syndicalist lines, to evolve ideas of sabotage and of direct action, ideas that were frowned upon by Social Democrats and Communists alike, but which might be considered by them as the sole means of asserting man's dignity within a terroristic system.

The picture is not very different in regard to the communist worker. The Communist party, as we have seen, has been prepared for social imperialism by the doctrine of National Bolshevism. It is therefore possible, and even likely, that some groups within the communist movement, especially the lowest paid workers, were susceptible to social imperialist theories up to the outbreak of the German-Russian war. But the National Bolshevist slogan of the Communist party was merely the formula of a corrupt leadership frantically searching for propaganda devices that would allow them to compete with nationalism, and National Bolshevism was never spontaneously accepted by the communist masses. It was accepted by the uprooted proletariat, by the *Lumpenproletariat*, especially by many groups belonging to the Red Fighting League, which, to a considerable extent, became absorbed by the Brown Shirts and the Black Shirts. Moreover, the National Bolshevist slogan was abandoned by the Communist party when it became clear that the communist masses turned against nationalism and National Socialism in spite of the attempted collaboration by the Communist party with the reactionary groups. The last remnants of National Bolshevism, especially among the lowest paid strata of the communist workers, were finally driven out by the actual social policy of National Socialism, which was most terroristic against these very groups. It is the unskilled, untrained worker, especially the road builder, who has probably received the worst treatment and whose rights and interests are sacrificed almost daily.

The social imperialist ideology is, however, probably fully accepted by the uprooted middle classes, so far as they have been organized within the National Socialist party. For these strata of the middle class are genuinely anti-capitalistic. For them, the new theory is really the formulation of a psychological demand for greater dignity. Under the Weimar Republic, to call a member of the middle class a proletarian was, in his view, to express contempt for him. But to call him a proletarian today is to invest his position with the highest possible dignity: that is, to name him a fighter for a greater proletarian Germany against the surrounding capitalistic world. The S.S. man is anti-capitalistic and today he seems proud to be called a proletarian. The former retailer or handicraft man, the dispossessed peasant, the unemployed intellectual who never had time or money to finish his studies, the elementary school teacher, all these groups dislike capitalism as much as Communists and Social Democrats did. For them, the doctrine of social imperialism is an adequate expression of their longings and an adequate formulation of their claims for dignity and security. For them, socialism is an untenable doctrine—since they hate the very basis upon which the socialist doctrine rests: that is, the equality of men. In addition, the doctrine of social imperialism is, as it has always been, a device of the ruling classes, a device as old as imperialism itself. Social imperialism is the most dangerous formulation of National Socialist ideology. It appeals to all those groups throughout the world who are in danger of proletarization: peasants, retailers, artisans, teachers and other intellectuals; it appeals to the unemployed, to all those who in the process of monopolization have lost security but do not want to be called proletarians. It becomes especially dangerous since it contains one element of truth: that the German economy is highly developed, is efficient, and contains many progressive elements. The amazing efficiency of Germany's technical apparatus, coupled with the social imperialist doctrine, is today Germany's greatest weapon. It is to the structure of this economic system that we now have to turn.

PART TWO

TOTALITARIAN MONOPOLISTIC ECONOMY

AN ECONOMY WITHOUT ECONOMICS?

1. STATE CAPITALISM?

IN summarizing the course of our investigation, the following points should be noted. The political structure of National Socialism exhibits a number of divergent elements. The concept of the strong, all-embracing totalitarian state, though now rejected in ideology, is by far the most characteristic. The rule of the bureaucracy and of the armed forces, represented by the ministerial council for the defense of the realm, is complete. The state is restricted only in the police and youth administrations, in which the party is sovereign. The underlying ideology is racism, the sovereignty of the racial people incarnated in the Leader. The whole structure is at the service of two ideas, the New Order and proletarian racism: the supremacy of the 'have-not' nation surrounded by plutocratic and hostile democracies.

Yet, the paramount question that urgently needs an answer is: what are the forces that keep National Socialist society together? We can by no means hope to give an exhaustive answer. We cannot provide a complete analysis of National Socialist society, and we must specifically omit culture and education. The third part of this book will deal with three outstanding problems: (1) The new economy—we shall attempt to lay bare the operation of the material forces that maintain National Socialist society. (2) The new society —an analysis of the social forces determining the structure of society; above all, class stratification and the formation of an élite. (3) Propaganda and terror as two aspects of a single development: the transformation of man into the passive victim of an all-inclusive force which flatters and terrorizes him, which elevates him and sends him into concentration camps. In the concluding chapter of this book, we shall try to depict the complete pattern of National Socialist society—the intertwining of state, law, economics, politics, and culture.

The achievements of the German economy are astounding. The abolition of unemployment, the increase in production, the development of synthetic industries, the complete subordination of economic activities to the needs of war, the rationing system before and during this war, the success of price control—these are achievements difficult to surpass. In that judgment all observers agree, but here the agreement ends. There is no agreement about how this miracle has been achieved, because there is no agreement about the nature of the economic system.

There is an increasing tendency to deny the capitalistic character of National Socialism.[1] It is called a system of brown bolshevism, of state capitalism, of bureaucratic collectivism, of the rule of a managerial bureaucracy. This school of thought believes that there are no longer entrepreneurs in Germany, but only managers; that there is no freedom of trade and contract; no freedom of investment; that the market has been abolished, and with it, the laws of the market. Prices are therefore administrative prices, wages only administrative wages. Consequently, the law of value is no longer operative. Values are use values throughout and no longer exchange values. Classes, if their existence is admitted, are no longer the outcome of production. The power to which the worker is subjected is not an economic power. His exploitation is political and is no longer a result of his position within the productive process. The appropriation of his labor is a political act, not economic. The new economy is, therefore, one without economics. Economics has become an administrative technique. The economic man is dead. The profit motive is supplanted by the power motive. Force, not economic law, is the prime mover of this society, ruled by an élite composed of industrial managers, party bureaucrats, high-ranking civil servants, and army officers.

Nearly all these theories are based on the view that the age of industrial revolution is over. That technological changes occur, is, of course, admitted. But it is denied that they result in fundamental changes in the structure of society. This view was first propounded before Hitler came to power, by the so-called *Tatkreis*, a group of romantic reactionaries who later turned into the most vicious National Socialists, connected with the monthly magazine, *Die Tat* (Action).[2] Their leader, Ferdinand Fried,[2] announced the end of the era of inventions, and thereby the end of capitalism. Lawrence

Dennis believes that 'as a capitalist dynamism, the industrial revolution is over' and that further technological changes are 'neither dynamic nor constructive.' [3] For Dennis, therefore, a totalitarian political revolution has to take the place of the industrial revolution.

The best formulation of this type of theory was given by the German theorist of the Social Democratic party, Rudolf Hilferding,[4] not with regard to Germany, but with regard to Russia.

What a government economy does is precisely to abolish the autonomy of economic laws; it is not a market economy, but an economy for use. What is produced, and how it is produced, is no longer determined by the price but by the state planning commission, which fixes the character and extent of production. To outward appearances, prices and wages still exist, but their function has completely changed. They no longer determine the course of production. That is directed by the central government . . . Prices and wages are now only instruments of distribution determining the share that each individual shall receive out of the sum total which the central government allots to the whole population. Prices have now become the technical means of distribution, a means simpler than would be a direct order stipulating the amount of the various products (which have ceased to be 'commodities') to be received by each individual. Prices have become symbols of distribution, but they are no longer the regulators of the nation's economy. While the form has been maintained, the function has been completely changed.

Those who believe that this theory holds good for Germany also accept the fascist interpretation of liberalism and democracy. They maintain that capitalism was characterized by private enterprise, by the capitalist-worker relation, by numerous politically sovereign states, parliamentary institutions, a ruling class composed of capitalists, and civil or natural rights for the individual. None of this exists any longer.

There are, of course, differences in the approach to the German situation. The German state does not own all the capital in the country. But that does not make any difference to the school of thought we have just discussed. In any case, so the school argues, the German state at least controls all the capital. For other writers, however, the Hilferding formulation presents an ideal type or model, and they believe that it is rapidly being realized.

This, then, is in brief outline the view held by many commentators on Germany. It is an enticing view, for it makes the differences between National Socialism and democracy appear not only political and ideological, but also economic: that is, it sees them as two economic systems, private capitalism and state capitalism, or capitalism and managerial dictatorship.

There are two different ways of refuting such a theory. The first would be theoretically to deduce the impossibility of such a structure. The second would be to show in detail the structure and operation of the German economy. It is the second course which we primarily propose to follow. A few preliminary remarks must be made.

The very term 'state capitalism' is a *contradictio in adiecto*. 'The concept of "state capitalism" cannot bear analysis from the economic point of view. Once the state has become the sole owner of the means of production, it makes it impossible for a capitalist economy to function, it destroys that mechanism which keeps the very processes of economic circulation in active existence.' [5] Such a state is therefore no longer capitalistic. It may be called a slave state or a managerial dictatorship or a system of bureaucratic collectivism—that is, it must be described in political and not in economic categories.

Theorists often speak of an ideal type or model, not yet fully realized, but in the process of becoming so. Germany admittedly has remnants of markets and therefore of prices. But the state-capitalist school maintains that these remnants have no basic importance, and that reality is rapidly approaching the model. Such a procedure is hardly legitimate and cannot be justified by reference to similar models, such as those constructed by Adam Smith and Karl Marx. Smith and Marx confined their analyses to prevailing trends within a given system and did not go beyond them. Marx even deliberately refused to depict the system of a classless society and kept strictly within the boundaries of one order: capitalism. The new theory violates the principle that the model or the ideal type must be derived from reality and must not transcend it. For its proponents describe a system that is utterly alien to capitalism, that is, in fact, its direct opposite, that necessitates a jump from one reality to another. This methodological objection does not, of course, make their theory untrue, but it compels them to show in detail that

German capitalism has ceased to exist. They cannot merely point to trends within capitalism in order to show that these trends must necessarily beget a system of power politics without economics, they have to prove their case for each of the systems concerned. Such proof has not yet been furnished. And in the present study we shall prove the contrary view.

One last question. What would this 'bureaucratic collectivism' mean for humanity? Would it bring peace and happiness or war and oppression?

In our view, these theorists must admit that their system may very well be the millennium. The maintenance of society is now based solely on politics. The obstacles that such a society meets are exclusively natural, no longer economic. Man-power and natural resources are the only factors that could possibly hinder the expansion of such a society. There is no longer any antagonism between the productive forces and the social conditions of production. The profit motive no longer fetters the productivity of labor. No plant can possibly refuse to expand, since there is no profit motive to keep it back. Technological progress, which in the capitalistic system springs from the profit incentive, now springs from the decision of a central governmental organ. Whether such a decision is made, whether production or consumption goods are produced, is no longer determined by the law of accumulation but by political expediency. Such a system may very well give everybody a house, an automobile, six suits and ten pairs of shoes a year. It could continuously raise the standard of living. It could shorten the hours of labor by installing labor-saving devices. It could, therefore, realize the dream of humanity. That would hold true even if National Socialism could not conquer the whole world. For, in the view of this school, every country is going the way of Germany. The New Deal is regarded as the forerunner of bureaucratic collectivism and of a managerial bureaucracy. The world will soon be divided into state-capitalistic empires, all of which are emancipated from economic necessities. But if that is true, then there is not even a world market, and if the world market is abolished, there may not even be a fight among the contending empires for a greater share in that market. What we have is the sole and exclusive rule of politics; and political expediency may very well exclude war for decades to come. Consequently, the state capitalistic view does not agree with the bolshevist view that Bukharin propounded in 1917,[6] that the capitalistic states would transform themselves into gigantic state trusts, and would compete in the world market so that the internal antagonisms would be reproduced at a higher level in the international sphere. That is not the view of the state capitalists, for if the whole world moves toward state capitalism or bureaucratic collectivism, the world market will be abolished and the relations between the states will become exclusively political, to be handled by exclusively political means.

If we share this view, we must also conclude that nothing but a series of accidents can destroy such systems. If the systems are held together only by political ties and not by any inescapable economic necessity, only political mistakes can destroy them. But why should political errors occur? Politics divorced from economics is a mere technique, an art. In the era of state capitalism it is a technique of mass domination, a technique that has indeed been highly developed. If the requirements of mass domination make it necessary, the standard of living can be raised. Consumption goods could be produced in abundance. If opposition arises within lower groups against that system, the lower groups may be taken into the élite. So skilful a system of mass domination may secure the stability of the system for a thousand years. That is, indeed, the promise that Hitler holds out to his people. Skilful political operations could exclude even war, since there are no economic necessities driving toward it.

But the state capitalists are not National Socialists. On the contrary, however much they may be fascinated by the efficiency of the German system and believe it to be the necessary outcome of the tendencies inherent in monopoly capitalism, they dislike it intensely, and are therefore prone to discover reasons for its decay. But are they able to detect such reasons? They say that the system cannot afford permanently to raise the standard of living, since, so they believe, this would inevitably produce dissatisfaction among the masses. The masses, they argue, would then begin to think and to question the compatibility of the high technical efficiency with the terroristic and repressive machinery. Whether it is true that fat bellies make for freedom of thought I do not know. The opposite thesis might just as well be true, that material satiety makes for political laxness and dullness. But even if the first hypothesis were true, nothing could prevent the system from silencing this sort of opposition by incorporating the opponents into the ruling élite. And if the masses themselves revolt, why should a classless society not be established, why should not the terrorists of today become the leaders of the classless society of tomorrow? No economic necessities make this transition impossible.

The state capitalists may argue that there are biological, morphological, or sociological laws that make for the disintegration of any social system after it has run its course. Many such laws have been 'discovered.' Cyclical theories of history are abundant, but their validity has never been proved; they are metaphysical categories.

Such then, might be the fate of mankind under a rule of bureaucratic collectivism. The world might not be exactly a pleasant place to live in for an intellectual, but for the large masses of society, it might turn out to be heaven.

But it might just as easily be hell. Mass domination might require oppression, the expansion of terroristic machinery, the lowering of the standard of living, and war against the other state capitalistic powers, in order to keep the masses in check. Both possibilities exist. We repeat that, if we accept the assumptions of the state capitalistic theory, the choice is determined solely by political expediency. The rulers are completely free to determine the character of their rule: their system of mass domination is so flexible that it seems potentially invulnerable from within.

The present writer does not accept this profoundly pessimistic view. He believes that the antagonisms of capitalism are operating in Germany on a higher and, therefore, a more dangerous level, even if these antagonisms are covered up by a bureaucratic apparatus and by the ideology of the people's community.

In analyzing the structure and operation of National Socialist economy, we must never rest content with the legal and administrative forms. They tell us very little. 'Anyone who wants to know the organization [of the economic system] cannot do so by merely studying the statutes, decrees, and rulings . . . Some provisions are practically obsolete, others have never become a reality.' [7] That is the judgment of the official commentator on the statutes on business organization. We go even beyond this statement. A careful study of the German newspapers and periodicals is far more important than that of the legal and administrative pronouncements. Our analysis is based entirely on German sources. Foreign studies are used only for occasional reference.

2. A National Socialist Economic Theory: * The Myth of the Corporate State

Does the economic theory of National Socialism coincide with the foregoing 'state-capitalistic' doctrines? The answer is no. There is no National Socialist economic theory except the slogan that general welfare is more important than self-interest, a slogan repeated on almost every possible occasion and used to cloak almost every economic decision. Aside from such meaningless phrases, we can find as many economic theories as there are groups within the National Socialist society. We must recognize once and for all that the structure of the National Socialist economic system does not follow any blueprint, is not based on any consistent doctrine, be it neo-mercantilism, any guild or 'Estate' theory, or liberal or socialist dogma. The organization of the economic system is pragmatic. It is directed entirely by the need of the highest possible efficiency and productivity required for the conducting of war. Of course, a definite pattern can be seen. But that pattern is not designed by a doctrine, but rather by the material structure of the economy.

The party program of 25 February 1920 contained a number of programmatic declarations concerning the economic reorganization of Germany. Points 11, 19, and 25 contain demands such as the breaking of the fetters of interest; the abolition of income without work and endeavor; the complete confiscation of war profits; 'the nationalization of [already] socialized [trusts] plants'; profit sharing in large enterprises; generous extension of old-age security; creation of a sound middle class, by communalization of department stores and by leasing them at cheap rents to small businessmen; more consideration for small businessmen in public contracts; agrarian reform; 'enactment of a statute for expropriation without indemnification for purposes of common welfare'; abolition of land rent; and a ruthless war on usurers. The program also contained one specific proposal for the organization of the economic system: it demanded

* See also pp. 320-27.

the creation of estate and occupational chambers for the execution of statutes enacted by the legislative authorities in order to implement the principle that public welfare comes before self-interest.

On 22 May 1926, the program was declared unalterable, and Gottfried Feder, the author of the economic theories during that stage of National Socialism, adds that Hitler demanded that the two major postulates of the program be printed in spaced type: the precedence of general welfare and the breaking of the fetters of interest.[8] These theories are elaborated in Feder's book,[9] which Adolf Hitler called 'the catechism of our movement.' Finally, in 1926 Hitler appointed Feder supreme arbiter of all disputes arising out of the interpretation of the party program. For a short time after Hitler's advent to power, Feder still had a role of some importance. He was appointed secretary of state in the federal ministry of economics. But his influence has long since waned and the once supreme ideological arbiter is now a nonentity.*

Feder's decline in importance indicates the complete abandonment of the economic sections of the party program, for there is not a single point in that unalterable program that has been carried out and every phenomenon denounced by the program has grown by leaps and bounds under the National Socialist regime. The unalterability of the program was suspended as early as 13 April 1928, when Hitler, anxious to win the support of the landed aristocracy, abandoned by way of 'an authentic interpretation' point 17 of the party program, which demanded the expropriation of land without indemnification. Instead, expropriation was restricted to 'Jewish real estate speculating corporations.'[10]

The economic theories developed during that stage of National Socialism were primarily directed against the supremacy of money capital, for the protection of the middle classes, and against Jewish enterprises. The entrepreneur was never attacked. On the contrary, men like 'Alfred Krupp, Mannesmann, Werner Siemens, Thyssen [father], Borsig, Krauss, Maffei,' received laudatory comments.[11]

Inspired by point 25 of the party program, some National Socialists elaborated comprehensive programs for a reorganization of the German economic system on a corporative basis.[12] Even after Hitler's accession to power,[13] a National Socialist institute for corpora-

* Feder died recently.

tive organization was founded,[14] but it had only a brief existence.

Many observers hold the erroneous view that the economic organ-ization of Germany is primarily determined by estate or corporative ideas. These ideas are closely associated with the German romantic movement, which represented the first protest against capitalism and English parliamentarism and tended to safeguard the German past. Adam Müller, whose economic theories are so muddled that it is almost impossible to bring any kind of order into them, came in the wake of the French Revolution, and was probably the first to pos-tulate estate organization as against class organization. He feared that the nation would split into two classes and sought to prevent the resulting antagonism by an estate system composed of an aris-tocracy, a clergy, industry, and merchants, which would integrate the industrial into the political system.[15] Hegel, in his *Philosophy of Right* (Sections 203, 205) conceived the estates as the mediators between the state and the civil society, as standing between the realms of public and private law. He believed that a system of cor-porations could fuse together civil society and the state. In the wake of the revolution of 1848, the greatest and at the same time least-known estate theorist, Karl Marlo (Karl Georg Winkelblech), elaborated a comprehensive and in many respects admirable critique of liberal economy and postulated an estate organization.[16] Winkel-blech was alarmed by the radicalization of the industrial proletariat, which he attributed to the cruel economic conditions of early indus-trialism. He was also horrified by the destruction of the artisan and of handicraft, and he therefore attacked free competition, liberal-ism, and the divorce of state from society, which is inherent in every liberal system. For him, the reconciliation of the two spheres lay in an estate organization in which the state itself appeared as an estate. His theories received practical significance in an address that he submitted to the Frankfurt parliament of 1848,[17] demanding the establishment of a 'social chamber [social parliament] which would have to consider the whole of social legislation and submit the reso-lutions passed by it to the political chamber [political parliament] for decisions.' 'The members of the social chamber were to be elected by all social estates according to an election statute which would fully guarantee the representation of all special occupations.' While Marlo's address demanded the coexistence of an occupational and of a political chamber and the subordination of the former to the latter, a requirement that was later fulfilled under the Weimar Republic, the reactionary movement soon seized upon the occupational idea for the purpose of suppressing parliamentary institutions, as for instance in Bismarck's political and social theory. Bismarck depicted his ideal political scheme as one of a strong monarchy, restricted by a system of corporate representation.[18] Nevertheless, the idea of occupational representation was never very important during the imperial period, probably because of the absence of syndicalist theories.

But it sprang up again in 1918 and 1919, when the revisionist group within the Social Democratic party (Max Cohen and Julius Kaliski) tried to convert it to the idea of a chamber of labor, that is, to occupational representation with equal rights to the political parliament. The plan was defeated by Germany's outstanding labor lawyer, Hugo Sinzheimer,[19] who, in two brilliant speeches, pointed out that occupational representation would lead to the stabilization of existing class relations, would destroy that elasticity which the parliamentary system offered, would establish a complete rigidity of the social system, and would thereby close the way to peaceful change. Sinzheimer's opposition was successful. All that remained of the corporate idea in the Weimar constitution was the provisional federal economic council composed of industry, labor, consumers, free professions, and experts, an organization with no achievements to boast of, possessing legislative initiative and certain advisory functions with which, however, the government, especially during the great depression, partly dispensed.

Ideologically, corporate ideas received a certain stimulus from Italian fascism and from Catholic social theory as expressed in the Papal encyclical, *Quadragesimo Anno* (1931), which was elaborated into the Catholic doctrine of solidarism.[20] Yet the German Catholics, in contrast to their Austrian brethren, were always careful to insist on the compatibility of their corporate ideas with parliamentary democracy. The strongly reactionary aspect of the corporate idea was advocated primarily by the Viennese sociologist, Othmar Spann, and by his school.[21] This group worked out, on the basis of a universalist doctrine, a radical-estate theory intended to supplant parliamentary institutions. The social 'whole is an independent reality existing prior to the individual . . . It is never tangible or visible to the outer eye. Deep spiritual concentration is necessary to perceive it with the inner eye.' [22] Even the state and the economy are conceived as estates, the state appearing as the supreme estate co-ordinating all others.

Although the Spann theories received a little more attention in 1932 and were pushed in 1933 by certain groups within the National Socialist orbit—by the institute for estate organization, by certain circles within the labor front, and by the leaders of the National Socialist retail and handicraft organization—they were nevertheless rejected and, according to Mr. Thyssen's letters in *Life* of 29 April 1940, the institute director was sent into a concentration camp.

In the early period, the labor front very strongly insisted upon a corporate organization of the German economic system. In a number of speeches, the leader of the front, Dr. Robert Ley, demanded such a basis: 'Citizenship is bound to the membership of an estate' (9 May 1933). 'Estate is that in which man stands as an occupational man, as a chemist, as an engineer . . .' (12 August 1933). 'The germ cell of the estate structure must be the plant where men know each other very well. The regulation of wage and labor conditions is the prerogative of the estate.' Feder was also allowed to postulate, in his speech to the party congress of 1933, a complete reorganization of the German economy on a corporate basis.[23]

In fact, corporativism and National Socialism are incompatible. For National Socialism, the primacy of politics is decisive. 'During its fighting years the party has never allowed itself to be induced . . . to put . . . the economic questions into the foreground and to announce comprehensive economic official party programs.' It has always insisted on the primacy of politics over economics and has therefore consciously remained a political party without any basic economic orientation. This is the view of Wilhelm Keppler, the Leader's deputy for economic questions.[24] The late Bernhard Köhler, formerly the chairman of the economic committee of the party, expressed the same opinion. 'From the very beginning, National Socialism was a revolt of the living feelings of the people against the fact that the whole life of the people was determined by economics, by material existence.' [25] Merely to change the economic structure will not produce 'a socialist structure of the life of the people' (p. 9). Only political changes can do so. These two speeches contain an uncompromising attack on corporate ideas, on the attempts of the corporate school, on groups within the labor

front, and others. Alfred Rosenberg had already attacked the philosophical basis of Spann's estate theories, namely, the abstract character of the universal conceptions and the failure to incorporate racial
ideas.[26] The leader of the labor front, Robert Ley, joined the
chorus,[27] abandoning his previous errors.

Moreover, the estate idea was quickly seized upon by the cartels
in order to strengthen their power and to destroy outsiders and
competitors. Immediately after the National Socialist revolution,
many cartels introduced the leadership principle into their organizations. They appointed National Socialist managers and, with the
power of the party behind them, compelled outsiders to join the
cartel organization or be destroyed. The estate idea was thus misused to bring about compulsory cartellization. This is one of the
reasons, according to National Socialists, why the whole estate
organization was stopped in 1933.[28]

The economic organization of Germany has, indeed, no resemblance to corporative or estate theories. Even the food estate and
the chamber of culture, which are both officially called estates,
do not have that character. They are not autonomous, but are
organs of the state. They do not operate from the bottom to the
top, but inversely. They do not regulate wages and labor conditions.
They are organizations of businessmen, excluding labor, controlled
by the state and performing certain administrative functions.

From this discussion it will be seen that there is no authoritative
body of National Socialist doctrines concerning the economic
organization of Germany. Hitler himself has repeatedly rejected
any blueprints, although, in *Mein Kampf*, he makes some flattering
remarks on estate ideology: 'We want to restore the primacy of
politics, which has the duty of organizing and leading the life battle
of the nation' (21 March 1933). 'Unemployment cannot be abolished
by economic committees, organizations, constructions, and theories'
(6 July 1933). The official commentator, mentioned above, formulates the attitude of the party in the following way: 'The freedom
from doctrines and dogmas . . . results in the fact that economic
policy in the national socialist state is determined by considerations
of expediency and, without prejudice, applies such means as are
necessary in every given case for the economic welfare of the
people.' [29]

There are, in consequence, considerable differences of opinion about the future structure of the National Socialist economy. Many see in the present regimentation of the economic system merely a transitional phase, conditioned by the requirements of war, and insist that after the war more economic freedom must be established. They believe this because, in their view, the economic organization of Germany is determined primarily by the specific situation of Germany, especially by its lack of raw materials.[30] Others are inclined to believe that perpetual state control may be the future of the German economic system. But no responsible National Socialist leader is out to expropriate private property and to substitute a socialist or a semi-socialist system (in the sense that we understand socialist) for that of a controlled or 'steered' capitalism. In short, no one adheres to the theory of state capitalism that we have discussed. This, of course, does not mean that the actual economic system is not non-capitalistic or that the inherent trends within the regime will not ultimately lead or have not already led to the dictatorship of the managerial bureaucracy. But such a goal is not the explicit aim of National Socialism.

II

THE ORGANIZATION OF BUSINESS

1. The Political Status of Business in the Weimar Republic

The extremely complex structure of National Socialist business organization can be much more easily understood if it is placed in an adequate historical context. By doing so, we shall at the same time find that National Socialism added little that is new to the already existing pattern of organization.

Ownership of the means of production exercises its function in a number of spheres,* especially in the labor market, the commodity market, and in the state. In the labor market, it operates as a hostile or friendly partner of labor organizations, either as an individual employer or as an employers' organization set up for the purpose of collective bargaining. In the commodity market, it operates as an individual entrepreneur, as a cartel, as a combine, or as a trust for fixing prices, sales, and purchasing conditions. In the state, business is organized in trade associations or estate associations for influencing the state's economic or financial policies. Business is in that case a political pressure group, which also elaborates machinery for advising and protecting its members and making their life within the increasing complexities of state regimentation more bearable than would otherwise be the case.

Corresponding to these three spheres of power are three different organizations, the prototypes of which are the employers' organization for the labor market, the cartel for the commodity market, and the *Fachverband* (trade association) for the political organization of business. In spite of the rather rigid distinction in the organizational set up, the three types are intertwined in personnel through interlocking management. In the small and medium-sized organizations, the cartel manager is, as a rule, at the same time manager of the employers' association and of the local or provincial *Fachverband*.

* See also p. 403.

This political organization of business was developed on a dual basis, territorial and functional. The territorial units were the chambers of industry and commerce (the chambers of handicraft), which were organizations under public law, in which membership was compulsory and the dues were collected like taxes. They possessed a considerable amount of self-government, and were supervised like any corporation under the public law, by the relevant state ministry. The officials of the chambers were elected by the members. The chambers represented the business in a particular territory, the president usually playing a considerable role in municipal life and in the organization of the stock exchange. The chambers were united in regional associations, which, however, had no public character, but were entirely private organizations—with the exception of the association of the handicraft chambers. The central organization of the chambers of industry and commerce in Germany was called the Diet of German Industry and Commerce. It was thus a so-called *Spitzenverband*,[1] that is, a top or holding organization, composed not of individual members, but of other, lower-ranking organizations.

The territorial organizations, were, therefore, the concern of every businessman. Whatever the size of his plant, he was accepted in the chambers, formally at least, on a basis of equality. His voting power was not in proportion to the size of his enterprise, and he could even play some role in the chamber, in some committee, as a publicly recognized expert before courts or administrative tribunals, and so on.

The real power of the political business organization did not, however, lie in the territorial, but rather in the functional division. Handicraft, agriculture, industry, trade, banking, and insurance were each organized in so-called *Spitzenverbänden*, composed of many affiliated associations. The most powerful among them was the *Reichsverband der Deutschen Industrie*, the Federal Union of German Industry, which, like most other *Spitzenverbände*, was founded in 1919 (3 February) as an attempt to safeguard business interests in what appeared to be a world torn by social revolution. The charter states that the Federal Union of German Industry is 'the representative of German industry in all questions of business and economic policy, and that it is in close collaboration with the federal union of German employers' organizations which is the representative of German industry in all social and socio-political questions.' It arose from the fusion of two industrial organizations, the Central Union of German Industry, founded in 1876, representing heavy industry, and the very ably led League of Industrialists, founded in 1895 and more or less identified with the light or processing industries. During the First World War, these two organizations came together in the war committee of German industry which, from 1918, was supported by the German industrial council. The composition of the *Reichsverband* was a mixture of functional and regional principles, but its largest affiliates were the so-called *Fachverbände*, amounting to 1,500 in 1931, which were embraced in 28 functional groups. But the union also incorporated individual entrepreneurs (1,400 in 1931) and very powerful territorial pressure groups such as the Bavarian union of industrialists, the association of Saxon industrialists, and, above all, the association for safeguarding the common economic interests of the Rhineland and Westphalia, popularly known as the 'long-name association.' * The *Fachverbände*, representing the kernel of the *Spitzenverbände*, were, in turn, the composite of many lower and smaller units. Each of them was, in fact, a network of many lower functional units. The size and significance of the Federal Union of German Industry may be gathered from the diversity and size of its organs. Besides the members' assembly, there was a *Hauptausschuss* or main committee, composed of 200 members, a directorate of between 205 and 220 persons with a presidency consisting of between 30 and 36, and a senate. The presidents were successively Dr. Sorge of the Krupp directorate, Dr. Duisberg of the dyestuff trust, and finally, Dr. Krupp von Bohlen and Halbach. The *Reichsverband* provided a number of services for its members, dealing with questions of economic policy, tariffs, imports, exports, money, finances, and reparations. One of the most important services was offered by the *Kartellstelle*, or cartel department, which functioned as an advisory and co-ordinating agency for all cartels, furnishing them legal and economic advice, working out master cartel agreements, and perpetually gearing the propaganda machine to the policy of the marketing organizations. The political organization of German business under the Weimar Republic was thus an imposing edifice, extending into almost every economic activity.

* See also p. 49.

COMMODITY MARKET
(*Marktregulierende* organizations)

LABOR MARKET

ENTER-PRISE	HORIZONTAL ORGANIZATIONS	VERTICAL ORGANIZATIONS	EMPLOYERS	EMPLOYEES
	the *cartel* The cartels are advised by the cartel department of the Federal Union of German Industry	the *Konzern* (combine) the *trust*	*Spitzenver-bände* in the following fields:	*Spitzenverbände* (also exercising 'political' f tions)
		Types:		*'Recognized'*

		a) combination of possessive functions: exchange of shares	a) Agriculture and Forestry	a) Socialists
				  I manual workers : ADGB
				  II salaried employees : Afa Bund
				  III civil servants : ADB—unimport

			b) Industry (*Vereinigung der Deutschen Arbeitgeber-verbände*)	b) Christian—National (DGB)
				  I manual workers : Gesamtverband
				  II salaried employees : Gedag (most in tant DHV)

		b) combination of administrative functions (interlocking directorates)	c) Trade	III civil servants : DBB c) Democrats (Hirsch-Duncker)—Gewerk-schaftsring
		c) combination of profits (pools—*Inter-essengemein-schaften*)	d) Banking	I manual workers : Verband deutsc Gewerkvereine unimportant
			e) Insurance	II salaried employees : GDA DBV (banking ployees) etc.

'Not Recognized'
a) RGO—communist
b) FAUD—revolutionary syndicalist
c) NSBO—national socialist
d) 'Yellow' organizations

STATE
(*Standes* organizations)

TERRITORIAL ORGANIZATION	FUNCTIONAL ORGANIZATION
) Chambers of *Agriculture* (in Bavaria: *easant Chambers). Public Law. Prussian entral Organization: *Preussische Haupt- ndwirtschafts-Kammer* (Prussian Main hamber of Agriculture). Public Law. Fed- ral Central Organization: *Deutscher Land- irtschaftsrat* (German Council for Agri- ulture). Private Law.	a) *Spitzenverband: Reichsausschuss der deutschen Landwirtschaft* (Federal Com- mittee of German Agriculture). Most impor- tant member: *Reichslandbund,* from merger of two organ- izations in 1921, composed of 30 functional organizations. Since 1929 member of Green Front, pres- sure group for higher agrarian tariffs
) Chambers of *Industry and Commerce.* ublic Law. Federal Central Organization: *eutscher Industrie-und Handelstag* (Diet German Industry and Commerce). Pri- te Law.	b) Spitzenverbände (1) *Reichsverband der Deutschen Industrie* (Federal Union of German Industry, 1919, composed of 'Fach- verbände') (2) *Reichsverband des Deutschen Gross- und Ueberseehandels* (Wholesale and Over- seas Trade) (3) *Hauptgemeinschaft des deutschen Ein- zelhandels* (Retail) 1919. Composed of 72 organizations. (4) *Zentralverband des deutschen·Bank-und Bankiergewerbes* (Bank) (5) *Reichsverband für Privatversicherung* (Insurance)
Chambers of *Handicraft.* Public Law. deral Central Organization: *eutscher Handwerks-und Gewerbetag* (Diet German Handicraft). Public Law. Super- ed by Federal Minister of Economics.	c) Spitzenverband: *Reichsverband des deutschen Handwerks.* 1919. (Handicrafts) Composed of: Guilds (organized under public law) free handicrafts organizations; and the cen- tral union of German handicrafts co-opera- tives
	d) *a—c* are co-ordinated in a super-*Spitzen- verband:* the *Zentralausschuss der Unterneh- merverbände* (Central Committee of Entre- preneurial Organizations) 1920. The Union of German Employers' Organizations is equally affiliated.

There was a very clear-cut division of labor between the political organizations and the employers' organizations. The employers' organizations were also organized in *Spitzenverbände*, five important ones, their leadership being vested in the industrial *Spitzenverband* of the employers' organizations, namely, *Die Vereinigung der deutschen Arbeitergeberverbände* (the union of German employers' organizations). The employers' 'peak' associations were not bargaining associations as such, since according to German law only labor-market organizations, composed of individual members, had the right to bargain collectively.[2] The union of German employers' organizations was thus a co-ordinating agency for all employers' associations in industry, advising them, working toward a common policy against the trade unions, and even offering the members financial protection against strikes by a strike-insurance corporation. The charter of the Federal Union of German Industry, which we have already mentioned, makes it clear that the two industrial peak organizations, one concerning the labor market and the other political, worked harmoniously with each other.

But even that centralization of associations did not go far enough. In 1920, all the peak organizations in agriculture, industry, trade, banking, insurance, and handicrafts, with the peak employers' organizations and some other industrial pressure groups, founded the central committee of entrepreneurial organizations (*Zentralausschuss der Unternehmerverbände*) in order to weld together all industrial activity in the face of the threat from the trade unions. The preceding picture will clarify the structure of German business organization.

2. The Political Organization of Business under National Socialism

The National Socialist structure of German business organization does not differ very much from that of the Weimar Republic. The provisional economic council, which had in reality ceased to operate long before, was formally dissolved on 23 March 1934, after a general council of economics (*Generalrat der Wirtschaft*) had been called together on 15 July 1933. It was a small body, having as its sole labor representative the leader of the German labor front, Dr.

Robert Ley. It met several times and listened to speeches, but did not develop any activity. The council soon became obsolete because of the new political organization of business.

This new form adhered to the already existing twofold division in territorial and functional units, streamlined the existing organization, expanded it, made it compulsory throughout, and introduced the leadership principle.[3] The structure of the National Socialist economic organization again rests on two pillars: a territorial and a functional one. The territorial units are once more the chambers of industry and commerce, and the chambers of handicraft, unchanged in composition. The functional units are, as before, the old *Spitzenverbände*, raised to the rank of compulsory bodies. The only exception is the organization of agricultural and food production, which has now a separate existence as the so-called food estate.

The basic law is that of 27 February 1934, for 'preparing an organic structure of the German economy,' authorizing the ministry of economics to dissolve and merge trade associations, to change their charters, to introduce the leadership principle, to take outsiders into the organizations, and to recognize the associations as the exclusive legitimate representatives of the relevant branches of trade and industry.

The first executive decree of 27 November 1934 created two new bodies. The first is the *national economic chamber*, the duty of which is to co-ordinate the territorial and the functional set-up. The same decree also created the *working community of the chambers of industry and commerce* as a peak association of the individual chambers. The chambers themselves were subjected to scarcely any change in this structure. The decree of 20 August 1934 merely laid down the leadership principle, and transferred the supervision of the chambers of industry and commerce to the federal ministry of economics.[4] The 7 July 1936 reform edict of the federal minister of economics streamlined the political organizations of business that had been created in the interval, and the 20 January 1937 ruling of the ministry instituted disciplinary courts within these organizations.* These edicts and decrees provide the basic legal structure for the autonomous political organization of business. The organization is now complete.

* See below, p. 425.

THE GROUPS

Every businessman must be a member of the national group (functional division) and of a chamber of industry (or handicraft) (territorial division). Even public enterprises, though in Prussia these do not belong to the chambers of industry, must join relevant groups, so that some groups such as those of the banks and public-insurance corporations consist entirely of public enterprises. Only the co-operatives are exempt. We should not, at this point, neglect to observe that the cartels, as organs of the commodity market, are not incorporated into this political structure of business. The relation between the cartel and the political organization will be discussed later.

The functional division rests on seven national groups that roughly correspond to the old *Spitzenverbände*. These groups are: (1) industry, (2) trade, (3) banking, (4) insurance, (5) power, (6) tourist industry, and (7) handicrafts. The six national transportation groups are separately organized. The national groups are divided into economic groups, 31 in industry, 4 in trade, 6 in banking, 2 in insurance, 2 in power, 1 in the tourist industry, while the handicrafts group is subdivided into 50 national guild organizations. While the national groups correspond roughly to the *Spitzenverbände*, the economic groups correspond to the *Fachverbände* within the federal union of German industry, or within the other peak associations. This identity and continuity is never hidden; on the contrary, it is stressed in the administrative pronouncements. Following is a sample of a decree of recognition issued by the federal minister of economics.[5]

Decree of the federal minister of economics for the recognition of the economic group of the wholesale import and export trade, 18 September 1934.

On the basis of paragraph 1 of the act of 27 February 1934 for preparing the organic structure of the German economy, I order: (1) the economic group of the wholesale import and export trade Berlin, W. 30, Mackensen Street 10 [national association of the German wholesale import and export trade; formerly national association of German wholesale and overseas trade] is to be recognized as the sole representative of its economic branch.

The recognition decree, therefore, simply takes over the existing trade association and recognizes it as the official representative of the whole branch.

The economic groups are further subdivided into branch groups (*Fachgruppen*), 327 now being in existence; and these, in turn, into sub-branch groups (*Unter-Fachgruppen*).

The organizational principle, as can readily be seen, is horizontal, and not vertical as in the food estate. The vertical principle combines everybody who is active in the production and distribution of certain commodities, down to the smallest retailer. By the recognition of the national trade group, therefore, the old horizontal principle is maintained. While the national and economic groups are constituted by statute of the federal ministry of economics, the branch and sub-branch groups are set up at the discretion of the national group. However, since the reform ruling of 1936, it is necessary to obtain permission from the federal minister of economics for the establishment of new branches and sub-branch groups and their provincial units.

The kernel of the whole structure is the economic group within the national group. The economic groups levy the contributions and finance the national groups on the one side and the branch and sub-branch groups on the other side. The differences in size and importance among the groups are, of course, considerable. While the economic group, which covers mining (within the national group embracing industry), has only 50 members, that covering the retail trade (within the national group embracing trade) comprises about 500,000 members.

THE CHAMBERS

This dual structure is now organized in three strata: an upper, a middle, and a lower.

At the top there is the national economic chamber, the successor, so to speak, to the provisional federal economic council. It is composed of the 7 national groups, 23 economic chambers, the 100 chambers of industry and commerce, and the 70 chambers of handicrafts.

Closely connected with the national economic chamber is the 'working community of the chambers of industry and commerce,' the successor, as can readily be seen, to the diet of German industry and commerce. This working community is, in fact, inactive, but it furnishes the personnel of the national economic chamber, and the leadership of the two top organizations is identical (the president of both is Pietzsch).*

The differences between the national economic chamber and the provisional economic council are, however, considerable. Labor and the consumers, the free professions, and the independent experts are completely excluded from the economic chamber, which is now exclusively a representative of business and handicrafts and is undisturbed by any alien influence. It is true that under the Leipzig agreement [6] of 1936,† concluded between the federal minister of economics, the federal minister of labor, and the leader of the German labor front, the national economic chamber entered the labor front as a corporate body, but, as we shall see later, this agreement was made merely to exclude labor from any voice in business control and regulation. In addition, the national economic chamber has been given what the federal economic council never had: executive machinery in the middle and lower strata. The most important members of the national economic chambers are the seven national groups.

The middle stratum, which is completely new, consists of the 23 economic chambers. They are composed of the chambers of industry and commerce in their province, of the chambers of handicrafts, and of the provincial economic groups. The economic chambers, therefore, also combine the functional and territorial principles. They represent all business in one province, creating a united front of business in relation to the provincial executive machinery of the state. In many cases the economic chambers are headed by the president of the largest chamber of industry in this province, and have become the decisive organs of industrial self-government since the decree of 27 October 1936. They are composed of six departments: (1) the department 'chambers of industry,' the co-ordinating agency for the chambers in the region; (2) the department 'industry,' which is the co-ordinating agency of the economic branch and sub-branch groups in the national group covering industry on the provincial level; (3) the department 'trade,' where the four subdivisions, retail, wholesale, import

* See below, p. 390.
† See below, p. 416.

and export trade, agents and peddling trade, are of greater significance than the department itself; (4) the department 'tourist industry'; (5) the department 'handicrafts chambers,' acting as the coordinating agency of the chambers of handicrafts in that province; (6) and finally, the provincial clearing office, which has assumed major significance, and which has a decisive influence on the distribution of public contracts among the members of the economic chambers. As a rule these clearing offices are directed by the president of the economic chamber and supervised by governmental commissioners. Each of the departments is presided over by a director, who is assisted by a council and acts through a manager; this manager is generally an industrialist who is the leader of the provincial group.

Side by side with the economic chambers are the provincial organizations of the economic groups (220), the branch groups (180), the sub-branch groups (270), the handicrafts, and the provincial guild organizations.

At the bottom are the chambers of industry and commerce (100), the chambers of handicrafts (70), the local bodies of the groups when such exist, and the guilds for handicraft.

The following chart clarifies this organizational set-up.

This whole structure is run in accordance with the leadership principle.* The leaders of the national economic chamber, of the economic chambers, of the chambers of industry, of the national groups and of the economic groups are proposed by the national group and appointed by the federal minister of economics, while the leaders of the branch and sub-branch groups are proposed by the leader of the economic groups and appointed by the leaders of their national groups. The members of the groups have to obey the orders of their leaders, and the leader of the economic group, as the central agency, can mete out disciplinary punishment to members breaking the law.

As in the political sphere, so in this economic activity the leadership principle is merely a euphemistic way of describing a centralized bureaucratic body, run on authoritarian principles. The leaders, mostly important businessmen, as we shall have occasion to see later,† do not, of course, manage the whole business; the groups

* See also p. 83.
† See below, p. 388.

THE AUTONOMOUS POLITICAL ORGANIZATION OF GERMAN BUSINESS

(Groups and Chambers—Except the Food Estate)

UPPER

National Economic Chamber ⟵⟶	Working Community of the Chambers of Industry and Commerce
Members: 1. National Groups (7) 2. Economic Chambers (23) 3. Chambers of Industry (100) 4. Chambers of Handicrafts (70)	Members: Chambers of Industry and Commerce (100) *inactive*

National Groups

1	2	3	4	5	6	7		
Industry	Trade	Banking	Insurance	Power	Tourist Industry	Handi-crafts	⟵⟶ Handi-crafts Diet	National Transport Groups (6)

Economic Groups

(31) (4) (6) (2)

National Guild Associations (50)

Branch Groups (328)
Sub-Branch Groups (327)

MIDDLE

The provincial organizations of the Economic, Branch, and Sub-Branch Groups	23 Economic Chambers	The Provincial Guild Organizations

MEMBERS
The Chambers of Industry
the Chambers of Handicraft
the provincial Economic Groups

DEPARTMENTS
1. Industry
2. Trade; with 4 sub-departments
3. Tourist Industry
4. Clearing (for public contracts)
5. Chambers of Industry
6. Chambers of Handicraft

LOWER

The local organization of the groups where such exist	100 Chambers of Industry and Commerce	70 Chambers of Handicrafts	The local Guilds

Members: Only individual firms

are run by managers who often are, in fact, the actual directors. Each of the leaders is surrounded by an advisory council composed of the group leaders, the presidents of the chambers of industry, representatives of the food estate, of the municipalities, and of the transport organization. Members' meetings no longer play any role, since the decree of 4 March 1935 permitted the leaders of the superior group to dispense with such meetings if the advisory council thought it appropriate.

This, in brief outline, is the autonomous political organization of German business as it had been shaped prior to the outbreak of the present war. From a juristic point of view, the organizations have a twofold task, as does every self-governing body in German law. They carry out genuine functions of self-government and they also carry out state functions that are delegated to them by the public authorities. Whether it is a municipality or a chamber of industry or a group, each operates in a twofold capacity: as a self-governing body and as an organ of the state.

This political organization of business faces in three directions: toward the commodity market, that is, the business activities carried out by individual enterprises, cartels, concerns, and trusts; toward the labor market; and toward the state.

THE EXECUTIVE MACHINERY OF THE STATE

The chief organ of the war economy is Göring. The two most important agencies are the Four Year Plan Office and the General Commissioner for Economics (Funk), who controls the whole economic life, except the armament industry. Funk, therefore, is not only minister of economics but at the same time is the chief of the ministers of labor, finance, food, and forestry. Prior to the outbreak of this war, the ministry of economics had no provincial and local executive machinery of its own. This defect has been remedied by the 'decree on the administration of the economy' of 27 August and 28 November 1939. It creates regional and executive machinery of the ministry of economics.

The general commissioner for economics has created *Führungsstäbe der Wirtschaft*, leadership staffs for the economy, which are attached to the provincial presidents in Prussia and to the federal regents and state ministries in the other states. These leadership staffs co-ordinate all activities in the realm of economics (outside the armament industries proper) and are made superior to the regional organizations of the ministries of labor, food, forestry, to the economic chambers, to all regional bodies of the groups and handicraft associations, and to the chambers of industry and handicraft. While the *Führungsstäbe* are mere co-ordinating agencies, the very same decree now creates a regional and local set-up for the ministry of economics in the eighteen *Bezirkswirtschaftsämter* (regional economic offices) and the local *Wirtschaftsämter*, primarily concerned with the rationing of consumers' goods.

The leadership of these eighteen offices has been entrusted to various officials, such as the Prussian provincial presidents, federal regents, or sub-provincial presidents. These provincial economic chiefs, who also head the *Führungsstäbe*, are subordinates of the minister of economics, may issue orders to all public authorities belonging to the middle stratum, to the groups, and to the chambers of industry and of handicrafts. The provincial economic offices form a part of the office in which they have been established. Thus no new organization has been set up, but the old machinery is utilized. The eighteen provincial economic offices can direct the whole economic activity in their province. This authoritarian trend has been facilitated by the creation of federal commissioners for each chamber of industry and commerce, and by the power of the minister of economics to delegate to the chambers any activity that he thinks suitable. Federal commissioners are subject to the commands of the provincial economic chiefs. Legally, therefore, there is now a complete centralization of the whole economic administration. The federal commissioner for economics is superior to the ministers of economics, finance, labor, food, forestry. He operates in the eighteen districts through the provincial economic offices, as well as locally through the federal commissioners of the chambers of industry and commerce.

But the decree goes still further. It creates, in addition, provincial food offices (*Landes-* or *Provinzernährungsämter*), set up in the offices of the supreme organs of the various states (in Prussia, in the office of the provincial presidents), and also subjects the whole food estate to the commands of the federal minister for food and agriculture. The same authoritarian organization is carried out in forestry by means of provincial forest and timber offices.

At the bottom, the same process is repeated.

The first executive decree (27 August, 22 September 1939) defines and clarifies the extent of power vested in the new organizations, the eighteen economic offices. They are made subject to various federal organs and may give orders to the following organizations: the state mining agencies; the economic chambers, including their clearing * departments; the chambers of industry; the chambers of handicrafts; the provincial groups (national, economic, branch, and sub-branch groups); the federal offices for foreign trade; and the currency offices. They are called upon to secure production, to protect indispensable trades and handicrafts, to co-operate in safeguarding the supply of electric power, to execute measures concerning the consumption of coal, oil, rubber, textile materials, and soap, and to organize the collection of used materials. The same decree makes the presidents of the chambers of industry and commerce federal commissioners for the chambers, which are thus transformed into executive agents for the whole field within the jurisdiction of the provincial economic offices.

It is evident that the most important agency in the state organization is the federal ministry of economics. Since February 1938, its chief has been Walther Funk, who is also president of the *Reichsbank*. The ministry is divided into five main departments.†

MACHINERY OF RATIONALIZATION

Parallel to the ministry, and in some ways still more important, is the office of the Four Year Plan, headed by the marshal of the *grossdeutsche Reich*, Hermann Göring, who, in this capacity, has the title of general deputy for the Four Year Plan. The Four Year Plan office carries out its functions partly within the ministry of economics, partly through general deputies (*Generalbevollmächtigte*) for specific branches of trade and industry, and partly through its own office.

This office was originally (in 1936) the central agency of a preparedness economy, a kind of planning organization. It has transferred most of its functions to other agencies and is now primarily concerned with two tasks: the rationalization of specific branches of German industry—which is mainly carried out through the general deputies—and the gaining of key economic positions for

* See p. 245.
† See below, p. 371, on its composition.

the party (such as the Hermann Göring works). Göring has appointed Funk as the supervising agent for the whole field of rationalization.

The general deputies are primarily organs for raising the efficiency of a specific trade, by recommending measures of rationalization, standardization, and reorganization. The most important are: the general deputies for power (at present Mayor Dillgardt of Essen, who is at the same time leader of the national power group No. 5); for motor vehicles (at present Colonel v. Schell); for machine production (at present Karl Lange, manager of the V.B.M.A. under the Weimar Republic and also manager of the economic group); for special functions in the chemical industry (at present Professor K. Krauch, member of the board of managers of the Dyetrust); and for iron and steel (Lieutenant General von Hanneken, also chief of the main department II of the ministry of economics).

There is also a special deputy for building construction, whose function is wider than those of the other deputies. As early as 9 December 1938 Göring appointed the inspector general for German roads, Dr. F. Todt, 'general deputy for the regulation of building constructions.'[7] (Dr. Todt is also munitions minister.) * His task was to adjust the civil building construction to military needs and to carry out such measures as were necessary to increase the efficiency of the building industry. He has very wide powers, and is also authorized to allocate building materials (iron, timber, cement) and to establish a system of priorities. The rationing of building materials has been simplified by making certain central offices quota offices. This means that the labor front, the labor ministry, the ministry of communications, and so on, are, as quota offices, entitled to receive supplies of building materials for their affiliated organizations and enterprises. If, for instance, a steel manufacturer wants to start building construction and needs building materials, he has to apply to his quota office, that is, in this case, the federal ministry of economics, main department number II.

The general deputy for the building industry also operates through regional deputies (21), who, according to the decree of 30 December 1939, are entitled to demand information from all

* Now also minister for electric power.

public and party authorities. The general deputy for the building industry also appoints confidential officials in certain lower-ranking territorial units.

CONTROL OF RAW MATERIALS

The supply of raw materials and the establishment of priorities have been completely taken away from the Four Year Plan office and transferred to the ministry of economics, which, for this task, has set up *Reichsstellen* for specific branches, based on the decree on commodity exchange (*Warenverkehr*) of 18 August 1939, which in turn had originated in 'supervisory boards' for imports and exports, based on the decree of 4 September 1934. The *Reichsstellen* are federal agencies, with legal independence, financed by fees or permanent contributions that the industries concerned have to pay for specific activities. They are headed by a federal deputy (*Reichsbeauftragter*). They are, to repeat, solely concerned with rationing and thereby also with foreign trade.

Some examples may clarify the nature of their task.

By a decree of 13 August 1934, a 'supervisory office for iron and steel' was created, which is now a *Reichsstelle*.[8] The 'federal agency for iron and steel' may issue orders for the registration of material. It may regulate production and issue a number of restrictions. The orders of the *Reichsstellen* are numbered. They fall into four categories, the most important of which are the so-called 'directives,' which establish quota systems. The directive number 25 of 25 January 1940 contains a codification of this quota system creating various types of quotas, and defining the bodies that act as quota agents. In this case, it is primarily the economic groups that are the quota agents. A steel industrialist who needs iron or steel or any other material has to submit his demand to his economic group, which then decides whether or not he is to receive the supply.

There is a similar agency for paper,[9] created in September 1934 as a supervisory agency, now simply a *Reichsstelle*. This federal agency began as an office for restricting the import of cellulose, but of necessity it soon became an agency for the complete control of imports and of production. It issues regulations for purchasing, processing, packing, and for the collection and utilization of old paper and packing material. It has, since the outbreak of the war, attached all paper stocks. It has finally caused the whole paper industry to organize into eight cartels. With the consent of the federal minister of economics, two 'war deputies for packing and paper material' have been appointed.

There are at present 31 *Reichsstellen*, 25 of them in industry proper.

Since the scarcity of raw materials was the most important problem of the German economy prior to this war, and, is especially so during the war itself, the function of the *Reichsstellen* has assumed paramount significance. They are the most influential federal offices for organizing specific branches of industry, and for war needs, especially for rationing of raw materials and for establishing a priorities system. But the *Reichsstellen* have no executive organs of their own, and they could not cope with the enormous amount of work involved. Since the fall of 1939, they have therefore begun to set up the so-called *Verteilungsstellen* or distributing agencies. The task of the agencies is to carry out the rationing system within each specific industrial branch—that is, to allocate to the various industrial enterprises such raw materials as may be needed and are at hand.

In the fall of 1939, the *Reichsstelle* for the coal industry created twelve such distributing agencies, corresponding to and having the same personnel as the twelve coal syndicates. The coal syndicates thereby became the distributing offices, determining how much coal is to be allocated to each consumer.[10]

In the paper industry, the *Reichsstelle* operates, as we have seen, through two war deputies, but also through the numerous distributing agencies, which are here, too, identical with the cartels,[11] so that we have a complete identity between the business organization of the paper industry (the cartels), the political organization of the paper industry (the branch groups), and the state agency for allocating paper (the distributing offices).

The set-up in the textile industry is somewhat different. In this industry there are six such *Reichsstellen*, which, however, are co-ordinated by a 'special deputy for yarn.' The six *Reichsstellen* have also set up distributing offices, but in this case the *Reichsstellen* could not fall back upon the cartels, since there are practically no price cartels. Because of this, the branch and sub-branch groups have been made distributing agencies.[12]

WAR ORGANIZATION OF THE GERMAN ECONOMY

Decree 27 Aug./28 Nov. 1939

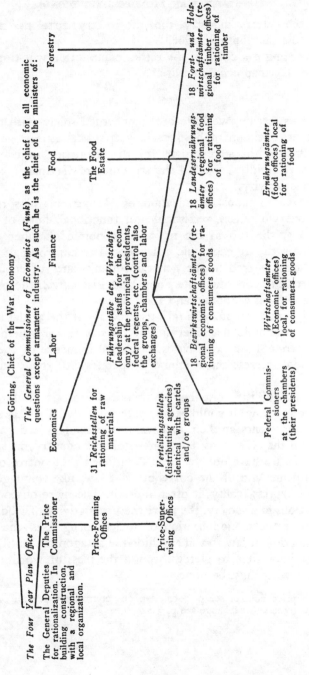

Göring, Chief of the War Economy

The General Commissioner of Economics (Funk) as the chief for all economic questions except armament industry. As such he is the chief of the ministers of:

Economics — Labor — Finance — Food — Forestry

The Four Year Plan Office

The Price Commissioner

The General Deputies for rationalization. In building construction, with a regional and local organization.

Price-Forming Offices

Price-Supervising Offices

31 *Reichsstellen* for rationing of raw materials

Verteilungsstellen (distributing agencies) identical with cartels and/or groups

Führungsstäbe der Wirtschaft (leadership staffs for the economy) at the provincial presidents, federal regents, etc. (control also the groups, chambers and labor exchanges)

Federal Commissioners at the chambers (their presidents)

The Food Estate

18 *Bezirkswirtschaftsämter* (regional economic offices) for rationing of consumers goods

18 *Landesernährungsämter* (regional food offices) for rationing of food

18 *Forst- und Holzwirtschaftsämter* (regional timber offices) for rationing of timber

Wirtschaftsämter (Economic offices) local, for rationing of consumers goods

Ernährungsämter (food offices) local for rationing of food

In the battery industry, too, the battery cartel has simply been made the distributing office.

Preceding is a chart of the rather complicated war-time organization of German economic life.*

SUMMARY

In this section, we have been concerned solely with the autonomous organization of business in its political aspects and with the structure of the state organs for the regulation of economic life. We have rigidly excluded the structure of German business in its business activity.

The autonomous organization of German business rests, as we saw, on two pillars, territorial and functional, both of which are united at the top in the national economic chamber and in the middle in the 23 economic chambers. The controlling influence of the state is vested in the general commissioner of economics, the ministry of economics, the Four Year Plan office, the new provincial, and local economic and food offices.

This structural analysis tells us little about the actual functioning of the economic machinery. Nor does it reveal whether markets still operate, how extensive is the actual influence of the state, and in whose interest the machinery operates. All these questions are basic.

In theory, the state has unlimited power. It could legally do almost anything; it could expropriate anybody. If we take such legal pronouncements at their face value we shall indeed gain the impression that Germany is a state-capitalist country, in spite of the fact that we have not yet even mentioned the control of labor, of investments, and of the currency. But law, like language, does not always express reality; it often hides it. The more obvious the contradictions in a society, the more the productivity of labor increases, the more the monopolization of society progresses—the more it is the function of law to veil and hide the antagonisms until it becomes almost impossible to pierce through the mass of words. Yet this is exactly what must be done.

* On price control see p. 305; on profit control see p. 316; on control of foreign trade and exchange see p. 327.

III

THE MONOPOLISTIC ECONOMY

1. PROPERTY AND CONTRACT

(ECONOMICS AND POLITICS)

To understand the nature of the National Socialist economic system, a few considerations on the relation between property and contract will prove helpful. What is capitalism? How do we define it? Many identify capitalism with freedom of trade and contract, that is, with free competition. Capitalism is defined as an economy that is continuously maintained by the free initiative of a large number of entrepreneurs competing in a free market. It is thereby identified with one phase of its development, competitive capitalism. In that phase, free competition is held to be the distinguishing mark. This theory of capitalism is to a certain extent the classical one, though it has highly significant differences.

We propose to illustrate the nature of the economic system by an examination of the institution of property.[1] By an institution, we mean an authoritarian or co-operative enduring association of men or of men and property, for the continuation of social life. This definition is purely descriptive. It has nothing to do with institutionalist philosophies, with pluralism, neo-Thomism, or syndicalism. Our definition covers all kinds of institutions: family, property, foundations, et cetera. Above all, it defines the major institution of modern society, private property in the means of production. Property, for a lawyer, is merely a subjective right that one man has against all others. It endows the proprietor with absolute defensive rights. The scope of man's power over the things he owns is, in principle, unlimited. The owner is a sovereign.

But the sociologist has to distinguish between various types of property. The man who owns a house in which he lives, furniture which he uses, clothes which he wears, food which he eats, an automobile which he drives, has no other power than the direct possession of the things he owns. He does not by virtue of his ownership control other men's lives. Houses, food, clothes, and automobiles are not institutions, are not intended to endure. They disappear or become valueless as they are consumed or used.

There is, however, a second type of property which is an institution, because it is an enduring and authoritarian organization for the perpetuation and reproduction of society: property of the means of production. In our language, domination over means of consumption and means of production is called by the same name: 'property'; the term has thus become the legal mask behind which the owner of the means of production exercises power over other men. The term property (and ownership) never indicates what kind of object and what kind of power lies behind it, whether it is restricted to control over things or whether it also gives control over the fate of men. Property in the means of production gives power: power over workers, power over the consumers, power over the state. Property in the means of production is enduring, it aids in the continuous reproduction of society, it is the primary institution of modern society.

According to liberal ideas, if society is continuously to reproduce itself, there must be a free market. The prime requisites of the free market are free entrepreneurs, freedom of contract, and freedom of trade. The owner must be able to sell and to purchase, to lend and to borrow, to hire and to dismiss. Freedom of contract is, therefore, a supplementary or auxiliary guarantee of private property. It makes it possible for the owner of the means of production to produce and distribute. A competitive society must also be based on freedom of trade, the right to carry on one's business without interference and to establish a competing business. Freedom of trade is therefore another supplementary or auxiliary guarantee of property during the era of free competition. It, too, aids in the reproduction of society. In the process of competition, unfit competitors are thrown out, new establishments arise. Disturbances in equilibrium eliminate entrepreneurs who are not sufficiently rational in the conduct of their business; higher profits in one branch attract capital from other branches, thereby preserving the dynamic quality of a competitive society. Freedom of trade and freedom of contract are thus integral elements in a competitive society.

Hence property is surrounded by supplementary and auxiliary

guarantees and by supplementary and auxiliary institutions, which make the operation of this major institution possible. They are at the service of the major institution, property, and are, in consequence, changed when the institution changes its function. Thus they are not merely juristic categories, as they are conceived to be today. The natural lawyers of the seventeenth century and the classical economists of the eighteenth century clearly realized that freedom of contract and freedom of trade are not simply legal categories but exercise specific social functions. Present-day apologists of economic liberalism maintain that freedom of contract implies the right to establish industrial combinations, to erect cartels, concerns, and trusts. They believe that freedom of trade exists even when a branch of industry is so completely monopolized that freedom of trade becomes a mere formal right. They maintain that competition implies the right to eliminate competing businesses and to establish the prerogative of a monopolistic group.

This was not the view held by the classical economists. 'One individual must never prefer himself so much even to any other individual as to hurt or injure that other in order to benefit himself, though the benefit of the one should be much greater than the hurt or injury of the other.' 'In the race for wealth and honor and preferment, each may run as hard as he can and strain every nerve and every muscle in order to outstrip all his competitors, but if he should justle or throw down any of them, the indulgence of the spectators is entirely at an end.' [2] In these statements, Adam Smith introduces a distinction between two kinds of competition, one based on efficiency and the other based on the destruction of the competitor. He does not tolerate unfettered competition, since, in the theory of Adam Smith, competition is more than a right of the entrepreneur: it is the basic device for the continuous reproduction of society on an ever higher level. But this necessarily presupposes the absence of monopolies. Freedom of contract does not imply the right to establish industrial combinations; freedom of contract is the form of 'free commodities.' Where the commodities are not free, where they are monopolized, governmental interference must take place. 'For a free commodity . . . there is no occasion for this [governmental interference], but it is necessary for bakers who may agree among themselves to make the quantity and prices what they please.' [3]

Yet the assumptions under which the classical economists are willing to guarantee freedom are still wider in character. They refer to the basic institution of society, to private property. Monopolies are repudiated as incompatible with the economic and social system, exceptions being allowed only for colonies, and even here only for a transitional period. As for the laws passed during the mercantilist period for protecting monopolies—'like the laws of Draco, these laws may be said to be written in blood.' [4] Even the joint stock corporation is rejected in principle and allowed only for four economic activities: banking, insurance, the building and navigation of canals, and the water supply of great cities.[5] It is characteristic of the profound sociological insight of Adam Smith that he considers joint stock corporations legitimate only because in these activities the initiative of the entrepreneur has become unnecessary since the economic activity has been reduced to a mere routine.

The mechanism of the classical system is based, therefore, on the assumption of a large number of entrepreneurs of about equal strength, freely competing with each other on the basis of freedom of contract and freedom of trade, with the entrepreneur investing his capital and his labor for the purpose of his economic ends, and bearing the economic risks involved.

In this stage of society, freedom of contract was indeed the means by which society was held together. The contract was then the form through which the owner exercised his liberty and it was at the same time the means of ending the isolation in which each owner finds himself. 'To bring about that I may own property, not only by means of a thing and my own subjective will but by means of another will and thereby a common will—this constitutes the sphere of contract.' [6] In Hegel's words, therefore, contract is the form in which society recognizes property and by which the property owners constitute society.

It is characteristic of the later development of capitalism that it completely divorced the juristic categories of freedom of contract and freedom of trade from the socio-economic background and thereby made the juristic categories absolute. Freedom of contract, the means by which free competition was secured, became the device by which it has been destroyed. Legal theory and practice, even more so in Europe than in the United States, separated the legal notion 'freedom of trade' from the socio-economic requirements. Freedom of contract became the means of and the justification for the formation of industrial combinations, announcing the end of free competition. In the same way, freedom of trade degenerated into a mechanism for maintaining economic privileges and prerogatives. Its existence was asserted even in those branches of industry in which, because of the immense capital investment in one plant, no outsider could hope to establish a competing business, since he could not put up the necessary capital. Freedom of trade was perverted into a slogan for the defense of economic prerogatives and against state intervention.

This is one side of the development, but there is a second which is perhaps still more characteristic. Freedom of contract, although long disputed, implies the right to form trade unions and to oppose the power of the monopolist by the collective power of labor. Freedom of trade also implies the right of any entrepreneur to leave a combination and to re-establish his economic freedom, thereby endangering monopolistic possessions. Although it has lost much of its actual content, it still allows the establishment of competing business, once again endangering monopolistic privileges. These rights assume an especially dangerous form of monopolistic privileges in periods of recession and depression. The more perfect and rigid the structure of the economy becomes, the more sensitive it is to cyclical changes. A severe depression will inevitably shatter monopolistic positions. Cartels will be dissolved, outsiders will remain aloof, labor unions will fight off cuts in wages, protected by the sanctity of contracts. In such periods, the free contract, the freedom to keep aloof from the monopolists, turns into a major weapon against them.

Moreover, the new technology requires enormous investments, which involve risks and may give but uncertain returns.* Only rich and powerful corporations will be able to make such investments, and their willingness to do so will depend upon what protection they receive—against cut-throat competition and the chiseler, even against competition as such. They may—and do—even demand specific guarantees from the state, in the form of guarantees of profit or turnover, of permission to write off investments in a short time, even in the form of outright subsidies. Outsiders, new competitors,

* See p. 277.

labor unions—all these manifestations of freedom of trade and contract are then a nuisance. They must be destroyed.

For both sides, therefore—for the large masses and the small businessman on the one hand and the monopolistic powers on the other—state intervention in economic life becomes the major problem. The large masses and the small businessman will call in the state machinery for their protection. They will demand interference in the freedom of contract and freedom of trade in order to halt monopolization or even to dissolve existing industrial combines. By that demand they are merely drawing the consequences of the views of the classical economists. But in this situation monopolists will demand abrogation of freedom of contract and freedom of trade. They will insist that the right of industrial enterprises to leave cartels or to stay aloof from them means ruin for the economic system. They will point out that the freedom of labor to organize increases the costs of production and thereby the price of commodities. They will therefore demand complete abrogation of economic liberty.

In the period of monopolization, the new auxiliary guarantee of property is no longer the contract but the administrative act, the form in which the state interferes. But because that is so, it is the form and the content of the interventionist measure that now assumes supreme importance. Who is to interfere and on whose behalf becomes the most important question for modern society. The possession of the state machinery is thus the pivotal position around which everything else revolves. This is the only possible meaning of primacy of politics over economics. Shall the state crush monopolistic possessions, shall it restrict them for the sake of the masses, or shall interference be used to strengthen the monopolistic position, to aid in the complete incorporation of all business activities into the network of industrial organizations? Shall the state become the weapon by which the masses will be made completely subservient to the policies of the industrial empires within it?

The aims of the monopolistic powers could not be carried out in a system of political democracy, at least not in Germany. The Social Democratic party and the trade unions, though they had lost their aggressive militancy, were still powerful enough to defend their gains. Their defensive strength made it impossible to place the whole machinery of the state at the service of one particular group in society. Similarly, the National Socialist party could not possibly carry out its economic policy on a democratic basis. Its propaganda and program were ostensibly aimed at protecting the small and medium-scale entrepreneur, handicraftsman, and trader—that is, those very groups that have suffered most under the National Socialist regime. The complete subjugation of the state by the industrial rulers could only be carried out in a political organization in which there was no control from below, which lacked autonomous mass organizations and freedom of criticism. It was one of the functions of National Socialism to suppress and eliminate political and economic liberty by means of the new auxiliary guarantees of property, by the command, by the administrative act, thus forcing the whole economic activity of Germany into the network of industrial combinations run by the industrial magnates.

The German economy of today has two broad and striking characteristics. It is a monopolistic economy—*and* a command economy. It is a private capitalistic economy, regimented by the totalitarian state. We suggest as a name best to describe it, 'Totalitarian Monopoly Capitalism.'

2. The Cartel Policy of National Socialism

THE BRÜNING DICTATORSHIP AND THE CARTEL

The first stage of the National Socialist cartel policy is a direct verification of our thesis. The cartel system, gravely endangered during the great depression, has been saved by National Socialism. Before analyzing National Socialist cartel policy, it will be helpful to make a few preliminary remarks about the depression policy of the Brüning, Papen, and Schleicher administrations.

In 1930, the government was faced with a dilemma. It could attack the existing cartel system, dissolve the cartels, and bring prices down to the world-market level, or it could maintain the existing system at the expense of the large masses of consumers. This dilemma could not be solved by the successive governments between 1930 and 1933 because none of them had a parliamentary majority. The cartel policy of the period 1930-33 was therefore characterized by the most contradictory features. It began with a presidental decree of 26 July 1930, which was directed against the system of bound or fixed prices. This decree gave the cabinet power to void existing cartel agreements or portions of them and to enjoin cartels from carrying out certain practices. This not only covered genuine cartel agreements but also, for the first time, vertical agreements, that is to say, individual contracts between producers, wholesalers, and retailers for the purpose of fixing and maintaining a price structure. Further, all agreements and devices with similar economic effects, even if they did not fall strictly within the range of the decree, were actually covered by it, and this included agreements between independent producers, or associations of entrepreneurs. Finally, the cabinet was empowered to lower or abolish tariffs in order to facilitate the dissolution of cartels or reductions in prices. The official press release that accompanied the decree stated: 'It is generally agreed that the real adjustment of artificially fixed prices to the altered economic situation and to the decline in purchasing power as well as to the burden of such business circles as are engaged in unrestricted competition, is proceeding at too slow a pace and in too limited a degree.' The release, besides, reproached the cartels for the dislocation in the relation between prices and services, and asserted that recovery was hindered by the cartel and price system. This emergency decree, taken at its face value, constitutes a considerable step toward an active economic policy. It freed the federal government from any control by the cartel tribunal, and the government could now act without filing a motion with the cartel tribunal. In this way the cartel policy could be completely co-ordinated with the general governmental economic policy. Yet the results of the decree were extraordinarily meager. Only one cartel was dissolved, the lignite cartel, and that because it had been attacked for many years and had been investigated by a special professorial commission which charged it with wholly unreasonable practices. The decisive power that the emergency decree gave to the federal government, to abolish or lower tariffs in order to break down cartel prices, was never utilized.

The failure of the emergency decree soon led the government to seek other ways of breaking the cartel price structure. On the basis of the presidential emergency act, the cabinet issued on 16 January 1931 a decree attacking the price structure of trade-marked articles. All price agreements on trade-marked articles were voided unless the prices were cut down by 10 per cent below the level of 1 July 1930. They were also voided if the price agreements prevented wholesalers and retailers from granting their customers such additional discounts as they were allowed to grant on 1 July 1930. Certain commodities were exempted from the decree, which also prohibited punitive measures against organizations, especially co-operatives, which granted their members certain rebates. Since this decree was restricted to trade-marked articles, it did not, of course, affect the price structure to any marked extent.

For this reason, on 8 December 1931 the president issued the fourth emergency decree, lowering all fixed prices to 10 per cent below their level on 30 June 1931; at the same time wages fixed by collective agreements were reduced proportionately. Brüning's ominous deflationist policy was now under way. This fourth emergency decree also appointed a price commissioner for supervising the prices of those commodities and services that were important in daily needs. An executive decree of the same date defined the precise powers of the commissioner. If prices were too high, he could lower them. Violators could be punished by imprisonment and fines. The commissioner could close down a plant if the owner was unreliable. He could order that prices in plants and stores be posted or that price tags be affixed to commodities. In a very small field of commodities and services, the commissioner thus had full powers to do whatever he thought best. But this system, too, proved a complete failure. The trade associations refused to co-operate, although they did not make an open attack. An analysis of the rulings of the commissioner shows, for instance, that he set maximum fees for chimney sweeps, a concession to the house owners whose support the cabinet needed. He lowered the price of bottled and draught beer, a concession to the separationist Bavarians, for whom beer is food. He lowered the price of wall paper, mineral water, and sea food. He issued a large number of rulings ordering the posting of price laws and labels. But that is all he did.

With the one exception of reducing the price level by 10 per cent no effective measures were or could be taken by the three pre-Nazi semi-dictatorial governments of Brüning, von Papen, and von Schleicher. Their policy was that of a tightrope walker over a deep abyss.

THE PURGE OF THE CHISELER

The National Socialist regime came to power 30 January 1933 and at once initiated a cartel policy that satisfied all the requirements of the industrial combines. The first cartel decree was issued on 15 July 1933. Whereas the cartel emergency decree of 26 July 1930 was merely an emergency act, the statute of 15 July 1933 permanently changed the cartel decree of 1923. It eliminated the cartel tribunal from all actions that the government intended to take against cartels, restricting its sphere to disputes between members, and members and outsiders. German industry had always attacked section 9 of the cartel decree, the so-called preventive censorship on boycotts, and similar measures. The statute of 1933 changed section 9 by adding a new paragraph:

No unreasonable restriction on economic freedom [of the firm against whom the boycott is threatened] exists, if the business of the party concerned is managed by persons who do not possess the reliability necessary in business. Unreliability exists if, in the business of the party concerned, commodities and services . . . are offered or sold at prices which must be held to be economically unjustified in view of the interests of the business as well as those of the national economy or of the common welfare, and if a continuation of such price practices is to be expected.

The new statute thus allows cartels to destroy unreliable competitors by means of boycotts or similar measures. It aims at the exclusion of all unreliable businessmen from the economic system, and it finds unreliability wherever a competitor sells below justified prices, even if he is not bound by any price agreement. The price-cutter can thus be exterminated by private power with the sanction of the state. However, the extermination of the price-cutter is not provided for in a planned or direct manner. It is not the state that purifies the economic system. The death sentence is pronounced by a private organization, although the president of the cartel tribunal has to give his consent.

This purification is directed exclusively against the small retailer, wholesaler, and handicraftsman. It is a regular feature of the National Socialist policy of elimination of the inefficient businessman, that is, the businessman whose plant is not big enough to give him a decent living or materially to contribute toward preparedness and war. At this stage, we shall confine ourselves to drawing attention to the purification carried out by the cartels sanctioned by the state, and not by the state itself; two such examples must suffice. The cartel agreement in the German radio industry of August 1934 and February 1936 [7] provides that only recognized wholesalers and retailers may be supplied with receiving sets and that no new traders may be admitted. In consequence, the number of wholesalers declined from about 800-900 in 1933 to 598 in 1939, while within the year 1938 the number of retailers declined from 31,800 to 27,590.[8] Recognition is given only to a reliable trader, that is, one who is personally, economically, and financially reliable. To be financially reliable, a wholesaler must have a capital of at least 30,000 marks and he must provide this out of his own means, and may not, therefore, borrow it. The solution in the cigarette industry is just as extreme. According to the cartel charter of 31 December 1938,[9] only retailers who have an annual average tobacco turnover valued at not less than 5,000 marks are entitled to be supplied directly by the manufacturer. In the case under review, the federal economic tribunal (which has taken the place of the cartel tribunal, now dissolved) denied that right to a grocer and innkeeper, although there was but one tobacco outlet in his village and although the application was supported by the local National Socialist leader. These two examples indicate clearly that the newly won organizational power of the cartel is utilized for 'combing out' the small businessman.

The position of the 'unreliable businessman' was further endangered by the weakening of the preventive censorship. An executive decree of 5 September 1934 declared that the filing of a motion with the cartel tribunal, whether by members or by outsiders, against intended boycotting measures no longer had suspensive effect. The organizational power of the cartel was, by the statute of 15 July 1933 enormously strengthened.

COMPULSORY CARTELLIZATION

On the same date, a second cartel statute was enacted, introducing compulsory cartellization. The federal minister of economics was given the power to create compulsory cartels, to compel outsiders to attach themselves to existing cartels, to prohibit the erection of new enterprises and the extension of existing enterprises either in size or capacity, and to regulate the capacity of existing plants. No indemnification is allowed for damages arising out of such acts.

Compulsory cartellization is nothing new in German economic history. We mention only the coal and potash cartels and compulsory cartels for starch, matches, milk, beet sugar, inland navigation, and corn. But the previous compulsory cartels were always based on special statutes, and thereby subject to parliamentary debate and parliamentary control, whereas the statute of 15 July 1933 gives the minister of economics unlimited and arbitrary power of compulsory cartellization. It is not surprising that we find identical laws in Italy (June 1932) and in Japan (April 1931).

What are the aims of this decree? The official press release bears out our view that cartels are organized forms of waste. It says: 'The severe depression hanging over the German economy has struck most severely at those branches of industry that have a productive capacity far in excess of present marketing possibilities. Intensified competition and the low price level resultant therefrom . . . have brought nearer the point at which the ruin of enterprises valuable to our national economy is threatened.' In consequence, compulsory cartellization is necessary. The state must receive greater power in order to prevent the closing down of plants and the slashing of prices, to preserve such enterprises and such industries that are endangered by competition because they are overcapitalized and have excess capacity. Three different powers are thus vested in the minister of economics—the creation of new compulsory cartels, the attachment of outsiders to existing cartels, and the prohibition both of new establishments and of the extension of existing plant capacity. Private organizations for restricting capacity and for subordinating whole industries to the wishes and commands of the monopolistic rulers have thereby received official sanction. The National Socialist state thus brought to its logical conclusion a development initiated many decades ago, namely, that the organization of industry in cartels is a better and higher form of industrial organization. An intelligent National Socialist economist summed up: 'The compulsory order, with the help of the state's sovereignty, gives the cartel a power which it could not obtain on a voluntary basis.' [10]

The compulsory-cartellization decree is again primarily directed against the small and medium-scale businessmen, who are often reluctant voluntarily to join the cartel and thus are now completely subordinated to the demands of the powerful concerns. Resistance to cartellization also arises out of the antagonism between pure and mixed plants, that is, between enterprises producing but a single type of commodity and vertical concerns turning out the whole range of raw materials, production goods, and consumer commodities. It is again against the independent businessman that the new power of the state is applied. This is a direct contravention of the official cartel ideology, which considers cartels as organizations for protecting small and medium-scale businessmen.

A National Socialist investigation into the application of the compulsory cartellization decree up to 1937 confirms our point of view.[10] There are dozens, nay, hundreds of such decrees prohibiting the establishment of new plants or the extension of existing ones or compulsorily creating cartels. In the cement industry, for instance, the old dream of the cement magnates has finally come true. For years, the cement cartels fought bitter and expensive fights against outsiders, who, attracted by the high profits that the cartel structure made possible, established new mills or merely threatened to do so, which they could easily do since the raw material is plentiful and the capital requirement low. Millions had to be sacrificed by the cartels to buy off such actual or would-be competitors. On 12 December 1940,[11] the four regional cement cartels were compulsorily joined to a German cement union covering the whole territory and comprising every manufacturer. The paper industry was protected by a decree prohibiting the creation of new or the expansion of existing plants.[12] The printing industry, which has suffered severely since Dr. Goebbels monopolized printing, was protected by a compulsory cartellization, thus prohibiting outsiders from underbidding.[13] In the course of the purification of the retail and wholesale business, which we shall discuss later, the order of 15 January 1940 prohibited with but a few exceptions the establishment or the taking over of commercial enterprises, and made such acts dependent upon previous consent.[14] The life of all iron cartels has been compulsorily extended. There are innumerable restrictions of this kind in almost every branch of trade and industry, duly reported by the *Kartell-Rundschau*.

We see, then, that the statute for compulsory cartellization maintains and solidifies the existing organizational patterns. In the first stage of National Socialist economic policy, the object was to secure the profits of the industrial combines even with the reduced volume of production. In this respect, therefore, National Socialist policy is not different from that of the pre-Hitler crisis cabinets. It merely carries their policies to a radical conclusion.

PREPAREDNESS, WAR, AND CARTELS

With the enactment of the Four Year Plan on 18 October 1936, the economic policy of National Socialism changed, now aiming at full employment and the utilization of all resources for preparedness. The place of the cartels in the preparedness and in the war economy has, consequently, also changed. The Four Year Plan decree is very brief and does not give any concrete indication of the course of the cartel policy. It runs:

The realization of the Four Year Plan, which I promulgated at the party conference for honor, requires a unified direction of all the forces of the German people and a rigid concentration of all the competences of party and state.

I entrust the carrying out of the Four Year Plan to Prime Minister Colonel-General Göring.

Prime Minister Colonel-General Göring will issue the measures necessary for the performance of the task assigned to him, and to that extent he has the right to issue executive decrees and general administrative regulations. He is entitled to hear and to give orders to all authorities, including the supreme federal authorities, to all offices of the party, to its organs and affiliated organizations.

The aim of the Four Year Plan is necessarily in contradiction to the traditional character of the cartels. For the essence of the cartel economy, the very reason for compulsory cartellization, is the restriction of productive capacity. For this reason, cartel organization was rejected by many leading German industrialists. Dr. Schacht, for instance, stated as early as 1903 that 'cartel means stagnation. Trust means progress and production. Cartels are nothing but mutual associations for the assurance of profit.' [15] Schacht conceived cartels to be organs of a declining economy and incompatible with an expanding economic system. The goal of the Four Year Plan on the contrary is increase in output and productive capacity and the full rationalization of German industry.

This very antagonism between the official aim of the economic policy and the traditional policy of the cartels found expression time and again in outbursts by National Socialist leaders. At a meeting of the federal peasant organization on 27 November 1938, Secretary of State for Agriculture Backe expressed a preference for vertical forms of organization, in other words for full trustification. Only such forms, he said, could solve Germany's economic problems.[16] An even more significant statement was made by Dr. Rudolf Brinkmann, secretary of state in the ministry of economics, on 21 October 1938.[17] His programmatic speech viewed the whole economic policy, the relation between the state and the economy, with unprecedented clarity. Brinkmann began from the assertion common to all liberal theory, that the state and the economy are two different systems with two different spheres of influence, two different tasks, and two different organizations. The economic policy of Germany was not that of mercantilism, although he admitted a similarity in the methods applied and in the extent of governmental activity in the economic sphere. National Socialism, Brinkmann continued, believes in the free personality working within the framework of an order that is not and must not be bureaucratic. However, he admitted that the state was forced to create 'a frightening abundance of administrative agencies.' But cartels, in his view, were equally subject to that evil. 'The more the genuine National Socialist economic spirit gains the upper hand—and it will be seen that it does get the upper hand—the more readiness there will be for free submission . . . to genuine economic necessities and *many bureaucratic agencies will be replaced by self responsibility of the economy* [italicized in the original]. True socialism, it must be stated, is a fight against arbitrariness and for true efficiency.' The profit motive is still strong and decisive. Free initiative, in Brinkmann's view, is bound up with the existence of small and middle businessmen. But he is forced to admit that small and medium-scale business is in a state of decline. Powerful private organizations continue to exist and to use the state sovereignty to solidify their powers. Monopolistic organizations dictating prices actually live on subsidies paid out of the pocket of the mass of the people.

From that point Brinkmann proceeds to a severe indictment of the cartel system. The stabilization of cartel prices leads, he believes, to a much greater sensitivity of free prices. It then becomes impossible to secure a sound relation between bound and free prices. High cartel prices do not contribute to the furtherance of rationalization. Quota cartels especially, by rigidly fixing the output of cartel members, compel their most rationalized members to work on unrationalized lines. Worst of all, in his view, is the fact that in a period of full employment, the cartel system prevents the automatic and complete reduction of the costs of production, hinders a higher standard of life for the mass of the people, and prevents the rise of a new generation of entrepreneurs. If the cartel system continues to fail, the state will have to resort to sterner measures. It will not nationalize industry, because National Socialism believes in a 'spiritual' and not in a 'materialistic' nationalization of the economy. That is why the state has retransferred to private corporations its holdings in private banks and in United Steel Trust. But the state must assume additional responsibility if the drive for high productivity and for the full utilization of all available resources is not to be hampered by the cartel system.

CARTELS AND GROUPS

Cartels have indeed become the organs for attaining full employment with the collaboration and under the pressure of the state. They have become so because now more than ever before they are simply the mask hiding the power of the industrial empires, which have thereby secured control of the political structure of business.

We have already mentioned that the corporative organization of business was stopped because the cartels used the new ideology for exterminating outsiders and extending their net over whole branches of industry and trade. Some National Socialist commentators have expressed their hatred of the 'process of degeneration and falsification caused by the corruption of the state by the cartels' [18] Though the corporative organization has been stopped, the delivery of the political organs to the cartels still goes on. One point of supreme significance has to be remembered in discussing the relation between business and its political organization. In the cartel organizations, in the trusts, in the combines, and in the joint stock corporations, the leadership principle does not prevail. In all these organizations, the majority decides. But in the cartels the majority is not a majority of the members, but one of quotas, either of production or of sales quotas. The bigger the quota, the bigger the voting power.* By logical necessity, therefore, cartels

* See below, p. 274.

are dominated by the biggest members. It is they who use the semi-democratic form of the cartels for seizing control of the political organization of business.

This situation has often been criticized. In fact, no facet of the economic organization has received so much attention as the power that the cartels exercise over public, political, estate, corporate, self-governing or autonomous bodies of business. 'It is true that in the trade associations [groups] the known identity of the personnel of trade associations and cartels has played an exceptionally important role and has, in practice, had the result that the influence and power of the public organizations which should not regulate the market, has been utilized to strengthen the private power of the cartels'—so writes the *Frankfurter Zeitung*.[19] One of the best observers of structural changes in the National Socialist economy comes to the conclusion:

There appears to be a union between trade associations and cartels, which implies that the organization in its lower and therefore in its decisive stage is bound from the very beginning to the further-ance of existing cartels. The present state has seriously weakened the position of the outsiders, since the leader of the trade association thus has authority as the representative of a compulsory organiza-tion and so contributes to the strengthening and domination of the cartel. Cartels have sometimes been directly organized by the groups [electrical industry and automobile trade] in order to be able to carry out cartellization measures. This procedure seems to have be-gun particularly in various sections of trade which were not previ-ously cartellized.[20]

Time and again has the complaint been received that the cartels dominate the groups and not vice versa.

The groups have obtained a number of rights over the cartels—and that constitutes primarily what the Germans understand by 'ordering of the market.' The groups are entitled to obtain in-formation from the cartels, to examine their prices, quotas, and sales conditions, and to veto all cartel decisions that are contrary to the economic principles evolved by the groups or by the federal gov-ernment.[21]

But the distinction between the regulation and the ordering of the market becomes less and less tenable since the groups 'may almost daily' [22] enter into marketing activities with the consent of the minister of economics, and are, besides, vitally concerned with questions of foreign trade, which certainly comes within the scope of market regulation.

So the groups have, indeed, become supervisory organs of the cartels, but at the same time some have also turned into cartels: it is therefore almost impossible to state where the task of the one begins and the other ends. One fact, however, remains decisive: it is still the cartel which, through interlocking personnel, rules the group.

As a result of this development, the federal minister of economics found himself compelled to issue a ruling demanding 'as far as possible' a separation of the functions of group and cartel. The statute of 27 February 1934 forbade the groups to engage in marketing activities, and the ruling of 2 July 1936 insisted that the cartels should avoid confusion with the groups. The famous reform decree of 12 November 1936 insisted that the offices of group and cartel leaders and managers should not remain in the same hands, in order 'to secure their impartiality.' The minister ordered the national economic chamber to report to him up till 1 April 1937 how far there was still the same personnel occupying the leading positions in the groups and cartels, and whether this identity of personnel was necessary. It is characteristic that nothing further has been heard of the reports of the federal economic chamber. The minister's ruling adds that the groups, 'built upon compulsory membership and the leadership principle, with their general economic tasks, stand above the marketing organizations and not beside them. I therefore intend to enlist the aid of the organizations of industry for supervising the marketing organization, which, up to the present, has been carried out by myself. This applies to the groups and chambers. The self-government of industry shall feel itself responsible for seeing that the marketing organizations, in all their measures, act in accordance with the economic policy of the federal government.' [23] Groups and chambers have indeed increasingly become supervisory agents of the state but their control by the cartels and trusts has not been lessened—on the contrary, it has been strengthened. The iron law of capitalistic concentration and the requirements of war have been far more powerful than the pious hopes of the minister of economics. For it is during the war itself that the intertwining of cartel and political authority has become more intensified and widespread than ever before. We have already discussed the composition and tasks of the distributive bodies that allocate raw materials and semi-finished products to consumers.* Although the distributive agencies are juristically organs of public law and agents of the *Reichsstellen*, they are either legally or factually identical with the cartels. The wish uttered by the minister of economics and by many well-meaning critics was incapable of fulfilment in the face of the cartel system. Today the most important politico-economic activity in Germany—the allocation of raw materials—is entrusted to private organizations run by powerful monopolists.

This is not all. German industry has sought to strengthen the organizational ties between the cartels and the groups. Two examples will indicate the trend. One of the most recent and comprehensive cartels is the German salt union.[24] The statement announcing its establishment says that the charter of the cartel introduces the leadership principle, adding however that the leader is elected and not appointed from above. The charter provides that the leader of the branch group covering the salt industry would automatically become the deputy leader of the cartel. In this case the close relation between cartel and group is accepted even in the charter of the cartel. Only one case known to the present writer shows an apparently genuine subordination of the cartels to the groups: the glass industry, which, owing to the incorporation of the most progressive European glass works of the Sudetenland, was faced with complete disruption. In order to bring order into the chaos, the federal deputy for the glass industry organized a glass trustee-corporation, which assumed leadership over all cartels and over the whole glass industry.[25]

It is not surprising that, owing to the subordination of the political structure of business to the cartels, the cartels have received a new name. They are alleged to represent a completely new type of organization.[26]

The cartellization of German business is almost complete. Cartels are fully recognized. They exercise public political functions but are nevertheless exempt from the political leadership principle and remain under the control of their own members. Statistics of the numerical growth of the cartels mean nothing. Between the outbreak of the present war and December 1940, twenty new cartels

* See p. 257.

were set up and between twenty and thirty dissolved.[27] These data are meaningless because they do not take into account the rationalization of the cartel system, the incorporation of smaller into larger cartels, the increase in size due to the incorporation of the Sudetenland, Austria, and the Protectorate. Though the number of cartels has not greatly increased, the range of activity of these cartels has become complete.

3. THE GROWTH OF MONOPOLIES

Who in turn rules the cartels? Are the cartels democratic organizations of approximately equally powerful businessmen? Definitely not. They are much more the democratic mask that the industrial magnates use to disguise their autocratic powers. Behind the powerful cartel movement there is a still more powerful trend of centralization, which has reached a scale never dreamed of before. The cartel structure is not democratic but autocratic. Cartel decisions are reached by a majority of quotas and not of votes. In the Upper Silesian coal syndicate, for instance,[28] 100,000 tons of production give one vote. The production in 1928 amounted to 26,000,000 tons, shared by four works, each producing between four and five million tons, by five works each producing between one and two millions, and by one work producing 200,000 tons. Of the 260 votes therefore, the four big works alone disposed of about 180 votes. This is not at all an extreme instance.[29]

The process of monopolization has received an enormous stimulus from a large number of factors. The study of structural changes seems to indicate that there is scarcely any economic measure, of whatever nature, which does not ultimately conduce to concentration and centralization.

In particular, the following factors are vital in that gigantic process: Aryanization; Germanization; technological changes; the weeding out of small and medium-scale businessmen; and the corporate structure. Apart from these factors, each of which will be discussed, there is inherent in the bureaucratic structure of state and of business and in the scarcity of numerous materials a trend toward the encouragement of the big and destruction of the small. The state bureaucracies prefer dealing with one big business or with a few big businesses instead of with hundreds of small and medium businesses, which have many divergent interests. If a system of priorities has to be established, if raw materials have to be allocated, the big businesses will inevitably fare better than the small enterprises, and the 'mixed combines,' which have their own raw-material basis, better than the 'pure' ones. It is obviously more important to secure the supply of a big corporation employing thousands of workers than to keep a smaller factory running.

This tendency will be more marked the closer the relation between business and the state, provided that, as in the case of Germany, big business runs the cartels and the groups.

ARYANIZATION

The role of Aryanization has already been mentioned.* National Socialist observers admit that the acquisition of Jewish property played a considerable role in the expansion of the industrial combines, and that, in the textile industry, for instance, it even gave rise to new industrial combinations.[80] The beneficiaries of Jewish industries have, without exception, been the most influential industrialists: Otto Wolff,[81] Friedrich Flick,[82] and Mannesmann.[88] The profits that thus accrued to the new owners apparently stank to heaven. A special decree had to be issued for the taxation of profits resulting from Aryanization. But this decree does not seem to have gone far enough. A special ruling of the minister of finance, on 6 February 1941, demanded the retroactive taxation of 'special cases of an especially aggravating kind.' [84] Specific cases in which the profits are considered excessive are thus to be reopened by the tax authorities, but the ruling explicitly prohibited any reopening of the general problem of profits derived from Aryanization.

GERMANIZATION

Still more important is the increase in the power of the industrial combines which accrues by including within their orbit all business in the conquered territories. A full survey would almost certainly bore the reader. Some of the techniques have already been mentioned before, the most important being the use of the cartel. The process is by no means complete. Only the surface of business in the conquered territories has as yet been touched. It is not only the Hermann Göring works which benefit from conquest, but also the

* See pp. 116-19.

industrial magnates. Two examples will show the extent to which private property secures the benefits of conquest and the domination of German capital throughout the realm of Europe. One is the establishment of the 'Continental Oil Corporation' in Berlin,[35] which has been called 'a model of a future organization of an enterprise.' The corporation is a holding corporation for all those oil interests outside German territory proper that Germany has already acquired or may acquire in the future. The official report remarks that the acquisition of the Rumanian oil holdings from French and Belgian holders is soon to be expected. The promoters [36] are the most important German banks and oil corporations. Two of them are state-owned corporations. The initial capital of the corporation is 80,000,000 marks, and this may be increased to 120,000,000 marks; 50,000,000 marks are divided in personal shares carrying plurality votes, 30,000,000 in bearer shares to be sold to the public. The personal shares, which are to be kept by the promoters, grant 50 times more voting power than the bearer shares, so that the domination of the promoters over the corporation cannot be broken even if the capital were increased to an inconceivable extent. The supervisory council of this new corporation reads like a list of the new German élite. Its members are representatives of the party, the Secretaries of State Keppler and Neumann; of the military bureaucracy, Generals Thomas and von Heemskerk; representatives of the civil service, of the natural oil and synthetic oil producers, of the coal and lignite industry, of the banks, and of the groups. It is headed by Minister of Economics Walther Funk. The supervisory council is therefore an amalgamation of industrial leaders, high party leaders, representatives of the armed forces and of the ministerial bureaucracy. The task of the new corporation is 'to control the production, utilization, and transportation of [Germany's] oil needs' (*Frankfurter Zeitung*). The National Socialist commentators are full of praise for this new body, especially for the collaboration between the government and business. They prefer it to the old form of a mixed corporation, in which public and private capital jointly entered into specific economic undertakings. They believe that by giving the government influence in the supervisory council, this organization can be made better to serve the interests of Germany than through the capitalistic interest of the government. They forget that this corporation, which, according to its charter, does not and will not drill oil wells in Germany proper and does not and will not produce synthetic gasoline in Germany so as not to compete with the German oil producers, is solely concerned with the exploitation of oil in the conquered territories, acquired by the labor of the German workers and the blood of the German people. The profits accrue solely to this giant corporation in which plurality votes are an absolute guarantee of the power of the capitalistic promoters.

As characteristic is the distribution of the French heavy industry in Lorraine. The five blocks: Heckingen, Rombach, Carlshütte, Kneuttingen and Hagendingen, have been equitably distributed among five German combines: Stumm, Flick, Röchling, Klöckner, and the Göring Works. The five industrialists are, it is true, at present merely trustees. But the official announcement adds that the trustees will have the opportunity to acquire their trusts after the establishment of peace.[37]

TECHNOLOGICAL CHANGES AND MONOPOLIZATION

Germanization and Aryanization opened up new fields for the centralizing trends of German business, but they are not the real source. Monopolization is primarily the result of profound technological changes made since about 1930.[38] We may go so far as to maintain that the technological changes during the past ten years have been of such an extent and profundity that they deserve the name industrial revolution. The basis of this industrial revolution is the new chemical processes.

In German industry, mixed plants, that is, a combination of iron and coal, mining, metallurgy, and engineering, were always decisive.[39] Coal was and is the basis of industrial production, and each steel mill, each big machine-tool construction plant, fought for a coal basis. Very soon the new methods of coal processing made the acquisition of a coal basis a vital concern of the chemical industry.[40] The heavy industries were overcapitalized—we have continually stressed this fact. Their expansion, even their further existence, was conditioned by state help and by the introduction of new technological processes. State help was readily given between 1930 and 1933. We have shown that the maintenance of the cartel and tariff structure during that period and directly afterward by subsidy amounted to saving the industrial structure. The new technology provided the second outlet for progress. But it did not start in the state bureaucracy; it originated within the very mechanism of capitalistic production, refuting the belief of those who hold that capitalism has lost its dynamism. While, however, the new technology originated within that mechanism, it could not be utilized within it. The initial costs involved are tremendous. The financial risks that an enterprise shoulders when, for instance, it embarks upon the construction of a new coal processing plant are considerable. The investment may be completely lost, or no returns may be expected for years. It thus follows that only rich enterprises, preferably those that engage in diverse economic activities, can risk such new investments and engage in new and untried processes. But once a process has started in one combine, others are compelled to follow suit. One instance may clarify the situation. The leading potash combine, Wintershall, a powerful and rich enterprise, embarked upon the erection of a coal hydrogenation plant at a time when the risks involved were extremely heavy. It could afford to do so, because its activities were extremely diversified (potash, coal, oil, lignite, and munitions). The Thyssen combine, however, primarily a metallurgic concern with a coal basis, was near financial collapse when compelled to start a hydrogenation plant of its own (Gelsenberg–Benzin). Its financial position became so difficult that it had to surrender its Austrian holdings to the Hermann Göring works, thereby preparing for the expropriation of all Thyssen's holdings after his flight from Germany. This example may make clear why, on the basis of so monopolized an economic system, huge new investments often cannot be made without state assistance. For that reason state assistance was demanded by German industry and that demand was fulfilled by the National Socialist state. True, the state gave it with reluctance: 'The endless claim for Reich guarantees is a downright *testimonium paupertatis* to private initiative and to private business's willingness to bear responsibilities. There surely remain today and will remain in the future tasks that may not be undertaken or carried out but as collective tasks. In the fulfilment of such tasks, private business must be given a big share. Besides this, however, a vast domain in which private business and the private businessman can exert their efforts will not only be preserved, but in addition found anew to the very largest extent after the war.' That is the view of Minister of Economics Walther Funk.[41]

The new methods of processing coal, wood, straw, nitrogen, oil, and metals, are the central features of the new technology and they all require considerable investments. Moreover, the results of the new technology are often unpredictable. Chemical synthesis is the transformation of the structure of high molecular combinations, in order to produce new substances in which the molecules, though of an identical atomic composition, comprehend differently constructed groups (polymers), that is, different chemical bodies with different chemical properties to be used for different manufacturing purposes. Polymerization is carried out under a pressure of hundreds of atmospheres, by an extremely costly machinery, and with uncertain results. The financial expenditure involved leads in the first place to a complete concentration of all chemical industries all over the world. As a second consequence, the combines entering those new fields claim and receive governmental support, thereby strengthening and enlarging their power.

But this very process also increases the power of all those combines that control coal. Coal is used for gasoline and oil production,[42] for the manufacturing of synthetic rubber (Buna),[43] and for the production of plastics, and it is also indispensable in making any other synthetic material. Coal, once an abundant commodity, has become a scarcity.

The new chemical processes have allowed the motorization of the transport system and have thereby provided the requisites of the lightning war. They have necessitated an enormous expansion of the machine-tool industry,[44] and at the same time have in turn compelled the introduction of considerable further technological changes, namely the replacement of heavy steel by new light metals. The result is, to take one example, that the weight of a Diesel engine of 50 h.p. could be reduced from 175 kilograms per h.p. to a mere 60 kilograms per h.p.[45]

There are, besides, many technological changes that, although not new, have now assumed considerable proportions. We have already mentioned the glass industry, which, in the judgment of a very careful observer,[46] is undergoing a second industrial revolution. The entire textile industry has been revolutionized. Rayon and cellulose wool have taken another great share. Filaments from straw and potato stalks are now beginning to be produced in considerable quantities.[47] All this, in turn, has made enormous demands upon the electrical, iron, steel, and machine industries which have again expanded.[48] This demand for more and more iron led to the establishment of the Hermann Göring works, with which we shall deal later.* But private industry followed and also turned to the exploitation of low-grade ores, thereby once more changing the metallurgical processes.

We cannot hope to present an adequate picture of the technological changes and the technological progress achieved. Capitalism has certainly not lost its dynamism. The era of inventions is not at an end. It is true that inventions are no longer, let us say, individualistic, and that the inventor is no longer as a rule a single person but a team of workers who are set to work for the very purpose of inventing. Nor does a single invention any longer change the technological pattern; it is more often a whole series of interconnected inventions that revolutionizes technology. The technological changes undoubtedly originate in capitalistic competition, in the necessity for each competitor perpetually to expand, lest he stagnate or die. Capitalistic economy, therefore, is not a mere routine, not a mere administrative technique; its original drives are still operating.

But the decisive difference lies in the fact that the very process of monopolization and the costliness and uncertainty of technological changes have made the help of the state indispensable. It is certainly true that the state could, if it wanted, utilize this situation for nationalizing at least the new industries. But National Socialism has not done that. On the contrary, the financial help given for the establishment of new enterprises redounded primarily to the benefit of the long-established monopolists.

THE FINANCING OF THE NEW INDUSTRIES

State financial help has taken various forms, such as guarantees of profit or turnover, or permission to write off investments in a short period. These devices are not very different from the methods that every modern capitalistic system uses in order to overcome the reluctance of businessmen to undertake unknown risks. But

* See p. 298.

Germany has also developed new methods of financing the new technological processes, which led to so-called 'community financing.' Its essence is the compulsion of the small and middle entrepreneur to finance the expansion of the big one.

The new technology has thus led to the creation of new types of enterprise, the most striking example of which is the corporate structure of the new cellulose wool industry. Originally only two such plants existed, one being run by the dye trust, the other by the Glanzstoff Bemberg rayon combine. New works appeared imperative, and their regional distribution was necessary since the consumers of cellulose wool are about equally distributed within the federal territory. The capital for the establishment of the new works was taken up under more or less pressure by the local textile factories. The state then appointed experts for the management of the new corporations and sometimes secured for itself a small share of the initial capital. The shares, taken up with reluctance by the promoters, soon turned into a boon, since they carried with them a quota for cellulose wool and thus secured raw material for the textile manufacturers. Because many small textile manufacturers bought the shares, they were fairly equally distributed, and the board of directors very soon became the real power,* the more so since the acquisition of new shares was dependent upon the consent of the minister of economics, who used his authority to strengthen the hold of the combines. In mid-1939, there were 11 cellulose wool plants. Very soon afterwards, they merged first into cartels, then into combines, and within a year after the foundation only four such combines remained. Besides the dye trust and the Glanzstoff Bemberg combine, there was the Phrix group, dominated by the textile combine of Christian Dierich, while the fourth group is still dominated by the small and medium-size textile factories.

The financing of the lignite hydrogenation industry is even more striking. The capital requirements are immense and only the wealthy dye trust could take the risk of constructing such a plant (Leuna). By a decree of 28 September 1934, therefore, a 'compulsory community of the lignite industry' was created, composed of all lignite mines with a yearly production of 400,000 tons or more. The community then set up a joint stock corporation for the

* See p. 284.

production of synthetic gasoline from lignite, the so-called *Braun-kohlen-Benzin* (Brabag). Ten enterprises were attached, in contrast to the organization of the cellulose wool industry, in which hundreds of factories are co-ordinated. The big ten control the whole production of synthetic gasoline from lignite. With the exception of two state-owned works, only the powerful combines are represented—Wintershall, Count Schaffgotsch, Flick, the steel trusts, and the dye trust. The supervisory body of the Brabag also reads like a list of the new élite. The party hierarch, Secretary of State Keppler, is surrounded by delegates of the combines, who are often leaders of their economic groups, by bankers, such as Kurt von Schröder, the broker of the Papen and Hitler understanding of January 1933, and by ministerial bureaucrats—but only four members of the supervisory body are civil servants or delegates of the state.

The new technology and the new financing methods have undoubtedly accentuated the process of monopolization.

THE ELIMINATION OF SMALL BUSINESS

While the cartel system has already eliminated inefficient and unreliable businessmen,* legislative measures have opened a frontal attack on the inefficient handicraftsman and retailer. Two such decrees have been enacted, one for the 'purification of retail trade,' on 16 March 1939,[49] the other 'for the carrying out of the Four Year Plan in the sphere of handicrafts,' on 22 February 1939.[50] The aims of the decrees are twofold: to solidify the position of the healthy entrepreneur and to gain labor power. Inefficient retailers and handicraftsmen can be compulsorily liquidated without indemnification. For retailers, the economic group carries out the liquidation in conjunction with the local party leader, the local labor exchange, and the trustee of labor. Handicrafts are 'purified' by the chambers of handicrafts. The 'purified' retailer and handicraftsman become manual laborers, thus sinking from the level of independence to the lowest scale of the proletariat. At the handicrafts conference of 7 May 1938, Minister of Economics Funk reported that 90,448 out of 600,000 one-man plants had been closed in 1936 and 1937, and that this process was by no means at an end (*Frank-*

* See p. 264.

furter Zeitung, 9 May 1938). In February 1939, Ministerial Councillor Dr. Münz mentioned a figure of 104,000 closed one-man workshops and also added that the trend would continue (*Rheinisch-Westphälische Zeitung*, 7 February 1939). These figures refer to the situation prior to the enactment of the purification decrees. Funk candidly stated that handicrafts had to bear the increase in the cost of production by a decrease in profits. The absolute number of handicrafts enterprises fell from 1,734,000 in 1934 to 1,471,000 [51] on 1 April 1939. Figures for the decline of the retail trade are difficult to gather. But the federal coal commissioner, appointed by Göring to raise the efficiency, has announced that the number of coal retailers (70,000) must be reduced by half in order to raise the profitability of the remaining members of the trade.[52]

This process is intensified by the price-control measures, which often shift burdens resulting from price cuts or price stabilization to the wholesale and retail trader by either cutting down or freezing the trade margin.[53]

The trend moved sharply upwards during the present war. Many plants in the consumers' goods industries (textiles, leather, soap, chocolate, and so on) have been shut down. Since spring 1940, hundreds of thousands of workers employed in the consumers' goods industries have been 'combed out' and transferred into producers' goods industries and into the auxiliary army (organization Todt and labor service). In 1940 alone, 480,000 men were thus set free.[54] Some of the closed plants receive community help on the basis of the decree of 19 February 1940, a financial assistance collected by and within the economic groups. Others have been allowed to continue as mere distributive agents. They had to give up production but are allowed to merchandise the products manufactured by the more efficient plants. The trend in the consumers' goods industries, produced by rationing, is thus in accordance with that in the producers' goods industries, namely the wiping out of small and medium-scale business.

This process is partly desirable, if it is carried out with sufficient safeguards. For the economic position of the enormously swollen distributive agencies and of small handicrafts has indeed become untenable and incurable. In his book on the social stratification of the German people, the German sociologist Theodor Geiger has distinguished three social types of handicraft and the retail trade:

the capitalist, the middle type, and the proletaroid. And, on the basis of the industrial census of 1925, he found the following ratio between them: [55]

Handicrafts: 4.5—65.5—30.0
Retail Trade: 2.4—65.0—33.5.

According to these statistics, about one third of all retailers and handicraftsmen are economically proletarians, although they are still independent businessmen. This antagonism between economic reality and the demand for social prestige could not be and had not been solved under the Weimar Republic. National Socialism was compelled by the necessity of securing the consent of at least some sections of the middle classes to restore to them a sound economic position by destroying the smallest and most impoverished groups of the middle classes. However bitter may be the descent into the stratum of the proletariat and however brutally the whole process may have been carried out, any other way was unthinkable. But the profits accrued not only to the remaining sections of the middle classes, but also to big business, which, by freezing or even cutting trade margins for the trader, was able to shift some of the burdens resulting from the price policy to the weakest groups in society. This whole process is not yet ended. In fact there seems to be a bitter discussion regarding the future of the retail and wholesale trades, as may be seen from the passionate defense of the function of trade by the general manager of the national group that covers trade.[56]

THE CORPORATION STRUCTURE

The legal form in which the process of monopolization is carried out is the joint stock corporation.

The American scholars, Berle and Means,[57] have shown in detail the techniques by which small amounts of capital are able to dominate large combines. These devices have been known and practiced in Germany ever since joint stock corporations played a major role. Even the form of the joint stock corporation is a departure from the principle of the free entrepreneur, and this was recognized by Adam Smith. The modern corporation, whether monopolistic or not, has already changed the function of property.[58] By the very form of the joint stock corporation, the capital function is divorced from the administrative one and thereby creates the germ for the development of a managerial bureaucracy, destroying that very cornerstone of free competition, the free entrepreneur, who risks his capital and labor in order to achieve certain economic ends. However, this divorce need not be harmful so long as the capitalists, the stockholders, obtain control of the management—that is, so long as the corporations are democratic bodies. But that is not and cannot be the case. It was Walther Rathenau, who, in a little pamphlet entitled *Vom Aktienwesen*, drew attention to the fact that the democratic structure of the joint stock corporation inevitably gives way to an authoritarian one.[59] Within the joint stock corporations the very same changes occur as in a political democracy. Just as the cabinet becomes independent of parliament, so the board of directors establishes its sovereignty over the stockholders. Preferential stocks, voting by proxy (where the power of attorney is already contained in the conditions of the banks in which the stockholder deposits his stock), the very size of the corporation, which makes it both impossible to convene meetings of thousands of stockholders and impossible for stockholders to attend, and a number of other devices have made the stockholder powerless. Just as in parliament the power of the individual deputy gives way to that of political parties bound by strict discipline, so the stockholders' meeting is no longer a discussion between industrial capitalists, but a struggle between powerful monopolistic groups, which bargain with the management and support it when their own ends are attained.

The power of the management under the Weimar Republic was in many cases used for entirely selfish purposes, even sacrificing the well-being of the corporation proper and leading to enormous capital destruction. Only a hint can be given how the authoritarian power of the management was misused. The famous Schultheiss Brewery in Berlin was financially ruined by the chairman of its *Vorstand* (president), who, with the help of the banks, acquired the stock of his own corporation in order to facilitate a merger with an overcapitalized concern, a mixture of factories, mills, cement works, and machine plants. The ensuing loss of 70,000,000 marks had to be borne by the brewery, though the stockholders and even the members of the supervisory board knew nothing of the transaction. The famous insurance corporation of Frankfort o.M. was reduced to complete bankruptcy by its directors, who considered the corporation merely a pot from which to rob as much as possible in as short a time as possible. The famous wool concern (Nordwolle) was also ruined by the criminal activities of its presidents, costing more than 200,000,000 marks. The directorate of the North German Lloyd bought shares in its own corporation in conjunction with members of its supervisory council and thrust the ensuing loss squarely on the North German Lloyd when the shares fell on the stock exchange. The famous industrialist Otto Wolff sold the shares of his own corporation to another one that he controlled at a price far exceeding the value, earning a sum of 10,000,000 marks. The managers of a leading department store, Karstadt, speculated violently. These are just a few examples of the misuse for selfish purposes of the independence of the management from control.

This phenomenon has a deep political significance, too. For just in that period the National Socialist party began violent propaganda against corruption within the Social Democratic party, because some of its leaders were, or were asserted to be, connected with speculators like the Barmats, Kutisker, and so on. But while the criminal activities of the small fry received enormous attention in the German press and led to severe political reverberations, really big cases of the misuse of the corporate structure for the furtherance of the egoistic ends of the managers had practically no such political consequence. The anti-corruption campaign of the National Socialist party was solely and exclusively directed against Jewish and Social Democratic corruption.

The rule of the board, by which we understand the board of managing officers and the supervisory council, was sanctified by the theory of the 'enterprise as such,' [60] that is, by the permeation of individualistic legal theory with the institutionalist doctrine. This theory maintains that a corporation, if it is economically and socially powerful, is divorced from its shareholders and the managing board, and that it constitutes an institution the fate of which must not be identified with that of the persons owning and directing it. Rathenau, for instance, had made the point that a bank like the Deutsche Bank, because of its size and national importance, must not be allowed to go into voluntary liquidation, since public interest demanded its continued operation.

From this institutionalist * point of view, the right of the indi-

* See p. 448 on institutionalism.

vidual shareholder was a mere nuisance and in consequence the theory became one of identifying the enterprise with its board, which was thus freed from any control by the shareholders.[61] The German courts slowly adopted this doctrine and the democratic ministry of justice, in its draft for a new company act, subscribed to the view that 'the interests of the enterprise as such are as worthy of protection as the individual interests of the shareholders.' It is worthwhile recalling the criticism by one of Germany's outstanding lawyers of this draft and of its underlying institutionalist philosophy.

It is surprising to see how, in an age of democracy and sovereignty of the people, an oligarchification of company matters is aimed at, degrading the shareholders to a mere *misera contribuens plebs*. Even the outworn stock phrase of the organism of the company had to be used to glorify a fascist tyranny of the board, not to speak of minorities for the benefit of which otherwise—in Geneva and elsewhere—such well-meant speeches are nowadays made. These bureaucratic tendencies cannot be sufficiently strongly resisted. They originate from a totally wrong principle. As in the case with the state, so, too, the company does not serve its own purposes, but those of its members, and the gentlemen of the board are not masters, but servants. *L'état, ce sont nous.*[62]

By a decree of the president of the Reich, on 19 September 1931, the German company law was changed under the impact of the financial scandals we have just mentioned. But the decree did not break the power of the board. It merely demanded more publicity (in balance sheets, profit and loss accounts, and reports of the directors). It instituted compulsory auditing by certified accountants, made the acquisition of the company's own shares more difficult, and allowed for the reduction of capital in an easier form.

The National Socialist company act of 1937 carries these principles still further. The middle-class ideology of National Socialism had frowned upon the joint stock corporation and its anonymous character. An act of 1934, therefore, allowed the conversion of joint stock corporations into partnerships or limited-liability companies in a more or less formless manner. The act of 1937 provides that the minimum capital of joint stock companies is 500,000 marks and that the nominal value of a share must be at least 1,000 marks. Exemptions are, however, admitted. The act further allows the dissolution of a company whose board 'grossly violates the law or the principles of responsible business methods.' The main feature of the new act, however, is the re-definition of the relation between board and shareholders. While the Academy for German Law desired the introduction of the leadership principle, however, not of an appointed, but of an elected leader, the statute itself does not go as far, but nevertheless strengthened the position of the board against 'the mass of irresponsible shareholders who largely lack the necessary insight into the position of business.' The shareholders have, in consequence, lost most of their rights. Normally now, the accounts are established by the supervisory council if it accepts them as they are prepared by the board of directors. The shareholders' meetings are thus deprived of the right to accept or reject the yearly accounts unless the board of managers and the supervisory council submits them to the meeting, or unless the supervisory council rejects the proposal of the board of managers. This change, of course, merely sanctifies a *de facto* practice, since in reality the meetings of the shareholders had usually been a mere formality. Besides, the shareholders' meeting is formally forbidden to decide questions of management. Plurality shares are admitted only with the permission of the federal minister of economics.

The National Socialist act thereby gives legal sanctions to a trend apparent in all modern corporations. It now lays the sacrificing of the rights of the shareholders to the very principle of company law.

Under National Socialism, the number of joint stock corporations declined, but the average capital invested in each corporation increased.[63] There is no doubt, therefore, that the new corporation law and the law allowing the conversion of joint stock corporations into partnerships materially contributed to the process of monopolization.[64] Shareholders are mere *rentiers*. Interlocking directorates, proxy voting, plurality votes, exchange of shares, pooling of profits, all these well-known devices have made possible the erection of a system of combines not surpassed in any country, not even the United States.

WHO ARE THE MONOPOLISTS?

Are the monopolists merely managers, or are they only or also genuine private capitalists? The outstanding achievement in building up an industrial empire is that of Friedrich Flick, industrial *condottiere* who outranked every industrial competitor, above all, Fritz Thyssen. His career is meteoric. From the middle German steel industry, he soon reached into the United Steel Trust, into the North German steel industry (blast furnace work, Lübeck). He acquired a coal basis (Harpen and Essen), he got control of a considerable lignite basis (formerly Petschek), and he finally again entered into manufactory.[65] This process started in 1936 and reached its height in 1937.

Perhaps still more surprising is the rise of the Quandt combine, though its size cannot be compared with the big ones. The Quandt family, originally small textile manufacturers, soon entered into machine construction (Accumulatoren Fabrik, Hagen), into armament and munitions, and from there into metallurgy (Dürener Metall), thence into electricity, transportation, building construction, lignite, and potash. In 1939 its general manager took over the management of parts of the Hermann Göring works.[66] The combine is a family affair, as is the Flick combine. How this phenomenal rise can be explained we do not know. Perhaps the fact that the leader of the combine was Mrs. Goebbels' first husband may help to explain it.

Rapidly rising to the fore is the Otto Wolff combine.* Wolff started in trade and then acquired minorities in the United Steel Trust and in the Mansfeld Copper combine. But he soon exchanged his minorities for acquisitions that he controlled exclusively, and rapidly built up a kingdom, if not an empire. From Jewish hands he acquired the steel mills of Thale. He then gained control of the Weser iron works and of the Bochum iron and steel mills. The *Anschluss* with Austria rounded off his kingdom, after he had already pushed into the Saar territory.[67] Otto Wolff had already played a considerable role under the Weimar Republic, closely collaborating with the right wing of the Center party, playing the cultured gentleman and even writing a biographical novel about *Ouvrard*, Napoleon's financial *condottiere*. His combine reached its height in 1937.

The Mannesmann combine is well known to all students of international relations. Under National Socialism it realized an old dream, its extension from a specialized to an all-embracing combine. It is

* Otto Wolff died in 1939.

the most distinguished beneficiary of Aryanization, but it went far beyond swallowing Jewish property. In 1935 its famous steel-pipe works acquired a rolling mill in the Saar. In 1936 it rounded off its holdings in the Kronprinz corporation. In 1938 it acquired further rolling mills.[68] It is not by chance that its general manager, W. Zangen,* is also the leader of the national group industry.

The Count Ballestrem [69] combine knew how to establish its absolute control in the Upper Silesian iron industry, pushing from there into lower Silesia and lower Austria. From the Prussian state it acquired the remaining capital of the Upper Silesian mill works. This expansion gave no rest to the other Upper Silesian, Count Von Schaffgotsch,[69] whose combine rounded off its holdings in the Upper Silesian coal and mining industry, profiting heavily from Aryanization.

Perhaps the most striking phenomenon is the rise of the Wintershall potash combine. It offers a convincing proof that the cartel system, by guaranteeing differential profits, gave rise to a combine that invested its savings in a large number of other branches. Even under the Weimar Republic the Wintershall combine accounted for about 50 per cent of all the potash produced in Germany. In 1936, it incorporated a competitor, the Burbach combine, and reached out into oil production, oil refining, coal and lignite mining,[70] and then into the production of synthetic gasoline. The only remaining potash competitor, the *Salzdethfurth* combine, followed suit.[71] It strengthened its position in potash, acquired the Otto Wolff holdings of copper shares, and finally entered into lignite mining, again profiting from Aryanization.

We cannot continue this story. We have not even mentioned the old combines, the Krupp, Haniel, Gutehoffnungshütte, Klöckner, nor have we mentioned the concentration in the textile, electrical, glass, cement, and ceramics industries. It is the same story repeatedly. It is not restricted to the production goods industry, but is equally true of consumption goods industries. In the cigarette industry, there is one combine, *Reemstma,* which had always supported National Socialism and had found financial support from the Weimar Republic, which had granted respites from the payment of cigarette taxes and had finally waived a considerable amount.

* See also p. 390.

This combine now produces 95 per cent of all cigarettes.[72] The same process is also true of banking, where it has taken on tremendous dimensions. Private banks rapidly decreased.[73] The big banks again expanded and soon entered industry, thus playing havoc with the National Socialist theory that creative capital should not be dominated by financial companies. According to an estimate of the German Business Cycle Institute,[74] all raw and semi-manufactured goods produced within Germany and about half of all finished industrial goods were bound by monopoly or cartel agreements.

This monopolistic structure is not maintained solely by the general managers (*Generaldirektoren*), but just as much by capitalists.* Otto Wolff, Friedrich Flick, and Günther Quandt are not managers, but powerful capitalists. They are not *rentiers* who at the end of the year cut the dividend coupons of their stock certificates and cash their dividends. Nor are the managers themselves simply managers, that is, salaried employees. They have long ago assumed the role of capitalists proper, investing their savings in shares and often speculating with the funds of their own corporations, thereby strengthening their personal financial power within them. Moreover, the managerial positions are often as hereditary as those of the capitalists proper.

At this stage we need only show that markets and competition have by no means been abolished. The conflicts are reproduced on a higher level and the incentives of competition remain operative. The defeat of Thyssen is a major example. His economic decline was an accomplished fact long before his flight from Germany, which, in reality, may have been merely the consequence of his defeat by his competitors, Friedrich Flick and the Göring combine.

Competition is even intensified by the scarcity of raw materials, and the state itself is drawn into the struggle between the competing combines. Cartellization and monopolization are not the negation of competition, but only another form of it. Following some National Socialist economists, we may distinguish three types of economies existing within Germany: a competitive economy, a monopolistic economy, and a command economy;[75] and, on the basis of our material, we may agree with their conclusion that the monopolistic economy is at least as powerful an element as the

* See also the chapter on the New Society, pp. 385-91.

command economy. We may even go beyond this statement and maintain that, far from negating competition, cartels assert it. The struggle for production or sales quotas within the cartel—for raw materials, for capital, for consumers—determines the character, the stability, and the durability of the cartel. It is true that the more monopolistic the system, the less it is open to scrutiny. The veils become thicker, the anonymity takes ever more complicated forms. But competition, even cut-throat competition, still goes on. Opponents are compelled to surrender not by price cutting or ruinous underbidding but by the cutting off of supplies of raw materials and capital.

Entrepreneurial initiative is not dead; it is as vital as ever before and perhaps even more so. Karl Lange, general deputy for machine building and general manager of the economic group covering the machine industry, in discussing the performance of the German machine industry in comparison with England and America,[76] again stressed the fact that without the energetic co-operation of private industry success could not have been attained. The motivating power of expansion is profit. The structure of the German economy is one of a fully monopolized and cartellized economy.

IV

THE COMMAND ECONOMY

THE foregoing picture of the German economy is, however, one-sided and therefore incomplete. It has not yet taken into account the command economy—the interfering and regimenting state. It is conceivable that the extent and depth of the command economy may decisively change the picture. Five such kinds of interference may shatter our construction: (1) the direct economic activities of the state; (2) of the party; (3) the control of prices; (4) of investment and profits; (5) of foreign trade; (6) and of labor. While the allocation of raw material, the rationing of consumer goods, and the rationalization by the general deputies have already been described, each of these six activities deserves closer scrutiny to determine whether Germany has already reached the stage of a managerial dictatorship or of state capitalism, or whether state regimentation is primarily designed to strengthen existing capitalism in spite of the fundamental changes that are the inevitable consequence of regimentation.

The economic policy of National Socialism may be divided into four stages: the initial phase, Schacht's new plan, the Four Year Plan, and the war.

In the initial phase, the economic policy was not very much different from any other depression policy. It tried to overcome unemployment by stimulating private enterprise and by extending the work-creation policy of the previous regimes.

A number of such work-creation programs had been started and largely completed when Hitler came to power: the Brüning program of June 1932 (165,000,000 marks), the Papen program of June and September 1932 (280,000,000 marks), the 600,000,000 marks emergency program of Gerecke in January 1933, which was topped by the Reinhardt National Socialist program, with a total cost of 1,070,000,000 marks.[1] The aim of all these programs was the abolition of unemployment by stimulating the upward trend of the business cycle, by 'kindling the initial spark,' that is, by pump priming—after which private business would be able to carry on the upward trend. Public works, state subsidies, tax remissions, and employment of workers outside of private industry were the devices to be applied. The major part of the money was spent on civil-engineering. New publicly owned financing institutions were founded and the financing was made possible by the issuing of loans, by taxation, or by the extension of credit. There is no doubt about the temporary success of these measures. Public investments undoubtedly stimulated the production goods industry and with it the whole economy.

But perhaps as important as the work-creation policy in this narrow sense were the strengthening of the monopolistic positions, which we have already discussed, and the open or hidden subsidies paid to industry,[2] which aimed at raising industrial profits. Investments for the replacement of old industrial and agrarian machinery were free from taxation (act of 1 June 1933), so that the entrepreneur could write off his new investment at once. Outstanding taxes could be remitted if new investments were made, and new industrial units received tax privileges for the development of new methods of production (15 July 1933). House owners received subsidies and tax exemptions for repairs, while industry as a whole received cheaper credits. In order to raise purchasing power and stimulate production, newly licensed motorcars and motorcycles were exempt from the motor vehicle tax (10 April 1933), while owners of old cars could compound the taxes by a lump-sum payment. The marriage loans, which we have already discussed, fell into this category, and the whole cartel policy (discussed previously) served this purpose. All these attempts were undoubtedly successful, as they were in almost every country in which they were applied. The national income rose from 45,175,000,000 marks in 1932 to 58,660,000,000 marks in 1935—that is, by 24.7 per cent (see note 113). The value of production rose by 63.2 per cent, while the turnover in the retail trade increased by only 11 per cent.[3] Unemployment was reduced by the absorption of labor in industry, in public-works programs, in the labor service, and in the land service, but prices began to rise, thereby endangering the success of the whole plan.

Whether this initial success would have ripened into a full boom is impossible to say, for late in 1934 the work-creation policy was overshadowed by the new phase of Germany's economy, the beginning of preparedness economy.

On 24 September 1934, Schacht's plan for controlling imports went into operation. On 5 November 1934, the first office of Reich commissioner for price control was created. The office was to expire on 1 July 1935. On 30 January 1935, Schacht succeeded Schmidt as minister of economics and on 16 March 1935 compulsory military service was introduced. On 21 October 1935, Germany left the League of Nations, thereby announcing her intention of regaining her former world position either with the help of, or in the face of opposition from, the great powers, and at the party conference held in September 1936 the Four Year Plan was promulgated.

1. The Nationalized Sector [4]

Has the command economy really superseded competition and monopoly? Among these questions the foremost is whether National Socialism has actually embarked upon the nationalization of business. Has the direct economic activity of the state been increased to such an extent as to make it a decisive factor? If it were so, state capitalism would really be operative in Germany. But it certainly is not so. The share of the public authorities in public utilities, industrial production, transportation, and insurance has always been great—greater than in any other country. The organizational forms differ—they do not concern us here. The state carried out its economic activity under public law or under private law, as a public institution or as a private corporation, or sometimes in the form of a mixed corporation, in which public and private capital participated. The federal government, the states, the provinces, municipalities, and associations of municipalities were and still are the bodies that carry on this economic activity.

The railroads have been and are a federal monopoly, with a capital equipment valued at 25,780,000,000 marks, and employing 713,119 men in 1929. Post and telegraphic services are also federal monopolies, capitalized at 2,334,000,000 marks and employing 331,766 men. The federal government runs canal and air transportation. The federal monopoly of railroads, post, and telegraph is a traditional German policy not challenged by any section of the country, whether industry, the middle classes, or labor. This public management was not inferior to private management and in one respect at least it was much superior, since it could and did take into account the interest of the community as a whole. In railroads and the postal service, therefore, the federal government has never been in a competitive position.

But the federal government soon turned toward industrial activity, partly by necessity, partly by accident. Up to 1914, for instance, Germany had no aluminum production of its own, but imported aluminum from Switzerland and France. The First World War helped to give birth to Germany's powerful aluminum industry. With the aid of several private industrial enterprises, which furnished capital and electricity, the United Aluminum Works were founded in 1917 with a capital of 50,000,000 marks, half of it subscribed by the Reich, half by private interests. The World War had ended before all the plants had fully started production and international competition threatened the profitability of the new aluminum plants. Private industry became frightened, and sold its share to the Reich, with the result that under the Weimar Republic practically the whole aluminum production of Germany derived from one government-owned corporation. There is no doubt that this corporation was run with marked efficiency. Being *the* producer of aluminum, the federal government was soon coerced to enter the field of electricity.

During the First World War, synthetic nitrogen plants were erected. Here, too, private industry was unwilling and unable to risk such huge investments and refused to expand. The federal government therefore constructed plants of its own, but left the operation to private industry (agreement of 31 March 1915).

Finally, after the First World War there were remnants of armament production by the military services. They were co-ordinated into the Deutsche Werke, A. G. (1920). The federal government also acquired a number of industrial holdings and in addition set up a bank of its own, which is the government's industrial bank (Reichs-Kreditgesellschaft). All these holdings were finally concentrated in one holding corporation known under the abbreviated name *Viag* (United Industrial Works).

But this is only a small fraction of the total field of public enterprise. States and municipalities followed. While the federal government's empire was built primarily on electricity, Prussia's combine was primarily built on coal, concentrated in one holding corporation, the United Electricity and Mining Corporation (abbreviated name *Vebag*), with a capital of 250,000,000 marks in 1929. Four industrial groups were attached to the Vebag, all reaching into many other industrial fields. The other states expanded similarly, especially Saxony. As a rule municipalities own the public utilities, gas, water, often electric power, bus, street car, and subway services.

The widespread public-insurance system, the holdings in land and forestry, health and sport organizations, milk distributions, and so on, further illustrate the extent to which public enterprise had spread under the Weimar Republic. There is not the slightest doubt that these enterprises were successful. Their success is due to the efficiency of the ministerial bureaucracy and to the ardor with which trade-union officials devoted themselves to municipal enterprises close to their hearts.

What happened to the nationalized sector under National Socialism?

The changes have not been fundamental. But in many cases the nationalized sector has been restricted. Holdings of the Reich have been returned to their previous owners. During the last years of the Weimar Republic, the Viag had acquired shares of the Steel Trust and of the Dresdner Bank, in order to save the shareholders from ruin. Although these shares had been paid for at a price far above the stock quotations, they were sold back to the original owners at a loss. The Viag also sold the Rheinmetall-Borsig corporation to the Hermann Göring works. The *Frankfurter Zeitung* of 1 January 1941 announced that the complete restoration of the great shipping lines to private owners is under serious consideration. Their shares had been acquired by the federal government in order to save them from bankruptcy. Aside from this trend, which merely indicates that nationalization is not and never has been the aim of National Socialism in spite of its party program, the nationalized sector has not undergone any changes. On 31 March 1937[5] the nominal capital of German joint stock corporations and limited-liability combines was 23,300,000,000 marks, while the corporations owned and controlled by the federal government and the states had a nominal capital of 1,774,000,000 marks, that is, about 7 per cent (this does not include railroads, postal service, telegraph and

roads). But still more important is the distribution of the capital
invested in publicly owned corporations among the various
branches. Only 345,000,000 marks were invested in holding corporations, 509,600,000 in heavy industry (299.8 millions in mines,
79 in water power, 75 in machines and armaments) while 611,000,-
000 were invested in public utilities. The total capital in all municipal enterprises of Germany amounted to merely 1,553,000,000
marks in 1936.

While the nationalized sector has certainly not grown at the
expense of the private one, that previously controlled by the public
authorities is now under the joint control of public and private
managers. There seems to be no reason for the change; it results
solely from the ever closer connection between private capitalists
and the state. In the supervisory board of the Viag, for instance,
we find Krupp, representatives of the Aryanized Berliner-Handels-
gesellschaft (bank), and other bankers. In the Reichs-Kreditgesellschaft the supervisory board contains only two officials; the
rest are representatives of private industry and banks. In some of
the operating corporations of the Prussian holding corporation,
we find similar arrangements.

We may sum up by saying that there is no reason to speak of
nationalization in Germany—on the contrary, there is a definite
trend away from nationalization. All industrial positions held by
public authorities had been established prior to National Socialism.
Wherever they expanded, they did so under the pressure of economic necessities. The power of private capital is certainly not
threatened or broken by public capital—on the contrary, in the
control of public corporations, private capital plays a decisive part.

2. The Party Sector [6]

(the göring combine)

Side by side with the nationalized sector there has arisen since
1937, with amazing rapidity, a party sector comprising: (1) the Hermann Göring combine; (2) the Gustloff Foundation; (3) the business corporations of the labor front; (4) the business activities
of the party (publishing, printing, real estate).

The establishment of a party economy follows the familiar pattern of American gangsters, who, after having accumulated money by blackmail and 'protection,' realize their dreams of becoming honorable by entering into legitimate business. In June 1937 a giant industrial enterprise was founded which now occupies the first place in Germany's industrial structure. It was first called the *Reichs-werke, A. G. für Erzbergbau und Eisenhütten, Hermann Göring,* with a capital of 75,000,000 marks.[7] When the Hermann Göring works were founded this act was at once interpreted as a step toward the socialization of the German iron industry, but the German officials at once sharply protested against such an interpre- tation and Major General von Hanneken, director of the main department II in the ministry of economics and general deputy for the iron and steel industry, declared on 10 January 1938 before a select assembly of iron producers that 'the works would be taken over as soon as possible' by private industry,[8] although five days later this statement was denied. What was not denied was the asser- tion that the federal government never had the intention of 'enter- ing into unbearable competition' with private industry. The pro- moters originally intended to utilize the low-grade iron ore which private industry allegedly did not want to touch, but which, in the view of the Four Year Plan office, was needed to fill a gap in the sup- ply. By a decree of 23 July 1937, the Salzgitter (near Brunswick) mining rights were compulsorily amalgamated and the Hermann Göring works were founded to mine the ores, build coke ovens, and complete steel works. Had the Göring works stuck to this program, they would undoubtedly have created something new, even if this new enterprise should have been merely a stop-gap measure for the duration of preparedness and war.

But the Göring works did not keep within the original program; in fact, they soon abandoned it and turned into a gangster organ- ization out to steal and rob as many organizations as they could, in every branch of industry. It is true that the Göring works really opened a new iron and steel plant at Brunswick. The ore production in 1938 amounted to 413,000 tons and the two first blast furnaces utilizing a new smelting process were opened in the fall of 1939.

But the great extension was carried out after the conquest of Austria. In June 1938, the works acquired a huge combine of ma- chine, armament, automobile and railroad-car factories, and mines.

In March 1939, the biggest industrial plant of Austria, the *Alpine Montan*, was taken over from Thyssen. The extension of the Hermann Göring works to its present scope was, in fact, carried out at the expense of Thyssen, just as Flick's empire would hardly have been conceivable without Thyssen's downfall. The robbery of the Alpine Montan is an altogether ironical occurrence, since the combine, which never paid high profits, was kept up by Thyssen with great sacrifices for patriotic reasons and had always been the spearhead of anti-unionism and National Socialism in Austria. A number of Austrian works were taken over from the former Austrian state, while the Viag supplied the Hermann Göring works with iron fields and the already mentioned *Rheinmetall-Borsig*. The Göring works thus entered the armament business in direct competition to Krupp. The Prussian state corporation furnished the Göring works with coal mines, and, last but not least, the expropriation of Thyssen supplied a marvelous opportunity for the acquisition of Thyssen's coal interests and other holdings, which were first administered by District Leader Terboven, Göring's henchman who was later appointed federal commissioner for Norway.

The moment the Austrian spoils were digested, the original purpose of the Hermann Göring works was dropped. A leading newspaper [9] declared it would be wrong to assume that the Göring works intended to build a new mining center. The national task was abandoned as soon as such spoils had been amassed. It would be arduous to follow the expansion of the works. The Sudetenland, the Protectorate, Norway, and Rumania supplied new opportunities.

The progress of the combine is amazing. The leading German economic journal [10] wrote: 'The Hermann Göring works have here in a short time passed through all the stages which private iron industry had taken several decades to pass. Only one essential difference still remains today: while the private iron combines dispose of coal and coke bases of their own, the Göring works, with the exception of the lignite mines of the *Alpine Montan* and of the old southeastern participation of the Danube steamship corporation, receive their coal from outside.' Since the expropriation of Thyssen, this 'essential difference' has ceased to exist.

The structure of the combine is not determined by any economic necessity. That an iron-ore work should want to own blast furnaces, steel mills, and a coal basis is understandable. But the

Göring works comprise machine construction, munition, transportation, shipping, finance, automobiles, potash, oil, building construction, in short, they enter into almost every economic activity. It is again true that nearly every German combine expanded in these directions. But a private combine usually does so because it becomes overcapitalized, as Hugo Stinnes's did during the inflation of 1923. But the Hermann Göring works expanded immediately after their foundation—without having any accumulated savings.

How, then, were the acquisitions financed? Very little is known about the method, but the little we know is this: partly it was simple robbery in the form of expropriation (especially against Thyssen), and partly by exchange of shares or by purchase. Who gave the money? The tax payer and private industry. Of the 400,000,000 marks capital which the Hermann Göring works had in 1939, 245,-000,000 marks were subscribed by the Reich and 155,000,000 had to be subscribed by private industry, especially by the iron-processing works, which were compelled to acquire shares to the amount of 50 marks for each employee. These shares do not receive any dividends until the steel mills in Salzgitter are fully completed, and they have no voting power until 1943. In 1948, the administrative board of the Göring works may redeem the shares. The financing was thus a typical case of gangsterism. The iron industry had to pay protection money and to finance its own competitor.

That private industry and Schacht were not enthusiastic about the new venture is well known.[11] But the threat of expropriation is too great to be disregarded. Besides, it is not known how much the big combines, Flick, Wolff, Mannesmann, the dye-stuff trust, Wintershall trust, have profited by their collaboration with the Hermann Göring works.

The Hermann Göring combine now has the following organizational structure. It is composed of three operating corporations, which are co-ordinated by a holding corporation. It must be understood, however, that the three operating corporations represent in turn a network of many affiliated enterprises. The most important operating corporation is the already mentioned *Reichswerke A. G. für Bergbau und Hüttenbetrieb, Hermann Göring,* with a capital of 560,000,000 marks and reserves of 118,000,000 marks. It comprises especially mines and foundries. The second operating corporation is called *Reichswerke A. G. für Waffen und Maschinenbau,*

Hermann Göring (guns, munitions, machines), with a capital of 80,000,000 marks and 13,500,000 reserves. The smallest is the *Reichswerke A. G. für Binnenschiffahrt, Hermann Göring* (canals and shipping), with a capital of 12,500,000 marks and reserves of 11,500,000 marks.[12] The holding corporation is called *A. G. Reichswerke, Hermann Göring,* originally equipped with a capital of 100,000,000 marks, now raised to 250,000,000 marks.

What is the reason for this giant enterprise? A comparison with gangster organizations will illustrate the problem. National Socialist officialdom has not been able to pierce the fortifications held by the ministerial and industrial bureaucracies in the nationalized sector. The overwhelming influence of these two groups is still as secure as it was under the Weimar Republic. Nor has the party been able to penetrate into the private industry, which, on the whole, is run by the very same set of people. The party has not succeeded in supplanting the power of the bureaucracies in the army and in the navy, in the judiciary, and in the administration. The party controls only the police, youth, and propaganda.

But that is not enough. A gangster can survive only if he becomes honorable. Terrorism alone may not give him sufficient security. Only an economic basis, providing him with a steady income and giving him social status, will open the way for him into society. The Hermann Göring works constitute the attempt of the party to provide the economic basis for the party's rule. The establishment of the works was economically unnecessary from the very beginning. The utilization of low-grade iron ore is not the privilege of the Hermann Göring works. Two other combines financed and organized by private industrialists do the same. Hermann Göring's irruption into private industry is a political, not an economic phenomenon. It intends to secure and fortify the political power of the party bureaucracy. It opens new careers for party officials. It creates new revenues for the party hierarchy and it puts them on the same social basis as the leaders in industry and in the civil service. More concretely, it is the Göring wing within the party that is trying to make its way into high society, and, to achieve this, will leave no stone unturned. That will become clear when we study the personnel of the corporations.

Who are their managers? The supervisory board of the holding corporation is headed by Secretary of State Paul Körner. Born in

1893, he studied law without completing his studies, has been a member of the party since 1936, and rose to the position of high S.S. leader, member of the Göring Prussian state council, member of the Reichstag, and Göring's proxy as deputy of the Four Year Plan. The other members are Secretary of State Dr. Landfried, whose name occurs again and again in many corporations and offices: born in 1884, the son of a wealthy merchant and manufacturer, he is a lawyer by profession, who served in the army, entered the Prussian administration in 1920, and rose rapidly. He is an absolutely reliable party member. We find Ministerial Councilor Brekenfeld, of the ministry of finance; Hans Kehrl, born in 1900, textile manufacturer, president of the economic chamber, leader of the textile industry group and district economic adviser of the party; Karl Lange, Germany's machine dictator; and Thomas, one of the economic generals. The two managers of the holding corporation are Röhnert, formerly with the Quandt combine, and Dr. Guido Schmidt, former Austrian foreign secretary and instrumental in the betrayal of Austria to National Socialism. In the operating corporation number 1, we have a still higher ratio of party hierarchs; besides Körner and Keppler, there is the prime minister of Brunswick, Dietrich Klagges, born in 1891, elementary school teacher and old party member. The managers are Paul Pleiger, a small iron manufacturer, district economic adviser of the party; and the State Councilor Wilhelm Meinberg, born in 1898, member of the party and of the Brown Shirts since 1929, organizer of the National Socialist peasant organization. In the operating corporation number 2, the manager is Dr. William Voss, certified accountant and old party member. In the *Alpine Montan*, affiliated with the operating company number 1, we have, in the supervisory board, Körner, the brothers Eigruber (Austrian National Socialists), Kehrl, Keppler, and Röhnert, the Bavarian Prime Minister Ludwig Siebert (lawyer by profession, old National Socialist), and some bureaucrats. The influence of the party officials is thus overwhelming.

While the legal status of the Göring combine is that of a federally controlled corporation, there exists another industrial combine which is even legally completely controlled by the party, namely, the Gustloff works, founded upon Aryanized property—the Suhl gun factory. In honor of Wilhelm Gustloff, the National Socialist agent for Switzerland, who was shot in 1934, the party established a Wilhelm Gustloff foundation, which soon turned into a not unimportant industrial combine, consisting of six corporations, among them the famous Austrian Hirtenberg munitions factory. This combine is run solely by the party, that is, by the Thuringian district leader, Fritz Sauckel, who has been affiliated with racial organizations since 1919. The finances of this foundation are in complete darkness, since it does not publish balance sheets or profit-and-loss accounts. It is subject solely to the control of the party hierarchy.

Equally surprising is the growth of the business activities of the German labor front. The German labor front now operates the following enterprises:

1. The Bank of German Labor, with a balance of 513,000,000 marks and 34 branches in 1938; now ranking among the four biggest German banks
2. The German Ring—life and health insurance
3. The *Volksfürsorge*—popular life insurance
4. The German Ring—Austrian life insurance
5. *Gehag* and *Einfa*—building and settlement corporations
6. 26 building and settlement corporations under the name of *Neue Heimat*
7. 'German Building Corporation'—a building construction firm
8. 16 printing and publishing houses, among them the famous trade-union book guilds
9. The People's Car Works ⎫
10. The People's Tractor Works ⎬ only in a preparatory stage
11. German National Theater Corporation

In 1938 it ran 65 corporations [18]—most of them (with the exception of Nos. 9 and 10) stolen from the trade unions. In 1941, the labor front finally took over the consumers' co-operatives, both in the old territory and in Austria.[14]

The expansion of the labor front's insurance business received a tremendous stimulus by the decree enjoining all occupations not covered by federal social insurance, to be insured. The lion's share went to the labor front's German Ring.

Is that development a negation of capitalism? I do not believe so.

On the contrary, it appears as an affirmation of the living force of capitalistic society. For it proves that even in a one-party state, which boasts of the supremacy of politics over economics, political power without economic power, without a solid place in industrial production, is precarious. There is no doubt that German capitalism dislikes this development. There is no doubt that this process has intensified the contempt in which the old bureaucracy and the industrial leadership hold National Socialist gangsterism, which, in less than four years, built up the biggest industrial empire of Europe by expropriation, outright theft, and 'shake-downs.'

3. PRICE CONTROL AND THE MARKET

The assertion that the market has been superseded by administrative regulation is, to a large extent, based on the existence of price control. There is, so the argument runs, a system of administrative prices which are determined from above and not by the market automatism. It is undeniable that the potential and actual power of the state over prices has increased. Price control exists and is on the whole efficient. But whether the pattern of control abolishes the operation of the market or whether the market mechanisms reappear in another form in the system of price control is a more decisive problem. We cannot, in this book, hope to present a comprehensive analysis of the price-control measures, their operation and economic effects. The enactments, rulings, regulations, and decisions amount to thousands. All we can do is give a short outline of the organizational structure and present a condensed survey of the principles and mechanism at work.

The legal basis of price control is the act for the execution of the Four Year Plan of 29 October 1936, creating the office of a federal commissioner for price formation. 'For the control of price formation of goods and services of every kind, especially for all needs of daily life, for the whole agricultural and industrial production, and for the transportation of goods and commodities of every kind, and for other compensations, a Federal Commissioner is appointed.' Subject to his authority are prices for commodities and services of any kind; rents; transportation rates; fees of doctors, dentists, and lawyers; admission tickets of theaters, cinemas, and concerts; dues to organizations; postal fees and railroad fares; com-

missions and school fees; and the whole sector of agricultural prices
with the exception of labor, which is subject to specific regulation.
On 3 June 1939, a penal decree was enacted, which calls for imprisonment (up to five years) and fines without limitation for intentional or negligent violation of the statute and rulings of the price
commissioner.

Price Commissioner Joseph Wagner, National Socialist district
leader and provincial president, explained his functions in a speech,[15]
which is interesting for his promise not to do violence to the economy, his view that supply and demand no longer regulate prices,
his desire for close collaboration with the groups and chambers, and
his insistence that the price policy should secure the living standards of the large masses.

The price commissioner carries out his functions either directly
or through two different regional organizations: the price-forming
and the price-supervising agencies. The former are attached to the
Prussian provincial presidents, to federal regents, or to other high
administrative agencies; the latter are attached to the sub-provincial
presidents and other administrative organs. Roughly speaking,
the former fix the prices, the latter see to it that the rulings of the
price commissioner and of the price-forming agencies are carried
out.

The underlying aim of any such price policy must be, of course,
to prevent inflation and thereby to secure the living standards of
the large masses of the people. Inflation in Germany—in contrast to
the United States—could already have been the consequence of the
war economy, since a sufficient supply of vital consumers' goods
did not and does not exist. Because effective demand far exceeds
the available supply, a comprehensive price control appears inevitable. For this purpose, the first decisive decree of the price commissioner was the so-called 'price freezing' (price stop) decree of
26 November 1936.[16] Price increases for goods and services above
the level of 18 October 1936 were prohibited. Prices as they were
on this date were thus frozen. Nevertheless, the decree authorized
the price offices to grant exemptions, which soon became the rule.
Ordinarily the price commissioner decides upon exemptions for
rates of public utilities if they operate in the whole federal territory,
upon price changes of organizations, including the food estate, upon
all cartel prices, and upon special cases of major importance. All

other exemptions have to be granted by the price-forming offices.[17]

We cannot follow the development of the price policy under the Four Year Plan, and shall concentrate entirely on the price policy pursued during the war. The basic enactment, which is not very illuminating, is the war economy decree of 4 September 1939 (Sections 22 to 28). 'Prices and compensations for goods and commodities of any kind must be calculated according to the principles of an economy committed to war.' [18]

In order to understand the operation of the price-control measures, the following distinctions have to be made, for, in spite of the price-freezing decree, there are several types of prices differently computed and differently controlled. We may distinguish the so-called 'bound' prices, that is, prices agreed upon (by cartels or in similar agreements), non-estimated prices, estimated prices, and prices for government orders.

Bound prices that are fixed by cartels or in similar agreements have been subject to special treatment since 1934. The decree of 12 November 1934 (as amended 11 December 1934) had already demanded the consent of the price commissioner for new price agreements and for changes in existing ones. The supplementary decree of 29 March 1935 had required the previous consent for any understanding among bidders for public works. This whole legislation has now been superseded and codified in the decree of 23 November 1940, in force since 12 March 1941.[19] The decree recognizes the price-regulating activities of the cartels and intends only to prevent abuses, those which run counter to 'National Socialist morals.' The principles of this decree are that private price agreements must secure sufficient profits to economically necessary plants. They must, therefore, make possible the existence of the good, middle-sized enterprises by giving them adequate profits and by preventing boundless competition; moreover, they must give to the good enterprise a 'just efficiency premium.' The differential profit inherent in every cartel structure, the so-called cartel rent, is therefore recognized, but it is supposed to be utilized to improve plant efficiency and thereby prepare for future price reduction. Future price agreements will be examined according to these standards. Three years after this enactment has come into operation (that is, on 12 March 1944) all price agreements already in existence on 12 March 1941 lapse unless they have been newly approved in the meantime. Each change in the agreed price structure needs the consent of the federal price commissioner.

The decree applies to all cartels, to the food estate, to so-called vertical price agreements between producers and wholesalers or wholesalers and retailers. It applies not only to prices but to sales conditions as well. The decree also enlarges the power of the price commissioner. He may make his consent to price changes dependent upon the fulfilment of certain conditions, primarily those aiming at rationalization and modernization of plants.

It is clear—and the commentators of that decree stress this point—that trusts and combines are exempt from it. They appear on the commodity market as individual enterprises and they do not agree upon prices but fix them for their plants. The exemption may, in the future, have a decisive consequence. Should the power of the price commissioner really be utilized for cutting down bound prices, the process of concentration and centralization within the economic system will again be favored. The lowering of bound prices is, by necessity, directed against sub-marginal plants, that is against less rationally working cartel members. The lower the cartel price, the less tenable becomes the competitive position of the weak cartel member, which is finally driven into the arms of its bigger and more efficient brother. Nevertheless, the retention of the differential rent is not attacked; it is rather approved. We have already mentioned the view of the official commentator; [20] others ceaselessly stress this point. Göring's periodical [21] reminds industry 'that plants with high costs have been granted lower profits.'

Yet we must not overlook the fact that by means of interfering with the differential rent, the structure of German business may be seriously affected. One official commentator [22] says the primary aim of the decrees is the wiping out of 'unjustified differential rents by lowering the price structure' of all cartels, if that price structure is too high because it is based on the production costs of sub-marginal members. Should such a policy be carried out, rationalization and monopolization would be still intensified.

The economic effects of the control of bound prices are thus relatively simple. If a high price level is maintained, efficient cartel members will receive high differential rents, which will be used for self-financing and as a result will strengthen the monopolistic hold. If the price structure is lowered, uneconomical members will be forced into combines. One example may clarify our assertion. The decree of the price commissioner of 23 March 1937 lowered the price of the potash syndicate by 30 per cent. This decree was hailed as a manifestation of truly socialist spirit. Agriculture was subsidized, not by the state and by the tax payer, but by one group of industry which was willing to make such sacrifices. But it is certainly not a coincidence that the unprecedented growth of the two potash combines, Wintershall and Salzdethfurth, occurred just in that period.

There is thus very little in the decree that makes it necessary to assume that cartel prices are administrative prices. They are agreed upon by the cartels and on the whole they are retained. It is true, of course, that in conjunction with the groups the prices of trade-mark articles have also been lowered.[23] But production costs, sales costs, tradition, and political influence with the price-control offices determine the competitive strength of each cartel member, and therefore determine the prices.

The price-freezing decree thus applies merely to so-called free prices, prices not agreed upon by organizations, and in fact it does not apply to all of them. It can logically apply only to such prices where a frozen price can be ascertained, which may be impossible. A textile factory may, for instance, not have any price as of 18 October 1936 for some or all commodities. Besides, new goods may have been produced that had not been manufactured on 18 October 1936. Wherever such frozen prices cannot be found, the price-freezing decree does not apply.[24] Its realm is thus narrowed. Moreover, it is steadily and continuously encroached upon by legislative enactments of the price commissioner. There are many price regulations for specific branches, such as the textile [25] and leather [26] industries. There are maxima, minima, and standard prices (in cases where the manufacturer may move within a maximum and a minimum price), and each of these types admits of further differentiations. But even in the very narrow margin still left to the operation of the price-freezing decree, exemptions may be granted if they are 'economically necessary or urgently required to avoid special harshness.' [27] Such applications must go through the economic groups that have to pass upon the formal correctness as well as the material justification of the application. The federal price commissioner may grant a general exemption for all commodities of one plant or he may grant it only to one commodity produced in a particular plant.

Wherever the price-freezing decree and special enactments do not apply, prices have to be estimated as of 18 October 1936. A plant must then estimate a price under the condition that existed on 18 October 1936 even if the basis for estimating should have completely changed.[28] If it is found that the estimate is too hard on the producer, he may apply for an exemption. If the basis for estimating is unavailable, the prices have to be established in accordance with principles laid down by the federal price commissioner.

These principles are ordinary business principles; they do not demand any sacrifices from the manufacturer. Raw material may be inserted in the cost sheet at cost price; wages, only in the legally permissible amounts. There is a provision for overhead costs, for special costs, even for contributions to the party and other organizations, and for 'adequate profits.' Also important is the insistence of the price commissioner on the following considerations: 'If a plant operates at costs which are high above the average, if it is badly organized or badly managed, only adequately lower profits may be granted to it, and, in this case, it must even be expected to bear a loss.' [29] Wherever the rulings allow adequate profits or average branch profits, the view of the economic groups is decisive.

The price policy, therefore, has clearly rationalizing and monopolizing functions; it compels unrationally working plants to modernize or to perish, and if modernization is impossible (for instance, because of lack of capital), the sub-marginal plant is driven into the fold of the monopolistic competitor.

As for government orders, a distinction is made between such commodities where the government competes with private entrepreneurs on the demand side (for instance, food and clothing for the armed forces) and where the demand is monoplized by the government. In the former case all price regulations are valid; in the latter the cost-plus basis becomes the rule. The principles are laid down in two decrees,[30] which follow, on the whole, ordinary business principles. The decrees do not violate the principles of competitive prices and even exempt cartel prices,[31] but since the bulk of public orders is not competitive by nature (there are no competing buyers for guns, tanks, and ammunition), the prevailing standard of measurement becomes the cost of production plus adequate profits.

But on what basis shall the costs be determined? If the most modern plant is selected, all others must go bankrupt; if the sub-marginal plant is picked out, the others must receive too-high differential profits; so that, as is usually the case in such situations, the practice follows a middle course, the American bulk-line method.

On the whole the price-fixing policy has been successful, although stabilization of prices has not been obtained, has perhaps not even been desired. The index of wholesale prices has risen from 90.7 in 1933 to 110.9 in December 1940 and 111.9 in April 1941 (1913 = 100).[32] This is not a decisive rise in wholesale prices, yet if we analyze the wholesale index we find that while the prices of producers' goods have remained relatively stable, those of consumers' goods have risen from 109.2 in 1933 to 145.0 in December 1940 and to 147.3 in April 1941, so that the price rise chiefly affects the last consumer. This, of course, is a deliberate policy of curtailing consumption. The wholesale index coincides with the index of the cost of living. It rose (without rents) from 115.9 to 134.7 in April 1941 (1913/14 = 100). The index for clothing rose from 105.6 to 153.1 in the same period.[33] The figures are, of course, of but little value. The deterioration of commodities is not and cannot be taken into account. Besides, prices in a rationed economy do not indicate whether goods are obtainable.

What is the function of the price control? *

In a purely competitive economy, prices crystallize as a result of supply and demand. Supposing a given level of prices, an arbitrary increase in the price of any particular commodity would contract the demand and an arbitrary price-cut would increase the demand. If the contraction of demand is not accompanied by a reduction in the supply, a surplus of commodities ensues that tends to exercise a pressure on the price and to re-establish the previous correlation of prices. Maintaining the increase in price presupposes a reduction in the volume of supply, alters therefore the proportions of production. Conversely, demand increasing with price-cuts can be satisfied only through increase in production; if more of the cheaper commodity can be produced, again the proportions of production are altered; when production cannot expand, an excess of buying capacity ensues that either tends to re-establish the previous correla-

* I am indebted to Dr. A. Gurland for his help in formulating the following paragraphs on price control.

tion of prices or flows into other spheres, disrupting the given concatenation of price relations.

It is obvious that this mechanism of prices can function without disturbance only in an economic system wherein no restrictions of any kind bar competition. The slightest check on competition—either as a result of a natural shortage in the supply of elements of production or of an artificial regulation of supply or demand in any particular sphere—must disrupt the system of functional equations that constitutes the 'price level,' and must prevent the proportions of production from directly following the price equations as well as preventing the price equations from exactly reflecting the proportions of production. This is the case both when monopolies bar competition in particular fields and when centralized controls are established to 'stabilize' any set of given correlations of several elements of production or even of all of them.

Yet, the disruption of the 'automatism' of market reactions does not abolish the market. The fact that the tendencies of the production agents to react accordingly are checked and are subject to restrictions does not annihilate them. When an individual production agent is prevented through monopoly or administrative regulation from making profits by raising prices, he will try to increase his sales or cut down his costs, or both, in order to achieve his goal as a producer of commodities for sale. When he is not allowed to market more than a definite quantum of goods, he will have to raise prices, and when both prices and marketing quotas are set by regimentation or monopoly he must recur to alternations in the set-up of the cost elements in the manufacturing processes through pressure upon the costs of raw materials, manufacturing equipment, labor and capital used, as well as through changes in the manufacturing process itself, both organizational and technological.

In doing so he again will modify the given correlations of the elements of production at all the stages of manufacture and marketing, at which changes in the previous set-up can be executed. The system of equations that appears at the surface of the production relations as 'the market' will undergo changes with any move the production agent is free to make. Thus, economic activities will constitute market activities and provoke 'movements in the market' as long as there are any activities at all that the production agents are free to undertake in their own right and upon their own decision.

Under totalitarian rule, of course, the automatism of market relations is disrupted in numerous fields. This does not mean, however, that market relations have ceased to exist. Even if it were true that the prices have been established and remain stabilized on a definite level (which it is not), there still would remain the tendency of the producers to find compensation through changes in the marketing possibilities, in the costs of production, in the manufacturing process. Any such change would alter the system of equations that underlies the set-up of 'stabilized prices' and change the economic meaning of the market relations, which would thus prove only superficially stabilized.

In reality, the centralized controls of prices as well as of other components of the economic process veil and dissemble economic facts, which by themselves revolutionize the 'automatic' interdependence of supply and demand. The system of totalitarian controls masks an economy that expands permanently on the basis of full employment. This means that there is an ever-increasing demand of commodities while supply is limited by the productive capacity of the economic apparatus as determined by the general economic set-up at any given moment. Therefore, all prices display the tendency to rise. General shortage produces a general increase in the price level.

In a competitive economy this would result in a final contraction of the demand that would not be able to follow the progressive increase in prices, and in a more or less general decline of prices. The expansion would be temporarily checked, and since neither the increase nor the decrease in prices would be uniform, the new expansion would start from a modified correlation of individual prices.

The principal aim of controls and restrictions under totalitarian rule is to prevent any such temporary checks on expansion. In preventing all prices from going up simultaneously, the system of price regimentation that culminates in the price-freezing legislation equally prevents a general slump, which would be inevitable when the buying capacity fell short of the exorbitantly priced supply. Yet, price freezing does not and cannot hamper intrinsic changes in the price correlations. On the contrary, the restrictions imposed upon the arbitrary raising of prices compel the production agents to hunt for compensations both in the manufacturing set-up and in the cost elements of production. Thus, the basic correlations of prices undergo permanent changes, permanently adjust themselves to the permanently changing conditions of production and marketing. The visible general readjustment taking place in the market after a general slump within a competitive system is replaced under the totalitarian regime by a steady subterranean current of readjustments modifying the system of price equations through scarcely visible convulsions every hour and every minute. The market, instead of being abolished by regimentation, functions invisibly underground and maintains, within the framework of regimentation, legions of unco-ordinated economic decisions that scorn planning and control.

Prices still play the decisive part in determining who shall produce, or better, who shall produce most. The expansion of a plant improves its competitive position and thereby increases its profits, in turn stimulating expansion. To be sure, the entrepreneur cannot arbitrarily expand or restrict production. To restrict production is, under conditions of full employment, unnecessary. But it is precisely the incessant excess of demand over supply that provides a powerful stimulus for expansion and higher profits. This is the motivating force of the National Socialist economy:

Still bigger tasks than the ones he has . . . to perform in peacetime devolve upon the head of the enterprise in the war economy. It is understood that the war demands thorough planning in the use of man power, raw material, and productive capacity and thus imposes certain planning restrictions upon business. However, this kind of planned economy must never lead to a situation in which the initiative and the working impulse of industrialists are hampered by executive agencies of the authorities. Extensive restriction of free market production does not mean obstructing the entrepreneurial initiative; *on the contrary, the more active, resourceful, and daring the head of the enterprise, the more will he be able to fulfill his war task.**

In these words Major General George Thomas, the head of the division of defense economy in the High Army Command, outlined the tasks of the entrepreneur.[34] It is the most daring and the

* Italics mine. F. N.

most ruthless competitor who wins and shall win. Price control organizes and speeds up the process of selection taking place in a competitive economy.

Price control does not negate the profit motive but rather intensifies it. Even if the volume and the kind of production were fully regimented, the entrepreneur would have no other aim than to produce profitably, and no price decree negates this principle.[35] In every economy in which the flow of commodities is punctuated by money transactions, the impossibility of making profits would be equivalent to being debarred from production. Since, besides, the raising or even the maintaining of a production level depends upon the supply of raw material and labor, and this in turn is easier to secure to the most efficient plant, profit making and accumulation become in fact more imperative than ever. Each restriction imposed upon the entrepreneur sharpens the sting of the profit motive. Each regimentation strengthens the need of business to have pull with the authorities. A good connection with the raw-material allocating agencies, the labor exchanges, the price-control agencies becomes in fact a priceless commodity—as one National Socialist economist frankly admits.[36] Even admitting that National Socialism has succeeded in stabilizing the prices—which it has not—there is no price control for either liquid or fixed capital. Even if the prices of commodities were completely freed from the pressure of supply and demand, the prices of capital, of quotas, of permits, of shares, of bonds, of patents, of licenses would still be definitely subjected to it. It is by this detour, so to speak, that the market laws are still operating.

Nor does the fact that the government is the major buyer change the pattern. It is again true that the government as the major buyer and distributor receives a huge part of the total demand and can thereby direct, contract, or expand it. Yet even there economic limits exist that cannot be transcended. If we assume—we shall have to prove it in the next chapter—that the social system of National Socialism is based upon full employment in order to ward off opposition of the working classes, then a contraction of government demand must be compensated for by an expansion of private industry; moreover, the buying capacity of the state is limited by the volume of production and the speed of the flow of commodities.

In an economy in full production, the printing of money will not increase production; it can only change the distribution.

4. PROFITS, INVESTMENTS, AND 'THE END OF FINANCE CAPITALISM'

Does the control of profits and investments change this picture? If they were rigidly controlled, if a planning machinery directed the flow of investments according to social principles, if profits were taxed away, then possibly the system would no longer be capitalistic.

But a profit control never has existed and does not exist today. Not even the celebrated Dividend Limitation Act of 1934 contains a profit control.[37] According to the act, which in German is called *Anleihestockgesetz*, a joint stock corporation should not distribute more than 6 per cent (in some cases 8 per cent) among its stockholders. Dividends in excess of 6 per cent or 8 per cent had to be paid into the Gold Discount Bank, which invested them, on behalf of the stockholders, in government bonds. The bonds were to be redeemed in 1938 and could be used for paying taxes in 1941 and the following years. The act, therefore, had no intention of cutting down profits but merely of restricting the distribution of dividends among the shareholders, who, in the view of German economists and lawyers, are a mere nuisance. The act thereby intended to make the stock market less attractive in order to divert the flow of capital into the government bond market. The act thus belongs to the policy of controlling investments. Up to 1936, the capital market was almost closed to private industry and reserved for the government, but in 1936 this ban was relaxed and in 1939 practically abandoned. The effect of the act was small. By the end of 1940 the accumulated dividends amounted to merely 108,000,000 marks.[38] Aside from price control and taxation, there was no profit control of any kind.

The situation changed in the spring of 1941. On 5 and 11 March 1941, the Four Year Plan office and the price commissioner jointly issued two decrees. I quote that of 11 March 1941:

The price-supervising offices are authorized to order that profits which have been made contrary to the provisions of the war economy decree of 4 September 1939 have to be delivered to the Federal

Government even if no infraction against the law has been committed. Against the order of the price-supervising offices an appeal can be lodged within a week with the price-forming offices.

The federal price commissioner and the price-forming offices may change the orders when such action is justified according to the principles of the national economy.[39]

Two rulings are in effect that concretize these measures, one for industry and one for trade.[40] The details do not concern us here. The basic principle is that wherever super-profits have been made in the past, they must be paid to the federal government, while, for the future, prices must be lowered. In both cases only the lower profits will be subject to corporate and income taxes. By profits the price commissioner understands the profits of a whole enterprise, not the profit deriving from specific commodities, so that losses and profits in different departments or commodities can be equalized. Expenses for investment are not deductible from profits except by special permission of the price commissioner. Plants with higher production costs ought to have smaller profits than those with lower costs. 'The differential rent is, therefore, admitted.'[41] All measures have to be carried out in conjunction with the competent economic groups.

The new enactments do not, therefore, abolish the previous price-control measures, they merely supplement them. Their primary aim is undoubtedly the lowering of the price structure. The social aims stand in the foreground; it is the prices of consumers' goods which should primarily be lowered. But the decrees do not demand 'economic suicide,'[42] they do not aim at destroying the profits of an enterprise, they are directed merely against super-profits made by super-prices. It is, however, very questionable whether and how far the rulings have been put into operation.

A speech of Minister of Economy Funk indicates the trend of the new legislative enactments.[43] Funk attacked the self-financing of German industry and also announced the intention of restricting the distribution of dividends to 6 per cent, at the same time the possibility that the nominal value of the shares could be raised was admitted. The decree of the Ministerial Council for the Defense of the Realm of 12 June 1941 translated Funk's announcement into practice.[44] For the duration of the war, dividends are limited to 6 per cent except in the cases of corporations having paid more than 6 per cent. A limitation to 8 per cent is introduced in regard to dividends paid in cash, but the excess earnings must be invested by the corporations in government bonds which the ministry of economics holds in trust. The decree, finally, imposes heavy taxes on excess dividends. But—and this is the big hole—the decree allows the revaluation of capital, and the reports of the *Frankfurter Zeitung* show that a large number of corporations have already availed themselves of this opportunity. The leader of the national group industry, W. Zangen, explained that dividend limitation and profit freezing are merely war measures, to be discarded after the war (*Frankfurter Zeitung*, 6 July 1941), and the official press release stresses that 'it does not lie in the interest of the economy or of the enterprise . . . to lay bare too much of the hidden reserves' of an undertaking—self-financing shall, therefore, not be tampered with.

The interpretations in the German periodicals and press are very contradictory. Some take the view that it would be sufficient to raise the nominal capital of the shares. This would lead to a higher amount of distributed dividends,[45] would raise the income taxes, and would, thereby, ultimately increase savings. Others direct the attention to self-financing, which robs the tax offices of taxes and makes a comprehensive investment control impossible.

As we already mentioned, the new decrees may be directed against internal financing (acting, therefore, as a kind of undistributed profit tax), and it is this phenomenon that we shall have to discuss, because it constitutes one of the decisive aspects of German economic life. We have seen that the capital market was closed to private business until 1939 so that expansion could be financed only internally, out of undistributed profits. The 1933 legislation had, as we have already seen, encouraged internal financing by tax privileges and tax exemptions. As a consequence, undistributed profits rose for the old territory from 175,000,000 marks in 1933 to 1,200,000,000 in 1935, and 3,420,000,000 in 1938, and have since risen considerably.[46] We have to add to this figure the internal investments of individual firms and partnerships, estimated at more than 1,000,000,000 marks, so that for 1938 we reach a figure of nearly 5,000,000,000 marks undistributed profits, while the total of savings accumulated in the savings banks in 1938 amounted to merely 2,000,000,000 marks and distributed dividends during that year to approximately 1,200,000,000 marks. These figures make us realize that a decisive change has taken place, a change even greater than the change in the United States revealed in the hearings before the Temporary National Economic Committee.[47] The *Frankfurter Zeitung* of 14 March 1941, says about this situation, that while balance sheets of the corporations became 'untrue' due to self-financing, 'many dividends have become "unnatural" to a still higher degree— of course, unnaturally low.' 'It cannot be overlooked,' so it says on 10 January 1941, 'that it is just the plants necessary for warfare which, in many cases, possess a considerable fortune for investments out of their own strength and a high and even ever-increasing liquidity.' Industry is no longer indebted to banks. The nominal capital of the corporations is low, the reserves are high and permanently increasing.

Yet even the shareholders cannot complain; not only did the stock-price index of the *Frankfurter Zeitung* (according to its issue of 10 January 1941) rise from 128.22 in September 1935 to 180.97 in November 1940, but even the average dividends rose from 4.20 per cent in 1935 to 6.49 per cent in 1939, while the average yield increased from 3.91 per cent in 1935 to 5.19 per cent in 1939.[48]

The victory of internal financing over the borrowing from banks, savings banks, and insurance institutions indicates the decline of the investment banks, and the decay of the role of banking capital. That decline is a universal trend and is as operative in the United States as it is in Germany. This trend seems to be determined by the decline in the pace of economic expansion; by the monopolistic and cartel structure, which, by granting differential rents, facilitates the internal accumulation of capital; by the growth of institutional investments, government spending, and financing.

The primacy of self-financing over borrowing is not the end of capitalism and is not even the end of finance capitalism. It merely indicates that the seat of finance capitalism has shifted from the banks to industry, or rather to a congruence of banks and industry. The *Bank-Archiv*,[49] a periodical issued by the economic group 'private banks,' quite openly ridicules the attempt of heavy industry to present internal financing as a kind of socialism, as a fight against capitalism and capitalistic principles of financing. What the *Bank-Archiv* attacks is the very basis of the National Socialist ideology, and this attack reveals the sham character of National Socialist anti-capitalism.

National Socialist anti-capitalism has always exempted productive capital, that is, industrial capital, from its denunciations and solely concentrated on 'predatory' (that is, banking) capital. We have already pointed to the party program of 1920.* But even the fight against banking capital was only a sham. On 14 October 1930, the National Socialist parliamentary group introduced into the democratic parliament a draft bill demanding the confiscation without indemnity of the 'entire property of the bank and stock exchange barons, of the eastern Jews, and of other foreigners who had entered after 1 August 1914, and of all additional property acquired through war, revolution, inflation, or deflation after that date.' When the Communists and Social Democrats declared their intention of voting for the bill, the National Socialists quickly withdrew their motion. Still the attack against 'predatory' as opposed to 'productive' capital did not cease; on the contrary, it increased by leaps and bounds. The slogan was no doubt popular—a bank is always a creditor of the small and little businessman and, therefore, hated as a creditor usually is. Interests on loans are no doubt not the outcome of productive labor, though they are necessary within the capitalistic system. Finance capital as identified with banking capital has always been the target of all pseudo-socialist movements, movements that never dared to touch the foundations of capitalist society but rather sought a reform that would break the poisonous teeth off the capitalist system and direct the deep resentment of the masses against exploitation toward certain concrete symbols. Whether the chosen symbol is John Pierpont Morgan or a Jewish banker is immaterial.

In singling out predatory capital, National Socialism treads in the footsteps of Proudhon, who, in his *Idée Générale de la Révolution au 19ᵉ Siècle*, demanded the liquidation of the Banque de France and its transformation into an institution of 'public utility' together with a lowering of interest to one-half or one-fourth of 1 per cent. The *Communist Manifesto* had already denounced that type of socialism, the so-called 'True Socialism,' as specifically Germanic. Marx, in a letter to Engels on 8 August 1851,[50] had, with supreme wit, denounced Proudhon's fight against banking capital and interest as a sham. He had already pointed out that the so-called 'social liquidation' is 'merely the means of starting afresh the

* See p. 228.

healthy bourgeois society.' The theory expresses the longing of every non-industrial capitalist to become an industrial capitalist—a quite understandable wish. The anti-finance capitalistic propaganda may have had even a certain amount of truth in it when banking capital really was decisive, when banks could control, merge, and acquire industries, when money alone really represented economic power. But, as we shall see, that period is far behind us, and it is important to realize that National Socialist anti-capitalism and its fight against predatory capital was raised to the rank of the supreme economic principle in a period when banking capital has lost its significance, when the investment banker has lost his power, when money alone cannot found economic empires, when, in short, industry has become financially almost self-sufficient, when it not only finances its own expansion by its own means but even penetrates into banks and insurance institutions and subjugates them to the needs of the industrial capitalists.

It is ironical that the exclusive concentration of National Socialist anti-capitalism on banking capital was preceded by the economic doctrine of the leading Social Democratic theorist, Rudolf Hilferding, who devoted a whole and deservedly famous book to showing how banking capital becomes the promoter 'and finally the ruler in industry.' [51] 'In the final instance,' he continues, 'this tendency would lead to the fact that one bank or one group of banks obtains the control over the whole money capital. Such a central bank, therefore, would control the whole social production' (page 218). As important as is his theoretical basis are the political consequences he draws. 'As soon as finance capital has achieved control over the most important branches of production, the seizure of finance capital by society, through its . . . executive organ, namely, the state which has been conquered by the proletariat, is sufficient to achieve immediate control over the major branches of production' (page 473). And already in 1910 he maintained that 'the seizure of six big Berlin banks would already mean today the seizure of the most important spheres of the great industries.'

The economic theory of the Social Democratic party, however, lagged behind reality even before the First World War. For in 1910, when Hilferding's book was published, the theory of the supremacy of the banks over industry was no longer completely true. Emil Kirdorf, one of the leaders of heavy industry, the representative of the most die-hard industrialists in Germany and a close friend of Hitler, who visited him on his 80th birthday and handed him the eagle shield of the Third Reich, had stated as early as 1905: 'Never has the power of the banks over us been as weak as it is today.' [52] Many competent economic observers in Germany shared Kirdorf's view.

The relation between industrial and banking capital passes through three stages; [53] in the early stage of large-scale industry, capital formation within industry is not sufficient for expansion. Industry needs large amounts of capital in single lumps. The banks organize the credit system by canalizing the savings of the masses, especially to the railroads. In this period the demand for money capital is indeed high, and correspondingly the power of the banks, whether in the form of the private investment banker as in the United States, or in that of the joint stock banks as in Germany. In the second phase, however, · the accumulation of capital within industry increases to such an extent that industry becomes almost independent of the banks and is able to finance expansion out of undistributed profits. In the final phase, that of National Socialist monopoly economy, industry is often incapable of investing all its savings in its plant. It begins to expand into almost any other economic activity, and even begins to conquer banks and insurance institutions—and thereby assumes the role of the finance capitalist.

The fight against banking capital is not anti-capitalism; it is, on the contrary, capitalism and indeed often fascist capitalism, not only in Germany but in almost every other country. Those who do not tire of attacking the supremacy of finance capital (by which they always understand banking capital) thereby play into the hands of the most powerful and most aggressive groups in modern society, the industrial monopolists. Whenever the outcry against the sovereignty of banking capital is injected into a popular movement, it is the surest sign that fascism is on its way. The *Bank-Archiv*, which is closely connected with the economic group 'private banks,' ridiculed, therefore, with full justice the so-called socialist character of internal financing as asserted by heavy industry. Unfortunately the *Bank-Archiv* stops here. One step further and it would have recognized the sham of the whole National Socialist economic philosophy.

Finance capitalism is not dead; it is a reality and a very powerful one, too. The accumulation of undistributed profits by the corporations was not merely used for plant expansion and for an increase in stock, but it was as much utilized for the extension of the power of the monopolies over other enterprises. That we have already showed in detail. But we have still to prove the congruence of industrial and banking capital and the extent to which industrial capital penetrated into the banks. We have no other means of ascertaining this except by analyzing the composition of the supervisory boards. We select two banks, the Deutsche Bank and the Dresdner Bank.

In the Deutsche Bank, the supervisory board consists of two chairmen and thirty members. Only three of them belong to the administration of the bank, among them the vice-president of the Reichstag, Dr. E. G. von Stauss; four are connected with other banks; one may be considered as somehow representing public interests; those remaining are delegates of industrial combines, of the Haniel combine (heavy industry), of the United Steel trust, of the Hoesch combine (heavy industry), of the Mannesmann combine (represented by the leader of the national group industry, W. Zangen), of the chemical industry (Henkel and Pietzsch, who is also the president of the national economic chamber), of the Quandt combine, of the Dye Stuff trust, of the cigarette industry (Reemtsma), of the potash industry (Salzdethfurth), and of the automobile industry (the Duke of Saxe Coburg-Gotha). Not much different is the board of the Dresdner, which formerly belonged to the federal government. Its supervisory board has one chairman, three deputies, and twenty-seven members. Only the chairman belongs to the Dresdner Bank proper; one is a member of the Reichsbank, five belong to other banks, three to insurance institutions, three to the Göring combine, and the rest to private combines such as Krupp, Junkers, Flick, North German Lloyd, automobile industry, Wintershall and Bosch.

Industrial capital also pushes into the insurance corporations; Krupp, Röchling, and Mannesmann into the famous Allianz; the steel trust, Quandt and Hoesch, into the Gerling combine, to name but a few. They are thus also trying to control institutional investments. Nor is this all. Private industry and allied big banks have also penetrated into the mortgage banks, which finance agriculture by the issue of mortgage bonds. In the Rhenish Mortgage Credit Bank, we find representatives of Röchling, of the Dresdner Bank and of a number of private banks. The automobile industry, Krupp, the Dresdner Bank, and a number of private banks have entered into the German Central Real-Estate Credit Bank. The chemical industry, the Deutsche Bank, the Dresdner Bank, and private banks have entered into the Rhenish Westphalian Real-Estate Credit Bank. There is, I believe, not a single fully autonomous bank in Germany. No independent financial combines as they exist in the United States —even if their power is reduced—are to be found in Germany—in contrast to Austria of 1931 where the Austrian Credit Bank dominated industry and its collapse seriously threatened the whole industrial structure of Austria.

But even as far as the banks proper are concerned, they have not become simple governmental agencies. They in turn have expanded not only in incorporating private banks, especially the Jewish banking business, but in acquiring a number of commercial and industrial holdings, partly in the process of Aryanizing, partly in that of Germanization. The Deutsche Bank, for instance, acquired 90 per cent of the capital of the Banca Commerciala Romana in Bukarest—French and Belgian interests had to withdraw. Two of the Czechoslovakian Banks have fallen prey to the Deutsche and Dresdner Banks, other Rumanian and Yugoslavian banks have been taken over by a number of other German banks—so the *Frankfurter Zeitung* proudly reports on 4 June 1941.

Nevertheless, it is in the control of the banks that the influence of the state is great, so great that indeed a change in the socio-political structure must be admitted. A special statute of 1934 created a credit supervisory board [54] composed of the president and vice-president of the Reichsbank directorate, a member appointed by Hitler, and the secretaries of state in the ministries of finance, economics, food and agriculture, and the interior. The leading influence belongs to the Reichsbank. The board enacts rulings which serve a dual purpose. They intend to prevent all those misuses in the banking system that had become apparent and were partly the cause of the banking crisis of 1931. The board may therefore issue rules fixing the amount of reserves, regulating the liquidity of the banks, controlling the granting of credits to employees of the bank. But the board exercises also an investment control. The actual supervision of the credit structure is carried out by a federal credit commissioner to whom is entrusted the actual supervision within the framework of the rulings of the supervisory board. O. C. Fischer's article [54] stresses the groups' supreme importance in exercising the control of credits. Not only has the power of the private banks decreased in view of the significance of internal financing, but the banks have also been superseded to a large extent by the public financial institutions and by institutional financing (savings banks and insurance institutions).

The center of the credit structure is, of course, the Reichsbank, no longer an autonomous body controlled by the shareholders and the directorate, but, since 30 August 1934, simply an executive agency of the federal government.[55] Section 6 of the new statute states that 'The bank is administrated by the Reichsbank directorate which stands directly under the Leader and Chancellor; it consists of a president acting as chairman, and the necessary number of members. The Reichsbank directorate especially determines the currency, discount, and credit policies of the bank.' By its power to discount bills the Reichsbank exerts considerable influence over the private banks. By closing the capital market to private industry it compelled the banks to invest primarily in government bonds— which the banks did without reluctance because of their high liquidity.[56] It is, therefore, true that the control of credits no longer rests with the banks. But this does not mean that it rests solely with the federal government, since internal financing sets up a definite limit, and besides, government spending flows to a large extent into private industry.

Credit control, nevertheless, indicates a new phase in the development of the political structure of society. Under conditions of liberal democracy, the control of the credit machinery gave the banks a stranglehold upon the political machinery, while the independence of the central banks more than once was utilized by powerful financial and industrial interests to break the neck of any government that threatened their privileges. The history of France, of Great Britain, and particularly of Germany in 1923 and 1924 provides a large number of instances.

This private money capital can no longer do. Banks, insurance institutions, and savings banks cannot invest where they please. They can no longer organize investors' strikes. The central bank can no longer sabotage the financial machinery, or paralyze a political system. In this field, the state has indeed absolute supremacy.

But this supremacy does not mean that the flow of investments is planned. Indeed it is impossible to say that investment planning exists in Germany. Too large a sector, self-financing, is completely free from regimentation. Neither does the state's sovereignty over the credit system mean that that control is exercised for the sake of universal interests. Nor does it mean that the banks are opposed to credit control. There is no longer any need for a banker to go on strike against the government since the short-term interests of the banks and of the government have become almost identical. The regime fulfils their expectations.

The supremacy of politics within the credit system, in spite of the reduced significance of that credit system for industrial capitalism, makes it again urgent to subordinate the political machinery to the needs of capital. The more the state regiments, the greater the urgency to eliminate the 'accidents' inherent in every democracy, that is, to make the political system safe for banking capital too. It is significant that some of the most powerful figures in the National Socialist hierarchy are outstanding bankers. Dr. E. G. von Stauss of the Deutsche Bank is a vice-president of the Reichstag; O. C. Fischer, originally of the *Reichskreditgesellschaft*, now a partner in a powerful private bank that greatly benefited from Aryanization, is the leader of the national group banking; Friedrich Reinhart, with the Commerz-Bank, is president of the Berlin stock exchange, leader of the economic chamber Berlin-Brandenburg, member of the central committee of the Reichsbank and of the advisory committee of the railroads; Kurt von Schröder of Cologne, the famous intermediary between Hitler, Papen, and Hindenburg in January 1933, sits in almost every important supervisory board. We may also mention again Kurt Weigelt, a member of the management of the Deutsche Bank, member of the colonial office of the National Socialist party and close collaborator of that arch-imperialist, Werner Daitz.* They are representatives of powerful banking interests and at the same time outspoken advocates of National Socialism.

The control of profits never has existed and does not exist today. The distribution of dividends has now been restricted to 6 per cent —it is even possible that some kind of undistributed profit tax might

* See p. 171.

be levied on the basis of the so-called profit-freezing decrees of the price commissioner. They would not change the picture.

There is a control of credits, which, however, halts before one of the essential sources, self-financing, where the mechanism of capitalistic society fully asserts itself. The existing credit control strengthens the necessity for business to get power and more power over the state machinery.

5. Foreign Trade, Autarky, and Imperialism

Foreign trade may be a means of enriching a higher and better-organized nation at the expense of a less industrialized. This is the essence of foreign trade even under conditions of free competition. That was not Ricardo's view. In the seventh chapter of his *Principles* he tries to prove that the profit rate can only be raised by the lowering of wages, while foreign trade, though beneficial to the country, never increases profits. We believe that on the world market commodities are not exchanged at their value, but that, on the contrary, a more industrialized country exchanges less labor for more. Foreign trade, under conditions of free competition, is thus the means of transferring profits. For this reason, foreign trade is one of the decisive means of counteracting the dangers arising from domestic over-accumulation and the saturation of the domestic market. The fight for a bigger share in foreign trade thus assumes paramount importance for every industrial nation. In addition, it brings in surplus profits that may even be, for a time, the sole source of profits. This fundamental impetus has not changed. What has changed are the methods.

As soon as Germany began to threaten England's trade monopoly, the whole situation on the world market underwent decisive changes culminating in what amounts to a state-regimented foreign trade.

England's supremacy was threatened when Germany achieved a monopolistic structure protected by tariffs. Monopoly and tariffs deeply affect the character of foreign trade; they give birth to dumping, that is, to a differential between domestic and export prices, to the cutting of export prices on the basis of a higher domestic price structure. 'Once monopoly control has been achieved in the domestic market, it may pay, if domestic orders do not fully occupy the productive facilities, to bid for orders in other markets at prices lower than those exacted at home,' [57] says America's foremost expert in the question of dumping.

This, indeed, was the situation in Germany as early as the turn from the nineteenth to the twentieth century. England, the 'have' nation, was the country of free trade; Germany, the 'have-not' nation, was the country of monopolies and protection. The cartel system made it possible for a time to sell on the world market without profits, even at a loss, since the cartel rent and protective tariffs operated as an indirect tax levied upon the domestic consumers and paid to the cartels, and thus compensated the domestic industries for the temporary losses on the international market. Cartels and protective tariffs thus changed from a device for the protection of the domestic market into one for the conquest of foreign markets.

Dumping as a practice of German monopolies was the subject of a federal investigation as early as 1902, namely during the first federal cartel inquiry, and became the standard practice of German industry when industry openly became imperialistic. But this very process creates counter-tendencies, above all the monopolization of raw materials in the 'have' countries. Rubber and tin, oil and copper are, as every raw material is, conducive to monopolization. International cartels and pools raise the prices, curtail production, and thereby impose taxes upon the have-nots that heavily reduce their profits. The monopolization of the raw-material market has often been discussed and the super-profits accruing to the monopolists have often been attacked. There is no doubt that the mastery over the raw-material market tends to diminish the profits that are derived from industrial production.

But the monopolization of raw material has a second, a political, function. If a country like Germany is committed to expansion, the control of raw material becomes a political as well as an economic necessity. International cartel agreements, even if Germany shares in them, will not be sufficient to protect her interests. The supply of raw material may be cut off and her industrial production may be jeopardized at any moment. The security of the raw material supply thus becomes a problem to be solved by the state. The political power of the state must get control over territories where such raw materials are found. Moreover, during the Weimar Republic, the government's gold reserves became depleted and raw-material imports could be paid for solely by the export of finished goods. But since the spread of protectionism made the export of finished goods more and more difficult, political control over territories producing raw materials seemed inescapable to a Germany committed to foreign expansion.

Not only the raw material supply, but also the export trade proper must ultimately rely upon political protection. Monopolies and tariffs in one country beget monopolies and tariffs in a competing country. Dumping by one state produces dumping by others, until a time comes when political power has to decide which competitor shall exploit the market.

This coalescence of foreign trade and politics receives a new stimulus by capital export. Capital export is not just one of the many phenomena of capitalism, it is the decisive phenomenon in the stage of modern capitalism. If the internal market is over-capitalized, if domestic investments do not yield returns, if the pace of economic expansion slackens, if domestic depression throws the economy out of gear, if the burdens cannot be fully thrown upon the large masses of the people because parliamentary democracy functions and trade unions operate, the need for capital export becomes more and more stringent. Capital export is the export not merely of money but also of industrial equipment. To secure a sufficient and stable return from investments, political means once again are necessary.

This is the secular trend of foreign trade: domestic monopolies and protective tariffs—dumping—monopolistic exploitation of raw-material producing countries—control of foreign trade to save gold for the payment of imports—capital export—demand for political guarantees of investments.

It is against this background that Germany's foreign trade has to be understood. It is foreign trade in name only. Foreign trade and currency manipulation now become predominantly the means of subjugating foreign countries.

It is, therefore, nonsense to maintain that Germany aims at autarky or self-sufficiency.[58] Autarky is not Germany's long-range aim but a political necessity for a country out to wage war against a world that controls most of the vital raw materials. Autarky is the philosophy of a fortress about to be beleaguered. Even during the Weimar Republic the debate on autarky raged among economists and the wide public. The discussions, when we re-read them today, betray a complete unreality. Those who advocated self-sufficiency as a 'new philosophy of life,' as a 'platonic idea' [59] (like Sombart and Fried), wanted Germany to devote its energies to internal reconstruction and even to undo part of its industrial development and turn to agriculture. The statistics that the advocates of autarky appended to their books intended to prove that once the domestic resources of Germany were fully utilized (like low-grade iron ore and synthetic industries), Germany would become nearly independent of the outside world and only a narrow margin of imports would be needed, which could be paid for by the export of finished goods. The advocates of autarky thus demanded a 'conscious withdrawal from the world economy.' Apparently they did not expect that only one year later Germany would be committed to a rearmament program such as the world has never seen before, that industrial capacity would be expanded to tremendous proportions, and that enormous quantities of raw material would have to be imported, in addition to the full utilization of domestic resources —while re-agrarization remained a pious dream that was certainly not even dreamed by the National Socialist leadership except perhaps by Dr. Darré.

Autarky in Germany is not a new philosophy of life, it does not express the wish of the leadership, it does not imply the undoing of industrialization, it is merely a war measure intended to make Germany as independent as possible in foodstuff, fodder, fats and raw material. Its ultimate aim is the conquest of raw material bases and of markets for export goods. Free trade no longer opens such vistas. The world is divided among powerful states, each of them committed to protect its own economy. The higher the industrial capacity of Germany, the more foreign markets will be needed to absorb production. Even a completely Nazified Europe will not be sufficient. The *grossdeutsche Reich* will not be able to absorb the goods unless the process of industrialization in the conquered territories and perhaps even in the old federal territory is deliberately reversed. Even assuming that Germany will retain control of the whole of Europe (excepting Russia), the new order must still rely upon imports of foods, fodder, and raw materials—as a Brookings Institution study has convincingly shown.[60] Yet even the figures this study mentions may be more or less meaningless, as the author admits. They do not and cannot take account of the amount of destruction wrought upon Europe. They cannot foresee whether Nazi Europe will receive co-operation or hostility from the rest of the world. One factor, however, will always remain. Germany will need enormous amounts of raw material to keep its industrial machinery going, and the greater the industrial machinery, the more it will need, and the more urgent will be the need for foreign trade with the rest of the world.

This is implied in Minister Funk's speech of 12 June 1941, given in Vienna before the Southeastern Europe Society, headed by Baldur von Schirach; he insisted that extreme autarky would lead to the impoverishment of Germany and must, therefore, be rejected was the extreme international division of labor. Large-space economies and world trade are, in his view, not incompatible, and Germany demands 'free access to the markets of all countries'— which, in his view, does not imply that other competitors should be arbitrarily excluded.[61] The most comprehensive analysis of Germany's foreign-trade policy yet undertaken [62] comes, indeed, to a wholesale refutation of the autarky philosophy.

Autarky is indeed incompatible with Germany's imperialist population policy. Autarky would imply the reduction of the standard of living to the lowest level and 'is thereby the means of making impossible an active population policy.' [63] Autarky is incompatible with the doctrine of social imperialism, which, as we have tried to show, is directed against the Anglo-American 'haves.' Therefore, it is merely a transitory phenomenon, and not even a complete one— whether it is a 'small' or 'large-space' autarky.

As a result Germany will be driven to the conquest of the world market, for it is an indisputable fact that the bulk of surplus goods is absorbed not by trade with colonial, semi-colonial, and non-industrial states, but by trade with industrial nations. To trade successfully with them, that is, to transfer from them more labor for less labor, can no longer be carried out by mere economic exchange but only with the help of political domination that incorporates the states into Germany's currency system.

National Socialism has always recognized the supreme importance of foreign trade.[64] 'We know that the geographic location of Germany, poor in raw materials, does not permit complete autarky for our Reich. It must be insisted again and again that the federal government is far from being hostile to exports. We know that we need connections with the world and that the sale of German commodities nourishes many million Germans.' This was Adolf Hitler's view on 23 March 1933.[65]

Germany's trade policy encouraged export trade wherever it could. A federal foreign-trade board was established (October 1933) as a liaison agency to the ministries of economics and foreign affairs. It is assisted by a foreign-trade council composed of the most powerful representatives in foreign trade. Federal export insurance, formerly the business of private insurance corporations, was now given by the state. Trade with Russia had always received favorable treatment, and Germany often advanced money to Russia. Similar agreements were made with the Balkans. Reduction of transportation rates, tax privileges, direct subsidies by blocked marks, and collective levies raised within the economic groups (28 June 1935) gave additional stimuli.

The policy was successful on the whole, though the annexation of Austria worsened the condition of foreign trade.[66] A number of methods were used for the purpose of securing raw material and of conquering foreign markets, namely the control of foreign currencies, the manipulation of clearing agreements, and barter-trade methods. It is these aspects of Nazi policy that are best known to the outside world.[67] Control of foreign currency proved an excellent means of getting rid of foreign debts. It is a well-known fact that the bigger the debt, the more powerful the position of the debtor. To owe huge debts gives power—this is one of the anomalies of every credit system. It makes it risky for a creditor to insist on the payment of a huge debt if that insistence might lead to the destruction of the very existence of the debtor. Big debtors must, therefore, be handled with care, they must be treated like hens laying golden eggs—in the future. To this general observation there must be added the solidarity of international capitalism. To insist on German payments might, in the view of the creditors, have driven National Socialism into Bolshevism. This was indeed the music that Schacht played with success.'

German indebtedness to foreign creditors was high. The Layton-Wiggin Committee appointed on recommendation of the London conference of 1931 established it at 23,000,000,000 marks—8,000,-000,000 in long-term, 9,000,000,000 in short-term loans, and 6,000,-000,000 in other investments.[68] The depression and the collapse of international trade (see note 66) made the flow of gold from Germany and the payment of reparations extraordinarily difficult. This difficulty was overcome, however, by the Hoover moratorium, which Congress ratified on 22 December 1931. Reparation payments ended in the middle of 1931. But these payments never were a considerable drain on German resources. From 1924 to July 1933, 11,400,000,-000 marks were paid,[69] though that figure is disputed as too high. How little the reparation payments amounted to may be gathered from the fact that domestic savings from 1925 to 1928 amounted to 25,000,000,000 marks and those from 1925 to 1930 to about 45,000,-000,000 marks.[70]

While reparation payments were thus ended, the payment of private debts still remained a problem. The legal means of stopping them was the decree for the control of foreign currency enacted by President von Hindenburg on the basis of Article 48 of the Constitution on 15 July 1931; this decree served in turn as the basis of a number of other decrees, which were ultimately codified in one comprehensive regulation.[71] Control of foreign currency was vested in the Reichsbank, which, together with the Gold Discount Bank, was exempted from control. All others had to have permission to acquire, sell, or otherwise dispose of foreign-currency holdings and securities above a certain amount. Exemptions were to be granted by the Reichsbank. Future trading in foreign currency was forbidden and securities acquired after a certain date were to be reported to the Reichsbank. The legislation proved only partly efficient. The drain on gold and foreign currency continued and the gold reserves of the Reichsbank fell from about 3,000,000,000 marks in the middle of 1930 to 991,000,000 in December 1932, and finally to approximately 78,000,000 in 1939. This, in spite of the various standstill agreements concluded between the German debtors and the foreign creditors, first in August 1931, and changed and renewed at various other dates.

The democratic government of Germany refused to go again the way of devaluating the mark, as Great Britain had done in 1931 with its own currency. This refusal was perhaps not so much a result of economic reasons as of psychological. The terror created by the inflation of 1923 was not yet forgotten. There even existed political groups thriving on the inflation and fighting for revaluation. The government tried to check the drain on currency by sharpening the foreign-currency control legislation.[72] Permission was now necessary for the paying of imports, foreign services, for the amortization and interest on foreign debts.

The new currency legislation, of course, affected foreign trade. The currency control authorities had already the power to control the flow of imports and thereby the allocation of raw materials.

This was the situation when National Socialism came into power. The reparation problem had ceased to exist, but the deficit in capital payments was still heavy. It could still be met by Germany's export surplus of about 1,000,000,000 marks (see note 66) but it was doubtful, indeed unlikely, that the export surplus could be maintained. The devaluation of the mark by National Socialism was still more out of question, since National Socialist propaganda had lived for years on the denunciation of the democratic parties as responsible for the 1923 inflation. The new regime started with a transfer moratorium, which was followed by a full moratorium in 1934. German debtors had to pay their international obligations into a conversion office for foreign debts, which, at discretion, could make payments to foreign creditors. Only the Reichsbank and the obligations arising from the standstill agreements were exempt, although certain concessions were wrought from time to time by one or other creditor nation. At the same time the control of foreign currency was transferred to a special agency, until, on 24 September 1934, Schacht's new plan went into operation and the manipulation of foreign currency became entirely a function of foreign trade. The supervisory boards and later the *Reichsstellen* * controlled the flow of imports. A clearing office was established, a number of obligations were denounced. By clever manipulation of the stock and bond market the standstill debts were heavily reduced (to 4,100,-000,000 marks in February 1933) while the subsequent standstill agreements and currency legislation tightened the control and closed existing leaks.

Control of foreign currency changed from a means of supporting the rather tottering German currency, into a powerful device for controlling foreign trade and thereby subjugating foreign countries. The currency-control offices and the *Reichsstellen* could, at

* See p. 251.

will, stop any imports from any country so as to soften it. The law for the protection of the German commodities export of 22 September 1933 made possible the establishment of import quotas, the quotas being regularly determined by the treatment accorded to German exports.

Within a very short time bilateral trade agreements became the rule. Export and import prices were often arbitrarily determined.[73] Prices for food-stuffs to be imported, especially those paid to the Balkan peasants, were certainly high in terms of local currency, but the aim, of course entirely propagandist, was to win the masses of the peasants for Germany. The hold that currency and import control gave Germany over most of the exporting European countries was strengthened by clearing agreements and barter contracts.

The essence of the clearing agreements, which soon became the condition without which trade agreements could not be concluded, is as follows: German debtors paid into the Reichsbank or into a clearing account while the foreign importers paid to their central agencies. The balances were then adjusted. If Germany had a surplus in relation to another country, that currency surplus was used to pay her debts to a third over-seas country for raw material. The agreements were made partly with central governments, partly with central banks. The function of the clearing agreements has been admirably described by Douglas Miller.[74]

Exporters in Germany would ship, for example, to Yugoslavia and be credited with the mark value of their shipments by the German Reichsbank. Yugoslav exporters to Germany would be credited in dinars by the central bank in Belgrade, with the two banks balancing accounts. Payment was credited to the exporters in each country in their local currency, and at the time of the year the balance would be carried forward in favor of one or the other country to apply against next year's transactions.

The aim of Germany's trade policy thus became exceedingly simple: to buy from a country as much as you can; acquire for instance the whole crop of a country—but without paying. The increase in imports even led to the importation of finished goods in competition with German industry.[75] As a result of this policy Germany was in the process of becoming a huge debtor nation— on clearing accounts. We have already mentioned the case of Den-

mark under German occupation.* Today the accumulation of debts
within Nazified Europe is a simple matter. But even previously the
economic position of certain countries, especially the Balkan states
and some Central and South American states, played into Germany's
hands.[76] There was no consumer for their agricultural over-produc-
tion except Germany. The western democracies, which still pursued
a policy of appeasement, were unable or unwilling to see that the
fight against National Socialism must be fought on all fronts, not
the least being the economic one, and that economic war could be
waged only by taking over the surplus production of the threatened nations.

Germany not only gained a supply of some raw materials and
food-stuffs by the clearing system, but also succeeded in economically subjugating the countries she traded with. The National Socialist economists have therefore described the clearing system as
the most powerful means of currency and trade politics.[77] Berlin
has become the clearing center and the Reichsmark has been deliberately overvalued in comparison with the currencies of Holland,
Czechoslovakia, Yugoslavia. Clearing thus became the basis for what
is called a 'planned exchange of commodities.' [78]

Barter and clearing also gave an excellent means of flooding a
country that had claims against Germany on the clearing account
with overvalued or depreciated export goods, the creditor nation
often being glad to receive at least that.

This then is, in the briefest possible outline, the course of Germany's trade policy. In it Germany's imperialist character is most
apparent. Here the change in the methods of German capitalism
is most manifest. Here the congruence of economics and politics
becomes a complete identity of interests and aims.

It is, we repeat, nonsensical to believe that Germany aims at
autarky and renounces foreign markets. Autarky is on the contrary
merely a preparation for the conquest of world markets. Since the
world market is divided among powerful contending states, it can
no longer be conquered by trade and investments but only by political means. And since trade between industrial states is the essence
of foreign trade, the political conquest of the world is and must be
the aim of National Socialist Germany if she wants to survive as a

* See p. 180.

highly industrialized nation. If Germany is willing to transform Europe into a primarily agricultural state, if she is willing to reduce the standard of living of the masses in Europe, she may indeed renounce the conquest of the world. But is it conceivable that a highly industrialized state should voluntarily abandon economic progress? In our opinion, it is not. Germany, if defeated, may be compelled to withdraw from the society of highly industrialized states, but that is certainly not the policy of her present government. It would be a complete negation of the whole history of German industrial capitalism. On the contrary, it is the high productivity of the industrial apparatus, the pressure for foreign markets, and the need for satisfying the vital material interests of her masses that have driven Germany into a policy of conquest and will continue to drive her to still further expansion until she is defeated or has fulfilled her aim. It is the dynamics of a fairly young, aggressive, monopolized country that is the prime mover of Germany's expansion.

6. THE CONTROL OF LABOR *

It is in the control of the labor market that National Socialism is most sharply distinguished from democratic society. The worker has no rights. The potential and actual power of the state over the labor market is as comprehensive as it can possibly be. The state has already reached the utmost limit of the labor market control.

It might, therefore, be argued that since the freedom of the labor contract has ceased to exist, capitalism has ceased to exist in Germany. For capitalism, one might say, is built on free labor, and free labor distinguishes capitalism from any previous economic system. That is the view of all economists, from Karl Marx to Max Weber. The view is certainly correct. But we have to define what we understand by free labor and the freedom of the labor contract. There are three different concepts of freedom of labor, expressing different stages in the development of capitalism.

Freedom can mean the individual right of the worker to bargain with his employer on the basis of legal equality. Such freedom characterized liberal capitalism and found its best expression in the *lex Le Chapelier* of the French Revolution. 'There is,' Le Chapelier

* On the legal and sociological aspects of the control of labor, see p. 413.

said on 14 June 1791, 'only the interest of the individual and the interest of the commonwealth, and no one is entitled to win over citizens to the pursuit of any interests that conflict with these and that alienate them from service to the state through the medium of corporate interests.' Such freedom, hostile to trade unions and collective bargaining, characterized European labor policies for decades—in France until 1864, in Germany until 1869, in England until 1871. It meant either outright prohibition of trade unions or their mere toleration. Such law gave the power to the worker to determine formally the price of his labor power—but it failed to take into account that, in relation to him, the employer always is a monopolist and that, in consequence, freedom also veils exploitation.

Freedom of the labor contract may also mean the material right of the laborer to determine the price of his labor power—by means of collective organization and bargaining. This material freedom does not negate the formal freedom, it merely fulfils it; formal and material freedom do not contradict but supplement each other. The material freedom of labor, to bargain with the employer on a basis of factual equality, was achieved by the triumph of trade unionism after the First World War. Neither of these two types of freedom exist under National Socialism.

But there is a third type of freedom, upon which the other two types rest—the freedom consisting in the mere rejection of slavery and servitude. This concept of free labor is polemical, directed against any kind of servitude. The feudal contract was a contract of faith, involving the whole personality of the worker without distinguishing between labor and leisure. Such contract is incalculable and unpredictable, it controls man in all his aspects, it demands complete subservience. In such a contract the worker does not sell himself for specific services and for a specific time, but for any service that might be required and for his whole time. In Prussia, remnants of such feudal labor relations existed until the end of 1918. The famous *Gesindeordnungen*, for domestic and agrarian personnel, granted the police the power forcibly to return the workers to their employers if and when they left their services in violation of their contractual obligations.

Freedom of the labor contract means, then, primarily a clear distinction between labor and leisure time, which introduces the element of calculability and predictability into labor relations. It means that the worker sells his labor power for a time only, which is either agreed upon or fixed by legislative acts. It also means, though not primarily, that laborers sell their time only for specific performances, which are defined by agreement, statute, or custom, and that they are not obligated to do any kind of work their employer might arbitrarily determine. This type of freedom prevails in the period of primary accumulation.

Such freedom of the labor contract still exists in Germany. The labor contract is still the form that rules labor relations. The distinction between labor and leisure is as sharp in Germany as it is in any democracy, even though the regime attempts to control the worker's leisure time. In the next chapter we shall have occasion to deal with the development of labor law and we shall try to prove that every attempt of the National Socialist lawyers to supersede the labor contract by another legal instrument (such as community relations) has failed, and that all relations between employer and employee are still contractual ones.

To be sure, the identity of the basic pattern does not say much about the actual operation of the labor market, and it is here that the sharpest possible difference exists between democracies and totalitarianism.

A free labor market does not, of course, exist when trade unions bargain collectively. The price of labor power is not merely the result of supply and demand, and the pressure from industrial reserve army is partly overcome. Wages are also determined by the social power of trade unions. Workers' organizations attempt to transform the mere legal fact of the free contract into genuine material freedom. Yet we must not overestimate the power of the unions. If all their activities are not subordinated to the interests of small aristocratic groups within the labor movement, and if they really strive to improve the wages and labor conditions of the working class, their power is extremely limited. We maintain that their power is primarily of a defensive character. This thesis cannot be proved here. I must content myself with the bare assertion which I believe to be true and which can be substantiated by research. In the upward business cycle, wages normally increase. But the increase is, as a whole, the natural outcome of improved economic conditions. It is rather in the period of contractions that the power of the trade unions manifests itself and that their influence makes itself felt. It is always easier to defend a position than to conquer a new one. The policy of the German trade unions during the depression of 1931-2 proves my contention.* Though they could not prevent wage cuts, they could and did prevent the complete adjustment of wages to the low of the business cycle, and it was their very defensive strength that made them the target of industry. It is this aspect of autonomous labor-market control that National Socialism has destroyed. Yet it is no longer necessary under conditions of full employment. If the effective demand for labor far exceeds the supply, no defensive organizations are needed to prevent the fall in wages; what is needed rather is offensive unions fighting to adjust the wage scale to full capacity. It is the function of the National Socialist policy to prevent such adjustment.

For in contrast to business, labor has no organization of its own. There is no autonomous organization of the working classes corresponding to that of business. There is no organization of labor for the control of the labor market, corresponding to the cartels. The German labor front is not an autonomous organization of labor, for it does not consist solely of workers and employees, nor is it a marketing organization. We shall deal with its functions later.†

The aims of the National Socialist labor-market policy are clear and directly expressed. Since two descriptions of that kind exist,[79] it is not necessary to add here a third one. We are primarily concerned with the functions performed by that policy and with its principles. They may be defined as: (1) the full utilization of manpower for productive purposes (*Arbeitseinsatz*); (2) the raising of the productivity of each individual worker and the simultaneous stabilization of the wage level.

THE UTILIZATION OF MAN-POWER

The utilization of man-power means two different things: the introduction into gainful employment of as many people as possible not yet gainfully employed, and the shift within the gainfully employed from industries and trades where labor is not needed into other branches suffering from a shortage.

The number of gainfully employed rose, of course, steadily from 17,817,000 in 1929 to 22,617,000 in January 1941.[80] Preparedness and

* See also p. 434.
† See p. 413.

war have also led to an increase in the employment of women, especially in transportation and industry. While in 1933 women constituted 37.3 per cent of all workers employed in industry and in 1936 their share was reduced to 31.8 per cent, it had already reached, in October 1940, 37.1 per cent. In absolute figures, the number of employed women rose from 4,700,000 in 1933 to 6,300,000 in 1938 and 8,420,000 in January of 1941.[81] The labor reserve, represented by women, is not yet exhausted, for the total number of women capable of working is estimated at between 10,000,000 and 12,000,-000, and for this reason, the ways and means of mobilizing the reserve of women are being increasingly discussed.[82]

The labor supply was further increased by the combing-out of handicraft and retail, already described,* and the closing down of plants producing consumption goods.† To these figures must be added the alien workers, partly composed of workers imported into Germany on the basis of international agreements (1,100,000 in October 1940) [83] and partly of war prisoners.[84]

There is no doubt that although the labor reserve is scarce, it is not yet exhausted and three more million women can be introduced into the productive process. More plants producing consumption goods can be closed down and more workers from the occupied territories can be shifted to Germany proper.

But the policy of utilizing the available man-power to the utmost equally implied the increase in the supply of skilled labor, and that in turn meant the repatriation of skilled labor from other branches in trade and industry, compulsory training and the shortening of the apprenticeship period.

The policy of transferring people to productive work has been brutally carried out, without regard to humanitarian considerations. The legal acts on which this power rests have become more and more stringent. They began with the decree for securing labor power of 22 June 1938, issued by the Four Year Plan office, which obligated every German citizen to work on a fixed place for a fixed period or to submit to compulsory vocational training. The decree did not go far enough. It was soon superseded by that of 13 February 1939,[85] extending the obligation to all inhabitants of the federal territory and making the service compulsory for indefinite periods.

* See p. 282.
† See p. 283.

Every inhabitant of the territory, foreigner or citizen, already employed or not, man or woman, juvenile or adult, may be summoned to do any kind of productive work for a fixed or an indeterminate period. If he is summoned for a definite period and already employed, the labor contract remains in force; if he is summoned for an indefinite period, it lapses. The compulsory service is carried out under a labor contract. The moment an individual receives an order that summons him to work for a specific employer, a labor contract between him and the employer is deemed to be concluded. This contract is regulated by all legislative and administrative provisions under which the free labor contract stands. It can be ended, however, only with the consent of the labor exchange.

The same decree also considerably reinforced the legislation intended to prevent the workers from changing their place of employment by empowering the minister of labor to make the dissolution of the labor contract dependent upon the consent of the labor exchange.[86] A later decree forbade the dissolution of the labor contract by both parties without the consent of the labor exchange; this consent is also required in the hiring of workers, except miners and domestic workers in households with children below 14 years of age.[87]

This comprehensive regulation is, however, supplemented by others equally far reaching. While this act aims at increasing the labor force in the economic sphere, the emergency service act of 15 October 1938 [88] gave the authorities the right to summon 'inhabitants of the federal territory in cases of public emergency or for training purposes for a limited time.' According to the ruling of the Four Year Plan deputy, it is primarily the police which has received these powers. The emergency service, being a political function, is not based upon the labor contract. The decree, incidentally, reveals that the regime places the workers above the National Socialist officials, civil servants, or free professions. If an employee is called for emergency service exceeding three days, the labor exchange has a right to protest. But if civil servants, political leaders of the party, its clerical and labor staff, employees of the health services, or lawyers are summoned, no notice even need be given to the labor exchange. Only persons of less than 15 and more than 70 years of age, mothers of minors under certain conditions, pregnant women, and invalids are exempt. In the protectorate, only the president of the protectorate and the president and members of the government are free from emergency service. The army, the two S.S. police troops, and the air raid protection workers are exempt by the very nature of their work.[89] The emergency workers receive certain emoluments and family support, which is finely differentiated according to the previous income of the worker summoned to service.

We may thus say, briefly, that the worker does not enjoy any freedom. He cannot choose his place of work or kind of work, he cannot leave at will, but, as a rule, he cannot be fired without the consent of the labor exchange—a protection quite unnecessary today.

The executive agency for the full utilization of man-power is the labor exchange whose work is co-ordinated with that of other agencies by the defense commissioner.* The labor exchanges have now (since 28 June 1935) absolute monopoly over employment service, thus completing a development that has started under the Weimar Republic.

Originally the Federal Institute for Labor Exchange and Unemployment Insurance was a semi-autonomous body (statute of 16 July 1927), run by the trade unions, the employers' organizations, and the representatives of public authorities, under the control of the minister of labor. It had a regional and a local set-up. National Socialism changed the structure from top to bottom. The provincial and local labor exchanges are now simply executive agencies of the ministry of labor (25 March 1939) while the head office has been incorporated into the ministry of labor. Its president (the inevitable Dr. Syrup) has been appointed secretary of state in the ministry of labor. Only the financial administration is under a separate body, serving merely accounting purposes.

The device by which that control is exercised is the work book that was gradually extended to cover every branch of trade and industry. Every employee must possess a work book in which all data relevant to his occupation are entered, such as apprenticeship training, former employment. It must indicate flying experience, and training, and experience in agricultural work. The work book has, of course, lost its significance as a condition necessary to procure employment, but it is a fully developed method for terroriza-

* See p. 59.

tion of the worker; at the same time it provides a means for statistically controlling the labor supply.

The regime also strengthened the power of the labor trustee, both as regards his power to issue wage regulations [90] and his authority to inflict fines for the violation of any of his rulings and orders.[91]

FIGHT FOR HIGHER PRODUCTIVITY

While the mobilization of the available labor supply has been achieved successfully, it is questionable, and far from being clear, whether the raising of the productivity of labor has been equally successful. For it is in this that the last remnants of the market mechanism are still operating. The regime cannot place behind each worker a S.S. man who at the point of his gun forces the worker to work harder and faster. Consequently, new methods of industrial warfare, hitherto unknown to German workers, have apparently risen methods more akin to revolutionary syndicalism than to German trade unionism. Passive resistance, the Ca' canny, or the slow-down, one of the decisive methods of syndicalist warfare, attempted on a large scale first in 1895 by Italian railroad workers, advocated by Emile Pouget and Fernand Pelloutier of the French syndicalist movement, applied successfully by the Austrian railroad workers in 1905, 1906 and 1907 in the form of scrupulous compliance with all traffic and security regulations, has seemingly come to the front in Germany. The slow-down staged by the German workers is certainly not an open or very marked policy, which would spell death for the leaders and concentration camps for the followers. It consists in the refusal to devote all energy to work, and sometimes in the determination to give much less than the normal.

It is, of course, difficult to prove our contention, since it is next to impossible to evaluate statistically the average output per man; and besides there is nothing so closed and so veiled in secrecy by the regime as the response the regime has evoked within the working classes. We have, however, one proof: the slow-down of the miners in 1938 and 1939 and the resulting changes of the regime's wage policy. The average productivity of the miners dropped in the Ruhr district from 2,199 kilograms in 1936 to 1,964 kilograms in 1939,[92] and with it the whole coal production. As a result a special deputy was appointed to raise the productivity in the coal industry. The labor time below ground was extended from 8 hours to 8 hours and 45 minutes, but piece work and over-time pay had to be increased by a special decree of 2 March 1939.[93] The decree granted the miners not only 25 per cent of the wage as overtime pay, but gave them an additional 200 per cent premium for additional increase in productivity.

But apparently a new and much greater victory was won by the masses of the workers during this war.

The war economy decree of 4 September 1939 provided not only for price freezing but also for wage freezing.[94] To understand the wage-freezing decree a few introductory words are necessary. The act for the regulation of national labor of 20 January 1934,[95] the German charter of labor, had created the office of the labor trustee, a federally appointed civil servant who replaced the collective agreements between trade unions and employers' organizations. The labor trustees received the right to enact tariffs, that is, rulings containing wage scales and labor conditions for a whole industry within their territory. The new tariffs were, on the whole, identical with the collective agreements, with the difference, however, that they applied not only to organized members of the contracting parties but to every employer and employee working in that specific branch of trade or industry. The tariffs were in consequence minimum regulations leaving it to the individual agreement between the employer and the employee or to agreements between a plant and its workers to improve the working conditions.

Already the decree of the Four Year Plan deputy of 25 June 1938 authorized the trustees to fix in certain trades (building and metal) not only minimum but also maximum wages in order to prevent the exploitation of the labor shortage by employers and employees alike. The wage-freezing provision in the war-economy decree now gave the trustees the power 'to adjust at once according to orders of the ministry of labor the earnings of labor to the conditions created by war and to enforce maximum wages, salaries, and other labor conditions.' The decree thus empowered trustees arbitrarily to interfere with the existing structure of wages and labor conditions without regard to existing obligations.

Since then, it is not the minimum but the maximum wage that has been the rule.

Soon, however, this new authority vested in the trustees was deemed insufficient. A large number of acts gradually shifted to labor the burdens caused by the exigencies of war. If, for instance, in the process of shutting down plants, dismissals appear necessary, the trustees may (and do so regularly) shorten the dismissal periods foreseen by statute, tariff regulation, or individual contracts.[96] It expressly forbade employers to pay the usual wage provisions for overtime, Sunday, holiday, and night work, and invalidated all provisions contained in statutes, tariff regulations, or individual agreements granting paid or unpaid holidays, thereby destroying an achievement of which National Socialism had so much boasted. Moreover, it empowered the minister of labor to change all provisions concerning labor time.

Nevertheless, at least one attempt has been made to prevent employers from reaping profits from the abolition of overtime pay and other regulations. They were compelled to deliver such additional profits to the federal tax offices, though later this duty was considerably abrogated.[97]

All this, however, was deemed insufficient, and another executive decree finally created a ceiling of wages [98] prohibiting raises of wages, salaries, and other compensations and changes in the piece work provisions. How rigidly the wage-freezing decree is carried out may be gathered from the tariff regulation of the labor trustee for Berlin, which fixes the salaries of Berlin commercial employees.[99] Not only is it prohibited to increase salaries, but even the adjustment of lower salaries to the new salary scale is expressly forbidden. Even Christmas bonuses must not exceed the amounts paid the previous year.[100]

The war legislation did not stop short at wages. It went out to destroy the whole protective legislation of labor, of which Germany was rightfully proud. Statutes and regulations fixing a maximum working time for male workers and salaried employees above the age of 18 were repealed by the decree of the ministerial council for the defense of the realm,[101] and the administrative agencies were entitled to deviate from the whole existing labor-time legislation with regard to juveniles between 16 and 18 years of ages. They may, in urgent cases, be employed up to 10 hours daily, not exceeding 50 hours a week.[102] Juveniles below the age of 16 may be employed in urgent cases, if they have to attend occupational training and trade schools, up to 10 hours, but when training does not take place, up to 48 hours a week; practically all regulations prohibiting Sunday and holiday work for juveniles have been rescinded.

Hand in hand with this downward revision of wages, salaries, and labor conditions went the destruction of unemployment insurance—which, though of little practical value in a period of full employment, may at any moment be of major significance. The new decree of the ministerial council for the defense of the realm [103] no longer considers the support of the unemployed as insurance but as help, and accordingly makes it dependent on a rigid means test. It is true that the new decree contains some improvements over previous legislation; the waiting period and the time limit are abolished. But since the benefits are considerably reduced, since the means test is rigidly carried out, and since assistance may be refused if the unemployed rejects an offer of employment, the financial obligations toward the unemployed are not great.[104] However, the profits that accrue to the government from the contributions to the unemployment assistance scheme are enormous. The joint contributions of employers and employees, raised in 1930 from 3 to 6½ per cent of the nominal wages, are retained. The total expense in 1937, at a time when full employment had not yet been reached, was already 1,058,000,000 marks, of which 9,600,000 marks were spent for incapacity insurance, 674,300,000 for work creation policy, 6,200,000 for subsidizing the Saar region, while 368,800,000 were paid to the federal government.[105] In late years practically the whole income has gone directly into the federal government treasury.

Thus, it is clear that the intention of the regime at the outbreak of the war was not only to establish a ceiling of wages but to abolish all social gains made in decades of social struggles.

But it is at this point that passive resistance seems to have begun on a large scale. The regime had to give way and to capitulate on almost every front. On 16 November 1939,[106] it reintroduced the additional payments for holiday, Sunday, night, and overtime work. On 17 November 1939,[107] it reintroduced paid holidays and even ordered compensation to the workers for previous losses. On 12 December 1939,[108] the regime had finally to enact new labor-time legislation, and strengthen the protection of women, juveniles, and workers as a whole. The regular working time is now 10 hours a day, or 60 hours a week, though an extension of the labor time is permitted in a number of cases. The employment of women and juveniles beyond the limits foreseen in the youth protection act of 30 April 1938 is prohibited. Night work is now possible only in extraordinary cases and then only with special permission. Over-time payment is 25 per cent. We cannot here go into the details of the new regulations, which have from time to time been modified.[109] They signify in my view a defeat of the regime and a victory of the working classes. This may be seen from the wording of the decree reintroducing payment for overtime. It justifies the reintro-duction of bonuses by the blackout; it asserts that Sunday work brings special hardships upon the workers; and that the abolition of additional payments was only a temporary measure. If the black-out had been more than a pretext, it would not have been necessary to reintroduce over-time payment for the whole territory. The wording of the decree is intended to veil the defeat of the regime.

It may be true that the partial restoration of the workers' rights has primarily been the result of the 'phoney' war of 1939, which made it unnecessary to demand high sacrifices. The enactment of a decree for assistance of part-time employed workers seems to sup-port this view.[110] The regime apparently expected that the war on the western front would necessitate the closing down of many plants in the west; that, as a result, production in other plants would have to be stepped up, labor time extended to the utmost, and provisions made for those who became fully or partly unemployed because of the closing down. This did not happen. The plants situated in west-ern Germany worked to full capacity and the stringent legislation could be relaxed.

To raise the productivity of labor, the regime used not only terror and propaganda, but also ordinary wage incentives.

It also used other methods. The shift from consumption to pro-duction goods [111] and the increase in the volume of production necessitated an occupational shift in the working classes. Appren-tices had to be trained and, as a result, vocational training was made compulsory. Certain branches like building and engineering were compelled to hire apprentices according to a fixed ratio between journeymen and apprentices. Skilled workers who, during the de-pression, had migrated to other professions had to return to their old ones. As a result, there was a considerable decline in the number of agricultural laborers. The census of 1939 showed that labor employed in agriculture and forestry dropped by 1,145,000, that is, by more than 10 per cent.[112] The gap had to be filled by war prisoners and foreign civilian workers.

Still the decisive question whether the average productivity of labor has increased cannot be answered. We believe that because of the exhaustion of the workers, the employment of too young or too old people, and of insufficiently trained workers, the average productivity of the worker will be lower than in 1929, despite rationalization and increased volume of production.

Labor has been delivered to authoritarian control, as completely as possible. The labor market is regimented.

7. Conclusion

We have come to the end of our tiresome journey through National Socialist economics. We have not explored every by-path. We have not touched the subjects of the agrarian market and the food estate. A discussion of the latter is today quite unnecessary, since it is now merely a governmental agency without any independence; the social position of the peasant will be dealt with in our next chapter.* We have not discussed war financing. Suffice it to say that the problems, although formidable, have been overcome. War financing is done by revenues consisting primarily of: the income tax plus a war surtax of 50 per cent, with the provision, however, that tax and surtax together must not exceed 65 per cent of the income; war surtaxes on consumption goods (beer, champagne, alcoholic beverages, tobacco); increased contributions by the states and municipalities to the federal government; the corporation tax, which had already been raised before the war; the issue of government bonds; the anticipation of future tax revenues; short-term borrowing. They all and more provide the financial basis for warfare. Full employment and the low exemptions in the income tax, the high liquidity of banks, mortgage banks, private and social insurance institutions, and the government's tight hold on the credit structure have made financing of the war not an exceedingly difficult task. Owing to full employment, national income rose consider-

* See p. 392.

ably.[118] It must be mentioned, however, that the surtax of 50 per cent does not affect the wage earners who earn less than 234 marks a month or 54 marks a week or 9 marks a day, and they are a huge section of the wage earners. In other words, the taxation policy has not shifted the burden of war financing upon the large masses, wage and salary earners. Indeed, the wage and salary tax levied since 1919 has not been increased by National Socialism. The contributions to social-insurance institutions have not been raised since 1930. Only the contributions to the party and its auxiliary organizations constitute a heavy burden, as shall be seen later. Anyhow, the curtailment of consumption has not been effected by taxation.

Though we have not aimed at completeness, we believe that we have covered the major phenomena of German economy and we are now able to piece the many parts together into a whole. Three problems have confronted us again and again.

How is the organization running?

What is the generating force of the economic system?

What is its structure?

EFFICIENCY

The present efficiency of the organization would have been impossible without the smoothness and completeness of the organizational structure of business already achieved under the Weimar Republic. The groups and chambers have here, for decades, acted as the centers in which industrial, commercial, financial, and technical knowledge has been pooled, deepened, and systematized. The groups and chambers are the mediators between the state bureaucracy and the individual enterprise. In the rationing of raw materials and of consumers' goods, in rationalization, in the allocation of public orders among businessmen, in price control, credit control, and foreign trade, the groups and chambers are active, partly as advisory bodies, partly as executive organs to which the state has delegated coercive power.

The completeness of the cartel organization, also achieved under the Weimar Republic, is another contributing factor. As marketing organizations, the cartels have for decades studied the markets closely, followed every fluctuation, and were thus able to place their long experience at the government's disposal. In consequence, the cartels have, during the war, become privately controlled public organs, especially in the allocation of raw material.

The efficiency of the organization also owes much to the ministerial bureaucracy and the complete absence of the 'heavy hand of the treasury.' The German ministerial bureaucracy has always been highly competent, and the experience it has gained in the railroad and postal services, in the Reichsbank and other public financial institutions, in the currency-control offices, in the federal- and state-owned industrial organizations has prepared it for the gigantic task of running a war economy of such size. Credit must also be given—perhaps more than to any other factor—to the high training and skill of the German worker and the system of occupational training during apprenticeship, in trade schools, technical schools—all of which was achieved under the Weimar Republic by the states, the municipalities, the trade unions, and, to a lesser degree, by industry.

The contribution of the National Socialist party to the success of the war economy is nil. It has not furnished any man of outstanding merit, nor has it contributed any single ideology or organizational idea that was not fully developed under the Weimar Republic.

To show in detail how the machine is operating is, however, much more difficult. I shall try to analyze a few typical cases.

Let us take a medium-size entrepreneur. He must be a member of his group and of his local chamber of industry and commerce, and he may or may not be a member of the cartel. If he works unrationally, that is, if his production costs are too high, a number of things may happen. The general deputy * under the Four Year Plan may ask his group to investigate. The group will report and submit its recommendation, to close down the plant or to modernize it or to let it continue as it is. If the report condemns the plant, the general deputy may execute the sentence indirectly or directly. If the entrepreneur desires raw material, the *Reichsstelle* † or the distributing agency ‡ (cartel or group) or the quota office § (which is, as a rule, the group) will refuse it to him. Or the general deputy may execute it directly. He or the group may approach the minister of economics and the minister of economics may make use of the powers vested in him by the cartel decree. If the entrepreneur

* See p. 249.
† See p. 251.
‡ See p. 252.
§ See p. 250.

is not a member of the cartel, he may be forced to join it and the cartel may then give him no quota or an insufficient quota; or the minister of economics may close down the plant.*

If the report of the group recommends modernization of the plant, negotiations will take place with a bank to obtain the necessary capital, which may or may not be found. The same result may be achieved by a lowering of the price structure by the price commissioner or the price-forming offices.† If the entrepreneur desires, or is even dependent upon government orders, he may or may not receive a share in public orders by the clearing office of the provincial economic chambers,‡ or even if the clearing office is willing to allocate government orders to him, he may not be able to accept because he cannot produce profitably at the prices allowed by government decrees.§

If the entrepreneur runs a consumers' goods factory (let us say, a shoe factory), his stock in leather will have been attached by the leather *Reichsstelle*.[114] If he wants to continue production, he has to apply to his quota agency, that is, to his *Reichsstelle* or to his branch group, for a leather cheque.[115] If the plant is sufficiently big and is running efficiently, the application may be granted. If it is refused, he must close down and may receive community help.|| If he is a soap manufacturer, he has to produce one of four kinds of soap, either the 'federal standard soap' for bodily culture, or shaving soap, or one of the two existing types of laundry soap.[116] If the *Reichsstelle* refuses him raw material because his group testifies that he is inefficient, he must cease production, but he may be allowed to continue as a trader living practically on a commission basis.[117]

But there are other ways by which the machine can be put into operation. If a new factory necessary for economic warfare must be established or if an existing one must be expanded, the labor exchange ¶ will make a survey within its territory in order to find out which other plants may be 'combed out.' It will ask the group to report, the defense commissioner ** will co-ordinate the activities, and some day the labor exchange will command workers in

* See p. 265.
† See p. 305.
‡ See p. 245.
§ See p. 310.
|| See p. 283.
¶ See p. 342.
** See p. 59.

unnecessary plants to leave employment and to start in another factory.*

If the entrepreneur is a shoe retailer and needs shoes for delivery to his customers, he will have to apply to his *Reichsstelle* for rationing cards, which will be given only in conjunction with the provincial economic office.† He may meet with refusal and be 'combed out' by the chamber of industry.‡ If he is a shoemaker and needs leather for repairs, he has to apply for order cards to the president of his handicraft guild, who may or may not give it to him.[118] He might then be 'combed out' by the chamber of handicraft and then be transferred to the proletariat.§

If the need for new industrial plants arises, the general deputy under the Four Year Plan for his specific industry will investigate the situation in conjunction with the ministry of economics and perhaps in collaboration with the federal bureau of spatial research.‖ The technical problems will be discussed with the group. The discussion will be continued with the leading combine. The combine may or may not desire to start construction of this new plant. If it expresses such a wish, the problem of financing will be discussed. The Reichsbank ¶ and private banks in conjunction with the combine will decide whether the plant should be financed out of undistributed profits ** or whether banks should advance the money, or whether the capital market should be approached, or, finally, whether a decree should be issued for community financing of the new undertaking.†† Problems of technical equipment, of location, and of financing will be discussed by the groups and cartels and combines and federal officials. The *Reichsstelle* in question will be asked to clarify the problem of raw material supply, and the relevant labor exchange that of labor supply. Once the decision has been reached, the machinery will be set into motion.

From this summary it will be clear that the intertwining of business, self-governmental agencies, and governmental agencies achieved what appears outwardly as a higher amount of organizational efficiency, though, of course, antagonisms and conflicts will be operative under the surface.

* See p. 341.
† See p. 248.
‡ See p. 282.
§ See p. 282.

‖ See p. 249.
¶ See p. 324.
** See p. 318.
†† See p. 280.

PROFIT MOTIVE

What, however, is the generating force of that economy: patriotism, power, or profits? We believe that we have shown that it is the profit motive that holds the machinery together. But in a monopolistic system profits cannot be made and retained without totalitarian political power, and that is the distinctive feature of National Socialism. If totalitarian political power had not abolished freedom of contract, the cartel system would have broken down. If the labor market were not controlled by authoritarian means, the monopolistic system would be endangered; if raw material, supply, price control, and rationalization agencies, if credit and exchange-control offices were in the hands of forces hostile to monopolies, the profit system would break down. The system has become so fully monopolized that it must by nature be hypersensitive to cyclical changes, and such disturbances must be avoided. To achieve that, the monopoly of political power over money, credit, labor, and prices is necessary.

In short, democracy would endanger the fully monopolized system. It is the essence of totalitarianism to stabilize and fortify it. This, of course, is not the sole function of the system. The National Socialist party is solely concerned with establishing the thousand-year rule, but to achieve this goal, they cannot but protect the monopolistic system, which provides them with the economic basis for political expansion. That is the situation today.

It is the aggressive, imperialist, expansionist spirit of German big business unhampered by considerations for small competitors, for the middle classes, free from control by the banks, delivered from the pressure of trade unions, which is the motivating force of the economic system. Profits and more profits are the motive power. It is, indeed, in the words of Major General Thomas, the most daring and the most enterprising industrialist who wins and shall win.* It is as though Mandeville's contention that private vices are public benefits had now been raised to the rank of supreme principle—not for the masses, not for the retailers, wholesalers, and handicraft men, not for the small and middle businessmen, but for the great industrial combines. As regimentation spreads, as price control becomes more efficient, as regulation of the credit and money market be-

* See p. 314.

comes more stringent, as the government strengthens the monopoly of the capital market, and as foreign trade evolves into a political operation, the need to make profits becomes increasingly urgent. Profits are not identical with dividends. Profits are, above all, salaries, bonuses, commissions for special services, over-valuated patents, licenses, connections and good will. Profits are especially undistributed profits.

Each of the regimenting measures tends to play into the hands of the monopoly profiteers. Each technological process, each invention, each rationalizing measure strengthens their power. German coal mining, for instance, seems to stand today before an industrial revolution, the introduction of the so-called 'iron miner,' but German periodicals insist [119] that only big plants will be able to carry out full mechanization.

With all this the party does not interfere. The period of party interference in economics has ended long ago.

The organization of the economy is an institution below the state. It is not a group or an affiliated organization of the party. This does not mean an expression of lack of interest by the party. Such interest follows principally from the fact that the whole economy, too, has to follow the National Socialist philosophy of life. But it means that the party restricts itself to questions of philosophy of life and, the selection of leading personalities in the organization of the economy, and that it leaves all technical questions of detail of the economic policy to the state. Whether one allocates foreign currency and grants claims for international clearing, whether one furthers compensation trade or ordinary export business, how and whether one exports . . . whether borrowing or self-financing is to be preferred—all these and many other questions of technical and organizational expediency must be decided by the state.[120]

That is the view of the official commentator of the National Socialist economic organization. The party receives a compliment, but it must not interfere with the economy. The relation between the party and the economy is identical with that between the party and the inner administration, which has found the best expression in the decree * that leaves the leadership of the morale of the people to the party and the coercive machinery to the civil service. It would, therefore, be wrong to assume that there exists a dual rule in the

* See p. 72.

economy, one of the party and one of the state. In our opinion, the very fact that the party is so completely excluded from the control of economic power positions led to the foundation of the Göring works.

STRUCTURE

What is the structure of the economic system? It might be instructive to translate an editorial in the *Deutsche Volkswirt*,[121] written on the occasion of the foundation of the Continental Oil Corporation: *

The most competent representatives of the new German state and the most faithful guardians of the National Socialist ideals have, from the very beginning, stressed the principle that the state should merely steer the economy, but leave economy itself to the private initiative of the entrepreneur, based on private property and the efficiency principle. To invoke such declarations would be tiresome if the unequivocal clarity of the principle did not stand in strange contrast to the permanently arising doubts about the actual fate of private economy.

A realistic study of the situation confirms that small business and, in fact, the whole trade (perhaps with the exception of special tasks in foreign trade) and handicraft are the exclusive domain of private activity. But even in the industrial sector, the position of the private entrepreneur including large middle-sized plants is practically uncontested and not endangered; from the beginning, the isolated activity of public authorities in this field has always been the exception which confirms the rule. Only in the realm of big enterprises and giant plants do phenomena appear which could induce us to express a fundamental concern over the fate of private economy.

. . . Two developmental trends cause in many places skepticism about the durability of the principle of private economy in big industry. The first comes from above and concerns its direct relation to the state. To execute its . . . program the *grossdeutsche Reich* had to demand from the economy performances which . . . exceeded the ability even of big private enterprises . . . The Hermann Göring works, the people's car works, and now the people's tractor works may be quoted as examples. It is, however, so it is very often argued, the solution of *new* economic problems . . . which forms the very field of activity of private entrepreneurial initiative . . . If the demands which the state has to make upon the giant industry sector exceed the possibilities of private activity, does

* See p. 276.

this not spell the end of private big industry? Is it possible that the industrial enterprises of the state, despite their limited number, are not mere exceptions from the rule, but the first symptoms of a fundamentally new development?

The second developmental trend . . . comes from below. It concerns the relation between the enterprise and the share-holder . . . It is a fact that the living ties between . . . the joint stock corporation and the broad stratum of the small and free share-holders have gradually loosened. The sole remaining tie is the yearly distribution of profits; but dividend policy has become more and more independent of the actual economic policy. New blood and new shares could hardly flow into the corporations. The share-holders' interest in the enterprises has been deprived of its living character and reduced to a mere phantom of a juristic construction . . .

Thus we witness from above the taking over of entrepreneurial tasks by the state: from below, the dissolution of the ties between big industry and the public, which are based on the concept of property.

However, the announcement of the federal minister of economics at the shareholder's meeting of the Reichsbank signifies a break in the development threatening the existence of private big industry. The clarification of the capital structure of joint stock corporations will abolish the unclear conceptions of the broad public . . . and will thereby increase its interests in the corporations.* *This break will be strengthened and widened* † by a remarkable positive measure which National Socialist economic policy now makes with the establishment of a giant corporation, namely *Continental Oil Corporation,*† in which the chairmanship of the supervisory board has been taken over by the minister of economics, and in which private big industry and small capital owners form a *unified* † front.

The view that the foundation of the Continental Oil Corporation has strengthened private economy actively in the sector of big industry is not contradicted by the fact that the state itself has actively participated in this foundation, because of two facts. The Continental Oil Corporation will not be concerned with the production of fuel in the old federal territory in the hand of private industry. The tasks of the new corporation lie beyond the frontiers of the

---

* Meant is the speech which we mentioned on p. 317, where Funk made it appear likely that the nominal value of capital could be raised.

† Italicized in the original. F. N.

Reich . . . These tasks require a settlement among private . . . and political interests . . . In addition, the political importance of oil and geological . . . factors create *risks* * which cannot be borne solely by the private economy . . .

The very reasons which justify the active participation of the state in the Continental Oil Corporation contribute additional clarity to the fundamental importance of the decisive participation of the German big enterprises in the oil and coal industry . . . For it is now obvious that the future *political* * new order . . . will give [private industry] possibilities and tasks for far-reaching collaboration . . .

We apologize for so long a quotation. It has the merit of indicating the trend so clearly that no comments are necessary.

THE FAILURE OF DEMOCRATIC PLANNING

The question arises why such steered or controlled economy, why such 'planning,' if we may use the word, has not been carried out under democratic conditions and by democratic methods. The reasons for the failure of democratic planning and collectivism in Germany seem to be both economic and political. 'Planning' becomes necessary (this, too, is indicated in the quotation above) because industry refuses to make new investments that require huge capital and that are, moreover, extremely risky. The risks involved are two-fold: political uncertainty, which leads to economic uncertainty, and economic depressions, which lead to the disintegration of political democracy.

The parliamentary system may at any time give rise to forces hostile to the monopolists, who are continually threatened by heavy taxes, above all, taxes on undistributed profit, by a loosening of the system of protection, by 'trust busting,' by the possibility of industrial disputes. All·this leads to the well-known investors' strike, the refusal to expand because political uncertainty may endanger returns on the investment. Political uncertainty creates economic instability. If the state does not fully control money, credit, and the foreign trade, the business cycle cannot be stabilized. A downswing would lead to the collapse of the overcapitalized monopoly structure. In these conditions the co-ordination of all regimentation measures by the state seems inevitable and necessary.

* Italicized in the original. F. N.

There existed, of course, an abstract possibility of entrusting such co-ordination to parliament. The German trade unions proposed a number of such plans; the French Popular Front and the Belgian Labor party developed similar plans, and Roosevelt's New Deal partly carried them out. All European attempts failed and Roosevelt's New Deal succeeded in part because the country is rich and its reserves, which have been only partially tapped, are far from being exhausted.

Democratic planning failed because democratic planning must satisfy the needs of the large masses—and that is the very reason why democracy should take up planning. To satisfy the demands of the large masses, however, means to expand or at least maintain the consumers' goods industry; this necessarily restricts the profits of heavy industry. Moreover, in the dynamics of the democracy one achievement of the masses will lead to further demands. One example: under democratic conditions, an arch reactionary and industrial die-hard like Krupp would never have granted his workers the concessions they demanded. They would have infringed upon his being master in his own house. They would have given rise, so he feared, to more and more dangerous demands. Under totalitarian conditions, he will not hesitate to fulfil certain demands, because democratic automatism has ceased to function.

Democratic planning must co-ordinate the many particular interests of retail and handicraft, of small, middle, and big businessmen, of the peasants, civil servants, workers, and salaried employees. A democracy cannot simply annihilate, 'comb out,' the inefficient producer and trader. It cannot enslave the workers. It cannot simply transfer the middle class into the proletariat; this would merely strengthen the anti-democratic trends and contribute to the growth of fascism.

Democratic planning, also, enlarges the power of the state; it adds the monopoly of economic coercion to the monopoly of political coercion. The more powerful an instrument becomes, the more precious it is. The monopolists could fear that if democratic groups had control over the state they would strive to increase the welfare of the masses and cut down profits.

In the case of Germany, additional reasons were: the bankruptcy of the leading political parties, of the social democrats, and of the trade unions who were motivated by cowardice, led by incompe-

tent leaders, and who preferred abdication to a fight. We must remember that the Catholic Center party, never a homogeneous group,
discovered in 1930 that it had a reactionary wing as well as a democratic; that political liberalism in Germany had died many years
ago; that the Communist party, incompetently led, wavered between
dictatorship of the proletariat, revolutionary syndicalism, and national bolshevism, and thereby weakened the working classes. It is
also significant that the army, the judiciary, and the civil services
organized a counter-revolution the very day on which the revolution of 1918 broke out.

The ruling classes refused to give the power over the economy
to a democracy. To them, democracy appeared 'as a species of social
luxury,' to use the words of Carl Becker [122]—but they did not hesitate to give all economic power to a totalitarian regime. Thyssen,[123]
Kirdorf, and others paid the debts of the National Socialist party
in 1932, and today it is no secret that industry financed the party
in the past; this is openly admitted by *Deutsche Volkswirt*.[124] The
homes of the industrial leaders were open to Hitler and Ley, to
Göring and Terboven. Baron von Schröder, the owner of the
Cologne Banking house J. H. Stein, arranged the reconciliation between Hitler, Papen, and Hindenburg on 4 January 1933. It is, of
course, correct to say that National Socialism failed to keep many
of the promises to the industrial leaders. So it appeared at least to
Thyssen, who, never very intelligent, accepted the nonsense of the
guild state and social monarchy at its face value.

National Socialism has co-ordinated the diversified and contradictory state interferences into one system having but one aim: the
preparation for imperialist war. This may now seem obvious. For
years it did not appear so to the outside world, and it gives a certain satisfaction to the author that as early as 1935 he formulated
the aim of National Socialism in the following terms: 'Fascism is
the dictatorship of the Fascist [National Socialist] party, the bureaucracy, the army, and big business, the dictatorship over the
whole of the people, for complete organization of the nation for
imperialist war.' [125] Once this aim is recognized, the economic structure is clear. Preparation for totalitarian war requires a huge expansion of the production-goods industry, especially of the investment-
goods industry, and makes it necessary to sacrifice every particular
economic interest that contradicts this aim. That involves the organ-

ization of the economic system, the incorporation of the total economy into the monopolistic structure, and, though we use the word with reluctance, planning. This means that the automatism of free capitalism, precarious even under a democratic monopoly capitalism, has been severely restricted. But capitalism remains.

National Socialism could, of course, have nationalized private industry. That, it did not do and did not want to do. Why should it? With regard to imperialist expansion, National Socialism and big business have identical interests. National Socialism pursues glory and the stabilization of its rule, and industry, the full utilization of its capacity and the conquest of foreign markets. German industry was willing to co-operate to the fullest. It had never liked democracy, civil rights, trade unions, and public discussion. National Socialism utilized the daring, the knowledge, the aggressiveness of the industrial leadership, while the industrial leadership utilized the anti-democracy, anti-liberalism and anti-unionism of the National Socialist party, which had fully developed the techniques by which masses can be controlled and dominated. The bureaucracy marched as always with the victorious forces, and for the first time in the history of Germany the army got everything it wanted.

Four distinct groups are thus represented in the German ruling class: big industry, the party, the bureaucracy, and the armed forces. Have they merged into a unit? Is the ruling class one compact body? Is their rule integrated within and accepted by the masses? What are their methods of mass domination? These are the final problems that we must consider.

PART THREE

THE NEW SOCIETY

I

THE RULING CLASS

IF one believes that Germany's economy is no longer capitalistic under National Socialism, it is easy to believe further that her society has become classless. This is the thesis of the late Emil Lederer.[1] A brief analysis of his book will serve to introduce our discussion of the new German society.

Lederer rejects attempts to define National Socialism as the last line of defense of capitalism, as the rule of the strong man, as the revolt of the middle classes, as domination by the army, or as the ascendency of the untalented. For him, it is a 'modern political system which rests on amorphous masses.' It is the masses 'which sweep the dictator into power and keep him there' (page 18). The masses are therefore the actors, not the tools of a ruling class.

But who are the masses? They are the opposite of classes. They can be united solely by emotions (page 31); they tend to 'burst into sudden action' (page 38), and being amorphous, they must be integrated by a leader who can articulate their emotions (page 39). As the very opposite of classes, the masses make up a classless society. The policy of National Socialism is to transfer a class-stratified society into masses by keeping the latter in a state of perpetual tension (page 105). Since the regime must also satisfy the material demands of the masses, it goes in for large-scale public spending and thus achieves full employment. National Socialism realizes that 'people are filled with envy, with hatred for the rich and successful' (pages 110-11). The emotions can best be kept alive in the field of foreign affairs; for an aggressive foreign policy and preparation for foreign war prevent 'the reawakening of thinking and of articulation into social groups' (page 123).

National Socialist society is thus composed of the ruling party and the amorphous masses (page 127). All other distinctions are removed. 'It is on this psychological basis that the Fascist party has been built up. With their success they attract active mass-men who

then are kept in a state of emotion and cannot return to their former ways of life. Even family cohesion is broken, the pulverization
of society is complete. Masses make dictators, and dictators make
masses the continuing basis of the state' (page 131). That is why the
social stratification of society is of the utmost importance and why
the Marxist theory of a classless society becomes so dangerous (page
138). National Socialism has completely destroyed the power of
social groups and has established a classless society.

Were Lederer's analysis correct, our earlier discussion would be
completely wrong. Social imperialism would then be not a device
to ensnare the masses but an articulation of the spontaneous longing
of the masses. Racism would not be the concern of small groups
alone but would be deeply imbedded in the masses. Leadership
adoration would be a genuine semi-religious phenomenon and not
merely a device to prevent insight into the operation of the social-
economic mechanism. Capitalism, finally, would be dead, since all
particular groups have been destroyed and only leaders and masses
remain.

Lederer is wrong, however, though a little of the truth sifts into
some of his formulations. Occasionally one feels that even he realizes that the so-called spontaneity of the masses and their active
participation in National Socialism are a sham and that the role of
the people is merely to serve as an instrument of the ruling group.
The problem is perhaps the most difficult of all in an analysis of
National Socialism. The difficulties lie not only in the paucity of
information and the inadequacy of the sociological categories but
also in the extraordinarily complicated character of the social relations themselves. Class structure and social differentiation are not
identical—failure to recognize this point is the basic error underlying Lederer's analysis. A society may be divided into classes and
yet not be socially differentiated in any other way. On the other
hand, a classless society may have sharp differentiations.[2]

The essence of National Socialist social policy consists in the
acceptance and strengthening of the prevailing class character of
German society, in the attempted consolidation of its ruling class,
in the atomization of the subordinate strata through the destruction
of every autonomous group mediating between them and the state,
in the creation of a system of autocratic bureaucracies interfering
in all human relations. The process of atomization extends even to

the ruling class in part. It goes hand in hand with a process of differentiation within the mass party and within society that creates reliable élites in every sector. Through these élites, the regime plays off one group against the other and enables a minority to terrorize the majority.[3]

National Socialism did not create the mass-men; it has completed the process, however, and destroyed every institution that might interfere. Basically, the transformation of men into mass-men is the outcome of modern industrial capitalism and of mass democracy. More than a century ago the French counter-revolutionaries, de Maistre and Bonald, and the Spaniard Donoso Cortes,* asserted that liberalism, Protestantism, and democracy, which they hated, bore the seeds of the emotionally motivated mass-man and would eventually give birth to the dictatorship of the sword. Mass democracy and monopoly capitalism have brought the seeds to fruition. They have imprisoned man in a network of semi-authoritarian organizations controlling his life from birth to death, and they have begun to transform culture into propaganda and salable commodities.

National Socialism claims to have stopped this trend and to have created a society differentiated not by classes but according to occupation and training. That is absolutely untrue. In fact, National Socialism has carried to its highest perfection the very development it pretends to attack. It has annihilated every institution that under democratic conditions still preserves remnants of human spontaneity: the privacy of the individual and of the family, the trade union, the political party, the church, the free leisure organization. By atomizing the subject population (and to some extent the rulers as well), National Socialism has not eliminated class relations; on the contrary, it has deepened and solidified the antagonisms.

National Socialism must necessarily carry to an extreme the one process that characterizes the structure of modern society, bureaucratization. In modern anti-bureaucratic literature, this term means little more than the numerical growth of public servants, and especially of civil servants.† Society is pictured as composed of free men and autonomous organizations on the one hand and of a bureaucratic caste, on the other hand, which takes over more and more political power. The picture is inaccurate, for society is not wholly

* See also pp. 195-6.
† See also pp. 77-9.

free and unbureaucratic nor is the public bureaucracy the sole bearer of political and social power.

Bureaucratization, correctly understood, is a process operating in both public and private spheres, in the state as well as in society. It means that human relations lose their directness and become mediated relations in which third parties, public or private functionaries seated more or less securely in power, authoritatively prescribe the behavior of man. It is a highly ambivalent process, progressive as well as reactionary. The growth of bureaucracy in public life is not necessarily incompatible with democracy if the aims of the democracy are not limited to the preservation of individual rights, but also include the furtherance of certain social goals. Even in the social sphere the growth of private organizations is not entirely retrogressive. It brings some kind of order into an anarchic society and thereby rationalizes human relations that would otherwise be irrational and accidental.

If members of a trade union decide to change their labor conditions, they do so by accepting the recommendation of their officials, in whose hands the decision is left. When a political party formulates some policy, it is the party hierarchy that does so. In athletic organizations, the machinery of presidents, vice-presidents, secretaries, and treasurers goes into operation in arranging matches and carrying on the other activities of the group. This process of mediation and depersonalization extends to culture as well. Music becomes organized in the hands of professional secretaries who need not be musicians. The radio prescribes the exact amount of culture to be digested by the public, how much classical and how much light music, how much talk and how much news. The powers extend to the most intimate relations of man, to the family. There are organizations for large families and for bachelors, birth-control associations, advisory councils for the promotion of family happiness, consumers' co-operatives, giant food chain stores making a farce of the consumers' supposedly free choice.

There is, in short, a huge network of organizations covering almost every aspect of human life, each run by presidents and vice-presidents and secretaries and treasurers, each employing advertising agencies and publicity men, each out to interfere with, and to act as the mediator in, the relations between man and man. Civil liberties lose many of the functions they had in a liberal society.

Even the exercise of civil rights tends more and more to be mediated by private organizations. Whether it is a problem of defense in a political trial or protection of the rights of labor or the fight against unjust taxation, the average man, lacking sufficient means, has no other choice but to entrust his rights to some organization. Under democratic conditions, such mediation does not destroy his rights, as a rule, since the individual still has a choice between competing organizations. In a totalitarian society, however, even if his rights are still recognized on paper, they are completely at the mercy of private bureaucrats.

What National Socialism has done is to transform into authoritarian bodies the private organizations that in a democracy still give the individual an opportunity for spontaneous activity. Bureaucratization is the complete depersonalization of human relations. They become abstract and anonymous. On this structure of society, National Socialism imposes two ideologies that are completely antagonistic to it: the ideology of the community and the leadership principle.

1. THE MINISTERIAL BUREAUCRACY

The total number of civil servants has increased considerably under the National Socialist regime.[4] The officers and professional soldiers of the new standing army are included in the civil service, as well as the enlarged police force (such as the two armed S.S. formations), the labor service leaders, and the officials of the new economic organizations. In addition, what has traditionally been known as the civil service also shows an increase.

The bureaucracy does not form one unified and integrated body. It never has, and the attempts of the National Socialists to break down the stratification have merely scratched the surface. There is a basic distinction between civil servants who exercise political functions and those who do not. Within the political civil service, a further distinction must be drawn between those who frame the political decisions and those who are merely organs of the executive. The former type is best exemplified by the ministerial bureaucracy, the latter by the police and the lower administrative agencies. The nonpolitical civil service includes a large section basically indistinguishable from other workers and salaried employees. Railroad and postal officials, for example, are classed as civil servants in German law, but they neither exercise political power nor perform tasks that could not be done equally well under the labor contract. They serve the public directly in vital economic and social tasks and therefore do not belong to the bureaucracy in the proper sense of the word.

Running through the whole structure of the civil service, there is a social antagonism between the so-called academic (university training and state examination) sections and the non-academic. This distinction is perhaps the most powerful of all in creating a gap between strata within the bureaucracy. The new regime has not touched it, though it is difficult to say whether that means wholehearted acceptance or capitulation. In 1933 the government took the revolutionary step of giving the Prussian ministry of justice to Hanns Kerrl, a middle-ranking, non-academic civil servant in the judicial administration. Kerrl soon had to give up his post and the academic monopoly of the judicial hierarchy has not been disturbed since.

The key positions within the academic civil service are held by the ministerial bureaucracy: assessors, government councillors, ministerial councillors, ministerial directors, secretaries of state. Their power had grown in the last years of Weimar as the decline of parliamentiary democracy brought in the practices of delegated legislation, emergency legislation, and the virtual immunity of the budget and administration from parliamentary control.*

The ministerial bureaucracy is a closed caste. In the Republic its personnel was ostensibly neither anti-democratic nor pro-democratic and cared little about the forms of state and government. The upper civil servant regards the state more or less as a business undertaking to be run efficiently. He has the successful businessman's cynicism except that administrative efficiency takes the place of profit as his highest goal. Political problems are reduced to technical administrative problems. The inefficiency of parliamentary control and the weakness or inexpertness of the ministerial chiefs strengthened this technocratic and somewhat nihilistic outlook. Essentially, of course, it is an anti-democratic and authoritarian outlook. It values success more than right or social justice. Power is revered because it guarantees efficiency. Efficient and incorruptible in the ordinary sense, the ministerial bureaucracy was the center of every anti-democratic movement in the Weimar Republic.

* See p. 24.

The number of Socialist officials in the federal administration was small. Only Socialist ministers would make such appointments and they were excessively timid in their personnel policy. They saw no reason to dismiss a ranking functionary unless he consorted with reaction openly. In the present National Socialist ministries, the bureaucracy consists of a startling number of functionaries holding the same, or higher, positions they held during the Republic. There are variations from ministry to ministry of course (the ministries of propaganda and air are entirely new). Where the change has been least, we can safely assume that the reactionary character of the ministry was greatest in the Republic. The most reactionary of all, the federal ministry of justice, is completely unchanged in personnel despite its consolidation with the Prussian office. Not one of the seven main- or three sub-department heads is new to the service. Only one of the two secretaries of state is new, the National Socialist Dr. Freisler.[5] The same holds true for the office of the president of the republic.[6] Dr. Meissner served Ebert as faithfully as he served Hindenburg and now Hitler. Only two members of his staff are new. Even in the chancellery, where the situation is different, the head is Hans Heinrich Lammers, an old civil servant, previously with the ministry of the interior (since 1922). Many changes have been made in the foreign office, but they are chiefly transfers from one post to another, characteristic of every foreign office. The one important political change is the appointment of Ernst Wilhelm Bohle to head the department of Germans abroad. Bohle, who was born in Bradford, England, and whose father was a professor at the University of Capetown, is also director of the party office for Germans abroad.

The story can be repeated for the ministry of the interior and for the *Kaiser Wilhelm Gesellschaft zur Förderung der Wissenschaften* (Kaiser Wilhelm Association for the Advancement of Science) attached to it, for the ministry of finance, the federal statistical office, and even for the ministry of labor, which had always had the reputation of being staffed by many staunch democrats.

A complete turnover has taken place at the top in the ministry of economics, which has also undergone a basic structural reorganization. According to the latest report it is now divided into five main departments: [7] (1) personnel and administration, headed by Hans Ilgner; (2) industry, under Lieutenant General Hermann von

Hanneken; (3) organization of the economy, directed by Schmeer; (4) finance, under Ministerial Director Klucki; and (5) commerce and currency, headed by the under-secretary of state, Gerhard von Jagwitz. The secretary of state for the ministry is Friedrich W. Landfried. The department chiefs are all new men. The rest of the personnel is practically unchanged.

The changes that have been made are not without significance. Most of the secretaries of state are new, like Landfried in the ministry of economics, Freisler in the ministry of justice, Backe in the ministry of food and agriculture, Fritz Reinhardt in the ministry of finance. They are appointees of the National Socialist ministers. In the ministry of labor the outstanding new figure is Dr. Werner Mansfeld, former counsel to the Ruhr employers' organizations and a member of the Stahlhelm organization, which had been headed and eventually delivered to the National Socialists by Minister of Labor Seldte. Mansfeld is a perfect specimen of the nihilistic post-war generation. As chief of the labor law division he has never betrayed his industrial masters.

In the ministry of economics the next in command to Landfried is Hanneken, the organizer of the iron and steel industry and a typical economic general. Hanneken is a brother-in-law of the German machine dictator, Karl Lange, the manager of the economic group 'machines.'[8] He too has faithfully pursued a policy of full support for the interests of private industry against party interference. The only outsider and the one genuine National Socialist in the ministry is the state councillor, Rudolf Schmeer, who is responsible for the economic organization. After working as an apprentice in the electrical industry, Schmeer became active in the party in 1922. He was convicted by the Belgian army of occupation for sabotage in the Ruhr district in 1923 but never served his sentence. In 1930 he was elected to the Reichstag and subsequently became deputy leader of the labor front. Yet even Schmeer follows the traditional policy of the ministry. In a preface to Barth's book on economic organization, he indicates his complete agreement with Barth's insistence that the party has no place in economic life.[9] *

A detailed comparison of the composition of the bureaucracies in

* See p. 355.

1931 and in 1936 (in some cases even for 1939) shows that the stability of the academic bureaucracy extends down to the heads of the provincial and local finance organizations, to the members of the federal and provincial financial tribunals, to the civil and criminal courts, and to a large percentage of the domestic administrative staffs (except for Prussia).

The ministerial bureaucracy is a closed caste that does not admit outsiders. Its members are excessively ambitious, and on the whole efficient, technicians who care little for political and social values. Their great desire is to remain where they are, or, more correctly, to be promoted as rapidly as possible. They are neither pro- nor anti-National Socialist, but pro-ministerial-bureaucracy. As in the past, they march with the strongest army—from monarchy through Republic to National Socialism. Nor will they hesitate to abandon the Leader if and when the present regime shows real signs of weakness.

The ministerial bureaucracy has never betrayed industrial capitalism. The few honest trust-busters (like Josten in the ministry of economics) played no role in the Republic and play none now. Faithful service to industrial interests might one day, perhaps after retirement, bring an appointment to a big industrial combine, with higher pay and better social position. Industrial supervisory boards are filled with former secretaries of state and ministerial directors. The bureaucracy is now the most important single agency in the formulation of policy, especially in the economic, financial, social, and agricultural fields. The normal legislator is the ministerial council for the defense of the realm,* and the council relies upon the draft decrees and executive orders prepared by the ministerial bureaucracy. Wider than ever before, the power of this bureaucracy is not unlimited, for it must compete with other bureaucracies of the party, the armed forces, and of industry.

2. THE PARTY HIERARCHY

The National Socialist party is before all else a huge bureaucratic machine. Its ruling group consists of Hitler, his deputy (now Bormann), the *Reichsleiter* at the head of the various departments within the central party administration, the Leader's heir, Hermann

* See p. 56.

The Party Hierarchy: THE REICHSLEITER

NAME	YEAR OF BIRTH	SCHOOLING	1914–1918	JOINED PARTY	PROFESSION OR OCCUPATION	SOME PRESENT POSITIONS
Max Amann	1891	elementary and trade school	n.c.o.	1921	none	Press; president, press chamber
A. Axmann	1912	?	–	?	?	Youth
Philipp Bouhler	1899	high school 'Kadettenkorps'	lieutenant	1921	apprentice, publishing houses	Deputy chief, Party Leader's chancellery
Walter Buch	1883	high school	lieutenant	1922	secretary to warrior organizations	Chief of the supreme party court
Otto Dietrich	1897	university Doctor of Econ.	lieutenant	?	chamber of commerce secretary	Federal press chief
Franz X. von Epp	1868	high school	lieutenant general	1928	professional officer; free corps leader	Colonial office; regent of Bavaria
Karl Fiehler	1895	middle school	lieutenant	1923	clerk	Municipalities
Hans Frank	1900	university J.D.	free corps Epp	1920	lawyer	Law; minister without portfolio; governor general of Poland
Wilhelm Frick	1877	university J.D.	–	1923	high civil servant	Chairman parliamentary group; minister of the interior
Joseph Goebbels	1897	university Ph.D.	–	1922	party journalist	Minister of propaganda
Wilhelm Grimm	1889	elementary and trade schools	n.c.o.	1920	professional n.c.o., later civil servant calls himself 'farmer'	Deputy chief, supreme party court
Heinrich Himmler	1900	technical college	some months 'Fahnenjunker'	1925	officer	SS, federal police chief
Konstantin Hierl	1875	high school	colonel; free corps leader	1929	officer	Labor service
Adolph Hühnlein	1881	?	officer	?	?	NS motor corps (NSKK)
Robert Ley	1890	university Ph.D.	lieutenant	1924	chemist	Chief of the organization (PO); leader, labor front

Name	Born	Education	War service	Joined party	Occupation	Function
Viktor Lutze	1890	high school	n.c.o.; free corps	1919	racial organizations (commerce, post, etc.)	SA chief; provincial president
Alfred Rosenberg	1893	technical college	—	1921	"architect"	Foreign policy, editor, Völkischer Beobachter (1921-)
Franz X. Schwarz	1875	elementary and trade schools	n.c.o.	1922	n.c.o. and middle civil servant	Treasurer; chief of the party administration
THE LEADER'S HEIR						
Hermann Göring	1893	Kadettenanstalt	captain	1922	officer	No party office
THE LEADER'S DEPUTY						
Martin Bormann	?	?	?	?	farmer	
THE LEADER'S AIDE-DE-CAMP						
Friedrich W. Brückner	1884	university (not completed)	officer; free corps	1923	officer	
NATIONAL SOCIALIST CABINET MINISTERS†						
Joachim von Ribbentrop	1893	university	officer	1930	commercial traveler	Foreign affairs
Walther Funk	1890	university	private (no front service)	1930	economic journalist	Economics
Richard W. Darré	1895	university and colonial college	lieutenant	1930	farmer	Federal peasant leader; agriculture
Bernhard Rust	1883	university	lieutenant	1922 (racial movement)	high school teacher	Education
Hanns Kerrl *	1887	high school	lieutenant	?	middle civil service	Churches
Fritz Todt	1891	technical college	officer	1923	building construction manager	Automobile roads; munitions; electricity

† If not mentioned above.

* Kerrl died recently,

The Party Hierarchy: THE REICHSLEITER—Continued

SECRETARIES OF STATE AND MINISTERIAL DIRECTORS

NAME	YEAR OF BIRTH	SCHOOLING	1914-1918	JOINED PARTY	PROFESSION OR OCCUPATION	SOME PRESENT POSITIONS
Herbert Backe	1896	university	Russian war prisoner	?	agrarian manager	Secretary of state, agriculture
Ernst Bohle	1903	university	—	1931	commercial manager	Secretary of state, foreign office
Kurt Daluege	1897	university	front; free corps	1922	building construction manager	Chief, order police
Wilhelm Keppler	1882	technical college	lieutenant	?	engineer	Secretary of state, and institute of soil research
Paul Körner	1893	university (not completed)	private(?)	1926	industrial manager	Secretary of state, Four-Year Plan office
Friedrich W. Landfried	1884	university J.D.	captain	1933(?)	high civil servant	Secretary of state, finance
Werner Mansfeld	1893	university J.D.	lieutenant	1934(?)	counsel, employers' organization	Ministerial director, labor
Erhard Milch	1892	university and technical college	officer	1933(?)	air transportation	Secretary of state, air
Reinhard Heydrich	1904	high school	—	1920 (racial movement)	navy officer	Chief, security police
Fritz Reinhardt	1895	middle and trade schools	civilian prisoner in Russia	1928	tax consultant	Secretary of state, finance
Wilhelm Stuckart	1902	university J.D.	—	1920	auxiliary judge SA and SS	Secretary of state, interior
Roland Freisler	1893	university J.D.	war	1924 (racial)	lawyer	Secretary of state, justice

Göring, Hitler's aide-de-camp, the *Gauleiter* (district leaders) and those National Socialist cabinet ministers and secretaries of state who do not have specific positions within the party hierarchy.

The influence of the *Reichsleiter* is decisive. A few are cabinet ministers, others hold high positions in the ministries, still others occupy leading administrative posts. One controls the press, another the youth, a third labor. Some, like Franz Schwarz, are concerned chiefly with inner party administration.* [10]

The thirty-three district leaders of the party are beginning to assume more and more importance.[11] Many of the new government offices are being filled from their ranks. They are sent to the conquered territories, and serve as governors, federal regents, provincial presidents, and state ministers. Today the most important of the district leaders are Julius Streicher, the most extreme Anti-Semite, Robert Wagner of Baden, Josef Bürckel of the Saar and Lorraine, Fritz Sauckel of Thuringia, Federal Price Commissioner Josef Wagner, Terboven in Norway, H. Lohse, the governor of the Baltic states, Baldur von Schirach, the former youth leader, now federal regent in Vienna. A composite picture of the district leader shows that he was born around 1890, attended elementary school, served as an officer in the First World War, was a school teacher— if he had any fixed profession—and joined the party in its early years. The number of elementary school teachers in the party hierarchy is surprisingly high: Rust, Streicher, the two Wagners, Bürckel, the district leaders of Silesia, and Himmler.[12] The leadership of the labor front and of the National Socialist food estate, the provincial peasant leaders, and the fourteen labor trustees bring the total in the party hierarchy to about 120. As a group, they have about the same background and general characteristics as the district leaders. All in all, they are professional politicians, skilled and trained in mass domination.

Though the party administration is centralized in Munich, there is a special center in Berlin under the deputy leader. To the Berlin organization are attached all those party offices that establish direct contact with the ministries and which are often headed by either a ministerial bureaucrat or other ranking civil servant. The foreign policy department is typical. It is headed by E. Bohle, secretary of

* See above p. 81.

state in the foreign office. Another is the department of technology under F. Todt, one of the most influential National Socialists. There are departments for racial questions, universities, finance and taxation (headed by Fritz Reinhardt, who is at the same time secretary of state in the ministry of finance), and party literature (under the leadership of the supreme censor, Bouhler).

The dualism of party and government bureaucracy serves a double purpose. The bureaucracy is not disturbed in its smooth functioning and retains full responsibility for administrative and political decisions. At the same time, the influence of the party is secured through the liaison officers.

The party hierarchy can hardly be considered a closed, well-integrated group. There are different wings, whose influence varies on different occasions. The lack of a consistent theory allows the party at any given moment to bring into the foreground 'radical' or 'moderate' leaders, 'socialistic' or 'capitalistic' elements, 'terrorists' or 'lovers of humanity.' The cabals and intrigues inevitably produced in a closed, hierarchic group centering around a leader prevent that homogeneity that is the prerequisite of popular rule.

3. The Civil Services and the Party *

The civil servants were never enthusiastic supporters of the Weimar democracy. They looked upon the Social Democratic party and trade unions as corrupt and job-hungry 'criminals' who had betrayed the monarchy in 1918 for entirely selfish reasons. Though not openly National Socialist, their own union, the DBB, became more and more reactionary as the prestige of the democracy declined.

The present position of the civil service is not at all clear. The National Socialist party apparently controls the elementary teachers' organization. In 1936 and 1937, 160,000 party political functionaries came from the teaching profession, primarily from the elementary schools (22.9 per cent of a total of 700,000 political leaders).[13] Many of these teachers had been trained during the imperial period, and their participation in the National Socialist

* On the constitutional relation between party and civil service, see above, p. 65.

regime demonstrates the complete deterioration of German philosophical idealism as it was taught officially. More than anything else,
the divorce of Kant's legal and political philosophy, with its insistence on duty, from the rest of his doctrine provided a means of
surrounding every perfidy with the halo of idealism. The high-
sounding phrases became empty shells to conceal the adoration of
power.[14] Such a trend is inherent in the very structure of German
idealism. By banishing the idea of law into the sphere of transcend-
ence, Kant left 'actual law and actual morals at the mercy of empiricism and the blind forces of tradition.'[15]

What is still worse, the majority of the National Socialist teachers
received their education under the Weimar Republic. There could
be no more terrible indictment of the educational philosophy and
policies of German democracy, perhaps of all so-called progressive education. Even during the Republic, sections of the elementary
school teachers had stood out as the most inveterate foes of the
system, as the most ardent chauvinists, the most passionate anti-
Semites. The elementary school teacher belongs to the non-academic
civil service and is separated by a deep social gap from the high
school teacher with his university education and his academic degree. His income is low and his social status no better than that
of any low-ranking non-academic civil servant. Under the empire,
however, army service gave him a certain compensatory dignity.
As a non-commissioned or reserve officer, he could exercise authority over men who stood higher in the social scale. Weimar removed
this compensation. So he turned to the SA, the SS, and the *Stahlhelm*, while the republican militia (the *Reichsbanner*) was left
largely to the workers. The pseudo-egalitarianism of the National
Socialist party and its private army thus provided an excellent outlet for all the resentments accumulated during the life of the pacifist
Republic.

The relation between the elementary teachers and the party does
not extend to the civil service as a whole. We unfortunately do not
possess adequate statistics of the differentiations within the party
membership. A report by Hermann Neef, the leader of the civil-
service organization, to the convention of 1939 shows that of the
one and a half million civil servants, all members of his organization,
28.2 per cent belong to the party;[16] 8.3 per cent of all civil servants
(102,619) were political leaders; 7.2 per cent (98,860) belong

to the S.A.; 1.1 per cent (14,122) belong to the S.S.; 1.1 per cent (13,144) belong to the National Socialist motor corps, and 1.6 per cent (19,857) to the National Socialist aviation corps.

The infiltration of the party into the service is accomplished by three devices, by the so-called revolutionary act of 1933 expelling non-Aryan and other unreliable elements, by indoctrination of personnel, and by party monopolization of all new openings in the service. The first of these devices led to the dismissal of 211 and the demotion or transfer of 258 of the higher civil servants in Prussia and of 1.13 per cent and 2.33 per cent respectively of the 2,339 in the remaining states.[17] These figures reveal how small the genuinely democratic element was.

Far more important is the indoctrination of the mass of civil servants, which seems to be very successful with the younger generation though apparently much less so with the older group. In a hierarchical structure like the civil service, the superior, if he has unlimited power, will mold the attitudes of his inferiors. The National Socialists have taken over the key positions in the Prussian ministry of the interior, the posts of the provincial and sub-provincial presidents, and of the rural county chiefs (*Landrat*). Every one of the twelve provincial presidents has been replaced by a party member (usually a district leader), all but one of whom had joined the party before 1933. Of the 34 sub-provincial presidents, 31 are new (19 having joined the party before 1933).[18] There are 264 new Prussian county chiefs, 247 of them party members antedating 1933.

Equally important are the figures for the *Referendare*, those who have passed the first state examination in the law or administration and who, after additional training for three or four years and a second state examination, become assessors and may then practice at the bar or join the civil service or judiciary. Of the 293 new appointees from 1933 to 1936, 99 per cent were party members, 66 per cent having joined between 1922 and 1933.[19] The legal basis for appointment is now the Civil Service Act of 26 January 1937, requiring the civil servant to 'be guided in his whole conduct by the fact that the party, in indissoluble union with the people, is the bearer of the German idea of the state' and to denounce every person and every action that 'might endanger the position of the Reich or of the party.'[20]

We have already seen (see p. 72) that the civil servant may, even without obtaining the consent of his superior, accept unpaid party posts, though in his administrative work he remains subject to the orders of his superior in the bureaucratic hierarchy and to no one else. This principle is stressed in the ruling of 28 December 1939 on administration of county offices,* which limits the role of the party to the leadership of the people, in other words, to problems of popular morale.

National Socialist morale is therefore the primary concern of the party in the civil-service organization. That task had originally been entrusted to the *Werkscharen,* plant brigades of National Socialism in each public plant, and to the *Politische Stosstruppen,* political shock troops in the administrative agencies and offices. This dual organization has now been abandoned. By an agreement between Dr. Ley, the leader of the political organization of the party, and Körner, leader of the office of 'power and transportation' in the party administration, all National Socialist forces in administrative agencies, offices, and public enterprises are now united.[21] They are organized into National Socialist cells, and further subdivided into 'blocks' if necessary. Cell and block leaders are appointed by the party leader (*Kreisleiter*) upon recommendation of the leader of the labor front, the local leader of the civil-service organization, and the local leader of the party. They must be selected either from the plant chairman of the labor front or from the local chairman of the civil-service organization, depending on which group has the majority.

The new organizational set-up is a step in two directions: the destruction of social differentiations and the formation of élites within the civil service. In a law court, for instance, the plant chairman will generally be a lower- or middle-ranking servant, rarely a judge. The National Socialist cell in that court will include the entire personnel, even the charwomen. There could hardly be a more thoroughgoing destruction of social differences in outward appearance. It is a false democratization, however, since differences in status and power remain completely unchanged. An even better example would be a railroad repair shop employing both academic and non-academic civil servants and manual laborers.

* See p. 72.

There will be two plant chairmen, one for the workers appointed by the local labor front, another for the civil servants designated by their local organization. According to the Ley-Körner agreement, all the employees form one cell and the leadership falls to the workers' chairman if the workers have the majority, which is likely to be the case. False democratization is thus not limited to the civil service but also extends to distinctions between manual worker and civil servant, again without changing the real financial, social, and political differences in the slightest degree. Over both groups, furthermore, there towers a reliable élite, acting as a terrorizing agency against anyone who slackens in his manifestations of faith in the party or who is unwilling to contribute to the winter help and similar undertakings.

The relation between the party and the civil service is thus not at all simple. The ministerial bureaucracies are relatively free from old party members. Their relation with the party is established either through liaison officers, or, as in the case of the police, youth, and propaganda agencies, by assigning state tasks directly to the party. In the middle and lower hierarchies, on the other hand, the key positions are in the hands of the party, while the non-party majority of the civil servants is terrorized and indoctrinated through the cells. The party has an unquestionable control over promotions and fills new positions from the ranks of its reliable members. The submergence of civil service in the party is in full swing.

4. THE ARMED FORCES AND THE PARTY

The German army leadership, like the ministerial bureaucracy, is probably not National Socialist, strictly speaking. No one really knows anything about the exact relation between the party and the armed forces. One guess is as good as another. An understanding of certain trends, however, may help us form an intelligent opinion.

It is not true that the army rules Germany. It has never done so and does not now. In fact, it does so less today than in any previous war. At the same time, the army is the sole body in present-day Germany that has known how to keep itself organizationally free from party interference. Through its economic generals, in fact, the army has encroached upon the party and the civil bureaucracies. The army bureaucracy is the most fervent advocate of 'free capitalism' against all attempts of the National Socialist party leaders to extend the power of the state. The German army (unlike the navy, perhaps) under the Kaiser was not the driving force in imperialism. Under the Kaiser, for example, it fought an army expansion program that threatened to entail democratization of the army.* The Weimar army was chiefly interested in playing the leading role in the state and in avenging the defeat of 1918. It is safe to assume that the present leadership fully agrees with National Socialism in so far as the restoration of Germany to its 1914 frontiers and reacquisition of the colonies are concerned. Its close contacts with industrial capital have tended to make of the present German army the most powerful arm of imperialist expansion.

The connections have always been extremely close between army, industrial, and agrarian leadership, so close as to give the appearance of an extensive caste. Industry found it useful to add admirals and generals (like former high civil servants) to its supervisory boards. Under National Socialism the short-term interests are identical: industry made profits, the bankrupt agrarian holdings were saved, the officer corps gained social standing and political power, and the sons of the agrarians and industrialists once again found occupations fitting their social status.

Earlier attacks on the Prussian officer corps had always been directed against the preponderance of the nobility, especially of the landed section. We now know that this criticism was not entirely correct. Though the landed aristocracy was probably the most unenlightened and most reactionary group in Prussian society, it was not, and is not now, the most aggressive. It retained some of the more decent characteristics of feudalism, the longing for culture, even though dilettante, for comradeship and faith. These attributes have disappeared, to be replaced by a pseudo-egalitarianism veiling a complete contempt for the masses and a brutal aggressiveness especially among the younger officers. Such experiences as the purge of 30 June 1934 should have destroyed the illusions common in the outside world about the honesty, comradeship, 'Prussian tradition,' and other laudable qualities of the German officer corps. The army officer of today is a technician, interested in keeping the army machine running. The reaction of the Reichswehr to the murder of

* See p. 6.

their comrades Schleicher and Bredow shows how profound a change has taken place. If a republican ministry had merely insulted a general, the whole officers corps would have risen in wrath. Yet the cold-blooded murder of two generals who had done more than anyone else to promote military interests during Weimar found the whole army kowtowing before the supreme judge, Adolf Hitler.

The army could not do anything else. The blood purge was directed primarily against the S.A. leader Röhm, who had advocated a second revolution and sought to introduce the whole body of his S.A. into the army, with himself as minister of war. Against these ambitions, Hitler organized the purge, most likely with the knowledge, and perhaps even with the support, of the army generals. 'Germanic faith' ended where selfish interests began. On 4 January 1938, the army leadership suffered a second major defeat when Blomberg's marriage to a social inferior led to the replacement of Fritsch and many other ranking officers by the more servile leadership of Keitel and Brauchitsch. The army also betrayed the church and the religiosity once the cornerstone upon which its spiritual power rested. The National Socialist army oath has no religious character: the Leader has been substituted for God.

The S.A. monopolizes post-military training (decree of 19 January 1939). The S.A. keeps the males bodily fit in the so-called *Wehrmannschaften*, while the army is restricted to military training proper. Pseudo-egalitarianism has also been introduced in the retired officers' organization, the National League for German Officers. In 1939 its name was changed to Officers' Welfare Community, and it was placed under the control of the National Warriors' League (*Reichskriegerbund*). The membership of the latter group is drawn largely from privates and non-commissioned officers.

There are limits, of course, beyond which the army cannot allow party interference. A certain rationality operates within the army making it impossible to deliver the army lock, stock, and barrel to the party leadership. The legally recognized incompatibility between army membership and party activity,* previously discussed in another connection, has survived frequent challenge by the younger officers. Himmler's attempts to gain jurisdiction over the army have failed completely. On the other hand, the S.S. operates alongside of,

* See p. 71.

and often in conflict with, the military authorities in the conquered territories, even where the political pattern is one of military rule.* Army objections to terroristic methods against the civil population may very well be the reason why civil rule has been preferred in most of the conquered lands.

In general, it is difficult to speculate about the attitude of the armed forces. The leadership has been submitting to political control by the party and has permitted the destruction of its most sacred traditions. One immediate aim dominates the party, the army, and industry: Now that the war has come, a German defeat must be prevented at all costs. Beyond that, however, it is doubtful whether any real identity of aims can be assumed. The army is out to preserve its existence, its social and political status, and it will not willingly surrender this position whatever course the war may take.

5. THE INDUSTRIAL LEADERSHIP

Contrary to the common belief in this country, industrial leadership in National Socialist Germany is by no means the monopoly of 'managers.' Throughout the industrial set-up, and particularly in certain vital divisions like the machine industry, control remains overwhelmingly in the hands of the private entrepreneur or family, and the managers are no more than salaried employees taking orders from the owners.

The continued existence of an influential group of private capitalists does not conflict with the trend toward bureaucratization of the economy. The two problems should not be confused. An economic system may be bureaucratic; it may be integrated into a network of organizations, of cartels, groups, and chambers controlled by permanent officials; these organizations may vie with each other for control; the modern corporation may be defined as an hierarchical structure in itself—and private capitalism still remains. Not only are private capitalism and bureaucratization of the economy not incompatible, they actually complement each other at a certain stage in the development of monopoly capitalism.

Bureaucratization of private life, as previously defined, means the interference of professional organizations in direct human relations.

* See p. 173.

In the economic sphere it means that a stratum of officials stands between the owner and the surrounding world of the state, consumer, worker, and competitor, exercising the function of the owner under the latter's control. Though it thus destroys the direct relations between property and the surrounding world, bureaucratization still does not destroy the institution of private property. Nothing could be more erroneous than to call National Socialism a feudal system,[22] for the essence of feudalism, sociologically speaking, is the directness of human relations expressed without mediation by a market. Bureaucratization of the economy entails the complete depersonalization of all property relations. Even the traditional market economy leaves a large number of direct human relations in existence. It is the essence of National Socialism to have destroyed those that remained.

Some measure of bureaucratization of the economy is inevitable in our society. The joint stock corporation, the cartel, the combine are all bureaucratic forms. As monopolization increases and as business seeks more and more control over the state, it must develop more highly organized forms of political pressure. In turn, the more the state interferes in the economic life, the faster will the pressure groups grow. All this means greater regimentation and the individual would be completely helpless without organizations to interpose between himself, the state, the competitor, the consumer, or the worker. The utmost of formal rationality is reached. Human relations are now fully abstract and anonymous. This depersonalization also serves to conceal the seat of economic power, the real economic rulers operating behind the plethora of organizations surrounding private property. It is responsible for the false interpretation of bureaucratization of the economy as the disappearance of private ownership.

There is also a second reason why the two processes are not incompatible. The manager may turn into a capitalist. Actually the term 'manager' is a loose one, meaning one of three things. He may be a highly paid employee and nothing else, directing the enterprise according to specific instructions. A second type is the manager who has risen from the ranks of the leading salaried employees or who was once a capitalist and has by one device or another captured control of an enterprise. We might call such a man a capitalist-manager. He soon is accepted by the capitalists proper, becomes virtually indistinguishable from them, and shares in the industrial leadership.

Even within the group of pure managers, finally, a clear distinction must be made between the entrepreneurial (or corporation) and the organizational type. The former directs an individual enterprise or combine and occupies a higher position than the manager of a professional business organization like the cartel, the association, or the chamber. The trade association official or the cartel secretary has one ambition—to transfer to an industrial enterprise, with a higher salary and an improved social status. With that objective constantly before him, he is a willing tool of the most powerful and the most wealthy members of the organization.

Here is one of the basic distinctions between the trade-union secretary and the organizational manager. The former is either an equal among equals or has a higher social status than the rank and file. He may flatter the members to strengthen his power, but frequently trade-union officials carry out their own policies as they see them with little concern for the desires and wishes of the membership. The organizational manager, on the contrary, is faced with huge differences in power and wealth among the members of his organization. He is a nonentity; his sole aim is to please the most powerful. His power is, therefore, far less than that of the trade-union functionary and he is much less independent. He is often far more capitalistically minded and far more employer-conscious than the capitalists themselves. What Max Weber called the 'advantage of small numbers' operates as a qualifying factor: The more numerous the membership, the more independent the leaders and professional organizers. That is why the executives of the retail trade associations, for example, are comparatively powerful, those in the mining and heavy industry fields decidedly unimportant.

These distinctions between *capitalist, capitalist-manager, corporation manager*, and *organization manager* must be kept in mind in analyzing the composition of the industrial leadership.[23] The composition of the leadership can best be studied in the groups and chambers. The organs of self-government are the mediating agencies between the state and business. They collaborate in the framing, or at least in the executing, of all economic decisions. They represent the attempt to incorporate all business into one single block, capable of carrying out any decision efficiently. They translate the economic power of big business into political power. The autonomous organizations of German business are thus run by a combination of capitalists, capitalist-managers, and corporation managers, supported by a body of experts, chiefly lawyers and economists, who had filled similar positions under the Republic.

The National Economic Chamber is headed by Albert Pietzsch, who is also president of the Munich Chamber of Industry and Commerce and of the Economic Chamber of Bavaria. Born in 1874, Pietzsch studied engineering at the technical college in Dresden, received his practical training in a chemical factory, invented various new processes, and in 1910 founded the Electro-Chemical Works in Munich, which he still controls and operates. He joined the party in 1925 out of resentment at his exclusion from Munich high society. From 1933 to 1936 he was the economic expert on the staff of the Leader's deputy. His executive secretary in the national organization, significantly enough, is a typical organizational manager, Dr. Gerhard Erdmann. A lawyer by profession and a party member, Erdmann served as an officer during the First World War and headed an important department in the Federation of German Employers' Organizations until its dissolution in 1933.

The following table presents the composition of the leadership of all national groups, of the six transportation groups, of all economic groups, and of the branch groups in the national group industry.

Representatives of public corporations	13
Capitalists (mostly leaders)	20
Capitalist-managers (mostly leaders)	17
Corporation managers (mostly leaders)	31
Organizational managers and secretaries	27
Civil servants	9
No biographical data available	56
Total	173
Former army officers 31	
Party membership declared 21	

Every important industrial combine is represented in the leadership of the groups. The most powerful figure is undoubtedly Wilhelm Zangen, the general manager of the Mannesmann combine and head of the national group industry, whose name is found on many important supervisory boards of industrial corporations, banks, insurance companies, and public or semi-public corporations. Next is the leader of the national group banking, Otto Christian Fischer, formerly associated with the *Reichskreditgesellschaft* and now a partner in a Munich private bank. Other combines represented in the leadership of the groups are the United Steel Trust, the Salzdethfurth potash combine, General Electric, the oil combine, the Göring combine, the Gutehoffnungshütte, Zeiss, the Portland Cement combine, the cellulose combine. A considerable number of the leaders come from middle-sized businesses, of course, since many of the groups are made up of smaller industries like machine, building, textile, leather, trade, handicraft.

The picture is different in the provincial economic chambers. Instead of analyzing the 100 chambers of industry and commerce and the 70 chambers of handicraft, it is better to study the leadership composition in the economic chambers because their functions are much more comprehensive. For example, it is they who distribute public orders among the businessmen in their territories.

The Leadership in 17 Provincial Economic Chambers

I. *Leaders*		II. *Managers*	
Capitalists	10	Civil servants	1
Capitalist-managers	3	Organizational managers	11
Corporation managers	3	Party officials	1
No biographical data available	1	No biographical data avail-	
	17	able	4
Party officials	2		17
Army officers	13	Officers	8 *
Party membership declared	14	Party membership de-	
Representatives of industrial		clared	7 *
combines	5		
Owners of independent en-			
terprises	7		
Bankers	2		

The leadership in the provincial chambers thus lies chiefly with independent businessmen of substantial means who joined the party before 1933 and who were reserve officers in 1914-18. Their appointment is their reward for faithful party service. Every president of a provincial chamber is at the same time the president of

* There may be other officers and party members but that cannot be determined from the available biographies.

Leaders and Managers of the Economic Chambers

DISTRICT	NAME OF LEADER MANAGER	C	Ca	Co	O	Of	P	OTHER POSITIONS	BUSINESS AFFILIATION
East Prussia	Ries	?	?	?	?	?	?	Pres., Chamber of Ind.	Zellstoff Waldhof
	Manager				✓	✓			
Silesia	Fitzner		✓			✓	✓	Leader: Economic Group 3	Giesche Coal
	Manager	?	?	?	?	?	?		
Berlin-Brandenburg	Reinhart	✓						Leader: Economic Group	Banker (Commerzbank)
	Manager	Civil Servant ✓							
Pomerania	Fengler	✓				?	?		Owner
	Manager	?	?	?	?	?	?		
Nordmark	de la Camp	✓				✓	✓	Pres., Chamber of Ind.	Owner
	Manager				✓	✓			
Bremen	Bollmeyer	✓				✓	✓	?	Owner
	Manager				✓	?	?		
Lower Saxony	Hecker			✓		✓	✓	Many Supervisory Boards	Ilseder Hütte
	Manager				✓		✓		
Düsseldorf	Zucker		✓			✓	✓		Hydro-Apparate
	Manager	?	?	?	?	?	?		
Westfalia	Franke		✓			✓	✓	District Economic Adviser of the Party	
	Manager				✓		✓	Party Official	
Cologne	v. Schröder	✓				✓	✓	Many Supervisory Boards	Banker (I. H. von Stein)
	Manager				✓	✓	✓		

Leaders and Managers of the Economic Chambers—Continued

DISTRICT	NAME OF LEADER MANAGER	C	Ca	Co	O	Of	P	OTHER POSITIONS	BUSINESS AFFILIATION
Hesse Nassau	Lüer			✓		✓	✓	Party Career	Adam Opel Automobiles
	Manager				✓		✓	Party Official	
Magdeburg	Fahrenholz	✓				✓	✓	Dep. Leader Economic Group	Owner
	Manager				✓	✓	✓	Author	
Thuringia	Thiel	✓				✓	✓		Owner
	Manager	?	?	?	?	?	?		
Saxony	Wohlfarth			✓		✓	✓		Zeiss-Ikon
	Manager				✓	✓	✓		
Bavaria	Pietzsch	✓				✓	✓	Leader, National Economic Chamber	Owner
	Manager	Party Official							
Badenia	Köhler	✓	Party Official					Prime Minister	
	Manager				✓	✓	✓		
Württemberg	Kiehn	✓				✓	✓		Owner
	Manager				✓	✓			

Explanation of Symbols:
C = Capitalist
Ca = Capitalist-manager
Co = Corporation manager
O = Organization manager or secretary
Of = Officer during first World War
P = Party member

his local chamber of industry and commerce. Only five leaders represent combines: two are party officials and two bankers (Friedrich Reinhart * and Kurt von Schröder.) † Most of the managers were also reserve officers and party members before 1933. Their previous experience was with chambers of commerce, cartels, or the old *Spitzenverbände*. Some are also party officials.

The industrial leadership today differs in three respects from that under the Weimar Republic. Commercial capital is no longer represented. The free trader is a phenomenon of the past. Trade has become a function of the monopolistic producers who have either set up their own distributing apparatus or have transformed the wholesaler and retailer into their administrative agents. Secondly, banking capital has lost its position as already indicated. And among the monopolistic producers, the formerly exclusive domination of heavy industry has been somewhat restricted. The chemical and certain metallurgical industries have come to the fore and have changed their character; they too have become heavy industries. The Dye Stuff Trust of today is as much a mining as a chemical combine. The vertical combine from coal (or lignite) to manufacturing is the type which best expresses the industrial leadership. This leadership is thus smaller in number, more closely integrated, and much more powerful than heretofore. By the device of self-government in industry, the whole economy has been incorporated into the rule of monopolistic producers not only factually but also legally.

6. The Agrarian Leadership

The most formidable allies of heavy industry in the struggle against democracy were owners of the large estates, and especially those in the rye belt of eastern and northern Germany. The inflation of 1921-3 had freed agriculture from its indebtedness, but only for a fleeting moment. After the unusually bad harvests of 1924 and 1925 the peasants were in debt again. In the late fall of 1925 they were selling their crops at any price to raise cash. Prices fell below the level of the world market, with long-term credits absolutely unavailable. Subsidies began to flow and the credit system was reorganized to try to stem the tide. Unfortunately, there was no

* See p. 326.
† See p. 326.

planning in the government program. High tariffs and the system
of subsidies prevented rationalization of the dairy and vegetable
industries, in contrast to Holland and Denmark, for example. One
illustration will suffice. By stimulating the production of fodder,
the German government could have given major assistance to the
dairy farmer. Instead, it retained the grain tariffs and thus protected
the most costly and most capitalistic of all branches of agricultural
production.

The Weimar policy of internal colonization also left large landowners untouched. A statute of 11 August 1919 gave the government the right to expropriate estates at rates below market value,
but the federal supreme court declared it unconstitutional. The re-
settlement administration then resorted to direct purchase. What
little they could accomplish for the peasants (19,000 families re-
settled from 1919 to 1925) was fully balanced by a proportionate
expansion on the part of the big estates. With their higher rate of
profit and their protected position, the latter could easily and
steadily acquire smaller farms. All the agrarian loan institutions,
furthermore, favored the larger estates with lower interest rates
(much as the banks made special concessions to the larger industrial
concerns).

The depression of 1929 undoubtedly hit agriculture more severely
than industry. Farm prices declined while industrial prices remained
rather stationary, thus widening the scissors. Peasants revolted and
the Junkers started their final offensive against the democracy. Hindenburg had close connections with the East Elbian Junkers and
not one of the last three pre-Hitler cabinets, Brüning, Papen, or
Schleicher, dared to take advantage of the agricultural depression to
divide the latifundia among the small farmers. On the contrary,
financial assistance from the federal and local governments was
used chiefly to maintain the privileges of the large estates. The
Eastern Help Act of 31 March 1931, for example, enacted by the
Brüning cabinet ostensibly to relieve the suffering population of
the eastern provinces, actually became a device to preserve the social
and economic status of the Junkers. When Schleicher ordered an
investigation into the subsidy system in order to win political support from the trade unions, he was denounced to the President as
an agrarian Bolshevik by the Junker camarilla and was forced to

resign. The immediate antecedent to Hitler's appointment was thus the revival of the political influence of the Junkers.

The National Socialist food estate has successfully organized food production and distribution on a vertical basis, neglecting no sphere of agriculture. Farm prices are fixed by the government. The peasant has been subsidized and anchored in 'blood and soil.' That is National Socialism's proudest boast. The peasant is to constitute the 'new nobility of blood and soil' and the 'path breaker of an organic exchange of commodities.' [24]

By the Hereditary Estate Act, in force since 1 October 1933, the peasant (only if racially a pure Aryan, of course) was tied to the land. Upon his death, it passes to one heir, undivided and unencumbered. The order of succession is fixed: the son, his offspring, the father, brothers or daughters and their offspring, sisters. To be a hereditary peasant one must be *bauernfähig*, that is, capable of managing the farm. The size of the estate must not exceed 125 hectares (about 300 acres) as a rule, although it is permissible for one peasant to own several farms exceeding this limit in total acreage. The minimum size varies according to the fertility of the soil, following the principle that the farm must be sufficient to support a family. The total number of hereditary estates in 1938 was 684,997, occupying 15,562,000,000 hectares of land, or 37 per cent of the whole agricultural and forest area under cultivation.[25]

A few figures will quickly dispel any notion that National Socialism has revised or even checked the process of agricultural centralization or realized the romantic ideal of a middle peasant rooted in his soil. As with industry, German agriculture has moved steadily toward bigger and bigger estates.[26] National Socialism can hardly be expected to sacrifice efficiency to an anachronism. Only the ideology remains romantic, opposed to the reality, as usual.

The structure of ownership has undergone a considerable change. The average size of the hereditary estates protected by the 1933 statute has increased from 12.3 hectares in 1933 to 22.5 in 1939.[27] Small peasants have been dispossessed, victims of the process of centralization. And even among hereditary peasants a process of concentration has been taking place.

Internal colonization has become too insignificant to mention. The number of new farms for peasants fell steadily from 4,931 in 1934 to 798 in 1939.[28] Nor does the earlier figure mean that the

Hereditary Farms

SIZE GROUPS (IN HECTARES)		NUMBER	PER CENT OF ALL HEREDITARY FARMS	TOTAL ACREAGE (IN HECTARES)	PER CENT OF ALL HEREDITARY FARMS
below 7.5		20,067	2.9	135,000	0.9
7.5 — below	10	99,786	14.6	875,000	5.6
10 — "	15	175,444	25.6	2,168,000	13.9
15 — "	20	118,741	17.3	2,053,000	13.2
20 — "	25	75,696	11.0	1,692,000	10.9
25 — "	50	145,057	21.2	4,969,000	31.9
50 — "	75	33,120	4.8	1,975,000	12.7
75 — "	100	11,320	1.7	965,000	6.2
100 — "	125	4,680	0.7	520,000	3.4
above 125		1,086	0.2	209,000	1.3
		684,997	100	15,561,000	100

anachronistic doctrine actually prevailed among the National Socialist leaders for a time. The total land acquired or placed at the disposal of the 4,931 new settlers was 148,000 hectares, of which 6,000 were moor land, 23,000 were carved out of state property, 109,000 acquired from private estates of more than 100 hectares, and 15,000 from the smaller private farms.[29] In 1934 the total acreage of farms of 100 hectares or more was approximately 20,000,000 hectares, so that the re-settlement figures even at the peak were depressingly insignificant. Net income increases in proportion to the size of the farm. Max Sering, the leading agricultural economist of Germany, has published figures showing that although big farms suffered losses in 1924, their net return in 1935 was 53 marks per cultivated hectare as against 49 marks for the middle-sized and only 28 marks for the small farm.[30]

The independent small farmer has not disappeared, however. He still makes up 40 per cent of the total of independents.[31] But within the peasantry the economic process of centralization is being paralleled by a social process of élite formation. National Socialism is deliberately creating a reliable élite of wealthy peasants at the expense of the small farmer. The 700,000 hereditary peasants form a privileged body: Their estates cannot be encumbered; they may extend their holdings; their prices are protected.

The peasant élite is being created without de-feudalizing or even dividing the entailed Junker estates. National Socialism has retained the inheritance system (the so-called *Fideikommisse*) abolished in France by the Revolution of 1789 and in the western parts of Germany after the Napoleonic conquest. The entailed estate belongs to the family as a super-owner while the head of the family owns and manages it, though he can neither encumber nor alienate it. The Weimar constitution had called for the dissolution of entailed estates and the Prussian government set up a special board in 1919 to carry out this provision. Nothing much happened, however. There is an obvious, though superficial, similarity between the entailed Junker estates and the hereditary peasant estates. The National Socialists have seized upon the law of entail in order to give the Junkers, the feudal lords, the protection of the Hereditary Estates Act, ostensibly passed to protect the peasant.[82] That is how they repaid the Junker class for its considerable assistance in bringing the new regime into power.

The political influence of the Junkers is still strong, though not decisive. They are powerful in the food estate, in the agricultural credit and finance corporations, in the army, in the ministerial bureaucracy, and even in the entourage of the Leader. Two anachronisms are preserved thereby: the Junker class and the hereditary peasantry. The one forms the remnants of a dying ruling class, the other the élite among the independent peasantry.

7. The Continental Oil Corporation as a Model for the New Ruling Class

The ruling class of National Socialist Germany is far from homogeneous. There are as many interests as there are groups. Nothing holds them together but the reign of terror and their fear lest the collapse of the regime destroy them all. Attempts have been made to merge the four hierarchical groups into one integrated élite, as in the supervisory board of the Continental Oil Corporation,* which under certain conditions might become the model of a new ruling class composed of the party, the army, the bureaucracy, and industry. But, as this corporation itself shows, the unity of the ruling groups rests on the oppression and exploitation of foreign countries and of the German people alike. Germany must conquer so that

* See pp. 276, 356.

the four groups may reap the benefits. That is the essence of the highly praised Continental Oil Corporation, the one tie that binds the ruling class together.

What if attempts at conquest fail? Will the identity of short-term interests be able to withstand the pressure of ruthless egoism on the one hand and of the popular hatred of National Socialism on the other? Probably not. Industry wanted to get rid of unrestricted competition and of the trade unions—but it was far from desiring a system of party control such as has developed. Retailers and handicraftsmen wanted to crush the power of the banks and of Jewish competitors—but they have no desire to be purged. The bureaucracy was grateful for the abolition of parliamentary control and for the elimination of Social Democratic trade-union officials— but they do not like the overlordship of zealous party hierarchs. The officers wanted a huge army expansion program—but they detest party meddling.

These various strata are not held together by a common loyalty. To whom could they give it, after all? Not to the state, for it has been abolished ideologically and even to a certain extent in reality. The ideological basis on which the army and bureaucracy formerly rested has been destroyed. Adoration of the Leader is no adequate substitute, because the Leader's charisma will be completely deflated if he does not prove his worth, that is, if he is not successful. Furthermore, leadership adoration is so deeply contradictory to the process of bureaucratization and depersonalization that a mere postulation of a community integrated by a Leader is insufficient. Racial proletarianism is similarly dependent on final victory. As for such concepts as freedom and equality, it is doubtful if they were ever the basis for common loyalty, certainly not now. The monarchical tradition is gone; even the leader of the reactionary Kapp Putsch in 1920 carefully separated himself from monarchist aims. Religion is but a minor concern of the party and there is a serious split in the ranks of the clergy.

Nothing remains but profits, power, prestige, and above all, fear. Devoid of any common loyalty and concerned solely with the preservation of their own interests, the ruling groups will break apart as soon as the miracle-producing Leader meets a worthy opponent. At present, each section needs the others. The army needs the party because the war is totalitarian. The army cannot organize society 'totally'; that is left to the party. The party, on the other hand, needs the army to win the war and thus to stabilize and even aggrandize its own power. Both need monopolistic industry to guarantee continuous expansion. And all three need the bureaucracy to achieve the technical rationality without which the system could not operate. Each group is sovereign and authoritarian; each is equipped with legislative, administrative, and judicial power of its own; each is thus capable of carrying out swiftly and ruthlessly the necessary compromises among the four.

8. The Renewal of the Ruling Class

The process of renewing the ruling class is becoming more and more of a party monopoly, organizationally at least. Though economic leadership is still largely inherited—and that is true of managerial positions in corporations as well as of ownership—the renewal of the political leadership is in party hands both in law and in fact. Every youth, for example, is a member of the Hitler Youth, controlled by party hierarchs who make use of the state machinery to carry out party aims. The family and the church still remain as counteracting agencies, however, living in the traditions of the past. And the antagonisms that National Socialism produces (to be discussed later) must also be considered as a competing factor.

Elementary schools, high schools, and universities are subject to increasing control.[33] For its own functionaries, the party has established Adolf Hitler schools (one for each district), schools for the labor services, for the S.A. and S.S. Then there are the so-called 'order castles' (*Ordensburgen*), established and run according to the principles laid down by the ideological oracle, Alfred Rosenberg:

> The National Socialist movement has decided to select and unify from the mass of 70 million a nucleus of men to whom the special task of state leadership will be entrusted, whose members grow from youth on into the idea of an organic politics . . . The National Socialist state is, therefore, if we wish to use old concepts to describe its structure, a monarchy on a republican basis.

All this is to be achieved by the creation of a National Socialist Order, says Rosenberg.[34] Such an order has not been created yet, however, and we do not know whether it ever will be, but the groundwork is being laid in the order castles where the élite of the party spends four years in training.

Nor is that all. There is a party university that concentrates on Anti-Semitism. There are schools for plant leaders (four-week courses),[35] and so on. It is in these undertakings that the middle classes and even sections of the working class find their compensation for the loss of economic prospects. The craftsman and the shopkeeper, the dispossessed peasant, the worker who can no longer rise within the circle of his own party and trade union, they may all be selected to rise in the new party hierarchy—if they are pure Aryans, physically outstanding, and politically docile.

A comparison of the social composition of the universities with that of the party is significant. During the Republic, 34.1 per cent of the university students came from the upper classes, 59.2 per cent from the middle, and only 5.9 from the lower classes, the workers furnishing only 3.2 per cent of all university students.[36] No analysis of the social composition under National Socialism is available,[37] but there is no reason to assume that it has changed. The university is no longer the crux of the educational system after all. Total enrolments have dropped sharply, as the result of a deliberate policy, from 97,576 in 1932 to 51,527 in 1938 (for women from 18,578 to 6,346 during the same period).[38] More than 90 per cent of the students are organized in the National Socialist students' association (*Deutsche Studentenschaft*).

According to official statistics, about one-third of the party members come from the working classes, about 20.6 per cent are salaried employees, and the rest are distributed among independents, peasants, officials, and others.[39] The proportion of civil servants rose from 6.7 per cent in 1933 to 13.0 per cent in 1935; the bureaucracy marches with the victors.*

---

* Professor Theodore Abel [40] has, on the basis of life histories of National Socialists, which he collected in Germany in 1933, found that his panel was composed of 35 per cent workers, 51 per cent members of the lower middle classes, 7 per cent of the higher middle classes and the aristocracy, and 7 per cent peasants. Though these figures are in no way representative for the party as a whole, they nevertheless indicate the large share of the lower classes, so that the rise in the social scale will benefit considerably these groups in society.

II

THE RULED CLASSES

1. National Socialist Principles of Organization

A DEMOCRATIC society operates on the pluralistic principle of competition among social organizations, the scope and character of which are determined by the natural differences modern society produces: class, occupation, ancestry, religion, cultural interests, and so forth. No matter how thoroughly the society may be organized, such competition still preserves some of man's spontaneity. Since there is no authority which can compel the behavior of the mass organizations, however, the establishment of a social equilibrium requires that the various organizations adjust their conflicting interests by agreements. Antagonisms, strikes, disputes, lock-outs, political disturbances can safely be allowed to exist in a democracy as long as the society can count upon the good will of the leaders and rank and file of the social organizations, upon their readiness to make adjustments and compromises.

National Socialism has no faith in society and particularly not in its good will. It does not trust the various organizations to adjust their conflicts in such a way as to leave National Socialism's power undisturbed. It fears even the semi-autonomous bodies within its own framework as potential nuclei of discontent and resistance. That is why National Socialism takes all organizations under its wing and turns them into official administrative agencies. The pluralistic principle is replaced by a monistic, total, authoritarian organization. This is the first principle of National Socialist social organization.

The second principle is the atomization of the individual. Such groups as the family and the church, the solidarity arising from common work in plants, shops, and offices are deliberately broken down. The treatment of illegitimacy and procuring, for example, reveals the complete collapse of traditional values. The birth of illegitimate children is encouraged, despite the fact that the sacredness of the family is supposed to be the cornerstone of National Socialism's 'domestic philosophy.' [1] Thus, when the federal supreme labor court had to decide whether an employer could dismiss an unmarried pregnant woman without notice, it ruled in the negative on the ground that such pregnancy need no longer be regarded as *ipso facto* 'immoral and reproachable.' [2] The commentator adds:

Our views of today, based on a concept of morality that is in unison with nature, living force, and the racial will to life, must, if it affirms the [sexual] drive, affirm the naturally willed consequence, or more correctly, the naturally willed aim. For it is solely the latter which justifies and sanctifies the drive.

This attitude, we must remember, is not part of a progressive social and eugenic policy. On the contrary, it is thoroughly hypocritical, an imperialistic attitude accompanying the ideological glorification of the family.

A second example is perhaps even more illustrative not only of the destruction of family life but also of the prostitution of the judiciary. Pre-National Socialist courts had generally ruled that toleration by the future parents-in-law of sexual intercourse between an engaged couple was punishable as procuring. Under pressure from the regime, particularly in the *Schwarze Korps*, organ of the SS, the courts have reversed themselves. One decision actually quotes the diatribes in the *Schwarze Korps* in justification of the reversal.[3] Again it is not a matter of a new and honest philosophy of society. It is merely a function of its imperialism, intensified by a bohemian desire to *épater le bourgeois*.

There must be no social intercourse outside the prescribed totalitarian organizations. Workers must not talk to each other. They march together under military discipline. Fathers, mothers, and children shall not discuss those things that concern them most, their work. A civil servant must not talk about his job, a worker must not even tell his family what he produces. The church must not interfere in secular problems. Private charity, even of a purely personal nature, is replaced by the winter help or by the other official (and totalitarian) welfare organizations. Even leisure time is completely organized, down to such minute details as the means of transportation provided by the authoritarian Strength through Joy organization. On the argument, purely, that the bigger the organization the less important the individual member and the greater the influence of its bureaucracy, National Socialism has set about increasing the size of its social organizations to the utmost limit. The Labor Front has about twenty-five million members. Of what account can the individual member be? The bureaucracy is everything.

The natural structure of society is dissolved and replaced by an abstract 'people's community,' which hides the complete depersonalization of human relations and the isolation of man from man. In terms of modern analytical social psychology, one could say that National Socialism is out to create a uniformly sado-masochistic character, a type of man determined by his isolation and insignificance, who is driven by this very fact into a collective body where he shares in the power and glory of the medium of which he has become a part.

So vast and undifferentiated a mass creates new problems. It cannot be controlled by an ordinary bureaucratic machine. National Socialism therefore seeks to carve out from the masses certain élites who receive preferred treatment, greater material benefits, a higher social status, and political privileges. In return the élites act as the spearhead of the regime within the amorphous mass. When necessary one group can be played off against the other. The racial Germans are the élite in contrast to the peoples living around them. The National Socialist party is the élite within the racial German group. Within the party, the armed forces (S.A. and S.S.) constitute further élites. And even within the S.S., there are élites within an élite.* The same is true of the Hitler Youth, the Labor Front, and the civil service. The élite principle not only preserves the distinction between manual and white-collar workers but goes still further and differentiates among the working classes as well. One small body of skilled workers is raised above the level of the unskilled and semi-skilled.† None of these stratifications are the natural outcome of a society based on division of labor. They are the product of a deliberate policy designed to strengthen the hold of the leadership over the masses. Differentiation and élite formation make up the third principle of National Socialist social organization.

To prevent the masses from thinking, they must be kept in a

* See p. 111.
† See p. 433.

permanent state of tension. That is accomplished by propaganda. The ideology is in an unceasing process of change and adaptation to the prevailing sentiment of the masses. The transformation of culture into propaganda and the transience of the slogans constitute the fourth principle of National Socialist social organization.

Propaganda wears out, however, and it wears out all the more rapidly the faster the slogans are changed. So it is supplemented by terror. Violence is not just one unimportant phenomenon in the structure of National Socialist society; it is the very basis upon which the society rests. Violence not only terrorizes but attracts. It is the fifth and final principle of National Socialist social organization.

2. THE WORKING CLASS UNDER THE WEIMAR DEMOCRACY

The position of the working class alone of the ruled classes will be analyzed to illustrate the methods of mass domination and the status of the subject population. Certain historical trends and general sociological consideration must be studied first, however, to provide the necessary background.

Property is not merely control over material things.[4] It is a relation between men through the medium of things and thus confers power over human beings as well. The owner of property in the means of production controls the individual as worker, consumer, and citizen. The worker's only property is his labor power. He is separated from the means of production and yet he can turn his labor power to useful account only by combining it with the means of production, which do not belong to him and concerning which he has no say. Property in the means of production, therefore, exerts a twofold influence upon the worker: It attracts him into its orbit and it controls him. From the moment the worker enters the factory gate he surrenders part of his personal freedom and places himself at the disposal of an outside authority.

The owner of property controls the worker as worker in five spheres: the plant (the technical unit), the enterprise (the economic unit where business decisions are reached), the labor market, the commodity market, and the state. The power of property to draw men into labor contracts and to dictate their behavior while at work sets a series of problems for the working class and for the

state. The major problem is how to replace the employer's dictatorial power by a democratic power in which the workers too shall
share. This is the task of the trade unions. Their function may be
divided under three heads. First, they act as friendly (or benefit)
societies. They provide sickness and accident benefits, unemployment benefits, strike and lock-out pay, old-age pensions, and legal
aid. Almost all the state systems of unemployment relief, labor exchanges, accident and sickness insurance are modeled after arrangements devised by the trade unions. This group of trade-union activities (the inner trade-union function) has been carried furthest in
England, whose example had a marked effect on German trade
unionism.

The second function of a union is its marketing function or
collective bargaining. The union seeks control of the labor market,
confronting the power of private property with the power of organized workers and either laying down the conditions of work
and pay or, where the state regulates these conditions, seeing to it
that the governmental regulations are actually carried into effect.
The more important of the two is the collective agreement backed
by the threat of a strike.

Finally, the trade unions are political bodies bringing pressure on
the state in all three of its functions, legislative, executive, and judicial. It is impossible to say which of the three types of union
activity is of greatest importance. The answer depends on the particular historical, political, and economic situation in each case. The
attempt to influence the state is always present and always basic,
however, partly because the state can so strongly affect the benefit
and market functions of the workers' organizations.

Four stages can be distinguished in the historical development of
the relation between the trade unions and the state, with some
overlapping and repetition. Trade unions were illegal in the early
period of capitalism. Every state prohibited any combination of
workmen formed for the realization of social aims, as in the French
Le Chapelier law passed early in the Revolution on 14 June 1791.
In England, the French Revolution frightened the governing class
to such an extent that they too suppressed the trade unions in order
to prevent revolution. The Prussian General Civil Code (*das
allgemeine Landrecht*) forbade stoppages on workdays and thus
blocked the use of the main trade-union weapon, the strike. Col-

lective contracts regulating conditions of employment were null and void during this early period. Trade unions were forcibly dissolved and membership became a punishable offense.

Despite all opposition, however, the trade-union movement continued to grow and at some point every state was forced to rescind its anti-combination laws. The earliest signs of this second stage appeared in England in 1824. In France, a law of 25 May 1864 gave recognition to labor's freedom to organize, though, as in the English statute of 1825, the restrictive criminal laws were retained. In Germany the period of prohibition lasted until 1869. The Industrial Code of the North German Federation, adopted in May of that year, lifted the ban on combinations for the first time, but only for industrial workers. Agricultural laborers, domestic servants, seamen, and state employees were excluded from the privilege. Criminal laws continued to impose heavy obstacles.

The repeal of Bismarck's anti-socialist laws and the enactment of the industrial code made possible the establishment in 1890 of the *Generalkommission der Gewerkschaften*, a central body of the 'free' or socialist trade unions. In 1919, this body was transformed into the *Allgemeine Deutsche Gewerkschaftsbund*, similar to the British Trades Union Congress or the American Federation of Labor.

The common characteristic of this second period, the era of toleration, was that the social power of the working-class movement had forced the state to abandon direct prohibition of trade unionism and to resort to indirect interference through a whole series of special provisions and with the help of the penal code, the courts of law, and particularly the police force. Philip Lotmar, pioneer in German labor law, summed the situation up in these words: 'The trade union is free, as free as an outlaw' (*Die Gewerkschaft ist frei, aber sie ist vogelfrei*).

The triumph of democracy brought with it recognition of the trade unions; it gave them a new status and their threefold function was acknowledged without qualification. The clearest expression of this stage was found in Germany, England, and Austria.[4]

The German trade-union movement had a short but stormy history dating from 1877. The German Constitution of 11 August 1919 gave the trade unions special recognition. Articles 159 and 165 acknowledged their existence as free bodies *vis-à-vis* the state.

Neither the cabinet, the legislature, nor the police was to have the right to dissolve the unions. In return, they were called upon to fulfil certain positive tasks. In the pluralistic collectivism of Weimar, the trade unions played the decisive role. More than the political parties, they were the bearers of the new form of social organization, the bridge between the state bureaucracy and the people, the agency for developing a political democracy into a social democracy.

A law of 11 February 1920 introduced the system of works councils restricting (to draw an analogy between factory and state) the employer's power and introducing the elements of constitutional government into the plant.[5] Like the state, an industrial enterprise has three powers: legislative, executive, and judicial. Prior to the works-council law, the employer exercised all three powers: he was the legislator because he issued the factory rules; the executor because he hired and fired; the sole judge because he inflicted the punishments for violations of the factory rules. The works-council act vested the legislative power jointly in the hands of the employer and the council. The members of the council were elected by secret ballot according to the principle of proportional representation, with various trade-union tickets competing and without any influence from either the state or the employer. If no agreement could be reached between the works council and the employer, a board of arbitration (later the labor court) issued the factory rules.

The works council also had a voice in factory administration, though only a limited one. If it upheld the protest of a dismissed worker, for example, the latter could sue in the labor court for reinstatement or for monetary damages. The council also supervised the execution of collective agreements and the observance of the factory rules, and generally protected the employees. It had the right to have two delegates attend meetings of the corporation's board of directors and to examine the balance sheets and profit-and-loss statements. These provisions had little practical importance, however.

The works councils were what the Germans called 'the elongated arms' of the trade unions. Though formally independent of the unions, they constantly relied on them for assistance in the fulfilment of their duties. Council members were trained in trade-union schools and supported by the unions in every conflict with the employers. The unions in turn leaned heavily on the councils for such functions as enforcement of maximum-hour legislation.

In general, the attempt to give the working class direct influence in the sphere of the private enterprise was not particularly successful. Reaction, impotent when the statute was enacted early in 1920, set in again too soon for that. Trade-union influence in the commodity market was equally weak—except in the coal and potash industries in which special laws (erroneously called socialization acts) provided for partial state management. The coal and potash unions could delegate representatives to the public boards of directors and were thus to a certain extent participants in management.

The most important influence of the unions was in the labor market. A decree of 23 December 1918, issued by the Council of People's Deputies, recognized collective agreements as the legal means of determining wages and conditions of employment. Whenever trade unions and employers' associations arrived at collective agreements, the provisions became part of the employment contract between the employer and each of his workers. They had the force of objective law. No deviation could be made in the individual labor contract unless it favored the employee. This statutory provision formed the cornerstone upon which the whole structure of Republican German labor relations rested. Only organized workers and employers were affected by such agreements, however. To meet the danger that employers would hire only non-union men, the same law authorized the minister of labor, at his discretion, to extend an agreement to the whole of an industry or trade by decree. Frequent use was made of this power until 1931.

When a voluntary agreement could not be reached, the supposedly neutral state could intervene. Arbitration boards were created by a 1923 decree.[6] The chairman was to be a state official and the members equally divided between employers and union representatives. If either party rejected a board decision, then an official of the Reich made an award that was binding, an imposed wage agreement between the employers' association and the trade union.

With a few unimportant exceptions, the famed German system of unemployment insurance was the creation of the Weimar constitution and of the trade unions. The basic law of 1927 also provided for the regulation of labor exchanges, placing the whole system under the Reich Board for Employment Exchanges and Unemployment Insurance, divided into one central, 13 regional, and 361 local boards. Each had an equal number of representatives of employers, workers, and public bodies (states, municipalities, etc.) under the chairmanship of a neutral official. Ultimate supervision rested with the minister of labor. We have here one more expression of collectivist democracy, with the state calling upon autonomous private groups to help execute the business of government efficiently.

The regulation of wage rates and conditions of employment can be effective only if accompanied by unemployment benefits sufficiently high to prevent a severe drop in wages. After many struggles and legal disputes, the trade unions eventually succeeded in establishing the principle that the union scale of wages should be paid to relief workers in order to prevent a downward pressure on the wages of employed workers. The whole system was supplemented by extensive insurance against accident, illness, and old age, applying to manual and professional workers alike.

The fifth and last domain in which the rule of property comes to the fore is the state. The trade unions could not participate directly in the legislative process because the framers of the constitution had rejected the proposal of a second chamber organized along professional and occupational lines of representation.* They could exert considerable influence, nevertheless. In 1920, for example, the trade unions defeated the Kapp Putsch by a very effective general strike. All the trade unions were attached to political parties, furthermore, and exercised a strong political role in that way. The free unions were attached to the Social Democratic party and the Democratic to the Democratic party. The Christian unions were linked with the Center party, though their white collar and professional wings were more closely allied with the German Nationalist party and later with the National Socialists.

The Social Democratic party was financially dependent on the unions, and the increasing frequency of elections increased this dependence. As a result, a large number of trade-union functionaries found their way into the Reichstag. There they naturally spoke for

* See p. 231.

the union policy, social reform, and at times created peculiar situations. In 1930, for example, the Reich cabinet, headed by the Social Democratic leader Hermann Müller, had to resign at the request of the free trade unions because the other parties in the coalition were unwilling to raise the unemployment-insurance contributions. No important political decision was made without the trade unions. In fact, their influence was invariably stronger than that of the Social Democratic party.

In the judicial sphere the trade unions participated actively in the administration of labor law. They had great influence in the labor courts created by act of 1927 to settle disputes between employers and employees, between employers and works councils, between the parties to a collective bargaining agreement, and among employees in group work. The three courts of the first, second, and third instance each consisted of a judge and an equal number of trade union and employers' association representatives. Only trade-union officials could represent the worker in the first court; in the second the worker could select either a union official or an attorney; but only lawyers could plead in the third. Thus, as the recognized representatives of workers, the unions were called on to advise in state affairs in this sphere as well.

It must be said in conclusion that this vast system of collectivist democracy was never carried through completely. The constitution promised it, but the continued and growing political power of reaction blocked fulfilment of the promise. The Weimar Republic, a democracy of the Social Democratic party and trade unions, did achieve two things. It won for the working man a comparatively high cultural level and it had begun to give him a new political and social status.

Two basic developments occurred during the period of trade-union recognition. The competitive capitalist economy was fully transformed into a monopolistic system and the constitutional state into a mass democracy. Both trends changed the whole structure of state and society. The influence of the state enjoyed uninterrupted growth. The state itself assumed extensive economic functions. With its representatives presiding on all parity boards, it acquired an increasingly decisive influence in the sphere of social policy, especially because the two sides could so rarely reach an agreement by themselves.

Mass democracy strengthened the political consciousness of the working class. The First World War had made the working class throughout the world conscious of its needs and its power and finally detached the working-class movement from the bourgeois political parties.

The functioning of the trade unions was seriously affected by each of these developments. The extensive introduction of improved scientific methods of production created technological unemployment. Growing standardization and rationalization of industry altered the composition of the working population. The rise of cartels, trusts, and combines created a new bureaucracy. The number of office workers, clerks, officials, and technical superintendents increased. There was a leap in the proportion of unskilled and semi-skilled workers (especially women) at the expense of skilled labor. Contracting markets and intense competition requires an enlarged distributive apparatus, increasing the number and proportion of workers engaged in this sphere.

Social legislation facilitated the trend toward the concentration of capital, with all that it brought in its train. A pattern of high wages, short hours, and good working conditions places the heaviest financial burden on medium and small-scale undertakings. Large-scale enterprises escape because they use relatively little labor and much machinery. Every enforced rise in wages and every increased expenditure imposed by the demands of social legislation forced the producer to save elsewhere. The 'saving' usually took the form of labor-saving devices.

The German trade unions deliberately fostered this rationalization process because they believed with undue optimism that the technological displacement of workers would lead to greater employment in the capital-goods industries and that the ensuing rise in purchasing power would increase production all around and lead to reabsorption of the unemployed in the industries producing consumers' goods.

Faced with powerful monopolist opposition, the trade unions needed the help of the state. But at the same time the growth in governmental economic activity led to a new conflict. By participating in industry as a producer and shareholder, the state itself frequently became the opponent of the unions in matters of wages and working conditions.

The altered composition of the working population and the chronic unemployment of the depression era measurably weakened the appeal of the trade unions. Their membership fell off and unemployment drained their treasuries. They had to reduce their benefit payments—at the very time when vast unemployment forced a sharp cut in the size and number of state unemployment payments.

Unskilled workers, inspectors, administrative officials, shop assistants, and women workers increased in proportion, and they are extremely difficult to organize. The increased role of the professions and salaried posts heightened the significance of their trade unions, but most of these unions were middle class in outlook. The salaried and professional employee did not want to 'be reduced to the level of the masses.' He fought to retain his tenuous middle-class status and his privileges, and he succeeded. White-collar and manual workers were treated differently in the social legislation. Social insurance benefits were higher for the former. The period of notice to which they were entitled before being dismissed was longer. No party dared oppose their demands nor those of the minor government officials, whose henchmen were present in every political faction. The attitude of capital was simple—divide to rule; grant privileges to a small group at the expense of the larger. The 'new middle class' thus became the stronghold of the National Socialists.

Even the trade unions' appeal to the vocational interests of the workers was weakened by the increased governmental activity in the regulation of wages and conditions of employment. The arbitration system, the legal extension of collective wage agreements to unorganized workers, unemployment insurance, and the entire paraphernalia of social insurance made the worker feel that he no longer needed his union. 'If the state takes care of all these things, of what use are the trade unions?' was a stock question in Germany.

The number of strikes diminished steadily. In 1931 not a single offensive strike was called by a German trade union. The risk involved became greater, success less certain. Only large sympathetic strikes could hold out any real prospect of victory. Every strike could easily have led to civil war, both because of the acute political crisis and because in a monopolistic economy every strike affects the entire economic system and the state itself.

A collectivist democracy, finally, binds the trade unions and the state in a closer relation. Though the unions remain independent and free, their close contact with the state leads them to develop a psychological attitude of dependence that discourages strikes.

Neither the trade unions nor the political parties were able to cope with the new situation. They had become bureaucratic bodies tied to the state by innumerable bonds. In 1928 the Social Democratic party boasted of its phenomenal achievements in government. The following statistical summary was captioned, 'Figures every official should know.' [7]

33 regional organizations
152 Social Democratic Reichstag deputies
419 Social Democratic provincial deputies
353 Social Democratic aldermen (*Stadträte*)
947 Social Democratic burgomasters
1,109 Social Democratic village presidents (*Gemeindevorsteher*)
4,278 Social Democratic deputies of the Kreistag (sub-provincial bodies)
9,057 Social Democratic deputies of the municipal diets
9,544 local organizations
37,709 Social Democratic village deputies
1,021,777 party members (803,442 men, 218,335 women)
9,151,059 Social Democratic votes (Reichstag election of 1928).

The Communist party indulged in similar boasts:

360,000 members
33 newspapers
20 printing houses
13 parliamentary deputies
57 deputies in state diets
761 municipal deputies
1,362 village deputies.[8]

Nor is this all. The trade-union bureaucracy was much more powerful than the corresponding party bureaucracy. Not only were there many jobs within the unions but there were jobs with the Labor Bank, the building corporations, the real-estate corporations, the trade-union printing and publishing houses, the trade-union insurance organizations. There was even a trade-union bicycle factory. There were the co-operatives attached to the Social Democratic party and trade unions. And there were innumerable state jobs: in the labor courts, in the social-insurance bodies, in the coal and potash organization, in the railway system. Some union officials held five, six, and even ten positions at the same time, often combining political and union posts.

Bound so closely to the existing regime and having become so completely bureaucratic, the unions and the party lost their freedom of action. Though they did not dare to co-operate fully with Brüning, Papen, or Schleicher, whose cabinets had severely curtailed civil liberties and the democratic process generally and had cut wages and living conditions, neither could oppose these regimes. Real opposition would have meant strikes, perhaps a general strike and civil war. The movement was neither ideologically nor organizationally prepared for drastic struggle. They could not even fulfil their inner trade-union functions. What little funds remained after the depression were invested in beautiful office buildings, trade-union schools, real estate, building corporations, and printing plants. There was not enough left for their unemployed members.

The pluralistic social system of the Weimar Republic had broken down completely by 1932. No organization could fulfil its aims. The social automatism no longer functioned. The spontaneity of the working classes had been sacrificed to bureaucratic organizations, incapable of fulfilling their promise to realize the freedom of each by pooling individual rights into collective organizations. National Socialism grew in this seed-bed.

3. THE LABOR FRONT

Upon seizing power, the National Socialist party planned to continue the trade-union organizations, merge the three different wings, and place the unified group under National Socialist leadership. Through their workers' cell organization (the NSBO), they began negotiations with the Social Democratic union leadership. The two chairmen of the free unions, Leipart and Grassmann, were co-operative. They agreed to abdicate if the trade-union structure were retained. They publicly dissolved the alliance of the unions with the Social Democratic party and promised the future political neutrality of the trade-union movement. When the new regime proclaimed May Day a national holiday in 1933, the free trade unions passed a resolution of approval. This action, they said, was the realization of an old working-class dream.

The betrayal of a decade-old tradition in an attempt to save the union organizations from complete destruction was more than just cowardice. It was a complete failure to appreciate the real character of National Socialism, and it opened the eyes of the National Socialists. They saw that even the little strength they had attributed to the trade unions was an illusion. Besides, German industry did not trust the National Socialist workers' cell organization too far. Had it not in the past instigated and supported strikes, though only for propaganda purposes? The ambitious Dr. Ley at the head of the party's political organization therefore decided to seize control of the trade unions.

On 1 May 1933, the new national holiday was celebrated. A number of trade-union officials and a few members, still hoping to save their organizational structure, participated side by side with the National Socialists. The next day truck-loads of Brown Shirts and Black Shirts raided all union headquarters, arrested the leaders, seized the funds, and placed National Socialists in charge. Dr. Ley had in the meantime set up a 'committee of action' composed of Brown Shirts, Black Shirts, party officials, and representatives of the NSBO, with himself at the head.[9] It took exactly thirty minutes for the huge trade-union structure to collapse. There was no resistance; no general strike, not even a demonstration of any significance. What further proof is needed that the German trade-union organizations had outlived their usefulness? They had become machines without enthusiasm or flexibility. They no longer believed in themselves.

On 12 May 1933, the property of the trade unions and their affiliated organizations was attached by the public prosecutor of Berlin—no one has ever been able to explain the legal basis for this action—and Dr. Ley was appointed trustee. He had been appointed leader of the German Labor Front two days before. On 24 June, the offices of the Christian unions were occupied and on 30 November, the Federation of German Employers' Organizations decided to liquidate.

Under the influence of corporative ideas, the National Socialists originally planned to organize the Labor Front on three pillars: salaried employees, workers, and employers. For this purpose a simplified organizational structure was announced on 1 July 1933, with the workers divided into fourteen organizations and the salaried employees into nine, each under a leader and council. The corporative set-up was quickly abandoned in Germany, however.* It was particularly dangerous to the regime in the field of labor because, by articulating the working class into bodies distinct and separated from the employers, it implicitly recognized the differences created in society by the division of labor. Italy has retained at least the outward forms of a syndical and corporate structure; Germany not a trace. The reasons seem to be that the German working class is far more numerous and highly trained than the Italian, and, though not so militant as some groups in the Italian labor movement, far less amenable to authoritarian control.

After the one false start, the German Labor Front was deliberately planned to destroy the natural differentiations created by the division of labor. The first change occurred on 27 November 1933, initiating the transformation to a system of 'federal plant communities' (*Reichsbetriebsgemeinschaften*). To prepare the way, no new members were admitted to the Labor Front.[10] On 7 December 1933, the old organizations were finally dissolved.

The Labor Front is now a body of approximately 25,000,000 members, including every independent and every gainfully employed person outside the civil service. It is the most characteristic expression of the process of complete atomization of the German working classes. It is divided into sixteen federal plant communities: food, textiles, cloth and leather, building, lumber, metal, chemistry, paper and printing, transportation and public enterprises, mining, banks and insurance, free professions, agriculture, stone and earth, trade, and handicraft. The important point is that the individual workers are not members of the federal plant communities. They are solely and exclusively members of the total body, the Labor Front itself. The plant communities are not lower organizational units out of which the Labor Front is formed. They are merely administrative departments within the Labor Front, organizing plants but not individuals. That is how much the regime fears that articulation along even occupational lines might lead to opposition.

The basic statute is the Leader's decree of 24 October 1934. The

* See above, pp. 228-34.

Labor Front was raised to the rank of a party grouping * and its leadership is party leadership. At the head is the leader of the political organization of the party, Dr. Ley, who appoints and dismisses the lower leadership selected chiefly from the NSBO, the S.A., and the S.S. The finances of the Labor Front are under the control of the party treasury.† It has a central office divided into a number of departments. Departments 1 to 5 comprise the closest collaborators of the leader, the central supervisory staff, the legal and information departments, the training department, and so on. Department 6 is called 'securing the social peace' and is subdivided into the offices for social policy, for social self-administration, for youth and women, and for the sixteen federal plant communities. Department 7 is concerned with 'raising the living standards.' Its most important sub-division is the Strength through Joy office with its own sub-departments. Departments 8 to 10 are concerned with vocational training, the disciplinary courts of the Labor Front, and the plant troops.

The central office also has a number of auxiliary offices, such as the Institute for the Science of Labor, an institute of technology, and an office for the execution of the Four Year Plan. There are regional and local organizations sub-divided along territorial (street blocks) and functional (plant blocks) lines.

Even this monstrous structure does not complete the picture. Aping the autonomous organization of business, the National Socialists have set up a national chamber of labor and regional chambers. The national body is composed of the leaders of the federal plant communities, the provincial chiefs and the heads of the main departments of the Labor Front, and certain other individuals. It has never functioned. The provincial chambers have a similar composition and are equally inactive.

The tasks of the Labor Front were defined by the famous Leipzig agreement of 21 March 1935 between the leader of the Labor Front and the ministries of labor and economics.[11] The minister of transportation entered the agreement on 22 July 1935 and the food estate on 6 October 1936. It is a most revealing document, for, by specific provision, it surrenders all the economic activities of the Labor Front to the national economic chamber and the ministry of eco-

* See p. 81.
† See p. 81.

nomics. The national economic chamber was admitted to the Labor Front as a body, which meant that all the economic groups, every chamber of industry and commerce, every chamber of handicraft, and all provincial economic chambers are also affiliated as a body. So are the six national transportation groups and the food estate.

In order to compensate the Labor Front for this loss of independence, another elaborate body was created on paper, a federal labor and economic council composed of the councils of the national economic chamber and of the national labor chamber. This body has never functioned. Its tasks were defined in the Leipzig agreement and in Dr. Ley's executive decree of 19 June 1935 as follows:

    a. To deal with those tasks that the federal government, the German Labor Front, and the National Economic Chamber delegate to it;

    b. to answer, clarify, and prepare . . . in joint discussions essential and fundamental questions of social and economic policy;

    c. to receive pronouncements of the federal government, the German Labor Front, and the National Economic Chamber.

There could be no more patent fraud. The sole purpose of this elaborate mechanism is to create the impression that the Labor Front has an organization and tasks similar to those of the employers. In actual fact, the Labor Front exercises no genuine economic or political functions. It is not a marketing organization, since it has nothing to do with the regulation of wages and labor conditions. It is not a political organization of labor. It is not even an organization solely of labor. It has five functions: the indoctrination of labor with the National Socialist ideology; the taxation of the German working class; the securing of positions for reliable party members; the atomization of the German working classes; and the exercise of certain inner trade-union functions. Business, on the other hand, does have a functioning organization of its own on a territorial and functional basis. Labor has none. The Labor Front is merely one more organization of the whole German people without distinction as to occupation, training, or social status.

The primary task of the Labor Front is the indoctrination of the German working class and the destruction of the last vestige of Socialism and Marxism, of Catholic and democratic trade-unionism. This task is entrusted to the Labor Front proper through its countless officials in the central, regional, and local offices, above all through the so-called plant troops, reliable party members in each plant acting as the agents of National Socialist terrorism, and through the political shock troops.[12] In the words of Dr. Ley, the shock troops are 'the soldier-like kernel of the plant community which obeys the Leader blindly. Its motto is "the Leader is always right." ' [13] The shock troops are not fused into a national organization. Each group is controlled by the local party organization in conjunction with the local Labor Front, and supervised by the main department of plant troops.

The NSBO, the original party organization in plants, shops, and offices, has been dissolved. Its fate was shared by the National Socialist handicraft and retail cell organizations (NS Hago). They had been the fighting outposts of the movement among the working classes and the small businessmen. Both were super-local organizations, and therefore out of harmony with the pulverizing policy of National Socialism. There was the danger that they could become centers of dissatisfaction and opposition through communication between workers of various plants and businessmen of different communities. They had to go.

What remains is only the Labor Front for party members and outsiders alike. Although there is no legal compulsion to join the Labor Front, the pressure is so strong that it is inadvisable for anyone to stay out. The members must attend meetings, but must not enter into discussion. They may put questions but have no right to insist on an answer. Its papers and periodicals are poor substitutes for the trade-union publications of the Republic. They are filled with pictures of the Leader and his entourage, war photographs, the speeches of the leadership, idyllic descriptions of life in the New Germany, glorification of the party and the Reich, and little else—certainly little information relevant to labor conditions.

The ties created by common work and common training are no longer articulated for the working classes. There are special organizations for doctors, dentists, lawyers; there are handicraft guilds, groups, chambers of commerce and industry, chambers of handicraft for businessmen—but the German worker and salaried employee alone of all the sections of the population have no organization built on the natural differences and similarities of work and occupation. The Labor Front has driven the process of bureaucratization to its maximum. Not only the relations between the enterprise and the worker but even the relations among the workers themselves are now mediated by an autocratic bureaucracy.

4. THE LABOR LAW [14]

PLANT COMMUNITY AND PLANT LEADER

In no other field has the National Socialist community and leadership ideology encountered so much trouble as in labor law. The basis of labor law and labor relations is the individual contract in which the employee sells his labor power for a specified time, price, performance, and place. Even in a completely collectivistic system of labor law in which every worker is organized, there are individual agreements upon which the collective contract rests. The individual agreement remains the indispensable basis of all labor relations. For a collective agreement becomes effective only if individual agreements exist, whether forced upon the employer or employee or upon both. The individual labor contract of course hides the fact that the employee is subject to the power of the employer, but it is none the less a rational instrument dividing labor from leisure and clearly limiting the power of the employer in space, time, and function. In any modern society it must consider labor power as a commodity, though not exclusively so.

This simple consideration has been hotly denied by National Socialism. Labor power is not a commodity, they insist.[15] The very concept of the individual labor contract is Romanistic.[16] 'The labor relationship is a community relationship based on honor, faith, and care, in which a follower utilizes his labor power for an entrepreneur, either in the latter's plant or otherwise in his service. The labor contract is the agreement which creates and molds the labor relationship.' [17]

The basis of labor relations is 'the ethical idea of faith.' [18] 'Not the materialistic Roman *locatio conductio operarum* but the Germanic structure of a contract of faith is decisive for the labor relationship . . . the follower enters the service of the entrepreneur and not only receives remuneration but above all protection and care. He not only performs work but promises faith and work, which is, so to speak, the materialization of it.' [19]

These quotations can be repeated endlessly. National Socialist politicians and philosophers provide a chorus chanting that labor is no commodity; labor is honor; the relation between employer and employee is a community relation.

The so-called charter of labor (the act for the regulation of national labor, 20 January 1934) begins with the following provision: 'In the plant, the entrepreneur as the plant leader and the salaried employees and workers as the followers work jointly for the furtherance of the aims of the plant and for the common benefit of people and state.' This plant community ideology bears a strong resemblance to the theory of the 'enterprise as such' * and has the same function. While the latter theory delivers the corporation to its board, the community plant doctrine delivers the workers into the power of the owner.

The community ideology in labor relations is one of the worst and one of the most significant of the heritages from the Republic. Section 615 of the imperial civil code had provided that every employee who offered his labor to an employer must receive wages even when the latter was unable to let him work either because of technical mishaps in the factory or because of economic conditions or a strike in another factory. The legislators argued that the employer, as the owner, had to bear the full risk involved in the operation of his enterprise. The federal supreme court reversed this statutory provision in 1921. It argued that the establishment of works councils had created a plant community in which the employee was a 'living link' and therefore had to share the risks.[20] Lower courts were advised to examine the equity in each specific case. If the disturbance is caused by strikes, for example, the employer is not obligated to pay wages even if the stoppage occurs in a wholly unrelated enterprise.

The so-called plant community was a very strange community even during the Republic. It was a community of losses but never of profits. Neither during the Republic nor after has a single court reached the logical conclusion that higher profits must automatically lead to higher wages. The plant-community theory was nothing but an anti-democratic doctrine by which the judiciary sabotaged progressive labor legislation.

* See p. 286, above.

Leadership in labor relations has a different meaning and function from leadership in politics or business. All political leaders are chosen from above. The employer is the leader of the plant simply because he is the owner or manager. Ownership of the means of production automatically means authoritarian control over the workers, and the 'community' thus established is comparable to a barracks. Section 2 of the National Socialist charter of labor makes that unmistakably clear:

'The leader of the plant decides as against the followers in all matters pertaining to the plant in so far as they are regulated by statute.

'He shall look after the well-being of the followers, while the latter shall keep faith with him, based on the plant community.'

All the attempts of the National Socialist legal experts to supplant the labor contract by a community theory have failed. They have been unable to find a legal basis for labor relations that will not resemble the condemned liberal, Romanistic, and materialistic individual labor contract. In despair the leading commentator has accepted the conclusion that the labor contract is essential for the establishment of the community.[21] The language of the community ideology remains—and the burdens upon the employee have been increased considerably.

The duty of the employer to look after the welfare of his workers is no innovation of National Socialism. It was stated in sections 616-18 of the civil code of 1900, based upon the insight that the labor contract is not a pure exchange relation but is a power contract placing one man under the sway of another. Power entails duties—that much was clear to the framers of the 'materialistic' and 'Romanistic' civil code. The obligation of the employer to prevent accidents and to look after the health and security of his employees does not follow from an alleged community, but from the fact that the owner controls the means of production. The community ideology of the National Socialists has added nothing here. I have been unable to find a single decision by the supreme labor court that substantially improves the protection of the worker by invoking the community ideology.[22] But I have found innumerable instances in which the new theory has been used to deprive workers and salaried employees of the remnants of those rights which the rational character of the individual labor agreement had granted to them.

The essence of rational law consists in clearly defining and de-limiting rights and duties. Such rationality has been almost com-pletely destroyed. In a liberal society the worker sells his labor power for a given time, place, performance, and price. Under Na-tional Socialism all limitations have disappeared unless defined by statute, or by the regulation of the trustee of labor, or by a plant regulation.* In the unanimous view of National Socialist lawyers, the new theory that the worker owes faith means that he is obliged to accept any work the employer demands within reason, whether previously agreed upon or not; that he must work at any place the employer determines within reason, whether previously agreed upon or not; that he must accept any wages that the employer equitably fixes, unless they are fixed in trustee or plant regulations.[28]

In sum, the community and leadership theory in labor relations uses a medieval terminology to conceal the complete surrender of the rights of the workers by the destruction of the rationality of the individual labor contract. How completely the ideology con-tradicts reality becomes still clearer when we remember the discus-sions of the control of the labor market.† Compulsory repatriation, compulsory training, and deportation are hardly devices to awaken a plant community spirit. The textile workers or the retail em-ployees who are carted off in trucks and freight trains to distant parts of the *grossdeutsche Reich* and then forced into new occupa-tions cannot possibly develop a plant community feeling.

THE PLANT

Through the works councils, the Weimar democracy permitted workers to choose plant representatives in secret competitive elec-tions. National Socialism has suppressed the works councils and replaced them by the so-called councils of confidence, chosen in typical National Socialist fashion. The leader of the plant (that is, the employer or his manager) jointly with the chairman of the NSBO cell names the slate (two to ten members according to the size of the plant) and every March the employees approve or re-ject it in so-called elections. No other slate is admitted, of course. The council, furthermore, is a 'leader council,'[24] and section 6 of the charter of labor defines that term to mean that it is directed by

* See p. 337.
† See p. 337.

the employer. The duty of the council is to 'deepen the mutual trust within the plant community'; to discuss measures 'pertaining to the improvement of efficiency' and to the creation and execution of the general conditions of labor; to concern itself with the protection of the workers and the settlement of disputes. A councilman may be deposed by the trustee of labor but can be dismissed from his regular job only if the plant closes or if his labor contract is terminated for an important reason. If an employer owns several plants belonging to the same technical or economic unit and if he himself does not manage all of them, he must set up an enterprise council from among the members of the various plant councils to advise him in matters of social policy.

The almost complete control of the Labor Front (assisted by the plant troops) and the employer over the composition of the 'council of confidence' would seem to guarantee against their becoming centers of opposition. In many cases, however, the councils were apparently dominated by old trade unionists and did become spearheads of opposition. National Socialism has not been able to conquer the manual worker or even the entire group of the salaried employees. To evaluate the sentiment of the Weimar working classes, particular attention should be given to the works-council elections. They are perhaps even more important than the parliamentary elections, for in choosing the council the workers based their decision almost exclusively upon actual social experience. The composition of the works councils in 1930 and 1931 is striking—not a single National Socialist in 1930 and only 710 out of 138,000 as late as 1931:

Composition of Works Councils for Manual Workers in 1930 and 1931

(Reported by the Socialist Trade Union ADGB) [25]

TYPE OF UNION	1930	1931
Social Democratic	135,689	115,671
Catholic	11,333	10,956
Democratic	1,561	1,560
Communist	2,374	4,664
National Socialist	...	710
Other Organizations	1,025	1,282
Unorganized	4,163	3,575
Total	156,145	138,418

When broken down properly, the parliamentary election figures show the same thing. In the election of 31 July 1932, when the National Socialist party achieved its biggest parliamentary victory under democratic conditions, the Social Democrats and Communists received 13,241,000 votes. There were about 18,267,000 manual and white-collar workers in Germany at that time. Although the left-wing voters were not all workers, the bulk was. This can be shown by comparing the results in a mixed industrial and agricultural district with a considerable Catholic minority (Hessen-Nassau), a highly industrialized and predominantly Protestant district (Saxony), a mainly agrarian and predominantly Protestant district (East Prussia), and a predominantly Catholic, agrarian district (Baden).[26] We may safely conclude that about 65 per cent of the workers and salaried employees voted for the Social Democratic and Communist parties in the middle of 1932. Even in the election of 5 March 1933, when the Communist party was illegal and the Social Democratic press completely suppressed, the two parties together mustered 30.6 per cent of the votes; the Catholic Center, 11.2; the Nationalists, 8.0; the Peoples party, 1.1; the Bavarian Peoples party, 2.7; and the National Socialists 43.9 per cent.

The National Socialist regime published official statistics of the elections to the councils of confidence, but they do not reveal the true results. We have a simple but sure indication of the results, however—there have been no elections since March 1936.[27] The terms of the existing councilmen have been extended year by year and the replacements are appointed by the trustees of labor. In other words, the workers have not even the shadow of plant representation, despite fine words in the charter of labor. The councils of confidence are mere tools of the plant troops and the Labor Front. They are used to terrorize both the workers and the employer and to increase efficiency. The articulation of opposition and criticism is impossible.

The process of isolating the worker and terrorizing him is carried still further by stretching the concept of treason. Any document, drawing, other object or 'fact or news about them' may be considered a state secret according to the penal code. Betrayal of such information to a third person, not necessarily a foreign government, constitutes treason to the country. Even preparation for betrayal is punishable by death, unintentional betrayal by imprisonment up to three years. Since most plants are engaged in war work in a preparedness and war economy, virtually all plant secrets become state secrets and the threat of imprisonment, the concentration camp, or death hangs over most workers and their families. The isolation of the worker is completed. Nor is that all. The war economy decree of 4 September 1939 orders imprisonment or death for anyone 'who destroys, puts aside, or retains raw material or products that belong to the vital needs of the people and thereby maliciously endangers the satisfaction of these needs' (Section 1).[28] Penal legislation has been tightened and special courts have been created.

We must come to the conclusion that community theory, plant leadership, councils of confidence, Labor Front, and plant troops have but one function: They are devices for the manipulation of the working classes, for the establishment of an authoritarian control, for the destruction of the natural differences created by work, training, and occupation, for the isolation of each individual worker from his family, and for the creation of élites. It is not merely the requirements of war that are responsible; it is the very structure of labor and other social relations.

THE HONOR OF LABOR AND THE LABOR COURTS

Entrepreneurs and managers who belong to groups and chambers, so the decree says, are duty bound to be decent and honorable in their economic activities. Gross violation is punishable by a warning, reprimand, or fine, or by loss of the right to hold office in the groups and chambers, penalties that do not hurt the entrepreneur economically but merely in his political status. Special disciplinary courts have been set up for each provincial economic chamber and one federal appeal court. They are peer courts, composed of two entrepreneurs or managers and a chairman appointed by the minister of economics upon recommendation of the president of the national economic chamber (the appellate court has four entrepreneurs or managers and a chairman).[29]

The contrast with the social courts of honor in labor relations is strikingly revealing. According to the Charter of Labor, each 'member of the plant community bears the responsibility for the conscientious fulfilment' of the community duties. Employers are guilty of violating the social honor if they 'maliciously misuse their power position in the factory to exploit the labor power of the followers or to injure their honor.' Employees are punishable when they 'endanger the labor peace by malicious sedition of the followers'; when councilmen consciously arrogate to themselves the right of illegal interference in management; when they disturb the community spirit; when they 'repeatedly make frivolous appeals . . . to the trustee of labor or strenuously violate his orders'; or when they betray plant secrets. Employers may be punished by a warning, a reprimand, a fine up to 10,000 marks, or loss of the right to be plant leaders. The maximum penalty for the employee is dismissal.

The social honor courts are not peer courts. The provincial courts are composed of a judge, appointed jointly by the ministries of labor and justice, and a plant leader and councilman selected from lists prepared by the Labor Front. The federal appellate court has three judges, a plant leader, and one councilman. The influence of the workers is non-existent. Their punishment is much more severe, for dismissal threatens their means of existence, whereas the maximum employer's penalty, loss of plant leadership, leaves ownership untouched. The federal honor court has further ruled that an employer may be deprived of plant leadership for a limited time only and only for one plant if he has several.[30]

Actually, this particular judicial machinery has been little more than an ornament. In 1937, 342 charges were filed, 232 in 1938, and only 142 in 1939. The 156 trials in 1939 were distributed as follows: [31]

> against plant leaders, 119
> deputies, 1
> superintendents, 19
> followers, 14

Lest the disproportionate number of employers and foremen tried by the honor courts be misleading, a further breakdown of these trials is necessary:

> against handicraft plants, 32
> agrarian enterprises, 32
> industrial plants, 12
> retailers, 9
> transportation firms, 4
> innkeepers and restaurant owners, 11
> building firms, 16
> others, 4

The overwhelming majority are obviously small businessmen. They are always the violators of labor legislation, not because they are especially malicious but because big plants are far more able to digest the burden of social reform. Only in seven cases, finally, were plant leaders actually deprived of their right to be plant leaders.

There were about 20,000,000 manual and white-color workers employed in 1939, and only 14 cases against 'followers.' That seems astounding, but the explanation is simple and significant. The terroristic machinery is far tighter and far more complete against the follower than against any other stratum in society. Why should the police, the Labor Front, or the employer initiate a cumbersome procedure before the honor courts when much cheaper, swifter, and more efficient means are available? There is the army service, the labor service, protective custody (a polite word for the concentration camp) requiring no procedure whatsoever, and, in emergency, the special criminal courts, which can render decisions within twenty-four hours. In so far as the social honor courts have any function, in other words, it is to reprimand an occasional offense by a small businessman and thus demonstrate to labor the social consciousness of the regime.

As for the labor law courts, the outstanding contribution of the Republic to rational labor relations, they remain in existence with hardly a change in structure.[32] Like every court, however, they have lost most of their functions. Since there are no collective agreements, there can be no law suits between trade unions and employers' organizations. There are no more works councils and so there can be no disputes between councils and employers. Only individual disputes between employee and employer remain. And since it is a major task of the legal-aid departments of the Labor Front to negotiate settlements, in fact no law suit can be brought before the courts without the consent of the Labor Front. When the Front does consent, it acts as counsel for both parties and has the sole decision whether or not to admit attorneys.[33]

The exclusion of professional attorneys from labor cases began under the Republic as a progressive step. The employee had either to act for himself or employ a trade-union secretary as counsel. The ensuing union monopoly of legal representation in the courts of first instance undoubtedly influenced workers to join unions (the closed shop did not exist), though they retained a choice between competing unions, and if they remained unorganized they often enjoyed the benefits of the collective agreements concluded between trade unions and employers' organizations. Today, the monopolization of legal aid by an authoritarian body leads to complete annihilation of the remnants of labor rights.

5. The Regimentation of Leisure

While liberal theories, and especially the utilitarian, hold that work is pain and leisure is pleasure, in modern society leisure is almost completely devoted to reproducing the strength consumed in the labor process. And in mass democracy, leisure has come under the full control of monopolistic powers. The major forms of entertainment—the radio, the cinema, the pulp magazine, and sports— are all controlled by financial interests. They are standardized in the selection and treatment of topics, and in the allocation of time.

Under democratic conditions, however, the family, the church, and the trade union continue to provide other incentives, diametrically opposed to the prevailing conditions of life—of labor and leisure. Such progressive trends were clearly apparent in the leisure-time activities of the German labor movement, both Catholic and Social Democratic. Unfortunately a conflicting trend was equally manifest—envy of petty-bourgeois culture and a desire to imitate it, and its worst elements at that. In the field of labor education, for example, the program of the central trade-union body, the ADGB, was geared primarily to romantic, petty-bourgeois incentives. It is not surprising therefore that nearly all ex-teachers in the ADGB school are now National Socialists; some of them were actually secret members of the National Socialist party as far back as 1931. The educational program of many of the affiliated unions, on the other hand, led by the metal-workers union, was diametrically opposed. For this group, education and leisure activities were designed to make men critical of the existing labor process. The conflict between the two principles within the workers' education movement was never solved.

The same situation prevailed in the other cultural activities of the labor movement. Some of the trade-union book guilds, theater guilds, and radio guilds were experimental. They did not consider leisure merely as the basis for reproducing labor power or culture simply as mass culture. Here too there were conflicts and a resulting instability. Nevertheless the German workers' educational and cultural groups retained a marked vitality. In both Catholic and non-Catholic circles they were the most powerful antidotes against a standardized mass culture dictated by private monopoly. As time went on, the leisure policy of the unions aimed more and more at changing the conditions of labor rather than at relaxation and the regaining of bodily strength for greater efficiency.

Free leisure is incompatible with National Socialism. It would leave too great a part of man's life uncontrolled. 'Of 8760 hours a year, only 2100 hours (24 per cent) are work hours, and 6660 are leisure. Even if we deduct 8 hours a day for sleep from this leisure time, there still remains an actual leisure time of 3740 hours a year.' [34] This is the official arithmetic of the Labor Front.

National Socialist theory of the relation between labor and leisure has been worked out fully. One example will serve for analysis—the vocational training of apprentices. A preliminary word of warning: The official statements of the Labor Front addressed to the workers betray considerable uneasiness on the question of leisure. Leisure is not merely a preparation for labor, they say; the two are not opposites but interrelated. 'Economic, social and cultural policy will have to work for this aim: that in the future one need no longer speak of the "working life of the people" but of racial life as such.' [35] In publications and communications addressed to professional educators and organizers, the language is very different. The leading expert on the social policy of the Labor Front writes: 'To win strength for daily work was therefore the final goal toward which the new creation strove. Thus the leisure organization "After Work" became the National Socialist community, Strength through Joy.' [36]

The co-ordinator of all vocational training in the Reich is K. Arnhold.[37] At the founding of the *Dinta*, the German Institute for Technical Work Training,[38] in 1925, Arnhold, its director, announced its aim to be to take 'leadership of all from earliest childhood to the oldest man, not for social purposes—and I must empha-

size this once more—but from the point of view of productivity.
I consider man the most important factor which industry must
nourish and lead.' [39] During the Republic, the Dinta, run by the most
reactionary of German psychologists and sociologists, was the inveterate foe of trade unionism of any kind. It promoted company
unions and they in turn compelled industrial apprentices to attend
the Dinta schools. The Dinta has been taken over by the Labor
Front and is now called the German Institute for National Socialist
Technical Work Training. By the end of 1936 there were 400
apprentice training centers in existence and 150 more under construction. There were 113 Dinta plant newspapers with a combined
circulation of 1,500,000 as compared with 95 Labor Front plant
publications with a circulation of only 350,000.[40] (There are also
other Labor Front papers published for whole branches of industry
or for the whole Labor Front.)

The work of the Dinta is supplemented by the Federal Institute
for Vocational Training in Trade and Handicraft and by a number
of scientific institutes attached to industrial combines. The latter
may be exemplified by the Siemens Society for Applied Psychology,
attached to the most powerful German electrical combine. Its publication formulates our problem this way: 'It is true that there is a
marked separation . . . between labor and leisure . . . Man often
uses . . . leisure for creative work . . . in the garden and for personal education. Fully recognizing the ardor and energy [of such
endeavors] . . . it must be pointed out, however, that the most
important aim of leisure is relaxation for the collection of strength.'
'It is impossible to shift the essence of our existence from the realm
of labor to another realm.' [41] Education must therefore be education for work. 'The concept of duty must be known even to the
ABCdarian.' [42]

The reduction of leisure to a mere auxiliary of work is the official
leisure philosophy of National Socialism. It is all the more brutal
because it coalesces with the National Socialist principle of social
organization: drive the workers into huge organizations where they
are submerged; lose their individuality, march, sing, and hike together but never think together. The Labor Front thus takes particular pride in one achievement of its Strength through Joy organizations; the yearly efficiency competition among boys and girls (in
1936, there were 720 professions with 1,500,000 participants; in 1937,

there were 1,800,000 participants). Plants developing the most successful vocational-training institutes receive from Dr. Ley an efficiency medal. The design is a cog-wheel enclosing a swastika above
a hammer with the initials DAF (German Labor Front) and below
the words 'recognized vocational training plant.' [48]

Strength through Joy makes full use of the findings of applied
psychology to prescribe in detail the correct methods, time, and
content of leisure for the one aim of enhancing the worker's productivity. The same purpose is served by the Beauty of Labor department of the Labor Front, whose function is to beautify factories
and canteens. These organizations have of course given material
benefits to many working-class groups. But much as glee clubs,
orchestras, and baseball teams may improve the lot of prisoners,
they do not tear down the bars.

6. WAGES AND INCOMES AS MEANS OF MASS DOMINATION

The wage policy serves the same purpose of controlling and
isolating man as the social policy. National Socialism is built on full
employment. That is its sole gift to the masses, and its significance
must not be underestimated. The business cycle has not been
brought to an end, of course, nor has the economic system been
freed from periods of contraction. But state control over credit,
money, and the labor market prevents slumps from taking the form
of large-scale unemployment. Even if production should sag after
the war and the inherent contradictions of monopoly capitalism
should make it impossible to direct the flow of capital back into
consumers' goods, there will probably be no mass dismissals. Women
will be sent back to the kitchen and invalids to their pensions.
Over-age workers will be compulsorily retired on meager old-age
grants. War prisoners and foreign workers will be repatriated. If
necessary, the work will be distributed and labor time shortened,
technical progress stopped or even reversed, wages lowered and
prices raised. There are dozens of such devices available in an
authoritarian regime. The crucial point is that unemployment must
be prevented so as to retain this one link that still ties the masses
to its ruling class.

Full employment is accompanied by an elaborate social-security
program. The system developed by the Weimar democracy has

been streamlined and brought under authoritarian control. Unemployment assistance, health and accident insurance, invalidity and old-age pensions—that is how National Socialism wins the passive toleration of the masses for the time being. Social security is its one propaganda slogan built on the truth, perhaps the one powerful weapon in its whole propagandistic machinery.

The wage policy of the Weimar Socialist trade unions was aimed at increasing the workers' share of the national income and at achieving a class wage. They sought to level wage differentials among unskilled, semi-skilled, and skilled workers in each branch of industry and within the economy as a whole. Even apprentices were included. Apprenticeship was transformed into a genuine labor contract, with genuine wages. The trade-union movement was hostile to such devices as family allowances, both because they might drive out the married man with dependants and because they conflicted with the class wage theory. Employers fought union policy bitterly. They tried deliberately to play off a labor aristocracy against the plebeians by granting concessions to the skilled workers and by extending special treatment to salaried employees.

Full employment and social security have been achieved by National Socialism at the expense of wage rates and hence of the standard of living of the masses, or at least of those who did not face unemployment during the Republic. Wages are cost elements. They are the basis for an adequate reproduction of labor power and a device for distributing workers among the various branches of trade and industry. The class wage of the Socialist trade unions has been replaced by the 'performance wage' (*Leistungslohn*) defined in Section 29 of the Charter of Labor.[44] 'It has been the iron principle of the National Socialist leadership,' said Hitler at the Party Congress of Honor, 'not to permit any rise in the hourly wage rates but to raise income solely by an increase in performance.' The rule of the wage policy is a marked preference for piece work and bonuses, even for juvenile workers.[45] Such a policy is completely demoralizing, for it appeals to the most egotistic instincts and sharply increases industrial accidents.

Apprentices have lost their status as workers and their contract is no longer a labor contract but an 'educational agreement.' The federal supreme labor court has therefore held that the apprentice is not entitled to overtime pay nor may the employer make pay deductions for lost time.[46] (The latter is no problem in a period of full employment anyway.) The power of the trustees of labor has been extended by the war economy decree of 4 September 1939, so that they may now not only issue tariff regulations for whole branches of industry but also specific regulations for each plant and even for subdivisions of a plant without regard to existing obligations.[47] Two decades of progress have been wiped out completely.

The preponderance of the performance wage brings the problem of wage differentials into the forefront of social policy. It is essential that this problem be understood not as an economic question but as the crucial political problem of mass control. Official wage statistics say nothing about it, but there is ample proof that the process of differentiation is in full swing.* Hourly wage rates reveal nothing about the process of differentiation [48] in a system that relies largely upon the performance wage. The indices of income from work [49] show that despite the stability of differentials in the hourly wage rates, the gap between actual earnings of skilled and semi-skilled workers has widened noticeably. The trend would become even clearer if the figures included the unskilled, for that group of wage earners has increased most. Within each of the three groups, furthermore, there is a great variety of differences.[50]

Wage differentiation is the very essence of National Socialist wage policy. That becomes clear from the debate of the past two years preparatory to an expected federal wage decree. 'The amount of wages is no longer a question of an adequate share of the followership in the plant profits but a problem of incorporating the folk comrade into the racial income order according to his performance for the people's community.' [51] Clearly Dr. Sitzler, once a democratic ministerial director in the ministry of labor and now editor of *Soziale Praxis*, has learned the language of National Socialism well. He leaves no doubt that the wage policy is consciously

* But even before the war the process of differentiation was already markedly developed. The Institute of Social Research has carried out an analysis on the basis of an inquiry secretly made in Germany in 1938. This inquiry covered certain regions of Germany and certain industries such as building, printing, engineering, blast-furnace works, wood-working, the chemical industry, the textile, the shoe, and the sugar industry. It shows that the differentials between unskilled, semi-skilled, and skilled workers have increased markedly from 1931 to 1938. I do not publish the figures here since it is my aim to rely exclusively on German sources.

aimed at mass manipulation. His successor in the ministry of labor, Mansfeld, who came to his post from an employers' organization, says flatly that the one problem for National Socialism in this field is to provide a legal basis for the performance wage. In a detailed study, another author proposes no less than seven wage groups, each to be further differentiated according to sex, age, family status, territory, and any other category that will divide the working classes.[52]

The preferential treatment of certain small groups must of course come out of the pockets of the large masses of workers and salaried employees. That is amply demonstrated by the distribution of the national income.[53] In the table below, the basis of comparison is the year 1929, the last boom year of the Weimar Republic. From 1929 to 1938, the number of employed rose by 9.2 per cent (column 2), the national income by 5 per cent (column 4), and the volume of production by 23.6 per cent (column 5). In other words, the productivity of labor increased more than the increase in the number of employed workers and still more than the national income. The national income per person fell by 1.8 per cent (column 7), and the distribution of that income shows that the economy expanded at the expense of the workers and salaried employees (column 8). In 1929, income from salaries and wages constituted 56.7 per cent of the total national income; in 1932, 56.9 per cent. Though 1932 was the worst depression year, income from capital fell much more than earnings from wages and salaries—clear proof of the defensive strength of the trade unions. Under National Socialism, on the other hand, despite the increase in the number of persons employed, in the volume of production, and in national income, the share of wages and salaries fell to 53.6 per cent. Because of the abolition of unemployment, pension and relief payments in 1938 constituted only 9.5 per cent of the national income as against 12.1 per cent in 1929 and 20.7 per cent in 1932 (column 9). In sum: the exploitation of the workers has been measurably intensified.

These figures do not mean that the level of consumption by the working classes declined prior to the outbreak of the war. This problem need not concern us here, for it is distinct from the problems of differentiation within the various groups in society.

The corollary to the decline in the wage and salary share of the

Income Distribution [54]

	1	2	3	4	5	6	7	8	9	10	11	12	13	14
	WORKERS AND SALARIED EMPLOYEES		AGGREGATE NATIONAL INCOME		VOLUME OF PRODUCTION	NOMINAL NATIONAL INCOME PER CAPITA		INCOME FROM					INCOME FROM	
								1 WAGES AND SALARIES	2 PENSIONS AND RELIEF	3 CAPITAL	4 INDUSTRY AND COMMERCE	5 CORPORATIONS UNDISTRIBUTED	1 + 2	3+4+5
	,000 omitted	1929=100	RM ,000,000 omitted	1929=100	1929=100	RM	1929=100	as percentage of aggregate national income %					as percentage of aggregate national income %	
1929	17,870	100.0	75,949	100.0	100.0	1,187	100.0	56.7	12.1	4.3	15.5	1.2	68.8	21.0
1932	12,580	70.4	45,175	59.5	58.2	696	58.6	56.9	20.7	5.1	13.3	-1.0	77.6	17.4
1937	18,370	102.8	72,590	95.6	115.8	1,070	90.1	53.6	10.2	3.9	17.9	3.4	63.8	25.2
1938	19,518	109.2	79,722	105.0	123.6	1,166	98.2	53.6	9.5	3.7	18.6	4.3	63.1	26.6

national income is the increase in another ratio. Column 10 of the table shows that income from capital fell as a consequence of the new dividend policy, whereas income from industry, trade, and undistributed profits rose considerably (columns 11 and 12). Even if we combine income from wages, salaries, and pensions (column 13) and compare them with income from capital, trade, industry, and undistributed profits (column 14), we find that the former dropped from 68.8 per cent in 1929 and 77.6 per cent in 1932 to 63.1 per cent in 1938, while the latter rose from 21.0 per cent in 1929 and 17.4 per cent in 1932 to 26.6 per cent in 1938.

The growing inequality becomes still clearer if the comparative year selected is 1932, the worst year in the history of the Republic.

YEAR	INCOME FROM				WAGE- AND SALARY-EARNERS EMPLOYED			VOLUME OF PRODUCTION	HOURS OF WORK (INDUSTRIAL WORKERS ONLY)
	salaries and wages		capital, industry and commerce, and un-distributed income of corporations		Workers	Employees	Total		
	RM ,000,000 omitted	1932 = 100	RM ,000,000 omitted	1932 = 100	1932 = 100			1932 = 100	
1932	25,711	100.0	7,848	100.0			100.0	100.0	100
1937	38,907	151.3	16,580	211.3			146.0	199.0	202
1938	42,717	166.1	19,340	246.4			155.2	212.4	217

Income from wages and salaries rose from 1932 to 1938 by 66.1 per cent, while other income rose by 146.4 per cent. The number of employed rose by 55.2 per cent in the same period. The manual and white-collar worker therefore received more per capita than in 1932, the worst crisis year—only because his working time was longer. The volume of production rose by 112.4 per cent and the total hours worked in industry by 117 per cent. That is, the productivity has more than doubled while income has risen by merely 66.1 per cent.

7. PROPAGANDA AND VIOLENCE

P. Janelle, the historian of Catholic England, remarks that Henry VIII got rid of the opposition to his claim for royal supremacy by *'violence faite aux âmes, c'est-à-dire propagande.'* [55] Propaganda is violence committed against the soul. Propaganda is not a substitute for violence, but one of its aspects. The two have the identical purposes of making men amenable to control from above. [56] Terror and its display in propaganda go hand in hand. That is the theme of the leading theorist of National Socialist propaganda and the dictator of the German radio, E. Hadamovsky.[57]

By itself, propaganda can never change social and political conditions; it acts in conjunction with other and far more important factors. National Socialist propaganda did not destroy the Weimar democracy. Nor could the best counter-propaganda of the democratic parties and groups have saved the Republic. Neither the Three Arrows invented by the Social Democratic party as a counter symbol to the swastika, nor the Hammer groups created within the democratic militia (*Reichsbanner*), nor the establishment of an 'iron front' of the *Reichsbanner* and other auxiliary organizations of the Social Democratic party could help. They did not symbolize a vital and realistic policy. The leadership was unwilling to take risks, and democratic policy had become petrified. National Socialist propaganda, we must not forget, went hand in hand with terror by the S.A. and by the S.S., tolerated by the German judiciary and by many of the non-Prussian states. A democratic movement cannot beat terror by counter-terror; it must rely on the state machine to suppress terror. That the republican leaders did not succeed in inducing the state machine to stop National Socialist terror will remain the most severe indictment of Weimar. The democracy collapsed chiefly because of the ineptness of the democratic movement and the strength of the reaction. More recently, France was not beaten by propaganda.[58] Its collapse was the result of the disintegration of French morale and of the military superiority of the German army.

What National Socialism has done and is doing with its propaganda is to take advantage of the soft spots in the social body. That is the technique it has developed to the fullest. Such soft spots are visible in any social organism. There is class struggle from above and from below; there are religious and racial antagonisms, clashing economic interests, competing political groups—all fertile grounds for a skilled propaganda machine.

The superiority of National Socialist over democratic propaganda lies in the complete transformation of culture into salable commodities. A democracy can never completely divorce propaganda from truth because there are competing propaganda machines and they must ultimately prove their value by actual performance in the social life of a nation. National Socialism has no political or social theory. It has no philosophy and no concern for the truth. In a given situation it will accept any theory that might prove useful; and it will abandon that theory as soon as the situation changes. National Socialism is both capitalistic and anti-capitalistic. It is authoritarian and anti-authoritarian. It will co-operate with any group in the army or bureaucracy that is amenable to National Socialist propaganda but it will not hesitate to flatter anti-authoritarian movements when that is more expedient. It will promise liberation to racial minorities and will sacrifice any minority if the government of the country involved is ready to co-operate with Germany. National Socialism is for agrarian reform and against it, for private property and against it, for idealism and against it.

Such versatility is unattainable in a democracy. National Socialist propaganda will always be superior because National Socialist culture is propaganda and nothing else, while democratic culture is a mixture. National Socialist propaganda cannot be beaten by a democratic super-propaganda, but only by a superior democratic policy that eliminates the soft spots.

Worse still, attempts to fight fascism primarily by propaganda methods are almost invariably connected with an abandonment of democratic convictions. A recent work by Serge Chakotin is a case in point.[59] He divides the population into 10 per cent possessing an active attitude and 90 per cent who are 'lazy minded or tired out or their whole attention is absorbed by the difficulties of every-day life,' and are thus reduced to a mere biological level. Should a democracy remain on this biological level, and the 90 per cent be nothing more than tools to be controlled by propaganda, force and power would be the prerequisite of success. Chakotin admits that.

Within Germany proper, National Socialist propaganda has other aims than the mere penetration of soft spots. Through its synchronization of all cultural activities, National Socialism subjects the German people to unceasing tensions. The insistence upon activism in place of thinking means that men shall never have the freedom and time to think for themselves. Action without thought is possible only if it is directed and controlled action, except in short periods of genuine mass spontaneity. Thus controlled it is pseudo-action, for it is not man who acts but a bureaucratic machine. That is the technique of National Socialism—to make the action of an authoritarian apparatus appear as the spontaneous activity of the masses. It was first developed in the National Socialist mass meeting. Hitler said in *Mein Kampf:*

The mass meeting is necessary if only for the reason that in it the individual, who in becoming an adherent of a new movement, feels lonely and is easily seized with the fear of being alone, receives for the first time the picture of a greater community, something that has a strengthening and an encouraging effect on most people . . . If he steps for the first time out of his small work shop or out of the big enterprise, in which he feels very small, into the mass meeting and is now surrounded by thousands and thousands of people with the same conviction . . . he himself succumbs to the magic influence of what we call mass suggestion.[60]

National Socialist propaganda is thus the expression of the same two phenomena that appear in every aspect of the regime: the destruction of whatever remnants of spontaneity are left and the incorporation of the population into a super-machine. The super-machine is allegedly driven by an irresistible force of nature, by providence, or by a fate that is stronger than any individual, any particular group, or any foreign nation—leading to the ultimate victory of Germany. Magic becomes the major concern of National Socialist culture. The world can be manipulated by techniques and formulas; in fact, if properly used these techniques and words automatically change things. And the secret is in the possession of the National Socialist leadership. Magical ceremonies are celebrated on many occasions, reminiscent of the practices of primitive tribes. The annual induction of the Hitler youth into the party is the equivalent of primitive initiation rites. The words used at mass meetings carry in themselves means for changing nature and society.[61] The touching of the blood flag of Munich and being touched by the Leader are thaumaturgical practices.

The emphasis on magic has even changed the language. The noun tends to supersede the verb. Things happen—they are not done. Fate, providence, objective natural forces produce things: German victories. The loss of man's active role in society is expressed by a language that negates activity and stresses the impersonality of the noun and of the 'it.' *

* I owe this insight to a paper by Dr. Henry Paechter, which he read at the Institute of Social Research in the summer of 1941. Dr. Paechter is now preparing an article on this point.

8. NATIONAL SOCIALIST LAW AND TERROR

The average lawyer will be repelled by the idea that there can be a legal system that is nothing more than a means of terrorizing people. He will point out that hundreds of thousands, perhaps millions, of transactions in Germany are handled according to calculable and predictable rules. That is true. Any society based on a division of labor will necessarily produce competences, jurisdictions, regularities, which give the appearance of a functioning legal system. Traffic must move to the right or the left; houses are to be painted green or white; groups and chambers may raise this or that fee. These and thousands of other questions are dealt with rationally, even in the so-called 'prerogative' state—the S.S., the S.A. and the Gestapo. But they are, in the words of my late teacher Max E. Mayer, 'culturally indifferent rules' of a predominantly technical character.[62] They may acquire political or economic relevance at any moment (for instance, traffic rules may play a considerable role in the economic struggle between the railroad and the automobile), but in normal cases they are culturally neutral. The body of such technical rules grows steadily with the increasing complexity of modern society, and, in consequence, the legal and administrative machinery will also grow.

Do we really mean such technical rules when we speak of law, however? Two notions of law must be distinguished, a political and a rational notion.[63] In a political sense, law is every measure of a sovereign power, regardless of its form or content. Declarations of war and peace, tax laws and civil laws, police measures and court attachments, court decisions and legal norms applied in the decisions, all these are law simply because they are expressions of sovereignty. Law is then will and nothing else. The rational concept of law, on the other hand, is determined by its form and content, not by its origin. Not every act of the sovereign is law. Law in this sense is a norm, comprehensible by reason, open to theoretical understanding, and containing an ethical postulate, primarily that of equality. Law is reason and will. Many natural-law theorists even go so far as to divorce law completely from will of the sovereign. For them, law is a system of norms which is valid even if the positive law of the state ignores it.

There are two ways of determining the reason inherent in law: the material and the formal. The one is that of natural law, which postulates that law should correspond to certain material demands: freedom, equality, security. The other maintains that law can be expressed only in general, universal terms.

Natural law began to disappear at the beginning of the liberal era (seventeenth-century England, late eighteenth-century France, early nineteenth-century Germany) with the spread of democracy and of the theory of the social contract. The general character of positive law then began to occupy the center of legal systems and doctrines. Only a law which had a general character was recognized as law. The formal structure of the law became decisive. If rights may be infringed upon only within the framework of the law or by due process of law, and if, as liberal constitutional theory never tires of repeating, law itself is nothing but an infringement upon freedom and property, then it must follow that the form of the infringement is as relevant as its content. In other words, the formal structure of the law receives a significance independent of its content.

In the liberal era, the general character of law is that element which alone embodies reason. The reasonableness of law is no longer determined by the reasonableness of the society in which the law operates, as in Thomistic natural law, but by its formal structure. Reasonableness thus becomes rationality, but a rationality that is formal and technical, that is to say, predictable and calculable.

'When I say that the object of laws is always general,' wrote Rousseau, 'I mean that law considers subjects *en masse* and actions in the abstract, and never a particular person or action. Thus the law may indeed decree that there shall be privileges, but cannot confer them on anybody by name. It may set up several classes of citizens, and even lay down the qualifications for membership of these classes, but it cannot nominate such and such persons as belonging to them . . .' [64]

Rousseau's determinant is insufficient, for the generality must be formulated in specific terms. In order to develop the second element, a distinction is to be drawn between legal rules (*Rechtssätze*) and general legal principles or legal standards of conduct (*Generalklauseln*). Contracts which are against public policy, unreasonable, or against good morals are void. 'One who performs an act which the statute declares to be punishable or which is deserving of punishment according to the healthy racial feeling shall be punished' (Section 2 of the German penal code in the formulation of 28 June 1935). Such sentences are not legal rules, for they are not rational and they represent a false universality despite the general character of the formulation. There can often be no agreement in contemporary society whether any given action is against good morals or is unreasonable, whether a punishment corresponds to a healthy racial sentiment or not. In other words, these concepts lack an unequivocal content. A legal system that constructs the basic elements of its rules out of these so-called general principles or legal standards of conduct is only a shell covering individual measures.

The formal structure of the general rule—this is the third element of universality—must contain a minimum of material concreteness. It guarantees the judge a minimum degree of independence, because it does not subordinate him to individual measures of the sovereign.

The corollary of such a theory of the formal structure of law is a specific theory of the relation of the judge to the law. When the law rules and rules alone, the judge's sole function is to perceive the law. In Montesquieu's formulation, the judge is nothing more than 'the mouth which announces the word of the law, an inanimate being.' Judicial acts are therefore 'in a certain sense nil.' [65] This 'phonographic' doctrine, as Morris Cohen calls it,[66] is closely tied up with the theory of the separation of powers, with the doctrine that the creation of law is identical with legislation and that law cannot be created outside the process of legislation, either by judges or by private lawmaking bodies. The doctrine of the separation of powers, it must be remembered, does not imply an equality among the three powers but rather the supremacy of the legislative. The right of judicial review of statutes was denied throughout most of the nineteenth century (in Germany until 1919). The legal system of liberalism is supposedly a complete system which the judge need merely apply.

What is the social significance of the theory of the rule of law, of the denial of natural law, and of the absolute subordination of the judge to the law?

The rule of law is necessary to satisfy the needs of a competitive capitalist system which seeks to create profit through continuous rational capitalist undertaking. Free competition requires general law because that represents the highest degree of formal rationality. Free competition rests upon the existence of a large number of more or less equal competitors who meet on a free market. Freedom of the commodity market, freedom of the labor market, free selection within the entrepreneur group, freedom of contract, and above all calculability of the administration of justice are the essential requirements. The primary task of the state is to create a legal system that will guarantee the fulfilment of contracts. The expectation that contracts will be fulfilled must be calculable. When there are many competitors of approximately equal strength, general laws are necessary for predictability. These laws must be sufficiently specific within their abstraction to limit the discretion of the judge as much as possible. The judge must not fall back upon general principles. When the state interferes with liberty and property, the interference must also be calculable. It must not be retroactive, for then it would nullify already existing expectations. The state must not interfere without law, for then the interference would not be predictable. Interference by individual measures is intolerable because it destroys the basic equality of the competitors. Finally, the judge himself must be independent, that is, the various powers in the state must be completely separate.[67]

The general law also has an ethical function, most clearly expressed in Rousseau's legal philosophy. Paradoxically enough, this ethical function lies in the rigid divorce of legality from morality. (The lasting achievement of liberalism is that it freed legal judgments from moral evaluations.) The common man will, in all probability, view the separation as reprehensible and the interpenetration of law and morals as ideal. The common man always criticizes the legal system for its formality, rigidity, and aloofness from moral considerations. And yet it is precisely this separation that permits law to become an instrument of social adjustment. It was a devoutly religious man, Hugo Grotius, the founder of modern natural law, who initiated this divorce. The laws of nature, he held, would be valid even if God did not exist. Hobbes, Pufendorf, and Christian Thomasius fully elaborated a legal system distinct from moral norms. In their view, the divine natural law was either an imperfect obligation or mere counsel. Kant completed the development and established legality and morality as separate values, the former dealing with the outer duties, the latter with the inner.

Indeed, an identity of law and morality can be maintained only in a fully homogeneous society, in a religious group, for example, that is ruled by a universally accepted system of values. Law could then regulate not only outer behavior but 'also inner conviction, and morals could organize both conscience and outer duties. Law and morals would then be identical. In an antagonistic society, however, in which moral convictions are always clashing, an alleged identity between the two normative systems is merely a way of terrorizing man's conscience. Karl Theodor Welcker, one of the founders of the *Rechtsstaat* theory, put this thesis very convincingly:

Were a one-sided law to be imposed on free men, whether by a single vote or by a majority of votes, and, as necessarily occurs in the state, were it to be imposed by coercion, that would be despotism. The pretext that one would be doing it for the sake of morality would prostitute reason. The enlightened people would only too soon tear the halo from about the false prophet and perceive behind it the tyrant.[68]

The generality and the abstractness of law together with the independence of the judge guarantee a minimum of personal and political liberty. Voltaire's statement that freedom means dependence on nothing save law has meaning only if the law is general in character.[69] The general law establishes personal equality. Law, after all, is the basis of all interference with liberty and property. Only when such interference is controlled by general laws is liberty guaranteed, since the principle of equality is preserved. If the sovereign is permitted to issue individual decrees, to arrest this man or that, to confiscate this or that piece of property, then the independence of the judge is at an end. The judge who must execute such decrees becomes a mere policeman. In sum, general law, judicial independence, and the separation of powers have purposes that transcend the requirements of free competition.

Equality before the law is merely formal or negative, to be sure, but it does contain a minimum guarantee of freedom and must not be discarded. Both functions of the generality of law, calculability of the economic system and guarantee of a minimum of freedom and equality, are equally important; not the first alone, as the theories of the totalitarian state maintain. If one accepts their view that the generality of law is nothing more than a way of satisfying the needs of free competition, then the conclusion is inevitable that the substitution of organized state capitalism for free competition requires the substitution of the command of the Leader or the general principle for the general law, the independent judiciary, and the separation of powers.

The generality of the law implies the negation of *ex post facto* laws. 'Retroaction is the most evil assault which the law can commit. It means the tearing up of the social contract, and the destruction of the conditions on the basis of which society enjoys the right to demand the individual's obedience, because it deprives him of the guarantees of which society assured him and which were the compensation for the sacrifice which his obedience entailed. Retroaction deprives the law of its real legal character. A retroactive law is no law at all.' These words of Benjamin Constant affirm the unanimous conviction of liberalism. The Weimar constitution, for example, specifically forbade retroactivity in criminal law. A retroactive law is not faced with an indeterminate number of concrete configurations, but with a definite number of cases fully materialized in the past. It is, therefore, an individual measure.

Legal theory and practice both undergo a decisive change in the period of monopoly capitalism. The rule of general law is no longer possible. When the state is confronted with but one party, a monopoly, it is meaningless to set up a general norm. The individual measure becomes the only appropriate expression of the sovereign. It does not destroy the principle of equality before the law, for the legislator is faced with an individual situation. German legislation in the Weimar period therefore introduced special measures for specific monopolistic enterprises, as in the Reich president's emergency decree of 13 July 1931, prohibiting the application of bankruptcy proceedings against the Darmstädter Bank. A special measure was introduced for one powerful monopoly because this bank alone was in danger and its continued existence was considered necessary.

Discussions over the formal structure of law in Germany before the First World War remained within the sphere of theory because judicial review of legislation was not recognized. After the war, however, the German supreme court suddenly assumed the right of review and what had been an academic discussion became a vital political problem.[70] The supreme court was motivated in its new path by a desire to sanction the existing property regime. Its decisions in this direction were all concerned with the question whether a given statute interfered with Article 153 of the Weimar constitution securing the rights of property.[71]

After the war, the positivist approach of the preceding period became a threat to the position of the monopolies. Natural law became a central point of discussion once again. Carl Schmitt, for example, sought to take over the American doctrine of the 'inherent limitations upon the amending power.' The justices of the German supreme court followed a similar line of thought in 1924, when, at a meeting (not a regular court session) to discuss the first emergency tax decree, they decided:

This idea of trust and faith stands outside the particular statute, outside of any single positive legal provision. No legal system which deserves that honorable name can exist without this principle. For that reason, the legislature must not use its power to thwart an action which is imperiously demanded by trust and faith. It would be a severe attack upon the prestige of the regime and upon the sense of justice if anyone who based his claim on a new law were to lose his case in court because his reference to the law would violate trust and faith.[72]

They then announced that a mortgagor who based his claim upon the emergency-tax decree would lose his case because his suit against the mortgagee would be immoral.

An unexpressed natural law came to be applied without restriction or inhibition. The period from 1918 to 1932 was characterized by the almost universal acceptance of the doctrine of free discretion (*Freirechtsschule*), by the breakdown of the rationality and calculability of law, by the limitation of the system of contract (replaced in part by the idea of command), by the victory of legal standards of conduct over true legal norms. The legal standards of conduct changed the whole legal system. By their reference to extra-legal values they destroyed the formal rationality of law. They gave the judge amazingly broad discretionary powers and they destroyed the line between the judiciary and the administration, so that administrative political decisions took on the form of normal court decisions.

Legal standards of conduct serve the monopolists. The individual

norm is calculable for the monopolist because he is strong enough
to dispense with formal rationality. Not only is rational law unnecessary for him, it is often a fetter upon the full development of
his productive force, or more frequently, upon the limitations that
he may desire; rational law, after all, serves also to protect the
weak. The monopolist can dispense with the help of the courts
since his power to command is a satisfactory substitute. His economic power enables him to impose his wishes upon consumers and
workers even within the contract form. The standard monopolistic
contracts transfer all conceivable risks to the consumer, who must
fulfil all the obligations of the law.

National Socialism completely destroys the generality of the
law and with it the independence of the judiciary and the prohibition of retroactivity. Legal standards of conduct acquire greater
significance than before because even the restrictions set up by parliamentary democracy against the demands of monopoly, insufficient
as they may have been, have been removed. By its very vagueness,
the legal standard of conduct serves to bring pre-National Socialist
positive law into agreement with the demands of the new rulers.
National Socialism postulates the absolute subjection of the judge
to the law, but the standards of conduct make it possible for him
to introduce political elements even when they conflict with positive law. 'The principles of National Socialism are immediately and
exclusively valid for the application and administration of general
standards of conduct through the judge, attorney, or teacher of
law.' [73] The judge has been reduced to the status of a police official.

There is complete agreement in the literature that the law is
nothing more than the command of the Leader, so that 'pre-revolu-
tionary' law is valid only through his will. 'All the political power
of the German race is united in the Leader, it rests in his hand.
All law, therefore, derives from him.' [74]

Many individual measures that have the character of privileges
are promulgated. Retroactivity is no longer forbidden. Even the
principle of equality before the law, the fundamental principle of
the *Rechtsstaat*, is rejected. National Socialist legal theory replaces
the legal person by the 'concrete personality,' [75] demagogically calling upon Hegel as its authority, forgetting that Hegel had refused
to discard formal equality before the law although he was clearly
aware of its purely negative character. Since law is identical with

the will of the Leader, since the Leader can send political opponents to their death without any judicial procedure, and since such an act is glorified as the highest realization of justice,[76] we can no longer speak of a specific character of law. Law is now a technical means for the achievement of specific political aims. It is merely the command of the sovereign. To this extent, the juristic theory of the fascist state is decisionism. Law is merely an *arcanum dominationis*, a means for the stabilization of power.

The juristic ideology of the National Socialist state is very different from this analysis, of course. It takes the form of institutionalism, or, as Carl Schmitt and many others call it, a 'concrete order and structure [or community] thought.'[77] Institutionalism is opposed to both decisionism and normative positivism. The positivists hold that all law is statutory law; that the legal system is a logically consistent and closed system of general norms; that the judge need only apply this system of norms in order to realize the will of the legislator; that these norms prevail in their full purity despite the fact that man is applying them. The fundamental concepts of the positivist system are the legal person, both natural and juristic; the subjective private right, expressing the freedom of the person that exists before objective law (its highest expression is the law of property); and the contract, to which all human relation must be reducible: state and association, marriage and sale, the church and the trade union. The state is a legal person, sovereignty does not rest in social groups but in the state-person itself operating through its organs. The individual has subjective public rights against the state.

Actually, the concept of the legal person is the economic mask of the property relationship. It conceals the fact that property is more than a subjective right, that it is also a relationship of domination and subordination. The contract, the auxiliary guarantee of property, is a contract between free and equal legal persons. But this freedom and equality are merely legal. The abstract equality of the partners to a contract conceals their economic inequality. The labor contract in particular is a contract between the legally equal worker and the legally equal employer. In its form, it does not give the slightest indication of the fact that the employer has domination over the worker. The state as such must be the sole bearer of sovereignty and the positivist theory thus refuses to admit of a sovereignty of the organs of the state. This conceals the fact that social groups and individuals rule over others.

Institutionalism takes a very different approach. The institution, according to Renard, the advocate of the school,[78] is an organism, a juristic structure serving the common good. It is more than a simple relation; it is a being. It is a whole in which the individual parts are integrated. 'The institutional relationship is an interiorization, a consortium, *invicem membra.*'[79] The plant is thus divorced from the owner of the plant, the enterprise from the entrepreneur, the joint stock company from the board of directors and the stockholders. Concepts like the state as such and its sovereignty are eliminated.[80] The state becomes an institution in which there is a parallelogram of forces. It becomes a community that rests organically upon lower communities. The power this state exercises is no external power but the power of the organized community itself, so that sovereignty disappears. There is no fundamental separation into public and private law. The whole legal system is an integrated system of community law.[81]

Since social law is the law of the social organization itself, called autonomous law, the theory of the sources of law must also be changed. The state was the sole source of law for positivism, whereas institutionalism includes autonomous law and also judicial law. Institutionalism discards the mechanistic view that the judge is only the mouthpiece of the law, and accepts the thesis that the judge creates law.

The changes in the theory of property are still more important. For positivism the plant is a technical unit in which the property owner produces, while the enterprise is an economic unit in which he pursues his business policy. Institutionalism transforms the plant into a social community. The enterprise becomes a social organization and the joint stock company changes from an association of legal persons with property into an *Anstalt*. In short, property changes from a subjective right belonging to a legal person into an institution, a reified social relation. The contract is not only excluded in practice, it even loses its role in the legal ideology. Rights and duties are no longer bound to the will of legally equal persons but to objective facts. The status of man in society becomes decisive. Sir Henry Maine's formula that law develops from status to contract has been reversed.

The basic concepts of legal positivism had concealing functions. The concept of the legal person, as we saw, is a social mask. It conceals—but it does not eliminate the bearer, he can still be surmised. In the period of competition it was not necessary that the property owner disappear, since he did not exercise any great economic or social power as an individual. Only an aggregate of individuals, the system, exercised power over men. In monopoly capitalism, on the other hand, an extraordinary power of command is concentrated into a few hands. This state of affairs would be quickly revealed if the mask were lifted.

Institutionalism, the legal theory of the monopoly state, allows the mask of legal theory to disappear, and its bearer, the property owner, along with it. The institutionalists do not speak of the property owner but of the institution. They do not speak of the legal person but of the plant and the enterprise. The state as such also disappears, for in positivism this concept concealed the fact that a social group actually exercised the sovereignty attributed to the state. When political power is concentrated as strongly as in the fascist state, it becomes advisable to replace the concept of the state and its sovereignty by the community and its Leader. The state is now characterized as a *Gestalt*, as 'the political *Gestalt*' of the German people.

Where a monopolistic economy exists under democratic forms of government, progressive elements, most notably the trade unions, may adopt the institutional theory as a justification for social reform, for it seems closer to reality than juristic positivism. When the plant, the enterprise, the joint stock company, and the monopoly are declared to be social institutions, that is a way of expressing the fact that property is no longer a private matter but a socially relevant institution. The approximation to reality is one-sided, however, since there is a danger that the institution will be divorced from the social power relation and become unintelligible. The labor law doctrines of all trade unions outside of the Soviet Union and National Socialist Germany have developed from institutionalist concepts. In England, under the influence of Gierke's *Genossenschafts* theory, both conservatives and Fabians took over the institutionalist theory to construct a new relation between the state and society. In France it was taken over primarily by the

Neo-Thomists under the impetus of the papal encyclical *Quad-ragesimo Anno*.

The divorce of the institution from the social relation is completed in National Socialism. The institutionalist's 'tendency to articulation,' writes a leading German theorist, 'is characterized by the fact that the destructive dialectical group formations in the body of the people: worker and entrepreneur, lessor and lessee, city and country, are sublated through synthetic, chiefly estate [*reichsständische*] articulations. A legal structure derived from this principle of construction finds its justification in the fact that fronts and occupations are articulations of the natural order of the people, in which a series of laws created by occupational and estate groups appears to be the optimum principle of a voluntary and orderly growth of law.' [82] The National Socialists avoid the word institutionalism, primarily 'in order to maintain a distance from Neo-Thomism.' [83] They prefer 'juristic order and structure [or community] thought,' or *Sachgestaltungsdenken*, that is to say, thought which is shaped by the needs of the concrete situation. Implicitly, at least, they admit to a close relation with monopoly capitalism.

Institutionalism does not hold the field alone in the fascist state, however. Elements of decisionism remain and acquire tremendous strength from the substitution of the political command for rational law. Institutionalism can never determine which institution is 'primitive' and which is merely 'purposive' in any given situation. It can never determine which interference and which norm are appropriate to the concrete situation. It cannot determine the concrete position of the racial comrades, for example. These decisions are made by the various machines, party, army, bureaucracy, and industry, through their leaders.

If general law is the basic form of right, if law is not only *voluntas* but also *ratio*, then we must deny the existence of law in the fascist state. Law, as distinct from the political command of the sovereign, is conceivable only if it is manifest in general law, but true generality is not possible in a society that cannot dispense with power. Even in such a society, however, the limited, formal, and negative generality of law under liberalism not only permits capitalist predictability, but also guarantees a minimum of freedom because general law is two-sided and allows the weak to retain some legal opportunity, at least. For that reason, the law and the

rights of freedom come into conflict with the needs of a monopolistic economy. Private property in the means of production remains untouched, but the general law and contract disappear at a
certain stage and are replaced by individual measures.

Absolute denial of the generality of law is the central point in
National Socialist legal theory. Consequently, there can be no separation of powers. The power of the state forms an undivided and
indivisible whole conceived under the category of the 'unity of
leadership.' [84] There are no two people and no two cases in which
the same rule applies. Every man and each concrete situation must
be dealt with by a particular rule, or, in our language, by individual
decisions. The main function of National Socialist law is to preserve
racial existence. It must therefore stress biological differences and
deny social or legal equality and civil rights. There can be no independent judiciary without general rules to guide them. The authority of the judge now rests upon the pronouncements of the Leader.

The ideological technique of the new legal theory is clear, as
always. National Socialism takes advantage of the incompleteness
of the liberal ideas of freedom and equality. It charges that freedom
and equality are cloaks behind which exploitation is hidden. But
National Socialism is out to destroy not the inequalities but what
little protection legal equality still offers. The new equality of
National Socialism is an equality of duties, and not of rights.

These principles are not yet fully developed. The law is still in a
state of flux, the judiciary not yet fully synchronized. The trends
are unmistakable, however, and during the war the law reached its
full development as an instrument of violence.

So-called 'protective custody' goes back to the 28 February 1933
decree of President von Hindenburg suspending civil liberties (the
Reichstag fire decree).[85] Section 7 of the Prussian decree of 10
February 1936 making the Gestapo an executive organ of the public
prosecutor's office provides that 'no order or affair of the Gestapo
is subject to control by the administrative tribunals.' The same
decree turned the concentration camps over to the Gestapo. They
may take anyone into protective custody, that is, send him to a
concentration camp, for as long a time as they please—even if a
criminal court had previously absolved him of guilt or if he had
already served his sentence in prison. The victim does not even have
recourse to so indirect a redress as suing the Prussian state for

damages.[86] At first some judges tried to restrain the discretionary power of the police. The Reichstag fire decree, they argued, was designed to protect the state 'against communistic state-endangering acts of violence' (a literal quotation from the introduction to the decree) and actions of the Gestapo that exceed this purpose are void. Needless to say, the absolute and arbitrary power of the Gestapo over all personal liberties is not disputed by any court today.[87]

To dignify such a decree with the name of law because it emanates from the sovereign power within the state seems nonsensical. As it is now interpreted, the Reichstag fire decree does not have a single concrete element that permits one to predict if, under what conditions, and for how long, a man may be deprived of his freedom. It simply says to the Gestapo: Do what you please; deal with each specific case as you think fit. Such a rule is not law but arbitrary decisionism.

The same process of mass manipulation by terror in the form of law is apparent in criminal law proper.[88] Like political theory, National Socialist criminal law has shifted from the idea of the totalitarian state to that of racial imperialism. In the first period, it was merely authoritarian. Its approach to crime was the volitional theory.[89] Not the objective fact but the subjective will makes man a criminal. No distinction exists, therefore, between a criminal attempt and the consummated act.

When the doctrine of the authoritarian state was abandoned, the simple volitional theory went too. The most important—though not yet completely official—school in criminal law today is the so-called phenomenological school, combining vitalism with Carl Schmitt's 'thinking in concrete orders.' [90] Take the example of theft. Traditional criminal law defines a burglar both by his acts and by the intent. The phenomenological school defines him by his personality. A burglar is one who is a burglar 'in essence' (*wer seinem Wesen nach ein Dieb ist*). The judge must decide by intuition whether to convict or not. There could be no more complete negation of the rationality of law, nor a better means of terrorizing the masses without the restraint of predictable rules.

The official theory, accepted until the outbreak of the war in 1939, is a mixture of traditional criminal law, authoritarian trends, and legal standards of conduct. Special consideration is given to the 'sound feeling of the people.' The dividing line between law and morality is destroyed and every act of the judiciary is invested with the halo of morality.

The federal supreme court tried to prevent the complete annihilation of rationality, especially where the churches were concerned.[91] For that very reason, however, its role declined steadily and rapidly. Step by step the judiciary has been deprived of the institutional guarantees of its independence. There was a purge in 1933, but it was not really significant, because the number of non-Aryans and genuine democrats among the judges had always been very small. Far more important was the abolition of judicial self-government, a trend culminating in a statute of 24 November 1937.[92] Previously the court president and representatives of members of the court distributed the offices among themselves without government interference. Now the ministry of justice not only appoints judges as it has always done, it allocates each office as well. As early as 18 June 1935, so-called 'great senates' were established within the federal supreme court. Appointments to the people's courts were made from the beginning by the chancellor on recommendation of the ministry of justice. With the decree of 1937, the leadership principle took full control of the judiciary.

In addition, judges are subject to Section 71 of the civil service act, providing that every official may be compulsorily retired or suspended if there is doubt that he always acts in the interest of the National Socialist state. The decision is made by the Leader upon recommendation of the ministerial chief after an investigation (but not a regular disciplinary trial). Theoretically, a judge cannot be compelled to retire because of the contents of one of his decisions, but it is obviously impossible to draw a clear-cut line.[93] Judges are not helped in this respect by the fact that the judiciary is the favorite object of attack by the S.S. organ, the *Schwarze Korps*. Since 26 August 1938, furthermore, they can be arbitrarily transferred at the discretion of the ministerial chief.

Nothing is left of the principle of *nulla poena sine lege, nullum crimen sine lege* (no punishment without a law and no crime without a law), the basic formula of any legal system. The German Supreme Court had once been rigid in its adherence to this formula. In an 1890 case, for example, it had refused to sentence men charged with the theft of electric power because the provision of the criminal code referred only to the theft of material things and electricity was then considered a mere force. Their reasoning was comparable to the argument of Justice Holmes in a case in which the United States Supreme Court refused to apply the Motor Vehicle Act of 1919 to aircraft. Justice Holmes wrote: 'When a rule of conduct is laid down in words that evoke in the common mind only the picture of vehicles moving on Land, the statute should not be extended to aircraft.' [94]

The German decision has been foolishly ridiculed as evidence of the complete sterility of legal positivism. It deserves the highest praise, however, since only strict application of the 'no crime without a law' principle can prevent the abuse of judicial power in criminal cases. In an advisory opinion of 4 December 1935, the Permanent Court of International Justice examined the question whether the Danzig penal code of 1 September 1935, which apes Section 2 of the new German code, is compatible with the Danzig constitution, which contains the usual guarantees of personal liberties. The court ruled that the two documents were incompatible because Section 2 'covers the whole extra-legal field of what is right and what is wrong according to one's ethical code or religious sentiments.' In other words, the German penal code destroys all guarantees.

The extensive departmentalization of the National Socialist judiciary and the dispersal of jurisdictions complete the picture. Innumerable special courts and tribunals have been created for specific cases and for specific strata of the population. Each of the four machines, party, army, state, and industry, has an extensive judicial system of its own, with statutes, decrees, courts, executioners, and bailiffs. The SS possesses the power not only to incarcerate but even to execute without a judicial decision. Increasingly, German newspapers contain the following stereotyped news: 'The Reich leader of the SS, and chief of the German police announces: On 30 April 1941 Ludwig Koch was shot to death because of resistance' (*Frankfurter Zeitung* 18 May 1941, 10 June 1941, etc.). Nothing else expresses so well the complete denial of the universality of law or offers a better means for treating each concrete situation and group differently so as to manipulate them at will. There are separate disciplinary courts for the party, for the S.A., for the S.S., for the Labor Front. There are social honor courts for employers and employees and disciplinary courts for business. The Labor Service has its own courts. Military courts have been re-established. And above all, there are the people's courts (statute of 24 April 1934) composed, said the vice-president of the Berlin people's court, of judges 'who are primarily politicians and only afterwards judges.' [95] It would be indeed difficult to call members of these courts judges; only two come from the ranks of the judiciary, the rest are high S.S. officials or army officers. The defendant has no right to select counsel, produce evidence, appeal, or obtain publicity. There are finally special courts called just that (*Sondergerichte*). Established on 20 November 1938, their jurisdiction has been continually expanded and the public prosecutor may now bring any case he wishes before them. Here too the rights of the defendant are almost non-existent.

All these developments have been accelerated since the outbreak of the war. A decree of 11 September 1939 created a special division within the federal supreme court before which the public prosecutor may, on order of the Leader, bring any criminal case he deems sufficiently important to warrant skipping the lower courts. He may also request this special division to reopen any case (unless tried by the people's court) within a year after the decision has become final if the leadership has serious objections to the judgment. Such a request is mandatory upon the court, so that it is the prosecutor who actually determines the final judgment, usually capital punishment. The first case that came before the special division was one of rape committed by a homosexual, and, as the official commentator states, the demand of the public prosecutor for the death penalty was granted in conformity with the leadership principle although the defendant had previously received a milder sentence.[96]

Lay judges have completely disappeared from the field of criminal justice, except in the people's courts. The so-called juries, consisting of three judges and six jurymen, no longer exist. The rights of defense counsel have been virtually abolished and criminal law has been brutalized even against juveniles (4 October 1939).[97] Many new crimes have been created, with capital punishment the rule. Every attempt at, or preparation for, a political crime is punishable by death. By decree of 1 September 1939, intentional listening to foreign radio broadcasts is punishable by imprisonment or death, and the federal supreme court has ruled that even listening to foreign music is a crime within the sense of the decree.[98] Another decree (5 December 1939), dealing with violent criminals (*Gewalt-verbrecher*), promises the death penalty to any 'criminal who engages his asocial egotism by means of violence and for this purpose uses certain weapons or other dangerous means.'[99] No distinction is drawn between the perpetrator and the accessory, between the attempt and the consummated act.

Retroactivity and the abolition of the territorial principle are now universal. In applying and interpreting the infamous Section 2, the federal supreme court, following the doctrines of racial imperialism, has pushed German criminal law far beyond the frontiers of Germany. A decree of 20 May 1940 allows the persecution of enemies of Germany who fall into its hands, regardless of their nationality or citizenship status.

The advocates of the phenomenological school have won out. They never define a crime; they describe types of criminals, such as the brutal criminal, the dangerous criminal, youth, the war profiteer, and punish accordingly. Thus, the special court in Stuttgart had to deal with a petty criminal who stole 65 marks, attacking the victim with his fist. The court deduced from the defendant's life history (punished twice previously for minor offenses) and from his method of attack that he was a typical gangster and professional criminal. Sentence of death was ordered, despite the fact that the decree of 5 December 1939 is applicable only if the criminal uses a dangerous weapon.[100]

The leading National Socialist authority on criminal law was certainly correct when he said that 'the activity of the criminal court has become more and more political.'[101] He was correct when he said that capital punishment no longer has the function of inflicting a just revenge for a specific crime; it is a deterrent, and the question of its justness in any specific case is no longer of primary importance. He is right in saying that it is becoming more and more difficult to distinguish between punishment and other measures, especially in the treatment of juveniles; that the 'intervention of high political authorities in the proceedings' is increasing steadily; that the most characteristic feature is a steady growth in the power of the public prosecutor; that the influence of the judiciary is declining, partly by the abolition of judicial self-government, even more by the dispersal of jurisdictions. He predicts that criminal law and procedure will soon change over completely into administrative justice and that the judge will become just another administrative official.

Does such a system deserve the name of law? Yes, if law is merely the will of the sovereign; definitely not, if law, unlike the sovereign's command, must be rational either in form or in content. The National Socialist legal system is nothing but a technique of mass manipulation by terror. Criminal courts, together with the Gestapo, the public prosecutor, and the executioners, are now primarily practitioners of violence. Civil courts are primarily agents for the execution of the commands of monopolistic business organizations.

BEHEMOTH

WE have finished our discussion. We have by no means covered the whole territory, but the evidence we have collected may be sufficient to warrant an interpretation of the decisive aspects of National Socialism.

1. HAS GERMANY A POLITICAL THEORY?

Every political system can be characterized by its political theory, which expresses its structure and aims. But if we were asked to define the political theory of National Socialism, we should be greatly embarrassed. National Socialism is anti-democratic, anti-liberal, and profoundly anti-rational. That is why it cannot utilize any preceding political thought. Not even Hobbes's political theory applies to it. The National Socialist state is no Leviathan. But Hobbes, aside from his *Leviathan* also wrote *Behemoth, or the Long Parliament*, which Ferdinand Toennies edited for the first time from the original manuscript in London in 1889. *Behemoth*, which depicted England during the Long Parliament, was intended as the representation of a non-state, a situation characterized by complete lawlessness. The Leviathan, although it swallows society, does not swallow all of it. Its sovereign power is founded upon the consent of man. Its justification is still rational and, in consequence, incompatible with a political system that completely sacrifices the individual. That was clear to Charles II, who had the *Leviathan* burnt; Clarendon had summed up the book for him in the following words: 'I never read a book which contained so much sedition, treason, and impiety.' That was also clear to Hobbes's contemporaries, especially Johann Friedrich Horn, the German reactionary political theorist, who perceived the revolutionary implications of a political theory that derived sovereign power from the consent of men. Hobbes's *Leviathan* also preserves remnants of the rule of law. The law should be general and should not be retroactive. The whole power of the sovereign is, for Hobbes, merely a part of a bargain in which the sovereign has to fulfil his obligations, that is, preserve

459

order and security so that there may be realized 'the liberty to buy and sell and otherwise contract with one another; to choose their own abode, their own diet, their own trade of life, and institute their children as they themselves think fit.' [1] If the sovereign cannot fulfil his side of the bargain, he forfeits his sovereignty. Such a theory has little in common with National Socialism, absolutistic as it may be.

Nor can National Socialism derive its philosophy from the French, Spanish, German, and English counter-revolutionary writers such as De Maistre, Bonald, Donoso Cortes, Burke, and F. J. Stahl. Their philosophies have certain common features with National Socialism, especially the pessimistic view of man. Burke considers the people 'miserable sheep' to be led by their shepherds; [2] if their shepherds desert them, the people will only become victims of another passion and 'the prey of impostors.' De Maistre shares with National Socialism the rejection of the democratic theory and the depreciation of the individual's effort: 'man, put on his own feet, would only cause filth, disorder, and destruction.' [3] 'Human reason, reduced to its individual forces, is only a brute which must be destroyed by all means.' [4] Bonald denies that political power resides in the people, and he regards the people as ambitious and wicked.[5] 'Liberty, equality, fraternity, or death have been in vogue during the revolution. Liberty has served to cover France with prisons; equality to multiply titles and decorations; fraternity to divide us; only death has succeeded.' [6] Such was his analysis of the accomplishments of the French Revolution. We have already discussed Donoso Cortes's condemnation of liberalism and democracy and its underlying philosophy of man.* Friedrich Julius Stahl, the founder of the Prussian monarchical theory, saw the whole of history as a struggle between two forces: revolutionary and counter-revolutionary, and he believed revolution to be inherent in any political theory that derives the power of the state from man's reason. 'It is revolutionary to oppose civil society to the state of nature and thereby to set man free from all traditions of law and custom, to reduce well-ordered society to the original chaos and to take from that chaos the standards by which the social order is measured. It is revolution to destroy the whole public body of the state, the whole

* See p. 195.

moral order of the nation and to leave nothing except the rights and mutual security of individuals. It is, finally, the essence of revolution to deny the authority power in its own right and to found it on the will of the people. The natural law from Grotius to Kant is the scientific foundation for revolution.' [7] This rejection of reason, civil rights, equality, and self-determination of the people—all this National Socialism shares with the counter-revolutionists and yet there is an unbridgeable gulf between the two. Burke did not want to change the foundations of English society, he wanted to preserve them. De Maistre, Bonald, and Donoso Cortes were ardent Catholics. For them sovereignty rested with the church and not with secular authorities, and consequently their theories, in spite of their Augustinian flavor, were rational. They could not and did not deny that man, although wicked today, might, after the realm of the church had been fully established, become essentially free. Stahl [8] was a legal positivist who believed that the monarchy and the protestant church had identical interests, who derived the validity of the state from this identity of interests, and who never denied the need for a *Rechtstaat*, a state based upon law, which would inviolably guarantee the rights of the individual. Christian counter-revolutionary theories are thus equally incompatible with National Socialism. As a result of the process of secularization it has become impossible to justify political power by reference to God and the church. The sole modern attempt to found political power on God is the Austrian constitution of 1 May 1934, promulgated by Dollfuss, who became, so to speak, 'God's vicar on earth.' This attempt collapsed internally even before Austria was conquered. But even aside from the process of secularization, Christianity and National Socialism are essentially incompatible. According to National Socialism, men are irrational and unequal, and this separates it even from the least rationalist theologies of St. Augustine and Calvin.

National Socialism comes closest to the political theory of the Restoration (the period after the French Revolution), especially to that of K. L. von Haller,[9] which regards the state as a natural fact and at the same time as a divine institution, which accepts the domination of the weak by the strong and rejects civil rights, parliaments, and human reason. Already Hegel had denounced that type of political philosophy as 'fanaticism, mental imbecility, and hypocrisy.' [10] Yet even Haller's imbecilities are, like all conservative traditional theories, still far too rational for National Socialism. Haller still recognizes a 'natural,' though out-dated and antiquated structure of society. This again stands in contrast to National Socialism's complete eradication of feudal remnants in society.

No known absolutistic or counter-revolutionary theory fits National Socialism, because National Socialism has traits that radically separate it from them and because it has no theory of society.

The ideology of National Socialism contains elements of idealism, positivism, pragmatism, vitalism, universalism, institutionalism—in short, of every conceivable philosophy. But these diverse elements are not integrated, they are merely used as devices to establish and extend power and to carry on propaganda. The prevalent interpretations of National Socialist ideology suffer from two great misunderstandings. The first is the identification of National Socialism with Hegelianism. We have shown the incompatibility of Hegel's rational political philosophy with National Socialism,* and Herbert Marcuse's [11] book supplies a brilliant refutation of this erroneous interpretation.

Nor must we fall into the second error, that of identifying National Socialism with relativism, positivism, or pragmatism. It is true that Mussolini has admitted his indebtedness to relativism and pragmatism:

In Germany relativism is an extraordinary daring and destructive theoretical construction (perhaps Germany's philosophical revenge which may announce the military revenge). In Italy, relativism is simply a fact. Fascism is a super-relativistic movement because it has never attempted to clothe its complicated and powerful mental attitude with a definite program but has succeeded by following its ever changing individual intuition. Everything I have said and done in these last years is relativism by intuition. If relativism signifies the end of faith in science, the decay of that myth, 'science,' conceived as the discovery of absolute truth, I can boast of having applied relativism to the analysis of socialism. If relativism signifies contempt for fixed categories and men who claim to be the bearers of an external objective truth . . . then there is nothing more relativistic than Fascist attitudes and activity . . . We Fascists have always expressed our complete indifference toward all theories . . . We Fascists have had the courage to discard all traditional political

* See above, pp. 77-8.

theories, and we are aristocrats and democrats, revolutionaries and reactionaries, proletarians and anti-proletarians, pacifists and anti-pacifists. It is sufficient to have a single fixed point: the nation. The rest is obvious . . . From the fact that all ideologies are of equal value, that all ideologies are mere fictions, the modern relativist deduces that everybody is free to create for himself his own ideology and to attempt to carry it out with all possible energy.[12]

This is, indeed, an extraordinarily illuminating quotation from Mussolini. It shows that his so-called relativism, which has next to nothing to do with either philosophic relativism or pragmatism, is nothing but cynicism and nihilism. What fascism means by its praise of relativism is that it uses theories as devices. We also know from Gaudens Megaro's biography [13] of Mussolini that the invocation of great models by the Fascist leader is pure eyewash and that they are invoked from time to time merely to give the Fascist doctrine an academic standing.

It is true that relativism and pragmatism contain authoritarian elements. By denying the validity of objective truth, they may pave the way for the adoration of the existing. But at the same time they are debunking theories; they are critical doctrines, deflating the arrogant claims of post-Kantian idealism, which, as we have shown,* veils the very same acceptance of given facts by transferring all decisive problems into the sphere of metaphysics. Positivism and pragmatism bow only to ascertained facts and, thereby, demand freedom to ascertain and analyze them. Such freedom is indeed granted by National Socialism—but only to the natural sciences, not to the humanities and not to the social sciences. No philosophy can be held responsible for National Socialism.

National Socialism is, we repeat, incompatible with any rational political philosophy, that is, with any doctrine that derives political power from the will or the needs of man. Why that should be so is, I believe, amply proved by the structure of National Socialist society. There exists a fundamental antagonism between the productivity of German industry, its capacity for promoting the welfare of the people and its actual achievements, and this antagonism is steadily deepening. For the past eight years huge industrial machinery in continuous expansion has been set to work exclusively for destruction. The promises given by the regime to the masses

* See above, pp. 378-9.

are certainly sweet, but many of them have been broken and every essential point of the party program has been sacrificed. This antagonism must be felt by the masses, which are not simply babes in the woods but have a long tradition behind them, a tradition that imbued them with a critical spirit and made them aware that the primary fact of modern civilization is this very antagonism between an economy that can produce in abundance for welfare but that does so only for destruction.

In such a situation, thought is fatal for the regime—on this point a leading positivist and a leading anti-positivist agree.[14] Thought, if allowed, would turn against oppression and injustice. When John Stuart Mill wrote his essay on Jeremy Bentham, he entitled one of his chapters 'The Danger of Asking the Why.'[15] Bentham's utilitarianism was rejected by a society which felt that critical analysis was dangerous to its existence. In National Socialist Germany thought of any kind, whether positivist or pragmatic, whether idealistic or not, must inevitably have a critical and revolutionary impact.

National Socialism has no rational political theory. But has it an anti-rational one, and is there such a thing as an anti-rational theory? We believe not. There are non-rational religious theories and there is a non-rational magic. But a political theory cannot be non-rational. If it claims to be non-rational, it is a conscious trick. 'And there has arisen . . . blood against formal reason; race against purposeful rationality; honor against profit; unity against individualistic disintegration; martial virtue against bourgeois security; the folk against the individual and the mass.'[16] This description of National Socialist philosophy by one of the leading National Socialist philosophers, Ernst Krieck, now professor at Heidelberg, may be considered authoritative. We have tried to show on many occasions that the so-called non-rational concepts, blood, community, folk, are devices for hiding the real constellation of power and for manipulating the masses. The charisma of the Leader, the superiority of the master race, the struggle of a proletarian race against plutocracies, the protest of the folk against the state are consciously applied stratagems. It may not be exaggerated to say that National Socialism acts according to a most rational plan, that each and every pronouncement by its leaders is calculated, and its effect on the masses and the surrounding world is carefully weighed in advance.

From the preceding political systems that lack theoretical justification and that were prevalent in the period of the foundation of the Italian city states and the early seventeenth century, National Socialism is distinguished by its appeal to the people.[17] We have seen that National Socialism has risen to power with the support of the masses. After society has passed the phase of large-scale democracy the appeal to the masses and their support become imperative. No political system can build on nothing or completely erase the past. Every new political system must incorporate certain aspects of the past. National Socialism has transformed institutional democracy of the Weimar Republic into a ceremonial and a magic democracy,[18] a development made necessary by the requirements of totalitarian war, in which the distinctions between civilians and soldiers are annihilated and in which the civilian suffers even more than the soldiers. The socialization of danger,[18] as Harold Lasswell aptly termed this situation, more than ever requires full control over the whole mass of the people and over each aspect of their individual lives. Finally, in order to manipulate the masses, in order to control, atomize, terrorize them, one must capture them ideologically.

National Socialism has revived the methods current in the fourteenth century, when the first modern states, the Italian city states, were founded. It has returned to the early period of state absolution where 'theory' was a mere *arcanum dominationis*, a technique outside of right and wrong, a sum of devices for maintaining power. The leaders of the Italian city states in the fourteenth century: Machiavelli, the early seventeenth-century German lawyers (like Arnold Clapmar); were masters of this art. A study of Arnold Clapmar's *De arcanis rerum publicarum* (1605) will reveal striking similarities with National Socialism in the transformation of thought into propaganda techniques.

It is noteworthy that the fourteenth century saw the first attempt to establish a kind of fascist dictatorship. This attempt was made in Rome at a time when the city was undergoing an acute economic crisis as a result of the removal of the papacy to Avignon, and was a prey to the German emperor and the ruler of Naples. Torn by the struggle between the two noble families of Colonna and Orsini, populated by a ragged impoverished mass that vividly remembered its glorious past, Rome became an ideal ground for the activities of the demagogue Cola di Rienzo. This son of a poor innkeeper and a washerwoman was an autodidact; by dint of hard work he became a scholar and was the first to explore the ruins of Rome. His plan to achieve power was financially backed by the wealthy; he also carefully cultivated, and as carefully hid, his connections with the Pope. At the same time he cleverly exploited the frustrations of considerable sections of the Roman populace, and propaganda was one of his most powerful weapons for mass domination. Huge allegoric paintings on house walls, street demonstrations, the celebration of magic ceremonies, passionate and violent speeches full of allegorical and historical reflections on the glory of Rome, promises of deliverance from the domination of the nobles were his stock-in-trade. Cola di Rienzo's whole career was marked by the same mixture of cunning and passion that can be observed in the recent history of Germany.

The Roman nobility refused to take him seriously, although—or perhaps because—he candidly expressed his aims. But the bourgeoisie saw in Cola di Rienzo its savior from destruction and unrest. The wealthy sons of the merchants, who had never been quite accepted by the nobility, went over to him. On Whit-Sunday 1347, Cola convoked a so-called Roman parliament of the people and proclaimed his dictatorship—constitutionally. His methods of seizing and exercising power closely follow the pattern made familiar by National Socialism: draconic laws, a drastic purge of the judiciary and the bureaucratic personnel, the creation of a strong army. He ordered corrupt civil servants to be led through the streets, dressing them ridiculously and exposing them to the mockery of the populace. Prisons were filled, special tribunals worked overtime, death sentences were multiplied. The nobility bowed to his rule and swore allegiance. Complete unity of the Roman people seemed restored, all the more so since the privileges of the nobility were abolished. In the end he was overthrown by the very classes he had promised to destroy but had actually strengthened. After his downfall, he conspired with the Franciscan monks and adopted the charismatic doctrine of Joachim of Floris, striving to realize the 'Third Empire,' the realm of the spirit.

There are other historical precedents, though none is as interesting as the brief reign of Cola di Rienzo, because it took place at the very dawn of the modern state. The dictatorship of Napoleon III proclaimed on 2 December 1851 was also characterized by the ideo-

logical flattering of the masses and their actual isolation and pulverization. Authoritarian control of the workers' associations, the
introduction of the work book, the creation of public works proj-
ects went hand in hand with the emperor's incessant declarations
of his love for the workers.

In these two cases—and in many others [19]—we are confronted with
masses whose position has become unbearable. These masses show
revolutionary tendencies, their resentment against their rulers increases as they realize their frustration. The modern fascist leader
canalizes the unrest in a manner that leaves untouched the material
foundations of society. In our time, this can be done only by substituting magic celebrations for thinking, not only in public ceremonies but also in daily life. To achieve that end, the isolation of
the individual characteristic of modern society is intensified to the
utmost limit with the help of an immense network of bureaucratic
organizations and an opportunistic, infinitely elastic ideology.

These considerations lead us to conclude that National Socialism has no political theory of its own, and that the ideologies it
uses or discards are mere *arcana dominationis*, techniques of domination. If that is true, it must, in my opinion, be granted that the
German leadership is the only group in present German society
that does not take its ideological pronouncements seriously and is
well aware of their purely propagandistic nature.

2. IS GERMANY A STATE?

But if National Socialism has no political theory, is its political
system a state? If a state is characterized by the rule of law, our
answer to this question will be negative, since we deny that law
exists in Germany. It may be argued that state and law are not
identical, and that there can be states without law. States, however,
as they have arisen in Italy, are conceived as rationally operating
machineries disposing of the monopoly of coercive power. A state
is ideologically characterized by the unity of the political power
that it wields.

I doubt whether even a state in this restricted sense exists in
Germany. It has been maintained that National Socialism is a dual
state, that is, in fact, one state within which two systems are operating, one under normative law, the other under individual measures,

one rational, the other the realm of prerogative.[20] We do not share
this view because we believe that there is no realm of law in Germany, although there are thousands of technical rules that are calculable. We believe that the monopolists in dealing with non-
monopolists rely on individual measures and in their relations with
the state and with competitors, on compromises which are determined by expedience and not by law. Moreover, it is doubtful
whether National Socialism possesses a unified coercive machinery,
unless we accept the leadership theory as a true doctrine. The party
is independent of the state in matters pertaining to the police and
youth,* but everywhere else the state stands above the party. † The
army is sovereign in many fields; the bureaucracy is uncontrolled;
and industry has managed to conquer many positions. One might
say that such antagonisms are as characteristic of democracy as they
are of National Socialism. Granting that, there is still one decisive
difference. In a democracy and in any other constitutional system,
such antagonisms within the ruling groups must be settled in an
universally binding manner. The absolutistic king is the real legislator, in his person, legislation, administration, and the judiciary are
actually unified. When his absolutistic claim comes into conflict
with reality, the state disintegrates, as France before the Revolution
of 1789 when the king was absolutistic in name only, while the
power was exercised by the bureaucracy, the feudals, the courts,
the high bourgeoisie, all of them bitterly fighting each other. In an
absolute monarchy, in a constitutional system, and in a democracy,
the compromises between various groups claim and have universal
validity. If it is necessary for the state to co-ordinate and integrate
hundreds and thousands of individual and group conflicts, the process must be accomplished in a universally binding manner, that is,
through abstract rational law or at least through a rationally operating bureaucracy. Under National Socialism, however, the whole of
the society is organized in four solid, centralized groups, each
operating under the leadership principle, each with a legislative, administrative, and judicial power of its own. Neither universal law
nor a rationally operating bureaucracy is necessary for integration.
Compromises among the four authoritarian bodies need not be expressed in a legal document nor must they be institutionalized (like

* See above, pp. 69-71.
† See above, pp. 71-5.

the 'gentlemen's agreements' between monopolistic industries). It is quite sufficient that the leadership of the four wings agree informally on a certain policy. The four totalitarian bodies will then enforce it with the machinery at their disposal. There is no need for a state standing above all groups; the state may even be a hindrance to the compromises and to domination over the ruled classes. The decisions of the Leader are merely the result of the compromises among the four leaderships. The ministerial council for the defense of the realm has no executive apparatus different from that of the four wings of the ruling class.

It is thus impossible to detect in the framework of the National Socialist political system any one organ which monopolizes political power.

The most advanced National Socialist's lawyers, Reinhard Höhn [21] and Gottfried Neesse,[22] reject the very concept of the state, and their ideas are widely approved.[23] Both reject the notion of the state's personality as a mere liberal construction, for if the concept of the state is accepted, they argue, those exercising its power are merely its organs. According to them, Germany's political power rests in in the Leader, who is not the organ of the state but who *is* the community, not acting as its organ but as its personification. Neesse distinguishes three independent powers of equal rank, the party, the army, and the state (by which he means the bureaucracy); above them is the Leader 'acting not only for the people and in its place but as the people.' [24] He utilizes the party, the army, and the state as his tools only because he cannot do everything personally. We are not concerned with the sophistry of this new theory of transubstantiation implied by the identification of the Leader and the people, but rather with the consequences that derive from such theory. This advanced National Socialist constitutional theory, although attacked even by Carl Schmitt,[25] clearly admits that it is not the state which unifies political power but that there are three (in our view, four) co-existent political powers, the unification of which is not institutionalized but only personalized. It may be readily admitted that in constitutional law, as in any other field, the theories of the people's community and leadership are a mere shield covering the powers of the enormously swollen bureaucratic machines. But at least a grain of truth may be contained in these theories; to wit, that it is difficult to give the name state to four groups entering into a bargain. In fact, except for the charismatic power of the Leader, there is no authority that co-ordinates the four powers, no place where the compromise between them can be put on a universal valid basis.

But if the National Socialist structure is not a state, what is it? I venture to suggest that we are confronted with a form of society in which the ruling groups control the rest of the population directly, without the mediation of that rational though coercive apparatus hitherto known as the state. This new social form is not yet fully realized, but the trend exists which defines the very essence of the regime.

3. What Are the Developmental Trends in this Structure?

That there are deep antagonisms within the ruling classes, we have already shown.* No common loyalties exist. The cement that binds them together is profit, power, and, above all, fear of the oppressed masses. But since that is so, it may come about that one group will swallow one or all of the others. It may very well be that National Socialism is on the way toward becoming a 'garrison state,' which Harold Lasswell [26] defines as a state run exclusively by practitioners of violence. It may come about that the party, in the event of a conflict, will expropriate industry. Does it mean the end of capitalism? I do not believe so. Germany would then re-enter a new period of primary accumulation, a period where capital is accumulated not by the process of production but by violence and terror alone, that is, by political means. Even today the system shows many features of primary accumulation, such as Aryanization, Germanization, and the foundation of the Göring works. A new class of capitalists will then arise and the political power of the party will then be fully anchored in the process of production. The ruling'class will then be a compromise structure not of four groups but perhaps of only two, the army and the party.

But while what we understand by primary accumulation once ushered in a process of gigantic expansion, an unheard-of unfettering of all productive forces, fascist primary accumulation indicates the end of this process. The conquest of economic power by pure

* See above, pp. 396-8.

terroristic means becomes necessary since it is impossible, for the many reasons we have given, to rise in the social scale merely by hard work and money.

Though that development is possible, it is not likely. The army is not a National Socialist group, however much army leaders may kowtow before Hitler. It is still subject to a rationality of its own. Its close connections with monopolistic industry, with the agrarians, and with the high ministerial bureaucracy are known and have been discussed. Should Germany win the war, the prestige and power of the army will be enormously enhanced and the party will not dare to go the way of wholesale expropriation. One or the other monopolist might fall, like Thyssen, as a warning to the others and as a concession to the party, but it is unlikely that in case of victory the present structure of German society will be materially changed.

Far more important are the antagonisms between the rulers and the ruled. There exists objectively a profound antagonism between the two classes. Whether and when it will explode we do not know. But within that universal and general class antagonism there exist innumerable cracks in the system, which we must mention. The most profound conflict will arise from the antagonism between the magic character of propaganda * and the complete rationality and depersonalization of society. The process of production is not magical, it is rational. Changes in the process of production are not created by the touching of the flag or by the uttering of ceremonial words, but by work. They do not just happen, they are man-made. The regime has tried and will try to prevent the rise of an ideology corresponding to the rational processes of labor, but that endeavor is hopeless. It can only arouse contempt and cynicism. According to some observers of National Socialist Germany, we have already reached the stage where leadership and community adoration are generally considered to be what they actually are: bunk.

Aside from this general antagonism there are other flaws in the system of mass domination, above all the conflict between the shock groups and the amorphous masses. That process is operative in the army and in industry and it may attain considerable proportions. Two of the most intelligent observers of modern warfare have

* See above, pp. 385-7, 436.

already pointed to the inherent conflict between the growing importance of the initiative of individual soldiers and the bureaucratization of the mass army.[27] National Socialist warfare must, to an ever greater extent, rely on the daring, the skill, and the initiative of the soldier and non-commissioned officer—but it practices at the same time complete authoritarianism, that is, rigid control from above.

A similar phenomenon is observable in the process of production. It has been argued that Germany is the land of engineers and that the inventive and organizational skill of the engineer is no longer hampered by the profit motive.[28] That is only partly true; above all it does not mean that the engineer is the ruler and that capitalism is at an end. It merely expresses the need of an economy lacking in raw materials and man-power to create substitute materials and to rationalize the productive process whatever the costs may be. But even if we assume that during these past eight years the engineer has not been fettered, he will later constitute (always assuming a German victory) the most serious break in the regime. The engineer exercises the most rational vocation and he knows what beneficent powers the productive machinery can wield. Every day sees how this machinery becomes an instrument of destruction rather than of welfare. The conflict between potentiality and actuality is, so to speak, taking place daily before his very eyes. Should Germany, even after the defeat of England and Russia, continue to rearm in order to conquer the world—and we have tried to prove that continuous aggressive expansion is inherent in the whole system *—that antagonism will become daily more threatening. But should Germany after the defeat of the opposition become domesticated and waive further expansion, then the powers of the engineer will again be fettered, technical progress will be most likely reversed in order to provide sufficient employment. We believe that the antagonism between the engineer, by whom we understand all technicians and foremen, and totalitarian monopoly capitalism is one of the decisive flaws in the regime.

That conflict goes deeper, it pervades the whole working class. The power of the skilled worker has grown. He has become, it is true, ever more interchangeable. The relation between the produced

* See above, pp. 178-83 and pp. 330-31, 336-7.

piece of work and his labor is completely dissolved in a highly rationalized machinery, but the relation between him and the labor process is not. The antagonism experienced by the engineer is repeated on a large scale. Though the number of skilled workers may decrease and the ratio of unskilled and semi-skilled workers continue to increase, the power of skilled labor grows, for it holds the key position in the industrial machinery. The regime can attempt to corrupt the skilled worker, it will try to satisfy his demands at the expense of the large masses of the unskilled. It will continue to destroy solidarity wherever it encounters it. It will annihilate all affinities arising from common work. But will it succeed? Will the higher skilled worker, knowing his interchangeability, understanding the potentialities of the industrial apparatus, be satisfied with a regime that uses these potentialities for oppression and terror? If we believe man to be essentially wicked, if egoism is the sole incentive of man, the prospects are rather black. But man is neither bad nor good, he will be molded by his cultural and political experience.

What is that experience? The transformation of culture into propaganda has far-reaching consequences for the regime—consequences it does not wish but from which it cannot escape. The conflict between the pseudo-socialist ideology and the naked facts of authoritarian monopoly capitalism must deepen. The anti-capitalist propaganda contains inner dynamics, which for a time can be halted by various devices but which cannot be permanently stopped. Even the nationalization of the economy will then not be sufficient. It will not do simply to transfer property to the state and to retain the socio-political system. The community ideology, fraudulent as it is, the anti-state ideology, fictitious as it may be, are, as we have mentioned, forms of the theory of a classless society—though, of course, degenerated forms.* By its anti-capitalistic and anti-state propagandas, the regime unwittingly furthers genuine socialist trends.

That applies to the pseudo-egalitarianism. Even fake egalitarianism will leave indelible impressions on those for whom it is practiced. William Shirer [29] has reported the equality of the treatment of sailors and officers on German battleships. Numerous reporters have told us that the rigid discipline of the German army outside the

* See above, pp. 191-3.

service time is a thing of the past, that officers and soldiers consort socially, that privates need no longer rise and stand at attention when officers enter a restaurant. We also know that many of the hierarchic orders have fallen to pieces, not only in the army but also in the civil service.* The soldier or non-commissioned officer, if entrusted with a task, is responsible to himself alone and need not tolerate any interference by any superior save the one who has issued the command. We have shown that the National Socialist cells in the civil service break down the barriers between the academic and non-academic civil services, and that the officers' organizations have been merged with military organizations primarily composed of privates. The S.A. and the S.S. are pseudo-egalitarian bodies; so is the army on a larger scale.

They all are pseudo-egalitarian bodies, because none of the demands of genuine equality are realized. And yet the daily repetition of 'equality by all racial Germans,' the complete annihilation of feudal remnants must ultimately lead to the demand for full and genuine equality. A non-academic civil servant with higher qualities than his academic superior will not be satisfied with just sitting in the same cell or with having even perhaps a higher rank in the civil-service organization—he will demand the destruction of all barriers and invoke the equality of all racial Germans. Privates may demand that the ultimate consequences be drawn from the fraternization between officers and soldiers. Nobody can call in the gods and remain unpunished.

This very same antagonism pervades culture. 'Strength through Joy' is a leisure organization that utilizes leisure for work,† but the organization will undoubtedly create a demand for genuine culture, which no garrison state can fulfil. Culture can breed only in freedom, and freedom will subject the labor process to criticism. Again the potentialities inherent in the 'Strength through Joy' movement are so immense and its actual fulfilments so regressive that the conflict must one day become fully apparent.

This is the cultural situation that will mold the consciousness of the working classes and among them, especially, the skilled worker, the foreman, and the engineer.

These antagonisms will be criss-crossed by the new nationalism

* See above, pp. 382-5.
† See above, pp. 429-30.

in the conquered territories, which will become more powerful and more dangerous every day. Now that Russia has entered the war, the 'national' and 'social' question will, for the impoverished masses in eastern and southeastern Europe, merge into one profound and deep hatred against the German conqueror.

Such are the flaws of this system, which must develop even if Germany wins the present war.

What if Germany is defeated? Can she be defeated? She certainly can. But the defeat must be planned, not merely as a military economic action but also as a psychological one. We have tried to indicate that Germany's revolution in 1918 was not merely due to the military superiority of the allied powers as a result of America's entrance into the war, but also to the superiority of Woodrow Wilson's new freedom over a monarchic political theory that had for long ceased to be believed.* Wilson was celebrated not only in Italy, France, and England, in Czechoslovakia and Poland, and not as President of the United States, but as the man who had given the liberal democratic idea its most precise and most concrete formulation. *Germany no longer believes in this ideology.* This is a fact that psychological warfare must take into account. The idea of the self-determination of the people has been betrayed not by Republican Germany but by the Western Powers. Minorities in eastern Europe were suppressed and the Western Powers have done nothing. The League of Nations has collapsed, but not through the fault of democratic Germany. Democracy has been betrayed by the German democrats—liberals, Social Democrats, Catholics. Political democracy alone will not be accepted by the German people, that much the Marxist and National Socialist criticism of liberalism and democracy have indeed accomplished. The German knows that behind political democracy, economic injustice may be hidden. Psychological warfare against Germany will not be successful if the mere *status quo* is the ultimate aim.[30] Europe must be reorganized. It cannot again be divided into hostile warring states. The potentialities of a unified Europe must be put to work for the welfare of the large masses. Germany cannot be divided and enslaved. We have tried to show that there is no specific German trait responsible for aggression and imperialism but that imperialism

* See above, pp. 8-9.

is inherent in the structure of the German monopolist economy, the one-party system, the army, and the bureaucracy.* To destroy aggression, the power of the monopolistic economy must be definitely broken and the economic structure of Germany must be profoundly changed, in addition to eradicating the power of the party, the army, and the high bureaucracy.

Much as the German longs for peace and freedom, for justice and equality, much as he abhors concentration camps, the executioner's axe and the S.S., much as he ridicules leadership and fake community—he will never be satisfied with a *status quo* which again delivers him to the anarchic conditions of the great depression.

National Socialism can in the psychological field be defeated only by a political theory that proves as efficient as National Socialism without sacrificing the liberties of man. That is the second postulate for psychological warfare against Germany, and the National Socialists know that, too. The incessant campaign against England and the United States waged daily by the National Socialist propaganda machine has but one aim: to convince the German people that England and the United States are not democracies, that behind their democratic façade lurks the power of capitalism, hunger and suffering, inequality and exploitation. The National Socialist leadership knows that once England and the American democracies will show themselves as efficient as, and perhaps more efficient than, National Socialism, while retaining or even deepening democracy, the belief in National Socialism, which is founded on fear and despair, will ultimately collapse. The primary condition for psychological warfare against Germany is, therefore, that the process of democratization in England and the United States be not sacrificed but that it be encouraged to progress. We know that that is difficult. It is much more strenuous to develop the potentialities of a nation on a democratic than on an authoritarian basis; and yet to uproot National Socialism in the minds of the German people, the model of an efficiently operated democracy will be worth as much as a powerful army.

The flaws and breaks in the system and even the military defeat of Germany will not lead to an automatic collapse of the regime. It can only be overthrown by conscious political action of the oppressed masses, which will utilize the breaks in the system.

* See above, pp. 149-50, 186-88, 199-210, 360-61.

NOTES

INTRODUCTION

THE COLLAPSE OF THE WEIMAR REPUBLIC

1. The Imperial message of 1881 announced the beginnings of a program of social legislation under which the following measures were put into effect:

   1883 Sickness-insurance law
   1884 Industrial accident-insurance law
   1889 Social-insurance law for invalids
   1891 Workers health law (providing for Sunday rest, etc.)

2. Sohm, *Kirchengeschichte im Grundriss*. 20th ed., n.d. (1st ed., 1867), pp. 216-17.

3. Eckart Kehr, 'Das soziale System der Reaktion in Preussen unter dem Ministerium Puttkamer,' in *Die Gesellschaft*, 1929 (II), pp. 253-74, esp. p. 269.

4. Puttkamer to his father in May 1859. Cited by Kehr, op. cit. p. 254.

5. An episode illustrates the kind of attempt made: Emperor Wilhelm I, in a letter written to Puttkamer on 11 September 1883 (Kehr, p. 256), protested a plan to celebrate Luther's birthday with a public feast. The idea terrified him because it would have enabled the liberals to take part in the celebrations.

6. Herbert Rosinski, *The German Army*, New York, 1939, p. 30.

7. Alfred Vagts, *A History of Militarism*, New York, 1937, p. 201.

8. Term coined by Carl Brinkmann, 'Die Aristokratie im kapitalistischen Zeitalter,' in *Grundriss der Sozialökonomik*, IX, 1, Tübingen, 1926, pp. 22-34.

9. Eckart Kehr, 'Zur Genesis des Kgl. preussischen Reserveoffiziers,' in *Die Gesellschaft*, 1928 (II), p. 492.

10. Vagts, op. cit. p. 11.

11. Ibid. p. 171.

12. The Prussian minister of war to the General Staff, 20 January 1913. Quoted in Hans Herzfeld, *Die deutsche Rüstungspolitik vor dem Weltkrieg*, Bonn, 1923, p. 63.

13. Vagts, op. cit. p. 340.

14. Max Weber, *Gesammelte Aufsätze zur Sozial- und Wirtschaftsgeschichte*, Tübingen, 1924, pp. 471-507.

15. Mention must be made of the fact that the poor state of Prussian agriculture was due largely to the lack of rationalization in East German farming and to the excessively high prices charged by the estates, deliberately kept high in order to secure an adequate luxury consumption to the estate owners. This problem is very well discussed by Eckart Kehr, *Schlachtflottenbau und Parteipolitik 1894-1901*, Berlin, 1930, p. 250.

16. A. B. Lindsay, 'The State in Recent Political Theory,' in *The Political Quarterly*, 1914 (I), p. 136.

17. The best exposition of the pluralist theory, and an excellent selected bibliography, may be found in Francis W. Coker, *Recent Political Thought*,

New York and London, 1934, pp. 497-520. The most trenchant criticism of the theory is made by W. Y. Elliott, *The Pragmatic Revolt in Politics*, New York, 1928.

18. Ernest Barker, *Political Theory in England from Herbert Spencer to the Present Day*, Everyman's Library, 1915, pp. 175-83.

19. The statement was made by General Gröner at a trial. The case involved a libel action brought by a Social Democratic editor against a Nationalist publisher who reproached the Social Democrats for their 'stab-in-the-back' of the army during the war. The quotation is taken from *Der Dolchstoss-prozess in München Oktober-November 1925*, München, 1925, p. 223. The eminent German, now American, historian, Arthur Rosenberg, in his work, *A History of the German Republic*, trans. by Morrow and Sieveking, London, 1936, p. 50 and pp. 324-5, denies that Gröner's statement is true. I cannot agree. Rosenberg has convincingly shown that Gröner erred when he testified that Ebert told him on 24 December 1918 that he was leaving Berlin and wanted to rest for three days. But this does not invalidate the rest of Gröner's statement, which is confirmed by objective and subjective facts. A secret telephone line existed between Ebert's and Hindenburg's headquarters in Hanover (Rosenberg, op. cit. pp. 60, 61). Hindenburg wrote Ebert on 8 December 1918 a letter in which he practically confirmed the agreement. Moreover, Ebert never concealed his hatred of social revolution. He even objected to Scheidemann's unauthorized proclamation of the Republic.

20. Otto Braun, *Von Weimar zu Hitler*, 2nd ed., New York, 1940, p. 5.

21. Thorstein Veblen, *Imperial Germany and the Industrial Revolution*, new ed., New York, 1939, p. 193.

22. Robert A. Brady, *The Rationalization Movement in German Industry*, Berkeley (Calif.), 1933, pp. 336-40.

23. Hilferding, 'Die Aufgaben der Sozialdemokratie in der Republik,' in *Sozialdemokratischer Parteitag Kiel*, Berlin, 1927, pp. 165-84.

24. Estimates are to be found in Kurt Mendelsohn, *Kapitalistisches Wirtschaftschaos oder sozialistische Planwirtschaft*, Berlin, 1932, p. 15, and Brady, op. cit. p. 139.

25. Estimates of subsidies paid to industry are given by Mendelsohn, op. cit. p. 55.

26. Excellent discussion by Hans Speier, 'The Salaried Employee in Modern Society,' in *Social Research*, 1934 (1), pp. 118-19.

27. *Jahrbuch der deutschen Sozialdemokratie für das Jahr 1930*, Berlin, 1930, p. 195.

28. William Ernest Hocking, 'Ways of Thinking about Rights: A New Theory of the Relation between Law and Morals,' in *Law: A Century of Progress*, New York, 1937, Vol. II, p. 261.

29. Excellent survey of republican justice: Philip Loewenfeld, *Das Strafrecht als politische Waffe*, Berlin, 1933.

30. *Hitler und Kahr, Die bayerischen Napoleonsgrössen von 1923*, ed. by the Landesvorstand der SPD in Bayern, 2 vols., Munich, 1928.

31.   I. Statistics of political murders 1924 to 1931:

1924	3		
1925	3	1928	6
1(?)	4	1930	20
1927	5	6 months 1931	18

From E. J. Gumbel, *Lasst Köpfe rollen*, Berlin, 1931.

II. Statistics of political murders 1918 to 1922:

COMMITTED BY	Left Groups	Right Groups	Total
	22	354	376
Not expiated	4	326	330
Partially expiated	1	27	28
Expiated	17	1	18

	Left Groups	Right Groups
Number of judgments against	38	24
Discharged despite plea of guilty	..	23
Promoted despite plea of guilty	..	3
Incarceration for murder	15 yrs.	4 mos.*
Number executed	10	..

* Average per person.

From E. J. Gumbel, *Vier Jahre politischer Mord*, Berlin, 1922, pp. 73-81. The Fehme murders totalled 17, of which 11 were committed in 1923; discharged or not prosecuted, 8; imprisoned hard labor, 3; imprisoned, 5. Compiled on the basis of E. J. Gumbel, *Verräter verfallen der Fehme*, Berlin, 1929, pp. 386-9.

32. The following statistics of crimes of treason to the nation are of great significance:

Year	Condemned for High Treason and Treason to the Country	Criminality per 100,000 of the Population Subject to Penal Law	Index of Criminality
1895	18	0.06	1.05
1900	6	0.02	0.35
1913	35	0.07	1.22
1921	111	0.23	4.01
1923	137	0.28	4.89
1924	516	1.10	19.20
1925	561	1.18	20.60

The criminality index is obtained by making equal to 1 the average criminality figure for the years 1893-1913, which is 0.0573.
Treason to the country committed through the press 1924-1927 (incomplete):

Information advanced against	360
Not prosecuted	45
Prosecuted	315
Nolle prosequitur	252
Pending	63
Sentenced	3

From E. J. Gumbel, 'Landesverratstatistik,' in *Die Menschenrechte*, Vol. III (1928), pp. 1-8.

33. Gustav Radbruch in *Die Justiz*, 1932 (6), p. 187; Loewenfeld, op. cit. p. 36.

34. Weber, 'Wirtschaft und Gesellschaft,' in *Grundriss der Sozialökonomik*, Vol. III, 1, Tübingen, 1921, p. 174.

35. Popitz, 'Finanzausgleich,' in *Handwörterbuch der Staatswissenschaften*, 4th ed., Jena, 1926, Vol. III, p. 1013.

36. Cf. the good survey by Frederick Mundell Watkins, *The Failure of Constitutional Emergency Powers under the German Republic*, Cambridge (Mass.), 1939.

37. Number of unemployed in thousands and the kind of support they received:

	Total Number	Supported by Unemployment Insurance	Supported by Emergency Unemployment Administration	Supported by Municipal Poor Relief or Unsupported *	Unsupported
1929 July	1,251	711	153	387	...
1932 January	6,042	1,885	1,596	1,713	847

* Up to July 1930, there was no statistical separation of those on municipal poor relief and those who were unsupported.
From W. Woytinsky, in *Internationales Handwörterbuch des Gewerkschaftswesens*, Berlin, 1931, p. 1563, and brought up to 1932 by the author from *Deutsche Wirtschaftskunde*, Berlin, 1933, p. 295.

38. Fritz Tarnow, 'Kapitalistische Wirtschaftsanarchie und Arbeiterklasse,' in *Sozialdemokratischer Parteitag in Leipzig*, Berlin, 1931, p. 45.
39. At the ECCI Plenum, in *Kommunistische Internationale*, 1931, p. 79.
40. Hilferding, 'Zwischen den Entscheidungen,' in *Die Gesellschaft*, January 1933, p. 4.
41. Quoted by Matthew Josephson, *The President Makers*, New York, 1940, p. 376.

PART ONE

THE POLITICAL PATTERN OF NATIONAL SOCIALISM

I: The Totalitarian State

1. Curzio Malaparte, *Coup d'Etat, the Technique of Revolution*, translated by Sylvia Saunders, New York, 1932.
2. Carl Schmitt, *Die geistesgeschichtliche Lage des modernen Parlamentarismus*, 2nd ed., Munich and Leipzig, 1926.
3. Hans Peter Ipsen, 'Vom Begriff der Partei,' in *Zeitschrift für die gesamte Staatswissenschaft*, 1940 (100), p. 490.
4. Ernst Rudolf Huber, 'Der Bedeutungswandel der Grundrechte,' in *Archiv für öffentliches Recht*, 1932 (23), pp. 1-98.
5. Franz Neumann, 'Gegen ein Gesetz über Nachprüfung der Verfassungsmässigkeit von Reichsgesetzen,' in *Die Gesellschaft*, 1929 (1), pp. 517-36.
6. Carl Schmitt, *Der Hüter der Verfassung*, Tübingen, 1931.
7. Carl Schmitt, *Der Begriff des Politischen*, new ed., Munich and Leipzig, 1932.
8. Ibid. p. 17.
9. Typical is the excellent little book by Otto Kirchheimer, *Weimar und was dann?*, Berlin, 1930.
10. Representative: Herman Heller, *Rechtsstaat und Dikatur*, Tübingen, 1930; also my own book: *Koalitionsfreiheit und Reichsverfassung*, Berlin, 1932.
11. Hans Kelsen has summed up his theory in *Reine Rechtslehre*, Leipzig and Vienna, 1934. English expositions are: Charles H. Wilson, 'The Basis of Kelsen's Theory of Law,' in *Politica*, 1934, pp. 54-82; and H. Lauterpacht, 'Kelsen's Pure Science of Law,' in *Modern Theories of Law*, Oxford, 1933, pp. 105-38.
12. Hans Kelsen, *Vom Wesen und Wert der Demokratie*, 2nd ed., Tübingen, 1929, pp. 27, 28.
13. Ernst Forsthoff, *Der totale Staat*, Hamburg, 1933, p. 29.
14. Otto Koellreuter, *Vom Sinn und Wesen der nationalen Revolution*, Tübingen, 1933, pp. 11, 12; also, his *Der deutsche Führerstaat*, Tübingen, 1934; and his *Volk und Staat in der Weltanschauung des Nationalsozialismus*, Berlin, 1935.
15. Hans Gerber, *Staatsrechtliche Grundlagen des neuen Reichs*, Tübingen, 1933, p. 15.
16. Ernst Rudolf Huber, 'Die Totalität des völkischen Staates,' in *Die Tat* (1934), Vol. 26, pp. 30-41.
17. The statement was made on 8 November 1933, as quoted by F. Poetzsch-

Heffter, C. H. Ule, and C. Dernedde, 'Vom Deutschen Staatsleben,' in the *Jahrbuch des öffentlichen Rechts* (1935), Vol. 22, p. 125.
18. Axel Friedrichs (ed.), *Die nationalsozialistische Revolution* 1933, Berlin, 1935, pp. 59-61.
19. *Völkischer Beobachter*, No. 185, 4 July 1933.
20. Ibid. 5 October 1933.
21. Dr. Frick, *Der Neubau des Deutschen Reiches, Vortrag gehalten vor Offizieren der Reichswehr am 15 November 1934*, Berlin (n.d.), p. 6.
22. Carl Schmitt, 'Starker Staat und gesunde Wirtschaft,' in *Volk und Reich*, 1933, pp. 81-94.
23. Published in Ernst Forsthoff (ed.) *Deutsche Geschichte in Dokumenten seit 1918*, 2nd ed., Stuttgart, 1938, pp. 290-99.
24. Poetzsch-Heffter, op. cit. pp. 119-20.
25. Frick, op. cit. p. 7.
26. *Life*, 29 April 1940.
27. A good analysis of the problem of separate powers occurs in Charles H. Wilson, 'The Separation of Powers under Democracy and Fascism,' in the *Political Science Quarterly* (1937), Vol. 52, pp. 481-504.
28. Frick, op. cit. p. 7. The enabling act was originally to expire on 1 April 1937. It was twice extended and now applies until 10 May 1943.
29. On the subject of the Harzburg front, consult Frederick L. Schuman, *The Nazi Dictatorship*, 2nd ed., New York, 1939, p. 149.
30. Franz Albrecht Medicus, *Programm der Reichsregierung und Ermächtigungsgesetz*, Berlin, 1933, p. 19.
31. Poetzsch-Heffter, op. cit. p. 63.
32. Huber, op. cit. p. 47.
33. The distinction has been propounded by Carl Schmitt in his *Legalität und Legitimität*, Munich and Leipzig, 1932.
34. Huber, op. cit. p. 97.
35. Erich Becker, 'Die Rechtsstellung der deutschen Länder in der Gegenwart,' in the *Zeitschrift für die gesamte Staatswissenschaft*, 1937 (97), pp. 462-98, esp. p. 494.
36. Italics mine. See F. Poetzsch-Heffter, op. cit. pp. 53-4. The quotation is also interesting because it admits that the exercise of presidential power during the last years of the Weimar Republic had been unconstitutional.
37. Ernst Rudolf Huber, 'Das deutsche Staatsoberhaupt,' in the *Zeitschrift für die gesamte Staatswissenschaft*, 1935 (95), pp. 202-29, esp. p. 204.
38. Carl Schmitt, *Das Reichsstatthaltergesetz*, Berlin, 1933.

II: The Revolt of the Party and the 'Movement' State

1. Frederick L. Schuman, *The Nazi Dictatorship*, 2nd ed., New York, 1939, p. 430.
2. Reprinted in Alfred Rosenberg, *Gestaltung der Idee. Blut und Ehre*, Vol. II, Munich, 1936.
3. Rosenberg, *Der Mythus des 20. Jahrhunderts*, 9th ed., Munich, 1933, especially pp. 525-7.
4. Adolf Hitler, *Mein Kampf*, Reynal and Hitchcock, New York, 1939, pp. 592, 594, 596, 122, 123. Although I have used this edition, I have changed a number of translations. The concept *Volk* must never be translated *nation*.

5. E. Koch (editor), *Nürnberg*, 1934.

6. *Völkischer Beobachter*, Munich ed., 8 September 1934 (No. 251).

7. Carl Schmitt, *Staat, Bewegung, Volk. Die Dreigliederung der politischen Einheit*, Hamburg, 1933.

8. Ernst Rudolf Huber, 'Die Totalität des völkischen Staates,' in *Die Tat*, 1934, pp. 30-42; also his 'Das deutsche Staatsoberhaupt,' in the *Zeitschrift für die gesamte Staatswissenschaft*, 1935, p. 210; and many others.

9. *Die Reden Hitlers am Parteitag der Freiheit* 1935, Munich, 1935, especially pp. 80, 81.

10. Otto Mayer, *Deutsches Verwaltungrecht*, 2nd ed., Vol. II, Munich and Leipzig, 1917, p. 591.

11. Anton Lingg, *Die Verwaltung der Nationalsozialistischen Deutschen Arbeiterpartei*, 2nd ed., Munich, 1940. Ernst Rudolf Huber, 'Die Rechtsgestalt der NSDAP,' in *Deutsche Rechtswissenschaft*, 1939, pp. 314-57; Gottfried Neesse, 'Die Rechtsnatur der NSDAP,' in the *Zeitschrift für die gesamte Staatswissenschaft*, 1935, pp. 709-18; also his 'Die verfassungsrechtliche Stellung der Einpartei,' in the same, 1938, p. 692.

12. Heinrich Himmler, *Die Schutzstaffel als antibolschewistische Kampforganisation*, Munich, 1936, especially p. 21.

13. *Juristische Wochenschrift*, 1938, p. 3289, decision of 14 November 1938.

14. *Verwaltungsblatt*, 1939, No. 147.

15. Werner Best, 'Die Schutzstaffeln der NSDAP und die Polizei,' in the *Deutsches Recht*, 1939, p. 47.

16. *Völkischer Beobachter*, 3 July 1939, No. 183, 184.

17. Hans-Helmut Dietze, 'Die verfassungsrechtliche Stellung der Hitler-Jugend,' in the *Zeitschrift für die gesamte Staatswissenschaft*, 1940 (100), pp. 113-56, especially pp. 132-7.

18. *Soziale Praxis*, 1939, p. 47.

19. Arnold Köttgen, 'Vom deutschen Staatsleben,' in the *Jahrbuch des öffentlischen Rechts*, 1937 (24); p. 58.

20. Lingg, op. cit. p. 113.

21. Prussian Court of Appeals (Stettin), 25 March 1936, in the *Juristische Wochenschrift*, 1937, p. 241; Prussian Court of Appeals (Kassel), 8 July 1936; especially, the Federal Supreme Court, 17 February 1939 in the *Deutsches Recht*, 1939, p. 1785. There is an extensive discussion of the problem in Lingg's book, pp. 278-303. Compare also Ernst Fraenkel, *The Dual State. A Contribution to the Theory of Dictatorship*, New York, 1941, pp. 34-7, in which decisions of many kinds are discussed.

22. Lingg, op. cit. p. 303.

23. 'Die Parteigerichtsbarkeit,' in the *Deutsches Recht*, 1934, No. 4.

24. Dr. Frick, 'Partei und Staat,' in the *Deutsche Verwaltung*, 1934, Nos. 15 and 16.

25. *Münchner Neueste Nachrichten*, November 1938, No. 319, 320.

26. Ibid. p. 21.

27. Hans Peter Ipsen, 'Vom Begriff der Partei,' in the *Zeitschrift für die gesamte Staatswissenschaft*, 1940 (100), pp. 309-36, and 477-510, especially p. 487.

28. Fritz Morstein Marx, *Government in the Third Reich*, 2nd ed., New York, 1937, pp. 67-8.

29. Mussolini, *The Political and Social Doctrine of Fascism*, trans. by J. Soames, London, 1933, pp. 21-2.

30. Sergio Panunzio, *Allgemeine Theorie des faschistischen Staates*, Berlin, 1934, p. 28.
31. Alfredo Rocco, *La dottrina politica del Fascismo*, Rome, 1925.
32. Giovanni Gentile, *Che cosa é il fascismo*, Firenze, 1924, p. 35.
33. V. Zangara, *Il partito e' lo Stato*, Catania, 1935, p. 37. More recently, opposition has begun to arise to the acceptance of the traditional view of a state personality and to the subordination of party to state. See C. Costamagna, *Storia e' Dottrina del Fascismo*, Turin, 1938, trans. into German under the title *Faschismus, Entwicklung und Lehre*, Berlin, 1939. As yet, I have been able to observe no practical consequences of the new opposition.
34. Editorial written by Mussolini on 6 April 1920 and quoted in A. Borgese, *Goliath*, New York, 1937, p. 224.
35. Ignazio Silone, *Der Faschismus*, Zurich, 1934, p. 73.
36. Erwin von Beckerath, *Wesen und Werden des faschistischen Staates*, Berlin, 1927, pp. 7-9.
37. There is an excellent analysis of the situation in agrarian Italy after the World War in Friedrich Vöchting, *Die Romagna*, Karlsruhe, 1927, p. 363 f., 418 f.
38. Silone, op. cit. p. 35.
39. L. T. Hobhouse, *The Metaphysical Theory of the State*, London, 1926.
40. We must make a distinction. There are some who maintain that Hegel is the greatest German political philosopher, but make no attempt to adapt his theory to National Socialism. These merely pay him a compliment and no more: for example, Hans Frank, president of the Academy of German Law, in his 'Die Aufgaben des Rechts,' in the *Zeitschrift der Akademie für Deutsches Recht*, 1938, p. 4. Others attempt to reconstruct Hegel's theory and make it useful to National Socialism, as, for the best example, Karl Larenz, 'Die Bedeutung der völkischen Sitte in Hegels Staatsphilosophie,' in the *Zeitschrift für die gesamte Staatswissenschaft*, 1938 (98), p. 110, where he says, 'It is not the state in the ordinary meaning of the term that was Hegel's most proper and original interest, but the community of life as a whole with a character and a most comprehensive activity of its own.' Hegel would have shuddered at such a definition. Finally, the most influential political theorists reject the Hegelian political philosophy because it glorifies the state. Among these, we can mention Alfred Rosenberg, *Mythus* . . . , pp. 525-7; Otto Koellreuter, *Volk und Staat in der Weltanschauung der Nationalsozialismus*, Berlin, 1935, pp. 12-15; and above all, Carl Schmitt, *Staat, Bewegung* . . . , pp. 31-2, in which he says, 'On this thirtieth of January [the day of Hitler's appointment] . . . the Hegelian civil service state of the nineteenth century . . . gave way to another state structure. On this day, one can therefore say, Hegel died.' Then follows the usual compliment to Hegel's greatness.
41. Herbert Marcuse, *Reason and Revolution. Hegel and the Rise of Social Theory*, New York, 1941. I am in complete agreement with Dr. Marcuse's analysis. As for Treitschke's denunciation of the Teutonism of the *Burschenschaften*, see Heinrich von Treitschke, *Deutsche Geschichte im neunzehnten Jahrhundert*, 3rd ed., 1886, Vol. II, pp. 383-443.
42. *Philosophy of Right*, trans. by W. Dyde, London, 1896, pp. 289-97.
43. Max Weber, 'Wirtschaft und Gesellschaft,' in *Grundriss der Sozialökonomik*, III, Tübingen, 1922.

44. Hans Gerth, 'The Nazi Party: Its Leadership and Composition,' in *The American Journal of Sociology*, 1940, No. XLV, pp. 517-41.
45. Lingg, op. cit. p. 83.
46. Franz Schwarz in a speech delivered 1 April 1939, as quoted by Lingg, op. cit. p. 17.
47. Oskar Redelsberger, 'Von der NSDAP betreute Organisation—ein neues Rechtsgebilde,' in the *Deutsche Verwaltung*, 1939, p. 132.
48. Gerth, op. cit. p. 522. Prior to the incorporation of Austria and the Sudetenland.

III: The Charismatic Leader in the Leadership State

1. C. A. Emge, *Ideen zu einer Philosophie des Führertums*, Berlin, 1936, p. 7.
2. Otto Koellreuter, *Der Deutsche Führerstaat*, Tübingen, 1934.
3. Ernst Rudolf Huber, 'Das Staatsoberhaupt des Deutschen Reichs,' in the *Zeitschrift für die gesamte Staatswissenschaft*, 1935, (95), pp. 202-29, especially 207. Also Reinhard Höhn, 'Der Führerbegriff im Staatsrecht,' in the *Deutsches Recht* (1935), p. 298; and his 'Führer oder Staatsperson,' in the *Deutsche Juristen-Zeitung* (1935), p. 66. Dr. Frick, *Der Neubau des Dritten Reichs*, Berlin (n.d.). Fritz Morstein Marx, *Government in the Third Reich*, 2nd ed., New York, 1937. Karl Loewenstein, 'Germany and Central Europe' in *Governments of Continental Europe*, ed. James T. Shotwell, New York, 1940. Hans Gerth, 'The Nazi Party: Its Leadership and Composition,' op. cit.
4. Arnold Köttgen, 'Vom Deutschen Staatsleben,' in the *Jahrbuch für öffentliches Recht*, op. cit.
5. Gottfried Neesse, *Führergewalt*, Tübingen, 1940; also Ernst Rudolf Huber, *Verfassung des Grossdeutschen Reichs*, Hamburg, 1939, p. 69.
6. 'Wirtschaft und Gesellschaft,' op. cit. pp. 140-48.
7. W. Tyndale, 'Obedience of a Christian Man,' published among the *Doctrinal Treatises*, ed. H. Walter (Parker Society), Cambridge, England, 1843, p. 178.
8. From early Tudor pamphlets contained in Franklin le van Baumer, *The Early Tudor Theory of Kingship*, New Haven, 1940, p. 86.
9. 'Admonition to Peace: A Reply to the Twelve Articles of the Peasants in Swabia 1525,' in *Works of Martin Luther*, Vol. IV, trans. by C. M. Jacobs, p. 240.
10. 'Whether Soldiers, Too, Can Be Saved,' 1526, Vol. V, p. 34.
11. 'Aus der Heerpredigt.'
12. 'Treatise on Good Works,' 1520, trans. by W. A. Lambert, Vol. I, pp. 184-286, p. 250, and p. 271.
13. 'An Open Letter Concerning the Hard Book against the Peasants,' 1525, Vol. IV, p. 272.
14. 'Against the Robbing and Murdering Hordes of Peasants,' 1525, Vol. IV, p. 249.
15. *Institution*; J. Bonnet's edition of the *Lettres Françaises de Calvin*, 2 vols., Paris, 1854; also, Marc Edouard Chenevière, *La Pensée Politique de Calvin*, Geneva and Paris, n.d. (1937).
16. From the *Catechism* of 1557, cited by Chenevière, op. cit. p. 50.
17. 'Confession à l'Empereur,' 1562, cited ibid. p. 50.
18. *Institution*, II, 2, 13.

19. Ibid.
20. Ibid.
21. Ibid. II, 2, 17; also II, 2, 14.
22. *Corpus Reformatorum*, Vol. 33, p. 542, cited by Chenevière, op. cit. p. 59.
23. *Institution*, II, 2, 15.
24. *Corpus Reformatorum*, Vol. 27, p. 409; cited by Chenevière, op. cit. p. 83.
25. *Institution*, Vol. II, 2, 24.
26. *Corpus Reformatorum*, Vol. 27, p. 412; cited by Chenevière, op. cit. p. 118.
27. G. de Lagarde, *Recherches sur l'esprit politique de la réforme*, Paris, 1936, p. 227.
28. Bonnet, op. cit. Vol. I, p. 346.
29. *Institution*, IV, 14, 17.
30. This has been convincingly shown by Kurt Wolzendorff, *Staatsrecht und Naturrecht in der Lehre vom Widerstandsrecht des Volkes gegen unrechtmässige Ausübung der Staatsgewalt*, Breslau, 1916.
31. *Institution*, IV, 20, 30.
32. Sir James Frazer, *The Golden Bough*; A. M. Hocart, *Kingship*, London, 1927, pp. 32-7.
33. W. O. E. Oesterly, *The Evolution of the Messianic Idea*, London, 1908, p. 41.
34. Lord Raglan, *The Hero, a Study in Tradition, Myth, and Drama*, New York, 1937, pp. 268-76.
35. Hocart, op. cit. p. 7.
36. Julius Kaerst, *Studien zur Entwickelung und theoretischen Begründung der Monarchie im Altertum*, Munich and Leipzig, 1898, pp. 40, 41.
37. August Freiherr von Gapp, βασιλεια του θεου (The Kingdom of God), *eine religionsgeschichtliche Studie zur vorchristlichen Eschatologie*, Heidelberg, 1926, pp. 452-3.
38. *Odes*, 1, 2, 42.
39. Fritz Kern, *Gottesgnadentum und Widerstandsrecht im früheren Mittelalter*, Leipzig, 1914, p. 20.
40. The most important publication in the field is that of Marc Bloch, *Les Rois Thaumaturges, étude sur le caractère surnaturel attribué à la puissance royale, particulièrement en France et en Angleterre*, Strasbourg, 1924. A very important letter is reprinted on page 123, addressed by Pope Gregory VII to Archbishop Hermann of Metz. I quote it here in English translation: 'Where among the emperors and kings does one find a man whose miracles can equal those of St. Martin, St. Anton, or St. Benoit, not to mention the Apostles or martyrs? Which emperor or king has resuscitated the dead, cured lepers, and given sight to the blind? Consider Emperor Constantine, of pious memory, Theodore and Honorius, Charles and Louis, all friends of justice, propagators of Christian religion, defenders of the church. The Holy Church praises and reveres them; it does not indicate that they have excelled through the glory of such miracles.'
41. *Policraticus*, ed. C. C. J. Webb, Oxford, 1909, Vol. I, p. 202 (3.10).
42. Bloch, op. cit. p. 129.
43. Ibid. p. 149.
44. Ibid. p. 377.
45. There is an interesting analysis in Ronald Syme, *The Roman Revolution*, Oxford, 1939, especially pp. 469-75.
46. Oesterley, op. cit.

47. Cf. Rudolf Otto, *The Idea of the Holy*, trans. by John W. Harvey, 3rd imp., London, 1925.
48. The early church reveals this quite clearly. The late Rudolph Sohm, the famous German legal historian (*Kirchenrecht*, 2 vols., Munich and Leipzig, 1923), based his studies in ecclesiastical law on the famous declaration that 'ecclesiastical law is at variance with the essence of the Church' (Vol. I, p. 1). According to Sohm, the early church organization was not legal but charismatic (Vol. I, p. 26), handed down by God. There was no abstract equality within it, only an ordering of superiority and inferiority, according to how God distributed his gifts (Vol. I, p. 27). The obedience required by the charisma was not based on formal laws, but was voluntary, born of the conviction that God willed it (Vol. I, p. 27; Vol. II, p. 178).

IV: The Racial People, the Source of Charisma

1. Ruth Benedict, *Race: Science and Politics*, New York, 1940, p. 11 f.
2. Arnold J. Toynbee, *A Study of History*, London, 1934, Vol. I, p. 245.
3. Ralph Linton, *The Study of Man*, New York, 1936, p. 34.
4. Benedict, op. cit. p. 241.
5. Otto Bauer, *Die Nationalitätenfrage und die Sozialdemokratie* (*Marx-Studien*, Vol. II), Vienna, 1924, p. 114.
6. Benjamin Disraeli, 'Whigs and Whigism,' in the *Political Writings* . . . , London, 1913, p. 343.
7. The most careful analysis of the meanings of the different terms appears in F. J. Neumann, *Volk und Nation*, Leipzig, 1888. For a short but precise account, see *Nationalism*, a report by a group of the Royal Institute of International Affairs, London, 1939, pp. xvi-xx.
8. Friedrich Hertz, 'Wesen und Werden der Nation,' in the *Ergänzungsband der Jahrbücher für Soziologie*, Karlsruhe, 1927, pp. 84-7.
9. *Social Contract* (Everyman's Library Edition), Book I, chapter 6.
10. Ibid. Book I, chapter 8.
11. Book I, chapter 3. For Rousseau's influence on the theory of the nation, compare *Nationalism*, pp. 27-8.
12. It is only in this sense that we can agree with Professor Barker's statement that 'It is possible for nations to exist, and even to exist for centuries, in unreflective silence' (see Ernest Barker, *The National Character and the Factors of its Formation*, London, 1917, p. 116). Until reflection has begun, we can only speak of a people.
13. Carré de Malberg, *Contribution à la théorie générale de l'Etat*, 2 vols., Paris, 1920, Vol. II, p. 168.
14. Neumann, op. cit. p. 124.
15. Ernest Renan, *Qu'est-ce qu'une nation?* Paris, 1882, p. 217. On the political significance of Renan's theory (reconquest of Alsace-Lorraine), see Hertz, op. cit. p. 56.
16. Fichte, *Address to the German Nation*, trans. by R. F. Jones and G. H. Turnbull, Chicago, 1922.
17. Friedrich Meinecke, *Weltbürgertum und Nationalstaat*, 6th ed., Munich, 1922, p. 39.
18. *Politik*, I, 280.
19. *Our Country*, New York, 1885, p. 179. Strong's other works include *Expansion*, 1900, *Our World*, 1913. On this phase of American intellectual

history, cf. Ralph Henry Gabriel, *The Course of American Democratic Thought*, New York, 1940, pp. 340-44.

20. Herder, *Outlines of a Philosophy of History of Man*, trans. by T. O. Churchill, London, 1800, p. 447. A good survey is given in Charles Callan Tansill, 'Racial Theories from Herder to Hitler,' in *Thought*, 1940, Vol. XV, pp. 453-68.
21. *Philosophy of History*, trans. by J. B. Robertson, London, 1888, pp. 310, 348; and Tansill, op. cit. pp. 456 f.
22. *Politics*, trans. by B. Dugdale and T. de Bille, New York, 1916, Vol. I, p. 50 f.
23. *Deutsche Geschichte im neunzehnten Jahrhundert*, 3rd ed., 1886, Vol. II, pp. 383-443.
24. *Politics*, Vol. I, p. 96.
25. Trans. by S. S. Lloyd, New York, 1909.
26. 'Über den Wert und die Bedingungen einer Allianz swischen Grossbritannien und Deutschland' (1846), in Friedrich List, *Schriften, Reden, Briefe*, Vol. III, Berlin, 1931, pp. 267-98.
27. Ibid. p. 283.
28. The reader will find an excellent analysis of Wagner's theories and influence in Evelyn A. Clark, 'Adolf Wagner: from National Economist to Nationalist Socialist,' *Political Science Quarterly*, 1940, Vol. LV, pp. 398-411.
29. Adolph Wagner, *Grundlegung der politischen Ökonomie*, 3rd ed., Vol. I, Leipzig, 1892, p. 6.
30. Ibid. p. 47.
31. *Preussische Jahrbücher*, 1868, Vol. XXI, pp. 379-402.
32. Adolph Wagner, *Elsass-Lothringen und ihre Wiedergewinnung für Deutschland*, 2nd ed., Leipzig, 187, p. 2 f.
33. *Die Grundlagen des neunzehnten Jahrhunderts*, trans. by John Lees, New York, 1912.
34. Trans. by A. Collins, New York, 1915.
35. William Langer, *The Diplomacy of Imperialism, 1890-1902*, 2 vols., New York, 1935, Vol. II, p. 417.
36. *Foundations*, Vol. I, lxvi-lxviii.
37. Tansill, op. cit. p. 464.
38. *Cosima Wagner und H. S. Chamberlain im Briefwechsel* 1888-1908, Leipzig, 1934.
39. Ibid. p. 36.
40. Ibid. p. 604 f.; p. 642 contains an attack on Mommsen.
41. Ibid. p. 641.
42. *König Ludwig II. und Richard Wagner im Briefwechsel*, 4 vols., Karlsruhe, 1936, Vol. III, p. 236.
43. The quotations are taken from the research project 'Antisemitism' of the Institute of Social Research, published in *Studies in Philosophy and Social Science*, 1940.
44. Cf. J. W. Parkes, *The Jewish Problem in the Modern World* (Home University Library), London, 1939, p. 60.
45. Clark, op. cit. p. 398 f. For the best survey of Anti-Semitic parties, Kurt Wawrzinek, *Die Entstehung der deutschen Antisemitenparteien*, Berlin, 1927, esp. pp. 18-30. The official National Socialist biography of Stoecker was written by Walter Frank (President of the Federal Institute for the

History of New Germany), *Hofprediger Adolf Stoecker*, 2nd ed., Hamburg, 1935.

46. See chapter XI, pp. 419-50.

47. For information on National Socialism's adoption of the *Protocols*, see Hitler, *Mein Kampf*, p. 423 f. The Protocols were the subject of a trial in Berne, Switzerland, where a publisher was indicted for having printed them. The basis of the indictment was the Berne statute of 10 September 1915 making the distribution of 'trash' (*Schund*) punishable. The charge was dismissed because the Protocols were not deemed to come under the provisions of the statute. The trial, however, remains important because for the first time an impartial agency clearly stated on the basis of exhaustive evidence that the Protocols constitute a mixture of bold plagiarism, falsification, and absurdity. Cf. the report of Emil Raas and Georges Brunschwig, *Vernichtung einer Fälschung. Der Prozess um die erfundenen 'Weisen von Zion,'* Zürich, 1938.

48. A Statute to Protect the Hereditary Health of the German People (*Ehegesundheitsgesetz*), 18 October 1935.

49. Statute against Habitual Criminals, 24 November 1933; Statute to Prevent Hereditarily Diseased Offspring, 14 July 1933, as amended 26 June 1935 and 4 February 1936.

50. I cite a few decisions. (1) A forty-year-old peasant who had been working all his life under the direction of his parents was ordered sterilized for imbecility. 'The peasant must be able to read and count correctly.' 4 April 1939 (Jena), *Deutsches Recht* (1939), p. 1400. (2) Sterilization was ordered although the specialist could not discover whether the case of epilepsy under observation was more than transitory. 22 March 1939 (Jena), *Deutsches Recht* (1939), p. 1400. (3) Even a single appearance of schizophrenia suffices for sterilization to be ordered. 4 June 1940 (Jena), *Deutsches Recht* (1940), p. 2031. (4) Strong and complicated short-sightedness is equal to blindness. 15 June 1938 (Jena), *Juristische Wochenschrift* (1938), p. 2914. (5) A cataract, even if successfully operated upon, is cause for sterilization, since the cataract may return. This decision is highly praised. 8 March 1938 (Berlin), *Juristische Wochenschrift* (1938), p. 2913.

51. Now in his book *Berlin Diary*, New York, 1941, pp. 569-75. This report is supplemented by the article of Michael Straight in *The New Republic* of 5 May 1941, reproducing in photostat the attacks of the Vatican against mercy killings. Similar facts are reported by J. C. Harsch in the *Christian Science Monitor* of 13 March 1941.

52. On the decline of the Jewish population, see *The American Jewish Year Book*, New York, 1940, p. 600. This volume contains the best statistics available on the distribution of Jews.

53. Alfred Marcus, *Die wirtschaftliche Krise der deutschen Juden*, Berlin, 1930.

54. Race betrayal outside of Germany: Decision of the Great Penal Senate, 23 February 1938, recorded in the *Zeitschrift der Akademie für Deutsches Recht* (1938), p. 349. Decision of the Penal Senate, 9 February 1940, recorded in *Deutsches Recht* (1940), p. 790. Decision of the Landgericht, Aachen, 23 October 1939, recorded in *Deutsche Justiz* (1939), p. 372. Decision of the Landgericht, Hamburg, 29 April 1938, recorded in the *Zeitschrift der Akademie für Deutsches Recht* (1938), p. 569.

55. Eduard Kohlrausch, 'Rasseverrat im Ausland,' in the *Zeitschrift der Aka-*

demie für Deutsches Recht (1938), pp. 335 and 569. For the opposite view, see Reichsgerichtsrat Dr. Schwarz (member of the federal supreme court), 'Das Verbrechen der Rassenschande,' in the *Zeitschrift der Akademie für Deutsches Recht* (1937), p. 459.

56. Decision of 28 March 1938 published in the *Juristische Wochenschrift* (1938), p. 1239. Decision of 21 March 1938, ibid. p. 1240.

57. Decision of 19 September 1938, ibid. p. 2952; Decision of the Great Penal Senate, 9 December 1936, reported in the *Juristische Wochenschrift* (1937), p. 160.

58. Decision of 28 November 1938, reported ibid. (1938), p. 228.

59. Decision of 5 January 1939, reported ibid. (1939) p. 340.

60. Decision of 14 October 1938, ibid. p. 34.

61. Federal supreme court in the *Juristische Wochenschrift* (1938), p. 1826; also Fraenkel, op. cit. p. 92.

62. Federal supreme labor court, ibid. (1937), p. 2310; Fraenkel, op. cit. p. 92.

63. Günter Keiser, 'Der jüngste Konzentrationsprozess,' in *Die Wirtschafts-kurve* 1939 (18), p. 148.

64. *Der Deutsche Volkwirt*, 1938 (XII), No. 41.

65. For example, the Bavarian Administrative Tribunal, as revealed in an article written by Otto Rilk, 'Judentum und Wirtschaft in der neuen deutschen Rechtsprechung,' in the *Juristische Wochenschrift* (1938), p. 2533.

66. Federal supreme court in the *Juristische Wochenschrift* (1936), p. 333.

67. Federal supreme court in the *Deutsches Recht* (1939), p. 437.

68. Federal supreme court in the *Juristische Wochenschrift* (1937), pp. 2310, 2707.

69. A good survey of material relative to this interpretation may be found in an article by Kammergerichtsrat Dr. Höver (member of the Prussian supreme court), 'Entjudungsfragen,' in the *Deutsches Recht* (1941), p. 12. For decisions, see those of the Prussian supreme court reported in *Deutsches Recht* (1940), pp. 820, 459, and 42.

70. Prussian supreme court in the *Deutsches Recht* (1939), p. 2110.

71. Höver, op. cit. p. 13.

72. *Die Rassengesetzgebung des Dritten Reiches*, Munich, 1934.

73. Term of Jacques Maritain, *Anti-Semitism*, London, 1939, p. 27.

74. Harold D. Lasswell, 'The Psychology of Hitlerism,' in *The Political Quarterly*, 1933 (IV), pp. 373-84. P. 374 is an excellent analysis of Anti-Semitism, even if I cannot accept L.'s theory that Hitler plays the 'maternal role for certain classes in German society' (p. 379).

75. Lasswell, op. cit. p. 380.

76. Wilhelm Grau, *Die Judenfrage als Aufgabe der neuen Geschichtsforschung*, Hamburg, 1935.

77. Grau, *Wilhelm von Humboldt und das Problem der Juden*, Hamburg, 1935.

78. Walter Frank, *Nationalismus und Demokratie im Frankreich der Dritten Republik*, Hamburg, 1933.

79. Frank, *Höre Israel! Harden, Rathenau und die moderne Judenfrage*, Hamburg, 1939.

80. *Das Judentum in der Rechtswissenschaft* (9 pamphlets), Berlin, n.d.

81. Italian Anti-Semitism is merely a device, a matter of convenience, although the former party secretary, Farinacci, and Paolo Orano (*Gli Ebrei in Italia*, 1937) developed an Anti-Semitic doctrine. Cf. Martin Agronsky,

'Racism in Italy,' in *Foreign Affairs*, 1939 (17), pp. 391-401, and Israel Cohen, 'Jews in Italy,' in *The Political Quarterly*, 1939 (10), pp. 405-18.
82. Op. cit. chapter xiv.
83. Eastern and Southeastern Jews under German rule (July 1940):

Country	Prior to Territorial Changes	Emigrated	Now Under German Rule
Austria .	181,778	117,000	56,000
Czechoslovakia	356,830		
Bohemia-Moravia	117,551	20,000	75,000
Slovakia	136,737	....	85,045*
Carpatho-Ukraine	102,542	....	....
Poland	3,325,000	....	2,200,000
Roumania	758,226	....	438,226
Bulgaria	48,398	....	48,398
	5,027,062	137,000	2,902,669

* 88,951, according to a report from Bratislava. *New York Times*, 21 March 1941. Source: 'Statistics of Jews, 1940' from *The American Jewish Year Book, 5701*, New York, 1940, pp. 589-632, especially p. 600.

84. Cf. Albert Weh (on the staff of the Generalgouvernement), 'Das Recht des Generalgouvernements,' in *Deutsches Recht*, 1940, pp. 1393-1403.
85. This is the main thesis of Maurice Samuel, *The Great Hatred*, New York, 1940.
86. Heinrich Härtle, *Nietzsche und der Nationalsozialismus*, Munich, 1937 (official), pp. 45-6.
87. All quotations are based on the edition of Oscar Levy, *The Complete Works of Friedrich Nietzsche*, 18 vols., London, 1903-13. *Genealogy of Morals*, 407 d, Aphorism 765.
88. *The Will to Power*, Aphorism 765. Vol. 15, p. 212.
89. Ibid. Aphorism 215. Vol. 14, p. 178.
90. *Twilight of the Idols*, Aphorism 43. Vol. 16, p. 186.
91. Ibid. Aphorism 39. Vol. 16, p. 230.
92. *The Will to Power*, 150-51, Aphorism 209.
93. Cf. Crane Brinton, *Nietzsche*, Cambridge (Mass.), 1941, esp. pp. 172-243. Unfortunately Brinton does not treat the actual dissemination of N.'s ideas among the various groups of the German people and the transformation of his ideas during this process of popularization. This important task is still to be done. That Nietzsche does not at all fit in an authoritarian order has been admirably brought out by Alfred von Martin, *Nietzsche und Burckhardt*, Munich, 1941, esp. p. 33.

V: The Grossdeutsche Reich

1. From R. R. Kuczynski, *Living Space and Population Problems* (Pamphlets on World Affairs, No. 8), New York, 1939, pp. 4-5.
2. *Frankfurter Zeitung*, 1 October 1939.
3. Fritz Kern, *Humana Civilitas*, Leipzig, 1913, esp. p. 33.
4. Excellent analysis of Stefan George: Paul Rosenfeld, 'The Nazis and Stefan George,' in *The New Republic*, 28 October 1940.
5. Alfred Rosenberg, 'Gegen Tarnung und Verfälschung,' in *Gestaltung der Idee. Blut und Ehre*, 11. Band, Munich, 1936, pp. 15-19.
6. Fedor Schneider, *Rom und der Romgedanke im Mittelalter*, München, 1926, p. 221.
7. F. Wolters, *Stefan George und die Blätter für die Kunst*, Berlin, 1930.
8. An excellent analysis of this aspect of George's philosophy: Herbert

Marcuse 'Der Kampf gegen den Liberalismus in der totalitären Staatsauffassung,' in *Zeitschrift für Sozialforschung*, 1934 (3), pp. 161-95, esp. p. 162.

9. *Das Dritte Reich*, 3rd ed.; ed. by Hans Schwarz (first ed. 1922), Hamburg, 1931, p. 300; partial trans. by E. O. Lorimer, *Germany's Third Empire*, New York, 1941.

10. Christoph Steding, *Das Reich und die Krankheit der europäischen Kultur*, Hamburg, 1938. Excellent review by Günther Stern in *Studies in Philosophy and Social Science*, 1939 (VIII), pp. 464-8.

11. *Stern*, op. cit.

12. Heinrich Triepel, *Die Hegemonie. Ein Buch von führenden Staaten*, Stuttgart and Berlin, 1938.

13. Roger Diener, 'Reichsproblem und Hegemonie,' in *Deutsches Recht*, 1939, pp. 561-6.

14. Otto Haussleiter, 'Rudolf Kjellens empirische Staatslehre und ihre Wurzeln in politischer Geographie und Staatenkunde,' in *Archiv für Sozialwissenschaft und Sozialpolitik*, 1925, Vol. 54, p. 157.

15. Survey by Charles Kruczewski, 'Germany's Lebensraum,' in *The American Political Science Review*, XXXIV, 1940, pp. 964-75.

16. Friedrich Ratzel, *Anthropogeographie*, Vol. I, 2nd ed., 1899, p. 21.

17. Op. cit. p. 33.

18. *Der Lebensraum. Eine biographische Studie* (Festgabe für A. Schäffle), Tübingen, 1911, p. 14.

19. *Anthropogeographie*, p. 211.

20. Ibid. p. 101.

21. Ibid. pp. 317-470, esp. p. 212.

22. Ibid. p. 12.

23. *Politische Geographie*, 2nd ed., Munich, 1903, p. 35.

24. Rudolf Kjellen, *Die Grossmächte vor und nach dem Kriege*, 22nd ed., ed. by K. Haushofer, 1930.

25. *Der Staat als Lebensform*, 4th ed., Berlin, 1924, p. 35.

26. Sir Halford MacKinder, 'The Geographical Pivot in History,' in *Geographical Magazine*, 1904, pp. 434-7.

27. Paul de Lagarde, *Deutsche Schriften* (new ed. by K. A. and P. Fischer under the title *Schriften für des deutsche Volk*), 2 vols., Munich, 1924.

28. Berlin, 1915; trans. by C. M. Meredith, London, 1916.

29. Survey of his writings in Kruczewski, op. cit.

30. K. Haushofer and K. Trempler, *Deutschlands Weg an der Zeitenwende*, Munich, 1932.

31. *Zukunftsweg einer deutschen Aussenpolitik*, Munich, 1927.

32. Ewald Banse, *Germany Prepares for War*, trans. by A. Harris, New York, 1934, p. 349.

33. *Was der Deutsche vom Ausland wissen muss*, Leipzig, 1934.

34. An excellent analysis is to be found in the paper by A. Whitney Griswold, 'Paving the Way for Hitler,' in *The Atlantic*, March 1941, pp. 314-21.

35. W. G. East, 'The Nature of Political Geography,' in *Politica*, 1937 (II), pp. 259-86.

36. D. V. Glass, *Population. Policies and Movements in Europe*, Oxford, 1940, pp. 458, 276, 278.

37. 'Ansprache des Herrn Reichsminister des Innern Dr. Frick,' in *Schriften-*

reihe des Reichsausschusses für Volksgesundheitsdienst, Heft 1, Berlin, 1933.

38. Dr. Stolzenburg, 'Entwicklung der Kriminalität,' in *Deutsche Justiz*, 1938, pp. 933-4, and Glass, op. cit. p. 285.
39. Glass, op. cit. p. 289.
40. R. R. Kuczynski, op. cit.
41. As reported by F. Thudichum, *Über unzulängliche Beschränkungen des Rechts der Verehelichung*, 1866, p. 66.
42. C. A. Weinhold, *Von der Überbevölkerung in Mitteleuropa und deren Folgen auf die Staaten und ihre Civilisation*, Halle, 1827.
43. Robert von Mohl, *Polizeiwissenschaft nach den Grundsätzen des Rechtsstaats*, Vol. 1. 1832.
44. H. Luden, *Über Sinn und Inhalt des Handbuchs der Weisheit*, 1811; K. H. Rau, *Lehrbuch der politischen Ökonomie*, 1826.
45. Günther Kraaz, 'Nationalsozialistisches Völkerrechtsdenken,' in *Reichs- und Preussisches Verwaltungsblatt*, 1934 (55), p. 7. Also Ernst Wolgast, 'Nationalsozialismus und internationales Recht,' in *Deutsches Recht*, 1934, p. 196, where he says: 'Also considerations of utility' make it advisable to accept international law, which always binds the stronger power.
46. Ludwig Schecher, *Deutsches Aussenstaatsrecht*, Berlin, 1933. Cf. especially the excellent discussion of Eduard Bristler (pen-name of John H. Herz): *Die Völkerrechtslehre des Nationalsozialismus*, Zürich, 1938.
47. Manfred Langhans-Ratzeburg, *Die grossen Mächte geojuristisch betrachtet*, Berlin, 1931.
48. Compare Bristler, op. cit. pp. 73-7.
49. *Nationalsozialismus und Völkerrecht*, Berlin, 1934.
50. Thus Professor Viktor Bruns (who was under the Weimar Republic, and still is Director of the Institute for Foreign Public Law and International Law, Berlin), *Völkerrecht und Politik*, Berlin, 1934, p. 24.
51. Franz Neumann, 'Types of Natural Law,' in *Studies in Philosophy and Social Science*, 1939 (VIII), pp. 338-61.
52. Carl Bilfinger, 'Gleichheit und Gleichberechtigung der Staaten,' in *Nationalsozialistisches Handbuch für Recht und Gesetzgebung*, 2nd ed., 1935, p. 100.
53. Bristler, op. cit. p. 83. Schmitt, op. cit. pp. 7, 8.
54. Heinrich Rogge, *Hitlers Friedenspolitik und das Völkerrecht*, Berlin, 1935, p. 10.
55. Lon L. Fuller, *The Law in Quest of Itself*, Chicago, 1940, p. 5.
56. Carl Schmitt, 'Sowjet-Union und Genfer Völkerbund,' in *Völkerbund und Völkerrecht*, 1934, 1935 (1), p. 263.
57. Carl J. Friedrich, 'Democracy and Dissent,' in *Political Quarterly*, 1939, pp. 571-82, attacked it quite recently.
58. Norbert Gürke, *Volk und Völkerrecht*, Tübingen, 1935, pp. 84, 99.
59. Bristler, op. cit. p. 134.
60. *The New York Times*, 28 March 1941. Compare the discussion by Philip C. Jessup, *Neutrality*, Vol. III, New York, 1936, p. 179.
61. Sir John Fisher-Williams, 'Sanctions under the Covenant,' and Arnold D. McNair, 'Collective Security.'
62. Carl Schmitt, 'Das neue Vae Neutris,' in *Völkerbund und Völkerrecht*, 1937-8 (4), pp. 633-8; *Die Wendung zum diskriminierenden Kriegsbegriff*, Munich, 1938.
63. Carl Bilfinger, 'Die Kriegserklärungen der Westmächte und der Kellogg-

pakt,' in *Zeitschrift für ausländisches öffentliches Recht und Völkerrecht*, 1940 (10), pp. 1-23.

64. Edwin Borchard and William Potter Lage, *Neutrality for the United States*, New Haven, 1937, p. 293.

65. Their letter: 21 September 1939.

66. H. A. Smith, 'Grossbritannien und die belgische Neutralität,' in *Völkerbund und Völkerrecht*, 1936-7 (3), pp. 513-18.

67. Dietrich Schindler (University of Zürich), 'Die schweizerische Neutralität,' pp. 413-44; and Edward Hambro, 'Das Neutralitätsrecht der nordischen Staaten,' in pp. 445-69, *Zeitschrift für ausländisches öffentliches Recht und Völkerrecht*, 1938 (8).

68. Carl Bilfinger, 'Englische Völkerrechtspolitik, ein Rückblick,' in *Deutsches Recht*, 1941, pp. 225-8.

69. Carl Schmitt, 'Raum und Grossraum im Völkerrecht,' in *Zeitschrift für Völkerrecht*, 1940 (24), pp. 145-79, p. 145.

70. S. S. Brigadeführer Dr. Werner Best, 'Rechtsbegriff und Völkerrecht,' in *Deutsches Recht*, 1939, pp. 1345-8.

71. Schmitt, op. cit. p. 145.

72. Ibid. p. 147.

73. Carl Schmitt, *Völkerrechtliche Grossraumordnung mit Interventionsverbot für raumfremde Mächte*, Berlin, Vienna, 1939, pp. 12, 13. The later editions were not accessible to me.

74. Ibid. p. 43.

75. Carl Schmitt, 'Der Reichsbegriff im Völkerrecht,' in *Deutsches Recht*, 1939, pp. 341-4. Carl Schmitt, 'Neutralität und Neutralisierung. Zu Christoph Steding . . .' in *Deutsche Rechtswissenschaft*, 1939 (4), pp. 97-118.

76. Ulrich Scheuner, 'Der Gedanke der Sicherheit Amerikas auf den Konferenzen von Panama und Habana und die Monroe-Doktrin,' in *Zeitschrift für Völkerrecht*, 1940 (24), pp. 273-92, esp. p. 275.

77. Ibid. p. 276.

78. 'Rights and Duties under International Law as affected by the U. S. Neutrality and the Resolution of Panama,' in *American Journal of International Law*, 1940 (34), p. 248.

79. Schmitt, *Völkerrechtliche Grossraumordung . . .*, p. 23; Heinrich Triepel, *Die Hegemonie*, pp. 298-301.

80. In 'Key,' 1940 (11), p. 116.

81. Art. 21 of the League Covenant. Compare James T. Shotwell, *War as an Instrument of National Policy*, New York, 1929, p. 20; and André N. Mandelstam, *L'interprétation du pacte Briand-Kellogg par les gouvernements et les parlements des Etats signataires*, Paris, 1934 (pp. 32-95 on the Monroe Doctrine).

82. In *Key*, 1940 (11), p. 118.

83. Max Hildebert Böhm, 'Minorities, national,' in *Encyclopedia of the Social Sciences*, Vol. x, p. 521; and Oscar I. Janowsky, 'The Treatment of Minorities,' in *International Conciliation*, 1941, No. 369, pp. 287-94.

84. An important document summarizing the situation of minorities is the memorandum transmitted to the House of Commons by Lord Cranborne, the then Under Secretary of State, and Mr. William Strang, then of the League of Nations. It is published in *The Congress of the European National Minorities*, H. M. Stationary Office, London, 1937.

85. The ideological basis has been primarily developed by Max Hildebert Böhm, *Das eigenständige Volk*, Göttingen, 1932. The most ardent advo-

cate is Werner Hasselblatt (counsel to the Union of German Folkish Groups in Europe). His contributions are: 'Die politischen Elemente eines werdenden Volksgruppenrechts,' in *Jahrbuch der Akademie des Deutschen Rechts*, 1938, Berlin and Munich, 1938, pp. 13-24; 'Volkspolitische Wende in Europa,' in *Europäische Revue*, 1939 (xv), pp. 28-34; 'Die sudetendeutschen Anträge über Volksgruppenrecht,' in *Zeitschrift der Akademie für Deutsches Recht*, 1937, pp. 353-61. Also: Herbert Kier, 'Über die Gestaltung eines Volksgruppenrechts,' in *Zeitschrift für ausländisches öffentliches Recht und Völkerrecht*, 1937 (vii), pp. 497-500; G. A. Walz, 'Grundlagen des Volksgruppenrechts,' in Paul Ritterbusch (ed.), *Politische Wissenschaft*, Berlin, 1940; and *Artgleichheit gegen Gleichartigkeit*, Hamburg, 1938, pp. 44, 45.

86. Frederick L. Schuman, *Europe on the Eve*, New York, 1939, p. 384.
87. '*Die sudetendeutschen Anträge* . . . ,' p. 353.
88. Ibid.
89. Schuman, op. cit. p. 387.
90. On the Hungarian-German and Rumanian-German minority treaties see Freiherr von Freytagh-Loringhoven, 'Politik und Recht,' in *Europäische Revue*, 1941 (xvii), p. 7.
91. *Deutsches Recht*, 1940, p. 1508.
92. The discussion is based on the following articles: Bälz (Ministerialrat, Prague), 'Die deutsche Gerichtsbarkeit im Protektorate Böhmen-Mähren in *Deutsches Recht*, 1940, pp. 1401-3. Krieser (Oberregierungsrat, Prague), 'Die deutsche Gerichtsbarkeit im Protektorate Böhmen-Mähren: Ausübung und Umfang,' ibid. pp. 1745-54; Dr. Nüsslein (Erster Staatsanwalt, Prague), 'Die deutsche Gerichtsbarkeit im Protektorate Böhmen-Mähren,' Strafrechtspflege,' ibid. pp. 2085-91.
93. *Bälz*, op. cit. p. 176.
94. 1. General: 14 April 1939. 2. Administration of penal justice: 14 April 1939, 18 September 1939. 3. Military justice: 8 May 1939. 4. Civil Justice: 14 April 1939, 3 May 1939, 5 September 1939, 20 March 1940. 5. The right of the protector to hand over cases to German courts: 4 April 1940. 6. Executive order of the federal minister of justice to establish branches of German courts outside their seats: 7 April 1939. (All decrees except No. 6 are published in the German *Reichsgesetzblatt*.)
95. Krieser, op. cit. p. 1745.
96. Freytagh-Loringhoven, op. cit.
97. Lawrence Preuss, 'National Socialist Conceptions of International Law,' in *American Political Science Review*, 1935 (29), p. 594; opposite view, Bristler, op. cit. p. 72.
98. Edwin M. Borchard, *Diplomatic Protection of Citizens Abroad*, New York, 1919, p. 17; Quincey Wright, 'Fundamental Problems of International Organization,' in *International Conciliation*, 1941, No. 369, pp. 468-92, esp. p. 485.
99. Professor Quincey Wright, who has been kind enough to make these points in an exchange of letters, has also pointed to the experiences of the Civil War, which from the Northern point of view was a 'war of rebellion' and 'not a War between the States' as it is called in Southern circles.
100. Hans K. E. L. Keller, *Das Recht der Völker, l. Abschied vom Völkerrecht*, Berlin, 1938, p. 118.

101. Heinrich Rogge, *Nationale Friedenspolitik*, Berlin, 1934; *Hitlers Friedens-politik und das Völkerrecht*, Berlin, 1935; Bristler, op. cit. p. 110.
102. *Nationale Friedenspolitik*, p. 657.
103. *Die rassengesetzliche Rechtslehre, Grundlinien einer nationalsozialistischen Rechtspilosophie*, 2nd ed., Munich, 1933.
104. *Volk und Völkerrecht*, Tübingen, 1935; *Grundzüge des Völkerrechts*, Berlin, 1936; 'Der Staats- und Volksbegriff im Völkerrecht,' in *Deutsches Recht*, 1934, p. 333.
105. *Volk und Völkerrecht*, p. 99.
106. 'Rechtsbegriff und Völkerrecht,' pp. 1345-8; 'Rechtsbegriff und Gesetzge-bung,' p. 673; 'Rechtsbegriff und Verfassung,' p. 1207, in *Deutsches Recht*, 1939.
107. 'Rechtsbegriff und Völkerrecht,' p. 1347.
108. *Das Selbstbestimmungsrecht Europas*, Dresden, 1940; 'Das neue Europa, seine Lebenseinheit und Rechtsordung,' in *Deutsches Recht*, 1940, pp. 2081-4; *Der Weg zur völkischen Wirtschaft und zur europäischen Gross-raumwirtschaft*, Dresden, 1938.
109. Rolf Fritzsche, *Aufbau der Wirtschaft im Dritten Reich*, Berlin, 1934, appendix.
110. 'Das neue Europa . . .'
111. Ibid. p. 2082.
112. Gustave Dumas, 'Documents from Occupied France,' in *Thought*, 1941 (16), pp. 133-41.
113. *Deutsches Recht*, 1941, p. 34.
114. Ibid. 1940, p. 1820.
115. *Norway Does Not Yield*, introd. by Mrs. J. Borden Harriman, publ. by the American Friends of German Freedom, New York, 1941; Josef Ter-boven, 'Neuordnung und Zusammenarbeit in Norwegen,' in *Europäische Revue* (17), 1941, pp. 13-20.
116. Decree of the federal commissioner, 26 October 1940, *Deutsches Recht*, 1940, p. 2100.
117. Ibid. p. 1819.
118. Werner Best, 'Die neue Gliederung und Verwaltung des emaligen pol-nischen Staatsgebiets,' in *Deutsches Recht*, 1939, pp. 2089-90. Julius von Medeazza (deputy of the governor general in Berlin), ibid. 1941, pp. 565-6. Julius von Medeazza, 'Ein Jahr Generalgouvernement,' ibid. 1940, pp. 1793-1807. Albert Weh (director of the department legislation in the office of the governor general), 'Das Recht des Generalgouvernements,' ibid. pp. 1393-1403.
119. Weh, op. cit. p. 1394.
120. *Deutsches Recht*, 1941, p. 913.
121. Weh, op. cit. p. 1396.
122. *Deutsches Recht*, 1940, p. 1819.
123. *In Europäische Revue* (15), pp. 238-43, pp. 337-42. See also K. Vowinckel, in *Zeitschrift für Geopolitik*, 1940 (17), p. 596.
124. The main German literature on the problem is: A. Predöhl, 'Die soge-nannten Handelshemmnisse und der Neuaufbau der Weltwirtschaft,' in *Weltwirtschaftliches Archiv*, 1940 (52), p. 193; Giselher Wirsing, *Zwi-scheneuropa und die deutsche Zukunft*, Jena, 1932; Ferdinand Fried, *Wende der Weltwirtschaft*, Leipzig, 1939; Ernst Wagemann, *Der neue Balkan, Altes Land — junge Wirtschaft*, Hamburg, 1939; Otto von Franges, 'Jugoslawiens Interesse am Vierjahresplan,' in *Der Vierjahresplan*, 1937

(1), 18; 'Der Vierjahresplan und die Industrialisierung der südosteuropäischen Agrarstaaten,' in *Europäische Revue*, 1939 (15), pp. 238; 'Die Donaustaaten Südosteuropas und der deutsche Grosswirtschaftsraum,' in *Weltwirtschaftliches Archiv*, 1941 (53), pp. 284-316; Bela Csikos-Nagy 'Zur Neuordnung der europäischen Wirtschaft,' in *Weltwirtschaftliches Archiv*, 1941 (53), pp. 126-35; and the studies of W. Daitz, see note 108 above.

125. Franges, 'Die Donaustaaten . . . ,' p. 515.

126. 'Die wirtschaftliche Gestaltung des europäischen Grossraumes,' in *Bank-Archiv*, 1941 (No. 3), p. 29.

127. Poland: see p. 180. In Belgium, 1941, 1 franc = 8 pfennig, 1 belga = 40 pfennig. *Deutsches Recht*, 1941, p. 1719. Denmark: Within four months, Germany succeeded in transforming a small German credit into a debt of 800,000,000 crowns. Only part of this debt is the cost of occupation. The largest part represents increased shipments of Danish goods to Germany. Cf. Henry Chalmers, 'Impact of War upon Trade Policies of Foreign Countries,' in *International Reference Service* (U. S. Department of Commerce), 1941 (1), No. 6.

128. W. Lepenies, 'Das Devisenrecht in den besetzten Gebieten und im Generalgouvernement,' in *Deutsches Recht*, 1941, pp. 89-91.

129. *Kartell-Rundschau*, 1940 (38), p. 41. See Louis Domeratzky, 'The German Cartel as an Instrument of Economic Control of the European Continent,' in *Foreign Commerce Weekly*, 1941 (3), No. 10.

130. i.e. the paper cartel in the Protectorate. *Kartell-Rundschau*, 1939 (37), p. 309.

131. Dresdner Bank acquires the *Nordböhmische Kohlenwerksgesellschaft* (mines) in Brüx: *Kartell-Rundschau*, 1939 (37), p. 255. The Allgemeine Deutsche Kreditanstalt (Bank), Leipzig, takes over the Länderbank, Prague: ibid. p. 259.

132. Sudetendeutsche Bergbau, A.-G.—a new combine. *Kartell-Rundschau*, 1940 (38), p. 351. Merger: Länderbank and Böhmische Escompte-Bank: ibid. p. 61. Concentration in the Bohemian iron industry: ibid. 1939 (37), p. 385.

133. Ibid. 1940 (38), p. 61.

134. Federal commissioner for the Unilever combine is Secretary of State Posse; see *Frankfurter Zeitung*, 2 July 1941.

135. Trustees are the big German combines; see page 277 of this book and *Frankfurter Zeitung*, 11 July 1941. On German banks in the New Order, see *Bank-Archiv*, 1941, No. 10, p. 214.

136. Julius von Medeazza, 'Ein Jahr . . . ,' p. 1776.

137. *Deutsches Recht*, 1940, p. 1874.

138. Ibid. p. 2100.

139. Terboven, op. cit. Foundation: 23 August 1940. The I. G. Farben participates, see *Frankfurter Zeitung*, 20 June 1941.

140. Terboven, op. cit.

141. *Vortrag Adolf Hitlers vor westdeutschen Wirtschaftlern im Industrieklub zu Düsseldorf am 27. Januar 1932.* 1st ed. Munich 1932, p. 13.

VI: The Theory of Racial Imperialism

1. General Ludendorff, *Der totale Krieg*, Munich, p. 87.

2. J. A. Hobson, *Imperialism*, London, 1938, p. xxi (introduction of 1938).

3. Albert K. Weinberg, *Manifest Destiny*, Baltimore, 1935, p. 286.
4. Ibid. p. 297.
5. William L. Langer, *The Diplomacy of Imperialism*, 1890-1902, 2 vols., New York, 1935, Vol. ii, p. 663.
6. Discussed for the U. S. in Mr. Weinberg's book; for England, cf. Langer, op. cit. Vol. i, pp. 67-100.
7. *New York Times*, 14 February 1940.
8. *Time Magazine*, 23 December 1940.
9. *New York Times*, 4 February 1940.
10. Peter Aldag, *Juden in England;* Vol. i: *Juden erobern England;* Vol. ii: *Juden beherrschen England*, Berlin, 1940.
11. Ibid. Vol. i, pp. 88-97.
12. Nibelungen-Verlag.
13. K. D. Schmidt (ed.), *Die Bekenntnisse des Jahres* 1933, Göttingen, 1934, p. 18.
14. *Frankfurter Zeitung*, 15 December 1940.
15. Ibid. 21 January 1941.
16. G. A. Borgese, *Goliath. The March of Fascism*, New York, 1937, pp. 248-9.
17. *Il Nazionalismo italiano*, Milano, 1914; *La Vita nazionale* (collected papers written in 1903, 1904), Siena, 1924. *Discorsi Politici*, Firenze, 1923. Illuminating discussion: Ignazio Silone, *Der Faschismus*, Zürich, 1934, pp. 267-72; Erwin von Beckerath, *Wesen und Werden des faschistischen Staates*, Berlin, 1927, pp. 18, 28-34.
18. *Il nazionalisimo*, p. 34.
19. *La vita*, p. 123.
20. Max Ascoli, *Georges Sorel*, Paris, 1921, p. 34.
21. *La vita*, p. 30.
22. *Discorsi*, p. 422.
23. Gaudens Megaro, *Mussolini in the Making*, Boston, 1938, p. 235.
24. Megaro, op. cit. pp. 86, 160, 250.
25. *Oeuvres* de Donoso Cortès, Marquis de Valdegamas, 3rd ed., Lyon, 1877 (L'église et la révolution, 1848; Discours sur la dictature, 1849), Vol. i, pp. 352 and 337.
26. Oswald Spengler, *Man and Technics*, trans. by C. F. Atkinson, London, 1932, p. 43. The translation is the text from Hans Speier, 'Germany in Danger. Concerning Oswald Spengler,' in *Social Research*, 1934 (1), p. 233.
27. *The Decline of the West*, trans. by C. F. Atkinson, New York, 1939, Vol. i, p. 452.
28. William L. Langer, op. cit. Vol. i, p. 85.
29. *Decline*, Vol. ii, p. 461.
30. Ibid. p. 463.
31. *Preussentum und Sozialismus*, Munich, 1920.
32. Ibid. p. 97.
33. Ibid. p. 98.
34. *The Hour of Decision*, trans. by C. F. Atkinson, New York, 1934, p. 145.
35. *Neubau des Deutschen Reiches*, Munich, 1924, p. 112.
36. *Decline*, Vol. ii, p. 454.
37. Ibid. p. 311.
38. Dr. Speier has drawn attention to it. Op. cit.
39. Excellent catholic critique of his social philosophy: Goetz Briefs, *Unter-*

gang des Abendlandes, Christentum und Sozialismus, Freiburg i. B., 1920. A survey of the Spengler discussion by theologians: Manfred Schroeter, *Der Streit um Spengler*, Munich, 1922, pp. 116-41.

40. *Das Dritte Reich*, 3rd ed., ed. by Hans Schwarz, Hamburg, 1931; *Das ewige Reich*, Vol. I, Die politischen Kräfte, Vol. II, Die geistigen Kräfte, Breslau, 1933 and 1934; *Sozialismus und Aussenpolitik*, Breslau, 1933.

41. Alfred Rosenberg, *Gestaltung der Idee*, Vol. I, 3rd ed., Munich, 1936, pp. 15-19.

42. On income from British investments overseas, see J. A. Hobson, op. cit. p. 375.

43. Sir Austen Chamberlain, *Politics from Inside*, New Haven, 1937.

44. Eckart Kehr, 'Englandhass und Weltpolitik,' in *Zeitschrift für Politik*, 1928 (7), pp. 500-26. 'Deutsch-englisches Bündnisproblem der Jahrhundertwende,' in *Die Gesellschaft*, 1928 (2), pp. 24-31.

45. Graf Westarp, *Konservative Politik*, Vol. I, 1904-14; Vol. II, 1914-18, Berlin, 1935.

46. Ibid. Vol. I, p. 168.

47. Ibid. Vol. II, p. 43.

48. Ibid. Vol. II, p. 50.

49. 'Die Deutsche Flotte,' in *Gedichte*, Zürich, 1844, p. 29.

50. Veit Valentin, *Geschichte der Deutschen Revolution von* 1848-9, Berlin, 1930, Vol. I, p. 268.

51. *A History of Militarism*, p. 208.

52. Ibid. p. 208; from Heyderhoff-Wentzke, *Deutscher Liberalismus im Zeitalter Bismarcks*, Vol. I, p. 71.

53. Franz von Liszt, *Ein mitteleuropäischer Staatenverband*, Leipzig, 1914, pp. 32-3. I owe this reference to Carl Becker, 'The Old Disorder in Europe,' in *The Yale Review*, 1941 (30), pp. 433-53, esp. p. 439.

54. Eckart Kehr, *Schlachtflottenbau und Parteipolitik*, 1894-1901, Berlin, 1930.

55. Felix Salomon (ed. Mommsen and Franz), *Die deutschen Parteiprogramme*, 4th ed., Leipzig, Vol. I, pp. 155-9.

56. Mildred Wertheimer, *The Pan-German League*, New York, 1924, p. 123.

57. Ibid. p. 133.

58. Ibid. p. 73.

59. Kehr, op. cit. pp. 307, 308.

60. Printed in Oscar Stillich, *Die politischen Parteien in Deutschland, II. Der Liberalismus*, Leipzig, 1911, p. 81.

61. William L. Langer, op. cit. Vol. II, p. 431. Alfred von Tirpitz, *My Memoirs*, 2 vols., New York, 1919, Vol. I, p. 77.

62. William L. Langer, op. cit. Vol. II, p. 436.

63. Kehr, op. cit. pp. 194-120.

64. Ibid. pp. 169, 170.

65. Ibid. p. 193.

66. Ibid. p. 205.

67. Ibid. p. 205.

68. Adolph Wagner, *Vom Territorialstaat zur Weltmacht*, Berlin, 1900.

69. Ernst von Halle, 'Weltmachtpolitik und Sozialreform,' in *Volks- und Weltwirtschaft*, Vol. II, pp. 229, 228, 204; and Kehr, op. cit. pp. 439, 440.

70. Kehr, op. cit. p. 101.

71. George Dunlap Crothers, *The German Elections of 1907*, New York, 1941.

72. Ibid. p. 105.

73. Election results: Crothers, op. cit. pp. 166 and 175.

74. Surveys of the various doctrines of imperialism in English: B. J. Houde, 'Socialistic Theories of Imperialism prior to the Great War,' in *Journal of Political Economy*, 1928 (36), pp. 569-691. E. M. Winslow, 'Marxian, Liberal and Sociological Theories of Imperialism,' in *Journal of Political Economy*, 1931 (39), pp. 713-58. William L. Langer, op. cit. Vol. 1, pp. 96-9, contains a full and excellent bibliography. Crothers, op. cit. pp. 151-4, and 211-29 on the actual policy of the Social Democrats. Two excellent German studies must be mentioned: Kurt Mandelbaum, *Die Erörterung innerhalb der Sozialdemokratie über das Problem des Imperialismus*, Frankfurt a/M., 1930 (Dissertation); Alfred Meusel, 'Der klassische Sozialismus' in *Die Wandlungen der Wirtschaft im kapitalistischen Zeitalter*, ed. G. Briefs, Berlin, 1932, pp. 36-79.
75. *Die Kolonialpolitik und der Zusammenbruch*, Leipzig, 1907.
76. Writing under the pseudonym Karl Emil, 'Der deutsche Imperialismus und die innere Politik,' in *Die Neue Zeit*, 1907/8 (26), Vol. 1, pp. 148-63.
77. Kehr, op. cit. pp. 306, 307.
78. R. Calwer, 'Der 25. Januar,' in *Sozialistische Monatshefte*, 1907 (11), pp. 101-7, 192-200. Max Schippel, *Grundzüge der Handelspolitik*, Berlin, Berne, 1902. 'Die Handels- und Wirtschaftspolitik der Arbeiter,' in *Sozialistische Monatshefte*, 1900 (4), p. 542. Ludwig Quessel, 'Der Wert unserer Kolonien,' in *Sozialistische Monatshefte*, 1912 (16), pp. 1124-31.
79. *Die Vorausetzungen der Sozialdemokratie;* 'Die heutige Sozialdemokratie in Theorie und Praxis,' in *Archiv für Sozialwissenschaft und Sozialpolitik*, 1907 (25).
80. Schippel, *Grundzüge*, pp. 336, 337.
81. Calwer, op. cit. pp. 101-7; 192-200, esp. p. 105.
82. Crothers, op. cit. pp. 214-20.
83. Cunow, *Parteizusammenbruch?*, Berlin, 1915.
84. Ibid. p. 14.
85. Lensch, *Die deutsche Sozialdemokratie und der Weltkrieg*, Berlin, 1915; *Drei Jahre Weltrevolution*, Berlin, 1917.
86. Meusel, op. cit. p. 62.
87. Winnig, *Vom Proletariat zum Arbeitertum*, Hamburg, 1930.
88. Nowack (ed.), *Die Aufzeichnungen des Generals Max Hoffmann*, Berlin, 1929, Vol. 1, p. 366; and Ernst Fraenkel, 'German-Russian Relations since 1918,' in *The Review of Politics*, 1940 (2), pp. 34-62.

PART TWO

TOTALITARIAN MONOPOLISTIC ECONOMY

For names of periodicals and newspapers, etc., the following abbreviations are used in the notes to this chapter:

BA—*Bank-Archiv*
DAZ—*Deutsche Allgemeine Zeitung*
DR—*Deutsches Recht*
DV—*Der Deutsche Volkswirt*
DZ—*Deutsche Bergwerkszeitung*
FZ—*Frankfurter Zeitung*

KR——*Kartell-Rundschau*
SJ——*Statistisches Jahrbuch für das Deutsche Reich*
SP——*Soziale Praxis*
VP——*Der Vierjahresplan*
WK——*Die Wirtschaftskurve*
WS——*Wirtschaft und Statistik*
ZA——*Zeitschrift der Akademie für Deutsches Recht*
ZS——*Zeitschrift für die gesamte Staatswissenschaft*

I have used the following collections of legislative materials: Posse-Land-fried-Syrup-Backe-Alpers (quoted *Posse*), *Kommentar zur Reichsverteidigungsgesetzgebung*, at present 4 vols., Munich, n.d.; Carl Mölders (ed.) (quoted *Mölders*), *Das gesamte Recht des Vierjahresplanes*, at present 2 vols., Berlin, n.d.; *Die Anordnungen zur Durchführung des Vierjahresplanes* (quoted *Anordnungen*), at present 3 vols., Berlin, n.d.

I: AN ECONOMY WITHOUT ECONOMICS?

1. Peter Drucker, *The End of the Economic Man*, New York, 1939. Frank Munk, *The Economics of Force*, New York, 1940. James Burnham, 'The Theory of the Managerial Revolution,' in *Partisan Review*, 1941 (May, June), pp. 181-97; *The Managerial Revolution*, New York, 1941. Dwight Macdonald, 'The End of Capitalism in Germany,' in *Partisan Review*, 1941 (May, June), pp. 198-220. Bruno R., *La Bureaucratisation du Monde. Le Collectivisme Bureaucratique. Quo Vadis America*, Paris, 1939. The last is the most important book of all those mentioned, written by a former Marxist. Also Frederick Pollock, 'State Capitalism' in *Studies in Philosophy and Social Science*, 1941 (9), pp. 200-226.
2. Ferdinand Fried, *Das Ende des Kapitalismus*, Jena, 1931.
3. *The Dynamics of War and Revolution*, New York, 1940, p. 66.
4. Quoted in Dwight Macdonald, op. cit. pp. 212, 213.
5. Hilferding, op. cit. p. 212.
6. Bukharin, *Imperialism and World Economy*, new ed., New York, 1929, and Macdonald, op. cit. p. 209.
7. Ministerialrat Dr. Eberhart Barth, *Wesen und Aufgaben der Organisation der gewerblichen Wirtschaft*, Hamburg, 1939, p. 9.
8. Feder, *Das Programm der NSDAP*, 116th-125th ed., Munich, 1937, pp. 20-21.
9. Feder, *Der deutsche Staat auf nationaler und sozialer Grundlage*, 13th ed., Munich, 1933.
10. Feder, *Das Programm* . . . , p. 7.
11. Feder, *Der deutsche Staat*, p. 60.
12. For an excellent analysis of the prehistory of the estate idea, see Taylor Cole, 'Corporative Organization of the Third Reich,' in *The Review of Politics*, 1940 (2), pp. 438-62. Professor Cole omits, however, to mention the influence of Karl Marlo (Winkelblech) and the discussion within the Social Democratic party in 1918 and 1919.
13. Max Frauendorfer, *Der ständische Gedanke im Nationalsozialismus*, 3rd ed., Munich, 1933.
14. Institut für Ständewesen, headed by Walter Heinrich. Cf. Cole, op. cit. p. 447.

15. Adam Müller, 'Staatswirtschaftliche Verlegenheiten und Reform der Geld-verhältnisse in Oesterreich,' in *Ausgewählte Abhandlungen* (J. Baxa ed.), 2nd ed., Jena, 1931, p. 200; and Cole, op. cit. p. 439.
16. Karl Marlo, *Untersuchungen über die Organisation der Arbeit*, Vol. i: Historische Einleitung in die Oekonomie, 1885; Vol. ii: Geschichte und Kritik der ökonomischen Systeme, 1884, 2nd ed., Tübingen. Cf. the great biography, E. Biermann, *Karl Georg Winkelblech* (Karl Marlo), 2 vols., Leipzig, 1909.
17. Published by Biermann, op. cit., Vol. ii, pp. 453-6.
18. Otto Fürst von Bismarck, *Gedanken und Erinnerungen* (Cotta ed.), 1898, Vol. i, pp. 15, 16.
19. Hugo Sinzheimer, *Das Rätesystem*, Frankfurt a. M., 1919.
20. Cole, op. cit. p. 444.
21. Othmar Spann, *Der wahre Staat*, 3rd ed., Jena, 1931.
22. Spann, *Gesellschaftslehre*, Leipzig, 1930, p. 98.
23. See the quotations in Walter Gehl (ed.), *Der nationalsozialistische Staat*, Breslau, 1933, pp. 116-27.
24. Wilhelm Keppler, 'Grundsätze nationalsozialistischer Wirtschaftspolitik,' in *Wirtschaftspolitik im Dritten Reich*, Munich, (n.d.), p. 3.
25. Köhler, 'Politischer Sozialismus,' op. cit. p. 7.
26. Rosenberg, *Der Mythus des 20. Jahrhunderts*, 7th ed., Munich, 1933, pp. 695-6.
27. *New York Times*, 2 January 1935. Cole, op. cit. p. 450.
28. Barth, op. cit. p. 26, and the Federal Minister of Economics Dr. Schmitt in a speech before leading industrialists published in Axel Friedrichs (ed.), *Die nationalsozialistische Revolution*, Berlin, 1935, p. 207.
29. Barth, op. cit. p. 11.
30. i.e. Leonhard Miksch, 'Brauchen wir noch Unternehmer?' in *WK*, 1941 (20), pp. 5-14, esp. p. 7.

II: THE ORGANIZATION OF BUSINESS

1. On Spitzenverbände, see the excellent contribution by Robert A. Brady, 'Manufacturing Spitzenverbände,' in *Political Science Quarterly*, 1941 (56), pp. 199-225.
2. Franz Neumann, *Tarifrecht*, Berlin, 1931, pp. 29-30.
3. The best survey of the National Socialist organizational forms is to be found in Robert A. Brady, *The Spirit and Structure of German Fascism*, New York, 1937. It is now partly outdated. My discussion is based primarily on Barth, op. cit., which, however, does not include the war organization which again has changed the picture. I have used many articles, statutes, decrees, and rulings, some of which I shall mention.
4. For handicraft chambers: Act concerning the structure of German handicraft of 29 November 1933; first executive decree 5 January 1934.
5. From Barth, op. cit. p. 107.
6. Brady, *The Spirit* . . . p. 146.
7. Posse, op. cit. Vol. ii, sect. iv (*Allgemeines-Bauwirtschaft*), p. 1.
8. Ibid. (*Auftragsregelung-Eisen- u. Stahlbewirtschaftung*), p. 1.
9. Ibid. (*Papier und Verpackungswesen*).
10. Leonhard Miksch, 'Bewirtschaftungskartelle,' in *WK*, 1940 (19), pp. 24-32.

11. 'Anordnung Nr. 1' of 8 January 1940, in Posse, op. cit. Vol. 11, sect. iv (*Papier* etc.), p. 81.
12. 'Anordnung Nr. 2' of 4 September 1939, ibid. (*Allgemeines-Spinnstoff-wirtschaft*), p. 11.

III: The Monopolistic Economy

1. The most important contribution in this field is Karl Renner, *Die Rechts-institute des Privatrechts und ihre soziale Funktion*, Tübingen, 1929 (1st ed. published under the pseudonym Josef Karner, 1904, in Vol. 1 of the *Marx-Studien*). I adapted these ideas to the German situation 1920-32 in my book *Koalitionsfreiheit und Reichsverfassung*, Berlin, 1932, and to National Socialism in my article 'Der Funktionswandel des Gesetzes im Recht der bürgerlichen Gesellschaft,' in *Zeitschrift für Sozialforschung*, 1937 (VI), pp. 542-96, trans. by the University of Chicago in *Second Year Course in the Study of Contemporary Society*, 8th ed., Chicago, 1939.
2. Adam Smith, A Theory of Moral Sentiments, 6th ed., 1790, Vol. 1, Part III, Ch. 3, p. 339; and Vol. 1, Part 11, sec. ii, Ch. 2.
3. Adam Smith, *Lectures on Justice, Police, Revenue and Arms* (Cannan ed.), Oxford, 1890, p. 177.
4. Adam Smith, *Wealth*, Book IV, Ch. 8.
5. Ibid. Book V, Ch. 1, p. iii, Art. I.
6. Hegel, *Philosophy of Right*, trans. by Dyde, sec. 71.
7. Reichswirtschaftsgerichtsrat Dr. W. Rittgen, 'Berufsanforderungen im Rundfunkgrosshandel,' in *KR*, 1940 (38), pp. 321-33.
8. A. Kaumann, 'Auswirkungen der An- und Aberkennungsrichtlinien,' in *Rundfunkhändler*, 12 April 1939, p. 297.
9. Decision of the federal economic tribunal of 12 July 1939, *KR*, 1940 (38), p. 13.
10. Claire Russell, 'Die Praxis des Zwangskartellgesetzes,' in *ZS*, 1937 (97), pp. 499-548, esp. p. 500.
11. *KR*, 1940 (38), p. 335.
12. *KR*, 1940 (38), p. 337 (Decree of 28 September 1940).
13. *KR*, 1940 (38), p. 82 (Decree of 27 January 1940).
14. *KR*, 1940 (38), p. 42.
15. In *Preussische Jahrbücher*, 1903 (110), p. 7.
16. *DAZ*, 27 November 1938.
17. *DAZ*, 2 November 1938.
18. Franz Böhm, *Wettbewerb und Monopolkampf*, Berlin, 1933, pp. x and 358.
19. *FZ*, 18 November 1938.
20. Leonhard Miksch, *WK*, 1936 (15), No. 4.
21. Barth, op. cit. p. 82.
22. Ibid. p. 75.
23. Ruling of 12 November 1936, *KR*, 1936 (34), pp. 753-60, and Barth, op. cit. p. 75.
24. *DV*, 1941, No. 22, p. 825.
25. Otto Suhr, 'Umwälzungen in der Glasindustrie,' in *WK*, 1940 (19), pp. 83-92.
26. Leonhard Miksch, 'Bewirtschaftungskartelle,' in *WK*, 1940 (19), pp. 24-32.

27. *KR*, 1940 (38), p. 95.
28. Karl Euling, *Die Kartelle im oberschlesischen Steinkohlenbergbau*, Jena, 1939.
29. In the Ruhr coal syndicate, 100,000 tons sale and 150,000 tons consumption secure one vote.
30. Günter Keiser, 'Der jüngste Konzentrationsprozess,' in *WK*, 1939 (18), pp. 136-56, 214-34; esp. p. 150.
31. Acquired the iron and steel work Thale; see *KR*, 1939 (37), p. 514.
32. Acquired Rawack and Grünfeld—now called A.-G. für Montaninteressen; see *KR*, 1939 (37), p. 514.
33. Acquired Wolff-Netter-Jacobi, see *KR*, 1938 (36), p. 179, and the Hahnsche Werke (capital 9,900,000 marks), *KR*, 1938 (36), p. 318.
34. *DV*, 1941 (15), No. 22, p. 820.
35. The account is based on the following sources: *FZ*, 30 March 1941, p. 15; *FZ*, 19 April 1941, p. 2; *BA*, 1941, No. 7, p. 151.
36. Borussia limited liability corp.; Deutsche Erdöl, A.-G.; Gewerkschaft Elwerath; Wintershall A.-G.; Preussische Bergwerks- und Hütten A.-G.; I. G. Farbenindustrie A.-G.; Braunkohle-Benzin A.-G.; Deutsche Bank; Dresdner Bank; Reichskreditgesellschaft; Berliner Handelsgesellschaft.
37. 'Der Montanblock im Westen,' in *FZ*, 11 July 1941. On the penetration of the German banks in the conquered territories, cf. 'Die deutschen Banken in Kontinentaleuropa,' in *BA*, 1941, No. 10, p. 214.
38. Cf. the excellent paper 'Technological Trends and Economic Structure under National Socialism,' in *Studies in Philosophy and Social Science*, 1941 (7), pp. 226-64, by Dr. A. R. L. Gurland, with whom I have discussed all the problems of this section of my book.
39. Such as: Krupp, Hoesch, Mannesmann, United Steel Trust, Flick, etc. Cf. *Deutsche Montankonzerne*, 1929 (Spezialarchiv der deutschen Wirtschaft), Berlin, 1929 (publication sponsored by the Dresdner Bank).
40. The connection between chemical industry and coal is discussed in detail in *Die grossen Chemie-Konzerne Deutschlands* (Spezialarchiv der deutschen Wirtschaft), Berlin, 1929.
41. *FZ*, 13 March 1941.
42. On coal output see Gurland, op. cit.; on gasoline and other oil production see General Loeb in *VP*, 1938, No. 2, and *FZ*, 18 April 1939.
43. According to Gurland, op. cit., the volume of buna production must be about one fourth or one third of the total German rubber requirements. See 'Chemie-Bilanz 1938,' in *DZ*, 1 January 1939.
44. On machine production, see Hans Ilau, 'Der Maschinenhunger,' in *WK*, 1939 (18), pp. 19-29.
45. Ibid. p. 24.
46. Otto Suhr, 'Umwälzungen in der Glasindustrie,' in *WK*, 1940 (19), p. 83.
47. On production of cellulose wool and rayon see Friedrich Sarow, 'Zellwolle,' in *WK*, 1938 (17), pp. 263-76; and *Wochenbericht, Institut für Konjunkturforschung*, 9 March 1939 and 15 March 1939. Cellulose wool production should be increased by 1939 to 200,000 and by 1940 to 275,000 tons. See *FZ*, 4 June 1939. Also: Friedrich Dorn, 'Die Zellstoff- und Papierwirtschaft in und nach dem Kriege,' in *VP*, 1940, No. 23, p. 1033.
48. On production of iron, steel and aluminum, see: Horst Wagenführ, 'Kontrollierte N.E.-[non-ferrous] Metalle auf dem Weltmarkt,' in *KR*, 1939 (37), p. 211.

49. *SP*, 1939 (48), p. 403.
50. *VP*, 1939 (3).
51. Handicraft statistics:

	Registration of New Plants	Extinction of Plants	Decrease
1936	104,234	132,109	27,875
1937	75,153	137,726	62,573
1938	59,700	122,642	62,942
	239,087	392,477	153,390

Source: *VP*, 1939 (3), p. 1029.

52. *FZ*, 9 January 1941.
53. *Mölders*, Vol. II, group 6, p. 69. Decree on prices and trade margins in the trade with automobiles and spare parts of 18 February, 17 April, 17 November 1937.
54. Erich Käsler, 'Stillegung und Wiederaufleben,' in *DV*, 1941 (15), No. 35/36, pp. 1254-9. For the soap industry, cf.: Decree of 6 October 1939 (Mölders, Vol. II, group 6, p. 413) and the ruling of the price commissar No. 115/39 of 28 October 1939 (Mölders, Vol. II, group 6, p. 414a) where the closing down of plants and their transformation into mere sales agencies is regulated.
55. Geiger, *Die soziale Schichtung des deutschen Volkes*, Stuttgart, 1932, p. 74.
56. Otto Ohlendorf, 'Kriegswirtschaftliche Gegenwartsfragen im Handel,' in *VP*, 1941 (5), pp. 513-15.
57. A. A. Berle and G. C. Means, *The Modern Corporation and Private Property*, New York, 1935.
58. Rudolf Hilferding, *Das Finanzkapital*, Vienna, 1923, p. 112.
59. Rathenau, *Vom Aktienwesen*, Berlin, 1918.
60. Excellent remarks on the German corporation law by F. A. Mann, 'The New German Company Law and its Background,' in *Journal of Comparative Legislation and International Law*, November 1937.
61. Excellent critique by Arthur Nussbaum (now at Columbia University), in *Juristische Wochenschrift*, 1932, p. 2585.
62. Hans Reichel, in *Juristische Wochenschrift*, 1930, p. 1459. Translation from Mann's article. On the reactionary character of the institutionalist theory, see Neumann, op. cit. pp. 587-95.
63. Concentration of capital in joint stock corporations:

	Number	Total Capital in Billion Marks	Average Capital in Million Marks
1931	10.437	24.6	2.25
1938	5.518	18.7	3.39

Source: *WS*, 1939, p. 237.

64. Keiser, op. cit. p. 154.
65. Ibid. p. 137.
66. From *Freies Deutschland*, 1939 (3), 27 July.
67. Keiser, op. cit. p. 215.
68. *KR*, 1939 (37), p. 448.
69. *KR*, 1938 (36), p. 116.
70. *KR*, 1938 (36), pp. 115, 234.
71. Keiser, op. cit. p. 142, and *KR*, 1938 (36), p. 114.
72. Keiser, op. cit. p. 147. Three plants in 1934 produced 83.3 per cent of all cigarettes. See *KR*, 1938 (36), p. 235. The cigarette industry is protected

by a decree of the minister of economics, prohibiting the establishment of new plants, of 11 March 1938. See *KR*, 1938 (36), p. 285.
73. On bank statistics, see *BA*, 1941, No. 4, p. 90.
74. *Wochenbericht, Institut für Konjunkturforschung*, 1936 (9), p. 198.
75. Willy Neuling, 'Wettbewerb, Monopol und Befehl in der heutigen Wirtschaft,' in *ZS*, 1939 (99), pp. 279-318.
76. 'Maschinenindustrie und Kriegspotential,' in *VP*, 1941 (9), p. 512.

IV: THE COMMAND ECONOMY

1. Excellent survey of the programs: Leo Grebler, 'Work Creation Policy in Germany 1932-1935,' in *International Labour Review*, 1937 (35), pp. 331-51 and 505-27.
2. Good survey: Gerhard Mackenroth, 'Deutsche Industriepolitik 1933,' in *Jahrbücher für Nationalökonomie und Statistik*, 1934 (140), pp. 54-70 and 204-24.
3. Grebler, op. cit. p. 518.
4. The two basic works on the subject of public enterprises in republican Germany are: Walter Pahl and Kurt Mendelsohn (eds.), *Handbuch der öffentlichen Wirtschaft*, Berlin, 1930 (a publication of the Social Democratic union of transport and municipal workers); and Julius Landmann (ed.), *Moderne Organisationsformem der öffentlichen Unternehmung*, Part II, *Deutsches Reich*, Munich and Leipzig, 1931 (Schriften des Vereins für Sozialpolitik, Vol. 176). My account is based primarily on the first publication because it is more comprehensive and because I have collaborated in it.
5. *SJ*, 1938, p. 525.
6. On the Hermann Göring Works, there are two excellent articles by A. R. L. Gurland (written under the pen-name of R. Lang), in *Freies Deutschland*, 30 March and 6 April 1939. In English: Kurt Lachmann, 'The Hermann Göring Works,' in *Social Research*, 1941 (8), pp, 24-40.
7. *KR*, 1939 (37), p. 513.
8. *DZ*, 12 June 1938.
9. *DAZ*, 2 March 1939.
10. *DV*, 1939, No. 23.
11. See *FZ*, 31 October 1937.
12. *FZ*, 18 January 1941.
13. *SP*, 1939 (48), p. 1070.
14. *SP*, 1941 (50), p. 215.
15. *Mölders*, Vol. ii, pp. 5-12.
16. Ibid. pp. 17-17a.
17. Ruling No. 60/39 of 29 June 1939. *Mölders*, Vol. ii, group 6, pp. 20c-20f.
18. Posse, Vol. i, *Kriegswirtschaftsverordnung*, p. 1.
19. *Mölders*, p. 451. A very thorough survey is in the article by W. Schütz (in the office of the Federal Price Commissioner), 'Neuregelung der Preisbindungen,' in *DV*, 1941 (15), No. 17, pp. 656-60.
20. Op. cit. pp. 658, 659.
21. *VP*, 1941 (5), No. 9, p. 527.
22. Ministerial Director Flottmann, according to *FZ*, 17 January 1941.
23. *Mölders*, Vol. ii, group 6, pp. 179, 180. *Anordnungen*, Vol. i, Sect. D, p. 10. The basic decree is of 27 October 1937.

24. Rulings of the price commissioner: No. 1/37 of 30 January 1937, *Mölders*, Vol. II, group 6, p. 19. No. 37/40 of 3 April 1940, ibid. p. 431.
25. Decree of 9 December 1937, ibid. p. 78a, and many others for almost any filament.
26. Decree of 29 April 1937 as amended 18 August 1937, 25 August 1938 and 4 July 1939, ibid. p. 119, with many executive decrees.
27. On procedure and principles, compare ruling No. 60/39 of 29 June 1939, ibid. p. 20c.
28. Ruling on 'estimated' prices: No. 137/40 of 8 November 1940, ibid. p. 20g.
29. ibid. p. 20n.
30. (1) 'Decree on the ascertaining of prices for governmental orders on the basis of the costs of production,' 15 November 1938 (*LSÖ*); *Anordnungen*, Vol. I, groups A and B, p. 36. New codification: 11 March 1941, *Mölders*, Vol. II, p. 384a-f. (2) 'Decree on the formation of prices for governmental orders,' 15 November 1938 (*RPÖ*); ibid. p. 52.
31. Theodor Kuhr, 'Der volkswirtschaftlich richtige Preis und die öffentlichen Aufträge,' in *Finanzarchiv*, 1940 (8), pp. 70-94; cf. p. 88.
32. Indexes of wholesale prices, April 1939–April 1941:

	April 1933	*April 1941*
All Commodities	90.7	111.0
Farm Products	87.8	111.8
Industrial raw material and semi-manufactured products	87.0	100.1
Coal	114.8	
Iron and iron ore	101.3	
Textiles	61.1	
Artificial fertilizer	71.9	
Industrial Manufactured Products	111.3	132.7
Producers } Goods	114.1	113.3
Consumers }	109.2	147.3

Source: *Statistisches Jahrbuch für das Deutsche Reich*, 1934, p. 259; *WS*, 1941 (21), p. 182.

33. Indexes of cost of living, April 1933–April 1941:

	April 1933	*April 1941*
All Items *	115.9	132.4
All Items without Rent	114.9	134.7
Food	109.5	128.6
Rent	121.3	121.2
Clothing	105.6	153.1

* Food, rent, fuel, light, clothing, miscellaneous (no taxes and social insurance contribution included).
Sources: *SJ*, 1938, pp. 331-2. *WS*, 1941 (21), p. 182.

34. *VP*, 1939, No. 20, p. 1178.
35. Cf. the illuminating discussion of Gurland, op. cit.
36. Kuhr, op. cit.
37. A brief survey of this act: C. W. Guillebaud, *The Economic Recovery of Germany*, London, 1939, pp. 77, 78, 252-3.
38. Ibid. p. 77.
39. *DR*, 1941, p. 917.
40. For industry: 1 March 1941, *Mölders*, Vol. II, group 6, p. 51v; and *FZ*, 15 March 1941. For trade: April 1941, *FZ*, 19 April 1941.
41. *Mölders*, op. cit. p. 52w.
42. *VP*, 1941 (5), p. 527.
43. *FZ*, 13 March 1941.
44. The discussion is based on the following publications: 1. E. W. Schmitt, 'Das Gesicht der Aktie,' in *SP*, 1941 (50), p. 501. 2. 'Selbstfinanzierung

und Kapitalmarkt,' in *BA*, 1941, p. 174. 3. *FZ* of 28, 29 June, 5, 6, 13 July. 4. 'Dividendenbegrenzung mit oder ohne Kapitalaufwertung,' in *BA*, 1941, p. 149. 5. 'Der Gewinn privat- und volkswirtschaftlich betrachtet,' in *SP*, 1941 (50), p. 321. 6. 'Germany's Limitation on Dividends,' in *Foreign Commerce Weekly* 1941 (4), 16 August 1941.

45. See the extensive discussion, 'Dividendenbegrenzung mit oder ohne Kapitalaufwertung?' *BA*, 1941, No. 7, pp. 149-51.

46. 'Selbstfinanzierung und Kapitalmarkt,' in *BA*, 1941, No. 8, p. 174.

47. *Investigation of Concentration of Economic Power*, Hearings, Part 9 (Savings and Investments), Washington, 1940.

48. *WK*, 1940 (19), pp. 219-22. The article (4) in *BA* (note 44 mentions the following figures: of the 852 shares quoted at the exchange, 336, that is, close to 40 per cent, distribute more than 6 per cent dividends.

49. Op. cit. (Note 46).

50. Marx-Engels *Gesamtausgabe*, Abt. III, Vol. I, p. 239. Cf. the note by Hans Speier, 'Marx und Engels über die Brechung der Zinsknechtschaft,' in *Die Gesellschaft*, 1931, Vol. I, pp. 117-119.

51. *Das Finanzkapital (Marx-Studien)*, reprint, Vienna, 1923, 1st ed., 1910, p. 282.

52. Quoted by Adolf Weber, *Depositenbanken und Spekulationsbanken*, Munich and Leipzig, 1915, p. 81.

53. Henryk Grossmann, *Das Akkumulations- und Zusammenbruchsgesetz des kapitalistischen Systems*, Leipzig, 1929, pp. 574-9.

54. Short survey, Guilleband, op. cit. p. 94. Otto Christian Fischer (formerly of the Reichskreditgesellschaft, now of Merck, Finck & Company, leader of the national group banking), 'Die Ausübung des Staatseinflusses im deutschen Kreditwesen,' in *ZA*, 1938 (5), pp. 408-10.

55. A. Koch and W. Roeder (ed.), *Das Recht der deutschen Bankwirtschaft*, Berlin, 1938, pp. 14-28.

56. Excellent discussion in Poole, op. cit. pp. 129-38.

57. Jacob Viner, *Dumping: A Problem in International Trade*, Chicago, 1923, p. 94; and the excellent discussion by M. Gilbert and P. D. Dickens, *Export Prices and Export Cartels* (TNEC Monograph No. 6), Washington, D. C., 1940.

58. The most enraged advocate of autarky as a new philosophy was the *Tat* circle, especially its leader, Ferdinand Fried, *Autarkie*, Jena, 1932, who had already predicted the end of capitalism. Also Werner Sombart, *Die Zukunft des Kapitalismus*, Berlin, 1932, who believed Germany's future to lie in re-agrarization. Against these distortions Herbert von Beckerath and Fritz Kern, *Autarkie oder internationale Zusammenarbeit*, Berlin, 1932. The contributions of the National Socialist party are not worth mentioning.

59. Fried, op. cit. p. 41.

60. Cleona Lewis, assisted by John C. McClelland, *Nazi Europe and World Trade*, Washington, 1941. Important is the table on p. 178:

1937	Old Territory (in billions of dollars)		Nazi Europe (including Germany and excluding Russia)	
Food, net imports	607.4		648.2	
Raw materials, net imports	931.4		2,594.7	
		1,538.8		3,242.9
Manufacturers' net exports	1,716.7		1,941.0	
Total net exports	177.9		......	
Total net imports	......		1,301.9	

61. See *FZ*, 13 June 1941, and *Neue Züricher Zeitung* (Handelsteil), 14 June 1941.
62. Albrecht Forstmann, *Der Kampf um den Aussenhandel*, Berlin, 1935.
63. Op. cit. p. 178.
64. A good survey: Charles Thomas Bonnell, *German Control over International Economic Relations*, 1930-1940, Urbana (Ill.), 1940, pp. 93-114. Excellent: Howard S. Ellis, *Exchange Control in Central Europe*, Cambridge (Mass.), 1941, pp. 191-269.
65. *Die Reden Hitlers als Kanzler*, 3rd ed., Munich, 1934, p. 21.
66. On statistics of German foreign trade from 1929 to May 1939, see *Wochenbericht, Institut für Konjunkturforschung*, 27 July 1939, p. 76; Bonnell, op. cit. p. 120, and Ellis, pp. 380-87.
67. See literature in Note 64 and the sound popular statement by Douglas Miller, *You Can't Do Business with Hitler*, Boston, 1941, esp. Chs. 4, 5, 6, 7. Also, Hans Staudinger, 'The Future of the Totalitarian Barter Trade,' in *Social Research*, 1940 (7), pp. 410-33. Thomas Balogh, 'Foreign Exchange and Export Trade Policy,' in *Economic Journal*, 1940 (50), p. 15. John C. de Wilde, 'Germany's Controlled Economy,' in *Foreign Policy Reports*, 1939 (14), 1 March 1939, esp. pp. 294-301. Excellent: Melchior Palyi, 'Economic Foundations of the German Totalitarian State,' in the *American Journal of Sociology*, 1941 (46), pp. 469-86. For the text of the report of the Wiggin Committee: *International Conciliation, Pamphlet* No. 280, May 1932.
68. Carl T. Schmidt, *German Business Cycles*, 1924-1933, New York, 1934, p. 87; and Bonnell, op. cit. p. 19.
69. Reparation payments from 1924-1932 = 11,464 million marks. *SJ*, 1931, pp. 534-5; 1933, pp. 498-9.
70. James W. Angell, *The Recovery of Germany*, New Haven, 1929, p. 326; *WK*, 1938 (7), pp. 301-5; and Schmidt, op. cit. p. 78.
71. Decree of 1 August 1931, in force since 4 August 1931.
72. Bonnell, op. cit. pp. 42-4.
73. Paul Einzig, 'Why Defend Nazi Trade Methods?' *The Banker*, 1941, No. 184, May 1941.
74. Miller, op. cit. p. 73.
75. Staudinger, op. cit. p. 415.
76. Balogh, op. cit. p. 15.
77. Friedrich Sarow, 'Verrechnungszentrum Berlin,' in *WK*, 1940 (19), pp. 181-90.
78. Ibid. p. 188.
79. L. Hamburger, *How Nazi Germany Has Mobilized and Controlled Labor*, Washington, 1940 (Brookings Institution); C. W. Guillebaud, *The Social Policy of Nazi Germany*, Cambridge (England), 1941.
80. Employment statistics:

I. Workers and Salaried Employees in 1000

1929	17.870
1932	12.580
1937	18.370
1938 (August)	19.518
1941 (January) estimated	22.670

II. Hours Worked in Industry

1936 = 100

		Total	Production Goods	Consumer Goods
1929		103.6	94.9	117.0
1932		54.8	42.6	74.7
1936		100.0	100.0	100.0
1938	(Aug.)	116.7	123.8	105.8
1939	(May)	128.2	131.4	124.0

Sources: *Halbjahrsberichte zur Wirtschaftslage* (Institut für Konjunkturforschung), 1938/39 (13), p. 119. For 1941: *WS*, 1941 (21), p. 100; and *Statistik des In- und Auslandes* (Institut für Konjunkturforschung), 1939/40 (14), p. 39.

81. *WS*, 1941 (21), p. 101.
82. 'Die Reserve an weiblicher Arbeitskraft,' in *WK*, 1941 (20), pp. 148-50.
83. Secretary of State Dr. Syrup, according to *WK*, 1940 (19), pp. 209-11. *WS*, 1941 (20), p. 101, mentions 820,000 foreign workers employed outside agriculture, 300,000 alone in building construction.
84. In agriculture, the following foreign workers are employed:

Polish (*not* war prisoners)	469,000
Other foreigners (during 1940):	
Italians	47,000
Slovaks	32,000
Jugoslavs	4,400
Dutchmen	4,650
Hungarians	2,000
Others	2,000
War prisoners from the Polish and Western campaigns (Sept. 1940)	650,000
Former Polish war prisoners (end of 1940)	180,000
	1,391,050

WS, 1941 (21), p. 100. According to *International Labour Review*, 1941 (43), No. 5, p. 584, the number of Italians employed in Germany will soon reach 264,000. Workers from Belgium: 83,000 (November 1941), see *Neue Internationale Rundschauder Arbeit*, 1941 (1), p. 201.

85. Posse, Vol. I, Part II, *Dienstpflicht*, pp. 3-66.
86. 1 September 1939; see Posse, Vol. I, *Arbeitsplatzwechsel*, pp. 1-4e.
87. First executive decree, see ibid. p. 14.
88. Posse, Vol. I, *Notdienst*.
89. Ibid. p. 5.
90. Decree of 1 September 1939, Posse, Vol. I, *Arbeitsrecht*, II, pp. 1, 2.
91. Third executive decree to the war wage decree, 2 December 1939; Posse, Vol. I, *Kriegslöhne*, II, pp. 23-30.
92. 'Die Bergarbeiterfrage,' *WK*, 1939 (18), pp. 303-9.
93. Mölders, op. cit. Vol. I, Group 4, pp. 31, 32.
94. Posse, Vol. I, *Kriegslöhne*, p. 1.
95. For an analysis, cf. Franz Neumann, *European Trade Unionism and Politics* (Preface by H. J. Laski), New York, 1936, pp. 43-9.
96. First executive decree to the war wage decree, 16 September 1939; Posse, op. cit. pp. 6-11.
97. Decree of 4 September 1939; ibid. pp. 12-14.
98. Second executive decree to the war wage decree, 12 October 1939; ibid. pp. 14-18a.
99. 4 February 1941; see *DV*, 1941 (15), No. 22, p. 822.
100. Ruling of the minister of labor, 16 November 1939; Posse, op. cit. p. 21.
101. Decree of 1 September 1939 of the ministerial council for the defense of the realm; see Posse, Vol. I, *Arbeitsschutz*, pp. 1-13.

102. 11 September 1939; ibid. pp. 12/13.
103. 1 September 1939; Posse, Vol. I, *Arbeitslosenhilfe*, II, pp. 1-74.
104. The system was again simplified and changed on 16 December 1940; see *International Labour Review*, 1941 (43), p. 586.
105. *WK*, 1938 (17), p. 292.
106. Posse, Vol. I, *Kriegslöhne*, p. 20.
107. Ibid. pp. 21, 22.
108. Posse, Vol. I, *Arbeitsschutz*, pp. 15-25.
109. i.e. for metal workers, where conditions have again been worsened. If the plant operates continuously 24 hours, the three-shift system has to be replaced by the two-shift system—that is, 12 hours a day and 72 hours a week. See *International Labour Review*, 1941 (43), No. 5, p. 585.
110. Decree 18 September 1939; Posse, Vol. I, *Kurzarbeiterunterstützung*, pp. 1-29.
111. See note 80, hours worked in industry.

I. Volume of Industrial Production

1928 = 100

	1933	1936	1938	May, 1939
Total	65.5	106.7	124.7	130.1
Without Food	61.5	107.8	128.0	132.6
Production Goods	53.7	112.9	135.9	148.9
Investment Goods	44.9	116.6	140.3	152.8
Consumption Goods	82.9	97.5	107.8	116.1

Sources: *Institut für Konjunkturforschung, Wochenbericht*, 1939, No. 8, 22 February, and *Statistik des In- und Auslandes*, 1939/40 (14), No. 2.

II. Share of Production Goods in the Industrial Production, in Prices of 1928

	Per cent
1929	61
1932	47
1936	63
1938	65

Source: *Institut für Konjunkturforschung, Vierteljahrshefte zur Wirtschaftsforschung*, 1939/40, No. 1.

112. 'Europas Menschenmagnet,' .in *WK*, 1940 (19), pp. 209-11. Cf. for a more detailed analysis of this legislation Hamburger, op. cit. pp. 14-31.
113. National income in millions of marks:

1929	75.449	1935 *	58.662
1932	45.175	1936	64.884
1933	46.514	1937	72.590
1934	52.710	1938	79.722

* Since 1935: including the Saar. Estimates for 1939 run into the neighborhood of 90 billion marks.
Source: *WS*, 1939, No. 21/22, p. 705. According to the speech of the former Secretary of State Brinkmann (*DAZ*, 2 November 1938), the share of taxes, tariffs, and contributions to social-insurance institutions in the national income rose from 11.3 per cent in 1913 to 22.2 per cent in 1925 to 30.6 per cent in 1932 to 33.5 per cent in 1937. See also the survey of the financial structure up to the middle of 1939 in *Economic Conditions in Germany in the Middle of the Year 1939*, presented by the Reichskreditgesellschaft, Berlin, 1939, pp. 42-59; and, critical: de Wilde, op. cit. pp. 301-3, and Thomas Balogh, 'The Economic Background in Germany,' in *International Affairs*, 1939 (18), p. 231.

114. Posse, Vol. II, *Lederwirtschaft*, IV, p. 3.
115. Ibid. pp. 11-13.
116. Posse, Vol. II, *Seife und Waschmittel*, p. 1.
117. For leather; i.e., Posse, Vol. II, *Schuhhandel, Lederwirtschaft* IV, p. 4.

118. Posse, Vol. II, *Schuhausbesserung*, p. 5.
119. *FZ*, 12 June 1941. The average productivity of a fully mechanized model mine is asserted to be 8.93 tons per man and shift, as against 2 tons in the Ruhr district, and 2.4 in Upper Silesia, non-mechanized.
120. Barth, op. cit. p. 12.
121. *DV*, 1941 (15), No. 27, pp. 995-6.
122. *Modern Democracy*, New Haven, 1941, p. 11.
123. See *Life*, 29 April 1940.
124. *DV*, 1940 (14), pp. 1712, 1713.
125. Neumann, op. cit. p. 35.

PART THREE

THE NEW SOCIETY

(For abbreviations, see pp. 499, 500)

I: The Ruling Clan

1. Lederer, *State of the Masses. The Threat of the Classless Society*, New York, 1940.
2. This has been pointed out by Goetz Briefs in his criticism of Lederer's book: see his 'Intellectual Tragedy,' in the *Commonweal*, 25 October 1940.
3. Franz Neumann, *European Trade Unionism and Politics* (Preface by H. J. Laski), New York, 1936 (British edition, London, 1935).
4. On population and occupational statistics for 1933 and 1939, see *WS*, 1940 (20), p. 336.
5. Ministerialrat Franz Sommer, *Das Reichsjustizministerium*, Berlin, 1939, pp. 54-60.
6. On the basis of a comparison between the *Handbuch für das Deutsche Reich* for 1931 and 1936 (Berlin). Later editions, if they exist, were not accessible to me.
7. *FZ*, 5 January 1941.
8. See note 23.
9. Eberhard Barth, *Wesen und Aufgaben der Organisation der gewerblichen Wirtschaft*, Hamburg, 1939, pp. 7, 8.
10. *Nationalsozialistisches Jahrbuch*, 1939.
11. According to op. cit. 1938 and 1939.
12. According to *Das Deutsche Führerlexikon*, 1933-1934, Berlin, 1934; and Hans Gerth, 'The Nazi Party: Its Leadership and Composition,' in *The American Journal of Sociology*, 1940 (45), pp. 517-41, esp. p. 525.
13. Gerth, op. cit. p. 525.
14. An excellent analysis of this phenomenon, H. Herrigel, 'Politik und Idealismus,' in *Kant-Studien*, 1921 (26), pp. 52-73.
15. Morris Ginsberg, 'Stammler's Philosophy of Law,' in *Modern Theories of Law*, London, 1933, p. 51.
16. *Deutsches Beamtenjahrbuch*, 1939, p. 171.
17. Ministerial director Dr. Schütze in *Dr. Wilhelm Frick und sein Ministerium. Aus Anlass des 60. Geburtstages des Reichs- und Preussischen Innenministers*, Munich, 1937, p. 48.

18. Ibid. pp. 54-6.
19. Ibid.
20. Trans. and introduction by James K. Pollock and Alfred V. Boerner, Jr., *The German Civil Service Act*, The Civil Service Assembly of the United States and Canada, 1938.
21. *FZ*, 12 January 1941.
22. I confess having been guilty of this interpretation too. See my op. cit.
23. The analysis is based upon the following publications: a. *Die Organisation der gewerblichen Wirtschaft. Verzeichnis der Mitglieder der Reichswirtschaftskammer und deren Untergliederungen*, ed. Reichswirtschaftskammer, Berlin, as of August 1939. This volume furnishes the names. b. Hermann Teschenmacher (ed.), *Handbuch des Aufbaus der gewerblichen Wirtschaft*, Vol. I, Leipzig, 1935; Vol. II, Leipzig, 1936; Vol. III, Leipzig, 1937. These volumes supply the biographical data. c. *Handbuch der deutschen Aktiengesellschaften* 1938 and 1939. These books furnish the data on the corporate affiliations of the personnel of the groups and chambers.
24. R. Walther Darré, *Neuadel aus Blut und Boden*, new ed. 1941. Darré, *Ziel und Weg der nationalsozialistischen Agrarpolitik*, Munich, 1934, p. 18.
25. *SP*, 1939 (48), p. 405.
26. On property relations in agriculture and forestry, see *SJ*, 1938, p. 85.
27. *DV*, 1941 (15), No. 20, p. 775.
28. *WS*, 1939, No. 5.
29. Figures from *SJ*, 1938, p. 90.
30. Net return on the hectar of cultivated land in marks:

	Small	Middle	Big
1924/5	9	9	−18
1928/9	36	41	25
1931/2	−10	5	8
1932/3	−4	19	28
1933/4	28	49	53

Small farm in Eastern Germany	5-50 ha
in Western Germany	5-20 ha
Middle farm in Eastern Germany	50-200 ha
in Western Germany	20-100 ha

Source: Max Sering, 'Die agrarischen Grundlagen der Sozialverfassung,' in *Probleme des Deutschen Wirtschaftslebens*, Berlin and Leipzig, 1937, p. 854.

31. In 1933, there were 5,337,900 independents (including leading salaried employees, leading civil servants), among them 2.188 million in agriculture and forestry. *SJ*, 1938, p. 27.
32. Decree 6 July 1938 and executive decree 20 March 1939.
33. There exists a large number of books dealing with National Socialist education. The latest is George Frederick Kneller, *The Educational Philosophy of National Socialism*, New Haven, 1941, who takes the National Socialist ideology quite seriously. Further: I. L. Kandel, *The Making of Nazis*, New York, 1936; H. L. Childs (trans.) *The Nazi Primer*, New York, 1938; for universities: E. Y. Hartshorne, *The German Universities and National Socialism*, Cambridge (Mass.), 1937. Kneller's book contains a comprehensive bibliography.
34. Alfred Rosenberg, *Der deutsche Ordensstaat*, Munich, 1934, p. 11.
35. *FZ*, 26 June 1941.
36. *Deutsche Hochschulstatistik Sommer-Semester 1931*, as published by Svend

Riemer, 'Sozialer Aufstieg und Klassenschichtung,' in *Archiv für Sozial-wissenschaft und Sozialpolitik*, 1932 (67), pp. 531-60, esp. p. 553.
37. Cf. Hartshorne, op. cit. p. 86, where only 'slight changes' are reported.
38. Statistics up to 1937 in the article by Charlotte Luetkens, 'Enrolments at German Universities since 1933,' in *The Sociological Review*, 1939 (31), pp. 194-209. For 1938: *SJ*, 1938, p. 602.
39. Social composition of the party in 1933 and 1935 (per cent):

	1933	1935
Manual workers	31.5	32.1
Salaried employees	21.1	20.6
Independents (excluding peasants)	17.6	20.2
Peasants	12.6	10.7
Officials	6.7	13.0
Others	10.5	3.4
	100	100

From Gerth, op. cit. p. 527.

40. Abel, *Why Hitler Came into Power*, New York, 1938, p. 5.

II: THE RULED CLASSES

1. Excellent discussion: Clifford Kirkpatrick, *Nazi Germany: Its Women and Family Life*, Indianapolis, New York, 1938.
2. *Juristische Wochenschrift* 1937, p. 3057 (Decision 21 August 1937).
3. Op. cit. 1937, p. 2387.
4. Cf. Neumann, op. cit. pp. 9-34. A reliable survey of German democratic labor relations is Nathan Reich, *Labour Relations in Republican Germany*, New York, 1938.
5. On works councils, see C. W. Guillebaud, *The Works Council. A German Experiment in Industrial Democracy*, Cambridge (England), 1928.
6. On arbitration: Frieda Wunderlich, *Labor under German Democracy. Arbitration*, 1918-1933, New York, 1940.
7. *Jahrbuch der deutschen Sozialdemokratie für das Jahr 1929*, Berlin, 1929, p. 187.
8. W. Pieck in *Jahrbuch für Wirtschaft, Politik und Arbeiterbewegung*, Hamburg, 1923, p. 649.
9. The text of Dr. Ley's order for the seizure of the trade unions is contained in Willy Müller, *Das soziale Leben im neuen Deutschland*, Berlin, 1938, p. 51.
10. Müller, op. cit. p. 78. A good survey of the development of the Labor Front is Taylor Cole's paper, 'The Evolution of the German Labor Front,' in *Political Science Quarterly*, 1937 (52), pp. 532-58; also Robert A. Brady, *The Spirit and Structure of German Fascism*, New York, 1937, pp. 127-39.
11. Brady, op. cit. pp. 147-9. Müller, op. cit. p. 129 and pp. 135-40.
12. *New York Times*, 14 February 1940.
13. Fraenkel, op. cit. p. 194.
14. My account is based upon the following sources: Rohlfing and Schraut (ed.), *Arbeitsgesetze der Gegenwart*, Berlin, 1938. Hueck, Nipperdey, Dietz, *Gesetz zur Ordnung der nationalen Arbeit*, Munich, 1939, 3rd ed. (the leading commentary). Rolf Dietz, *Gesetz zur Ordnung der nationalen Arbeit*, Munich, 1936. Arthur Nikisch, *Arbeitsrecht*, 2 vols., Tübingen, 1936 and 1938. Gerhard Hachtmann, *Die Wandlungen des industriellen Arbeitsverhältnisses*, Bleichrode, 1936. Burchhardt and others, *Zehn Jahre*

Arbeitsrecht, Berlin and Leipzig, 1937. Werner Mansfeld, *Die Ordnung der nationalen Arbeit,* 3rd ed., Munich, 1934. *Deutsche Sozialpolitik,* report of the German Labor Front, Berlin, 1937. *Entwurf eines Gesetzes über das Arbeitsverhältnis* (Akademie für Deutsches Recht), Hamburg, 1938. Fritz Meystre, *Allgemeine Sozialpolitik,* Munich, 1934. Fritz Seldte, *Sozialpolitik im Dritten Reich* (report of the minister of labor), Berlin, 1935. Wolfgang Siebert, *Das Arbeitsverhältnis in der Ordnung der nationalen Arbeit,* Hamburg, 1935. Wolfgang Siebert, 'Grundfragen des Arbeitsverhältnisses im Lichte der neueren Rechtsprechung,' in *Juristische Wochenschrift,* 1937, pp. 1103-11. Angela Meister, *Die deutsche Industrie-arbeiterin,* Jena, 1939. *Jahrbuch,* 1938 and 1939 (2 vols.), ed. by the institute for the Science of Labor of the German Labor Front, Berlin, 1938, 1939. Further, a number of articles and court decisions, some of which are mentioned, and the collection of legislative material mentioned on p. 500. There are two reliable English discussions of specific problems: Taylor Cole, 'National Socialism and the German Labor Courts,' in *The Journal of Politics,* 1941 (3), pp. 169-97. Nathan Albert Pelcovitz, 'The Social Courts of Honor of Nazi Germany,' in *Political Science Quarterly,* 1938 (53), pp. 350-71.

15. Meystre, p. 42.
16. Seldte, p. 31.
17. Section 1 of the *Entwurf* . . .
18. Mansfeld, p. 12.
19. Dietz, p. 5.
20. Cf. the analysis of this trend in Franz Neumann, *Die politische und soziale Bedeutung der arbeitsgerichtlichen Rechtsprechung,* Berlin, 1929, pp. 29-33.
21. Hueck, etc., note 17 to Section 1, and note 1 before Section 26.
22. Typical is the decision of the supreme labor court of 30 October 1940 (*DR* 1941, p. 893), which refuses to grant wages to a tuberculous for the first three days after his illness, arguing that the new National Socialist theory of plant community must not lead to a reinterpretation of Section 616 of the civil code, which provides for the duty of the employer to pay wages if the employee cannot work for 'a relatively insignificant time.' According to the court this provision cannot today be put aside.
23. Hueck, etc., notes 19-22 to Section 2; Nikisch, Vol. II, p. 78.
24. Hueck, etc., note 15 to Section 5.
25. W. Woytinsky in *Internationales Handwörterbuch des Gewerkschafts-wesens* (Ludwig Heyde, ed.), Berlin 1930-2, p. 1590. For similar results in the metal industry see: *Protokoll der 11. Konferenz des Reichsbeirats der Betriebsräte und Konzernvertreter der Metallindustrie,* Berlin, 1932, p. 142.
26. On the ratio of Social Democratic and Communist votes to working class population see *SJ,* 1932, p. 542 and p. 18.
27. Hueck, etc., Note 1 a to Section 9.
28. Posse, Vol. I, *Kriegswirtsschaftsverordnung,* p. 2.
29. *Ehrengerichtsordnung der gewerblichen Wirtschaft,* of 20 January 1937. I have used the commentary by Rolf Dietz, *Ehrengerichtsordnung der gewerblichen Wirtschaft,* Munich, 1937.
30. Decision 17 January 1940, *DR,* 1940, p. 2125.
31. 'Soziale Ehrengerichtsbarkeit 1939,' *SP,* 1940 (49), pp. 458, 459.
32. They are reported by Taylor Cole, op. cit.
33. On the activity of labor law courts, see *SJ,* 1938, p. 617.
34. *Jahrbuch* 1938, Vol. I, p. 91.

35. Ibid. p. 99.
36. Müller, op. cit. p. 176.
37. *SP*, 1940 (49), p. 687.
38. Cf. Brady, op. cit. pp. 151, 152; 161, 162.
39. K. Arnhold, *Der Betriebsingenieur als Menschenführer*, Berlin, March 2, 1937, p. 3. See Brady, op. cit., p. 164. K. Arnhold, 'Lehrling—einst und jetzt,' in *SP*, 1937 (July 23).
40. Müller, op. cit. p. 175.
41. Werner Fritzsche, *Das Arbeitsethos. Der Mensch und seine Arbeit*, Bad Homburg v. d. H. (publication of the Siemens-Studien-Gesellschaft für praktische Psychologie), n.d. (apparently 1938), pp. 87, 88.
42. Op. cit. p. 96.
43. In 1938, the Strength Through Joy theaters were attended by 14 million, libraries numbered 5,260, sports were attended by 22.5 million, excursions were attended by 10 million. Source: *SP*, 1939 (48), p. 911.
44. Used literature: Werner Mansfeld, 'Grundsätze der Lohngestaltung,' *VP*, 1938 (2), pp. 520-22; Werner Mansfeld, 'Leistungssteigerung und Sozialpolitik,' *VP* 1939 (3), pp. 656-9; *Jahrbuch* 1939, p. 77; Dr. Sitzler, 'Probleme der Lohngestaltung,' in *SP*, 1941 (50), pp. 3-7; G. Horedt, 'Zur Neugestaltung der Löhne,' in *SP*, 1941 (50), pp. 259-63.
45. *SP* 1941 (50), p. 251.
46. Federal Supreme Labor Court of 13 September 1939 in *SP*, 1940 (49), p. 372.
47. Posse, Vol. 1, *Kriegslöhne*, p. 1.
48. *SJ*, 1938, p. 339, for 1938 *WS*, 1939 (19), p. 24.
49. *SJ*, 1938, p. 338. For wages of women see also: Meister, op. cit. pp. 93-100. The book complains about the discrimination against female work but is based entirely on hourly tariff wages and, therefore, without value.
50. The differentiation becomes also apparent from the statistics of the weekly contributions to the invalidity insurance, and the monthly contributions to the salaried employees insurance. See: *Vierteljahrshefte zur Statistik des Deutschen Reiches*, 1937, p. 97; *WS*, 1938, p. 652; and Maxine Yaple Sweezy, 'Distribution of Wealth and Income under the Nazis,' in *The Review of Economic Statistics*, 1939 (21), pp. 178-84.
51. Sitzler, op. cit. p. 3.
52. Horedt, op. cit.
53. Sweezy, 'Distribution of Wealth and Income under the Nazis,' op. cit. pp. 178-84.
54. For the figures on number of employed workers and salaried employees, see p. 508. For figures on volume of production, see p. 510. For the remaining figures, see: *WS*, 1939, No. 8, and 1939, Nos. 21, and 22.
55. Janelle, *L'Angleterre Catholique à la Veille du Schisme*, Paris, 1935, p. 185. I owe this reference to the excellent book of Franklin le van Baumer, *The Early Tudor Theory of Kingship*, New Haven, 1940, p. 211.
56. Harold D. Lasswell, 'The Study and Practice of Propaganda,' in *Propaganda and Promotional Activities: An Annotated Bibliography*, Minneapolis, 1935, pp. 3-27, esp. p. 3.
57. Hadamovsky, *Propaganda und nationale Macht*, Oldenburg, 1933.
58. Cf. the excellent analysis of Edmund Taylor, *The Strategy of Terror*, Boston, 1940. Taylor's book is an outstanding example of what an American reporter can do.
59. *The Rape of the Masses*, New York, 1940.

60. *Mein Kampf,* pp. 715 and 716, and Erich Fromm, *Escape from Freedom,* New York, 1941, p. 223.
61. Clifford Kirkpatrick, *Nazi Germany: Its Women and Family Life,* Indianapolis, New York, 1938, p. 32.
62. Mayer, *Rechtsnormen und Kulturnormen,* Breslau, 1903, p. 27.
63. The following discussion follows closely my article, 'Der Funktionswandel des Gesetzes im Recht der bürgerlichen Gesellschaft,' in *Zeitschrift für Sozialforschung,* 1937 (6) pp. 542-96, trans. by Klaus Knorr and Edward Shils under the title, 'The Change in the Function of Law in Modern Society,' and published in *Second Year Course in the Study of Contemporary Society,* 8th ed., University of Chicago, Chicago, Ill., 1939. An excellent and detailed analysis of the National Socialist legal system is Ernst Fraenkel, *The Dual State,* trans. by E. A. Shils, E. Lowenstein, and K. Knorr, New York, 1941. I do not agree with the theoretical analysis of Fraenkel, as can readily be seen. The material and many discussions make the book valuable.
64. *Social Contract* (Everyman's Library).
65. Montesquieu, *L'esprit des lois,* xi, 6.
66. Cohen, *Law and the Social Order,* New York, 1933, p. 112.
67. Max Weber, 'Wirtschaft und Gesellschaft,' op. cit. p. 166.
68. Welcker, *Die letzten Gründe von Recht, Staat und Strafe,* Giessen, 1812, p. 31.
69. 'La liberté consiste à ne dépendre que des lois,' in *Pensées sur le gouvernement* (ed. Garnier, Paris, 1877-85), xxiii, p. 526.
70. Decision of the Federal Supreme Court in Civil Matters. Official collection, Vol. 102, p. 161.
71. An excellent analysis by Otto Kirchheimer, *Grenzen der Enteignung,* Berlin, 1932.
72. *Juristische Wochenschrift,* 1924, p. 90.
73. Carl Schmitt, *Fünf Leitsätze für die Rechtspraxis,* Berlin, 1933 (Rule 4). Wolfgang Siebert, *Vom Wesen des Rechtsmissbrauches,* Berlin, 1935, p. 15. The view has been fully adopted by the courts: i.e. Decision of the Great Senate of the Federal Supreme Court of 13 March 1936 in *Juristische Wochenschrift,* 1936, p. 1281.
74. Hans Frank, *ZA,* 1936 (4), p. 290.
75. Karl Larenz, *Rechtsperson und subjektives Recht,* Berlin, 1936, p. 9.
76. Carl Schmitt, 'Der Führer schützt das Recht,' in *Deutsche Juristenzeitung,* 1934 (29), p. 945.
77. Universally accepted. See Schmitt, *Über die drei Arten des rechtswissenschaftlichen Denkens,* Hamburg, 1934.
78. Georges Renard, *L'institution: fondement d'une renovation de l'ordre social,* Paris, 1931.
79. Op. cit. p. 178.
80. Reinhard Höhn, *Die Wandlung im staatsrechtlichen Denken,* Hamburg, 1934.
81. H. Lange, *Liberalismus, Nationalsozialismus und bürgerliches Recht,* Tübingen, 1933. F. Wieacker, *Wandlungen der Eigentumsverfassung,* Hamburg, 1935, p. 23.
82. Wieacker, op. cit. p. 126.
83. Schmitt, Ueber die . . . p. 57.
84. Siegfried Grundmann, 'Die richterliche Nachprüfung von politischen

Führungsakten nach geltendem deutschen Verfassungsrecht,' in *ZS*, 1940 (100), pp. 511-44, p. 513.

85. I use the convenient book by Werner Spohr, *Das Recht der Schutzhaft*, Berlin, 1937, and my own book, *Das gesamte Pressenotrecht*, Berlin, 1933, prohibited by the secret state police on the day of its publication.

86. A number of such decisions are printed in Spohr's book, pp. 67-111; also Fraenkel, op. cit. pp. 20-32.

87. See Spohr, op. cit. p. 16.

88. The best analysis of criminal law is by Otto Kirchheimer, 'Criminal Law in National Socialist Germany,' in *Studies in Philosophy and Social Science*, 1939 (8), pp. 444-63. On the penal policy of National Socialism: Otto Kirchheimer and Georg Rusche, *Punishment and Social Structure*, New York, 1939, pp. 177-82.

89. Roland Freisler in *Das kommende deutsche Strafrecht. Allgemeiner Teil*, 2nd ed., Berlin, 1935, p. 26; and Kirchheimer, 'Criminal Law, etc.,' p. 444.

90. The main representatives are: Georg Dahm, *Grundfragen der neuen Rechtswissenschaft*, Hamburg, 1935; and Friedrich Schaffstein, *Politische Strafrechtswissenschaft*, Hamburg, 1934. The most active opponents are: Erich Schwinge and Leopold Zimmerl, *Wesensschau und konkretes Ordnungsdenken im Strafrecht*, Bonn, 1937; see my review in *Zeitschrift für Sozialforschung*, 1937 (6), pp. 706, 707.

91. Interesting decision of 9 September 1937 (Civil Matters), in *ZA*, 1938, p. 25: the obligation of a municipality to continue payments to a church community cannot be ended by invoking the principles of the party program.

92. Eduard Kern, 'Die Selbstverwaltung der Gerichte,' in *ZA*, 1939, pp. 47-50.

93. Kirchheimer, op. cit. p. 452.

94. McBoyle *v.* U. S. 283 U. S. 25; excellent analysis by Jerome Hall, 'Nulla Poena sine Lege,' *Yale Law Journal*, 1937 (47), pp. 165-93.

95. Karl Engert (vice president of the People's Court, Berlin), 'Stellung und Aufgaben des Volksgerichtshofes,' in *DR*, 1939, p. 485. Also interesting: Lämmle (member of the People's Court, Berlin), 'Die Rechtsstellung der Volksgerichtshofs in der deutschen Rechtspflege,' in *Juristische Wochenschrift*, 1938, pp. 2569-72.

96. Decision of 6 December 1939 in *ZA*, 1940, p. 48.

97. Survey by Edmund Mezger, 'Kriegsstrafrecht und Kriegsstrafverfahrensrecht,' in *ZA*, 1940, pp. 59-62.

98. Decision of 27 August 1940, *ZA*, 1940, p. 376.

99. Alfred Kayser, 'Schärfster Kampf dem Gewaltverbrecher,' in *DR*, 1940, p. 345.

100. 1 February 1940, *DR*, 1940, p. 441.

101. Georg Dahm, 'Richtermacht und Gerichtsverfassung im Strafrecht,' in *ZS*, 1941 (101), pp. 287-308, esp. p. 292.

BEHEMOTH

1. Thomas Hobbes, *Leviathan*, Molesworth ed., Vol. III, Part II, ch. 21, p. 199. The following remarks on the political thought of National Socialism are based upon my unpublished manuscript, *The Governance of the Rule of Law*, written in 1936, available at the University of London, pp. 561.

2. Burke, *Works*, Vol. III, p. 63.

3. de Maistre, *Oeuvres complètes*, Lyon, 1891-2, Vol. II, p. 167.
4. Ibid. Vol. I, p. 367.
5. Bonald, *Mélanges Littéraires* . . . Vol. II, Paris, 1854, p. 410.
6. Ibid. 'Pensées sur divers sujets,' in *Du Divorce*, Paris, 1858, p. 360.
7. Stahl, *Uber die gegenwärtigen Parteien in Staat und Kirche*, Berlin, 1883, p. 23.
8. On Stahl cf.: Herbert Marcuse, *Reason and Revolution, Hegel and the Rise of Social Theory*, New York, 1941, pp. 360-73.
9. Haller, *Restauration der Staatswissenschaft*, first published in 1816.
10. *Philosophy of Right* (transl. S. W. Dyde), London, 1896, sec. 258, Note (p. 244).
11. Note 8.
12. *Diuturna*, Milano, 1924, pp. 374-7 ('Relativismo e Fascismo'). (The Diuturna are a selection of leading articles written by Mussolini and edited by V. Morello.)
13. *Mussolini in the Making*, Boston and New York, 1938.
14. Bertrand Russell, 'The Revolt against Reason,' in the *Political Quarterly*, 1935, p. 5. Max Horkheimer, 'Zum Rationalismusstreit in der gegenwärtigen Philosophie,' in *Zeitschrift für Sozialforschung*, 1934 (3), p. 1.
15. *Dissertations and Discussions*, 3rd ed., Vol. I, p. 332.
16. Ernst Krieck, *Nationalpolitische Erziehung*, 14th ed., Leipzig, 1933, p. 68.
17. This phenomenon has been observed by Carlton J. H. Hays, 'The Novelty of Totalitarianism in the History of Western Civilization,' in *Symposium on the Totalitarian State* (American Philosophical Society), Philadelphia, 1940, pp. 91-102.
18. Harold D. Lasswell, 'The Garrison State,' in *The American Journal of Sociology*, 1941 (46), pp. 455-68, esp. p. 462.
19. Compare the excellent analysis of Max Horkheimer, 'Egoismus und Freiheitsbewegung,' in *Zeitschrift für Sozialforschung*, 1936 (5), pp. 161-231.
20. Ernst Fraenkel, *The Dual State*, New York, 1941.
21. Höhn, *Die Wandlung im staatsrechtlichen Denken*, Hamburg, 1934.
22. Neesse, *Führergewalt*, Tübingen, 1940.
23. Roger Diener, 'Reichsproblem und Hegemonie,' in *Deutsches Recht*, 1939, pp. 551-66.
24. Neesse, op. cit. p. 54.
25. 'Der Reichsbegriff im Völkerrecht,' in *Deutsches Recht*, 1939, pp. 341-4.
26. Lasswell, op. cit.
27. Max Werner, *Battle for the World*, New York, 1941, p. 12; Tom Wintringham, *New Ways of War*, London, 1940.
28. Carl Dreher, 'Why Hitler Wins,' in *Harper's Magazine*, October, 1940.
29. Shirer, *Berlin Diary*, New York, 1941.
30. Cf. the excellent analysis 'War Aims in War Propaganda' in *Propaganda Analysis*, 1941 (Vol. IV), No. 27, March 1941.

APPENDIX

The major chapter of the text to which each Appendix chapter refers is indicated by the various chapter titles and the page references beneath them. For a detailed Table of Contents, see page xvii.

PART ONE

THE POLITICAL PATTERN OF NATIONAL SOCIALISM

I

THE TOTALITARIAN STATE IN THE WAR

(follows page 61)

1. THE NATIONAL LEADERSHIP

THE changes in the national leadership of the *grossdeutsche Reich* are of minor significance. Legislative power still rests with the agencies discussed on page 58. The hierarchy is as follows:

Reich Leader: Hitler
Presidential office: Meissner
Office of the Chancellor: Lammers
Chancellory of the Party Leader: Bormann
Chancellory of the Party: Bouhler
Reich Marshal and heir: Göring

Ministerial Council for the Defense of the Realm:
Chairman: Göring
Members: Lammers (managing), Keitel, Himmler, Funk, Bormann
Reich Commissioners, Inspector Generals and Chief of Civil Administration in Occupied Europe.

There is also a Privy Cabinet Council and a Reichstag, but both are mere ornaments.

2. THE FORMATION OF THE POLITICAL WILL

One important fact must not be forgotten: none of the institutions—Ministerial Council, Cabinet, Privy Council—are operating. Meetings of these committees hardly ever take place. Apart from Hitler himself, there is no institution where political power can be said to reside. The Reichstag is a mere ornament, and Mr. Fritz

Thyssen even reports in his book that when the famous Reichstag meeting was called for the declaration of war, party officials were invited to take the place of those Reichstag members who were unable to attend. Legislation emanating from the ministerial council is as a rule prepared by that member who has jurisdiction over the special field; the draft is sent to Lammers, who circulates it and then issues the decree.

German constitutional life is thus characterized by its utter shapelessness, in contrast to Italy prior to Mussolini's downfall. The Grand Council of Fascism and the Monarchy were institutions quite separate and distinct from the Duce; and it was there that Mussolini's overthrow was engineered. In Germany, it is impossible to place one's finger on any one Nazi institution and designate it as *the* agency in which political decisions are made.

How, then, are they arrived at? It is clear that only major decisions are made by Hitler, and even in those he merely expresses a compromise between different forces within the ruling class. Political decisions are made by contract. That may seem surprising in view of the anti-liberal ideology and the totalitarian character of the regime. But it follows that from our point of view (see pp. 467-70) it is doubtful whether Germany can be called a state. It is far more a gang, where the leaders are perpetually compelled to agree after disagreements. Indeed, innumerable agreements are made between the chiefs. We may mention the following:

(1) The Leipzig agreement between the leader of the labor front (Ley) and the ministries of labor and economics, followed by similar agreements (see pp. 416-17).

(2) Agreement between the leader of the Reich labor service (Hierl) and the supreme command of the armed forces whereby, for the duration of the war, the labor service is placed at the disposal of the armed forces.

(3) Agreement between the Organization Todt and the supreme command of the armed forces whereby the OT is placed at the army's disposal for the duration of the war.

(4) Agreement between the party's foreign office (Rosenberg) and the supreme command of the armed forces whereby the education of the members of the armed forces must be carried out in accordance with principles of the party.

(5) Agreement between the commissioner general for labor supply (Sauckel) and the leader of the labor front (Ley) concerning the care and control of foreign laborers.

(6) Agreement between the leader of the Hitler Youth (Axmann) and the Reich leader of the S.S. (Himmler) whereby recruits for the S.S. shall be taken primarily from the Hitler Youth.

(7) The 'Honor Agreement' between the party judge (Buch) and the supreme army command, providing that disputes between officers and party officials should be amicably settled, that no duels should be fought, and that a joint honor committee should be established.

(8) Agreement between the party and the armed forces, that for the duration soldiers be allowed—in spite of Section 26 of the armed-forces statute (see p. 71)—to attend political meetings of the party and its affiliates.

(9) Agreement between the Hitler Youth and the army high command, providing for auxiliary military service of the Hitler Youth and the appointment of liaison army officers. The Hitler Youth concluded similar contracts with the navy and air force.

There are many more such contracts. They are usually announced in the Nazi press, sometimes even published in the official ministerial gazettes, and are all considered as 'law.'

We have mentioned pluralism as the disease of the Weimar Republic (see pp. 10, 11, 13, 17, 44), and have pointed out that the German reaction and especially the Nazi party greatly benefited from a state of affairs in which a unified political will was lacking and where political parties, social organizations, and other power agglomerations constituted almost sovereign entities within the body politic. We have also shown that Nazi constitutional theory, especially that of Carl Schmitt (pp. 42-5), denounced the Weimar Republic for its pluralism and praised Nazism for its unity. Now, even Nazi constitutional lawyers occasionally express grave doubts. 'The German people,' says one,[1] 'has fought long enough for its full legal unity. Shall the field of the constitution of the courts be now dominated by—I venture to say—vertical pluralism?' The author refers to the extensive departmentalization of the judiciary (see pp. 455-6), the co-existence of many jurisdictions and court systems, phenomena that express the same shapelessness of Nazi constitutional life.

1. Fritz Baur, *Die Bindung an Entscheidungen*, Tübingen, 1941.

It would be fatally wrong to consider this shapelessness a weakness. It is, indeed, a strength of the system. It makes it impossible for any opposition to overthrow the regime merely by occupying one institution or even several. None has power, each is powerful only if synchronized with a large number of others. It also allows the Leader to play off one group against another without being compelled to resort to any one institution or even having to change the institutional arrangements.

The regime relies besides on other mechanisms for making this political system workable. In importance, these rank somewhat as follows: (1) The terror against the German people. The terror machine is fully centralized and utterly unpredictable. (2) Material benefits from spoils of Aryanization and Germanization. Considerable groups, including the most powerful, are tied to the regime because they have benefited from it. (3) Terror against foreign peoples inside and outside Germany. More and more groups of Germans are compelled to practice terror. The larger the group that does so, the larger the willing or unwilling supporters of the regime. Fear then compels even those who abhor terror to go along with it. (4) The destruction of traditional groups in society (especially political parties and labor unions). (5) The atomization of all human relations (see pp. 400-402), the impossibility for those who feel and think alike to organize. (6) The permeation of all groups by Nazis —open or hidden—making it impossible for anyone to rely on anyone else.

In such a situation, political society can be utterly unorganized, political institutions can be formless and shapeless. The manipulators at the top are favored by the absence of any institutional limitations upon their arbitrary power. The drawbacks will become apparent only when the system collapses. It may then most likely give way to complete chaos.

3. Inspector Generals, Commissioners, and the Cabinet

It follows that the high-sounding titles and even ministries do not give the slightest indication of the power that is actually wielded. Among the subordinates of Hitler, Bormann is certainly powerful, more so than Hess used to be,[2] while Lammers undoubtedly man-

2. On Bormann, see Konrad Heiden, *Der Fuehrer,* New York, 1944, p. 742.

ages all administrative and legislative matters with which Hitler must be concerned. Göring's power does not rest on a party office but on the agglomeration of power in the air ministry, the Four Year Plan, and his close relations with Himmler on the one hand and industry on the other.

The Commissioners and Inspector Generals have varying powers. Werlin has no executive machinery. He merely advises Hitler in questions of the motor-vehicle industry and has the right to investigate. Speer, on the other hand, as Inspector General for Roads, Water, and Power, chief of the Organization Todt, Minister for Armaments and War Production, has unlimited power over the economy that will be described below. Ley, as housing commissioner, has merely limited functions, and Kaufmann, as shipping commissioner, merely technical tasks. None of the chiefs of civil administration or commissioners for occupied territories wields power. The chapter on the *Grossdeutsche Reich* will make clear that the economic, labor, and police controls over occupied Europe are manipulated centrally from Berlin.

The cabinet as an institution does not exist. The members often rule over empty shells. Only Ribbentrop, Goebbels, Himmler, and Speer are powerful as cabinet ministers. The ministry of finance is today a 'technical' ministry, without policy-making power. The chief is a mere figurehead, while the little power concentrated there is exercised by his secretary of state, the Nazi Fritz Reinhardt. The justice ministry is an adjunct of Himmler's police. The labor ministry is a shell; its section concerned with housing is under Ley; those concerned with labor supply, wages, and labor standards are under Gauleiter Fritz Sauckel as labor supply dictator in the Four Year Plan (see below). The transportation ministry has lost its sections dealing with road transportation, power, and water, to the omnivorous Speer, and is besides a 'technical' ministry. The chief is overshadowed by the ardent Nazi secretary of state Ganzenmüller. The church ministry has not even a cabinet minister as chief and the agriculture ministry is merely the handmaiden of Speer.

The sole powerful ministry for all matters except propaganda, foreign affairs, and economics is the Reich Ministry of the Interior. It is here that all strands for the control of the administrative machinery in Germany and occupied Europe come together.

4. THE INTERIOR MINISTRY

The Interior is not only the police ministry—as such it will be discussed below (p. 541). It provides the framework for the whole administration. The powers of Reich Minister Himmler are unlimited. His chief assistant (outside of police matters) is the secretary of state, Wilhelm Stuckart.

A considerable number of institutions are attached to the Ministry: The Reich Administrative Tribunal; the Reich Kinship Office; the Reich Health Office under Reich Health Leader Dr. L. Conti; the Reich Archives; Reich Geodetic Service; the Reich Chambers of Doctors, Veterinarians, Apothecaries; the German Red Cross; the Diet of German Municipalities. All of these—including the Red Cross—are staffed with high S.S. leaders and thus bound to Himmler by civil service and S.S. bonds. The departments I and II are, besides, agencies for the administrative integration of all occupied, annexed, and appended territories with the Reich. This will be discussed below.

5. THE REGIONAL ORGANIZATION OF THE REICH

Yet it is not on the national level that administration is made; it is rather the regional and local levels that are all-important. Here the Ministry of the Interior exercises the greatest and most concentrated power. This was structurally achieved by the destruction of Prussia as a state, the complete emasculation of the other states (*Länder*), the creation of the Reichsgaue, and the appointment on 16 November 1942 of all 42 Gauleiter as National Defense Commissars.

Prussia has ceased to exist as a state and has been dissolved into her provinces. There is only one Prussian ministry, that of Finance, which administers the sorry remains of Prussian state property and the building administration. There is, it is true, nominally a Prussian prime minister, but Göring, who fills this position also, has no cabinet and no functions. All other Prussian ministries were merged with the corresponding Reich ministries, especially the justice and interior departments.

The Reich Ministry of the Interior directly controls the Prussian *Oberpräsidenten*, the provincial presidents, without the intermediary of either Göring or the Prussian Minister of Finance. The 11 [3] Prussian provinces are thus political divisions of the Reich.

The fourteen *Länder* have a position equal to that of the Prussian provinces and the federal regents are subject to the orders of the Reich Ministry of the Interior to the same degree as are the provincial presidents.

Reichsgaue are the third and new type of regional organization. The following have been created:

Westmark (Saarbrücken)—Gauleiter and federal regent Bürckel
Vienna (Vienna)—Gauleiter and federal regent v. Schirach
Carinthia (Klagenfurt)—Gauleiter and federal regent Dr. F. Rainer
Lower Danube (Vienna)—Gauleiter and federal regent Dr. H. Jury
Upper Danube (Linz)—Gauleiter and federal regent A. Eigruber
Salzburg (Salzburg)—Gauleiter and federal regent G. A. Scheel
Styria (Graz)—Gauleiter and federal regent Dr. S. Uiberreither
Tirol-Vorarlberg (Innsbruck)—Gauleiter and federal regent F. Hofer
Sudetenland (Reichenberg)—Gauleiter and federal regent Adolf Henlein
Danzig-West Prussia (Danzig)—Gauleiter and federal regent Albert Forster
Wartheland (Poznan)—Gauleiter and federal regent A. K. Greiser

The Reichsgaue thus comprise new territory, which has not been added to the existing political divisions of Germany (except in certain cases to be discussed in the chapter the Grossdeutsche Reich), and are a completely new type of political division. This new type shows two very distinctive features: the full co-ordination of party and government control, and the centralization of all powers in the hands of the Gauleiter-federal regents. Government and party structure is almost identical. All administrative agencies within a Reichsgau, no matter whether they come under the jurisdiction of the Reich Ministry of the Interior or under that of any other ministry, and all self-government agencies come under the authority of the Gauleiter-regent. Whereas, in the Prussian provinces and in the *Länder*, say, the Reich Minister of Labor can pass orders directly to his labor exchanges, he cannot do so in the Reichsgaue. He has to get clearance from the Gauleiter-regent.

3. There are now 13 provinces. Hessen-Nassau and Sachsen have been divided into two provinces.

6. Unification, the Encroachment of the Gau, and National Defense Commissars

This threefold distinction—province, Land, Reichsgau—is undoubtedly unsatisfactory, and only the exigencies of the war have prevented the Nazis from abolishing provinces and *Länder* and transforming all political units into Reichsgaue on the basis of the party Gau division.

Transitional measures had to be introduced in order to equalize the three types. The Statute on the Unification of the Structure of Administrative Agencies of 5 July 1939 was the first decisive step in this direction. It declared that the administrative organs of the *Länder* were at the same time organs of the Reich. The Statute also prohibited the establishment of separate administrative organs on the regional level and insisted that new administrative tasks had to be transferred to the existing organs (provincial and government presidents and *Länder* administrations). But the weak Frick was not able to achieve this. New administrative agencies mushroomed on the regional level. Then came the appointment of 16 Gauleiter as National Defense Commissars (see p. 59), organs of the Ministerial Council for the Defense of the Reich. But these were appointed for each corps area (*Wehrkreis*), a territory considerably larger than the established political divisions of Germany. This made effective control of the established political divisions difficult, and many Gauleiter who were thus not defense commissars were dissatisfied. In October 1939, therefore, 14 more Gauleiter were made defense deputies.

The confusion on the regional level was considerable. Slowly and steadily, the party Gau was chosen as the model for the co-ordination of all administrative activities. Ley, as housing commissioner, made the 42 Gauleiter his deputies; Sauckel, as labor supply commissioner, followed; the Economic Chambers were transformed into Gau Economic Chambers (see below, p. 598), and the Regional Labor Exchanges into Gau Labor Exchanges (see below).

By a decree of 16 November 1942, all 42 Gauleiter were finally appointed National Defense Commissars and established 42 War Economy Staffs (*Kriegswirtschaftsstäbe*) in succession to the dissolved defense committees (see p. 59). As defense commissars, the

Gauleiter are political commissars over the established administrative agencies, and co-ordinate labor supply, housing, the Gau labor exchanges, the trustees of labor, the Gau administration of the labor front, the Regional Economic, Food and Forest and Timber Offices, the Deputies for Suburban Transportation, the Armament Commissions (see below, p. 594). The necessity for full co-ordination of all powers created by defeats in Russia, in Italy, and in the air has necessitated complete and fully centralized political supervision over the administration. Yet the moment these political controls were established, a serious competitor arose in the new machinery of the Speer ministry (see below, p. 590).

II

THE PARTY AS A MACHINE

(follows pages 82 and 378)

THE N.S.D.A.P. is today the organization that maintains German society. Without the party, Germany would collapse. Party, State, and Society are, under war conditions, identical. The party provides the ideological leadership; it supplies the huge system of terror; it runs the occupied territories; it provides bread, shelter, clothing, and medical services for air-raid victims; it controls the administration; it administers labor and housing supply; it supervises millions of foreign laborers. In short, it controls all but two fields: the fighting fronts and the economy. It is thus necessary to provide a clear picture of its structure and composition. Apart from the party, there are its formations, affiliates, and supervised organizations (see pp. 81-2).

1. THE REICH LEADERS

While the Leader of the party is Adolf Hitler, administrative power is exercised by the deputy leader Martin Bormann, Hess's successor, and the treasurer Franz Schwarz. The power of the Reich organization leader (P.O.) Robert Ley is doubtful. Nor can it be said that the *Reichsleiter* exercise profound political influence, just because they direct national bureaus in the top party machinery.

The Hitler Youth Leader, Baldur von Schirach, has limited influence, the more so since the Hitler Youth today is in the army, in army auxiliaries, in the air-raid protection service under the police, or at work. Schirach is, besides, no longer actually the leader of the Hitler Youth (his successor is A. Axmann), but is federal regent and Gauleiter of Vienna.

The N.S.K.K. leader Erwin Kraus is equally unimportant. The Motor Corps is today either incorporated into the Organization Todt, whose supplies it organizes, or is in the army, where it is part of the training program for Panzer Troops.

The S.S. leader Heinrich Himmler's supreme power has been described above.

The S.A. leader Wilhelm Schepmann, who succeeded Lutze, has but little power, because of the steady decline of the Stormtroops—in spite of many attempts made to revive this proletarian guard. On 19 January 1939,[1] the S.A. was put in charge of all pre- and post-military training except for those joining or belonging to the S.S., the N.S.K.K., or the N.S.F.K. All potential soldiers and all former soldiers must undergo training by the S.A., though they need not join it. A previous decree had already given to the S.A. special courts. Yet neither this power nor the protectorship of Göring could stem the decline of the S.A. The establishment of rural and city guards described below, though using the power of the 1939 decree, fell again to the S.S. and police. The S.A. tries desperately to revive the tradition and esteem. But today it does merely dirty handiwork: collection of junk and of winter help, and the guarding of foreign laborers. The terror apparatus remains safely in the hands of the S.S.

The *Reichsleiter* in charge of municipal policy, Karl Fiehler, is only a nonentity.

The Reich Labor Service (R.A.D.) leader, Konstantin Hierl, though raised to the rank of a cabinet minister by the edict of 24 August 1943, nevertheless remains without great power. With the outbreak of the war, the members of the Reich Labor Service were placed at the disposal of the supreme command of the armed forces and the huge majority of the boys were sent to the fronts to assist the army, especially in solving the supply problems in the Eastern Front. The R.A.D. is thus almost entirely under military jurisdiction, though remaining in its own formations. It has a dual structure: in Germany, it is divided into Labor Service *Gaue;* for front service, the division is according to construction staffs (*Abschnitts-baustäbe*) and corresponding lower units.

It need hardly be stated that the Reich leader of the Nazi parliamentary group in the Reichstag, Wilhelm Frick, is a mere ornament. The Colonial office under the federal regent Franz Ritter von Epp was closed in 1943 for the duration.

Alfred Rosenberg still exerts considerable power as Reich leader

---

1. The following according to Hans Snyckers, *S.A.,* —*Wehrmannschaften,* 5th ed., Munich, 1941.

in charge of spiritual training and foreign policy. His influence was strengthened by his appointment as Reich Minister for the Eastern Occupied Territories, but is declining as his empire shrinks under the might of Rumanian attacks.

The Reich leader of the rural population (*Landvolk*), Walther Darré, has been on leave since 1942 and is never mentioned—either as Reich leader or as Minister for Food and Agriculture. It is likely that his place is being filled by Herbert Backe, secretary of state in the ministry (see pp. 269, 372, 376; now appointed minister).

The press chief, Otto Dietrich, has committed conspicuous blunders, described in Howard Smith's *Last Train from Berlin*, yet his power seems to be undiminished. He occupies, moreover, the important position of the Reich Cabinet Press Chief, with the rank of a cabinet minister.

The press leader and chief publisher, Max Amann, wields enormous power over the party press, whose influence was increased when, in January 1943, the labor mobilization act put an end to many non-party newspapers, among them the *Frankfurter Zeitung*. Nor can the power of Walter Buch, the Supreme Party Judge, be sufficiently emphasized.

Joseph Goebbels combines the position of a Reich leader in charge of propaganda with that of Minister for Enlightenment and Propaganda, and of a Gauleiter and defense commissar for Berlin. He is and will remain an indispensable tool of a regime that, more than ever before, has to rely on the manipulation of the masses. The undisputed mastery of this art makes him next to Himmler, Göring, Bormann, and Speer the best-known figure among the paladins of Hitler.

Philipp Bouhler's power as Reich leader in charge of the Hitler chancellory, as party leader, and as supreme party censor is hardly measurable.

It may thus be said that among the supreme officials in the party leadership only Bormann, Schwarz, Himmler, Rosenberg, Amann, Goebbels, Buch, and Bouhler—and possibly Ley—can be said to have genuine political power. But in almost every case (excepting Schwarz, Buch, and Bouhler) this power is based not only on the political position within the party, but also on positions within the government or control of property (Schwarz and Amann).

2. Prominent Nazis in the Government

Apart from the few Reich leaders and the Gauleiter, to be discussed below, there are Nazis who wield tremendous power because they constitute the link between the party and the other sectors in the ruling class. Foremost among them is Hermann Göring. He is a simple party member—but Hitler's designated heir. His power derives from the government positions he holds and the intimate relation with the services and industry. He is a *Reichsmarshal*—the only one; Hitler's deputy for the Four Year Plan, in charge not only of the German but of the European economy as well; chairman of the Ministerial Council for the Defense of the Realm and thus, next to Hitler, the highest legislator; air minister and supreme commander of the German air force; protector of the Göring combine.

Next to him in power is Albert Speer, Todt's successor. He is Hitler's favorite city builder and today in charge of all production.

Joachim von Ribbentrop, the foreign minister, has no party position and may yet be considered one of the most influential Nazis. Thierack, justice minister, may not be of first-class importance, but still controls—though not fully—the German judiciary. Ganzenmüller is secretary of state in the ministry of transportation. Fritz Reinhardt is secretary of state in the ministry of finance. Franz Hayler is S.S. Brigade leader and the new secretary of state in the ministry of economics.[2] Paul Körner is secretary of state in the Four Year Plan office. Wilhelm Stuckart is secretary of state in the interior ministry. Roland Freisler is president of the people's court. Günter Korten is chief of staff of the German air force, one of the few generals whose Nazi convictions are well established. Erhard Milch is field marshal and secretary of state in the air ministry. H. H. Lammers is cabinet minister, chief of the chancellory, and member and secretary of the ministerial council. Walther Funk, minister of economics, may still be powerful, though he had to hand over to Speer his jurisdiction over production. Jakob Werlin, commissioner general for motor vehicle transportation, derives his influence primarily from friendship with Hitler. Dr. Karl Brandt, the German health czar, is also Hitler's personal physician.

With the chiefs of the two police branches, Daluege and Kalten-

2. Succeeded F. W. Landfried in 1944. On Landfried see pp. 303, 372, 376.

brunner, and some other S.S. leaders, we have a fairly complete picture of Nazis in national party leadership and/or in the government leadership.

In addition there are nationally known Nazis whose power does not lie in government or party positions, but in the control of the means of production. With these, we shall deal later.

3. THE GAULEITER

The kernel of the Nazi party is the Gauleiter. There are 43 Gaue, one, however, identical with the Foreign Organization of the party (A.O.) under E. W. Bohle. It will be discussed below.

The present Gaue and Gauleiter are:

GAU	GAULEITER	GAU CAPITAL
1. Baden	Robert Wagner	Karlsruhe
2. Bayreuth	Fritz Wächtler	Bayreuth
3. Berlin	Joseph Goebbels	Berlin
	Arthur Görlitzer, deputy	
4. Danzig-Westpreussen	Albert Forster	Danzig
5. Düsseldorf	Friedrich K. Florian	Düsseldorf
6. Essen	Josef Terboven	Essen
7. Franken	Karl Holz, acting	Nürnberg
8. Halle-Merseburg	Joachim Eggeling	Halle
9. Hamburg	Karl Kaufmann	Hamburg
10. Hessen-Nassau	Jakob Sprenger	Frankfort o.M.
11. Kärnten	Dr. Friedrich Rainer	Klagenfurt
12. Köln-Aachen	Josef Grohé	Koln
13. Kurhessen	Karl Gerland, acting	Kassel
14. Magdeburg-Anhalt	Rudolf Jordan	Dessau
15. Mainfranken	Dr. Otto Hellmuth	Würzburg
16. Mark Brandenburg	Emil Stürtz	Berlin
17. Mecklenburg	Friedrich Hildebrand	Schwerin
18. Moselland	Gustav Simon	Koblenz
19. München-Oberbayern	Paul Giesler	München
20. Niederdonau	Dr. Hugo Jury	Wien
21. Niederschlesien	Karl Hanke	Breslau
22. Oberdonau	August Eigruber	Linz
23. Oberschlesien	Fritz Bracht	Kattowitz
24. Osthannover	Otto Telschow	Lüneburg
25. Ostpreussen	Erich Koch	Königsberg
26. Pommern	Franz Schwede-Coburg	Stettin
27. Sachsen	Martin Mutschmann	Dresden
28. Salzburg	Dr. Gustav Adolf Scheel	Salzburg
29. Schleswig-Holstein	Hinrich Lohse	Kiel
30. Schwaben	Karl Wahl	Augsburg

GAU	GAULEITER	GAU CAPITAL
31. Steiermark	Dr. Siegfried Uiberreither	Graz
32. Südhannover-Braunschweig	Hartmann Lauterbacher	Hannover
33. Sudetenland	Adolf Henlein	Reichenberg
34. Thüringen	Fritz Sauckel	Weimar
35. Tirol-Vorarlberg	Franz Hofer	Innsbruck
36. Wartheland	Arthur Karl Greiser	Posen
37. Weser-Ems	Paul Wegener	Oldenburg
38. Westfalen-Nord	Dr. Alfred Meyer	Münster
39. Westfalen-Süd	Albert Hoffmann	Bochum
40. Westmark	Josef Bürckel	Neustadt a.d.H.
41. Wien	Baldur von Schirach	Wien
42. Württenberg	Wilhelm Murr	Stuttgart
43. A.O.	E. W. Bohle	Berlin

It is obviously the regional and not the national level that is of supreme importance in regard to party membership and the people. As Gauleiter in charge of the regional party apparatus, they already control *Menschenführung*, mass manipulation. Political leadership is vested exclusively in them. It has been shown (p. 72) that the party should not assume administrative functions proper. Indeed, the distinction between administration and *Menschenführung* is frequently drawn and the principle of the decree of 28 December 1939 often repeated. But successful *Menschenführung* in a totalitarian society nevertheless necessitates control of all administrative key positions —and the more the prospects of victory dwindle, the more important it becomes to control all spheres of administration so as to be able to steer the state machinery in the right direction and to utilize its terror and welfare functions for mass control.

As a consequence, the Gauleiter have become more powerful the more the military situation has deteriorated. More than 30 are provincial presidents and federal regents. That, however, is no new development.

In the Reichsgaue, namely Wien, Niederdonau, Oberdonau, Kärnten, Steiermark, Salzburg, Tirol, Sudetenland,[3] Wartheland, Danzig-Westpreussen, and Westmark, the Gauleiter are all federal regents and the approximation of Gau and government administration is closest. It is difficult here to distinguish party and state. Yet this may be considered an exceptional case, because the 11 Reichsgaue comprise annexed territory.

3. This is somewhat an exception.

But the Gau has also become the unit for the Chambers (see below) and the Labor Exchanges (see below) so that the old administrative divisions have been destroyed. The party economic adviser
in the Gau (*Gauwirtschaftsberater*), usually an influential businessman, controls the Gau Economic Chambers to a considerable degree. In addition, all Gauleiter have been made national defense
commissars (*Reichsverteidigungskommissare*) in charge of so-called
war economy staffs (*Kriegswirtschaftsstäbe*) (to be discussed below; for the previous functions of the defense commissars see pp.
58-9). When the labor supply problem became crucial in the spring
of 1942, all Gauleiter were Gau Labor Supply Deputies, charged
with co-ordinating labor supply in the Gaue. When air raids mag-
nified the housing problem, they were appointed Gau housing commissars. Control of occupied Europe requires personnel. Wherever
civilian control was established, Gauleiter were called upon to represent German sovereignty: in Norway, Josef Terboven; in the
Ostland, Hinrich Lohse; in the Ukraine, Erich Koch. Rosenberg's
deputy as minister for the eastern occupied territories is Gauleiter
Dr. Alfred Meyer. Robert Wagner is chief of the civil administration for Alsace, Josef Bürckel for Lorraine, Gustav Simon for Luxembourg, S. Uiberreither for Lower Styria, F. Rainer for the Upper
Carniola.

Some Gauleiter are figures in the national administration. Goebbels as propaganda minister, Sauckel as commissioner general for
labor supply, Schirach as leader of the party Youth Office, and
Scheel as students' leader.

A few of the original Gauleiter have disappeared. Streicher may
be in a sanitarium; Adolf Wagner of Bavaria has died; Josef
Wagner, after his unhappy experience as price commissioner, was
sacrificed to business early in 1942 and has never been heard of
since. As a whole, however, the paladins are the same as they were
when Hitler took power. There are more today, because of the increase in territory.

The Gauleiter are the kernel of the party. They have their ears
close to the ground, they carry the burden of the propaganda cam-
paigns, they centralize air-raid assistance, in short, they provide the
political drive behind German society at war. There are only two
fields where their power has definite limits: business and the armed
forces.

The months of air war have doubled and trebled the powers accumulated in the regional level. Decisions can no longer be centrally made and enacted. Decentralization of execution and even of policymaking is vital in order to cope with the terrific problems created by bombing. Not all Gauleiter have been able to dominate the situation, but most of them, assisted by the N.S. Welfare Organization and the regional stratum of the economic control apparatus, have been able to provide a minimum of recuperation.

4. THE PARTY OUTSIDE GERMANY

THE FOREIGN ORGANIZATION [4]

Within the Reich leadership of the party, as part of the chancellory, a Foreign Department exists, called *Auslandsorganisation* (A.O.). Regionally, the A.O. is called Gau 43 under Gauleiter E. W. Bohle, under-secretary of state in the ministry of foreign affairs. The A.O. organizes only German citizens of German blood residing abroad, but not non-German citizens of German blood—not, therefore, *Volksdeutsche*. Every German party member who transfers his residence from Germany abroad has to join the appropriate regional unit of the A.O. while he is transferred from the A.O. in one of the other 42 Gaue when he returns to Germany. The insistence on membership of German citizens only is entirely owing to considerations of foreign policy, in order to avoid complications with foreign powers.

The connection between the A.O. and the Reich government is extremely close. It is not only secured by Bohle's dual position, but by the incorporation in 1935 of the German diplomatic and consular staff into the A.O., so that the German foreign service actually looks after the interests of the Reich as well as after those of the party. In 1937, the diplomatic and consular staff was co-ordinated into one local of the A.O.

The A.O. is regionally divided into *Landesgruppen* (groups), subdivided into *Landeskreise* (counties), *Ortsgruppen* (locals), *Zellen* (cells), and *Stützpunkte* (base points). Seamen are organized

4. This chapter is partly founded on Emil Ehrich, *Die Auslandsorganisation der N.S.D.A.P.*, Berlin, 1937.

by a seamen's department, and the ships are considered (according to size) either as locals or base points.

There is an intimate liaison between the A.O. and all other party affiliates, especially the Labor Front, which conducts the social work for the A.O. abroad. Many other functional divisions within the A.O. (government employees, foreign trade, culture, press, law, speakers department, department for returning Germans) round out the task of this spearhead for the creation of fifth columns all over the world.

THE PARTY IN OCCUPIED EUROPE

The control of vast areas of occupied Europe has placed new tasks before the party. It contributes considerably to the elaboration of policies and the actual administration. The party foreign department (under A. Rosenberg), with its *Ostamt* (office for eastern affairs), its *aussenpolitisches Schulungshaus* (foreign political training school), and its *Amt für Sonderaufgaben* (office for special tasks) under Werner Daitz (see pp. 171-3, 326, 495-6), has almost bodily been transferred into the ministry for eastern occupied territories, and many of the administrators for the eastern territories are graduates of Rosenberg's training school.

This, however, did not solve the problem of cementing party control of the hundreds and thousands of Germans employed in occupied Europe as government and party officials, businessmen, and employees. The A.O. could not cope with this task—and was probably not allowed to do so. To achieve this and to attain full integration of government and party activities in occupied Europe, a new regional division, the *Arbeitsbereiche*, activity spheres of the N.S.D.A.P. were created. These are not under Bohle, but directly under Hitler—that is, the party chancellory under Martin Bormann. Each activity sphere is under a *Bereichsleiter* (activity-sphere director). The first activity sphere was established in the Government General on 6 May 1940 and is directed by Governor General Hans Frank. It is divided into districts, corresponding to those of the Government General, further into locals, blocks, cells, and base points. Almost without exception, the chiefs of the activity sphere are officials of the Government General administration.

The establishment of the activity sphere does not, of course, exclude the existence of party formation, affiliates, and supervised associations in occupied Europe. On the contrary, it encourages them, and all (S.A., Hitler Youth, etc.) are operating.

In the occupied East, the activity sphere East is directed by Rosenberg and has two divisions, in accordance with the division of the Rosenberg ministry: Ostland and Ukraine. In the Netherlands the activity sphere has grown out of a well-developed *Landesgruppe* of the A.O., which existed before the invasion. The director of this activity sphere, Willi Ritterbusch, is also Commissioner General for Special Tasks in the office of Reich Commissar for the Occupied Netherlands. In Norway, no activity sphere has been formed, but the *Landesgruppe* of the A.O. continues to exist. The reason for this is probably the flirtation (not voluntary but necessitated by stubborn Norwegian resistance) with Quisling and his Nazi party, the *Nasjonal Samling* (see p. 175).

The Protectorate has been divided among four Gaue: Sudetenland, Upper and Lower Danube, and Bayreuth.

No activity spheres, though *Landesgruppen* of the A.O., exist in France and Belgium, because those countries are under military government proper. Denmark also has no activity sphere but a *Landesgruppe*, because, according to German ideology which will be explained below, Denmark is under 'alliance administration.'

5. THE PARTY MEMBERSHIP

In December 1943, the *Völkische Beobachter* revealed the party's strength. It did so in order to demonstrate that the party had fulfilled its duty during the war and that membership and still more official functions within it imposed war duties beyond those of the non-party member. The paper maintained that the party had 6,500,-000 male members, 40 per cent of whom were in the armed forces. Of the 85,500 officials of the party's central offices, 48,600 were serving in the armed forces. If we estimate the number of organized women to be about 3,000,000, it would mean that the party now has almost 10,000,000 members—an extraordinarily high figure.

THE RISE OF HIMMLER. THE POLICE AND S.S.

(*follows page* 82)

ON 24 August 1943, Hitler relieved of his office Reich Protector of Bohemia and Moravia von Neurath, appointed the minister of interior, Wilhelm Frick, in his place, and made Heinrich Himmler, Reich Leader S.S. and Chief of the German Police, Minister of the Interior and General Commissioner for Administration in the Ministerial Council for the Defense of the Realm (see pp. 56-7). The chief of the Order Police, S.S. Leader Daluege, was withdrawn from the Protectorate; the under-secretary of state in the Ministry of the Interior, Pfundtner, was relieved of his duties; while at the same time Reich Labor Leader Konstantin Hierl was given the title of a Reich minister and placed under the direct authority of Hitler—not, as heretofore, under the interior ministry.

The decree sanctioned Himmler's rise to supreme power over domestic politics, and marked the demotion of Frick. A demotion it was; Frick is a mere figurehead in the Protectorate, where power has been vested in Karl Hermann Frank, the Sudeten German who was made German minister of state in the Protectorate government, with a rank equal to that of a Reich minister.

As Minister of Interior, Himmler is in charge of the whole civil-service apparatus, not only in the Reich proper but also in the annexed and appended territories. Through this position, he controls the whole party machinery—since the Gauleiter are provincial presidents, prime ministers, federal regents, and defense commissioners (among other positions), and local leaders control city mayors and rural councilors (*Landräte*). He retains the control of the most important instrument of the Nazi system: the police.

As Reich Leader of the S.S., Himmler controls the widespread machinery of domestic terror and, through the Combat S.S. (*Waffen S.S.*), reaches into the jurisdiction of the supreme command of the army. As Commissioner General for Reich Administration, he has decisive voice in all legislative matters and is the political chief of the Reich Ministry of Justice. As Reich Commissar for the Strengthening of German Folkdom (*Reichskommissar für die Festigung des deutschen Volkstums*), he is responsible for the Germanization of occupied, annexed, and appended territories and controls the *Volksdeutschen* in Europe, that is the non-German citizens of German blood.

1. THE POLICE [1]

The German police is now divided into two wings: the Order Police (*Ordnungspolizei*) and the Security Police (*Sicherheitspolizei*).

The Order Police, under Colonel General of the Police and S.S. *Oberst Gruppenführer* Kurt Daluege,[2] comprises: the Protective Police (*Schutzpolizei*); the Gendarmerie; and the Administrative Police (*Verwaltungspolizei*).

The Protective Police is the uniformed police for cities, the Gendarmerie that for rural areas, while the administrative police fulfils a variety of functions, largely stemming from the German conception of a police state.

The Security Police, under S.S. *Ober Gruppenführer* Franz Kaltenbrunner, an Austrian who succeeded Reinhard Heydrich after the latter's murder in the Protectorate, is divided into: the Criminal Police (*Kriminalpolizei*); the Secret State Police (*Geheime Staatspolizei*); and the Security Service of the Reich Leader of the S.S. (*Sicherheitsdienst des Reichsführer S.S.*).

The Chief of the German Police operates through three main offices, those of the Order Police, the Security Police, and Budget and Buildings. He is not satisfied, however, with an indirect hold over the lower echelons of the police personnel. He directly controls all police and S.S. formations in the regional level through the Higher S.S. and Police Leaders (*Höhere S.S. und Polizeiführer*). Three types of Higher S.S. and Police Leaders exist: in Germany, for each corps area (*Wehrkreis*); outside of Germany, for almost each occupied territory; and those for special purposes. They con-

1. This section is based on Werner Best, *Die Deutsche Polizei*, Darmstadt, 1940.
2. Daluege appears to have taken over the leadership of the whole police. Himmler now reigns as Reich Leader S.S. and Reich Minister of the Interior. Chief of the Order Police is now probably Wünnenberg.

trol, within their regions, all Order and Security Police formations, the Security Service, and the General S.S. They may assume direct command of any one of these formations, or of all of them, whenever they deem it necessary. The fullest concentration of police and S.S. powers in any corps area is thus assured.

THE ORDER POLICE

The Command of the Order Police is divided into the main office Order Police (*Hauptamt*), and the office Administration and Law. The main office is subdivided into: the Reichoffice Technical Emergency Help (*Technische Nothilfe*); the office for Voluntary Fire Brigades; the State Hospital for Police; the Office for Police Sanitariums; State Training Stations for Police Dogs; and Order Police Schools. The Chief of the Order Police secures his power over all his subordinates through Inspector Generals (*Generalinspekteure*) of the Protective Police, the Gendarmerie, the Municipal Police, and the Police Schools. In addition he assures control of all Order Police formations in any corps area through Inspectors of the Order Police (*Inspekteure der Ordnungspolizei*) in charge of all Order Police branches in his territory. The Inspector belongs (as does the Inspector of the Security Police and Security Service) to the staff of the Higher S.S. and Police Leader.

In cities, the mayor as the head of local government is the police chief. In larger cities, however, state police administrations had already been established under the Weimar Republic. In these cities, all that remains to the mayors is the administrative police. The state police administrations are either police presidencies—in the largest cities—police directories—in the medium-sized ones—or police offices.

Above the local police authorities stand the higher police authorities, namely the rural councilors, the district presidents (*Regierungspräsidenten*) in Prussia and Bavaria, and the federal regents in the remaining *Reichsgaue* (see above, p. 527). The higher police authorities are topped by the Reich Minister of the Interior.

All Order Police activities come under the control of the higher police authorities, who may directly exercise police functions and often do so when authorized by law. As a rule, however, they are assigned either to state police authorities (*Landespolizeibehörden*)— district presidents, state governments, or federal regents—or county police authorities (*Kreispolizeibehörden*)—rural councilors in rural areas, mayors in cities, and state police administrations; so that they are at the same time local and state police authorities.

The Uniformed Police is employed by the Reich (*Schutzpolizei des Reiches*), or employed by the municipalities, or is the Gendarmerie or the Fire Protection Police (*Feuerschutzpolizei*). All these formations are militarized and, during the war, under military law, enforced by S.S. and Police Courts. They are all heavily Nazified, since replacements come exclusively from the Combat S.S. and the Armed Forces, while all police officers must be graduates of the S.S. Junker schools. As an outward sign of S.S. domination of the police, the S.S. collar patches are worn by the uniformed police.

Though the uniformed municipal police is probably less Nazified than the state police, it is nevertheless a reliable Nazi body. A central agency now allocates personnel to the municipal police that can be transferred to state police formations, while members of the latter may be shifted to the municipal police. The differences between the state and municipal police formations are thus reduced to purely fiscal considerations: the former is paid by the Reich, the latter by the municipalities.

It is likely that the least Nazified sector is the Gendarmerie, because appointment to this rural police corps requires 10 years' service in the protective police, a condition that but few can have fulfilled.

The Fire Protection Police is under Reich control since the Fire Protection Statute of 13 November 1938. All members of the fire brigades (professional and voluntary) are under Reich control, the professionals being policemen; the voluntary, auxiliary policemen. All officers now graduate from a special school at Eberswalde, near Berlin. In consequence of an agreement between the Hitler Youth Leader and Himmler, Hitler Youth is now trained for fire-protection police service. It is they who usually fight fires caused by air raids. After proper training, a Youth Fire Badge is awarded to them.

Air-raid Protection Police is provided by all the above-mentioned police formations, assisted by the party, the air-raid protection warning service, and the air-raid protection warning union, co-ordinated by an air-raid protection leader. The whole air-raid protection police is now under Himmler and no longer under Göring.

The Technical Emergency Help was founded in 1919 as a kind of strike-breaking organization composed mainly of technical students and technicians for the operation of railroads and utilities during industrial disputes. It was one of the many counterrevolutionary cells in the body of the Republic. It is now part of the Order Police, though still primarily composed of volunteers of the same kind and for the same purpose, especially for the repair of utilities after aerial destruction and in occupied Europe. It is commanded by S.S. Brigade Leader Schmelcher.

The Order Police has jurisdiction over a huge variety of affairs: traffic control, road maintenance, and cleaning; control of canals, rivers, and ports; fire fighting and air-raid protection; control of public work and of construction; the issuance and withdrawal of permits and licenses for licensed trades and occupations; veterinary and health control; supervision and censorship of theaters and movies; registration of Germans. It assists, of course, the Security Police, Gestapo, and the Criminal Police in the execution of their tasks. It controls and trains the Auxiliary Police Formations created by the Himmler decree of 11 February 1942, namely the rural guards (*Landwacht*) and the city guards (*Stadtwacht*).

Special Police Formations, like the Railroad Police and the Water Protection Police, appear to have been subordinated to Himmler, while the former was previously under the Ministry for Transportation and the latter under various lower administrative agencies.

THE SECURITY POLICE AND THE SECURITY SERVICE

The ominous implications of the Nazi term police derive not so much from the Order Police but from the Security Police and its intimate relation with the Security Service of the S.S.

The Command rests with the Chief of the Security Police and Security Service, who is not only the direct commander of all the branches to be described below, but indirectly controls the municipal police forces, whose training and activities as political and criminal police agents he supervises. He operates on the national level through the Main Office for the Security of the Reich (*Reichssicherheitshauptamt*), divided into six sections: (1) administration and law; (2) investigation of enemies (*Gegnererforschung*); (3) German spheres of life (*Deutsche Lebensgebiete*); (4) fight against enemies (*Gegnerbekämpfung*); (5) fight against crime; and (6) foreign countries. Section 4 was previously called Secret State Police (*Geheime Staatspolizei*) and still directs the work of the Gestapo. Training schools are attached to the main office.

The chief of the Security Police operates regionally through the Inspectors of the Security Police and Security Service for each corps area, who belong to the staff of the Higher S.S. and Police Leaders.

The Security Police thus comprises the Criminal Police, nationally controlled by Section 5 of the main office, regionally operating through 18 Criminal Police Directorates (*Leitstellen*), 46 Criminal Police Offices (*Kriminalpolizeistellen*), and 64 Criminal Departments. While the former two regional bodies are placed under the state police administration units in whose region they are located, the last are simply administrative departments of the state police units.

The Criminal Police tends to overshadow the role of the public prosecutor. Criminal police agents are, according to the Code of Criminal Procedure, simply 'auxiliary agents of the public prosecutor,' and thus subject to his direction. Their function is merely to supply his office with information to be used for the public prosecutor's indictment. This dependent position roused the ire of Dr. Werner Best, formerly in charge of Section 1 of the main Security office, now Hitler's plenipotentiary in Denmark. He aimed at the elimination of the public prosecutor and at the preparation and the defense of the indictment during trial by the criminal police. This has not been done and legally, therefore, the Code has not been changed, probably because with Himmler's appointment as Commissioner General for Administration, the Ministry of Justice (where the public prosecutors are incorporated) came under his control. But there is no doubt that the Criminal Police completely overshadows the public prosecutor, who is now only a stooge of the police.

The Secret State Police (*Gestapo*) is co-ordinated by Section 4 of the Security main office and operates regionally through 17 State Police Directorates (*Leitstellen*) and 52 State Police offices (*Staatspolizeistellen*). The powers of the Gestapo are unlimited, as has been shown on pp. 455-6.

The Gestapo also operates the Frontier Police (*Grenzpolizei*), who for this function are trained at a special school, while all Gestapo officers are, of course, graduates of the *S.S. Junkerschulen*.

The Security Service of the S.S. Reich Leader is far more than its name indicates. It was originally Himmler's intelligence and espionage service. But on 9 June 1934, Hitler gave it the monopoly for the party and all its formations and affiliates, while later it was also made the intelligence and espionage organization for the government—except for the military intelligence, which is still concentrated in the famous *Abwehr* under Admiral Canaris. Thus a branch of the S.S. has the monopoly of intelligence and espionage both for the party and the government, and nothing indicates better its paramount importance.

Nationally, the Security Service operates through the main Security office (*Sicherheitshauptamt*), regionally through 57 sections (S.D. *Abschnitte*). The personnel is to a large extent non-professional, composed of thousands of agents all over Europe, charged with reporting the slightest variations in the moods of the people, reporting to the Gestapo and the local, regional, and national officials of the party either for repressive action or for the purposes of elaborating new propaganda lines.

This is the Police System in Germany. Its soul is that of the S.S. It is this all-important party formation that we have to discuss.

2. THE S.S.[3]

The S.S. traces its history back to 1923. It came under Himmler's leadership on 6 January 1929. On 30 January 1933, it numbered 52,000. On 20 July 1934 it became an independent formation of the party, whereas before it had been merely a special branch of the S.A. Röhm's murder paved the way for the ascent of the S.S.

In the National Command, the Reich Leader S.S. operates through the following bureaus (main offices):

(a) The personal staff of the Reich Leader S.S., developed from the *Adjutantur*. It is composed of the following offices: the chief adjutant; the police adjutant; press; culture (affiliated is the chinaware factory at Allach); S.S. barracks; co-ordination of all S.S. students; economic assistance; cultural research (i.e. excavations—excavations in Tibet were indeed carried out by S.S. scholars); *Ahnenerbe*—the heritage of the past; association *Lebensborn*, for mothers with many children; office of Four Year Plan (for the co-ordination of the S.S. economic activities with the Reich Four

3. The description of the S.S. structure is based on Gunter d'Alquen, *Die S.S. Geschichte, Aufgabe und Organisation der Schutzstaffeln der N.S.D.A.P.*, Berlin, 1939.

Year Plan); and liaison officers with government and party and the command of the General S.S., the Combat S.S., and the Security Service.

(b) The Chief of the S.S. Court. The powers of the S.S. courts go far beyond those of the normal party, S.A., or Labor Service Courts. According to the decrees of 17 October 1939 and 17 April 1940, S.S. and police formations fighting as S.S. or police units within the German army are exempt from army tribunals and come exclusively under S.S. courts. So do the full-time employees of Himmler, the Higher S.S. and Police Leaders, the members of the troops at disposal of the Death Head formations, of the Junker schools, and specially used police. In fact, therefore, only members of the General S.S. in Germany or S.S. men as soldiers in army— not S.S.—formations, fall under the general or military courts.

(c) The main office of the S.S. (*Hauptamt* S.S.). It had (and may still have) 13 sub-offices, concerned with training, administration, supply, mobilization, reserves, physical training, etc. Within the S.S. main offices are: the inspector of the Troops at Disposal; the leader of the Death Head Formation; the inspector of the frontier and guard units; the inspector of the S.S. cavalry; the inspector of the S.S. Junker schools; and the inspector of the S.S. cavalry schools.

(d) The main office for Race and Settlement. This office plays a major role in the determination of occupation policies in Europe. It disposes of huge properties, especially in the East, due to the fact that Himmler occupies the position of a Reich Commissar for the strengthening of German Nationhood.

(e) and (f) The main offices for Personnel and Administration and Economics, whose functions are self-explanatory.

(g) The main office Security, identical with the Security Service, mentioned above.

The Regional Command is centralized in the Higher S.S. and Police Leaders for each corps area. They are in command of the General S.S.—with a chief of staff for the General S.S., they command the Combat S.S., the Special Units of the S.S., the Security Service, directed by an inspector, and operate through leaders of S.S. sections (*Abschnitte*). Since Higher S.S. and Police Leaders exist in all occupied Europe, their powers are probably not matched by any official on the regional level.

The lower echelon of the S.S. is divided into 20 *Oberabschnitte*

(main sectors—corresponding to the army corps in a corps area)
and 43 *Abschnitte* (sectors). The leaders of these units range from
Oberführer to *Obergruppenführer*.[4] The lower units, with leaders,
are:

Standarte (144)	(regiment)	—*Standartenführer* (colonel)
Sturmbann	(battalion)	—*Sturmbannführer* (major)
Sturm	(company)	—*Sturmführer* (captain)
Trupp	(platoon)	—*Truppführer* (lieutenant)
Schar	(squad)	—*Scharführer* (N.C.O.)

The General S.S. has but minor significance today. It serves now
primarily as a reservoir for the Combat S.S. It is composed of men
between 18 and 35 who, in their leisure, undergo some military
training and fulfil a number of minor functions. After 35, they join
the S.S. reserve; after 45, the S.S. *Stammabteilung*.

The Combat (*Waffen*) S.S.[5] arose from the Death Head (*Toten-
kopf*) formations and the S.S. Troops at Disposal (*Verfügungstruppen*). The Troops at Disposal, in turn, originated in Hitler's
own S.S. regiment, the *Leibstandarte* S.S. Adolf Hitler, under the
late Sepp Dietrich. Similar units were organized for his protection
throughout the Reich, namely the S.S. regiments Deutschland in
Munich, Germania in Hamburg, the S.S. engineer battalion (*Pionier-
sturmbann*) in Dresden, the communications battalion (*Nachrichten-
sturmbann*) in Tölz and Brunswick, and, in 1938, the fourth regiment *Der Führer* in Vienna, Klagenfurt, and Graz. The Death
Head formations were and still are the concentration camp guards.

Up to 1939, therefore, these two combat S.S. branches were concerned with the security of the Leader and the insecurity of political opponents inside the camps, and provided a mobile arm for
crushing internal disorder. In spite of conflicts with the army, the
arming and expansion of the combat S.S. continued, especially when
it showed its worth in the occupation of Austria and Czechoslovakia. In 1939, it thus started its equipment with artillery. When
the war broke out it resisted its incorporation into the army, and
expanded until it reached a number of divisions, each composed of
3 regiments, some of them recorded in the German press: the S.S.
Death Head Division; the S.S. Division *Leibstandarte Adolf Hitler*;

4. Only Daluege and Schwarz seem to be *Oberstgruppenführer*.
5. For details, see the excellent study by Alfred Vagts, *Hitler's Second Army*,
Washington, D. C., 1943.

the S.S. Panzer Grenadier Division *Das Reich;* the S.S. Division *Wiking;* and the S.S. Police Division. However, the German armed forces proved formidable competitors for recruits. As a consequence, the S.S. began to look for recruits outside Germany. It found them first in the *Volksdeutschen* (see pp. 160-66 on the folk groups). Some of the *Volksdeutsche* were incorporated into the existing S.S. regiments; others, especially from the Balkans, were organized in a special division, *Prince Eugen.* But even foreigners of non-German blood were taken into S.S. regiments, Norwegians and Swedes into the S.S. regiment *Nordland* (now part of the Wiking division), and the S.S. *Panzergrenadierregiment Norge.* Dutchmen are being organized (regiment *Westland*), while Danes form a special corps *Schalburg.* Not only has every country of German-occupied Europe contributed to the combat S.S., but also neutrals like Sweden, Switzerland, Spain; there is even a Moslem detachment.

While the combat S.S. fights, it does so under its own commanders, though within the framework of the normal army corps. It is, as has been shown, exempt from military tribunals so as fully to retain its identity and its sole allegiance to Himmler.

IV

ANTI-SEMITISM

(follows page 129)

HITLER's speech of 30 January 1944 brought again into the lime-light the supreme importance attached to Anti-Semitism. The anti-Jewish legislation is now concluded. Only a few new measures have been introduced since 1941. A decree of 25 March 1942 [1] requires the permission of the Ministry of the Interior to leave the Jewish community. Another decree of 1 July 1943 [2] outlawed the Jews. Crimes committed by Jews fall no longer under the jurisdiction of the courts but under that of the S.S. and police courts. The Reich is also made the heir of Jewish estates, though indemnification is provided for Aryan heirs of Jews. Radical anti-Jewish legislation has been enacted in all European states under Nazi control.

The decline of the Jewish population and the fate of the deficit population can be seen from two tables prepared by the Institute of Jewish Affairs. [3] The estimates appear reliable, since German publi-cations, though more scattered, give a similar picture.

The ruthlessness of this policy and the intransigence of Anti-Semitic propaganda again raise the question, Why?

An understanding of Anti-Semitism is impaired by the widely ac-cepted scapegoat theory, according to which the Jews are used as scapegoats for all evils of society. The slaughter or the expulsion of the scapegoat, however, marks in mythology the end of a process, while the persecution of the Jews, as practiced by National Social-ists, is only the prologue of more horrible things to come. The ex-propriation of the Jews, for instance, is followed by that of the Poles, Czechs, Dutch, French, anti-Nazi Germans, and middle classes. Not only Jews are put in concentration camps, but paci-fists, conservatives, socialists, Catholics, Protestants, Free Thinkers, and members of the occupied peoples. Not only Jews fall under

1. *Reichsgesetzblatt*, I, p. 161.
2. Ibid. I, p. 372.
3. See Institute of Jewish Affairs, *Hitler's Ten-Year War on the Jews*, New York, 1943.

the executioner's ax but so do countless others of many races, nationalities, beliefs, and religions. Anti-Semitism is thus the spearhead of terror. The Jews are used as guinea pigs in testing the method of repression.

It is, however, only the Jews who can possibly play this role. National Socialism, which has allegedly abolished the class struggle, needs an enemy who, by his very existence, can integrate the antagonistic groups within this society. This foe must not be too weak. If he were too weak, one could not make him the supreme foe in the eyes of the people. He must clearly not be too strong, because otherwise the Nazis would become involved in a serious struggle with a powerful enemy. It is for this reason that the Catholic Church has not been raised to the rank of the supreme foe. But the Jews admirably fill the role.

It follows that in this Anti-Semitic ideology and practice the extermination of the Jews is only the means to the attainment of the ultimate objective, namely the destruction of free institutions, beliefs, and groups. This may be called the spearhead theory of Anti-Semitism.

While Anti-Semitism has thus been a constant and consistent policy of National Socialism, its manifestations have changed considerably from 1933 to 1943. The physical extermination of the Jews in the spring of 1943 proves the thesis developed on pp. 125-7. The Labor Mobilization Act of 27 January 1943 again deprived hundreds of thousands of middle-class men of their independence. The political situation was as difficult as can possibly be imagined. The antagonisms within German society are only concealed by an all-comprehensive terrorist machine. The denunciation of bolshevism, socialism, democracy, liberalism, capitalism as Jewish, together with the planned extermination of the Jews, has the following purposes:

1. Dr. Werner Best, in 1942, clearly defined the function of Anti-Semitism for consumption abroad. A country, he said, that surrenders to Anti-Semitism has thereby already surrendered its liberal tradition. It has abandoned its bulwark against totalitarianism and is on its way to becoming a totalitarian society.

2. Domestically, Anti-Semitism is the testing ground for universal terrorist methods directed against all those groups and institutions not fully subservient to the Nazi system.

3. Persecution of the Jews, which is practiced at the order of the Nazis by ever larger strata of the German people, involves these strata in a collective guilt. The participation in so vast a crime as the extermination of the Eastern Jews makes the German army, the civil service, and large masses perpetrators and accessories in that crime and makes it therefore impossible for them to leave the Nazi boat.

V

THE SCOPE AND CHARACTER OF THE GROSSDEUTSCHE REICH

(follows page 183)

THE dreams of the New Order are over. Defense of the Fortress Europe and now even of Germany alone has replaced the fantastic ambitions of the Nazi ideologists. The Red Army, the invasion of North Africa and of Italy, the RAF, and the American air fleet have shattered the hope of transforming Europe into the field of exploitation of the German master race. The whole theory of the German New Order has collapsed and it is thus already possible to write its history.

1. TYPES OF TERRITORY UNDER GERMAN CONTROL—SURVEY

The *grossdeutsche Reich* consists of Germany, Austria, and certain annexed territories. The term 'Austria' is, of course, banned. But even the word *Ostmark* (Eastern Mark) is now forbidden and only the designation *Alpen* and *Donau Reichsgaue* is permitted, thus indicating that no reference must be made to Austria as a political entity.

(a) Annexed and incorporated territories are: the Sudetenland (Czechoslovakia); Memelland (Lithuania); Suwalki, Ciechanow, Danzig, Pomorze, Poznan, Silesia (Poland); Eupen, Malmedy, Moresnet (Belgium). Some of these territories are incorporated into the existing administrative divisions of Germany and are thus added to Prussian provinces, namely the Memelland, Suwalki, Ciechanow, Polish Silesia, and Eupen, Malmedy, and Moresnet. The rest are organized into new Reichsgaue, which do not form part of the Prussian state, but are integral parts of the German Reich. This is true of the Sudetenland, now the Reichsgau Sudetenland. The Free City of Danzig and Pomorze have been made into the Reichsgau Danzig-Westpreussen. Poznan and parts of Lodz and Warsaw constitute the Reichsgau Wartheland.

(b) Six territories have virtually been incorporated into the Greater German Reich. Their legal, administrative, social, and economic systems have been almost completely altered to resemble those prevailing in Greater Germany, although their administrations are still headed by chiefs of civil administration directly responsible to Hitler. The following territories fall under this category: (1) The District of Bialystok, under Erich Koch, the provincial president of East Prussia. Virtually half the district was incorporated into the Prussian province of East Prussia on 4 March 1942, with the status of a Government District. (2) Luxembourg, under Gauleiter Gustav Simon. (3) Alsace, under Gauleiter and Reich Governor Robert Wagner. (4) Lorraine, under Gauleiter Josef Bürckel, Reich Governor of the Westmark. (5) Lower Styria, under Gauleiter and Reich Governor Dr. Uiberreither. (6) Upper Carniola, under Gauleiter and Reich Governor of Carinthia Dr. F. Rainer.

(c) There are two territories which, in German constitutional law, are designated as *Nebenländer*, that is, auxiliary lands. These are the so-called 'Protectorate,' comprising the provinces of Bohemia and Moravia, and the Government General, comprising part of the Polish Republic. They are *Nebenländer* because, according to German constitutional theory, the republics of Czechoslovakia and Poland have ceased to exist as states. The Protectorate and the Government General are thus part of the Greater German Reich, although they do not have the status of the *Länder* or the Reichsgaue, but possess a definitely inferior status. The territories may thus be called 'appended territories.'

This category must be divided because the treatment of the two territories shows a considerable difference. While the Protectorate is more or less under what may be called indirect rule, the Government General is under the direct rule of the German authorities. In the Protectorate there is a division of labor between the so-called autonomous government and the German authorities, represented by the Reichsprotector and the German minister of state.

(d) The largest bulk of the territory under German control is represented by the category 'Occupied Territories.' This category shows four major divisions:

1. Territory under civil administration. Norway and the Netherlands are under German civil administration. Sovereign power rests with the Reich commissars directly responsible to Hitler. The

German army in these two territories has a status similar to that it enjoys in Germany proper. Although German control in Norway is exercised partly through an indigenous national government, this is not the case in Holland, where an autonomous government does not exist, even though the indigenous central administrative machinery is fully retained.

2. Territories under military government: (a) Belgium and Northern France under the military commander of Belgium and Northern France General Alexander von Falkenhausen;[1] (b) Occupied France, under the military commander General Otto von Stülpnagel; (c) Serbia, Greece, and the Channel Islands.

Although France, Serbia, and Greece possess autonomous governments, Belgium and the Channel Islands do not, although here again the German authorities utilize the indigenous central administrative machinery.

3. Territory under military occupation but without military government: Denmark, which is militarily occupied by forces under the command of General Hermann von Hanneken, but is not under German military government; and 'unoccupied' France.

4. Colonial administration in the Reichcommissariats Ostland and Ukraine. The two Reich Commissars Hinrich Lohse and Erich Koch, respectively, are under the jurisdiction of the Ministry for the Occupied Eastern Territories, with Alfred Rosenberg at the head.

2. The Nazi Theory of Military Government

In surveying the various types briefly mentioned above, the question arises why the Germans have so many different kinds of administration for the areas under their control. It seems certain that military-strategic considerations do not determine German controls of occupied Europe. This becomes clear if we study the difference between Holland and Belgium. The coastlines of Holland and Belgium show striking similarities; strategic considerations would demand identical treatment for both countries, and yet two different types of government have been chosen.

It is likely that the model of the British Empire has been one of

1. Replaced July 1944 by Gauleiter Grohé.

the determining factors. Alfred Rosenberg's influence in the planning of military government has been very marked. Hitler's and Rosenberg's *Hassliebe* for England is well known. British imperial conceptions always had a tremendous attraction for the German ruling classes.

In the British Empire, two major concepts have been developed, that of the Commonwealth of Nations and that of Indirect Rule. Great Britain and the Dominions form a Commonwealth of Nations. 'They are autonomous communities within the British Empire, equal in status, in no way subordinate one to another in any aspect of their domestic or external affairs, though united by common allegiance to the Crown and freely associating as members of the British Commonwealth of Nations.'[2] The preferential status given to Norway and the Netherlands can be explained by the desire of the Nazis to bind these Nordic brethren to the German Reich by allegiance to Hitler, who is considered as having a status similar to that of the British Crown.

The second major concept is that of indirect rule as developed by Lord Lugard:

The essential feature of the system [of indirect rule] is that the native chiefs are constituted as an integral part of the machinery of administration. There are not two sets of rulers—British and native —working either separately or in co-operation, but a single government in which the native chiefs have well-defined duties and an acknowledged status equal with British officials. Their duties should never conflict and should overlap as little as possible. They should be complementary to each other and the chief himself must understand that he has no right to place and power unless he renders his proper service to the state.[3]

It becomes apparent at once that the Protectorate's 'autonomous government' has pretty much the same functions as have the native chiefs in Lord Lugard's scheme. Later developments in Germany's occupation policy which will be described below show a partial extension of this principle to the eastern states. It is also somewhat applicable to newly created satellite states, like Slovakia, Croatia, and

2. A. Berriedale Keith, *The King and the Imperial Crown*, London, 1936, p. 425.
3. Lord Lugard, 'Representative Forms of Government and Indirect Rule,' in *British Africa*, 1928.

Serbia, so of course no general rule can be made regarding the actual political power exercised by any autonomous government.

The concept of British imperial rule is, moreover, compatible to the Nazi race theory, which has largely determined the pattern of German military government. According to this conception, the blood of the Germans, Dutch, Norwegians, and Danes is identical. As a consequence, they occupy the highest rank in the Nazi hierarchy of races. These countries must therefore also occupy the highest rank in the pattern of military government and must have a status that marks them off from all other countries. The Romance-language peoples are, according to Nazi concepts, racially different, although not necessarily inferior. Consequently, France and Belgium must come under military government, which represents merely a transitional state of affairs. The Romance-language peoples were to be united into one Romance block, which was to have a political life all its own, although, of course, under German hegemony. The Slavic peoples are racially inferior, with the Russians occupying the lowest rank in the ladder of races. As a result, they should be treated primarily as colonials to whom the blessings of German culture must be brought. In addition, the Slavic peoples constitute a direct threat to Germany's existence, owing to the heavy population pressure exercised by these countries, while no such danger arises from countries with a declining birth rate, like the Romance peoples.

In accordance with this theory, Belgium ought to have been divided into two sections—the Flemish and the Walloon. The Flemish, of course, are racially akin to the Germans and precedence for their preferential treatment can be traced back to the First World War, when the Germans actively supported the Flemish separatist movement against Walloon domination. This has not been repeated. It is most likely that the division of Belgium has not been carried out because of the existence of the Belgian colonial empire. If Belgium had been divided, the legal fate of the Belgian empire would have been uncertain and since the Germans hoped to achieve control, through Belgium, of the colonies, the division of Belgium was avoided.

The German race theory has merged, however, with geopolitical conceptions.[4] Haushofer's theory already shows a considerable trend

4. See above, pp. 136-83.

toward racialism, in contrast to the pure geopoliticians.[5] This merger of racialism and geopolitics has led to a redefinition of German international law. All three conceptions—racialism, geopolitics, and the new international law—are finally synthesized in the writings of Werner Daitz.[6]

On the basis of these discussions a specific theory of military government over Europe has been developed by Werner Best.[7] *Grossraum*, large space, means, according to Best, the whole space beyond its racial space (*Volksraum*) that a people consciously transforms into new units and which is delimited from other large spaces or brought into relations with them.

Best starts with the observation that it is impossible for the leading people to find within its own ranks enough administrators for the *Grossraum*. Since, therefore, only leading positions in the *Grossraum* can be occupied by administrators taken from the ranks of the leading people, the concept of the separation of powers must be completely abandoned. Lawgiving and administration must thus be concentrated in one person. The distinction between political and executive powers, which has already dwindled in Germany, must be abandoned as utterly unsuitable for the needs of large-space administration. The leading people, or *Grossraum* people, should conserve its own life without being absorbed by other peoples. This is one of the major functions of administration. The principle on which administration should be based is Freiherr von Stein's maxim, 'as little as possible, as cheaply as possible, and in the interests of the people.' Administration should be nothing but making the necessary corrections and giving directions to the autonomous governments. They have to be conserved and strengthened. If that were not done, there would remain only two equally undesirable alternatives for the subject peoples: slavery or assimilation.

From these introductory theoretical statements the following typology for the administration of large-space empires is developed.

(a) *Bündnisverwaltung*—alliance administration. Although the

5. Pp. 143, 145.
6. Pp. 171-2.
7. 'Grossraumordnung und Grossraumverwaltung,' in *Zeitschrift für Politik*, 1941, and 'Grundfragen einer deutschen Grossraumverwaltung,' in *Festgabe für Heinrich Himmler*, Darmstadt, 1941, pp. 33 ff. On Best, see the references in this book.

nominal independence of a state forced into such an alliance is supposed to remain intact, it must, according to Best, be clearly established that foreign relations are the prerogative of the 'leading' nation. The representative of the leading nation with the allied nation should not excel by his diplomatic abilities but rather by his administrative genius. Great reserve must, however, be exercised by the leading state, and no strong measures should be resorted to provided, of course, the native administration meets all the necessary duties required by its incorporation into the 'large space order.' The allied nation may have an army of its own under the leadership of the leading state.

It is clear that this category fits German control of Denmark, and Best has apparently devised a theory for his own policy in Denmark—a policy which failed lamentably.

It applies also to Slovakia, which, like Denmark, is considered a *Schutzstaat*, a protected state,[8] since the president and prime minister of the Slovak state put Slovakia under Germany's protection by his telegram to Hitler of 16 March 1939 and the treaty of 23 March 1939.

(b) *Aufsichtsverwaltung*—supervisory administration—is not derived from a treaty but from a onesided order of the leading nation's government. The leading nation's commissioner represents the political leadership. This representation must be unified. The native government cannot, as a matter of principle, maintain an army, but citizens of the supervised nation may, with adequate controls, enter the army of the leading nation.

This type is obviously applicable to Norway and Holland, both considered as *Schutzstaaten*.

(c) *Regierungsverwaltung*—government administration—is the type of control where the leading nation occupies the key administrative positions but leaves the lower administrative agencies to natives. Best warns, however, that the leading nation's policy must take care to awaken the amity of the governed people which still lives and feels as a nation, and which will strongly react against measures inimical to its existence. As to the army, the same principles should apply as under (b). This type clearly is applicable to the Protectorate.

8. Wilhelm Stuckart, *Neues Staatsrecht II*, Leipzig, 1943, p. 121.

(d) Colonial administration, the fourth and last type, concentrates all administrative powers in the hands of the leading nation. The natives do not retain any administrative powers. This is the policy to be pursued against peoples who are not nations. But the leading nation should take into consideration that, though the native people cannot exercise active resistance, they may react by 'dying off.' Since the racial abyss between the leading nation and the natives is too wide, no natives can be taken into the army of the former. This type is obviously meant to apply to the eastern occupied territories and to the Government Géneral.

Best's theory had, and still has, considerable influence. It is characteristic that in his theory territories under military government in the narrower sense do not appear at all—for reasons that we have already explained.

3. THE ADMINISTRATIVE CONTROL OF THE OCCUPIED TERRITORIES

TH REICH MINISTRY OF THE INTERIOR AS THE CO-ORDINATING AGENCY

In spite of the diversity of types for the control of occupied Europe, economic, labor, and police controls are quite uniform. There is, in addition, one institution that provides unification in all fields of administration. That is the Reich Ministry of the Interior. The ministry first appeared as the unifying link for the co-ordination of administrations in occupied countries at the time of the incorporation of Austria. By a ruling of 16 March 1938 a *Zentralstelle des Reichs für die Wiedervereinigung* (Central Office of the Reich for Re-unification) was established and the Reich Ministry of the Interior was charged with the functions of the Central Office. Its task was the co-ordination of all legal and organizational measures enacted by the Reich for the incorporation of Austria. The Central Office was charged especially with establishing a unified administrative structure, and with securing the uniformity of all the measures enacted by the Reich in the legal field. Its duty was to prepare the legislative and administrative rulings in the incorporated territory and, finally, to assure agreement with the Reich Commissar for Austria. The Central Office is, therefore, not a special organization but is the ministry of 'interior. It continued to exist after the abolition of the post of Reich Commissar for

Austria, and has retained this function for all annexed, appended, and occupied territories until today.

The annexed and incorporated territories form part of the *grossdeutsche Reich*.

(a) Sudetenland. According to German constitutional theory, the Munich agreement of 29 September 1938 creates the legal basis for the incorporation of the Sudetenland into Germany. This agreement provided for the evacuation of Czechoslovaks and for the occupation by German troops. The prerequisite of a plebiscite was waived by a decision of an international committee of 13 October 1938. The Czech government was obliged to release within four weeks all Sudeten Germans from the Czech military and political organizations, and to free all Sudeten German prisoners incarcerated for political crimes.

German troops started the occupation on 1 October 1938 and by 10 October 1938 the five German army groups had completed it. According to German theory, 10 October marks the incorporation of the Sudetenland into Germany. As a consequence, this date determines the change in citizenship. The incorporation was legalized by the Statute on the Re-unification, of 21 November 1938, and the Reichstag elections of 4 December 1938, which, according to the German view, gave the population the opportunity to confirm the incorporation; 98.78 per cent gave their votes for 'the Führer and the *grossdeutsche Reich*.' Consequently, it is the German contention that the Sudetenland has become part of the German Reich in accordance with all principles of international and domestic law.

During the so-called military operations, executive power rested with the commander of the German army, who operated through the commanders of the five army groups. By a Hitler decree of 1 October 1938, a Reich Commissar at Reichenberg was put at the head of the Sudetenland. The functions of the Reich Commissar were similar to those of the Reich governors in the Reichsgaue: he was the head of the administrative apparatus and he provided the political leadership. He could co-ordinate all administrative activities in the region and could give orders to autonomous and semi-autonomous corporations. He was in charge not only of the general, but also of the special administrations like judicial, fiscal, post, and railroad administrations, and was assisted by specialists in these fields. The Reich Commissioner was directly subject to the Führer. At the same time, however, by means of the decree of 1 October 1938, the Reich Ministry of the Interior was again made Central Office for the co-ordination of the measures taken by the Reich Commissar with those of the German government. Legislation passed in the German Reich proper was, therefore, not directly applicable in the Sudetenland so long as it was under the Reich Commissar, but became valid only if the Reich Commissar enacted it for his own area. Whether or not he would enact it was dependent upon the directives received from the Central Office.

The final incorporation of the Sudetenland was achieved by the Statute of 25 March 1939. By it the Sudetenland became a Reichsgau, identical with the party Gau. A number of territorial changes were made. The structure of the Reichsgau Sudetenland was determined by the so-called *Sudetengaugesetz* of 14 April 1939.

(b) Memelland. The incorporation of the Memelland was achieved by an international treaty between Lithuania and Germany. Memel was governed by the Memel Statute of 8 May 1924, approved by the Lithuanian parliament on 30 July 1924. The statute granted to the Memel government a so-called autonomous administration, culminating in a constitution of its own. The German contention was that the Lithuanian government never honored the Memel statute. Under German pressure, the Lithuanian government decided on 21 March 1939 to return Memel to Germany. On 23 March 1939, German troops occupied the country on the basis of the international treaty of 22 March 1939. A German statute covering re-unification of Memel with Germany was enacted on 23 March. The unification was, again, achieved by the Reich Ministry of the Interior as Central Office, and the president of the province of East Prussia was appointed *Überleitungskommissar* (transitional commissar). Both Lithuania and Germany appointed so-called *Übergabekommissare* (transfer commissars), the German operating under the authority of the *Überleitungskommissar*. Memelland was incorporated into the Prussian province of East Prussia and belongs to the district of Gumbinnen. As a consequence, there was no interim regime between the cession of Memelland by Lithuania and her incorporation into Germany. The Memelland became at once part of the German Reich and on 1 May 1939 the whole body of German and Prussian law became valid in the Memelland.

(c) Danzig. While there is at least a semblance of legality in the incorporation of the Sudetenland and the Memelland, there is none for the incorporation of Danzig. The semi-official German writer, Wilhelm Stuckart, formulated it in the following way: 'When the crisis with Poland approached its height, Danzig, by a statute of 23 August 1939, discarded the confining provisions of international and constitutional law and created a head of the state who was not provided for in the present constitution and to whom the exercise of sovereign powers of the state was delegated.'[9] It is clear from this that the incorporation of Danzig into the Reich does not rest upon law but upon violence. The newly appointed head of the state of Danzig, Gauleiter Forster, enacted on 1 September 1939 a basic constitutional law (*Staatsgrundgesetz*) providing for the re-unification with Germany. This Danzig constitutional law was passed on the same date by the German Reichstag, and the two laws provided that Danzig become a part of the German Reich, and that the constitution of the Free City of Danzig was thereby abrogated. All German laws were automatically applicable in Danzig unless special provisions were made to the contrary. The Reich Ministry of the Interior was, again, made Central Office for the co-ordination of the Reich and Danzig administrations.

After the conquest of Poland Danzig was incorporated into the Reichsgau Danzig-Westpreussen.

(d) Incorporated Eastern Territories. There is no legal basis for the incorporation of former Polish territories into Germany. According to German theory, 'This incorporation could be made, from the point of view of municipal and international law, because the Polish state has perished.'[10] The basis, therefore, is exclusively German municipal law, namely the edict of Hitler of 8 October 1939, following the completion of military government over Polish territory. The incorporation was carried out by the Reich Ministry of the Interior as the Central Office.

The new administrative form is, again, the Reichsgau except for Upper Silesia and certain smaller areas. The Reichsgau Danzig-West-

9. Op. cit. p. 68.
10. Stuckart, op. cit. p. 72.

preussen is divided into the government districts of Danzig, Bromberg, and Marienwerder. The latter was taken out of the Prussian province of East Prussia. The Reichsgau Wartheland is divided into the government districts of Hohensalza, Posen, and Lodz (Litzmannstadt). The Silesian industrial region was co-ordinated into the government district of Katowice and incorporated into the Prussian province of Upper Silesia. The area around the city of Zichenau was made into the government district Zichenau and incorporated into the Prussian province of East Prussia. The area around Sudanen (Suwalki) was incorporated into the government district of Gumbinnen of the Prussian province of East Prussia. Citizenship in these incorporated areas is determined by the decree of the 'German *Volkliste* and German Citizenship in the Incorporated Eastern Territories' of 4 March 1941.

(e) Eupen, Malmedy, and Moresnet. There is no legal basis for the incorporation of these Belgian territories into Germany. The semi-official statement says:

> In evaluating the 'Edict of the Führer and Chancellor on the Reunification of the Territories of Eupen, Malmedy, and Moresnet with the German Reich' of 18 May 1940, from the point of view of international and municipal law one has to consider that they are territories which have been illegally torn away from Germany and which were always innately connected with Germany. There was, therefore, no reason to treat these territories as occupied enemy territories even for only a transitional period, but the factual reunification with the Reich could be anchored at once in constitutional law.[11]

It follows from the above that the whole legal basis for the incorporation of Eupen, Malmedy, and Moresnet is the well-known German view about the character of the treaty of Versailles.

The incorporation was achieved by the above-mentioned edict of the Leader, and the Reich Ministry of the Interior was, again, charged with the functions of a Central Office. Eupen, Malmedy, and Moresnet are, therefore, part of the German territory and are (Statute of 4 February 1941) represented by a Reichstag deputy. All territories were incorporated into the government district of Aachen of the Prussian Rhine province. The inhabitants became

11. Op. cit. p. 78.

German citizens,[12] and German and Prussian law became valid on 1, September 1940. There was, therefore, no intermediate step between military occupation, lasting only a few days, and the total incorporation of the territories into Germany.

TERRITORIES IN THE PROCESS OF ANNEXATION AND INCORPORATION

The legal basis of the incorporation of the following territories is nonexistent, and even German constitutional lawyers are embarrassed when discussing the actual·legal status of territories Alsace, Lorraine, and Luxembourg. In the case of Poland, they at least have the excuse that the Polish state has ceased to exist. In the case of France, no such ideology can be supplied, all the more so since France surrendered to Germany on the basis of an armistice agreement covering the international relations between the two countries. The German theory is, therefore, the following:

An incorporation on the basis of constitutional law has not yet taken place, since the international relations between the Reich and France were heretofore determined by the armistice agreement. The Reich has, however, given to understand that it considers the re-occupation of Alsace and Lorraine not merely a transitory state of affairs, caused by the losses of war, but as a part of the future final order.[13]

It is for this reason that Germany considers Alsace and Lorraine as incorporated territories (*eingegliederte Gebiete*).

Nevertheless, the administration of the territories shows marked legal differences from that of the above-mentioned incorporated territories. We can say roughly that the administration of the territories in the process of annexation is identical with that of the Sudetenland prior to the statute of 25 March 1939, that is, comparable to the administration of the Sudetenland by a Reich Commissar. German legislation therefore does not automatically apply to them. German laws must be separately enacted by each of the Chiefs of Civil Administration.

(a) Alsace. Alsace is administrated by a Chief of Civil Adminis-

12. For details, see ,the decrees of 23 September 1941 and 28 September 1942 and the executive rulings of the Reich Ministry of the Interior 'of 10 February 1942 and 28 September 1942.
13. Op. cit. p. 80.

tration (*Chef der Zivilverwaltung*), Gauleiter Robert Wagner of Baden, who is directly responsible to Hitler. The Reich Ministry of the Interior, however, co-ordinates the administration of Alsace with that of the German Reich. All branches of public administration in Alsace are unified in the person of the Chief of Civil Administration, in contrast to the traditional administrative structure of Germany. It is the Chief of Civil Administration who, as already mentioned, enacts legislation published in the *Verordnungsblatt des Chefs der Zivilverwaltung.* Politically, Alsace and Baden form one Gau of the National Socialist party. The Chief of Civil Administration operates on the local level through *Landkommissare*, corresponding to the rural councilors in the rest of the Reich. The three largest cities, Strasbourg, Mulhouse, and Colmar, form city counties (*Stadtkreise*), administered by senior city councilors (*Oberstadtkommissare*).

(b) Lorraine. Lorraine is administered by a Chief of Civil Administration, Gauleiter Josef Bürckel. Together with the Saar, it forms one party Gau. The seat of the civil administration is, however, not Metz, but the German city of Saarbrücken. Its Chief of Civil Administration operates through rural councilors. Only the city of Metz is a city county.

(c) Luxembourg. The legal basis for the incorporation of Luxembourg is as shaky as that for Alsace and Lorraine. Consequently, the Germans consider that Luxembourg has been incorporated 'administratively into the German Reich and that she considers this territory as part of the German Reich.' [14] It is governed by a Chief of Civil Administration, Gauleiter Simon, in Luxembourg. Politically Luxembourg and the Gau Coblenz-Trier form Gau Moselland. Luxembourg is divided into three rural counties, administered by rural councilors, and the city county of the city of Luxembourg. Citizenship follows the pattern of Lorraine.

(d) Lower Styria and Upper Carniola. After the Balkan War of 1941 Germany incorporated the two parts of Jugoslavia as of 14 April 1941. The two territories are administered by two chiefs of civil administration and are organized after the model of the Reichsgau. All Jugoslav citizens of German descent (*Volksdeutsche*) have become German citizens, other Jugoslavs of Jugo-

14. Op. cit. p. 86.

slav blood have received revocable citizenship, all others are 'protected citizens.' [15]

APPENDED TERRITORIES

(a) The Protectorate of Bohemia and Moravia. Little has been changed in the structure of the Protectorate since the first edition of this book was published. A summary of the present status will thus be sufficient. The basic law, the Führer edict of 16 March 1939, is unchanged. The principles are: The Protectorate is an 'original' [16] creation of National Socialism. It has no status in international law but is regulated exclusively by German municipal law. Bohemia and Moravia belong to the *grossdeutsche Reich*. Sovereignty over them rests with the Reich, represented by the Führer. Customs between Germany and the Protectorate are thus abolished. The Protectorate is nevertheless 'independent' but under the 'protection' of the Reich. It has thus a head of state, called State President, who is dependent upon the Führer's confidence. Foreign affairs are handled by Germany. The Protectorate is represented in Germany by a minister who, however, has no diplomatic status. 'Military protection' is afforded by Germany. German interests in the Protectorate are represented by the Reich Protector and, since 1943, by the German Minister of State.

The present Reich Protector is the former Reich Minister of the Interior, Wilhelm Frick, who succeeded Neurath in 1943. Neurath, apparently a sick man, never did much. As a consequence, power rested with his deputy, Chief of the German Security Police and S.S. Senior Group Leader R. Heydrich. After Heydrich's assassination in May 1942, the Chief of the Order Police, S.S. Supreme Group Leader Kurt Daluege, was appointed deputy protector. The appointment of Himmler as Minister of the Interior on 24 August 1943 led to a complete reorganization. Frick was made protector, but the Sudeten German, Karl Hermann Frank, formerly merely secretary of state in the protector's office, was made German State Minister in the Protectorate and thus became the actual political boss of the Protectorate, while Daluege [17] was recalled.

15. Decrees of 14 September 1941 and executive rulings 10 February and 19 June 1942.
16. Stuckart, op. cit. p. 91.
17. His status is not clear. He may be the Chief of the Police.

Frank also retained his position as Higher S.S. and Police Leader in the Protectorate.

The Protector operates regionally through *Oberlandräte* (senior rural councilors) in seven districts. These councilors supervise the administration in the regional level. The Protector's powers are virtually unlimited. He is the representative of Hitler; he confirms and dismisses, according to his discretion, the members of the 'autonomous government'; he must be informed of all measures; he can veto all measures; he can issue directives and, if necessary, resort to direct administrative measures superseding all powers of the autonomous government.

There is below him an 'autonomous' government, composed of the state president (Dr. Emil Hacha), a prime minister, and several departmental ministers. The key position, the ministry for economics and labor, is held, however, by a Reich German, while the others are Czechs.

The Protectorate is divided into the *Länder*, namely Bohemia (administrative capital Prague) and Moravia (Brünn). The *Länder* are divided into districts (63 in Bohemia and 27 in Moravia) corresponding to the German rural counties.

The autonomous administration executes, at the same time, 'delegated' German administration (*Auftragsverwaltung*), so that, apart from the general supervisory function exercised by the Protector, they are, at the same time, German administrative organs. As a consequence, German civil servants are attached to the autonomous administration, making it a more or less complete fake.

There are two kinds of citizenship in the Protectorate:

Czechoslovak citizens of German descent (*Volksdeutsche*) became Germans as from 16 March 1939—with certain exceptions. Czechs became Protectorate citizens.[18] On the legal system, see pp. 164-5. The organization of the Protectorate indicates that it is an occupied country and that the autonomy is about as comprehensive as that of a German municipality under the Nazi statute on municipalities.

(b) The Government General. While the Protectorate is considered to belong 'directly' (*unmittelbar*) to the Reich, the Gov-

18. Ruling of the Reich Minister of the Interior 7 June 1940. On Jews, see decree of 2 November 1942.

ernment General is only an 'indirect' (*mittelbar*) part of Germany. It has thus no 'autonomous' administration, and is already constitutionally an object of rule, that is, a German colony.

Very little has changed in the administration of the Government General, which, schematically, appears as follows:

Central administration at Krakow

Governor General: Hans Frank
    chief of government: Buehler
    deputy chief: Boepple
Secretariat of state: Buehler
    deputy: Boepple
    director of the chancellery of the governor: Keith
    director of the chancellery of the government: Wolsegger

In addition there are: offices of the press chief; for foreign trade; legislation; price control; regional planning; personnel; maintenance; archives; statistics.

Each of the main departments is subdivided, so that the central administration of the Government General fully resembles that of Germany. This central government operates regionally through five District Governors (Warsaw; Krakow; Radom; Lublin; Lwow), who are assisted by a smaller or larger number of German officials. The districts are subdivided into counties, directed either by county chiefs or city chiefs. Below them are the local government units. According to the decree of 28 November 1939 the chiefs of the lowest local units shall be appointed from among that national group that has the majority, so that on the lowest level, Poles, Ukrainians, White Russians, and Gorales are represented.

The Governor General is Hitler's representative, and is thus a kind of 'territorial Reich Minister.' His powers are unlimited. He concentrates all powers in his hands and there is, therefore, no special administration that is not under his orders. So it is in theory —though the subsequent chapter will show that the practice is quite different. The Governor General is, moreover, the leader of the party in the Government General, and the party operates, as has been shown above (p. 538), in an activity sphere. So is the German youth organized in the Hitler Youth.

OCCUPIED TERRITORIES

(a) Civilian-Controlled Territories–Norway and the Netherlands. The Norwegian administration has changed in one basic point: the emergence of Vidkun Abraham Quisling as head of the state and party.

The Office of the Reich Commissar for Occupied Norwegian Territories (Josef Terboven) is now organized as follows: the Deputy is Hans H. Neumann, also leader of the N.S.D.A.P. in Norway. There are departments for administration; economics; propaganda; construction and technology; labor service; post and telegraphs; and police. The most powerful person is probably the Chief of the Police and S.S. in Norway, General of Police Rediess. Regionally the Reich Commissar operates through a number of branch offices in the major Norwegian cities.

On 1 February 1942 at a special ceremony (the so-called 'state act') Quisling was finally made prime minister and began to set up his own autonomous government–modeled after Hitler's. He is now, as is Hitler, head of the state and of the *Nasjonal Samling* party, and thus has two chancelleries. His cabinet consists of not less than 13 members. Since then, Dr. Best's category of supervisory administration applies to Norway, if we understand by this term that direct German intervention is not resorted to, provided that the Quisling government itself carries out the wishes of the German conqueror. This was made possible because Quisling, on the basis of a decree of 16 April 1942, engaged in a wholesale purge of the Norwegian administration and transformed it from a democratic into an authoritarian one.

The *Nasjonal Samling* party is, according to the laws of 12 March 1942, 'the Government Party in Norway and is firmly bound to the State. The party's organization and activities shall be decided upon by the Leader of the *Nasjonal Samling*.' The phrasing of the act is thus identical with the German statute on the unity between party and state (see p. 67). The Norwegian Nazi party has copied all features of 'the bigger German brother. There is a party tribunal, a woman's organization; a Youth; a labor service; a land service; and, above all, the para-military organization, the *Hird*, under Thorvald Thronsen, composed of the *Hird* proper, a *Hird* marine, a *Hird* air corps; it also has its S.S., the *Germanske S.S.*

Norge. The position of the *Nasjonal Samling* is, as is well known, extremely tenuous, since only a small fraction of the Norwegian people support it.

The situation in the Netherlands [19] is different from that in Norway because an autonomous government does not exist. Otherwise, the set-up is quite similar. Germany installed 'supervisory' administration. The Reich Commissar still is the Austrian Nazi, Dr. Seyss-Inquart, assisted by German Commissars General for administration and judiciary; police, finance and economics; and for special tasks. The indigenous administration is centralized in Dutch Secretaries General in charge of the various Dutch ministries, possessing the right to issue decree laws. An indigenous Nazi organization led by Mussert attempts to give support to the German rule.

(b) Territories under Military Control. Military government in Belgium and Northern France (under General von Falkenhausen) [20] and Occupied France (General von Stülpnagel·) has not changed since the publication of this book. A few details will round off the picture. The staff of the military commanders is divided into two sections: command staff and administrative staff. The latter is usually subdivided into departments dealing with general problems, administration, and economics. The administrative staff is composed of army civil servants and deals with all problems not of a military or police nature. This division is repeated on the lower regional levels.

(c) Territories under Military Occupation but without Military Government. Denmark was the ideal type of what Best called 'alliance' administration. When the German troops crossed the Danish borders on 9 April 1940, the German minister von Renthe-Fink submitted the note of his government whereby Germany assumed military protection of Denmark but promised not to interfere with the political institutions. Under duress and protest, the King and government accepted German protection. From then on, until 29 August 1943, 'alliance' administration was a partial reality. King, parliament, and government continued to function and German interests were cared for by Best as Hitler's plenipotentiary to the

19. See the complete German description by Seyss-Inquart and R. Kreiss 'Der Reichskommissar fur die Besetzten Niederlandischen Gebiete,' in *Zeitschrift fur völkische Verfassung und Verwaltung*, 1942, Vol. III.
20. Now Gauleiter Grohé.

Danish King, and the industrialist-general Hermann von Hanneken (see pp. 299 and 372) as commander of the German armed forces. German demands on Denmark were submitted through the normal diplomatic channels.

On 29 August 1943, after Danish sabotage had reached a new high, the Danish military units were disarmed and Hanneken declared a state military emergency. The Danish government under Scavenius resigned. When it became clear that Hanneken measures were of no avail, and no Quisling could be found in Denmark, the Germans regretted their steps. But the regret proved equally ineffective. Since then, German rule over Denmark can best be described as a clandestine form of military government. There is no military government as we know it in France and Belgium, the fiction of an alliance administration is still maintained, Danish administrative agencies still operate—but there is no cabinet to which Best can submit German demands. The Germans have to submit, almost clandestinely, their requests to the Danish administrative agencies.

(d) German Administration in Occupied Russia. The Reich Ministry for Occupied Eastern Territories, under Reich Minister Rosenberg and his permanent representative, Meyer, has been entrusted with general sovereign powers by the Führer. The ministry is composed of a number of miscellaneous officials for liaison or special purposes, on the staff directly under the Reich Minister, and of a regular departmental breakdown. This breakdown is into a Central Department and three Main Departments, for politics, administration, and economy. The Central Department fills the function of administration within the ministry. The Main Department Politics is broken down both functionally and regionally. The Main Department Administration has sections that handle the more routine aspects of civil affairs—finance, justice, health, popular welfare, science and culture, trustee administration. The Main Department Economy was evidently projected originally as a regular unit for economic control on a permanent basis, but for the duration of the war the direction of economic matters in the ministry has been placed under a Leadership Staff for Economic Policy, organized to parallel the Economic Staff East.

The Reich Commissariats *Ostland* and *Ukraine* represent the authority of the Reich Ministry in the territories concerned. The

Reich Commissariat Ostland is led by a Reich Commissar (Gauleiter H. Lohse) who possesses sovereign powers in the territory by delegation from the Reich Minister for the Occupied East. The organizational breakdown of the Reich Commissariat parallels that of the Reich Ministry. The Reich Commissariat Ukraine under Gauleiter E. Koch was originally organized similarly, but on 1 February 1943 it was reorganized into 11 Main Departments for more intensive exploitation.

General Commissars in Ostland and Ukraine represent Reich Commissars in their respective territories.

There are four General Districts in the Ostland, with administrative organizations similar to that for the Reich Commissariat Ostland. The General Districts are organized on the national level and constitute the focal point of the German administration. National native administrations, appointed by the German civil administration and delegated certain advisory and executive powers by it, exist in each general district. They form the basis of national liberation policy, centering around national military conscription in Estonia and Latvia.

There were six General Districts in the Ukraine, named after former Soviet oblasts which they include without attempting to follow their boundaries. The organization of the General Commissariats parallels that of the Reich Commissariat Ukraine.

There are 31 Regions (*Gebiete*) in the Ostland, organized under Regional Commissars, who appear to dispense with the usual functional organization of the higher levels and to utilize officials for special purposes rather than departments. There were 114 Regions in the Ukraine; these are arbitrary creations and form the focus of the German administration. The Regional Commissariat forms the lowest level of German administration.

In both the Ostland and the Ukraine local administration is in the hands of native leaders, who are responsible to the Regional Commissars for the fulfilment of their functions and who, in the top categories, are appointed to their posts by the Germans. The regional and local German agricultural leaders also exercise important administrative functions.

Certain fields have been removed from the jurisdiction of the territorial administration and placed directly in the hands of central agencies of the Reich. There is a regular territorial military organization under a *Wehrmachtsbefehlshaber* Ostland and *Wehrmachts-befehlshaber* Ukraine into field, county, and local commanders. In addition to its share in this regular military administration, Lithuania has been given the appellation of *Sicherungsgebiet* and an office of commander-in-chief of the *Sicherungsgebiet* Lithuania has been created.

Speer, as Reich Minister for Armaments and War Production, General Inspector for Roads, General Inspector for Water and Energy, General Inspector for Construction, and head of the Organization Todt, has been charged with all technical affairs.

The Reich Transport Ministry has been entrusted with the administration of railways, motor transport, and shipping. The Reich Post Ministry has been charged with the administration of postal and telegraph service.

The most important functions of the civil administration are carried out by central agencies of the Reich acting through the framework of the territorial administration. The N.S.D.A.P. controls citizens and *Volksdeutsche* through organization of the activity sphere East. The party acts through the territorial organization of the administration, since there is a complete identification between the party regional leaders and the administrative commissars down through the *Gebiet*.

The *Reichsleiter* S.S. and Chief of Police is represented on all the commissarial staffs in the occupied East. His representatives are, at the same time, subordinated to the respective commissars concerned. The organization of the German police in the occupied East is on the same pattern as the Reich, since each S.S. and Police Leader has a commander of the Order Police and of the Security Police under him. Native police units are under the control of the German police.

The Reich Commissioner for the strengthening of German Nativehood and the German Re-settlement Administration Company are active in Lithuania and the Ukraine for colonization activities.

There are various agencies of economic control. General control is exercised by the Office for the Four Year Plan, which is co-responsible with the Reich Minister for the Occupied East for all property held in trust, with special emphasis on raw material allocation, for the purpose of which it has established as special commissioner within the Office an Inspector General for the Collection and Contribution of Raw Materials in the Occupied Eastern Territories. General control is exercised as well by the Reich Ministry of Economics. Various other Reich agencies have jurisdiction, through the territorial administration, over the integration of the various economic activities in the occupied East with their own fields in the Reich. The Reich Ministry for Food and Agriculture has authority over agricultural production through personnel loaned to the territorial agricultural departments, through its supervision over the Eastern German Agricultural Administration Company, and through its Department for River Fishery in the *Ostraum*. Speer has jurisdiction over the relation of the economy to the *Wehrmacht* through his control over the *Wirtschaftsstab Ost* (Economic Staff East) which controls the whole economy of the territory under military administration and maintains close liaison with the civil administration; he also has authority over industrial reconstruction through his various technical capacities and leadership of the organization Todt. Industrial production is dominated by the respective Reich Groups through Eastern Committees, such as the Industry Committee Stone and Earth, Glass, and Ceramic. Trade is centralized in the Reich Group for Trade, banking and finance is under the control of the *Reichsbank*. Labor controls are exercised by the Organization Todt, the Labor Service, and the Commissioner General for Labor Supply.

Economic activities are directly administered by trustees for the Reich. While the trustee principle is formally based upon the taking over of the national property of the U.S.S.R. by the Reich, the preponderant weight of this property in the economic life of the area has made it possible for the trustees to take over the general direction of their respective fields. While at first many of the trustees were *ad hoc* administrators, eventually a network of monopoly trustee companies covering all branches of production and distribution has been established by the joint action of the central Reich agency concerned, and has territorial administration. Private German enterprise has been introduced into the occupied East within the framework of the trustee companies. They are called *Patenbetriebe* (guardianship plants) and work on the basis of a contract with the trustee company concerned. Native economic effort is limited to the sphere of handicraft and retail trade. German private enterprise was introduced into the Baltic countries much earlier than elsewhere in the occupied Soviet territory, since there remained a basis for private economy. The *Patenbetriebe* operated on a different basis in the Baltic countries also: whereas in occupied Russia the German companies were made responsible for general trading activities over a certain district, in the Baltic countries they were made responsible for particular branches of trade over the whole area. Supervision is exercised by the Reich Commissar, who has set up whole systems of economic organization and self-administration for the purpose. In the Ostland this takes the form of *Wirtschaftsverbände* (economic associations) for functional organization and economic chambers for geographical organization. In the Ukraine economic associations have been formed on a functional basis for the administration of industry. All these organizations are controlled by Germans and are under direct Reich Commissarial supervision. The handicrafts in the Baltic countries have been reorganized from the Soviet Artel into a Central for artisan associations, based on the leadership principle, under the control of a Special Commissioner on the staff of the Reich Commissar. Other native organizations of Baltic economic life on a small scale, like the co-operatives, have also been maintained, and also under a re-organization creating centrals responsible to the Germans for certain routine administrative tasks.

Financial activities are under the control of a twofold German banking system organized on the Reich Commissarial level. Each Reich Commissariat has a bank of issue and a general economic banking system, both organized directly under the Reich Commissar but connected through identity of personnel and currency and clearance arrangements with the Reichsbank.

On the legal basis of general conscription decrees enacted by the Reich Minister for the Occupied Eastern Territories and supplemented by executory decrees by the respective Reich Commissars, labor offices and recruiting commissions recruit native and German workers for service in the Organization Todt, the labor service, and service both in Germany and in the occupied East. In the Ukraine a native labor service (*Werkdienst*) for service on the spot has been organized. It is composed of natives, but Germans are the unit leaders.

Matters of routine administration that have no immediate relation to the interests of the Reich are cared for entirely within the framework of the territorial administration. Most of these matters are administered directly by the commissarial departments concerned.

At the seat of each Reich Commissar a German *Obergericht* (Supreme Court) has been set up, with a German court at the seat of each *Generalkommissar*. In addition a special court has been established next to each normal German court. These German courts are competent for both civil and penal cases in every instance in which a Reich or racial German or the interest of the German Reich is concerned, and for every type of jurisdiction allotted to them by decree. They apply Reich law. Moreover, the General and Regional Commissars have judicial powers in minor penal cases. In addition, the *Wehrmacht* operates courts martial and the Security Police operates summary courts martial. In the Baltic countries the whole pre-Soviet judicial structure has been restored, working on the basis of native law, but the decree establishing it provided definitely that it work within the framework allowed by the German judicial system. In Estonia the military court, set up on the basis of the laws of the former independent state of Estonia, has been reopened under the control of the Inspector General of the Estonian armed forces, who is a German appointee. In the old Russian areas, a start in the direction of reopening native courts has been made but only on the local level, and even this has not progressed far; Tsarist law is applied. For the rest, native legal administration in the Ukraine has been placed in the hands of local mediators who are competent only in minor cases, and in doubtful instances they apply German law. By decree, the German courts in the Ukraine try every important civil and penal case, and the legal offices of the civil administration can assign any case to them.

4. The Exploitation of Occupied Europe

POLITICAL CONTROLS

The diversity of types established for the control of occupied Europe must not for a moment lead us to believe that the aims of the various schemes are different. All forms serve but one purpose: the utilization of Europe's resources in raw materials, manpower, and productive capacities for Germany. Even the most minute description of administrative details will not reveal this. But the patterns of control over labor and economies clearly show that they transcend the differences in the types of administration and that labor and economic controls are centrally manipulated from Berlin without regard to the beautiful theories of military government and new order that have been described here and in the body of the text.

In order to insure the fullest exploitation of labor and economic resources, political control must be total, secure, and unified. This is not achieved by the administrative machineries that have been described, but by two agencies: the N.S.D.A.P. in occupied Europe, assisted by the Folk Groups of racial Germans, and the S.S. and Police.

The operation of the Folk Groups has been discussed in detail (see pp. 160-71). The role of the Nazi party in occupied Europe has been analyzed in this appendix (p. 537). It remains to add briefly to the analysis of the Police and S.S. in occupied territories (see also p. 540). Himmler operates in Germany as well as in occupied Europe through Higher S.S. and Police Leaders for each corps area. They are to be found in each occupied territory, where they fill usually two positions: that of a Higher S.S. and Police Leader, and that of the official in charge of public safety in the central administrative machinery of the occupied area. In the Government General, the secretary of state for public safety in the Governor General's office is the Higher S.S. and Police Leader. In the Protectorate, State Minister K. H. Frank is the Higher S.S. and Police Leader. In Norway, the role of Police General Rediess has already been stressed. In the Netherlands, the Commissar General for Special Tasks is the Higher S.S. and Police Leader, and so forth. (For occupied Russia, see above.) The Higher S.S. and Police Leaders are, however, under the direct control of Himmler, without mediation of the central machinery in occupied territory—no matter who rules there. This is clearly stated [21] in German periodicals. The same situation prevails with regard to the German armed forces in occupied Europe.

21. i.e. *Neue Ordnung* 29 August–5 September 1943.

ECONOMIC CONTROLS [22]

This is, however, also true of German economic controls in occupied Europe. They are uniform, transcend the legal differences in the status of the various territories, and are centrally manipulated from Berlin. Their detailed description would exceed the scope of this appendix and only the outline can thus be indicated.

German economic controls in Germany are based on the integration of government and self-government institutions. Chambers and groups which are compulsory for every businessman and operate under the leadership principle give the Nazi government the possibility of executing its policies with a minimum of personnel and the maximum of efficiency. In view of this dual character of Nazi economic controls in Germany, an adaptation of the economic institutions in the occupied countries was mandatory and, indeed, carried out. This adaptation had to extend to the government and self-government sectors of the indigenous economic systems. Everywhere, therefore, two things had to be done, either by the Germans themselves (as in Poland and Russia) or by the native governments: raw-material allocating agencies had to be installed; and compulsory chambers and/or trade associations had to be established. Both measures were executed.

In Holland, a council for Industrial Organization (*Raad van Bedrijfsleven*) was set up composed of six industrial groups and the chambers of commerce. The council obviously corresponds to the German National Economic Chamber. The industrial groups are subdivided according to the German model: compulsory membership and the leadership principle. *Ryksbureaus* were set up for the allocation of raw materials—corresponding to the German *Reichsstellen*. Following the Food Estate, a *Landstand* was created, divided into four departments (people and soil; production; food supply; administration, instruction and statistics), while allocations of food are made by an agricultural *Ryksbureau*.

In Belgium, the *Comité Central Industriel* is the counterpart of the German National Economic Chamber. It is composed of groups. The *Corporation Nationale de l'Agriculture et de l'Alimentation* (C.N.A.A.) is the Belgian Food Estate. *Offices Centraux de Marchandises* are the raw-material allocating offices.

22. For occupied Russia, see above.

Under the direction of Bichelonne, as minister for production (and temporarily also for labor), Vichy France has set up a system of allocation bureaus and a complicated network of authoritarian trade associations after the German model, the so-called Organization Committees (about 190), and has also transformed her chambers of commerce into economic chambers.

In Norway, ten professional groups (for merchants, artisans, industry, banking, building, fishery, insurance, hotels and restaurants, shipping, and transportation) were set up. Agriculture is compulsorily organized in the *Bondesamband*, the agrarian association.

The Polish Central Chamber for the Entire Economy is composed of four main groups, namely industry and transport; food and agriculture; lumber and woodworking; labor. Each of the main groups is broken down into more specialized trade associations (economic groups). Raw-material control is centralized in boards (iron and steel; coal; metals; leather and furs; textiles; chemical products; gold and other precious metals; used materials; building materials; paper and other goods).

The *Protectorate* has a dual organization. In the German Ministry of State (Frank) there is a coal board for the allocation of coal and timber and deputies for the allocation of other materials and the control of transportation. The autonomous government has a supervisory board under the minister of economics, Bertsch. Business is compulsorily organized in central unions (for industry, trade, handicraft, banks, etc.), subdivided in economic and trade groups. The peak agricultural organization is the Central Association of Agriculture and Forestry, composed of two regional associations for Bohemia and Moravia with functional subdivisions.

These examples may suffice. The reorganization of the native economic institutions provides the soil in which direct German controls could grow.

German controls are, again, of two kinds: through the self-governing organs of German industry and through German government agencies.

German industry is represented in each occupied country through a German Chamber of Commerce Abroad. The most important German business firms are represented on their managing boards; 37 such German Chambers exist abroad, 15 alone on the European continent. Their function is obvious. The German Chamber in the

Netherlands frankly admits that it considered as one of its main tasks to transfer Dutch labor to the occupied eastern territories.[23] Their central organization is the German National Economic Chamber (see pp. 243-7).

The activities of the German Chambers are supported by the German Groups. Many of the groups maintain offices in occupied Europe to assist German agencies to establish relations with their native counterparts and to secure business for their own members. The German *Reichsvereinigungen*, the national compulsory peak cartels in the fields of coal, iron and steel, chemical fibers, and hemp (to be discussed below, p. 601) have been designed for the very purpose of 'organizing' European resources. It need hardly be mentioned that individual German firms, if size and business allow it, continue to operate their branches, while occupied Russia, as has been shown above, was a completely new field for exploitation. To all these German business organizations—chambers, groups, cartels, corporations—an important addition was made in 1942: the Main Committees of Speer's Ministry for Armaments and War Production (see below, p. 590). These committees of private corporation engineers have to 'streamline' production by standardizing and rationalizing it and many such committees maintain delegations abroad. In many fields, all self-governing organs of German industry are co-ordinated in a single body.

Innumerable German government agencies are concerned with the spoliation of occupied Europe. There are, of course, first the economic departments in the civilian or military administration of the occupied territory. But they are primarily executive organs for policies determined by German national agencies, which also maintain direct representation abroad.

First in importance rank the Armament Inspectors, since 1942 under the jurisdiction of the Speer Ministry for Armaments and War Production. As a rule, there is one inspector for each occupied area. In France, however, there are three. They are co-ordinated in the War Economy and Armament Staff France. The armament inspectorates are subdivided into armament commands. Both are headed by officers, mostly retired officers with training in economics or engineering. Central control of them rests with the Armament Office of the Speer Ministry.

23. *Deutsche Bergwerkszeitung*, 6 April 1943.

Most of the commissioners and inspector generals have their agents in occupied Europe, the commissioner general for building construction in every country, the inspector general for ocean shipping at every foreign port. So have the ministries for transportation and post. It would serve no useful purpose to list all the agencies.

Germany pursued two major aims in occupied Europe: she transferred raw materials and machinery to Germany and she utilized the productive capacities of occupied Europe. The transfer of goods from France was demanded partly on the basis of the armistice agreement and the demands are then raised by the armistice commission, which uses the machinery of German military government for the execution of its requests. But this is most likely the minor aspect of the exploitation problem. Economically more important are the transactions clad in the form of contracts between Germany and occupied Europe.

Full authority for the exploitation of occupied Europe is vested in Göring as Hitler's Delegate for the Four Year Plan. The authorization of 26 August 1940 is entitled 'Decree on the Planned Utilization of the Occupied Western Territories for the German War Economy,' and that of 15 August 1941 'Decree on the Utilization of the Occupied Eastern Territories for the German War Economy.' A large number of executive decrees have been enacted on the basis of these two authorizations. They center around two main problems: the shifting of German orders from Germany to occupied Europe and the transfer of raw materials.

For the purpose of placing orders (*Auftragsverlagerung*), so-called Central Order Agencies (*Zentralauftragsstellen*) were established at Brussels—for Belgium and Northern France; Paris—for France; The Hague—for the Netherlands; Oslo—for Norway; Belgrade—for Serbia; Copenhagen—for Denmark.

These *Zasts*, as they are commonly called, are set up at the highest civil or military authorities in the occupied area but are centrally directed from Berlin. Without their consent, no orders can be placed. German businessmen are exhorted to transfer orders to occupied Europe. But they are forbidden to do so directly. They have first to approach their trade association (group), which applies to the *Zast*, which, in turn, opens negotiations with the native trade association in its territory, which finally allocates the order to its members. The supreme importance of the self-governing agencies in Germany and occupied Europe thus becomes clear. Without their mediation, the *Zasts* would have to have an enormous staff, while, owing to the delegation of power to the groups and chambers, the personnel is and can be very small.

The control of the placement of orders led by necessity to that of the flow of raw materials. On 21 August 1942, the *Zasts* were thus made the supreme agencies for the following transactions: control of the flow of raw materials from occupied Europe to Germany; from Germany to occupied Europe; between occupied territories; and between occupied territories and abroad. Each raw-material transaction requires the consent of the *Zast*.

It follows that German national agencies, especially the Ministry of Armaments and War Production, have full control of the economic life of occupied Europe, while the civil and military commanders of occupied territories are mere agents who have to assist the German national agencies with all their powers and personnel.

Similar methods are applied in the field of labor controls. The first concern of the Germans is either the creation or the transformation of labor exchanges. In Poland and Russia, German labor exchanges had to be set up. In the remaining parts of occupied Europe, the existing exchanges were given greater powers by their own governments and placed under more stringent controls from above. The Germans were much less lucky in their attempts to foster the creation of indigenous labor fronts. The U.T.M.I. in Belgium and the N.A.F. in the Netherlands are pale shadows of the German labor front, while the Norwegian attempt completely failed. The German Commissioner General for Labor Supply, F. Sauckel (see below, p. 619) maintains agents in each occupied territory and uses the economic or labor departments in the military or civil administration for the deportation of native labor to Germany (see below on the foreign worker in Germany, p. 623).

Germany is continuously receiving contributions and credits from occupied and allied Europe, now totaling approximately 20 billion Mark per year. These revenues are composed of occupation costs, taxes, increase in German clearing debts, and the sale of German government paper to foreign banks. Since Germany cannot maintain adequate exports, the clearing balances continue to increase.

5. In Search of Co-operation with Occupied Europe

No matter what aspect of German military government we touch —all serve the one purpose: to exploit Europe. Other methods are, of course, much subtler than those described. Property passes from foreign to German owners by any of the devices described above (see pp. 180-82). Propaganda flows endlessly into occupied Europe—by devices similar to those used for the control of the economies, namely by establishing culture chambers and by the operation of German agents. Indigenous groups or individuals are being systematically corrupted. Anti-Semitism and the appropriation of Jewish property are baits for the corrupt groups in western occupied Europe. Money flows freely to Quislings. Businessmen and farmers in Denmark, Norway, Belgium, and France are freely invited to share the spoils of eastern occupied Europe as traders, industrialists, or farmers. Foreign bankers are invited to join in the financial exploitation of their own and of foreign peoples. Gangsters and uprooted intellectuals are absorbed by the S.S., while native Fascist parties provide havens for those who would never have been able to make a living under normal conditions.

The Germanic and Romance nations were flooded day after day with promises of a glorious future as partners of Germany in the establishment of a new order. While the history of the European Quislings will eventually be written—this much is clear now: The German theory of the New Order and of military government suffered shipwreck in just those countries for which it was devised: in Denmark, Holland, and Norway. The 'Germanic brethren' opposed Nazism in all its forms—imported and native. Peaceful people were transformed into passionate and determined haters and fighters.

The defeats suffered by Russia, the invasion of North Africa and Italy, and the air raids led not only to the abandonment of the New Order Ideology and its replacement by the Defend the Fortress Europe, but also the scrapping of the practice of military government.

We have conquered and developed all who opposed us but we have not yet won them over. If we want to be honest and not exaggerate the number of people on our side, we must admit this. Some might say, 'Let them hate us as long as they fear and obey us.

Has spirit a chance in a process decided by might?' We say yes, but with reservations. The governments of Germany and Japan acknowledge this approval without neglecting the military and political. The degree of independence of our countries depends on their readiness to co-operate with Germany. Croatia is an ally; Holland and Belgium have supervisory administrations [*Aufsichtsverwaltungen*] based on pro-German movements such as those of Mussert, Elias, Degrelle; Norway has a Quisling government exclusively of Norwegians; France and Serbia have been granted self-government; even in the East our policy is to win over and not only conquer and develop. The special character of the Polish people necessitates quarantine. The Baltic peoples have been given back a great part of their autonomy. Of course Napoleon succeeded in starting the Russian campaign with former enemy soldiers, but he did not manage to keep them. If it is at all possible to win over conquered and occupied souls, the question arises whether it is not already too late or still too early. The answer is that it is rather late for some measures, but not yet too late. However, it is too early for great political and economic decisions and until then the task of mastering comes before that of winning over. We are quite clear about the fact that winning over of people's hearts is a question which is still more. difficult than conquest and development of countries and requires much time and still more patience . . .

This is the leader in an official Nazi newspaper published on 5 September 1943 and entitled Conquer, Develop, Win Over.

Indeed, attempts are being made to win over despoiled peoples, even those who are considered as almost subhuman.

PART TWO

Totalitarian Monopolistic Economy

INTRODUCTION

The Reorganization of 1942 and the Edict of 2 September 1943

The defeats suffered by Germany at the hands of the Red Army during the winter of 1941-2 led to a reorganization of the German economy, which started late in 1941 and ended in the early summer of 1942. Subsequent defeats on the Eastern front, the landings in North Africa and Italy, and the intensified air warfare caused another total reorganization of the economy in September 1943. The following chapter, while outlining the organizational changes of 1942, will discuss in greater detail the legislation of 1943.

The problem Germany faced in 1941-2 was briefly this: The losses in manpower and war material rapidly increased and began to deplete Germany's available reserves. As a consequence, additional men had to be called up. Care was taken, however, to avoid the draft of war-essential workers. As a consequence, shopkeepers, artisans, civil servants, and salaried employees were called, and another' closing-down campaign was imperative. This reduced the staffs available to the economic control agencies, while, in turn, severer restrictions upon entrepreneurial freedom became necessary. The solution was found in the strengthening of the 'self-governing' sector of German business, simplification of price and profit controls, more intense rationalization, and, above all, a reorganization of the raw-material allocation apparatus by delegating more functions to the Groups and to the newly created national cartels, so-called *Reichsvereinigungen.*

At the same time, however, the Ministry of Armaments and Munitions began to reorganize its own machinery. Albert Speer, who succeeded F. Todt (see pp. 72, 250, 375-7), took over the War Economy and Armament Office (*Wehrwirtschafts und Rüstungs-amt,* abbreviated Wi Rü) of the Supreme Command of the Armed Forces with its regional machinery, and began to build up his own 'self-governing' sector—namely the 'Main Committees' (*Hauptaus-schüsse*) and Industrial Rings (*Industrieringe*), composed of engineers and construction men drawn from the most powerful industrial corporations. From 1942 on, two rival organizations thus existed: the Organization Funk, with its ministry of economies, groups, *Reichsvereinigungen*, national boards for raw-material control, and economic offices; and the Organization Speer, with its ministry of armament and munitions, *Wi Rü*, and main committees.

No wonder that jurisdictional disputes arose. Very soon neither the outside observer nor apparently the German businessman could tell who had to determine the allocation of raw materials, allocate orders, or comb out workers.

This was ended on 2 September 1943 by an edict of Hitler,[1] which entrusted Speer with the control of production and left to Funk merely finance, credit, and foreign trade.

1. *Reichsgesetzblatt*, 1, p. 529.

I

CONTROL INSTITUTIONS

1. The Central Economic Controls and the Ministry for Armaments and War Production

PLANNING OFFICES

THE title of the Speer Ministry was in consequence changed into the Ministry for Armaments and War Production and a number of personnel changes were made. The most important of these are:

Hans Kehrl,[1] who had succeeded von Hanneken in 1942 as chief of Main Department No. II in the Ministry of Economics, was transferred from the Speer Ministry and put in charge of Speer's new office for raw materials. Dr. Friedrich Walter Landfried,[2] Secretary of State in the Ministry of Economics, was relieved of his duties in December 1943 and was succeeded by S.S. Brigade Leader Dr. Franz Hayler, the leader of the National Group 'Trade.' Hans Kehrl's place in the Ministry of Economics was filled by S.S. Leader Otto Ohlendorf, the chief manager of the National Group 'Trade.'

Under Göring as Delegate for the Four Year Plan, a Central Planning Office exists (*Zentrale Planung*). It is composed of: Göring as Chairman; Paul Körner, Secretary of State in the Four Year Plan Office; Erhard Milch, Secretary of State in the Air Ministry and Field Marshal; Walther Funk, Minister of Economics; and Albert Speer, Minister for Armaments and War Production. The functions of this committee will continue to be very circumscribed. Long-range planning is hardly possible in a period where economic decisions are forced upon Germany and speed is the essence of administration. Still it may be assumed that basic decisions (i.e. the transfer of whole industries, etc.) may be reached in the Central Planning.

Speer operates in a dual capacity. As Minister for Armaments and War Production, he is in charge of those factories and installations engaged in war production. The German newspapers asserted that Funk controlled 95,000 and Speer 90,000 establishments,

---

1. P. 303.　　　　2. Pp. 303, 372, 376.

though even the Funk-controlled sector was actually working for armaments production. Speer is, however, also Commissioner General for Armament Tasks in the Four Year Plan, the title now being 'for Armament Tasks and War Production.' As such, his function is to adapt the economy in sectors not directly under his control to the requirements of the war economy. It is for this office that Göring created a planning office (*Planungsamt*). Its management has been entrusted to the above-mentioned Kehrl. Here final decisions on the allocation of raw material are made on the basis of requests from the main quota claimants, such as armed forces, Organization Todt, S.S. and Police, the ministry of economics for the civilian sector, etc.

THE MINISTRY FOR ARMAMENTS AND WAR PRODUCTION

The Ministry is divided into an administrative sector (comprising the Central Office, Armament Office, and an office for Economic and Financial matters) and the so-called Production Departments. Generally the functions of the ministry are said to revolve around three things: co-ordination, production, and liaison. Speer's liaison officer with other agencies, especially with the Ministry of Economics, is K. A. Hettlage of the *Commerzbank*.

The Groups and *Reichsvereinigungen* become, though they remain under the administrative supervision of Funk, agents of the Speer Ministry. But not only the Groups but also the regional organs of the Economies and Food Ministries—namely the Regional Economic Offices and the Regional Farmers' Association—are made subject to the Speer Ministry, which thus controls all organs in the regional level. So are all organs concerned with raw-material control, a fact already expressed in Kehrl's appointment as chief of the department Raw Material. The *Reichsvereinigung* Coal has been put fully under Speer. He has also assumed control of Labor by the appointment of a Reich Labor Supply Engineer, G. Friedrich, of Regional Labor Supply Engineers and Labor Supply Engineers, for all plants employing 800 workers or more (see also below, p. 621).

Hand in hand with the strengthening of the bureaucratic controls in the Speer Ministry went an expansion of its self-governing sector. The Main Committees, divided into and composed of special committees, and the Industrial Rings have assumed greater powers and now completely overshadow the Groups and Chambers.

Quite important changes have been made and are being made on the regional level. It becomes increasingly clear that the key political unit for the control of the economy is becoming the *Rüstungsbezirk*, the armament inspection which, in turn, coincides with the *Wehrkreis*, the corps area. An exception has been made for the regional jurisdiction of the Labor Supply Engineers. As a consequence, all regional agents of Speer, in his capacity as Minister and Inspector General for Water and Power and Roads, operate in and for the area of an armament inspection. Since it is the production controls that are decisive in a war economy, the *Wehrkreis* has emerged as the key political unit.

Survey of the Reich Ministry for Armaments and War Production
　　Minister: Albert Speer
　　Secretary of State: Schulze-Fielitz
The Organization of the Ministry on the National Level
　　Bureaucratic Organization:
　　　　Central Office—Mayor of Nuremberg, Liebel
　　　　Armament Office—Lieut. Gen. Waeger
　　　　Economic and Financial Matters—Dr. K. A. Hettlage (*Commerzbank*)
Production Departments
　　Raw Materials—Hans Kehrl
　　Armament Supplies—Dr. Walther Schieber
　　Engineering in Relation to Finished Combat Materials—Saur
　　Production of Consumption Goods—Ing. Seebauer
　　Building—Stobbe-Dethleffsen [3]
　　Power Supply—Schulze-Fielitz
Self-Government Sector
　　Main Committees (divided into Special Committees)
　　　　1. Armed Forces and General Equipment—Wilhelm Zangen (*Mannesmann*)
　　　　2. Armored Vehicles and Tractors—Ing. Walter Rohland (*Aug. Thyssen Huette*) co-operating with:
　　　　Armored Vehicle Commission (*Panzerkommission*)—Dr. Porsche and Guderian
　　　　3. Shipbuilding

3. Removed.

4. Munitions—Prof. Dr. Albert Wolff (*Deutsche Waffen und Munitionsfabriken*)
5. Aircraft Hulls—Ing. Karl Frydag (*Henschel Flugzeug-werke A.G.*)
6. Aircraft Engines
7. Aircraft Equipment
8. Engines (*Triebwerke*)—Dr. William Werner (*Auto Union*)
9. Machines—Karl Lange (Economic Group, Machine Industry)
10. Electrical Installations is also *Industriering*—Dr. Lueschen (*Siemens* combine)
11. Rail Vehicles—Gerhard Degenkolb
12. Wood Construction and Barracks
13. Building Construction—Ing. Bruno Gaertner (*Wayss* and *Freytag*)
14. Power and Explosives
15. Committee for Armament Trade (*Arbeitsgemeinschaft Ruestungshandel*)—with rights equal to those of the main Committees—Consul Hommel (*Hommelwerke*)

Corporations

Rüstungskontor, limited liability company. Manager: Dr. Hettlage, for the clearing of steel allocation and financial transactions resulting from the periodic attachment of stock.

Generatorkraft A.G.—founded primarily by the former, but owned by the timber industry (50%), the Reich (22.5%), the coal industry (10%), the peat and oil industry (17.5%).

Festkraftstoff A.G.—founded by 1 and 2, for the promotion of solid fuels for motor vehicles.

Heeres—Rüstungskredit A.G., for the administration of long term credits to industry.

The bureaucratic pillar is strengthened by the 'self-government' pillar of the ministry, represented by the committees and rings. Just as the ministry of economics operates through bureaucratic agents and through the self-government of industry (groups and chambers) so does the Speer Ministry.

The establishment of the committees and rings was the outcome of the failure of the German control system, which was becoming apparent during the winter 1941-2, that is, under the impact of the defeat suffered on the Russian front. All efforts were then directed towards rationalizing the German war economy, that is, to achieve higher output with a lesser investment of labor, machinery, and raw materials.

In order to achieve this aim the Speer Ministry established the main committees and industrial rings. The organizational principles underlying the German economic system were formerly determined by industrial branches and still are determined by them in so far as raw-material control goes. The Main Committees and Rings, however, are determined by products (tanks, diesel engines, ball-bearings, rivets, etc.). If the finished product, e.g. a tank, is composed of a number of different parts, which are produced by several branches of industry, a main committee is established for it.

If, however, an article is used in a number of industrial enterprises (for instance, ball-bearings are used in tanks and other products), then industrial rings are created. While a main committee thus embraces the industries manufacturing parts for a finished product, a ring cuts across all the industries that are using a specific article. Committees and rings are composed exclusively of engineers and construction men, and no lawyers, administrators, or financial experts are admitted.

The composition of these bodies has been considered as proof that capitalism is dead in Germany and that the profit motive is nonexistent. It may be wise, however, to remember that according to an investigation carried out under the auspices of W. Zangen, the leader of the National Group Industry and president of the Mannesmann combine, 143 members of the directorates of 35 industrial corporations in the Ruhr District were composed as follows: 85 technicians, 47 merchants, and 11 jurists. It follows that engineers were and are predominant in the managing boards of German industrial corporations because the first-generation capitalists always took care to give their sons a technical rather than a commercial education. Many of these men now sit in the committees and rings.

Twenty-one main committees are operating at present. The most important is the main committee Armed Forces and General Equipment, headed by Zangen. This main committee deals with three fields: (1) armaments generally; (2) requirements of the armed forces in so far as they are identical with civilian requirements (spades, hammers, barracks); and (3) general principles of rationalization of armament production.

The aim of the committees and rings is to get the utmost out of production. It is these organizations that now discuss the technical aspects of armament orders with the representatives of the armed forces. They have also received a regional organization in order to enable the government to establish co-operation between the Speer Ministry and other ministries and industrial organizations on the regional level. The chairman of the committees and rings in the regional level are called *Rüstungsobmänner* (Armament Chairmen), and are appointed to this position by Speer. Below them are *Bezirksobmänner*. The committees and rings have field offices in occupied territory.

2. THE WAR ECONOMY AND ARMAMENT OFFICE OF THE SUPREME COMMAND OF THE ARMED FORCES

Until Hitler's access to power, all German armed forces were under the *Reichswehr* Ministry. The Nazis established in 1935 three separate service commands, an Army Command (*Heeresleitung*), a Navy Command (*Marineleitung*), and an Air Ministry. Co-ordination of the three services was achieved by the Reich War Ministry. In it there was an office called *Wehrmachtamt*, composed of officers of all three services and charged with the unity of planning and command. The decree of 4 February 1938 transformed the *Wehrmachtamt* into the *Oberkommando der Wehrmacht* (O.K.W. —Supreme Command of the Armed Forces). The ministry ceased to exist, its functions being taken over by the heads of the O.K.W. and of the three services, who rank as cabinet ministers and attend cabinet meetings.

Within the thus constituted Supreme Command of the Armed Forces, an *Amtsgruppe Wehrwirtschaftsstab* (Office War Economy Staff) was established. It was transformed on 22 November 1939 into the *Wehrwirtschafts und Rüstungsamt* (abbreviated *Wi Rü*), the Office for War Economy and Armaments under General George Thomas. The functions of this office were considerably increased and it became fully responsible for the war sector of the German economy until the expansion of the Speer Ministry in the spring of 1942. The Armaments Division is now under the Speer Ministry and its Price Control Division operates jointly with the Price Commissioner's Office.

The most important organs of the *Wi Rü* are the Armament Inspectors (*Rüstungsinspekteure*), now under the jurisdiction of the Speer Ministry. They also serve, however, as War Economy Inspectors, under the *Wi Rü*. They are, in conjunction with the committees and rings, in charge of production of combat material, of scheduling, and of contract letting. They also preside over the Armament Commissions.

3. THE FOUR YEAR PLAN OFFICE

A distinction must be made between the Four Year Plan and the Four Year Plan Office. The former is a principle that embodies the need to utilize the German economy for the preparedness and conduct of war. The latter is a specific institution. The execution of this plan is by no means confined to the Four Year Plan Office. The Four Year Plan Office is merely one of the institutions through which the adaptation of the German economy to preparedness and war has been carried out. Indeed, it is correct to say that the significance of the Four Year Plan Office has declined as compared with that, for instance, of the Ministry of Economics for the Civilian Sector and the Ministry of Armaments and Munitions for the Military Sector.

4. COMMISSIONERS DIRECTLY RESPONSIBLE TO HITLER

There are six national commissioners directly subordinated to Adolf Hitler. They may be conceived as agents for the reconciliation of military and civilian requirements. They are:

Professor Karl Brandt, Hitler's personal deputy in matters of public health. Jakob Werlin, a successful engineer and businessman and allegedly administering Hitler's investment in the Daimler-Benz Automobile Works, who has been made Inspector General for Motor Transportation. Albert Speer, who, in succession to Todt, has been made Inspector General of Roads, the oldest inspector generalship under the direct responsibility of Hitler. Robert Ley, leader of the Labor Front, made National Housing Commissioner (*Reichswohnungskommissar*) on 23 October 1942. The creation of this position was made necessary by the tremendous destruction of housing through aerial bombardment. The co-ordination of all efforts in this field was indispensable. Dr. Ley uses for his functions the old housing organization within the ministry of labor, main department 'IV'), all institutions of the Prussian provinces, the states, the municipalities, all public and semi-public housing organizations. He has ultimate responsibility for settlement, allotment, and town planning, and the allocation of funds for these purposes. He operates in the regional level through the Gauleiter, who have received the title of *Gauwohnungskommissare* (Gau Housing Commissars).

On 5 July 1942, the Hamburg Gauleiter Karl Kaufmann was made *Reich Commissioner for Ocean Shipping* for the co-ordination of all agencies engaged in the construction of ocean-going ships, to speed up loading and unloading.

Speer is also Inspector General for Water and Power, which office is now combined with the ministry proper.

5. The Ministry of Economics

Under Funk, this ministry has suffered a decisive decline in power. The structural changes need not be mentioned. The leading personnel is now fully Nazified.

6. The Ministry for Food and Agriculture

The Food Estate, at the outbreak of the war, was taken over by the Ministry of Food and Agriculture. It is divided functionally into cartels and regionally into 30 regional peasant organizations (*Landesbauernschaften*), which in turn are subdivided into smaller units, the *Kreisbauernschaften* (710) and *Ortsbauernschaften* (60,-000). In the summer of 1942, main Department 1 (*Der Mensch*) of the Food Estate, dealing with the indoctrination of the peasants, was dissolved.

Agricultural producers and distributors are compulsorily joined by the Minister for Food and Agriculture in *Hauptvereinigungen*, subdivided into regional *Wirtschaftsverbände*, for the regulation of the market (prices, sales conditions, price margins, etc.). The *Hauptvereinigungen*, compulsory cartels, are the organs for the planning of production and distribution. With the consent of the Minister for Food and Agriculture, they establish the plans for civilian supply as well as for that of the armed forces. They also supply the necessary agricultural products to plants (for production) and to the distributing apparatus. There are nine *Hauptvereinigungen*, as follows: Grain Economy; Milk, Fat, and Egg Economy; Cattle Economy; Potato Economy; Sugar and Candy Economy; Gardening and Viticulture; Brewing Industry; Wine and Brandy; Fish Economy.

7. TRANSPORTATION, POWER, AND BUILDING CONTROLS

These three fields are extremely important in every war economy. They assume supreme importance in Germany and have thus come under the authority of Speer. Speer's increased power over production led by necessity to a strengthening of his influence over the transportation sector. The Office for the Organization of Transport was incorporated into the Ministry and charged with organizing an 'effective' organization of transportation.

The new office operates through 32 Transport Main Commissions organized after the model of the main committees. They authoritatively fix 'marginal distances' which must not be exceeded. Such maximum transport distances have already been fixed for all major commodities. Transport deputies for each area of an armament inspection co-ordinate the activities of the transport facilities.

Speer has endeavored for a long time to compel the conversion of all liquid fuel vehicles to solid fuel or producer gas. However, before compulsory conversion could be decreed, adequate generators had to be designed, appropriate fuels had to be developed, and a system of distribution for solid fuel and producer gas had to be planned. A central Office for Generators was established in the Four Year Plan Office under state councilor Dr. Schieber to fulfil these tasks. On 4 October 1943 Speer as Commissioner General for Armament Tasks in the Four Year Plan ordered the conversion of all liquid-driven vehicles.

The control of power is divided between: (1) the National Board for Electricity; (2) the Inspector General for Water and Power (Speer); and (3) the Office for Power in the Speer Ministry. Though 2 and 3 retain a nominal identity, they are practically merged, and the chief of the Section Power in the Inspector General's Office is also the head of the corresponding department in the Speer Ministry.

The National Board Electricity has since the decree of 3 September 1939 the function of a *Reichslastverteiler*, primarily engaged in expanding and improving the grid system. To this have been added the repair of damage to power stations and the operation of old or shut-down power plants. The *Reichslastverteiler* operates through regional and local organs. The actual planning of production and of consumption, however, rests exclusively with the Inspector General and thus with the Speer Ministry. He operates through the Office for the Planning of Power, composed of outstanding experts in the field of power, and the main and special committees primarily engaged in the production of power plants and cables. For purposes of bureaucratic control, Germany is divided into power districts; there are 13 of these, directed by deputies. They are in turn co-ordinated by Speer's Special Deputy for the Saving of Power, who co-ordinates the Power Engineers that must be employed by all plants consuming·more than 5,000 tons of coal, or 200,000 KWH of electricity, or 100,000 ohms of gas.

The increased powers given to engineers led to a complete reorganization of the controls over building construction. The powers of the Commissioner General under the Four Year Plan for Building Construction were severely [4] curtailed and, as a consequence, Speer resigned this position; at the same time those of the main committee construction were increased. As a further consequence, the distinction between industrial building entrepreneurs (organized in the Economic Group Building) and the handicraft builders (organized in the Reich Guild) became meaningless and the two organizations were transformed into mere agents of the main committee.

8. THE SELF-GOVERNMENT OF INDUSTRY

The traditional forms of self-government have been largely superseded by the main committees and rings. Decisive changes have also occurred in the Chamber organization. By a decree of 30 May 1942, a completely new Chamber organization was created. So-called *Gauwirtschaftskammern* (Gau Economic Chambers) were instituted, and the Minister of Economics was authorized to abolish such Chambers of Industry and Commerce, Chambers of Handicraft, and Economic Chambers as he saw fit. As a consequence of

4. See p. 250.

this decree the following changes were made: instead of the 209 Chambers (111 Chambers of Industry and Commerce, 71 Chambers of Handicraft, and 27 Economic Chambers), only 42 Gau Economic Chambers and 18 Economic Chambers remained. The Economic Chambers operate more or less as branches of the Gau Economic Chambers. Many of the old Chamber presidents (see pp. 389-92) have been retained, but the new leaders are all reliable Nazi businessmen closely connected with the Gau economic advisers, who, in turn, must be invited to the Chamber meetings. Yet the sociopolitical power of the Chambers remains insignificant. It is probably true to say that the Chambers have been Nazified because they were the agents for the closing down of retail and artisan shops. Tighter party control of this business sector was thus indicated.

The personnel of the Groups has largely remained unaffected by the frequent reorganization, though the Groups have lost power to the technocratic organs. The power of the Group direction has been curtailed by the appointment of councils composed of the most active businessmen. The Groups are today primarily auxiliary organs for raw-material allocation.

9. CARTELS

Stronger state control over stronger cartels is the idea behind the cartel legislation of 1941-3. On 20 November 1942, the following decree was enacted:

The Minister of Economics is authorized . . . to give general or individual orders to enterprises which essentially influence the market due to their legal or factual position . . . if, by the use of their influence, they injure the national economy or any specific enterprise.

The Minister of Economics is further authorized to make the conclusion of cartel agreements dependent upon his consent.

The Minister of Economics may interfere with existing cartel agreements.

The legal controls are thus complete. Trusts, cartels, monopolies, in whatever form they are organized, may now be given general or individual orders. The minister may interfere with existing cartel agreements.

The new powers have been used to 'rationalize the cartel system.' Many of the 2,300 cartels have been dissolved, or rather incorporated into larger units; that is, the cartel system is being streamlined. Only 500 cartels are expected to remain.

The most important change occurred in the steel cartel, the kernel of industrial power. The old *Rohstahl gemeinschaft* founded by Emil Kirdorf has been dissolved. The *Eisen und Stahlwerkgemeinschaft in der Reichsvereinigung Eisen* (abbreviated E.S.G.E.) has been founded as a central syndicate that will sell iron and steel to consumers, fix the prices, control exports and imports, and enter into cartel agreements with other cartels. The new steel cartel is incorporated in the National Association Iron but remains more or less independent. The change in the leadership is remarkable. The president of the United Steel Trust (Poensgen) is out. He had already been deposed as leader of the Economic Group Iron-Making Industry and had not been made president of the National Association Iron, a position assumed by the Saar industrialist, H. Röchling. The steel cartel leader is Wilhelm Zangen, president of Mannesmann. He is assisted by a younger generation of steel captains from the biggest combines: Steel Trust, Flick, Hoesch, Arbed, and one Protectorate combine. Poensgen has been made honorary chairman.

Another decree by Zangen abolished the cartel quotas. It was justified by the fact that quotas had lost their meaning in a period of full production. Only the productivity of the cartel member and not an acquired right should henceforth be the standard for the allocation of production within the cartels. The decree does not create a new economic situation, because the quota system had long given way to the requirement of full employment. It had severe consequences for the internal financial action of the cartels. It no longer compels those cartel members who exceed their quotas to pay indemnifications into the cartel treasury, while those cartel members who do not reach their quotas are no longer entitled to indemnification from the cartel treasury. Since the comb-out has affected primarily small and medium-sized firms, it is they who have to bear the financial burdens resulting from the abolition of the quotas.

The rationalization of the cartel structure has entailed a redefinition of the relation between cartel and Group. This was achieved by a decree concerning the purification of cartels of 20 May 1943. It has been mentioned that while the cartels were not allowed administrative functions, the Groups were forbidden to engage in marketing activities.[5] This prohibition has fallen and the groups have assumed the functions of the dissolved cartels. The distinction between cartels and groups has thus practically come to an end.

10. REICHSVEREINIGUNGEN

The merger between cartel and group is fully realized in the *Reichsvereinigungen*, which may best be designated as compulsory national peak cartels, covering whole industries. The following have been created:

The National Association Coal, directed by Paul Pleiger of the Göring combine, appointed directly by Göring. He is assisted by a supervisory board consisting of 13 members. The major functions of the *Reichsvereinigung* Coal are to increase productivity; to control distribution and transportation; and to execute all government measures in the field of coal mining; it is the main agency for concluding international agreements in the field of coal.

The National Association Iron is directed by the Saar industrialist Röchling. He is assisted by a council composed of the most important steel industrialists, and by an administrative council where a lesser number of industrialists are represented. The *Reichsvereinigung* Iron has the task of rationalizing and increasing production. It also establishes the plans for production and for raw-material allocation and for imports and exports of iron, steel, scrap, etc. It is engaged in planning the transportation of its products. It supervises the existing steel cartels; it regulates prices, settles disputes between members, and decides upon the closing down of superfluous enterprises in its field. In order to further technological developments the *Reichsvereinigung* has abolished the so-called 'plant secrets' so as to make technological experiences of one member accessible to all other members.

The National Association Chemical Fibers is controlled by Dr. E. H. Vits, president of the *Vereinigte Glanzstoffwerke*. He is assisted by a presidential council of 8 members. This *Reichsvereinigung* is a holding cartel for the existing cartels in the field of rayon and cellulose wool fibers. It regulates the marketing and standardization

5. See pp. 270-74.

of products, is engaged in price control and concludes international agreements.

The National Association Hemp is directed by Dr. Gruber. It has functions similar to those of the *Reichsvereinigung* Chemical Fibers.

The National Association Textile Processing is different from the previous ones in that the control of the Minister of Economics over it is weakest. Its primary aim is the rationalization of the cartel system in the textile finishing branch, especially the amalgamation of existing cartels, a task which has been successfully carried out by this *Reichsvereinigung*.

Apart from these five German *Reichsvereinigungen* there have been established a number of similar organizations which, though not having the name *Reichsvereinigung*, have for all practical purposes identical functions. We may mention the Association of German Wire Rope Works effective as of 1 January 1943, the Association Forestry for the purpose of promoting the mechanization and the better exploitation of the material, the *Gemeinschaft* Shoes, and similar organizations.

The *Reichsvereinigungen* fulfil a number of functions. They are like cartels in that they engage in the regulation of marketing conditions. They are to some extent raw-material allocation agencies and thus have taken over some of the functions of the *Reichsstellen* (the National Boards for Raw Material Control). They have also assumed the functions of Groups in that they control the cartels below them. And they are finally agencies for the allocation of orders, especially of government orders, among their members. They constitute thus the culmination of five trends that have become apparent in the German economy since 1939, namely: to integrate an excessive number of cartels in any one industrial branch into a national holding or peak cartel, that is, doing away with over-cartelization; to create national cartels in such branches where free cartelization was found to be lagging, that is, to do away with under-cartelization; to transfer raw material control to the cartels; to utilize the cartel for community production; and to integrate the cartel and the Group.

II

METHODS OF CONTROL

1. Raw-Material Control

On 25 February 1943, the whole system of raw-material control was put on a new basis and so-called *Lenkungsbereiche*, 'spheres of steering,' were established. It was preceded by two other decrees: that of 11 December 1942, making the former chiefs of the raw-material boards National Commissioners (*Reichsbeauftragte*), and that of 12 December 1942, instituting the *Bewirtschaftungsstellen*.

The National Boards were originally the sole agents for raw-material control. Instituted in 1934 under Schacht's New Plan, they were then called Supervisory Boards and were primarily agencies for currency control through the establishment of import quotas. The spheres of steering are no longer oriented at the raw material but at the finished product and thus organized the whole German economy vertically. The aim of the *Bewirtschaftungsstellen* is that in the future a factory should have dealings only with one agency. The *Bewirtschaftungsstelle* should thus be the only agency with which a factory should deal in order to secure raw materials. The directors of the spheres of steering were authorized to delegate to the *Bewirtschaftungsstelle* a number of functions, namely (a) the allocation of raw material and semi-finished goods; (b) the elaboration of plans of production which were established by the directors of the spheres of steering; (c) the standardization of commodities for the purpose of allocating specific production tasks to specific factories; (d) the control of the sale; and (e) the giving of specific orders to specific plants in regard to production. The *Bewirtschaftungsstellen* are as a rule either cartels or economic, trade, or sub-trade Groups.

Many of the *Bewirtschaftungsstellen* have in time created *Auftragslenkungsstellen* (Order Distribution Offices) for their fields. These agencies distributed orders received from government agencies or private firms among the members of the cartel or group according to their ability to produce efficiently, speedily, and cheaply.

There are three types of spheres of steering: Type 1 is controlled by National Commissioners (*Reichsbeauftragte*). They are, as a rule, the former directors of the National Boards, although in the spring of 1943 many National Board directors have been replaced by businessmen. The National Commissioners are, so to speak, sovereign in their field. They are not dependent upon their advisory councils. Type 2 is controlled by the directors of the Economic Groups, who, in this capacity, have received the title *Bevollmaechtigte* (Deputies). Type 3 is controlled by the *Reichsvereinigungen*.

The ultimate reconciliation of military and civilian requirements and the broad outlines of the production plans are established in Speer's office by his raw-material chief, the Nazi textile magnate, Hans Kehrl. Once these decisions are made, the direction of the 22 spheres of steering work out the production and allocation plans for their respective fields. So do the marketing associations of the Food Estate. The procedure now valid in the allocation of iron and steel is generally being introduced, though the steel allocation has certain specific features. The *Rüstungskontor* has founded a clearing office for the establishment of iron and steel quotas. Each agency that orders iron and steel obtains an account. The firms that use iron and steel dispose of the accounts by means of iron checks (*Eisenscheine*). These checks are certified by the clearing office of the *Rüstungskontor*. With this transaction, the activity of the government agency ends. The remaining transactions are private. The owner of the iron checks issues under his own responsibility iron-transfer-checks (*Eisenübertragungsscheine*) to his sub-contractors. If the sub-contractor, in turn, needs smaller quantities of iron and steel products, he must acquire from his Chamber iron stamps. The accounts are established on a quarterly basis. The iron check, however, contains a note (*Vormerkung*) indicating the need for iron and steel for the coming quarter.

This is the method most commonly applied in all spheres of planning. It reduces governmental interference to a minimum and actually gives power over raw materials to the big combines.

2. PRICE AND PROFIT CONTROL

In the text (p. 317) it was questioned whether the former price commissioner, Josef Wagner, would put his profit-control rulings in operation. He had enacted them in order to skim off the super-profits made by German industry. Late in 1941, Wagner was deposed and Dr. Hans Fischboeck, Austrian banker and Commissioner General in occupied Holland, was put in charge. He abrogated Wagner's legislation totally and replaced it by enactments that an organ of German industry, the *Deutsche Allgemeine Zeitung*, frankly called 'A Pleasant Surprise.' Both the price- and profit-control legislations were completely overhauled.

The main problem was that of prices for government orders. Leaving out all irrelevant problems, three basic pricing systems exist today for government orders: (1) administrative prices fixed by decrees of the price commissioner, i.e. for textiles and leathers; (2) cartel prices which cannot be changed without previous consent of the Price Commissioner; and (3) uniform and group prices, as established by the decrees of 6 November 1941 and 2 February 1942. An explanation of the operation of uniform and group prices is necessary, because they have become major agents in effecting plant concentration. Prior to the group price decrees, the cost-plus price was the rule for government orders. The viciousness of this pricing system is well known. Two considerations led the government to abolish it. The lack of manpower made it necessary to close down inefficient plants, and the mounting war expenditure made it necessary to lower prices.

Uniform prices are thus fixed jointly by a liaison committee (*Arbeitsstab*) composed of officials from the price commissioner's office and the Speer Ministry for the whole territory and for a large number of articles. The prices are based on the production costs of the 'good' entrepreneur and no longer on those of the median producer. He who cannot produce at the new prices has to close down. There are exceptions, however, if the differences in production costs are too great. They may be conditioned, i.e. by an uneconomical location of the plant which, however, is highly desirable for strategic reasons. Therefore, Group prices are introduced (up to five groups), Group I representing the lowest price, Group v, the highest. Wherever group prices are established, the entrepreneur may choose which group he wants to join. If he adheres to Group I, that is, the lowest group, he is exempt from the excess-profit tax introduced 31 March 1942 for all deliveries made under Group I prices. The new profit-control legislation is thus closely integrated with the new price system.

The failure of Wagner's profit taxation is now universally recognized. A considerable part of the price commissioner's staff was busy with profit taxation so that the original function of the office was increasingly neglected. In addition, jurisdictional disputes broke out between the Ministry of Finance and the price commissioner, and there is no doubt that industry joined forces with the finance ministry, not only because industry naturally dislikes a profit tax, but also because this type of highly individualized profit tax created an enormous amount of administrative work. The new profit-tax legislation aims at: cutting red tape; establishing the authority of the Ministry of Finance over taxation; and providing an incentive for rationalization. The result of the old profit-control measures was financially disappointing, besides.

The new excess-profit tax is laid down in the first executive decree of 31 March 1942. Subject to the profit tax is the income of entrepreneurs from their entrepreneurial activities to the extent that this income is subject to the income or corporation tax. Entrepreneurs are taxed if: (1) their income in 1941 has exceeded 30,000 (now 20,000) Marks; and (2) the income for 1941 as compared with that of 1937-8 is 'extraordinarily' high; (3) incomes are considered 'extraordinarily' high only if they exceed 150 per cent of the income of 1938 or a minimum of 30,000 (now 20,000) Marks.

The tax rate is 25 per cent for individuals and so-called personal corporations (that is, partnerships and limited partnerships); and 30 per cent for 'capitalistic' corporations (namely: limited liability companies; joint-stock corporations; limited partnership-joint-stock corporations). Not subject to the tax, if application is made, are profits made on deliveries under Uniform or Group 1 prices in so far as prices have been fixed jointly by the Minister of Armament and Munitions and the Price Commissioner. The new tax is thus deliberately designed in such a way as to induce entrepreneurs to deliver at uniform and Group 1 prices that are lower than the old prices. If they want to enjoy the exemptions of the decree, they must sell more cheaply. This, in turn, requires a greater exploitation of the working class plus a more efficient organization of the plant. If they do so, they receive a financial reward. Consequently nearly all entrepreneurs have joined Group 1, the lowest price group.

III

CONCENTRATION OF CAPITAL

CONTINUED and intensified government intervention, above all the system of uniform and group prices, the new profit-control measures, combing-out, and rationalization stimulated the process of concentration of capital. All measures leading to concentration are frequently termed 'rationalization' in the German literature. A closer analysis of this term is thus advisable.

1. RATIONALIZATION

Five different problems are usually encompassed by the term 'rationalization,' a term of which the Germans are very fond. It means: (a) scientific management in factories; (b) the simplification of social and economic controls; (c) the installation of labor-saving devices; (d) the standardization of commodities; (e) the physical concentration of plants, that is, transfer of quotas from less efficient to more efficient plants. Within these five categories, two different types of rationalization must be distinguished. We might call them: inner-entrepreneurial, and supra-entrepreneurial rationalization.

The first is confined to one specific plant, enterprise, or combine, and is usually the outcome of competitive compulsion. It is, thus, unplanned; that is, it is carried out, or not carried out, according to the demands of competition. Considerations for the whole of the economy do not enter into such rationalization policies. Inner-entrepreneurial rationalization is stimulated by the regimentation of the Nazi economy. Rigid price control, i.e. the lowering of cartel prices, compels the enterprises to increase their profits by rationalization. Scarcity of raw materials compels the elimination of waste. Scarcity of labor is probably the greatest stimulus to scientific management and the installation of labor-saving devices. We need hardly add that by this very token, centralization and concentration are furthered. The capital requirements for installing labor-saving devices tend to increase, so that only rich enterprises can afford to do so and, among them, vertical combines are still in the most favorable position to do so.

While this aspect of rationalization presents no new problems, it is the second, the supra-entrepreneurial one which has come to the fore under Nazism. However, this encounters serious obstacles, unless the control of business is total. Rationalization of a whole branch of industry or of the whole industrial apparatus would have been inconceivable in the Weimar Republic.

The obstacles to a nation-wide rationalization will disappear when the business organizations are absolutely stable and nobody can leave them, and when no outsider can threaten the once-made rationalization agreement. Both conditions have been fulfilled by National Socialism. The compulsory cartel act, compulsory membership to the Groups, and the leadership principle have created that security under which monopolies could come to such agreements.

The task of supra-entrepreneurial rationalization rests with a number of agencies, among them the Four Year Plan Office. Göring has made Funk Commissioner General for Rationalization—merely a formal appointment. Funk has transferred these powers to W. Zangen, leader of the National Group Industry. The real power to rationalize rested originally with the General Deputies in the Four Year Plan.[1] Other equally important agencies for rationalization are the National Boards for Raw Material Control. They have enacted in innumerable cases prohibitions and orders. The use of certain materials or the manufacture of certain goods was prohibited, or manufacturers were ordered to use certain material and certain compositions.

In 1921 private combines and the government established the National Board for Efficiency (*Reichskuratorium für Wirtschaftlichkeit*) to promote rationalization and to advise business how best to carry out rationalization measures. The various trade associations within the peak associations established a number of *Normenausschüsse*, standardization committees, which from time to time recommended to their members specific measures regarding scientific management, labor-saving devices, and the standardization of goods. All economic and many of the trade and sub-trade groups now possess such committees, which continue to work in this direction. Their recommendations, however, could not be translated into leg-

1. See pp. 249-51.

islation until, in 1939, the Minister of Economics enacted a decree authorizing him to declare them valid for all producers, wholesalers, and retailers. As a consequence, a large number of such decrees have been issued by the Minister of Economics. There is hardly a field, especially in the civilian sector of the economy, which has not been affected by the standardization committees of the Groups.

The most important agencies today for the rationalization of combat material and related commodities are the *main* committees and *industrial* rings, discussed above. One can say today that the main committees and rings have assumed exclusive responsibility for the standardization of commodities in the military sector of the economy. They have also responsibility for the concentration of production in more efficient plants. Since the foundation of the five *Reichsvereinigungen,* these national associations have become very important in the field of rationalization.

All the above-mentioned agencies surveyed in standardization have now been integrated into the *Deutsches Normenwerk.* The interests of the various government agencies in this body are represented by a newly created Ministerial Committee for Standardization.

2. THE COMB-OUT

Within the whole sphere of rationalization, the concentration of plants, the closing of inefficient factories, and the transfer of their machinery and quotas to more efficient plants are of utmost importance and therefore deserve special mention. Two aspects must be distinguished in this field. Concentration has been going on in German industries for many decades and has taken a very rapid turn under National Socialism. It is the outcome of the structure of the German economy and is not the result of orders imposed upon the economy by the German government. This aspect of the concentration has been discussed on pp. 274-94, and will be amplified below.

There are industries, like the textile industry, where closing down has little effect because of the absence of large-scale industrial plants. In such cases the full utilization of existing plants, even of small ones, is of great significance. To achieve this purpose, the productivity of the smaller plants has to be improved. One means of doing this was the establishment of 'model factories,' *Leitbetriebe*, namely factories whose output exceeds that of their competitors. The model factories are compelled to assist the other plants by giving them technical advice and making accessible to them technological achievements. In return, the model factories obtain preferential treatment in regard to raw materials, machines, and labor.

The compulsory cartel act of 15 July 1933 vested in the Minister of Economics the power to establish compulsory cartels, etc. (see pp. 263-73).[2]

On other direct measures see pp. 282-3.

Sharply distinguished from these decrees under the Four Year Plan are the decrees closing handicraft and retail shops issued under the Labor Mobilization Decree of 27 January 1943. In this case, the execution of the decree rests with the National Defense Commissars (the *Gauleiter*), who order the Economic Groups to make proposals and who execute the proposals or amend them according to their discretion. The main purpose of the labor mobilization decree of 1943 is to win additional labor supply. There is a sharp difference between the above-mentioned measures of 1939 and those of 1943. The 1939 measures aim at excluding the purged retailer and handicraft men definitely from economic life. The labor mobilization act, however (so at least official statements maintain), is merely a temporary measure. The retailers, wholesalers, and handicraft men purged under the decree of 1943 have been promised restitution of their businesses after the war. Legal enactments therefore provide that the firm name should not disappear. While the purge of 1939 .did not provide support (some kind of mutual aid) for the closed-down retailers and handicraft men, the Labor Mobilization Act of 1943 and executive decrees do provide for such assistance.

The Labor Mobilization Act of 1943 does not affect industry proper because the process of industrial concentration has been much more severe than that of trade and handicraft concentration. It had started with vigor in the spring of 1942 when the reorganization of the German economy was undertaken. The procedure for the closing down preserved originally the rights of the smaller in-

2. See A. Gurland, O. Kirchheimer, and F. Neumann, *The Fate of Small Business in Nazi Germany* (United States Senate Committee to Study Problems of American Small Business), Government Printing Office, 1943, for details on the whole problem.

dustrialist. A complicated machinery had to be put in motion in order to obtain a closing-down order. But later in 1943, when air warfare against Germany rose to new heights, the whole protective machinery was scrapped and the power to close down vested in the main committees while the power to order the transfer of plants to safer regions was given to the big quota claimants (army, navy, air force, etc.).

Shut-down industrial plants are authorized to obtain aid (*Gemein-schaftshilfe*) [3] collected by the National Group Industry from among its members and given to the victims for repair and maintenance of buildings and machinery, for heating, light, rent, insurance premiums, and the guarding of the plants. It is clear that the assistance does not amount to much.

3. COMBINES AND CORPORATIONS

(a) Combines. The combines have experienced a further growth. It is impossible to record this process, but a few random examples may suffice to demonstrate its magnitude. The main result is the disappearance of 'free' coal mines with the acquisition of the *Gelsen-kirchen* mines by Krupp. While in 1914 still 50 per cent of all mines were free, today less than 10 per cent are so; the huge bulk is owned by the combines—not only the steel combines, but also by I. G. Farben, which has become not only a chemical but also a heavy-industry trust. The following transactions are worth recording.

Klöckner acquired from Göring combine the Simmering-Pauck-Grazer works. Krupp acquired the Gelsenkirchen mines from Wintershall combine. The two combines also agreed on common policy. A new combine is the Michel corporation, which has succeeded in consolidating its holdings in ignite and coal mines. The Stolberger Zinc extended its holdings. The General Electric (AEG) merged with the Corporation for Electric Enterprises (Gesfürel). The Elin and Schorch corporations in Vienna merged and became the fourth largest electrical combine. The Fendel and Rhenania inland navigation combines were consolidated.

(b) Corporations and Self-financing. The process of concentration finds but an inadequate expression in the corporation statistics.

3. Decree of 19 February 1940, *Reichsgesetzblatt*, I, p. 395.

A survey in *Wirtschaft und Statistik*[4] shows that the founding of new enterprises diminished throughout Greater Germany during 1942. In that year 14,180 new commercial firms were registered (including Ostland), as against 15,764 during the previous year, and 11,429 in 1940. By far the greater number are organizations with individual responsibility, and only 1,093 firms (1,193 in 1941) are limited corporations. On the other hand, 201 (318 in 1941) corporations were converted into firms with personal responsibility. Only 41 (46) stock companies were founded, while 170 (221) were dissolved and 19 (35) became individually owned firms. In all, 226 companies have refinanced their capital from foreign currency to German Reichsmark. The total number of enterprises at the end of 1942 amounted to 353,373, as against 347,061; 342,477; and 337,243, respectively, for the preceding 3 years.

The stock companies show an increasing trend toward the concentration of capital. In 1938 there were 5,518 stock companies with a total capital of 18.75 billion Reichsmark, and an average capital of 3.4 million. By 1941 the number of such companies had fallen to 5,418, while their total capital had risen to 24.91 billion and the average capital to 4.6 million. At the end of 1942 there were only 5,404 stock companies, with a total capital of about 29 billion, and an average capital of 5.4 million. Many concerns have undergone 'purges' and many branch firms were merged with the mother concern.

Naturally the total capital has been affected by the policy of capital increases, whereby up to the middle of 1943 a total number of 1,256 stock companies increased their capital by an average of 48½ per cent, from 9,020 to 13,397 million Reichsmark, at the expense of the open and secret reserves; in addition, there were true capital increases in 1942 amounting to 1,293 (954) million Reichsmark. The extent of the concentration of capital can be seen from the fact that 107 (89 in 1941) stock companies, with Rm. 50 million of stocks, control about half of the total stock capital.

Under war conditions, only large enterprises can survive, for they can raise their own finances when the capital market is almost entirely taken up with government needs. Aside from advance payments, which today average only about 1.5 billion Reichsmark per month, as against a former average of 5 billion, the Reich also con-

4. From *Neue Zürcher Zeitung*, 4 May 1943.

tributes to industrial financing to the extent of about 1.5 or 2 billion Reichsmark by making available machinery owned by the Reich. This amount is compensated by the lowering of prices, which gives the Reich an annual saving of about Rm. 2 billion. In spite of the enormous demands which the war economy makes on industry, the total of industrial indebtedness has increased only slightly above the 1939 level. From the end of 1939 to the end of 1941, the circulation of industrial loans and kindred obligations in Germany has gone up from 3.2 billion to 3.9 billion Reichsmark. (It stood at 4 billion in 1940.) Of this amount only 647 million are in the form of foreign loans, while in 1939 foreign loans amounted to 827 million. The overwhelming majority of all wartime investments was thus covered by industry's own financing, and not by recourse to the capital market or to the Reich itself (see for closer analysis pp. 316-26). Table 1 shows the development of joint-stock corporations

Table 1

JOINT STOCK CORPORATION ACCORDING TO CAPITAL (MARKS)	1927 NUMBER	1931 NUMBER	1941		1942	
			NUMBER	CAPITAL IN MILLION MARKS	NUMBER	CAPITAL IN MILLION MARKS
To 5,000	604	342	23	.0	19	.1
5,000-50,000	1,635	1,126	137	3.3	127	.3
50,000-100,000	1,367	1,252	208	12.3	182	10.9
100,000-500,000	3,802	3,340	1,645	392.6	1,515	354.0
500,000-1,000,000	1,482	1,352	845	542.3	841	546.8
1,000,000-5,000,000	2,378	2,255	1,781	3,758.5	1,843	3,978.3
5,000,000-20,000,000	540	578	549	4,913.3	617	5,699.6
20,000,000-50,000,000	98	121	141	4,076.7	153	4,417.6
50,000,000 and over	60	71	89	11,209.2	107	14,140.6
Total	11,966	10,437	5,418	24,908.2	5,404	29,058.2

in Germany. Three-fourths to four-fifths of the capital of all corporations is today held by large shareholders and the combines.

(c) Limited Liability Companies and Partnerships. A similar development took place with regard to the limited corporations. Many armament firms adopted this form of organization in order to evade the obligatory publicity. At the end of 1942 there were in Germany 23,498 (23,195 the year before) limited companies with original capital totaling 7.3 (6.1) billion Reichsmark. The tendency toward larger limited companies is evident from the fact that 1,091 new firms in 1942 had a total capital of 335 million Reichsmark, as against the previous year when 1,193 new firms had a total capital of 255 million.

The following list presents but a modest selection of the limited liability companies either newly founded or transformed from joint stock corporations:

> Mittelstahl (Flick combine), capital 50 million
> Godulla (Schaffgotsch combine), capital 40 million
> Tobis-Tonbild Syndikat, capital 5.4 million
> Deutsche Wollmanufaktor
> Demag (machine building)
> Bank für Industriewerte
> Mannesmann affiliates

Among the older companies in GmbH form is the Röchling combine.

Other corporations have preferred the still more personal partnership or limited partnership. The outstanding example is that of the biggest German combine, that of Friedrich Flick, outstanding 'finance' capitalist and close friend of Göring. He transformed his holding corporation, the Siegener Eisenindustrie, into the limited partnership Friedrich Flick KG, which owns 99 per cent of the Mittelstahl (now a limited liability) Company, which in turn owns machine and locomotive factories, 90 per cent of the Maximilianshütte, coal mines, and lignite mines.

His competitor, Alfred Krupp, found even a better way. Hitler himself, in 1943, issued a decree giving the Krupp family the right to divest themselves of the form of the joint-stock corporation, to determine the line of succession, and to maintain the enterprise henceforth as a family enterprise. Young Krupp, Alfried Krupp von Bohlen und Halbach, now owns the Krupp works as a hereditary estate.

The reasons for the preference of the limited liability company and the partnership are not far to seek. It is to avoid public control —a vital consideration in a time when the power of the combine grows and the small businessman is purged. Besides, the joint stock corporation becomes unnecessary when internal financing has reached such proportions as to make appeals to the capital market unnecessary.

This is what small industrialists think of the process of capital concentration.[5] This letter, addressed to a German newspaper, in reply to an article on 'The Giants,' explains better than a statistical analysis the changes in Germany.

Some months ago six industrialists—owners of small and medium-sized plants—were sitting together in a Russian fox hole north of Smolensk—almost all of them had volunteered—and talking about what would become of them, or at least of the plants they owned or managed, after the war. I was reminded of the long and serious discussion among these men, all of whom were fundamentally activistic optimists (they had proved this by the reconstruction or extension of their plants in the years between 1918 and 1939), when I set eyes on your article The Giants. In the first place it should be stated that no private and responsible industrialist who is possessed of his task (and you had to be that all through the last years if you wanted your enterprise to stand up against the pressure of the giant combines and the bureaucracy of the economic administration) would ever demand measures for his protection against big enterprise and combines. This would contradict his basic conceptions of the equal justification and equal value of all economic activities, which is an essential assumption. On the other hand, he demands emphatically identical treatment for all, meaning that there should be no one-sided sponsoring and furtherance of big industry as it actually exists, if not de jure, certainly de facto.

THE SOLDIER WATCHES THE DEVELOPMENTS

We, who are soldiers at present, but follow with open eyes the recent economic developments, recognize very clearly the inevitable consequences of the decrees and measures of the last years, and we understand them better now that we are sufficiently aloof. Whether we deal with the closing down of plants, or the appointment of leaders of the industrial rings, or the extension of the function and powers of certain economic groups, or the founding of Reichs organizations—again and again we find that we deal with measures which in the last analysis run counter to the interests of the small- and medium-sized enterprises. Or, has anyone ever heard that, when an unprofitable enterprise has been closed down, its machines, labor, and orders have been assigned to a medium or small plant? Or that the leader of an industrial ring has allotted interesting and profitable work to small and medium-sized plants and less profitable work to large-scale enterprises? It serves no purpose to talk about it. Above

5. *Deutsche Allgemeine Zeitung,* 16 November 1942.

all, we are at war and our personal desires must end in this war. Secondly, the men who work on the so-called economic self-administration are only human . . .

There is not one sensible industrialist who will deny that the existence of large-scale enterprise is necessary and justified, and we are in full agreement with you when you write that in many important fields of production the large enterprise is the only possible solution. But it is quite different with the combine. We have all gone with open eyes through Russia and have seen the horrible result of the elimination of the independent entrepreneur. Moreover, it is uncontested that a great many products, machines, and tools can be produced technically better and more economically in the small and medium-sized enterprises. From this it follows that all forms of enterprise are of equal value and that they will continue to exist if they all receive equal and just treatment.

However, all this will be possible only after the end of the war. We believe, in spite of this, that the political leadership has, at present, an opportunity to use for its ends the whole activism and idealism, the positive constructiveness and the fanatical drive to work, the great energy and the will for unconditional self-responsibility of the small and medium entrepreneur. It could use them in the reconstruction of the East. This is where the political leadership has a great chance. At the same time, the real entrepreneur could prove that his existence is still justified.

Is it absolutely necessary that the new Russian plants, which are being built up in the form of sponsored enterprises, must again become affiliated to large combines and big enterprises? And do the responsible authorities think that employees of large-scale enterprises, theoretical economists, and lawyers, can accomplish the pioneering task facing us in a better way than we, the entrepreneurs? We believe that many industrialists who owned or managed closed-down plants and who are at present employed in large-scale enterprises would be very happy if they could further this reconstruction through their knowledge, experience, ability, and energy, while they regard their present duties as mere slave labor . . .

ADAPTABILITY AND ABILITY TO FACE NEW SITUATIONS

It may be argued that only a large-scale enterprise or combine can guarantee rapid reconstruction as it is necessary today. To this we reply that the responsible entrepreneur, through his great adaptability and his ability to adjust himself quickly to new situations, is practically always superior to the employee of large-scale enterprises. He will also be content with a much smaller staff than the employee of big industry who is used to red tape . . .

(d) Control of Shares. A decree of 26 February 1942 provided that shareholders had to register their holdings of shares acquired between 1 September 1939 and 15 March 1942, that is since the outbreak of the war, if their total market value according to quotations on 31 December 1941 exceeded Rm. 100,000. Purchases of shares after 15 March 1942 must be reported to the Reichsbank if the total value of shares acquired by a person since the outbreak of the war reaches or exceeds 100,000 Reichsmark. Registered shares and newly acquired shares of this category may be sold only after they have been offered to and refused by the Reichsbank. The Reich Minister of Economics was given the right to requisition the registered shares; payment at the official quotations of 31 December 1941 to be made in Treasury Bonds deposited with the Reichsbank and the sale of these bonds to be allowed only on good grounds. Since market prices advanced noticeably after 31 December 1941, the requisitioning would necessarily cause losses to the holders.

In June 1942 it was announced that the government would now proceed to requisition registered shares, considering each case on its merits. The acquired shares would be used to manipulate the trend of quotations or would be released in small quantities for investment purposes.

The registration affected only 5 per cent of all shares, according to official statement. The percentage of shares held in fixed possession used to be estimated at 80 per cent, and, as a rule, these holdings were not subject to registration, since it can be assumed that they were acquired before the war. It follows that the object of the measure was not to assure for the state control of the industry, but that it had in view only the speculator who wanted to escape the devaluation of the currency by purchase of equity values. In fact, the measure rather affected the small capitalist, because the acquisition of a majority holding after outbreak of the war would probably be considered justifiable. The established control of majority holders over corporations was rather strengthened by making large-scale share acquisitions impossible. On the other hand, the sale of requisitioned shares by the Reichsbank opened various possibilities to exercise favoritism, influence the distribution of control, etc. The measures resulted in a substantial reduction of the trading volume on the stock exchange, but it became necessary nevertheless to put a price stop on all share dealings inside and outside the market. This price stop was introduced on 29 September 1943. It indeed succeeded in stabilizing the quotations. The policy testifies, however, to the failure of the Dividend Surrender Decree of 1941. This decree limited dividends to 6 per cent, but allowed corporations to increase their capital and to distribute the 6 per cent on the increased capital. It was hoped that the capital increases would supply the market with new stock, would thus alleviate the scarcity of stocks and shares, and that the new shares would be taken up by private investors. This, however, did not happen. We have already shown to what extent German corporations resorted to capital increases, but the overwhelming amount of new stock was absorbed by the large shareholders and combines. Wherever there was any danger that the new shares would be taken up by private investors, no capital increases were made, especially not by I. G. Farben, navy heavy industry, electrotechnical and heavy engineering combines, or, of course, by the limited liability companies (the shares of which cannot be traded on the exchange) and the partnerships.

IV

LABOR CONTROLS

FUNDAMENTAL changes have been made in the system of labor control. Labor constitutes the most important single vulnerable factor in the Nazi system, both as a commodity as well as politically.[1]

Eight stages in the development of the legislative and administrative powers granted to government agencies over labor power may be distinguished: (1) The general struggle against unemployment, 1933-4; (2) the statute of 15 May 1934 for the Regulation of Labor Supply and the decree of 10 August 1934 on the Distribution of Labor Forces; (3) the seven decrees of 7 November 1936 issued under the authority of Four Year Plan Office; (4) the decree of 22 June 1938 for Securing an Adequate Labor Supply for Tasks of Major Political Significance; (5) the war decree of the Ministerial Council for the Defense of the Realm of 1 September 1939; (6) the appointment of a General Deputy for Labor Supply under the authority of the Four Year Plan on 28 March 1942; (7) the labor mobilization act of January 1943 (total mobilization); (8) the appointment of a Reich Labor Supply Engineer in the Speer Ministry.

1. THE SUPREME CONTROL AGENCIES

Supreme control of labor (outside the field of social security) is vested in three agencies: (1) the German Labor Front (Robert Ley); (2) the Commissioner General for Labor Supply in the Four Year Plan (Fritz Sauckel); (3) the Reich Ministry for Armaments and War Production (Albert Speer).

Each of these agencies controls one specific aspect of labor relations. The Labor Front is supreme in the field of *Menschenführung*. The Commissioner General for Labor Supply is the supreme slave driver for both German and foreign labor. His appointment was

1. For detailed information, see F. Neumann, 'Labor Mobilization in the National Socialist New Order,' in *Law and Contemporary Problems*, vol. IX, pp. 544-66; R. Livchen, 'Wartime Development in German Wage Policy,' in *International Labor Review*, vol. LVI, pp. 136-65.

made in a Führer decree of 21 March 1942.[2] This decree appointed
Fritz Sauckel supreme agent in the field of labor supply in the Four
Year Plan and subjected to his authority the Main Departments III
(wages and labor conditions, and v (labor supply) in the Reich
Ministry of Labor and its subordinate agencies.

An executive ruling by Göring of 27 March 1942 dissolved, as a
consequence, the division Labor Supply in the Four Year Plan Office
and made it clear that Sauckel's authority was extended over wages
and labor conditions so that the work of the trustees of labor came
under Sauckel's direction and supervision. Thus Sauckel controls
German and foreign labor. He is superimposed on the existing controls, namely the Ministry of Labor, the former regional and local
labor exchanges, and the trustees of labor. He acts as a kind of political commissar over the civil service. Sauckel acts through the
following agencies:

He has appointed Professor Jung Inspector General for Labor
Supply. Jung is, therefore, the actual administrative head of the
Commissioner General's office. For the central control of foreign
labor, a Central Inspection for the Supervision of Foreign Labor
has been established by an agreement with the German Labor Front.
On 6 April 1942 Sauckel appointed the Gauleiter as his labor supply deputies for the region of the Gau and charged them with the
co-ordination of all labor supply measures under their jurisdiction.
The then Regional Labor Exchanges were directed to heed the orders of the Gauleiter.

The appointment of the Commissioner General for Labor Supply
thus put a party man in the supreme position of labor control. As a
consequence, the party controlled labor not only politically, through
the Labor Front, but also administratively, through the Commissioner General. Labor mobilization and labor control in general are
undoubtedly the most unpopular measures in Germany. Their execution requires complete ruthlessness and utter disregard for acquired rights and human considerations. It was Gauleiter Sauckel
who had to assume this responsibility and in an extremely dangerous moment, namely after the winter campaign of 1941-2, when
the Germans had suffered serious defeats on the Eastern Front.

Intensified air raids and further reverses on the Eastern Front, the

2. RGBI 1, 179.

landings in Italy, and the conquest of Sicily, however, created additional problems for the German Labor Supply organization.

In the same period that Sauckel assumed control over labor, Speer began to ascend to the supreme power over industry. It appeared likely that ultimately Speer would assume control over labor, too. This was achieved on 26 June 1943. The Reich Ministry for Armaments and War Production appointed a Reich Labor Supply Engineer. Below the Reich Labor Supply Engineer stand Regional Labor Supply Engineers. Below the Regional Labor Supply Engineers come Labor Supply Engineers. Each plant employing 300 or more workers is compelled to appoint such an engineer, while flying engineers supervise a number of smaller plants. The labor supply engineers are appointed by the chairmen of the Armament Commissions upon the proposal of the employers. They are, therefore, employed by the factories where they work and are not officials of the Speer Ministry. They may be compared to the power engineers (see above, p. 598).

The relation between Sauckel and the Reich Labor Supply Engineers has been defined in the following manner: 'The Commissioner General supplies the men, the Reich Labor Supply Engineer must see that they are properly utilized.'[3] This statement reveals very clearly the ascendance of Speer over Sauckel, for it means essentially that Sauckel's sole aim is to comply with the requests of the new labor-control machinery, that is, to supply workers wherever they are asked for, and to transfer them at the request of the labor supply engineer.

2. LABOR EXCHANGES AND TRUSTEES OF LABOR

The exigencies of *Menschenführung* led to two reorganizations of the labor exchanges. A decree of 16 November 1942 provided that the districts of the Labor Trustees and the Regional Labor Exchanges were to be adapted to the Regional Economic Districts, of which there were about 30, but that in certain cases one labor district could be provided for several economic districts. This plan was never put into practice in its entirety, but a beginning was made during the following months by dividing up some of the

3. *Deutsche Allgemeine Zeitung,* 25 October 1943.

larger areas, such as the Rhineland, Bavaria, and Southwest Germany, with the result that the number of districts rose to 26. In the summer of 1943, shortly after Sauckel had been made Commissioner General, it was announced that regional labor administration would be adapted to the party Gaue. This not only meant that the previous system of larger economic areas would be given up in favor of a division into 42 differently shaped districts, but also that there would be a close connection between party and state administrations as such, i.e. a stronger influence of the party Gauleiter and his bureaucracy upon labor administration. First, the offices of trustees and heads of the regional exchanges were now officially merged; that is, with the exception of factory inspection, the entire realm of labor administration was now brought under the uniform direction of one agency. Second, it was officially declared that, since the regulation of labor conditions and the allocation of labor constituted not purely administrative but eminently 'political' tasks, they should henceforward form a branch of 'political administration.' These measures meant that the party was to be given an important part in the shaping of labor policies, and also that the trustees were at all times to maintain close and personal contact with the Gauleiter of the district and to keep him informed about all developments of labor in the district. Labor administration, while not formally merged with the party, has thus become a branch of state administration in which the personal and political amalgamation with the party has achieved a far-reaching stage.

The destruction of the old regional labor exchanges was hardly completed when Sauckel discovered that the small area of the party Gau was not adequate. Early in 1944, therefore, several Gau labor exchanges were co-ordinated into labor inspectorates under the above-mentioned Inspector General Jung.

3. The Labor Chambers of the German Labor Front

We have already discussed the Leipzig Agreement of 19 June 1935 (pp. 417-19) and the system of labor chambers established under it. It never functioned. It was allegedly awakened to new life by a decree of Ley of 2 March 1943. This decree provides for an entire reorganization of the system of Labor Chambers. Each party Gau has a Gau Labor Chamber, headed by the Gau Chief of the Labor Front. There is an Advisory Council, the members of which are important persons of party and state administration, such as a labor trustee, chief of the Gau economic chamber, chief of the armament inspectorate, chiefs of the departments of the Gau labor front office, etc., and three leaders of 'model enterprises' from the district, as members. They are appointed by the Gauleiter and are empowered to deliberate upon important questions concerning economic and labor conditions in the Gau, e.g. those created by an air raid.

Each chamber is divided into four sub-chambers, which, in turn, are organized into working Communities or Working Committees. These are said to constitute the foundation of the entire structure but, strangely enough, nothing is said about their composition. These subdivisions are uniformly organized for the entire Reich and obtain their assignments uniformly from the Reich Labor Chamber, whose reorganization has been announced as near. The central supervision of the organization and activities of the chambers and their subdivisions is exercised by a special department of the central office of the Labor Front, called Department for Social Self-Responsibility (*Amt für soziale Selbstverantwortung*). Thus far there is no evidence that the new system has acquired any more practical importance than that which it has replaced.

4. Foreign Labor

Sauckel's appointment presaged intensified recruitment of foreign laborers for Germany. On 2 November 1942 the Nazis allegedly employed 5,000,000 foreigners. In December 1942, 17 per cent of all industrial workers were foreigners. In January 1943, 6-7,000,000 were said to be employed. There may today work in Germany (Greater Germany) 8,000,000 foreign workers, including working prisoners of war. The largest national groups are the French (about 1,200,000), the Poles (about 1,300,000), and the Russians (about 1,500,000). The conditions of employment were originally influenced by the Folk Group theory (see p. 160) and conditions varied according to racial descent. At the bottom of the hierarchy were the so-called *Ostarbeiter* (Eastern Workers).[4] They are all those

4. Küppers-Bannier, *Einsatzbedingungen der Ostarbeiter*, Berlin, 1942.

workers who come from the commissariats 'White Ruthenia,' the Reich commissariat Ukraine, and certain territories east of Estonia and Latvia. All Eastern workers have to wear a badge with the word 'East.'

The second category is composed of workers from the Government General, Poles, and others up to the Axis and pro-Axis nationals.

The responsibility for the foreign workers rests with the German Labor Front, and the 20,000 camps in which they are housed are now exclusively under its jurisdiction. Foreign workers other than those from the East receive the same wages as German workers, whereas Eastern workers, those from the Baltic States, and the Government General do not. A marked change has, however, taken place in the treatment of foreign workers. The previous decree of 20 January 1942 provided that the contract of Eastern workers is not the normal labor contract, but a 'special employment relationship.' As a consequence, prevailing wages and labor standards were not applicable to Eastern workers unless specifically enacted for them, and a heavy tax was enacted with the purpose of preventing a net income exceeding 15-17 Marks per week. From this amount 10.50 Marks were deducted for board and upkeep, so that the net money income amounted to only 6.50 per week.

The Germans admit that their legislation failed to provide sufficient incentives. The Ministerial Council for the Defense of the Realm therefore issued a new decree on 30 June 1942 with wage scales which considerably improve this economic situation. Since then the conditions of employment have improved, though rigid segregation and a complete denial of all rights are still practiced.

In April 1944, the Ministerial Council finally rescinded discriminatory wage legislation against the Eastern workers who are now to receive wages equal to those of the German workers without, however, belonging to the 'Plant Community.'

PART THREE

THE NEW SOCIETY

WHILE the economic changes are great, the social changes are revolutionary. They have a preponderant importance for any reconstruction of Europe and for any policy that an occupation army might want to pursue. The reconstruction of Europe is clearly dependent upon the character of social stratification, the ideological trends, and the psychological equipment of European peoples.

A liberal democratic society (which from the American point of view would be the ideal form of social and political organization) operating with a minimum of coercion requires one type of stratification, which may be explained in the following way. If we have a class-stratified society (and Germany is class-stratified), which besides is fairly class conscious, a liberal-democratic social and political system can be established only if society is organized in the form of a pyramid, so that between the base (the large masses) and the apex (the ruling classes) there exist a large number of middle classes to mediate between the two. This is a fairly common knowledge. The German masses and rulers are, however, class conscious, and the Nazis have tried desperately to eradicate class-consciousness by pseudo-egalitarian measures. It has already been explained (pp. 473-4) why the pseudo-egalitarianism of the Nazis is dangerous to them.

There is a second condition for the operation of a liberal democratic society (under modern conditions). There must be a civil service that operates not only efficiently but also objectively, bound only by a concept of duty, subject to abstract, general rules, and not to arbitrary commands. There must be, thirdly, a judiciary that conceives as its duty the preservation of the rights of the individuals —and not service to the state or any alleged community.

1. Social Stratification according to the Census of 1939

Table 1.*—Germany—Economically Active and Nonactive Population

	1882	1895	1907	1925	1933	1939 (NEW TERRITORY) [1]
TOTAL POPULATION IN THOUSANDS						
Gainful workers	16,885	19,756	25,156	32,009	32,296	39,792
Economically independent persons without occupation [2]	1,225	1,937	3,078	3,844	5,821	7,461
Dependents [3]	21,724	24,232	26,757	26,557	27,101	30,819
Persons drafted in armed forces and labor service [4]	......	......	......	......	......	1,303
Total population	39,834	45,925	54,991	62,410	65,218	79,375
PER CENT DISTRIBUTION OF TOTAL POPULATION						
Gainful workers	42.4	43.0	45.7	51.3	49.5	50.1
Economically independent persons without occupation [2]	3.1	4.2	5.6	6.2	8.9	9.4
Dependents [3]	54.5	52.8	48.7	42.5	41.6	38.9
Persons drafted in armed forces and labor service [4]	......	......	......	......	......	1.6
Total population	100.0	100.0	100.0	100.0	100.0	100.0

[1] Greater Germany as of May 1939, including Austria and Sudetenland, excluding Memel, Danzig, and territories annexed during the war.
[2] Persons living on social-security, old-age and other pensions, inmates of penal institutions, asylums, etc.
[3] Dependents of economically active and nonactive persons together.
[4] Data on service people, excluding permanent officers and noncommissioned officers of armed forces and labor service, computed from excess of resident over permanent population. Figures inexact and subject to correction.

* From Gurland, Kirchheimer and Neumann, *The Fate of Small Business in Nazi Germany*, Government Printing Office, 1943. The tables have been prepared by Dr. Gurland.

The tables on pages 626-7 show the familiar picture of a heavily monopolized and bureaucratized society where salaried employees, civil servants, and persons without occupation (receivers of pensions) show by far the greatest increase. This picture is, of course, considerably changed by the war.

2. The Middle Classes

Middle classes of independent small and middle businessmen (artisans, industrialists, retailers, wholesalers) have ceased to exist or will cease to exist within a very short period. The letter written

Table 2.—Germany—Total Population, by Social Groups of Gainful Workers

	1882	1895	1907	1925	1933	1939 OLD TERRITORY	1939 NEW TERRITORY [1]
TOTAL POPULATION (GAINFUL WORKERS AND DEPENDENTS) IN THOUSANDS							
Owners, managers, etc.	14,732	15,038	13,868	12,161	11,446	9,612	11,437
Unpaid family workers	1,721	1,862	3,871	5,565	5,446	5,837	6,950
Salary earners and civil servants	2,721	4,532	6,966	10,632	10,193	12,095	13,561
Wage earners	17,327	20,117	24,274	27,001	28,074	} 31,742	35,762
Domestic workers [2]	1,482	1,555	1,572	1,389	1,252		
Independent without occupation	1,851	2,821	4,440	5,662	8,807	8,842	10,361
Total population [3]	39,834	45,925	54,991	62,410	65,218	68,128	78,072
PER CENT DISTRIBUTION OF TOTAL POPULATION (GAINFUL WORKERS AND DEPENDENTS)							
Owners, managers, etc.	37.0	32.7	25.2	19.5	17.6	14.1	14.4
Unpaid family workers	4.3	4.1	7.0	8.9	8.4	8.6	8.9
Salary earners and civil servants	6.8	9.9	12.7	17.0	15.6	17.8	17.4
Wage earners	43.5	43.8	44.1	43.3	43.0	} 46.6	45.7
Domestic workers [2]	3.7	3.4	2.9	2.2	1.9		
Independent without occupation	4.7	6.1	8.1	9.1	13.5	13.0	13.3
Total population [3]	100.0	100.0	100.0	100.0	100.0	100.0	100.0
TOTAL POPULATION (GAINFUL WORKERS AND DEPENDENTS), INDEX NUMBERS 1882 = 100							
Owners, managers, etc.	100	102.1	94.1	82.5	77.7	65.2	77.6
Unpaid family workers	100	108.2	224.9	323.4	316.4	339.2	403.8
Salary earners and civil servants	100	166.6	256.0	390.7	374.6	444.5	498.4
Wage earners	100	116.1	140.1	155.8	162.0	} 168.8	190.1
Domestic workers [2]	100	104.9	106.1	93.7	84.5		
Independent without occupation	100	152.4	239.9	305.9	475.8	477.7	559.8
Total population [3]	100	115.3	138.1	156.7	163.7	171.0	196.0

[1] Greater Germany as of May 1939, including Austria and Sudetenland, excluding Memel, Danzig, and territories annexed during the war.
[2] Domestic service workers have not been counted separately in the 1939 census. The sum of previously enumerated wage earners and domestic workers does not exactly correspond to the category 'wage earners' in the 1939 census since a minor part of persons formerly counted as domestic workers have been included in the group 'salary earners.' For all practical purposes of comparison, however, the divergencies may be neglected.
[3] Permanent population only, excludes persons drafted in the armed forces and in the Labor Service in 1939.

Sources: For 1882 to 1933: 'Berufszählung. Die berufliche und soziale Gliederung des deutschen Volkes (Volks-, Berufs- und Betriebszählung vom 16. Juni 1933),' in Statistik des deutschen Reichs, vol. 458 (Berlin. 1937), p. 20. For 1939: Wirtschaft und Statistik, vol. 20, No. 16 (August 1940), p. 336; vol. 21, No. 3 (February 1941), passim. Per cent figures and index numbers for 1939 computed from data given in the sources above.

Table 3.—*Germany—Gainful Workers, by Social Groups*

	1882	1895	1907	1925	1933	1939 OLD TERRITORY	1939 NEW TERRITORY [1]
GAINFUL WORKERS IN THOUSÁNDS							
Owners, managers, etc.	4,331	4,619	4,749	5,095	5,303	4,784	5,679
Unpaid family workers	1,676	1,790	3,773	5,437	5,312	5,628	6,747
Salary earners and civil servants	1,183	2,115	3,311	5,442	5,513	6,482	7,360
Wage earners	8,344	9,804	11,874	14,709	14,950	} 17,375	20,007
Domestic workers [2]	1,351	1,428	1,449	1,326	1,218		
All gainful workers	16,885	19,756	25,156	32,009	32,296	34,269	39,793
PER CENT DISTRIBUTION OF GAINFUL WORKERS							
Owners, managers, etc.	25.7	23.4	18.9	15.9	16.4	14.0	14.3
Unpaid family workers	9.9	9.1	15.0	17.0	16.4	16.4	17
Salary earners and civil servants	7.0	10.7	13.2	17.0	17.1	18.9	18.5
Wage earners	49.4	49.6	47.2	46.0	46.3	} 50.7	50.2
Domestic workers [2]	8.0	7.2	5.7	4.1	3.8		
All gainful workers	100.0	100.0	100.0	100.0	100.0	100.0	100.0
GAINFUL WORKERS, INDEX NUMBERS, 1882 = 100							
Owners, managers, etc.	100	106.6	109.7	117.6	122.4	110.5	131.1
Unpaid family workers	100	106.8	225.1	324.4	316.9	335.8	402.6
Salary earners and civil servants	100	178.8	279.9	460.0	466.0	547.9	622.1
Wage earners	100	117.5	142.3	176.3	179.2	} 179.2	206.4
Domestic workers [2]	100	105.7	107.3	98.1	90.2		
All gainful workers	100	117.0	149.0	189.6	191.3	203.0	235.7

[1] Greater Germany as of May 1939, including Austria and Sudetenland, excluding Memel, Danzig, and territories annexed during the war.
[2] Domestic service workers have not been counted separately in the 1939 census. The sum of previously enumerated wage earners and domestic workers does not exactly correspond to the category 'wage earners' in the 1939 census since a minor part of persons formerly counted as domestic workers have been included in the group 'salary earners.' For all practical purposes of comparison, however, the divergencies may be neglected.

by independent industrialists from the Russian front (see p. 615) demonstrates the decimation of the middle classes and their moral degeneration. Characteristic for small business is not only their economic fate—but their mortal attitude. The letter shows that small business hopes to get again on its feet *by the spoliation of Eastern Europe. Let us exploit, at least, Poles and Russians—if you rob us of our economic independence. But even that you do not allow us to do!* Thus can the sentiment of the middle classes in Germany be expressed. This is, in no way, a surprise. There is in

Germany no group more corrupt than the middle classes. They have never stood for liberalism. Throughout the history of Germany the 'burgher' has attempted to achieve a good life at the expense of other peoples—whether of the German worker or of other nations. At every crucial situation in Germany (1813, 1848, 1862-6, 1914) the burghers have sold liberalism for foreign conquest and counter-revolution.

Indeed there will soon be but few independent artisans, retailers, wholesalers—and almost no independent industrialist. Not only will they have lost their businesses, but their plants will have physically ceased to exist.

What happened to the dispossessed middle classes?

The largest sector has become workers. Many of them may even be happier in their new professions, provided they continue to have employment. The transformation of burghers into workers applies to all European countries and means that the size of the working classes has considerably increased. This increase will become still more marked if the soldiers return home.

A smaller sector has joined the group of the practitioners of violence—to use Harold Lasswell's happy term. The German S.S. has taken in many dispossessed businessmen, frustrated professionals, second sons of hereditary farmers. But the same holds true of occupied Europe. The Flemish S.S., the Norsk S.S., the Danish S.S., the Baltic S.S., the Fascist groups all over Europe are mostly composed of these groups.

Another small group has joined the parasites. While they formerly used to trade in commodities, they now trade in good will, pull, Aryan certificates, vice, and in the black market.

The middle classes will have ceased to exist as a stratum out of which a democratic society can be rebuilt. Where remnants of true middle-class spirit still exist (in the professional groups and the intelligentsia—especially in Nazi-occupied Europe) their extermination by the Nazis may be expected when defeat is near.

3. THE CIVIL SERVICE

Nazism is out to destroy the traditional civil service in Europe. Sentimentally, Nazism had its strongest hold among the so-called middle civil service, that is the 'non-academic' civil servant who stands between the mere stenographer and the academic civil servant (usually a jurist). Many Nazi leaders come from this stratum. The large mass of civil servants—railroad, postal workers—is hardly distinguishable from a normal salaried employee. The pre-Nazi academic civil servant is probably neither pro- nor anti-Nazi. One may call the higher German civil servant a nihilistic technocrat, who is willing to serve any government that is strong and guarantees an efficient administration.

There is no question that the whole civil service is not, never has been, and never shall be a force for a liberal democracy. The civil-service tradition has, however, made this group somewhat immune to the most cruel and arbitrary measures of Nazism. The civil service has retained a rationality of its own. Some remnants of the Prussian tradition are still active, and they have made it possible to retain within the framework of Nazi arbitrariness some kind of a rational administration, based on the concept of duty.

It is exactly this remnant that is being wiped out now—since September 1942. This new development started early in 1942 with Sauckel's appointment as General Deputy for Labor Supply. Up to that time, the party was confined to *Menschenführung*, mass manipulation,[1] while administration was the prerogative of the civil service. Sauckel's appointment made it clear that the trend would be reversed. The measures taken in the fall of 1942 have wiped out the last fortress of the traditional structure of the civil service. The model for its organization is now the party Gau. Defense Commissars, Provincial Labor Exchanges, Provincial Economic Offices for the rationing of consumer goods, District Economic Chambers —all are now modeled on the Gau. In almost all spheres of administration, it is the Gauleiter who now reigns supreme. The sole exception are the Armament Commissions, still controlled by the Armament Inspectors under Speer.

4. THE JUDICIARY

In 1941, Reich Minister of Justice Gürtner died. For a considerable length of time, his post was not filled, but the ministry was temporarily administered by the Secretary of State, Dr. Schlegel-

1. See p. 72

berger, a residue from the Weimar period, an efficient, narrow-minded, reactionary civil servant—but almost certainly no Nazi. Contrary to expectation, Hans Frank, the leader of the German jurists and Governor General of Poland, was not appointed, though he had first claim as Hitler's counsel during the Weimar Republic. In August 1942 the president of the People's Court, Georg Thierack, was made Reich Minister; the Secretary of State in the Ministry, Roland Freisler, took over the former's position; and C. F. Rothenberger, president of the Hamburg court of appeal, was appointed Secretary of State, but resigned early in 1944. His successor is Dr. Klemm from Bormann's office. Frank had also to give up his position as president of the Academy of German Law, which was also taken over by Thierack.

The leading idea for the reorganization of the German judiciary was exposed in Hitler's speech of 26 April 1942. Hitler denounced the leniency of the German judiciary and, in quite threatening words, demanded a reorganization. From 1942 on, the process of Nazification of law and of the judges has rapidly progressed. Many new Nazi presidents have been appointed to courts of appeal and to the positions of public prosecutors. Since Himmler's appointment as Commissioner for Reich Administration (see p. 540), death sentence follows death sentence. The 'crisis of the German judiciary,' which Thierack quite candidly expressed, has been solved by the almost complete abandonment of rational law in all spheres, and the substitution of arbitrary dictation.

To achieve this, Thierack proposed the reduction of the number of judges from 14,000 to 5,000 and an increase in salary and status of the remaining ones. Thus a mass purge of unheard-of proportions was announced. The gap was to be filled by various methods: the merger of the many small local courts (*Amtsgerichte*) into larger ones; further restrictions on appeal; the introduction of laymen as justices of peace to deal with petty matters. This bold policy has been carried out only to a limited extent in spite of an avalanche of speeches by Rothenberger. It seems clear that Rothenberger's failure to live up to his promises caused his downfall and his replacement by a pure party man. Far-reaching reforms of the judiciary may now be expected.

Far-reaching changes have already been made in the treatment of juvenile delinquency. By a decree of 4 October 1940 [2] juvenile detention (*Jugendarrest*) was introduced. Fines and short-term sentences could be replaced by the administrative detention of juvenile offenders from a week-end to a month. The Hitler Youth also introduced Youth Service Detention (*Jugenddienstarrest*). A series of decrees strengthened criminal provisions against juvenile offenders and the Youth Criminal Law Decree of 6 November 1943 [3] finally codified all changes and proclaimed a new Reich Youth Court Act. Juvenile courts usually have jurisdiction over juveniles from 14 to 18 years. Twelve-year-olds can, however, be brought to trial if the seriousness of the crime makes prosecution imperative 'for the protection of the people.' A police decree for the Protection of the Youth of 9 March 1940 [4] had already authorized the police to restrict the freedom of the youth. Police and court control of the youth is thus watertight—in theory—though in practice youth delinquency now presents a major problem to the regime.

5. The Ruling Class

The ruling class is composed of those who command the means of violence (physical and moral) and the means of production, and those who possess the administrative skill. There are thus four groups: the Nazi leadership, which controls the police and propaganda; the army leadership; the industrial hierarchy; and the high civil service.

Among these, the power of the high civil service has steadily declined and can be completely ruled out of the picture.

The army leadership is still quite distinct from the party, though this by no means implies antagonism between army and party. The relation among army, party, and big business is still determined by the statement on pp. 397-8. The independence of the army from the party is true in spite of the fact that there may be now more party favorites in the army leadership (such as Zeitzler as chief of staff of the army, Korten as chief of staff in the air force, and Dönitz as supreme commander of the navy), that the Combat S.S. is outside of army jurisdiction and the Organization Todt is under

2. *Reichsgesetzblatt*, I, p. 336.
3. Op. cit. I, p. 635.
4. Op. cit. I, p. 499.

Speer. Leadership in the field still rests with officers who are officers first and last, and not party bosses.

Considerable changes have occurred, however, within the industrial leadership. Many of the outstanding old capitalists remain quiet, or have left their positions (such as Blohm, the shipbuilder). Others have clearly identified themselves with the Nazis and all they stand for, especially the Krupp family and the Röchlings. The Nazi group of businessmen has considerably increased through the establishment of Gau Economic Chambers. All their presidents, vice presidents, and members of advisory councils are party members.

The practitioners of violence tend to become businessmen, and the businessmen become practitioners of violence. Many leading industrialists become high S.S. leaders, chiefly Senior Group Leaders, corresponding to corps commanders: Baron v. Schroeder (Banker); W. Meinberg (Göring combine); H. Tengelmann (Hibernia); W. Zangen (Mannesmann), and many more could be mentioned. Many terrorists have assumed powerful industrial positions, such as Hans Kehrl (Phrix Cell Wool combine and Speer Ministry); P. Pleiger, W. Roehnert (Göring combine); F. Sauckel (Gustloff combine); F. Hayler (Retail and Ministry of Economics). This coalescence is not accidental but inherent in the structure of Nazi Germany. Nazism is interested in maximum production. There are two ways to achieve this. It could strengthen the bureaucratic controls and then compel more production. But this the Nazis could not do even if they wanted to. They lack trained personnel and will lack still more, as more manpower is absorbed by the armed forces. But the only feasible way for them was, therefore, to entrust the operation of the economy to the most powerful monopolists, to strengthen their powers, and to incorporate the whole industrial life into monopolistic and authoritarian organizations. This is the essence of the changes since the spring of 1942, the *raison d'être* of the *Reichsvereinigungen*.

But this very development creates new grave social problems. Small and middle business must suffer more. Workers must be still more terrorized to achieve higher performance. This is why Sauckel was appointed. One of the first decrees that he enacted was to give employers additional disciplinary powers. This is the significance of the Gau Economic Chambers and the disappearance of the Artisan Chambers. The Chambers 'combed-out' retailers and artisans and thus had to come under party control in order to put the full authority of the party behind them. This is the significance of the destruction of the civil service and of the judiciary. The ascendance of the practitioners of violence is thus inherent in the most intense monopolization that a modern society has ever witnessed. But the terrorists want to anchor their power not only in violence, but in industrial production. Hence the Göring combine. That is why high S.S. leaders become businessmen.

German society is thus composed of:

A small group of powerful industrial, financial, and agrarian monopolists tending to coalesce with a group of party hierarchs into one single bloc disposing of the means of production and the means of violence.

A large mass of workers and salaried employees without any kind of organization and without any means of articulating their views and sentiments.

The mediation between the two classes is assured by an ever-increasing number of terrorists; and an ever-increasing number of parasites trading in pull and vice.

INDEX

DATE DUE

D C 13			
NO 20 '67			
MY 9 '69			
MY 21 '69			
APR. 1 6 1984			
3/18/84			
MAR 20 84			
GAYLORD			PRINTED IN U.S.A.